CONCISE CHURCH HISTORY

AMG Publishers

CONCISE CHURCH HISTORY

JOHN HUNT

Concise Church History

Published by AMG Publishers.
6815 Shallowford Road
Chattanooga, TN 37421

ISBN 13: 978-0-89957-696-1
ISBN 10: 0-89957-696-6

First Printing, January 2008
Cover Design by Daryle Beam
Edited and proofread by Dan Penwell and Warren Baker

Printed in the United States of America
13 12 11 10 09 08 –Sh– 8 7 6 5 4 3 2 1

CONTENTS

INTRODUCTION

The Bible and history

The Bible is full of historical records of how God dealt with his followers, as well as with those who opposed him. The Old Testament and New Testament frequently encourage its readers to remember, learn from, and take encouragement from past events and people, both the godly and the ungodly. While no other book is divinely inspired like the Bible, *Concise Church History* does provide the record of hundreds of events in Christian history which can also encourage, challenge, and teach us.

There are scores of seemingly insolvable problems confronting Christian fellowships and denominations today. But there are countless lessons to be drawn from the history of Christianity which can guide us as we tackle our contemporary problems. For example, when we face heresy within our own ranks we can turn to the time when the whole church was in danger of embracing some of the errors of Jehovah's Witnesses. From the Arian controversy we may recall how Christians in the past survived and dealt with the threats of false teaching.

Why study Christian history?

According to Pastor David F. Reagan there are twelve good reasons to study the history of Christianity:

1. To obey God in studying history (Deuteronomy 32:7; Job 8:8–10; Psalm 78:2–3)
2. To understand God's plan for the ages (Ephesians 1:9–10)
3. To more fully understand the Bible (Daniel 8; Revelation 2–3)
4. To understand people: biography (James 5:11,17)
   a. Individuals
   b. Groups
5. To understand Christian experience (Hebrews 11:33,38) – through reading spiritual biography or autobiography
6. To provide illustrations and see biblical principles exemplified (Romans 15:4; 1Corinthians 10:6–11)
7. To see error and how it develops (Galatians 5:9)
8. To see God's providence (Psalm 75:6–7; Isaiah 46:9–11; Daniel 2:21; Romans 8:28)

9. To give the believer stability and roots (Psalm 11:3)
10. To explain present conditions (Deuteronomy 8:11–18; Isaiah 51:1)
11. To foresee future conditions and events (Ecclesiastes 1:9)
12. To follow the example of Christ and the apostles (Matthew 23:35; Luke 13:1–4; Acts 7)

The scope of Christian history

Reagan also lists ten branches of church history:

1. History of Revivals
2. History of Missions
3. History of Persecution
4. History of Denominations
5. History of Church Leaders
6. History of Worship
7. History of Christian Life
8. History of Doctrines
9. History of Heresies
10. History of Bible Believers

All these branches of church history are found in *Concise Church History*. Additionally, there are sections entitled, "History of Bible translations with examples of Bible translations."

Also included in *Concise Church History* are scores of extracts from Christian devotional writers from each era of Christian history. As well as being spiritually uplifting, these writings give us great insight into the thinking and Christian devotion of the time.

People

In *Concise Church History* biographical sketches of a wide variety of Christian leaders from every century are found. These include:

- Apologists
- Authors
- Bible translators
- Christian philosophers
- Church fathers
- Evangelists
- Hermits
- Historians of Christianity

- Missionaries
- New Testament scholars
- Old Testament scholars
- Pastors
- Popes
- Preachers
- Reformers
- Saints
- Teachers
- Theologians
- Visionaries

Eye-witness accounts

Concise Church History contains dozens of eye-witness accounts of historical events. So as well as relying on and quoting from the most learned historians of Christianity, *Concise Church History* is peppered with first hand accounts of the events themselves. Such accounts help us not only to understand the event but to feel it and experience it for ourselves.

Learning from the history of Christianity

Some people believe that Henry Ford's infamous quotation that, "History is bunk" may correctly be applied to Christian history. Their sympathy lies with George Bernard Shaw's observation that, "We learn from history that we learn nothing from history."

There are also plenty of cynical ideas around about history, such as Ambrose Bierce's definition of history: "HISTORY, n. An account mostly false, of events mostly unimportant, which are brought about by rulers mostly knaves, and soldiers mostly fools."

It is probably true that the average Christian knows more about the history of his or her country than he does about the history of Christianity.

Set alongside such negative thoughts are the following positive quotations, which perhaps apply equally, if not more strongly, to Christian history than they do to secular history.

> There is nothing that solidifies and strengthens a nation like reading the nation's history.
> *Joseph Anderson*

> History, despite its wrenching pain, cannot be unlived, but if faced with courage, need not be lived again.
> *Maya Angelou*

If history records good things of good men, the thoughtful hearer is encouraged to imitate what is good: or if it records evil of wicked men, the good, religious listener or reader is encouraged to avoid all that is sinful and perverse, and to follow what he knows to be good and pleasing to God.
Venerable Bede

The study of History is the beginning of wisdom.
Jean Bodin

History is the torch that is meant to illuminate the past to guard us against the repetition of our mistakes of other days. We cannot join in the rewriting of history to make it conform to our comfort and convenience.
Claude Bowers

Study history, study history. In history lies all the secrets of statecraft.
Winston Churchill

Not to know what happened before one was born is always to be a child.
Cicero

Study the past if you would divine the future.
Confucias

What are all histories but God manifesting himself, shaking down and trampling under foot whatsoever he hath not planted?
Oliver Cromwell

Whoever neglects learning in his youth loses the Past, and is dead to the Future.
Euripides

History maketh a young man to be old, without wrinkles or gray hairs, privileging him with the experience of age, without either the infirmities or inconveniences thereof.
Thomas Fuller

History is the only laboratory we have in which to test the consequences of thought.
Etienne Gilson

I have but one lamp by which my feet are guided, and that is the lamp of experience. I know no way of judging of the future but by the past.
Edward Gibbon

Unless we learn from history, we are destined to repeat it. This is no longer merely an academic exercise, but may contain our world's fate and our destiny.
Alex Haley

We can learn from history how past generations thought and acted, how they responded to the demands of their time and how they solved their problems. We can learn by analogy, not by example, for our circumstances will always be different than theirs were. The main thing history can teach us is that human actions have consequences and that certain choices, once made, cannot be undone. They foreclose the possibility of making other choices and thus they determine future events.
Gerda Lerner

Consciousness of the past alone can make us understand the present.
Herbert Luethy

History is a people's memory, and without memory man is demoted to the lower animals.
Malcolm X

History is a guide to navigation in perilous times. History is who we are and why we are the way we are.
David C. McCullough

Nothing worth doing is completed in our lifetime,
Therefore, we are saved by hope.
Nothing true or beautiful or good makes complete sense in any immediate context of history;
Therefore, we are saved by faith.
Nothing we do, however virtuous, can be accomplished alone.
Therefore, we are saved by love.
No virtuous act is quite as virtuous from the standpoint of our friend or foe as from our own;
Therefore, we are saved by the final form of love which is forgiveness.
Reinhold Niebuhr

There are three things every preacher needs to know: the English language, the English Bible and history.
J. Frank Norris

Dwell in the past and you'll lose an eye.
Forget the past and you'll lose both eyes.
Russian proverb

Those who cannot learn from history are doomed to repeat it.
George Santayana

A lawyer without history or literature is a mechanic, a mere working mason; if he possesses some knowledge of these, he may venture to call himself an architect.
Sir Walter Scott

History is Philosophy teaching by examples.
Thucydides

In history one is absolutely sickened, not by the original crimes that the wicked have committed, but by the punishment that the good have inflicted.
Oscar Wilde

Reading *Concise Church History* is one way to learn from Christian history so that we may live more Christian lives in the present.

CHAPTER 1

THE START OF THE CHRISTIAN CHURCH

From Jesus Christ to Clement of Rome
AD 30–100

Important dates in the start of the Christian Church

33 Death and resurrection of Jesus Christ
33 Descent of the Holy Spirit on the Day of Pentecost
33–65 The Acts of the Apostles recounts the story and expansion of the Christian church from its birth in Jerusalem, through the empire, all the way to Rome
39 Cornelius, the Gentile, converted by the apostle Peter, signalling the expansion of the Church to the world outside Judaism
42 Persecution of Christians in Palestine under Herod Agrippa
44 Many Christians flee persecution to Antioch; beginning of dispersion of Church; called Christians for the first time; Peter imprisoned
45 Paul the Apostle begins his missionary journeys
49/50 Council of Jerusalem
62 Martyrdom of James the Less
64 Persecution by Nero begins
68 Martyrdom of Peter and Paul
70 Destruction of Jerusalem by Titus
95 Persecution by Domitian
100 Death of the apostle John

Introduction

The first chapter in the two thousand year long story of Christian history covers the period from the coming of the Holy Spirit at Pentecost to the end of the first century.

Many of these events are recorded by the meticulously accurate historian, Dr Luke, in his New Testament book of Acts (Acts of the Apostles).
Important events recorded in Acts:

The Jewish response to the Christian message
Non-Jews respond to Christianity
The first Christians face opposition
The martyrdom of Stephen

The conversion of Paul
The spread of the Gospel: from Jerusalem to Rome

Important events recorded outside the New Testament:
The Romans sack Jerusalem, AD 70
Christians persecuted by Emperor Nero
Christians persecuted by Emperor Domitian

Events
Important events in the early church

The writing of the New Testament
The spread of Christianity
Persecution of Christians

People
Christian leaders in the early church

Peter (?-c. 65)
Paul (c. 1-?65)
John (?-c. 100/101)

Historians' overview of the early church

1. The Miracle of Pentecost and the Birthday of the Christian Church. AD 30

Acts 2:4

"The first Pentecost which the disciples celebrated after the ascension of our Savior, is, next to the appearance of the Son of God on earth, the most significant event. It is the starting-point of the apostolic church and of that new spiritual life in humanity which proceeded from Him, and which since has been spreading and working, and will continue to work until the whole humanity is transformed into the image of Christ."—Neander (*Geschichte der Pflanzung und Leitung der christlichen Kirche durch die Apostel.*, I. 3, 4).

The ascension of Christ to heaven was followed ten days afterwards by the descent of the Holy Spirit upon earth and the birth of the Christian Church. The Pentecostal event was the necessary result of the Passover event. It could never have taken place without the preceding resurrection and ascension. It was the first act of the mediatorial reign of the exalted Redeemer in heaven, and the beginning of an unbroken series of manifestations in fulfillment of his promise to be with his people "always, even unto the end of the world." For his ascension was only a withdrawal of his visible local presence, and the beginning of his spiritual omnipresence in the church which is "his body, the fullness of him that filleth all in all." The Easter miracle and the Pentecostal miracle are continued and verified by the daily moral miracles of regeneration and sanctification throughout Christendom.

We have but one authentic account of that epoch-making event, in the second chapter of Acts, but in the parting addresses of our Lord to his disciples the promise of the Paraclete who should lead them into the whole truth is very prominent, John 14:6, 26; 15:26; 16:7. The preparatory communication of the Spirit is related in John 20:22. and the entire history of the apostolic church is illuminated and heated by the Pentecostal fire. Comp. especially the classical chapters on the gifts of the Spirit, 1 Cor. 12, 13, and 14, and Rom. 12.

Pentecost was the fiftieth day after the Passover-Sabbath.... It was one of the three great annual festivals of the Jews in which all the males were required to appear before the Lord. Passover was the first, and the feast of Tabernacles the third. Pentecost lasted one day, but the foreign Jews, after the period of the captivity, prolonged it to two days. It was the "feast of harvest," or "of the first fruits," and also (according to rabbinical tradition) the anniversary celebration of the Sinaitic legislation, which is supposed to have taken place on the fiftieth day after the Exodus from the land of bondage....

This festival was admirably adapted for the opening event in the history of the apostolic church. It pointed typically to the first Christian harvest, and the establishment of the new theocracy in Christ; as the sacrifice of the paschal lamb and the exodus from Egypt foreshadowed the redemption of the world by the crucifixion of the Lamb of God. On no other day could the effusion of the Spirit of the exalted Redeemer produce such rich results and become at once so widely known. We may trace to this day not only the origin of the mother church at Jerusalem, but also the conversion of visitors from other cities, as Damascus, Antioch, Alexandria, and Rome, who on their return would carry the glad tidings to their distant homes. For the strangers enumerated by Luke as witnesses of the great event, represented nearly all the countries in which Christianity was planted by the labors of the apostles. The list of nations, Acts 2:8–11, gives a bird's eye view of the Roman empire from the East and North southward and westward as far as Rome, and then again eastward to Arabia. Cyprus and Greece are omitted. There were Christians in Damascus before the conversion of Paul (9:2), and a large congregation at Rome long before he wrote his Epistle (Rom. 1:8).

The Pentecost in the year of the Resurrection was the last Jewish (i.e. typical) and the first Christian Pentecost. It became the spiritual harvest feast of redemption from sin, and the birthday of the visible kingdom of Christ on earth. It marks the beginning of the dispensation of the Spirit, the third era in the history of the revelation of the triune God. On this day the Holy Spirit, who had hitherto wrought only sporadically and transiently, took up his permanent abode in mankind as the Spirit of truth and holiness, with the fullness of saving grace, to apply that grace thenceforth to believers, and to reveal and glorify Christ in their hearts, as Christ had revealed and glorified the Father....

The Sinaitic legislation was accompanied by "thunder and lightning, and a thick cloud upon the mount, and the voice of the trumpet exceeding loud, and all the people that was in the camp trembled." Exod. 19:16; comp. Hebr. 12:18, 19. The church of the new covenant war, ushered into existence with startling signs which filled the spectators with wonder and fear. It is quite natural, as Neander remarks, that "the greatest miracle in the inner life of mankind should have been accompanied by extraordinary outward phenomena as sensible indications of its presence."

There came a supernatural sound resembling that of a rushing mighty wind. It came down from heaven and filled the whole house in which they were assembled; and tongues like flames of fire, distributed themselves among them, alighting for a while on each head. . . . It is not said that these phenomena were really wind and fire, they are only compared to these elements. John Lightfoot writes: "as the form which the Holy Spirit assumed at the baptism of Christ is compared to a dove." . . . These audible and visible signs were appropriate symbols of the purifying, enlightening, and quickening power of the Divine Spirit, and announced a new spiritual creation. The form of tongues referred to the *glossolalia*, and the apostolic eloquence as a gift of inspiration.

"And they were all filled with the Holy Spirit." This is the real inward miracle, the main fact, the central idea of the Pentecostal narrative. To the apostles it was their baptism, confirmation, and ordination, all in one, for they received no other. They were baptized with water by John; but Christian baptism was first administered by them on the day of Pentecost. Christ himself did not baptize, John 4:2. To them it was the great inspiration which enabled them hereafter to be authoritative teachers of the gospel by tongue and pen. Not that it superseded subsequent growth in knowledge, or special revelations on particular points (as Peter received at Joppa, and Paul on several occasions); but they were endowed with such an understanding of Christ's words and plan of salvation as they never had before. What was dark and mysterious became now clear and full of meaning to them. The Spirit revealed to them the person and work of the Redeemer in the light of his resurrection and exaltation, and took full possession of their mind and heart. They were raised, as it were, to the mount of transfiguration, and saw Moses and Elijah and Jesus above them, face to face, swimming in heavenly light.

They had now but one desire to gratify, but one object to live for, namely, to be witnesses of Christ and instruments of the salvation of their fellow-men, that they too might become partakers of their "inheritance incorruptible, and undefiled, and that fadeth not away, reserved in heaven." 1 Pet. 1:3, 4.

But the communication of the Holy Spirit was not confined to the Twelve. It extended to the brethren of the Lord, the mother of Jesus, the pious women who had attended his ministry, and the whole brotherhood of a hundred and twenty souls who were assembled in that chamber. Comp. Acts 1:13, 14. They were "all" filled with the Spirit, and all spoke with tongues; Acts 2:3: "it (a tongue of fire) sat upon each of them." and Peter saw in the event the promised outpouring of the Spirit upon "all flesh," sons and daughters, young men and old men, servants and handmaidens. Acts 2:3, 4, 17, 18.

It is characteristic that in this spring season of the church the women were sitting with the men, not in a separate court as in the temple, nor divided by a partition as in the synagogue and the decayed churches of the East to this day, but in the same room as equal sharers in the spiritual blessings. The beginning was a prophetic anticipation of the end, and a manifestation of the universal priesthood and brotherhood of believers in Christ, in whom all are one, whether Jew or Greek, bond or free, male or female. Gal. 3:28.

This new spiritual life, illuminated, controlled, and directed by the Holy Spirit, manifested itself first in the speaking with tongues towards God, and then in the prophetic testimony towards the people. The former consisted of rapturous prayers and anthems of praise, the latter of sober teaching and exhortation. From the Mount of Transfiguration the disciples, like their Master, descended to the valley below to heal the sick and to call sinners to repentance.

Philip Schaff, History of the Christian Church,
Volume I: Apostolic Christianity. AD 1–100

Acts

It is easy to observe from a glance at the following outline of the book of Acts how Dr Luke pictures the expansion of Christianity, from being a handful of people in Jerusalem, to its arrival in the city of Rome.

Outline of Acts

I. Preaching the Gospel "in Jerusalem" and Judea.

(1) Preparation for the work (1:1–26).

(2) Events of Pentecost (2:1–47).

(3) The Church unfolding in miracle and endurance of persecution (3:1-4:37).

(4) The Church unfolding in penal power (5:1–16).

(5) The Church in the second persecution (5:17–42).

(6) The Church forming its economy (6:1–8).

(7) The Church in last struggle and dispersion (6:8–8:4).

II. Preaching the Gospel "in Samaria" and about Palestine.

(1) The deacon Philip evangelizes Samaria (8:5–25).

(2) The new Apostle of the Gentiles called (9:1–30).

(3) Gentile induction; new Christian center, Gentile Antioch (10:1–11:30).

(4) Desolation of Jerusalem Church by Herod; its avenging (12:1–25).

III. Preaching the Gospel "in the Uttermost Parts of the Earth".
   (1) Paul's first mission from Antioch (13:1–14:28).
   (2) Jerusalem Council on Circumcision (15:1–34).
   (3) Paul's second mission from Antioch (15:35–18:23).
   (4) Paul's third mission from Antioch (18:23–21:17).
   (5) Paul in council with James—Arrest—Sent to Cæsarea (21:18–23:35).
   (6) Paul's two years at Cæsarea (24:1–26:32).
   (7) Paul en route for Rome; at Rome (27:1–28:31).

The first expansion (Acts 6—9)

The first century of the Christian Church was characterized by its expansion into the world known at that time.

Early on in the history of the Christian Church the Gospel message is no longer confined to Jerusalem. Soon Jews from Greece joined the Aramaic Jews. The apostles appointed seven men to take care of the Hellenists. Thus the new community of Jews included those from the Diaspora; i.e., those who lived outside the limits of Palestine.

The second expansion (Acts 10—11)

The question soon arose: "Did you need to be a Jew to be Jesus' disciple?" The highly significant story of the conversion of Cornelius and his household answers this question. Through a vision Peter realized that the gospel was for everyone. He saw the Holy Spirit come upon the Roman Centurion Cornelius, who was not a Jew, and he welcomed him into the church without embracing Judaism.

Called "Christians" for the first time

In Antioch the disciples of Christ were first given the name Christians. From then on this would be the name that separated them from other religious groups.

"... and when he found him, he brought him to Antioch. So for a whole year Barnabas and Saul met with the church and taught great numbers of people. The disciples were called Christians first at Antioch." Acts 11:26 NIV

Antioch became the starting block for evangelization of the Roman Empire.

Perversions of the apostolic teaching

Introduction

The heresies of the apostolic age are caricatures of the several types of the true doctrine.

The three fundamental forms of heresy were:

- Judaizing
- The Gnostic heresy
- Syncretism

There heresies reappear, with various modifications, in almost every subsequent era of Christian history

1. The Judaizers

The Judaizing tendency is the heretical counterpart of Jewish Christianity. It so insists on the unity of Christianity with Judaism, as to sink the former to the level of the latter, and to make the gospel no more than an improvement or a perfected law. It regards Christ as a mere prophet, a second Moses; and denies, or at least wholly overlooks, his divine nature and his priestly and kingly offices.

The Judaizers were Jews in fact, and Christians only in appearance and in name. They held circumcision and the whole moral and ceremonial law of Moses to be still binding, and the observance of them necessary to salvation. Of Christianity as a new, free, and universal religion, they had no conception. Hence they hated Paul, the liberal apostle of the Gentiles, as a dangerous apostate and revolutionist, impugned his motives, and everywhere, especially in Galatia and Corinth, labored to undermine his authority in the churches. The epistles of Paul, especially that to the Galatians, can never be properly understood, unless their opposition to this false Judaizing Christianity be continually kept in view.

The same heresy, more fully developed, appears in the second century under the name of Ebionism.

Philip Schaff, History of the Christian Church,
Volume I: Apostolic Christianity. AD 1–100

Jerusalem Council, AD 49

The problem of the Judaizers is discussed under the leadership of the Apostles in Jerusalem, Acts 15:6,12.

James, Simon Peter, Barnabas and Paul all speak and come to an agreement that Gentiles as well as Jews are free from the Jewish ceremonial law.

However they must be sensitive to their Jewish Christians and stop eating food sacrificed to idols. Leviticus 17:10–14; 19:26; 1 Corinthians 8:7–13

The issue of sexual immorality was also raised because this was a problem with many Greeks.

Thus the first Church council set out the practical outworking of relations between Jewish and Greek Christians. The Jews were cautioned against legalism while the Gentiles were cautioned against immorality. Compassion and sensitivity were set over against legalism and hedonism. A letter and two personal witnesses in the person of Judas and Silas are sent back to Antioch to calm the Church there. Acts 15:22–29. The letter sent from the Jerusalem Council follows:

> [22]Then the apostles and elders, with the whole church, decided to choose some of their own men and send them to Antioch with Paul and Barnabas. They chose Judas (called Barsabbas) and Silas, two men who were leaders among the brothers. [23]With them they sent the following letter: The apostles and elders, your brothers, To the Gentile believers in Antioch, Syria and Cilicia: Greetings. [24]We have heard that some went out from us without our authorization and disturbed you, troubling your minds by what they said. [25]So we all agreed to choose some men and send them to you with our dear friends Barnabas and Paul—[26]Men who have risked their lives for the name of our Lord Jesus Christ. [27]Therefore we are sending Judas and Silas to confirm by word of mouth what we are writing. [28]It seemed good to the Holy Spirit and to us not to burden you with anything beyond the following requirements: [29]You are to abstain from food sacrificed to idols, from blood, from the meat of strangled animals and from sexual immorality. You will do well to avoid these things. Farewell.
> *Acts 15:22–29 NIV*

2. The Gnostic heresy

The opposite extreme to the Judaizers is a false Gentile Christianity, which may be called the Paganizing or Gnostic heresy. It is as radical and revolutionary as the other is contracted and reactionary. It violently breaks away from the past, while the Judaizing heresies tenaciously and stubbornly cling to it as permanently binding.

It exaggerates the Pauline view of the distinction of Christianity from Judaism, sunders Christianity from its historical basis, resolves the real humanity of the Savior into a Doketistic illusion, and perverts the freedom of the gospel into antinomian licentiousness.

Note on Docetism

Docetism taught that Jesus only appeared to have a body, that he was not really incarnate. The word "docetism" comes from the Greek, word *dokeo* when means "to seem".

This error developed out of the dualistic philosophy which viewed matter as inherently evil. This heresy taught that God could not be associated with matter, and that God, being perfect and infinite, could not suffer. Therefore, God as the word, could not have become flesh as is stated in John 1:1,14, "In the beginning was the Word, and the Word was with God, and the Word was God . . . And the Word became flesh, and dwelt among us" (NASB).

This denial of a true incarnation meant that Jesus did not truly suffer on the cross and that He did not rise from the dead.

The basic principle of Docetism was refuted by the Apostle John in 1 John 4:2–3. "By this you know the Spirit of God: every spirit that confesses that Jesus Christ has come in the flesh is from God; and every spirit that does not confess Jesus is not from God; and this is the spirit of the antichrist, of which you have heard that it is coming, and now it is already in the world." John also wrote in 2 John 7, "For many deceivers have gone out into the world, those who do not acknowledge Jesus Christ as coming in the flesh. This is the deceiver and the antichrist."

The second and third century Christian writers, Ignatius of Antioch, Irenaeus, and Hippolatus all wrote against this heresy.

Docetism was condemned at the Council of Chalcedon in 451.

The author, or first representative of this Gnostic heresy, this baptized heathenism, according to the uniform testimony of Christian antiquity, is Simon Magus, who unquestionably adulterated Christianity with pagan ideas and practices, and gave himself out, in pantheistic style, for an emanation of God.

Plain traces of this error appear in the later epistles of Paul (to the Colossians, to Timothy, and to Titus), the second epistle of Peter, the first two epistles of John, the epistle of Jude, and the messages of the Apocalypse to the seven churches.

This heresy, in the second century, spread over the whole church, east and west, in the various schools of Gnosticism.

3. Syncretism

As attempts had already been made, before Christ, by Philo, by the Therapeutae and the Essenes, etc., to blend the Jewish religion with heathen philosophy, especially that of Pythagoras and Plato, so now, under the Christian name, there appeared confused combinations of these opposite systems, forming either a Paganizing Judaism, i.e., Gnostic Ebionism, or a Judaizing Paganism i.e., Ebionistic Gnosticism, according as the Jewish or the heathen element prevailed.

This Syncretistic heresy was the caricature of John's theology, which truly reconciled Jewish and Gentile Christianity in the highest conception of the person and work of Christ. The errors combated in the later books of the New Testament are almost all more or less of this mixed sort, and it is often doubtful whether they come from Judaism or from heathenism. They were usually shrouded in a shadowy mysticism and surrounded by the halo of a self-made ascetic holiness, but sometimes degenerated into the opposite extreme of antinomian licentiousness.

Conclusion

Whatever their differences, however, all these three fundamental heresies amount at last to a more or less distinct denial of the central truth of the gospel—the incarnation of the Son of God for the salvation of the world. They make Christ either a mere man, or a mere superhuman phantom; they allow, at all events, no real and abiding union of the divine and human in the person of the Redeemer. This is just what John gives as the mark of antichrist, which existed even in his day in various forms. It plainly undermines the foundation of the church. For if Christ be not God-man, neither is he mediator between God and men; Christianity sinks back into heathenism or Judaism. All turns at last on the answer to that fundamental question: "What think ye of Christ?" The true solution of this question is the radical refutation of every error.

Philip Schaff, History of the Christian Church,
Volume I: Apostolic Christianity. AD 1–100

A universal message

As a result of the Council of Jerusalem, it became apparent to the apostles that the Christian faith was no longer tied to Judaism. No one had to be uprooted from their culture to receive the gospel. The early Christians now realized that the Christian message was a global message for the whole world.

Expansion under Paul

Paul carefully planned and led three extensive missionary tours in his quest to spread the Christian message and to strengthen new believers.

Paul's fourth journey led him back to Jerusalem to give James a collection for the church. In order to prove his faithfulness to Jewish traditions he showed himself in the temple and caused a riot and he was arrested. After two years in prison in Caesarea he appealed to the Roman Emperor and was sent to Rome to serve two more years in prison under house arrest where he preached about the kingdom of God and Jesus Christ quite openly. (Acts 28:30–31)

Dr Luke ends his history of the early church with this scene of the most famous missionary-theologian spreading the message of the Christian faith in the capital of the known world—Rome.

The record of expansion in Acts

The two main leaders of the expansion of the Church in Acts were Peter and Paul.

Barnabas and Silas accompanied Paul, and Mark the Evangelist was a disciple of Peter, while Luke the evangelist was a disciple of Paul. Acts

Timothy and Titus were the leaders in Ephesus and Crete, 1Timothy, Titus. Stephen's preaching cost him his life. Phillip preached in Samaria (Acts 8:5).

The record of expansion according to tradition

While the record of the expansion of Christianity is totally trustworthy, the record of the preaching activities of the early Christians, according to tradition, is often uncertain.

According to tradition:

- James the Great went to Spain to evangelize.
- Lazarus was the first bishop of France.
- Andrew and Bartholomew went to evangelize in Greece.
- Andrew went to Kurdistan and preached in the cities of Aksis, Aregnas and Henefores, as well as in Kiev, Russia.
- Bartholomew was martyred in Kalyana, a city state on the west coast of India, near modern-day Bombay.
- Thomas founded Christian churches in Palestine, Mesopotamia, Parthia, Ethiopia and India.
- While many of the above details are not verifiable, it is clear that the early church engaged in continuous evangelization.

The formation of the Christian scriptures

The words and sayings of Jesus are collected and preserved. By the end of the first century the New Testament books are completed.

The twenty-seven New Testament books are:

Historical Books

Matthew

Mark

Luke

John,

Acts

Thirteen letters written by Paul

Romans

1 Corinthians

2 Corinthians

Galatians

Ephesians

Philippians

Colossians

1 Thessalonians

2 Thessalonians

1 Timothy

2 Timothy

Titus

Philemon

Letters not written by Paul
Hebrews
James
1 Peter
2 Peter
1 John
2 John
3 John
Jude
Revelation

The fall of Jerusalem
When the Jews revolted against Roman authority, which resulted in the sacking of Jerusalem in AD 70 Christians do not join in. Rather, they relocated to Pella in Jordan.

Persecution
The Christians in the early church endured severe persecutions from the Roman emperors. Some of them may have taken refuge in the underground Catacombs in Rome.

Catacombs of Rome
The Catacombs of Rome are ancient Jewish and Christian underground burial places near Rome, Italy. Christians revived the practice because they did not want to cremate their dead due to their belief in bodily resurrection. Hence they began to bury their dead, first in simple graves and sometimes in burial vaults of pro-Christian patricians.

The first large-scale catacombs were excavated from the 2nd century onwards. Originally they were carved through soft rock outside the boundaries of the city, because Roman law forbade burial places within city limits. At first they were used both for burial and the memorial services and celebrations of the anniversaries of Christian martyrs (following similar Roman customs).

There are forty known subterranean burial chambers in Rome. They were built along Roman roads, like the Via Appia, the Via Ostiense, the Via Labicana, the Via Tiburtina, and the Via Nomentana. Names of the catacombs – like St Calixtus and St Sebastian alongside Via Appia – refer to martyrs that might be buried there.

Wikipedia

Dreadful persecutions of Christians were inflicted by the Roman Emperor Nero. He blamed Christians for a devastating fire that ravaged the city in AD 64. He used Christians as human torches to illuminate his gardens.

Nero's persecution of Christians

Nero, Claudius Caesar, was emperor from Oct. 13, 54, to June 9, AD 68. During his early reign Christianity was unmolested and seems to have spread rapidly at Rome. No doubt it received a great impetus from the preaching of St. Paul during the two years after his arrival, probably early in 61. But before long a terrible storm was to burst on the infant church.

Fires in Rome

On the night of July 16, AD 64, a fire broke out in the valley between the Palatine and the Aventine. That part of the city was crowded with humble dwellings and shops full of inflammable contents. The lower parts of the city became a sea of flame. For six days the fire raged till it reached the foot of the Esquiline, where it was stopped by pulling down a number of houses.

Soon after a second fire broke out in the gardens of Tigellinus near the Pincian, and raged for three days in the northern parts of the city. Though the loss of life was less in the second fire, the destruction of temples and public buildings was more serious. By the two fires three of the 14 regions were utterly destroyed, four escaped entirely, in the remaining seven but few houses were left standing.

Nero was at Antium when the fire broke out, and did not return to Rome till it had almost reached the vast edifice he had constructed to connect his palace on the Palatine with the gardens of Maecenas on the Esquiline.

The horrible suspicion that Nero himself was the author of the fire gained strength. Whether well founded or not, and whether, supposing it is true, the emperor's motive was to clear away the crooked, narrow streets of the old town in order to rebuild it on a new and regular plan, or whether it was a freak of madness, need not be discussed here. At any rate Nero found it necessary to divert from himself the rage of the people and put the blame upon the Christians.

Tacitus's account

The only author living near the time of the persecution who gives an account of it is Tacitus. After describing the origin of Christianity he proceeds:

> ". . .neither human resources, nor imperial generosity, nor appeasement of the gods, eliminated the sinister suspicion that the fire had been deliberately started. To stop the rumor, Nero, made scapegoats—and punished with every refinement the notoriously depraved Christians (as they were popularly called). Their originator, Christ, had been executed in Tiberius' reign by the Procurator of Judaea, Pontius Pilatus (governor from 26 to 36 AD). But in spite of this temporary setback, the deadly superstition had broken out again, not just in Judaea (where the mischief had started) but even in Rome.

First were arrested those who confessed, then on their information a vast multitude was convicted, not so much on the charge of arson as for their hatred of the human race. Their deaths were made more cruel by the mockery that accompanied them. Some were covered with the skins of wild beasts and torn to pieces by dogs; others perished on the cross or in the flames; and others again were burnt after sunset as torches to light up the darkness. Nero himself granted his gardens (on the Vatican) for the show, and gave an exhibition in the circus, and, dressed as a charioteer, mixed with the people or drove his chariot himself. Thus, guilty and deserving the severest punishment as they were, yet they were pitied, as they seemed to be put to death, not for the benefit of the state but to gratify the cruelty of an individual.

Tacitus, The Annals of Imperial Rome, Book XV, chapter 47 (AD 64)
Henry Wace (1836–1924), Dictionary of Christian Biography and Literature to the End of the Sixth Century AD, *with an Account of the Principal Sects and Heresies*

Foxe's Book of Martyrs

John Foxe opens his famous book with a chapter recording the martyrdoms of Stephen, most of the twelve apostles and other early Christians.

His second chapter is entitled, "The ten primitive persecutions." The first of these is devoted to those who died under the persecution of Nero. The second of these "primitive persecutions" gives details of those martyred during Emperor Domitian's reign. Domitian demanded that everyone, including Christians, should worship him as "Lord and God."

Early persecutions in Foxe's Book of Martyrs

Chapter 1

History of Christian Martyrs to the First General Persecutions

Under Nero

1. St. Stephen

St. Stephen's death was occasioned by the faithful manner in which he preached the Gospel to the betrayers and murderers of Christ. To such a degree of madness were they excited, that they cast him out of the city and stoned him to death. The time when he suffered is generally supposed to have been at the Passover which succeeded to that of our Lord's crucifixion, and to the era of his ascension, in the following spring.

Upon this a great persecution was raised against all who professed their belief in Christ as the Messiah, or as a prophet. We are immediately told by St. Luke, that "there was a great persecution against the church which was at Jerusalem;" and that "they were all scattered abroad throughout the regions of Judaea and Samaria, except the apostles."

About two thousand Christians, with Nicanor, one of the seven deacons, suffered martyrdom during the "persecution that arose about Stephen."

2. James the Great

The next martyr we meet with, according to St. Luke, in the History of the Apostles' Acts, was James the son of Zebedee, the elder brother of John, and a relative of our Lord; for his mother Salome was cousin-german to the Virgin Mary. It was not until ten years after the death of Stephen that the second martyrdom took place; for no sooner had Herod Agrippa been appointed governor of Judea, than, with a view to ingratiate himself with them, he raised a sharp persecution against the Christians, and determined to make an effectual blow, by striking at their leaders. The account given us by an eminent primitive writer, Clemens Alexandrinus, ought not to be overlooked; that, as James was led to the place of martyrdom, his accuser was brought to repent of his conduct by the apostle's extraordinary courage and undauntedness, and fell down at his feet to request his pardon, professing himself a Christian, and resolving that James should not receive the crown of martyrdom alone. Hence they were both beheaded at the same time. Thus did the first apostolic martyr cheerfully and resolutely receive that cup, which he had told our Savior he was ready to drink. Timon and Parmenas suffered martyrdom about the same time; the one at Philippi, and the other in Macedonia. These events took place AD 44.

3. Philip

Was born at Bethsaida, in Galilee and was first called by the name of "disciple." He labored diligently in Upper Asia, and suffered martyrdom at Heliopolis, in Phrygia. He was scourged, thrown into prison, and afterwards crucified, AD 54.

4. Matthew

Whose occupation was that of a toll-gatherer, was born at Nazareth. He wrote his gospel in Hebrew, which was afterwards translated into Greek by James the Less. The scene of his labors was Parthia, and Ethiopia, in which latter country he suffered martyrdom, being slain with a halberd in the city of Nadabah, 60 AD.

5. James the Less

Is supposed by some to have been the brother of our Lord, by a former wife of Joseph. This is very doubtful, and accords too much with the Catholic superstition, that Mary never had any other children except our Savior. He was elected to the oversight of the churches of Jerusalem; and was the author of the Epistle ascribed to James in the sacred canon. At the age of ninety-four he was beaten and stoned by the Jews; and finally had his brains dashed out with a fuller's club.

6. Matthias
Of whom less is known than of most of the other disciples, was elected to fill the vacant place of Judas. He was stoned at Jerusalem and then beheaded.

7. Andrew
Was the brother of Peter. He preached the gospel to many Asiatic nations; but on his arrival at Edessa he was taken and crucified on a cross, the two ends of which were fixed transversely in the ground. Hence the derivation of the term, St. Andrew's Cross.

8. St. Mark
Was born of Jewish parents of the tribe of Levi. He is supposed to have been converted to Christianity by Peter, whom he served as an amanuensis, and under whose inspection he wrote his Gospel in the Greek language. Mark was dragged to pieces by the people of Alexandria, at the great solemnity of Serapis their idol, ending his life under their merciless hands.

9. Peter
Among many other saints, the blessed apostle Peter was condemned to death, and crucified, as some do write, at Rome; albeit some others, and not without cause, do doubt thereof. Hegesippus saith that Nero sought matter against Peter to put him to death; which, when the people perceived, they entreated Peter with much ado that he would fly the city. Peter, through their importunity at length persuaded, prepared himself to avoid. But, coming to the gate, he saw the Lord Christ come to meet him, to whom he, worshipping, said, "Lord, whither dost Thou go?" To whom He answered and said, "I am come again to be crucified." By this, Peter, perceiving his suffering to be understood, returned into the city. Jerome saith that he was crucified, his head being down and his feet upward, himself so requiring, because he was (he said) unworthy to be crucified after the same form and manner as the Lord was.

10. Paul
Paul, the apostle, who before was called Saul, after his great travail and unspeakable labors in promoting the Gospel of Christ, suffered also in this first persecution under Nero. Abdias, declareth that under his execution Nero sent two of his esquires, Ferega and Parthemius, to bring him word of his death. They, coming to Paul instructing the people, desired him to pray for them, that they might believe; who told them that shortly after they should believe and be baptized at His sepulcher. This done, the soldiers came and led him out of the city to the place of execution, where he, after his prayers made, gave his neck to the sword.

11. Jude
The brother of James, was commonly called Thaddeus. He was crucified at Edessa, AD 72.

12. Bartholomew

Preached in several countries, and having translated the Gospel of Matthew into the language of India, he propagated it in that country. He was at length cruelly beaten and then crucified by the impatient idolaters.

13. Thomas

Called Didymus, preached the Gospel in Parthia and India, where exciting the rage of the pagan priests, he was martyred by being thrust through with a spear.

14. Luke

The evangelist, was the author of the Gospel which goes under his name. He traveled with Paul through various countries, and is supposed to have been hanged on an olive tree, by the idolatrous priests of Greece.

15. Simon

Surnamed Zelotes, preached the Gospel in Mauritania, Africa, and even in Britain, in which latter country he was crucified, AD 74.

16. John

The "beloved disciple," was brother to James the Great. The churches of Smyrna, Pergamos, Sardis, Philadelphia, Laodicea, and Thyatira, were founded by him. From Ephesus he was ordered to be sent to Rome, where it is affirmed he was cast into a cauldron of boiling oil. He escaped by miracle, without injury. Domitian afterwards banished him to the Isle of Patmos, where he wrote the Book of Revelation. Nerva, the successor of Domitian, recalled him. He was the only apostle who escaped a violent death.

17. Barnabas

Was of Cyprus, but of Jewish descent, his death is supposed to have taken place about AD 61–63.

And yet, notwithstanding all these continual persecutions and horrible punishments, the Church daily increased, deeply rooted in the doctrine of the apostles and of men apostolical, and watered plenteously with the blood of saints.

Chapter 2

The Ten Primitive Persecutions

The First Persecution, Under Nero, AD 67

The first persecution of the Church took place in the year 67, under Nero, the sixth emperor of Rome. This monarch reigned for the space of five years, with tolerable credit to himself, but then gave way to the greatest extravagancy of temper, and to the most atrocious barbarities. Among other diabolical whims, he ordered that the city of Rome should be set on fire, which order was executed by his officers, guards, and servants. While the imperial city was in flames, he went up to the tower of Macaenas, played upon his harp, sung the song of the burning of Troy, and openly declared that 'he wished the ruin of all things before his death.' Besides the noble pile, called the Circus, many other palaces and houses were consumed; several thousands perished in the flames, were smothered in the smoke, or buried beneath the ruins.

This dreadful conflagration continued nine days; when Nero, finding that his conduct was greatly blamed, and a severe odium cast upon him, determined to lay the whole upon the Christians, at once to excuse himself, and have an opportunity of glutting his sight with new cruelties. This was the occasion of the first persecution; and the barbarities exercised on the Christians were such as even excited the commiseration of the Romans themselves. Nero even refined upon cruelty, and contrived all manner of punishments for the Christians that the most infernal imagination could design. In particular, he had some sewed up in skins of wild beasts, and then worried by dogs until they expired; and others dressed in shirts made stiff with wax, fixed to axletrees, and set on fire in his gardens, in order to illuminate them. This persecution was general throughout the whole Roman Empire; but it rather increased than diminished the spirit of Christianity. In the course of it, St. Paul and St. Peter were martyred.

To their names may be added, Erastus, chamberlain of Corinth; Aristarchus, the Macedonian, and Trophimus, an Ephesians, converted by St. Paul, and fellow-laborer with him, Joseph, commonly called Barsabas, and Ananias, bishop of Damascus; each of the Seventy.

The Second Persecution, Under Domitian, AD 81

The emperor Domitian, who was naturally inclined to cruelty, first slew his brother, and then raised the second persecution against the Christians. In his rage he put to death some of the Roman senators, some through malice; and others to confiscate their estates. He then commanded all the lineage of David be put to death.

Among the numerous martyrs that suffered during this persecution was:

Simeon, bishop of Jerusalem, who was crucified; and
St. John, who was boiled in oil, and afterward banished to Patmos.
Flavia, the daughter of a Roman senator, was likewise banished to Pontus; and a law was made, "That no Christian, once brought before the tribunal, should be exempted from punishment without renouncing his religion."

A variety of fabricated tales were, during this reign, composed in order to injure the Christians. Such was the infatuation of the pagans, that, if famine, pestilence, or earthquakes afflicted any of the Roman provinces, it was laid upon the Christians. These persecutions among the Christians increased the number of informers and many, for the sake of gain, swore away the lives of the innocent.

Another hardship was, that, when any Christians were brought before the magistrates, a test oath was proposed, when, if they refused to take it, death was pronounced against them; and if they confessed themselves Christians, the sentence was the same.

The following were the most remarkable among the numerous martyrs who suffered during this persecution.

Dionysius, the Areopagite, was an Athenian by birth, and educated in all the useful and ornamental literature of Greece. He then traveled to Egypt to study astronomy, and made very particular observations on the great and supernatural eclipse, which happened at the time of our Savior's crucifixion.

The sanctity of his conversation and the purity of his manners recommended him so strongly to the Christians in general, that he was appointed bishop of Athens.

Nicodemus, a benevolent Christian of some distinction, suffered at Rome during the rage of Domitian's persecution.

Protasius and Gervasius were martyred at Milan.

Timothy was the celebrated disciple of St. Paul, and bishop of Ephesus, where he zealously governed the Church until AD 97. At this period, as the pagans were about to celebrate a feast called Catagogion, Timothy, meeting the procession, severely reproved them for their ridiculous idolatry, which so exasperated the people that they fell upon him with their clubs, and beat him in so dreadful a manner that he expired of the bruises two days later.

John Foxe, Book of Martyrs, edited by Forbush, William Byron, 1868–1927

PEOPLE

Peter (?-c. 65)
Paul (c. 1-?65)
John (?-c. 100/101)

Peter

Dates

AD ?-c. 65

Famous for being

The impetuous, courageous follower of Jesus and first leader of the apostolic church

Important writings

Two New Testament letters, 1 Peter and 2 Peter

One of his quotations
"Lord, I am ready to go with you to prison and to death."
Luke 22:33 *NIV*

The Chief of the Apostles was a native of Galilee like Our Lord. As he was fishing on its large lake he was called by Our Lord to be one of His apostles. Peter was poor and unlearned, but candid, eager, and loving. In his heart, first of all, his conviction grew, and then from his lips came the spontaneous confession: "Thou art the Christ, the Son of the living God!" Our Lord chose him and prepared him to be the Rock on which He would build His Church, His Vicar on earth, the Head and Prince of His Apostles, the center and indispensable bond of the Church's unity, the unique channel of all spiritual powers, the guardian and unerring teacher of His truth.

All Scripture is alive with Saint Peter; his name appears no fewer than 160 times in the New Testament. But it is after Pentecost that he stands out in the full grandeur of his office. He sees to the replacement of the fallen disciple; he admits the Jews by thousands into the fold and in the person of Cornelius, opens it to the Gentiles; he founds and for a time rules the Church at Antioch.

J. Dominguez, M.D.

Paul

Dates
c. AD 1-?65

Famous for being
Apostle, missionary, teacher of the Christian faith

Important writing
Paul wrote thirteen letters in the New Testament.

One of his quotations
"So then, King Agrippa, I was not disobedient to the vision from heaven." Acts 26:19

Paul's life in the words of the New Testament

[The King James Version of the Bible is used in this section about Paul's life.]

Apart from Jesus, there is more about Paul in the New Testament than any other person.

1. Paul's background

- Paul was born into a Jewish family in the capital of Cilicia, Tarsus.

I am verily a man which am a Jew, born in Tarsus, a city in Cilicia, yet brought up in this city Jerusalem) at the feet of Gamaliel. Acts 22:3
. . . and taught according to the perfect manner of the law of the fathers, and was zealous toward God, as ye all are this day. Acts 5:34–39

• Paul's original name was Saul. Saul is renamed in Acts 13.
Then Saul, (who also is called Paul,) filled with the Holy Ghost, set his eyes on him . . . Acts 13:9

• He was a member of the tribe of Benjamin.
I say then, Hath God cast away his people? God forbid. For I also am an Israelite, of the seed of Abraham, of the tribe of Benjamin. Rom 11:1

• He kept the laws of Moses perfectly
Concerning zeal, persecuting the church; touching the righteousness which is in the law, blameless. Phil. 3:6

• Paul was a Pharisee, a son of a Pharisee.
But when Paul perceived that the one part were Sadducees, and the other Pharisees, he cried out in the council, Men and brethren, I am a Pharisee, the son of a Pharisee: of the hope and resurrection of the dead I am called in question. Acts 23:6

• He was a tent maker by trade.
And because he was of the same craft, he abode with them, and wrought: for by their occupation they were tentmakers. Acts 18:3

2. Saul the persecutor of Christians

• Saul, the Pharisee, persecuted the early Christians and was responsible for having some of them put to death.
And I persecuted this way unto the death, binding and delivering into prisons both men and women. Acts 22:4
And Saul, yet breathing out threatenings and slaughter against the disciples of the Lord, went unto the high priest, Acts 9:1

Saul's reputation for persecuting Christians went before him.
• *Then Ananias answered, Lord, I have heard by many of this man, how much evil he hath done to thy saints at Jerusalem: And here he hath authority from the chief priests to bind all that call on thy name.* Acts 9:13–14

• Saul silently supported the martyrdom of Stephen. This is the first time Saul is mentioned in the New Testament.
And cast him out of the city, and stoned him: and the witnesses laid down their clothes at a young man's feet, whose name was Saul. Acts 7:58

• Paul, later in life, recalls this incident with great remorse.
And when the blood of thy martyr Stephen was shed, I also was standing by, and consenting unto his death, and kept the raiment of them that slew him. Acts 22:20

3. Saul sees the light

Paul's conversion is recounted three times in Acts.

• On his way to harass the Christians in Damascus Saul is overcome by a seeing a great light.
And as he journeyed, he came near Damascus: and suddenly there shined round about him a light from heaven: Acts 9:3

And it came to pass, that, as I made my journey, and was come nigh unto Damascus about noon, suddenly there shone from heaven a great light round about me. Acts 22:6

• Saul was blinded.
And Saul arose from the earth; and when his eyes were opened, he saw no man: but they led him by the hand, and brought him into Damascus. And he was three days without sight, and neither did eat nor drink. Acts 9:8–9

• Jesus rebukes Saul.
And he fell to the earth, and heard a voice saying unto him, Saul, Saul, why persecutest thou me? And he said, Who art thou, Lord? And the Lord said, I am Jesus whom thou persecutest: it is hard for thee to kick against the pricks. Acts 9:4–5
And I fell unto the ground, and heard a voice saying unto me, Saul, Saul, why persecutest thou me? And I answered, Who art thou, Lord? And he said unto me, I am Jesus of Nazareth, whom thou persecutest. Acts 22:7–8

• Jesus tells Saul to go to Damascus.
And he trembling and astonished said, Lord, what wilt thou have me to do? And the Lord said unto him, Arise, and go into the city, and it shall be told thee what thou must do. Acts 9:6

• In Damascus Saul fasts. and prays.
And he was three days without sight, and neither did eat nor drink. Acts 9:9

• Ananias is used to restore Saul's sight.

And Ananias went his way, and entered into the house; and putting his hands on him said, Brother Saul, the Lord, even Jesus, that appeared unto thee in the way as thou camest, hath sent me, that thou mightest receive thy sight, and be filled with the Holy Ghost. And immediately there fell from his eyes as it had been scales: and he received sight forthwith, and arose, and was baptized. Acts 9:17–18

4. The persecutor Saul becomes the preacher Paul

• Saul is baptized and starts to preach the Christian message.

And straightway he preached Christ in the synagogues, that he is the Son of God. Acts 9:20

• Paul goes to Arabia

Neither went I up to Jerusalem to them which were apostles before me; but I went into Arabia, and returned again unto Damascus. Galatians 1:17

• Paul visits Jerusalem.

Then after three years I went up to Jerusalem to see Peter, and abode with him fifteen days. Galatians 1:18

• Paul goes to Antioch.

And when he had found him, he brought him unto Antioch. And it came to pass, that a whole year they assembled themselves with the church, and taught much people. And the disciples were called Christians first in Antioch. Acts 11:26

5. Paul's three missionary journeys

• Paul's first missionary journey

And when they (Paul & Barnabas) were at Salamis, they preached the word of God in the synagogues of the Jews: and they had also John to their minister. Acts 13:5

And thence sailed to Antioch, from whence they had been recommended to the grace of God for the work which they fulfilled. Acts 14:26

• Paul's second missionary journey

And he went through Syria and Cilicia, confirming the churches. Acts 15:41

And when he had landed at Caesarea, and gone up, and saluted the church, he went down to Antioch. Acts 18:22

- Paul's third missionary journey

And after he had spent some time there, he departed, and went over all the country of Galatia and Phrygia in order, strengthening all the disciples. Acts 18:23

And the next day we that were of Paul's company departed, and came unto Caesarea: and we entered into the house of Philip the evangelist, which was one of the seven; and abode with him. Acts 21:8

6. House arrest

The last picture Luke gives us of Paul depicts him under house arrest, preaching the Christian message to all who visited him, in the most important town of the day—Rome.

See Acts 28:30–31

From sources outside the Bible we learn Paul was released from his house arrest and then visited Spain. He was again arrested and executed by Nero in AD 67.

Clement records the martyrdom of apostles Peter and Paul

Introduction

The *Letter of the Church in Rome to the Church in Corinth* is probably the earliest text in Christian literature after the New Testament. Tradition attributes it to Clement, leader of the church in Rome in AD 95.

Peter's death

Through jealousy and envy the greatest and most righteous pillars of the church were persecuted and contended to their deaths. Let us set before our eyes the good apostles: Peter, who because of unjust jealousy suffered not one or two but many trials, and having thus given his testimony went to the glorious place which was his due.

Paul's death

By reason of jealousy and strife, Paul by his example pointed out the prize of patient endurance. After that he had been seven times in bonds, had been driven into exile, had been stoned, had preached in the East and in the West, he won the noble renown which was the reward of his faith, having taught righteousness unto the whole world, and having reached the farthest bounds of the West and when he had done his testimony before the rulers, so he departed from the world and went unto the holy place, having been found a notable pattern of patient endurance.

Clement, Letter of the Church in Rome to the Church in Corinth 5.

The tombs of Peter and Paul in Rome

[The Christian historian, Eusebius, alludes to Peter and Paul's tombs.]

They say that in the reign of Nero Paul was beheaded at Rome itself, and that Peter likewise was crucified, and this story is confirmed by the association of the names of Peter and Paul with the cemeteries there, which has lasted to this day. That is also affirmed by a churchman called Gaius, who lived in the time of Zephyrinus (AD 199–217), Bishop of the Romans. When discoursing in writing with Proclus, the head of the sect of the Phrygians, Gaius in fact said this of the places where the sacred tabernacles of the said apostles were laid: 'But I myself can point out the trophies of the apostles. For if it is your will to go to the Vatican or to the Ostian way, you will find the trophies of those who founded the church.

Eusebius of Caesarea, Church History, II, 25,5–7.

John

Dates
AD-c. 100/101

Famous for being
"The apostle of love," "the beloved disciple," Jesus' close friend

Important writings
The Gospel that bears his name, three New Testament letters and the book of Revelation

One of his quotations
"Dear friends, since God so loved us, we also ought to love one another."
1 John 4:11

John the Apostle (Theologian)

With Peter and James, St. John belonged to the inner circle of disciples who witnessed such events as the Transfiguration and who fell asleep in the garden of Gesthemane. Thought to have been the youngest of the twelve apostles, John was the son of Zebedee and of Salome, one of the women who went to the tomb to anoint the body of Jesus.

John was a disciple of John the Baptist before being called, with his brother James, to follow Jesus, who gave them the name Boanerges. Many speculations why the two are called sons of thunder exist: the name may refer to their tempers or to the force of their faith.

The gospel of St. John records that John (the disciple whom Jesus loved) stood at the foot of the cross [and was entrusted with the safe-keeping of Jesus' mother, Mary: "When Jesus saw his mother there, and the disciple whom he loved standing nearby, he said to his mother, 'Dear woman, here is your son,' and to the disciple, 'Here is your mother.' From that time on, this disciple took her into his home." John 19:26–17.]

After the Pentecost, John and Peter worked together in the community at Jerusalem. John was a participant in the Council of Jerusalem, at which the church determined that Gentiles are not subject to Mosaic practices.

John is thought to have left Jerusalem after this event to preach in Asia Minor. Polycarp of Smyrna is said to have told Irenæus that John lived in Ephesus until the reign of Trajan. C. AD 95, during the reign of Domitian, John was taken to Rome to stand trial for his faith.

Legends recount that John was sentenced to death by being placed in boiling oil, and that he miraculously escaped.

Domitian exiled John to Patmos, where he had the vision described in the book of Revelation. In addition to his Gospel, John also wrote the three letters, 1 John, 2, John, and 3 John.

According to tradition, when Domitian died in 96, John was released and allowed to return to Ephesus, where he became bishop.

John died c. AD 99 or 100. He was the last of the apostles to die and the only one to have died a natural death.

Copyright © 1998, Karen Rae Keck

John's last words

St. John lived until he was about one hundred years old. In the end he was at last so weak that he could not walk into the church; so he was carried in, and used to say continually to his hearers, "Little children, love one another." Some of them, after a time, began to be tired of hearing this, and asked him why he repeated the words so often, and said nothing else to them. The Apostle answered, "Because it is the Lord's commandment, and if this be done it is enough."

Robertson, J. C., Canon of Canterbury, Sketches of Church History, from 33 AD to the Reformation

Other leading Christians in the apostolic age

Matthew
Luke
Stephen
Clement

Matthew

Apostle and evangelist.

Matthew, the author of the Gospel that bears his name, is spoken of five times in the New Testament; first in Matthew 9:9, when called by Jesus to follow Him, and then four times in the list of the Apostles, where he is mentioned in the seventh (Luke 6:15, and Mark 3:18), and again in the eighth place (Matthew 10:3, and Acts 1:13). The man designated in

Matthew 9:9, as "sitting in the custom house", and "named Matthew" is the same as Levi, recorded in Mark 2:14, and Luke 5:27, as "sitting at the receipt of custom".

The account in the three Synoptics is identical, the vocation of Matthew-Levi being alluded to in the same terms. Hence Levi was the original name of the man who was subsequently called Matthew; the *Maththaios legomenos* of Matthew 9:9, would indicate this. The fact of one man having two names is of frequent occurrence among the Jews. It is probable that *Mattija*, "gift of Iaveh", was the name conferred upon the tax-gatherer by Jesus Christ when He called him to the Apostolate, and by it he was thenceforth known among his Christian brethren, Levi being his original name.

Matthew, the son of Alpheus (Mark 2:14) was a Galilean, although Eusebius informs us that he was a Syrian. As tax-collector at Capharnaum, he collected custom duties for Herod Antipas, and, although a Jew, was despised by the Pharisees, who hated all publicans.

When summoned by Jesus, Matthew arose and followed Him and laid on a feast in his house, where tax-collectors and sinners sat at table with Christ and His disciples. The Pharisees protested about this. But they were rebuked by Jesus with these consoling words: "I came not to call the just, but sinners". No further allusion is made to Matthew in the Gospels, except in the list of the Apostles. As a disciple and an Apostle he then followed Christ, accompanying Him up to the time of His Passion and, in Galilee, was one of the witnesses of His Resurrection. He was also amongst the Apostles who were present at the Ascension, and afterwards withdrew to an upper room, in Jerusalem, praying with Mary, the Mother of Jesus, and with his brethren (Acts 1:10 and 1:14).

Of Matthew's subsequent career we have only inaccurate or legendary data. St. Irenæus tells us that Matthew preached the Gospel among the Hebrews, St. Clement of Alexandria claiming that he did this for fifteen years, and Eusebius maintains that, before going into other countries, he gave them his Gospel in the mother tongue. Ancient writers are not as one as to the countries evangelized by Matthew, but almost all mention Ethiopia to the south of the Caspian Sea (not Ethiopia in Africa).

E. Jacquier, Catholic Encyclopedia, Volume 10

Luke

Luke the Evangelist

Inspired by the Holy Spirit, Luke wrote what has been acclaimed: "the most beautiful book in the world."

In the third Gospel we have the setting of Christ's life in the Roman world, and historical data is given which links our Lord's life with the society in which He lived. Most of the information that we have of the birth and early years of Jesus are in Luke's record. He it is also who depicts our Master in the home and family life of His day. The religious trend of the first century was to keep women and children in a place of inferiority and it is mainly Luke who showed that Jesus ignored the fashion. He emphasizes the place of the gentle and simple things in the purpose of God. All this gives evidence of Luke's wide sympathies, which extend still further when consideration is given to the parables and miracles that are peculiar to his record.

He was interested in the poor and despised, and our Lord's appearance in the synagogue at Nazareth (Luke 4) is an appropriate opening for His ministry. But for Luke's pen we should not have had the great illustrations of compassion given in our Lord's parables of the Good Samaritan and the Prodigal Son. He too retold the striking contrasts between Pharisee and Tax Collector praying in the Temple and the real life study of Simon and the "sinful woman". Luke recognized the evil of racial and class distinction in the parable of the "rich fool" and Dives and Lazarus, and of Jesus' tolerance towards the Samaritans.

As a medical doctor he would be intimately acquainted with human suffering, and his method of recording miracles of healing reflects his knowledge and his sympathy. This is apparent in his description of "a man full of leprosy" in Luke 5.12. In writing of the woman in the crowd who touched the hem of Jesus' garment (Luke 8. 46) he uses a more professional term for the word "virtue" than Mark although this is not clear from the English version. His reference to Peter's mother-in-law as having a "great fever" is similarly the distinguishing mark of a physician. His delicate and restrained treatment of our Lord's experience in Gethsemane is masterly and again there is a singularly professional reference to the "drops of blood" (Luke 22. 44).

However he was not only a scientist and historian; he had great interest in the devotional aspect of the Christian life, and he has been called the first Christian hymnologist. The remarkable poems of Mary in the Magnificat, and of Zachariah at the birth of John the Baptist are a tribute to Luke's diligence. The third Gospel provides us with the greatest insight into our Lord's prayer life, recording some of His prayers and teaching upon the subject. Several of these were at critical points in His ministry, for example when He spent all night in prayer prior to selecting the disciples. In narrating the Transfiguration on the mount, Luke alone informs us that Jesus was praying. Finally, on the cross, the prayer of forgiveness was a precious reflection of our Savior preserved only by Luke.

Bible Fellowship Union

Stephen

First Christian Martyr. Deacon. Preacher.

All we know of him is related in the Acts of the Apostles. While preaching the Gospel in the streets, angry Jews who believed his message to be blasphemy dragged him outside the city, and stoned him to death. In the crowd, on the side of the mob, was a man who would later be known as Saint Paul.

The love that brought Christ from heaven to earth raised Stephen from earth to heaven; shown first in the king, it later shone forth in his soldier. His love of God kept him from yielding to the ferocious mob; his love for his neighbor made him pray for those who were stoning him. Love inspired him to reprove those who erred, to make them amend; love led him to pray for those who stoned him, to save them from punishment.

Love, indeed, is the source of all good things; it is an impregnable defense, and the way that leads to heaven. He who walks in love can neither go astray nor be afraid: love guides him, protects him, and brings him to his journey's end.

My brothers, Christ made love the stairway that would enable all Christians to climb to heaven. Hold fast to it, therefore, in all sincerity, give one another practical proof of it, and by your progress in it, make your ascent together.

Saint Fulgentius of Ruspe, from one of his sermons

John Chrysostom on Stephen's martyrdom

"He mentions the cause of his angelic appearance: `But he, being full of the Holy Spirit, looked up steadfastly into heaven, and saw the glory of God and Jesus standing on the right hand of God. And when he said, "I see the heavens opened, they stopped their ears, and ran upon him with one accord.' And yet in what respect are these things deserving of accusation? `Upon him,' the man who has wrought such miracles, the man who has prevailed over all in speech, the man who can hold such discourse! As if they had got the very thing they wanted, they straightway gave full scope to their rage. `And the witnesses,' he says, `laid down their clothes at the feet of a young man, whose name was Saul. Observe how particularly he relates what concerns Paul, to show thee that the Power which wrought in him was of God. But after all these things, not only did he not believe, but also aimed at Him with a thousand hands: for this is why it says, `And Saul was consenting unto his death.' And this blessed man does not simply pray, but does it with earnestness: `having kneeled down.' Mark his divine death! So long only the Lord permitted the soul to remain in him `And having said this, he fell asleep.'"

John Chrysostom

Clement

Introduction

Clement was bishop of Rome during the last decade of the first century AD. Because he wrote during the apostolic era and may well have personally known St. Peter and St. Paul,. Clement is known as one of the Apostolic Fathers.

Clement is counted as the third bishop of Rome (after the apostles). His predecessors are Linus and Cletus (or Anacletus, or Anencletus), about whom almost nothing is known. They are simply names on a list. Clement is a little more than this, chiefly because he wrote a letter to the Corinthians, which was highly valued by the early church, and has been preserved to the present day. The letter itself does not carry his name, but is merely addressed from the congregation at Rome to the congregation at Corinth. However, a letter from Corinth to Rome a few decades later refers to "the letter we received from your bishop Clement, which we still read regularly." Other early writers are unanimous in attributing the letter to Clement. Perhaps because this letter made his name familiar, he has had an early anonymous sermon (commonly called *II Clement*) attributed to him, and is a character in some early religious romances (e.g. the *Clementine Recognitions*).

One story about Clement is that he was put to death by being tied to an anchor and thrown into the sea. Accordingly, he is often depicted with an anchor, and many churches in port towns intended to minister chiefly to mariners are named for him.

The Epistle of St. Clement to the Corinthians (also called *I Clement*) is commonly dated around 96 AD. The letter is occasioned by the fact that a group of Christians at Corinth had banded together against their leaders and had deposed them from office. Clement writes to tell them that they have behaved badly, and to remind them of the importance of Christian unity and love. He speaks at length of the way in which each kind of official in the church has his own function for the good of the whole. The letter is an important witness to the early Christian understanding of Church government, but an ambiguous witness in that we are never told precisely why the Corinthians had deposed their leaders, and therefore the letter can be read as saying that presbyters ought not to be deposed without reasonable grounds, or as saying that they cannot be deposed on any grounds at all.

James Kiefer

Classic Christian devotional books from the start of the Christian Church

The Epistle of St. Clement to the Corinthians

The Didache

Extracts from Classic Christian devotional books from the start of the Christian Church

The Epistle of St. Clement to the Corinthians: Chapters 16–19

The Didache

The Epistle of St. Clement to the Corinthians

Chapter 17

The Saints as Examples of Humility

17:1 Let us be imitators also of them which went about in goatskins and sheepskins, preaching the coming of Christ.

17:2 We mean Elijah and Elisha and likewise Ezekiel, the prophets, and besides them those men also that obtained a good report.

17:3 Abraham obtained an exceeding good report and was called the friend of God;

17:4 and looking stedfastly on the glory of God, he saith in lowliness of mind, {But I am dust and ashes}.

17:5 Moreover concerning Job also it is thus written;

17:6 {And Job was righteous and unblameable, one that was true and honored God and abstained from all evil}.

17:7 Yet he himself accuseth himself saying, {No man is clean from filth;

17:8 no, not though his life be but for a day}.

17:9 Moses was called {faithful in all His house}, and through his ministration God judged Egypt with the plagues and the torments which befell them.

17:10 Howbeit he also, though greatly glorified, yet spake no proud words, but said, when an oracle was given to him at the bush, {Who am I, that Thou sendest me?

17:11 Nay, I am feeble of speech and slow of tongue}.

17:12 And again he saith, {But I am smoke from the pot}.

Chapter 18

David as an Example of Humility

18:1 But what must we say of David that obtained a good report?

18:2 of whom God said, {I have found a man after My heart, David the son of Jesse:

18:3 with eternal mercy have I anointed him}.

18:4 Yet he too saith unto God;

18:5 {Have mercy upon me, O God, according to Thy great mercy and according to the multitude of Thy compassions, blot out mine iniquity.

18:6 Wash me yet more from mine iniquity, and cleanse me from my sin.

18:7 For I acknowledge mine iniquity, and my sin is ever before me.

18:8 Against Thee only did I sin, and I wrought evil in Thy sight;

18:9 that Thou mayest be justified in Thy words, and mayest conquer in Thy pleading.

18:10 For behold, in iniquities was I conceived, and in sins did my mother bear me.

18:11 For behold Thou hast loved truth the dark and hidden things of Thy wisdom hast Thou showed unto me.

18:12 Thou shalt sprinkle me with hyssop, and I shall be made clean.

18:13 Thou shalt wash me, and I shall become whiter than snow.

18:14 Thou shalt make me to hear of joy and gladness.

18:15 The bones which have been humbled shall rejoice.

18:16 Turn away Thy face from my sins, and blot out all mine iniquities.

18:17 Make a clean heart within me, O God, and renew a right spirit in mine innermost parts.

18:18 Cast me not away from Thy presence, and take not Thy Holy Spirit from me.

18:19 Restore unto me the joy of The salvation, and strengthen me with a princely spirit.

18:20 I will teach sinners Thy ways, and godless men shall be converted unto Thee.

18:21 Deliver me from bloodguiltiness, O God, the God of my salvation.

18:22 My tongue shall rejoice in Thy righteousness.

18:23 Lord, Thou shalt open my mouth, and my lips shall declare Thy praise.

18:24 For, if Thou hadst desired sacrifice, I would have given it:

18:25 in whole burnt offerings Thou wilt have no pleasure.

18:26 A sacrifice unto God is a contrite spirit, a contrite and humbled heart God will not despise}.

Chapter 19

Imitating These Examples, Let Us Seek After Peace

19:1 The humility therefore and the submissiveness of so many and so great men,

19:2 who have thus obtained a good report, hath through obedience made better not only us but also the generations which were before us, even them that received His oracles in fear and truth.

19:3 Seeing then that we have been partakers of many great and glorious doings, let us hasten to return unto the goal of peace which hath been handed down to us from the beginning,

19:4 and let us look stedfastly unto the Father and Maker of the whole world, and cleave unto His splendid and excellent gifts of peace and benefits.

19:5 Let us behold Him in our mind, and let us look with the eyes of our soul unto His long-suffering will.

19:6 Let us note how free from anger He is towards all His creatures.

The Epistle of St. Clement to the Corinthians
Translated and edited, J. B. Lightfoot

The Didache

Alternate title: The Teaching of the Twelve Apostles

Introduction

No document of the early church has proved so bewildering to scholars as this apparently innocent tract which was discovered by Philotheos Byrennios in 1873. The Didache (Teaching") is the common name of a brief early Christian treatise (c. 50–160). Some scholars date its writing to as early as 60 AD and so place it as the oldest surviving extant piece of non-canonical literature. Other scholars believe that it was written in Egypt or Syria early in the second century.

It is not so much a letter as a handbook for new Christian converts, consisting of instructions derived directly from the teachings of Jesus. The book can be divided into three sections—the first six chapters consist of catechetical lessons; the next four give descriptions of the liturgy, including baptism, fasting and communion; and the last six outline the church organization.

The famous church historian, Phillip Schaff, ranks the Didache as first among the works of the post-apostolic age.

The Didache

CHAPTER 1

1:1 There are two paths, one of life and one of death, and the difference is great between the two paths.

1:2 Now the path of life is this—first, thou shalt love the God who made thee, thy neighbor as thyself, and all things that thou wouldest not should be done unto thee, do not thou unto another.

1:3 And the doctrine of these maxims is as follows. Bless them that curse you, and pray for your enemies. Fast on behalf of those that persecute you; for what thank is there if ye love them that love you? Do not even the Gentiles do the same? But do ye love them that hate you, and ye will not have an enemy.

1:4 Abstain from fleshly and worldly lusts. If any one give thee a blow on thy right cheek, turn unto him the other also, and thou shalt be perfect; if any one compel thee to go a mile, go with him two; if a man take away thy cloak, give him thy coat also; if a man take from thee what is thine, ask not for it again, for neither art thou able to do so.

1:5 Give to every one that asketh of thee, and ask not again; for the Father wishes that from his own gifts there should be given to all. Blessed is he who giveth according to the commandment, for he is free from guilt; but woe unto him that receiveth. For if a man receive being in need, he shall be free from guilt; but he who receiveth when not in need, shall pay a penalty as to why he received and for what purpose; and when he is in tribulation he shall be examined concerning the things that he has done, and shall not depart thence until he has paid the last farthing.

1:6 For of a truth it has been said on these matters, let thy almsgiving abide in thy hands until thou knowest to whom thou hast given.

CHAPTER 2

2:1 But the second commandment of the teaching is this.

2:2 Thou shalt not kill; thou shalt not commit adultery; thou shalt not corrupt youth; thou shalt not commit fornication; thou shalt not steal; thou shalt not use soothsaying; thou shalt not practice sorcery; thou shalt not kill a child by abortion, neither shalt thou slay it when born; thou shalt not covet the goods of thy neighbor;

2:3 thou shalt not commit perjury; thou shalt not bear false witness; thou shalt not speak evil; thou shalt not bear malice;

2:4 thou shalt not be double-minded or double-tongued, for to be double tongued is the snare of death.

2:5 Thy speech shall not be false or empty, but concerned with action.

2:6 Thou shalt not be covetous, or rapacious, or hypocritical, or malicious, or proud; thou shalt not take up an evil design against thy neighbor;

2:7 thou shalt not hate any man, but some thou shalt confute, concerning some thou shalt pray, and some thou shalt love beyond thine own soul.

CHAPTER 3

3:1 My child, fly from everything that is evil, and from everything that is like to it.

3:2 Be not wrathful, for wrath leadeth unto slaughter; be not jealous, or contentious, or quarrelsome, for from all these things slaughter ensues.

3:3 My child, be not lustful, for lust leadeth unto fornication; be not a filthy talker; be not a lifter up of the eye, for from all these things come adulteries.

3:4 My child, be not an observer of omens, since it leadeth to idolatry, nor a user of spells, nor an astrologer, nor a traveling purifier, nor wish to see these things, for from all these things idolatry ariseth.

3:5 My child, be not a liar, for lying leadeth unto theft; be not covetous or conceited, for from all these things thefts arise.

3:6 My child, be not a murmurer, since it leadeth unto blasphemy; be not self-willed or evil-minded, for from all these things blasphemies are produced;

3:7 but be thou meek, for the meek shall inherit the earth;

3:8 be thou longsuffering, and compassionate, and harmless, and peaceable, and good, and fearing alway the words that thou hast heard.

3:9 Thou shalt not exalt thyself, neither shalt thou put boldness into thy soul. Thy soul shall not be joined unto the lofty, but thou shalt walk with the just and humble.

3:10 Accept the things that happen to thee as good, knowing that without God nothing happens.

CHAPTER 4

4:1 My child, thou shalt remember both night and day him that speaketh unto thee the Word of God; thou shalt honor him as thou dost the Lord, for where the teaching of the Lord is given, there is the Lord;

4:2 thou shalt seek out day by day the favor of the saints, that thou mayest rest in their words;

4:3 thou shalt not desire schism, but shalt set at peace them that contend; thou shalt judge righteously; thou shalt not accept the person of any one to convict him of transgression;

4:4 thou shalt not doubt whether a thing shall be or not.

4:5 Be not a stretcher out of thy hand to receive, and a drawer of it back in giving.

4:6 If thou hast, give by means of thy hands a redemption for thy sins.

4:7 Thou shalt not doubt to give, neither shalt thou murmur when giving; for thou shouldest know who is the fair recompenser of the reward.

4:8 Thou shalt not turn away from him that is in need, but shalt share with thy brother in all things, and shalt not say that things are thine own; for if ye are partners in what is immortal, how much more in what is mortal?

4:9 Thou shalt not remove thine heart from thy son or from thy daughter, but from their youth shalt teach them the fear of God.

4:10 Thou shalt not command with bitterness thy servant or thy handmaid, who hope in the same God as thyself, lest they fear not in consequence the God who is over both; for he cometh not to call with respect of persons, but those whom the Spirit hath prepared.

4:11 And do ye servants submit yourselves to your masters with reverence and fear, as being the type of God.

4:12 Thou shalt hate all hypocrisy and everything that is not pleasing to God;

4:13 thou shalt not abandon the commandments of the Lord, but shalt guard that which thou hast received, neither adding thereto nor taking therefrom;

4:14 thou shalt confess thy transgressions in the Church, and shalt not come unto prayer with an evil conscience. This is the path of life.

CHAPTER 5

5:1 But the path of death is this. First of all, it is evil, and full of cursing; there are found murders, adulteries, lusts, fornication, thefts, idolatries, soothsaying, sorceries, robberies, false witnessings, hypocrisies, double-mindedness, craft, pride, malice, self-will, covetousness, filthy talking, jealousy, audacity, pride, arrogance;

5:2 there are they who persecute the good—lovers of a lie, not knowing the reward of righteousness, not cleaving to the good nor to righteous judgment, watching not for the good but for the bad, from whom meekness and patience are afar off, loving things that are vain, following after recompense, having no compassion on the needy, nor laboring for him that is in trouble, not knowing him that made them, murderers of children, corrupters of the image of God, who turn away from him that is in need, who oppress him that is in trouble, unjust judges of the poor, erring in all things. From all these, children, may ye be delivered.

CHAPTER 6

6:1 See that no one make thee to err from this path of doctrine, since he who doeth so teacheth thee apart from God.

6:2 If thou art able to bear the whole yoke of the Lord, thou wilt be perfect; but if thou art not able, what thou art able, that do.

6:3 But concerning meat, bear that which thou art able to do. But keep with care from things sacrificed to idols, for it is the worship of the infernal deities.

CHAPTER 7

7:1 But concerning baptism, thus baptize ye: having first recited all these precepts, baptize in the name of the Father, and of the Son, and of the Holy Spirit, in running water;

7:2 but if thou hast not running water, baptize in some other water, and if thou canst not baptize in cold, in warm water;

7:3 but if thou hast neither, pour water three times on the head, in the name of the Father, and of the Son, and of the Holy Spirit.

7:4 But before the baptism, let him who baptizeth and him who is baptized fast previously, and any others who may be able. And thou shalt command him who is baptized to fast one or two days before.

CHAPTER 8

8:1 But as for your fasts, let them not be with the hypocrites, for they fast on the second and fifth days of the week, but do ye fast on the fourth and sixth days.

8:2 Neither pray ye as the hypocrites, but as the Lord hath commanded in his gospel so pray ye: Our Father in heaven, hallowed be thy name. Thy kingdom come. Thy will be done as in heaven so on earth. Give us this day our daily bread. And forgive us our debt, as we also forgive our debtors. And lead us not into temptation, but deliver us from the evil: for thine is the power, and the glory, for ever.

8:3 Thrice a day pray ye in this fashion.

CHAPTER 9

9:1 But concerning the Eucharist, after this fashion give ye thanks.

9:2 First, concerning the cup. We thank thee, our Father, for the holy vine, David thy Son, which thou hast made known unto us through Jesus Christ thy Son; to thee be the glory for ever.

9:3 And concerning the broken bread. We thank thee, our Father, for the life and knowledge which thou hast made known unto us through Jesus thy Son; to thee be the glory for ever.

9:4 As this broken bread was once scattered on the mountains, and after it had been brought together became one, so may thy Church be gathered together from the ends of the earth unto thy kingdom; for thine is the glory, and the power, through Jesus Christ, for ever.

9:5 And let none eat or drink of your Eucharist but such as have been baptized into the name of the Lord, for of a truth the Lord hath said concerning this, Give not that which is holy unto dogs.

CHAPTER 10

10:1 But after it has been completed, so pray ye.

10:2 We thank thee, holy Father, for thy holy name, which thou hast caused to dwell in our hearts, and for the knowledge and faith and immortality which thou hast made known unto us through Jesus thy Son; to thee be the glory for ever.

10:3 Thou, Almighty Master, didst create all things for the sake of thy name, and hast given both meat and drink, for men to enjoy, that we might give thanks unto thee, but to us thou hast given spiritual meat and drink, and life everlasting, through thy Son.

10:4 Above all, we thank thee that thou art able to save; to thee be the glory for ever.

10:5 Remember, Lord, thy Church, to redeem it from every evil, and to perfect it in thy love, and gather it together from the four winds, even that which has been sanctified for thy kingdom which thou hast prepared for it; for thine is the kingdom and the glory for ever.

10:6 Let grace come, and let this world pass away. Hosanna to the Son of David. If any one is holy let him come (to the Eucharist); if any one is not, let him repent. Maranatha. Amen.

10:7 But charge the prophets to give thanks, so far as they are willing to do so.

CHAPTER 11

11:1 Whosoever, therefore, shall come and teach you all these things aforesaid, him do ye receive;

11:2 but if the teacher himself turn and teach another doctrine with a view to subvert you, hearken not to him; but if he come to add to your righteousness, and the knowledge of the Lord, receive him as the Lord.

11:3 But concerning the apostles and prophets, thus do ye according to the doctrine of the Gospel.

11:4 Let every apostle who cometh unto you be received as the Lord.

11:5 He will remain one day, and if it be necessary, a second; but if he remain three days, he is a false prophet.

11:6 And let the apostle when departing take nothing but bread until he arrive at his resting-place; but if he ask for money, he is a false prophet.

11:7 And ye shall not tempt or dispute with any prophet who speaketh in the spirit; for every sin shall be forgiven, but this sin shall not be forgiven.

11:8 But not every one who speaketh in the spirit is a prophet, but he is so who hath the disposition of the Lord; by their dispositions they therefore shall be known, the false prophet and the prophet.

11:9 And every prophet who ordereth in the spirit that a table shall be laid, shall not eat of it himself, but if he do otherwise, he is a false prophet;

11:10 and every prophet who teacheth the truth, if he do not what he teacheth is a false prophet;

11:11 and every prophet who is approved and true, and ministering in the visible mystery of the Church, but who teacheth not others to do the things that he doth himself, shall not be judged of you, for with God lieth his judgment, for in this manner also did the ancient prophets.

11:12 But whoever shall say in the spirit, Give me money, or things of that kind, listen not to him; but if he tell you concerning others that are in need that ye should give unto them, let no one judge him.

CHAPTER 12

12:1 Let every one that cometh in the name of the Lord be received, but afterwards ye shall examine him and know his character, for ye have knowledge both of good and evil.

12:2 If the person who cometh be a wayfarer, assist him so far as ye are able; but he will not remain with you more than two or three days, unless there be a necessity.

12:3 But if he wish to settle with you, being a craftsman, let him work, and so eat;

12:4 but if he know not any craft, provide ye according to you own discretion, that a Christian may not live idle among you;

12:5 but if he be not willing to do so, he is a trafficker in Christ. From such keep aloof.

CHAPTER 13

13:1 But every true prophet who is willing to dwell among you is worthy of his meat,

13:2 likewise a true teacher is himself worthy of his meat, even as is a laborer.

13:3 Thou shalt, therefore, take the firstfruits of every produce of the wine-press and threshing-floor, of oxen and sheep, and shalt give it to the prophets, for they are your chief priests;

13:4 but if ye have not a prophet, give it unto the poor.

13:5 If thou makest a feast, take and give the firstfruits according to the commandment;

13:6 in like manner when thou openest a jar of wine or of oil, take the firstfruits and give it to the prophets;

13:7 take also the firstfruits of money, of clothes, and of every possession, as it shall seem good unto thee, and give it according to the commandment.

CHAPTER 14

14:1 But on the Lord's day, after that ye have assembled together, break bread and give thanks, having in addition confessed your sins, that your sacrifice may be pure.

14:2 But let not any one who hath a quarrel with his companion join with you, until they be reconciled, that your sacrifice may not be polluted,

14:3 for it is that which is spoken of by the Lord. In every place and time offer unto me a pure sacrifice, for I am a great King, saith the Lord, and my name is wonderful among the Gentiles.

CHAPTER 15

15:1 Elect, therefore, for yourselves bishops and deacons worthy of the Lord, men who are meek and not covetous, and true and approved, for they perform for you the service of prophets and teachers.

15:2 Do not, therefore, despise them, for they are those who are honored among you, together with the prophets and teachers.

15:3 Rebuke one another, not in wrath but peaceably, as ye have commandment in the Gospel; and, but let no one speak to any one who walketh disorderly with regard to his neighbor, neither let him be heard by you until he repent.

15:4 But your prayers and your almsgivings and all your deeds so do, as ye have commandment in the Gospel of our Lord.

CHAPTER 16

16:1 Watch concerning your life; let not your lamps be quenched or your loins be loosed, but be ye ready, for ye know not the hour at which our Lord cometh.

16:2 But be ye gathered together frequently, seeking what is suitable for your souls; for the whole time of your faith shall profit you not, unless ye be found perfect in the last time.

16:3 For in the last days false prophets and seducers shall be multiplied, and the sheep shall be turned into wolves, and love shall be turned into hate;

16:4 and because iniquity aboundeth they shall hate each other, and persecute each other, and deliver each other up; and then shall the Deceiver of the world appear as the Son of God, and shall do signs and wonders, and the earth shall be delivered into his hands; and he shall do unlawful things, such as have never happened since the beginning of the world.

16:5 Then shall the creation of man come to the fiery trial of proof, and many shall be offended and shall perish; but they who remain in their faith shall be saved by the rock of offence itself.

16:6 And then shall appear the signs of the truth; first the sign of the appearance in heaven, then the sign of the sound of the trumpet, and thirdly the resurrection of the dead

16:7—not of all, but as it has been said, The Lord shall come and all his saints with him;

16:8 then shall the world behold the Lord coming on the clouds of heaven.

Didache, translated by Charles H. Hoole

CHAPTER 2

EXPANSION AND PERSECUTION

From Ignatius of Antioch to Cyprian
AD 101–310

Important dates in the time of expansion and persecution

110 Marcion, the heretic, is born
116 Martyrdom of Ignatius
117 Persecution of Christians under Hadrian begins; lasts 21 years
150 Justin Martyr writes his *First Apology*
166 Martyrdoms of Justin and Polycarp
168 Montanus publishes his heresy
177 Persecution at Lyons and Vienne
177 Irenaeus becomes bishop of Lyons and combats developing heresies within the Church
190 Tertullian flourishes
202 Persecution by Severus begins
206 Martyrdom of Perpetua and her companions
248 Cyprian, bishop of Carthage
249 Persecution by Decius
251 Paul, the first hermit
251 Troubles at Carthage; Novatian schism
254 Death of Origen
254 Disagreement between Cyprian and Stephen of Rome
257 Persecution by Valerian
258 Martyrdom of Cyprian
260 Conversion of the Goths begins
270 Manes publishes his heresy
270 Antony gives away his possessions and begins life as a hermit
298 Diocletian requires idolatry from soldiers
303 The last general persecution begins

Introduction

This chapter on the expansion of Christianity and the persecution of Christians contains the history of Christianity from the end of the Apostolic age to the beginning of the Nicene.

The first Edict of Toleration, 311, brought the persecution on Christians to an end; the second Edict of Toleration, 311, prepared the way for legal recognition and protection; and the Nicene Council, 325, marks the solemn inauguration of the imperial state-church.

EVENTS

Important events during the time of expansion and persecution

Crusades
Great schism (*Filioque* clause)
Scholasticism

PEOPLE

Christian leaders during the time of expansion and persecution

Ignatius of Antioch (? – c. 98/110)
Justin Martyr (100–165)
Irenaeus (c. 130–202)
Tertullian (155–230)
Origen (185–254)
Cyprian (200–258)

An historian's overview of the time of expansion and persecution

General character of Ante-Nicene Christianity

We now descend from the primitive apostolic church to the Graeco-Roman; from the scene of creation to the work of preservation; from the fountain of divine revelation to the stream of human development; from the inspirations of the apostles and prophets to the productions of enlightened but fallible teachers. The hand of God has drawn a bold line of demarcation between the century of miracles and the succeeding ages, to show, by the abrupt transition and the striking contrast, the difference between the work of God and the work of man, and to impress us the more deeply with the supernatural origin of Christianity and the incomparable value of the New Testament.

There is no other transition in history so radical and sudden, and yet so silent and secret. The stream of divine life in its passage from the mountain of inspiration to the valley of tradition is for a short time lost to our view, and seems to run under ground. Hence the close of the first and the beginning of the second centuries, or the age of the Apostolic Fathers is often regarded as a period for critical conjecture and doctrinal and ecclesiastical controversy rather than for historical narration.

Still, notwithstanding the striking difference, the church of the second and third centuries is a legitimate continuation of that of the primitive age. While far inferior in originality, purity, energy, and freshness, it is distinguished for conscientious fidelity in preserving and propagating the sacred writings and traditions of the apostles, and for untiring zeal in imitating their holy lives amidst the greatest difficulties and dangers, when the religion of Christ was prohibited by law and the profession of it punished as a political crime.

The second period, from the death of the apostle John to the end of the persecutions, or to the accession of Constantine, the first Christian emperor, is the classic age of the ecclesia pressa, of heathen persecution, and of Christian martyrdom and heroism, of cheerful sacrifice of possessions and life itself for the inheritance of heaven. It furnishes a continuous commentary on the Savior's words: "Behold, I send you forth as sheep in the midst of wolves; I came not to send peace on earth, but a sword." Matthew 10:16; Rom. 8:36; Phil. 3:10 sq. Col. 1:24 sq.; 1 Pet. 2:21 To merely human religion could have stood such an ordeal of fire for three hundred years. The final victory of Christianity over Judaism and heathenism, and the mightiest empire of the ancient world, a victory gained without physical force, but by the moral power of patience and perseverance, of faith and love, is one of the sublimest spectacles in history, and one of the strongest evidences of the divinity and indestructible life of our religion.

But equally sublime and significant are the intellectual and spiritual victories of the church in this period over the science and art of heathenism, and over the assaults of Gnostic and Ebionitic heresy, with the copious vindication and development of the Christian truth, which the great mental conflict with those open and secret enemies called forth.

The church of this period appears poor in earthly possessions and honors, but rich in heavenly grace, in world-conquering faith, love, and hope; unpopular, even outlawed, hated, and persecuted, yet far more vigorous and expansive than the philosophies of Greece or the empire of Rome; composed chiefly of persons of the lower social ranks, yet attracting the noblest and deepest minds of the age, and bearing, in her bosom the hope of the world; "as unknown, yet well-known, as dying, and behold it lives;" conquering by apparent defeat, and growing on the blood of her martyrs; great in deeds, greater in sufferings, greatest in death for the honor of Christ and the benefit of generations to come, as well as affection; for theirs was the fervor of a steady faith in things unseen and eternal; theirs, often, a meek patience under the most grievous wrongs; theirs the courage to maintain a good profession before the frowning face of philosophy, of secular tyranny, and of splendid superstition; theirs was abstractedness from the world and a painful self-denial; theirs the most arduous and costly labors of love; theirs a munificence in charity, altogether without example; theirs was a reverent and scrupulous care of the sacred writings; and this one merit, if they had no other, is of a superlative degree, and should entitle them to the veneration and grateful regards of the modern church. How little do many readers of the Bible, nowadays, think of what it cost the Christians of the second and third centuries, merely to rescue and hide the sacred treasures from the rage of the heathen!"

The condition and manners of the Christians in this age are most beautifully described by the unknown author of the *Epistle to Diognetus* in the early part of the second century.

The Christians are not distinguished from other men by country, by language, nor by civil institutions. For they neither dwell in cities by themselves, nor use a peculiar tongue, nor lead a singular mode of life.

They dwell in the Grecian or barbarian cities, as the case may be; they follow the usage of the country in dress, food, and the other affairs of life. Yet they present a wonderful and confessedly paradoxical conduct.

They dwell in their own native lands, but as strangers.

They take part in all things as citizens; and they suffer all things, as foreigners. Every foreign country is a fatherland to them, and every native land is a foreign. . . .

They marry, like all others; they have children; but they do not cast away their offspring.

They have the table in common, but not wives.

They are in the flesh, but do not live after the flesh.

They live upon the earth, but are citizens of heaven.

They obey the existing laws, and excel the laws by their lives.

They love all, and are persecuted by all.

They are unknown, and yet they are condemned.

They are killed and are made alive.

They are poor and make many rich.

They lack all things, and in all things abound.

They are reproached, and glory in their reproaches.

They are calumniated, and are justified.

They are cursed, and they bless.

They receive scorn, and they give honor.

They do good, and are punished as evil-doers.

When punished, they rejoice, as being made alive. By the Jews they are attacked as aliens, and by the Greeks persecuted; and the cause of the enmity their enemies cannot tell.

In short, what the soul is in the body, the Christians are in the world. The soul is diffused through all the members of the body, and the Christians are spread through the cities of the world. The soul dwells in the body, but it is not of the body; so the Christians dwell in the world, but are not of the world. The soul, invisible, keeps watch in the visible body; so also the Christians are seen to live in the world, but their piety is invisible. The flesh hates and wars against the soul, suffering no wrong from it, but because it resists fleshly pleasures; and the world hates the Christians with no reason, but that they resist its pleasures. The soul loves the flesh and members, by which it is hated; so the Christians love their haters. The soul is enclosed in the body, but holds the body together; so the Christians are detained in the world as in a prison; but they contain the world. Immortal, the soul dwells in the mortal body; so the Christians dwell in the corruptible, but look for incorruption in heaven. The soul is the better for restriction in food and drink; and the Christians increase, though daily punished. This lot God has assigned to the Christians in the world; and it cannot be taken from them.

The community of Christians thus from the first felt itself, distinct from Judaism and from heathenism, the salt of the earth, the light of the world, the city of God set on a hill, the immortal soul in a dying body; and this its impression respecting itself was no proud conceit, but truth and reality, acting in life and in death, and opening the way through hatred and persecution even to an outward victory over the world.

The ante-Nicene age has been ever since the Reformation a battle-field between Catholic and Evangelical historians and polemics, and is claimed by both for their respective creeds. But it is a sectarian abuse of history to identify the Christianity of this martyr period either with Catholicism, or with Protestantism. It is rather the common root out of which both have sprung, Catholicism (Greek and Roman) first, and Protestantism afterwards. It is the natural transition from the apostolic age to the Nicene age, yet leaving behind many important truths of the former (especially the Pauline doctrines) which were to be derived and explored in future ages. We can trace in it the elementary forms of the Catholic creed, organization and worship, and also the germs of nearly all the corruptions of Greek and Roman Christianity.

In its relation to the secular power, the ante-Nicene church is simply the continuation of the apostolic period, and has nothing in common either with the hierarchical, or with the Erastian systems. It was not opposed to the secular government in its proper sphere, but the secular heathenism of the government was opposed to Christianity. The church was altogether based upon the voluntary principle, as a self-supporting and self-governing body. In this respect it may be compared to the church in the United States, but with this essential difference that in America the secular government, instead of persecuting Christianity, recognizes and protects it by law, and secures to it full freedom of public worship and in all its activities at home and abroad.

The theology of the second and third centuries was mainly apologetic against the paganism of Greece and Rome, and polemic against the various forms of the Gnostic heresy. In this conflict it brings out, with great force and freshness, the principal arguments for the divine origin and character of the Christian religion and the outlines of the true doctrine of Christ and the holy trinity, as afterwards more fully developed in the Nicene and post-Nicene ages.

The organization of this period may be termed primitive episcopacy, as distinct from the apostolic order which preceded, and the metropolitan and patriarchal hierarchy which succeeded it. In worship it forms likewise the transition from apostolic simplicity to the liturgical and ceremonial splendor of full-grown Catholicism.

The first half of the second century is comparatively veiled in obscurity, although considerable light has been shed over it by recent discoveries and investigations. After the death of John only a few witnesses remain to testify of the wonders of the apostolic days, and their writings are few in number, short in compass and partly of doubtful origin: a volume of letters and historical fragments, accounts of martyrdom, the pleadings of two or three apologists; to which must be added the rude epitaphs, faded pictures, and broken sculptures of the subterranean church in the catacombs. The men of that generation were more skilled in acting out Christianity in life and death, than in its literary defense. After the intense commotion of the apostolic age there was a breathing spell, a season of unpretending but fruitful preparation for a new productive epoch. But the soil of heathenism had been broken up, and the new seed planted by the hands of the apostles gradually took root.

Then came the great literary conflict of the apologists and doctrinal polemics in the second half of the same century; and towards the middle of the third the theological schools of Alexandria, and northern Africa, laying the foundation the one for the theology of the Greek, the other for that of the Latin church. At the beginning of the fourth century the church east and west was already so well consolidated in doctrine and discipline that it easily survived the shock of the last and most terrible persecution, and could enter upon the fruits of its long-continued sufferings and take the reins of government in the old Roman empire.

Philip Schaff, History of the Christian Church,
Volume II: Ante-Nicene Christianity. AD 100–325

An introduction to the Fathers

As Christianity is primarily a religion of divine facts, and a new moral creation, the literary and scientific element in its history held, at first, a secondary and subordinate place. Of the apostles, Paul alone received a learned education, and even he made his rabbinical culture and great natural talents subservient to the higher spiritual knowledge imparted to him by revelation. But for the very reason that it is a new life, Christianity must produce also a new science and literature; partly from the inherent impulse of faith towards deeper and clearer knowledge of its object for its own satisfaction; partly from the demands of self-preservation against assaults from without; partly from the practical want of instruction and direction for the people. The church also gradually appropriated the classical culture, and made it tributary to her theology. Throughout the middle ages she was almost the sole vehicle and guardian of literature and art, and she is the mother of the best elements of the modern European and American civilization.

The ecclesiastical learning of the first six centuries was cast almost entirely in the mould of the Graeco-Roman culture. The earliest church fathers, even Clement of Rome, Hermas, and Hippolytus, who lived and labored in and about Rome, used the Greek language, after the example of the apostles, with such modifications as the Christian ideas required. Not till the end of the second century, and then not in Italy, but in North Africa, did the Latin language also become, through Tertullian, a medium of Christian science and literature. The Latin church, however, continued for a long time dependent on the learning of the Greek. The Greek church was more excitable, speculative, and dialectic; the Latin more steady, practical, and devoted to outward organization; though we have on both sides striking exceptions to this rule, in the Greek Chrysostom, who was the greatest pulpit orator, and the Latin Augustin, who was the profoundest speculative theologian among the fathers.

The patristic literature in general falls considerably below the classical in elegance of form, but far surpasses it in the sterling quality of its matter. It wears the servant form of its master, during the days of his flesh, not the splendid, princely garb of this world. Confidence in the power of the Christian truth made men less careful of the form in which they presented it. Besides, many of the oldest Christian writers lacked early education, and had a certain aversion to art, from its manifold perversion in those days to the service of idolatry and immorality. But some of them, even in the second and third centuries, particularly Clement and Origen, stood at the head of their age in learning and philosophical culture; and in the fourth and fifth centuries, the literary productions of an Athanasius, a Gregory, a Chrysostom, an Augustin, and a Jerome, excelled the contemporaneous heathen literature in every respect. Many fathers, like the two Clements, Justin Martyr, Athenagoras, Theophilus, Tertullian, Cyprian, and among the later ones, even Jerome and Augustin, embraced Christianity after attaining adult years; and it is interesting to notice with what enthusiasm, energy, and thankfulness they laid hold upon it.

The term "church-father" originated in the primitive custom of transferring the idea of father to spiritual relationships, especially to those of teacher, priest, and bishop. In the case before us the idea necessarily includes that of antiquity, involving a certain degree of general authority for all subsequent periods and single branches of the church. Hence this title of honor is justly limited to the more distinguished teachers of the first five or six centuries, excepting, of course, the apostles, who stand far above them all as the inspired organs of Christ. It applies, therefore, to the period of the oecumenical formation of doctrines, before the separation of Eastern and Western Christendom. The line of the Latin fathers is generally closed with Pope Gregory I. (d. 604), the line of the Greek with John of Damascus (d. about 754).

Besides antiquity, or direct connection with the formative age of the whole church, learning, holiness, orthodoxy, and the approbation of the church, or general recognition, are the qualifications for a church father. These qualifications, however, are only relative. At least we cannot apply the scale of fully developed orthodoxy, whether Greek, Roman, or Evangelical, to the ante-Nicene fathers. Their dogmatic conceptions were often very indefinite and uncertain. In fact the Roman church excludes a Tertullian for his Montanism, an Origen for his Platonic and idealistic views, an Eusebius for his semi-Arianism, also Clement of Alexandria, Lactantius, Theodoret, and other distinguished divines, from the list of "fathers" (*Patres*), and designates them merely "ecclesiastical writers" (*Scriptores Ecclastici*).

In strictness, not a single one of the ante-Nicene fathers fairly agrees with the Roman standard of doctrine in all points. Even Irenaeus and Cyprian differed from the Roman bishop, the former in reference to Chiliasm and Montanism, the latter on the validity of heretical baptism. Jerome is a strong witness against the canonical value of the Apocrypha. Augustin, the greatest authority of Catholic theology among the fathers, is yet decidedly evangelical in his views on sin and grace, which were enthusiastically revived by Luther and Calvin, and virtually condemned by the Council of Trent. Pope Gregory the Great repudiated the title "ecumenical bishop" as an antichristian assumption, and yet it is comparatively harmless as compared with the official titles of his successors, who claim to be the Vicars of Christ, the vice-regents of God Almighty on earth, and the infallible organs of the Holy Ghost in all matters of faith and discipline. None of the ancient fathers and doctors knew anything of the modern Roman dogmas of the immaculate conception (1854) and papal infallibility (1870). The "unanimous consent of the fathers" is a mere illusion, except on the most fundamental articles of general Christianity. We must resort here to a liberal conception of orthodoxy, and duly consider the necessary stages of progress in the development of Christian doctrine in the, church.

On the other hand the theology of the fathers still less accords with the Protestant standard of orthodoxy. We seek in vain among them for the evangelical doctrines of the exclusive authority of the Scriptures, justification by faith alone, the universal priesthood of the laity; and we find instead as early as the second century a high estimate of ecclesiastical traditions, meritorious and even over-meritorious works, and strong sacerdotal, sacramentarian, ritualistic, and ascetic tendencies, which gradually matured in the Greek and Roman types of catholicity. The Church of England always had more sympathy with the fathers than the Lutheran and Calvinistic Churches, and professes to be in full harmony with the creed, the episcopal polity, and liturgical worship of antiquity before the separation of the east and the west; but the difference is only one of degree; the Thirty-Nine Articles are as thoroughly evangelical as the Augsburg Confession or the Westminster standards; and even the modern Anglo-Catholic school, the most churchly and churchy of all, ignores many tenets and usages which were considered of vital importance in the first centuries, and holds others which were unknown before the sixteenth century. The reformers were as great and good men as the fathers, but both must bow before the apostles. There is a steady progress of Christianity, an ever-deepening understanding and an ever-widening application of its principles and powers, and there are yet many hidden treasures in the Bible which will be brought to light in future ages.

In general the excellences of the church fathers are very various. Polycarp is distinguished, not for genius or learning, but for patriarchal simplicity and dignity; Clement of Rome, for the gift of administration; Ignatius, for impetuous devotion to episcopacy, church unity, and Christian martyrdom; Justin, for apologetic zeal and extensive reading; Irenaeus, for sound doctrine and moderation; Clement of Alexandria, for stimulating fertility of thought; Origen, for brilliant learning and bold speculation; Tertullian, for freshness and vigor of intellect, and sturdiness of character; Cyprian, for energetic churchliness; Eusebius, for literary industry in compilation; Lactantius, for elegance of style. Each had also his weakness. Not one compares for a moment in depth and spiritual fullness with a St. Paul or St. John; and the whole patristic literature, with all its incalculable value, must ever remain very far below the New Testament. The single epistle to the Romans or the Gospel of John is worth more than all commentaries, doctrinal, polemic, and ascetic treatises of the Greek and Latin fathers, schoolmen, and reformers.

The ante-Nicene fathers may be divided into five or six classes:

The apostolic fathers, or personal disciples of the apostles. Of these, Polycarp, Clement, and Ignatius are the most eminent.

The apologists for Christianity against Judaism and heathenism: Justin Martyr and his successors to the end of the second century.

The controversialists against heresies within the church: Irenaeus, and Hippolytus, at the close of the second century and beginning of the third.

The Alexandrian school of philosophical theology: Clement and Origen, in the first half of the third century.

The contemporary but more practical North African school: of Tertullian and Cyprian.

Then there were also the germs of the Antiochian school, and some less prominent writers, who can be assigned to no particular class.

Together with the genuine writings of the church fathers there appeared in the first centuries, in behalf both of heresy and of orthodoxy, a multitude of apocryphal Gospels, Acts, and Apocalypses, under the names of apostles and of later celebrities; also Jewish and heathen prophecies of Christianity, such as the Testaments of the Twelve Patriarchs, the Books of Hydaspes, Of Hermas Trismegistos, and of the Sibyls. The frequent use made of such fabrications of an idle imagination even by eminent church teachers, particularly by the apologists, evinces not only great credulity and total want of literary criticism, but also a very imperfect development of the sense of truth, which had not yet learned utterly to discard the *pia fraus* as immoral falsehood.

The "apostolic," or rather post-apostolic "fathers"

The usual name is probably derived from Tertullian, who calls the followers of the apostles, *Apostolici.* Westcott calls them sub-apostolic, Donaldson, ep-apostolic. They were the first church teachers after the apostles, who had enjoyed in part personal intercourse with them, and thus form the connecting link between them and the apologists of the second century. This class consists of Barnabas, Clement of Rome, Ignatius, Polycarp, and, in a broader sense, Hermas, Papias, and the unknown authors of the Epistle to Diognetus, and of the Didache.

Of the outward life of these men, their extraction, education, and occupation before conversion, hardly anything is known. The distressed condition of that age was very unfavorable to authorship; and more than this, the spirit of the primitive church regarded the new life in Christ as the only true life, the only one worthy of being recorded. Even of the lives of the apostles themselves before their call we have only a few hints. But the pious story of the martyrdom of several of these fathers, as their entrance into perfect life, has been copiously written. They were good men rather than great men, and excelled more in zeal and devotion to Christ than in literary attainments. They were faithful practical workers, and hence of more use to the church in those days than profound thinkers or great scholars could have been. "The most striking feature of these writings," says Donaldson,"is the deep living piety which pervades them. It consists in the warmest love to God, the deepest interest in man, and it exhibits itself in a healthy, vigorous, manly morality."

The extant works of the apostolic fathers are of small compass, a handful of letters on holy living and dying, making in all a volume of about twice the size of the New Testament. Half of these (several Epistles of Ignatius, the Epistle of Barnabas, and the Pastor of Hermas) are of doubtful genuineness; but they belong at all events to that, obscure and mysterious transition period between the end of the first century and the middle of the second. They all originated, not in scientific study, but in practical religious feeling, and contain not analyses of doctrine so much as simple direct assertions of faith and exhortations to holy life; all, excepting Hermas and the Didache, in the form of epistles after the model of Paul's. Like the N. T. Epistles, the writings of the Apostolic fathers generally open with an inscription and Christian salutation, and conclude with a benediction and doxology. The Ep. of Clement to the Corinthians beginning thus (ch. 1.): "The church of God, which sojournes in Rome to the church of God which sojournes in Corinth, to them that are called and sanctified by the will of God, through our Lord Jesus Christ: Grace and peace from Almighty God, through Jesus Christ, be multiplied unto You." (Comp. 1 Cor. 1:2, 3; 2 Pet. 1:2.) It concludes (ch. 65, formerly ch. 59): "The grace of our Lord Jesus Christ be with you, and with all men everywhere who are called of God through Him, through whom be glory, honor, power, majesty, and eternal dominion unto Him from the ages past to the ages of ages. Amen."

The Ep. of Polycarp begins: "Polycarp, and the presbyters that are with him, to the church of God sojourning in Philippi: Mercy unto you and peace from God Almighty and from the Lord Jesus Christ our Savior, be multiplied;" and it concludes. "Grace be with you all. Amen." The Ep. of Barnabas opens and closes in a very general way, omitting the names of the writer and readers. The inscriptions and salutations of the Ignatian Epistles are longer and overloaded, even in the Syriac recension. Yet they show the germs of the apologetic, polemic, dogmatic, and ethic theology, as well as the outlines of the organization and the cultus of the ancient Catholic church. Critical research has to assign to them their due place in the external and internal development of the church; in doing this it needs very great caution to avoid arbitrary construction.

If we compare these documents with the canonical Scriptures of the New Testament, it is evident at once that they fall far below in original force, depth, and fullness of spirit, and afford in this a strong indirect proof of the inspiration of the apostles. Yet they still shine with the evening red of the apostolic day, and breathe an enthusiasm of simple faith and fervent love and fidelity to the Lord, which proved its power in suffering and martyrdom. They move in the element of living tradition, and make reference oftener to the oral preaching of the apostles than to their writings; for these were not yet so generally circulated but they bear a testimony none the less valuable to the genuineness of the apostolic writings, by occasional citations or allusions, and by the coincidence of their reminiscences with the facts of the gospel history and the fundamental doctrines of the New Testament.

The epistles of Barnabas, Clement, and Polycarp, and the Shepherd of Hernias, were in many churches read in public worship. Some were even incorporated in important manuscripts of the Bible. Their authority, however, was always but sectional and subordinate to that of the Gospels and the apostolic Epistles. It was a sound instinct of the church, that the writings of the disciples of the apostles, excepting those of Mark and Luke, who were peculiarly associated with Peter and Paul, were kept out of the canon of the New Testament. For by the wise ordering of the Ruler of history, there is an impassable gulf between the inspiration of the apostles and the illumination of the succeeding age, between the standard authority of holy Scripture and the derived validity of the teaching of the church.

Samuel M. Jackson, Biographical Sketches of Ecclesiastical Writers, 1882

Persecution of Christianity and Christian martyrdom

Contents

The Diocletian Persecution, 303–311
The Edicts of Toleration. 311–313

General survey

The persecutions of Christianity during the first three centuries appear like a long tragedy: first, foreboding signs; then a succession of bloody assaults of heathenism upon the religion of the cross; amidst the dark scenes of fiendish hatred and cruelty the bright exhibitions of suffering virtue; now and then a short pause; at last a fearful and desperate struggle of the old pagan empire for life and death, ending in the abiding victory of the Christian religion. Thus this bloody baptism of the church resulted in the birth of a Christian world. It was a repetition and prolongation of the crucifixion, but followed by a resurrection.

Our Lord had predicted this conflict, and prepared His disciples for it. "Behold, I send you forth as sheep in the midst of wolves. They will deliver you up to councils, and in their synagogues they will scourge you; yea and before governors and kings shall ye be brought for My sake, for a testimony to them and to the Gentiles. And brother shall deliver up brother to death, and the father his child: and children shall rise up against parents, and cause them to be put to death. And ye shall be hated of all men for My name's sake: but he that endureth to the end, the same shall be saved." These, and similar words, as well as the recollection of the crucifixion and resurrection, fortified and cheered many a confessor and martyr in the dungeon and at the stake.

The persecutions proceeded first from the Jews, afterwards from the Gentiles, and continued, with interruptions, for nearly three hundred years. History reports no mightier, longer and deadlier conflict than this war of extermination waged by heathen Rome against defenseless Christianity. It was a most unequal struggle, a struggle of the sword and of the cross; carnal power all on one side, moral power all on the other. It was a struggle for life and death. One or the other of the combatants must succumb. A compromise was impossible. The future of the world's history depended on the downfall of heathenism and the triumph of Christianity. Behind the scene were the powers of the invisible world, God and the prince of darkness. Justin, Tertullian, and other confessors traced the persecutions to Satan and the demons, though they did not ignore the human and moral aspects; they viewed them also as a punishment for past sins, and a school of Christian virtue. Some denied that martyrdom was an evil, since it only brought Christians the sooner to God and the glory of heaven. As war brings out the heroic qualities of men, so did the persecutions develop the patience, the gentleness, the endurance of the Christians, and prove the world-conquering power of faith.

Number of persecutions

From the fifth century it has been customary to reckon ten great persecutions: under Nero, Domitian, Trajan, Marcus Aurelius, Septimius Severus, Maximinus, Decius, Valerian,

Aurelian, and Diocletian. But the number is too great for the general persecutions, and too small for the provincial and local. Only two imperial persecutions-those, of Decius and Diocletian-extended over the empire; but Christianity was always an illegal religion from Trajan to Constantine, and subject to annoyance and violence everywhere.

The result

The long and bloody war of heathen Rome against the church, which is built upon a rock, utterly failed. It began in Rome under Nero, it ended near Rome at the Milvian Bridge, under Constantine. Aiming to exterminate, it purified. It called forth the virtues of Christian heroism, and resulted in the consolidation and triumph of the new religion. The philosophy of persecution is best expressed by the terse word of Tertullian, who lived in the midst of them, but did not see the end: "The blood of the Christians is the seed of the Church."

Religious freedom

The blood of persecution is also the seed of civil and religious liberty. All sects, schools, and parties, whether religious or political, when persecuted, complain of injustice and plead for toleration; but few practice it when in power. The reason of this inconsistency lies in the selfishness of human nature, and in mistaken zeal for what it believes to be true and right. Liberty is of very slow, but sure growth.

The ancient world of Greece and Rome generally was based upon the absolutism of the state, which mercilessly trampled under foot the individual rights of men. It is Christianity which taught and acknowledged them.

The Christian apologists first proclaimed, however imperfectly, the principle of freedom of religion, and the sacred rights of conscience. Tertullian, in prophetic anticipation as it were of the modern Protestant theory, boldly tells the heathen that everybody has a natural and inalienable right to worship God according to his conviction, that all compulsion in matters of conscience is contrary to the very nature of religion, and that no form of worship has any value whatever except as far as it is a free voluntary homage of the heart.

Trajan. AD 98–117

Martyrdom of Symeon of Jerusalem, and Ignatius of Antioch

Symeon, bishop of Jerusalem, and, like his predecessor James, a kinsman of Jesus, was accused by fanatical Jews, and crucified 107, at the age of a hundred and twenty years.

In the same year the distinguished bishop Ignatius of Antioch was condemned to death, transported to Rome, and thrown before wild beasts in the Coliseum. The story of his martyrdom has no doubt been much embellished, but it must have some foundation in fact, and is characteristic of the legendary martyrology of the ancient church.

The coveted crown came to him at last and his eager and morbid desire for martyrdom was gratified. The emperor Trajan, in 107, came to Antioch, and there threatened with persecution all who refused to sacrifice to the gods. Ignatius was tried for this offence, and proudly confessed himself a "Theophorus" ("bearer of God") because, as he said, he had Christ within his breast. Trajan condemned him to be thrown to the lions at Rome. The sentence was executed with all haste. Ignatius was immediately bound in chains, and taken over land and sea, accompanied by ten soldiers, whom he denominated his "leopards," from Antioch to Seleucia, to Smyrna, where he met Polycarp, and whence be wrote to the churches, particularly to that in Rome; to Troas, to Neapolis, through Macedonia to Epirus, and so over the Adriatic to Rome. He was received by the Christians there with every manifestation of respect, but would not allow them to avert or even to delay his martyrdom. It was on the 20th day of December, 107, that he was thrown into the amphitheater: immediately the wild beasts fell upon him, and soon naught remained of his body but a few bones, which were carefully conveyed to Antioch as an inestimable treasure. The faithful friends who had accompanied him from home dreamed that night that they saw him; some that he was standing by Christ, dropping with sweat as if he had just come from his great labor. Comforted by these dreams they returned with the relics to Antioch.

Hadrian. AD 117–138

The Christian apologies, which took their rise under this emperor, indicate a very bitter public sentiment against the Christians, and a critical condition of the church. The least encouragement from Hadrian would have brought on a bloody persecution. Quadratus and Aristides addressed their pleas for their fellow-Christians to him, we do not know with what effect.

Later tradition assigns to his reign the martyrdom of St. Eustachius, St. Symphorosa and her seven sons, of the Roman bishops Alexander and Telesphorus, and others whose names are scarcely known, and whose chronology is more than doubtful.

Antoninus Pius. AD 137–161

Antoninus Pius protected the Christians from the tumultuous violence which broke out against them on account of the frequent public calamities. But the edict ascribed to him, addressed to the deputies of the Asiatic cities, testifying to the innocence of the Christians, and holding them up to the heathen as models of fidelity and zeal in the worship of God, could hardly have come from an emperor, who bore the honorable title of Pius for his conscientious adherence to the religion of his fathers.

Polycarp was a personal friend and pupil of the Apostle John, and chief presbyter of the church at Smyrna, where a plain stone monument still marks his grave. He was the teacher of Irenaeus of Lyons, and thus the connecting link between the apostolic and post-apostolic ages. As he died 155 at an age of eighty-six years or more, he must have been born 69, a year before the destruction of Jerusalem, and may have enjoyed the friendship of St. John for twenty years or more. This gives additional weight to his testimony concerning apostolic traditions and writings.

Polycarp steadfastly refused before the proconsul to deny his King and Savior, whom he had served six and eighty years, and from whom he had experienced nothing but love and mercy. He joyfully went up to the stake, and amidst the flames praised God for having deemed him worthy "to be numbered among his martyrs, to drink the cup of Christ's sufferings, unto the eternal resurrection of the soul and the body in the incorruption of the Holy Spirit." The slightly legendary account in the letter of the church of Smyrna states, that the flames avoided the body of the saint, leaving it unharmed, like gold tried in the fire; also the Christian bystanders insisted, that they perceived a sweet odor, as of incense. Then the executioner thrust his sword into the body, and the stream of blood at once extinguished the flame. The corpse was burned after the Roman custom, but the bones were preserved by the church, and held more precious than gold and diamonds. The death of this last witness of the apostolic age checked the fury of the populace, and the proconsul suspended the persecution.

Persecutions under Marcus Aurelius. AD 161–180

Marcus Aurelius, the philosopher on the throne, was a well-educated, just, kind, and amiable emperor, and reached the old Roman ideal of self-reliant Stoic virtue, but for this very reason he had no sympathy with Christianity, and probably regarded it as an absurd and fanatical superstition. He had no room in his cosmopolitan philanthropy for the purest and most innocent of his subjects, many of whom served in his own army.

Belonging to the later Stoical school, which believed in an immediate absorption after death into the Divine essence, he considered the Christian doctrine of the immortality of the soul, with its moral consequences, as vicious and dangerous to the welfare of the state. A law was passed under his reign, punishing every one with exile who should endeavor to influence people's mind by fear of the Divinity, and this law was, no doubt, aimed at the Christians.

About the year 170 the apologist Melito wrote: "The race of the worshippers of God in Asia is now persecuted by new edicts as it never has been heretofore; shameless, greedy sycophants, finding occasion in the edicts, now plunder the innocent day and night."

The empire was visited at that time by a number of conflagrations, a destructive flood of the Tiber, an earthquake, insurrections, and particularly a pestilence, which spread from Ethiopia to Gaul. This gave rise to bloody persecutions, in which government and people united against the enemies of the gods and the supposed authors of these misfortunes. Celsus expressed his joy that "the demon" [of the Christians] was "not only reviled, but banished from every land and sea," and saw in this judgment the fulfillment of the oracle:

"the mills of the gods grind late." But at the same time these persecutions, and the simultaneous literary assaults on Christianity by Celsus and Lucian, show that the new religion was constantly gaining importance in the empire.

In 177, the churches of Lyons and Vienne, in the South of France, underwent a severe trial. Heathen slaves were forced by the rack to declare, that their Christian masters practiced all the unnatural vices which rumor charged them with; and this was made to justify the exquisite tortures to which the Christians were subjected. But the sufferers, "strengthened by the fountain of living water from the heart of Christ," displayed extraordinary faith and steadfastness, and felt, that "nothing can be fearful, where the love of the Father is, nothing painful, where shines the glory of Christ."

The most distinguished victims of this Gallic persecution were the bishop Pothinus, who, at the age of ninety years, and just recovered from a sickness, was subjected to all sorts of abuse, and then thrown into a dismal dungeon, where he died in two days; the virgin Blandina, a slave, who showed almost superhuman strength and constancy under the most cruel tortures, and was at last thrown to a wild beast in a net; Ponticus, a boy of fifteen years, who could be deterred by no sort of cruelty from confessing his Savior. The corpses of the martyrs, which covered the streets, were shamefully mutilated, then burned, and the ashes cast into the Rhone, lest any remnants of the enemies of the gods might desecrate the soil. At last the people grew weary of slaughter, and a considerable number of Christians survived. The martyrs of Lyons distinguished themselves by true humility, disclaiming in their prison that title of honor, as due only, they said, to the faithful and true witness, the Firstborn from the dead, the Prince of life (Rev. 1:5), and to those of his followers who had already sealed their fidelity to Christ with their blood.

About the same time a persecution of less extent appears to have visited Autun (Augustodunum) near Lyons. Symphorinus, a young man of good family, having refused to fall down before the image of Cybele, was condemned to be beheaded. On his way to the place of execution his own mother called to him: "My son, be firm and fear not that death, which so surely leads to life. Look to Him who reigns in heaven. To-day is thy earthly life not taken from thee, but transferred by a blessed exchange into the life of heaven."

From Septimius Severus to Philip the Arabian. AD 193–249

With Septimius Severus (193–211), who was of Punic descent and had a Syrian wife, a line of emperors (Caracalla, Heliogabalus, Alexander Severus) came to the throne, who were rather Oriental than Roman in their spirit, and were therefore far less concerned than the Antonines to maintain the old state religion. Yet towards the close of the second century there was no lack of local persecutions; and Clement of Alexandria wrote of those times: "Many martyrs are daily burned, confined, or beheaded, before our eyes."

In the beginning of the third century (202) Septimius Severus, turned perhaps by Montanistic excesses, enacted a rigid law against the further spread both of Christianity and of Judaism. This occasioned violent persecutions in Egypt and in North Africa, and produced some of the fairest flowers of martyrdom.

In Alexandria, in consequence of this law, Leonides, father of the renowned Origen, was beheaded. Potamiaena, a virgin of rare beauty of body and spirit, was threatened by beastly passion with treatment worse than death, and, after cruel tortures, slowly burned with her mother in boiling pitch. One of the executioners, Basilides, smitten with sympathy, shielded them somewhat from abuse, and soon after their death embraced Christianity, and was beheaded. He declared that Potamiaena had appeared to him in the night, interceded with Christ for him, and set upon his head the martyr's crown.

In Carthage some catechumens, three young men and two young women, probably of the sect of the Montanists, showed remarkable steadfastness and fidelity in the dungeon and at the place of execution. Perpetua, a young woman of noble birth, resisting, not without a violent struggle, both the entreaties of her aged heathen father and the appeal of her helpless babe upon her breast, sacrificed the deep and tender feelings of a daughter and a mother to the Lord who died for her. Felicitas, a slave, when delivered of a child in the same dungeon, answered the jailor, who reminded her of the still keener pains of martyrdom: "Now I suffer, what I suffer; but then another will suffer for me, because I shall suffer for him." All remaining firm, they were cast to wild beasts at the next public festival, having first interchanged the parting kiss in hope of a speedy reunion in heaven.

The Passion of the Holy Martyrs Perpetua and Felicitas

The young catechumens, Revocatus and his fellow-servant Felicitas, Saturninus and Secundulus, were apprehended. And among them also was Vivia Perpetua, respectably born, liberally educated, a married matron, having a father and mother and two brothers, one of whom, like herself, was a catechumen, and a son an infant at the breast. She herself was about twenty-two years of age. . . .

The day of their victory shone forth, and they proceeded from the prison into the amphitheatre, as if to an assembly, joyous and of brilliant countenances; if perchance shrinking, it was with joy, and not with fear. Perpetua followed with placid look, and with step and gait as a matron of Christ, beloved of God; casting down the luster of her eyes from the gaze of all. Moreover, Felicitas, rejoicing that she had safely brought forth, so that she might fight with the wild beasts; from the blood and from the midwife to the gladiator, to wash after childbirth with a second baptism.

And when they were brought to the gate, and were constrained to put on the clothing-the men, that of the priests of Saturn, and the women, that of those who were consecrated to Ceres-that noble-minded woman resisted even to the end with constancy. For she said, "We have come thus far of our own accord, for this reason, that our liberty might not be restrained. For this reason we have yielded our minds, that we might not do any such thing as this: we have agreed on this with you."

Injustice acknowledged the justice; the tribune yielded to their being brought as simply as they were. Perpetua sang psalms, already treading under foot the head of the Egyptian; Revocatus, and Saturninus, and Saturus uttered threatenings against the gazing people about this martyrdom.

When they came within sight of Hilarianus, by gesture and nod, they began to say to Hilarianus, "Thou judgest us," say they, "but God will judge thee."

At this the people, exasperated, demanded that they should be tormented with scourges as they passed along the rank of the venatores. And they indeed rejoiced that they should have incurred any one of their Lord's passions. . . .

For the young women the devil prepared a very fierce cow, provided especially for that purpose contrary to custom, rivaling their sex also in that of the beasts. And so, stripped and clothed with nets, they were led forth. The populace shuddered as they saw one young woman of delicate frame, and another with breasts still dropping from her recent child-birth. So, being recalled, they are unbound.

Perpetua is first led in. She was tossed, and fell on her loins; and when she saw her tunic torn from her side, she drew it over her as a veil for her middle, rather mindful of her modesty than her suffering. Then she was called for again, and bound up her disheveled hair; for it was not becoming for a martyr to suffer with disheveled hair, lest she should appear to be mourning in her glory. So she rose up; and when she saw Felicitas crushed, she approached and gave her her hand, and lifted her up. And both of them stood together; and the brutality of the populace being appeased, they were recalled to the Sanavivarian gate.

Saturus at the other entrance exhorted the soldier Pudens, saying, "Assuredly here I am, as I have promised and foretold, for up to this moment I have felt no beast. And now believe with your whole heart. Lo, I am going forth to that beast, and I shall be destroyed with one bite of the leopard."

And immediately at the conclusion of the exhibition he was thrown to the leopard; and with one bite of his he was bathed with such a quantity of blood, that the people shouted out to him as he was returning, the testimony of his second baptism, "Saved and washed, saved and washed."

Manifestly he was assuredly saved who had been glorified in such a spectacle. Then to the soldier Pudens he said, "Farewell, and be mindful of my faith; and let not these things disturb, but confirm you." And at the same time he asked for a little ring from his finger, and returned it to him bathed in his wound, leaving to him an inherited token and the memory of his blood. And then lifeless he is cast down with the rest, to be slaughtered in the usual place. And when the populace called for them into the midst, that as the sword penetrated into their body they might make their eyes partners in the murder, they rose up of their own accord, and transferred themselves whither the people wished; but they first kissed one another, that they might consummate their martyrdom with the kiss of peace. The rest indeed, immoveable and in silence, received the sword-thrust; much more Saturus, who also had first ascended the ladder, and first gave up his spirit, for he also was waiting for Perpetua.

But Perpetua, that she might taste some pain, being pierced between the ribs, cried out loudly, and she herself placed the wavering right hand of the youthful gladiator to her throat. Possibly such a woman could not have been slain unless she herself had willed it, because she was feared by the impure spirit.

Translated by R. E. Wallis

Persecutions under Decius, and Valerian. AD 249–260

Decius Trajan (249–251), an earnest and energetic emperor, in whom the old Roman spirit once more awoke, resolved to root out the church as an atheistic and seditious sect, and in the year 250 published an edict to all the governors of the provinces, enjoining return to the pagan state religion under the heaviest penalties. This was the signal for a persecution which, in extent, consistency, and cruelty, exceeded all before it. In truth it was properly the first which covered the whole empire, and accordingly produced a far greater number of martyrs than any former persecution. In the execution of the imperial decree confiscation, exile, torture, promises and threats of all kinds, were employed to move the Christians to apostasy.

"Multitudes of nominal Christians," says Cyprian, "especially at the beginning, sacrificed to the gods or procured from the magistrate a false certificate that they had done so, and were then excommunicated as apostates (lapsi); while hundreds rushed with impetuous zeal to the prisons and the tribunals, to obtain the confessor's or martyr's crown.

The authorities were specially severe with the bishops and officers of the churches. Fabianus of Rome, Babylas of Antioch, and Alexander of Jerusalem, perished in this persecution. Others withdrew to places of concealment; some from cowardice; some from Christian prudence, in hope of allaying by their absence the fury of the pagans against their flocks, and of saving their own lives for the good of the church in better times.

Among the latter was Cyprian, bishop of Carthage, who incurred much censure by his course, but fully vindicated himself by his pastoral industry during his absence, and by his subsequent martyrdom. He says concerning the matter: "Our Lord commanded us in times of persecution to yield and to fly. He taught this, and he practiced it himself. For since the martyr's crown comes by the grace of God, and cannot be gained before the appointed hour, he who retires for a time, and remains true to Christ, does not deny his faith, but only abides his time."

Under Gallus (251–253) the persecution received a fresh impulse thorough the incursions of the Goths, and the prevalence of a pestilence, drought, and famine. Under this reign the Roman bishops Cornelius and Lucius were banished, and then condemned to death.

Valerian (253–260) was at first mild towards the Christians; but in 257 he changed his course, and made an effort to check the progress of their religion without bloodshed, by the banishment of ministers and prominent laymen, the confiscation of their property, and the prohibition of religious assemblies. These measures, however, proving fruitless, he brought the death penalty again into play.

The most distinguished martyrs of this persecution under Valerian are the bishops Sixtus II. of Rome, and Cyprian of Carthage.

When Cyprian received his sentence of death, representing him as an enemy of the Roman gods and laws, he calmly answered: "Deo gratias!" Then, attended by a vast multitude to the scaffold, he proved once more, undressed himself, covered his eyes, requested a presbyter to bind his hands, and to pay the executioner, who tremblingly drew the sword, twenty-five pieces of gold, and won the incorruptible crown (Sept. 14, 258). His faithful friends caught the blood in handkerchiefs, and buried the body of their sainted pastor with great solemnity.

Temporary Repose. AD 260–303

Gallienus (260–268) gave peace to the church once more, and even acknowledged Christianity as a religio licita. And this calm continued forty years; for the edict of persecution, issued by the energetic and warlike Aurelian (270–275), was rendered void by his assassination; and the six emperors who rapidly followed, from 275 to 284, let the Christians alone.

The Diocletian Persecution. AD 303–311

The forty years' repose was followed by, the last and most violent persecution, a struggle for life and death.

"The accession of the Emperor Diocletian is the era from which the Coptic Churches of Egypt and Abyssinia still date, under the name of the 'Era of Martyrs.' All former persecutions of the faith were forgotten in the horror with which men looked back upon the last and greatest: the tenth wave (as men delighted to count it) of that great storm obliterated all the traces that had been left by others. The fiendish cruelty of Nero, the jealous fears of Domitian, the unimpassioned dislike of Marcus, the sweeping purpose of Decius, the clever devices of Valerian, fell into obscurity when compared with the concentrated terrors of that final grapple, which resulted in the destruction of the old Roman Empire and the establishment of the Cross as the symbol of the world's hope." So Arthur James Mason begins his book on the Persecution of Diocletian.

Diocletian (284–305) was one of the most judicious and able emperors who, in a trying period, preserved the sinking state from dissolution. In the first twenty years of his reign Diocletian respected the toleration edict of Gallienus. His own wife Prisca his daughter Valeria, and most of his eunuchs and court officers, besides many of the most prominent public functionaries, were Christians, or at least favorable to the Christian religion.

In 303 Diocletian issued in rapid succession three edicts, each more severe than its predecessor. Maximian issued the fourth, the worst of all, April 30, 304. Christian churches were to be destroyed; all copies of the Bible were to be burned; all Christians were to be deprived of public office and civil rights; and at last all, without exception, were to sacrifice to the gods upon pain of death.

The persecution began on the twenty-third day of February, 303, the feast of the Terminalia (as if to make an end of the Christian sect), with the destruction of the magnificent church in Nicomedia.

The number of martyrs cannot be estimated with any degree of certainty. The seven episcopal and the ninety-two Palestinian martyrs of Eusebius are only a select list bearing a similar relation to the whole number of victims as the military lists its of distinguished fallen officers to the large mass of common soldiers, and form therefore no fair basis for the calculation of Gibbon, who would reduce the whole number to less than two thousand.

The Edicts of Toleration. AD 311–313

Galerius, the real author of the persecution, brought to reflection by a terrible disease, put an end to the slaughter shortly before his death, by a remarkable edict of toleration, which he issued from Nicomedia in 311, in connexion with Constantine and Licinius. In that document he declared, that the purpose of reclaiming the Christians from their willful innovation and the multitude of their sects to the laws and discipline of the, Roman state, was not accomplished; and that he would now grant them permission to hold their religious assemblies provided they disturbed not the order of the state. To this he added in conclusion the significant instruction that the Christians, "after this manifestation of grace, should pray to their God for the welfare of the emperors, of the state, and of themselves, that the state might prosper in every respect, and that they might live quietly in their homes."

This edict virtually closes the period of persecution in the Roman empire.

Christian Martyrdom

To these protracted and cruel persecutions the church opposed no revolutionary violence, no carnal resistance, but the moral heroism of suffering and dying for the truth. But this very heroism was her fairest ornament and staunchest weapon. In this very heroism she proved herself worthy of her divine founder, who submitted to the death of the cross for the salvation of the world, and even prayed that his murderers might be forgiven.

Men and women of all classes, noble senators and learned bishops, illiterate artisans and poor slaves, loving mothers and delicate virgins, hoary-headed pastors and innocent children approached their tortures in no temper of unfeeling indifference and obstinate defiance, but, like their divine Master, with calm self-possession, humble resignation, gentle meekness, cheerful faith, triumphant hope, and forgiving charity. Such spectacles must have often overcome even the inhuman murderer. "Go on," says Tertullian tauntingly to the heathen governors, "rack, torture, grind us to powder: our numbers increase in proportion as ye mow us down. The blood of Christians is their harvest seed. Your very obstinacy is a teacher. For who is not incited by the contemplation of it to inquire what there is in the core of the matter? And who, after having joined us, does not long to suffer?"

The martyrdom of the first three centuries still remains one of the grandest phenomena of history, and an evidence of the indestructible divine nature of Christianity.

No other religion could have stood for so long a period the combined opposition of Jewish bigotry, Greek philosophy, and Roman policy and power; no other could have triumphed at last over so many foes by purely moral and spiritual force, without calling any carnal weapons to its aid. This comprehensive and long-continued martyrdom is the peculiar crown and glory of the early church; it pervaded its entire literature and gave it a predominantly apologetic character; it entered deeply into its organization and discipline and the development of Christian doctrine; it affected the public worship and private devotions; it produced a legendary poetry; but it gave rise also, innocently, to a great deal of superstition, and undue exaltation of human merit; and it lies at the foundation of the Catholic worship of saints and relics.

Finally, while the Christian religion has at all times suffered more or less persecution, bloody or unbloody, from the ungodly world, and always had its witnesses ready for any sacrifice; yet at no period since the first three centuries was the whole church denied the right of a peaceful legal existence, and the profession of Christianity itself universally declared and punished as a political crime. Before Constantine the Christians were a helpless and proscribed minority in an essentially heathen world, and under a heathen government. Then they died not simply for particular doctrines, but for the facts of Christianity. Then it was a conflict, not for a denomination or sect, but for Christianity itself. The importance of ancient martyrdom does not rest so much on the number of victims and the cruelty of their sufferings as on the great antithesis and the ultimate result in saving the Christian religion for all time to come. Hence the first three centuries are the classical period of heathen persecution and of Christian martyrdom. The martyrs and confessors of the ante-Nicene age suffered for the common cause of all Christian denominations and sects, and hence are justly held in reverence and gratitude by all.

Philip Schaff, History of the Christian Church,
Volume II: Ante-Nicene Christianity. AD 100–325

Two Christian heresies: Marcionism and Montanism

Marcionism

Marcion of Sinope (c. 110–160), was a major 2nd century Early Christian theologian, founder of what would later be called Marcionism, and one of the first to be strongly denounced by other Christians (who would later be called Catholic as opposed to Marcionite) as heretical. He created a strong ecclesiastical organization, parallel to that of the Church of Rome, with himself as Bishop.

Marcion's endeavor to call the Roman Church back to what he deemed the Gospel of Christ and of Paul resulted in his own excommunication about 144. He now gathered followers into a separated church. For their use he compiled a canon of sacred books, composed of the epistles of Paul (omitting the Pastorals), and the Gospel of Luke, shorn of all passages which implied that Christ regarded the God of the Old Testament as His Father, or was in any way related to Him. As far as is known, this was the first attempt to form an authoritative collection of New Testament writings.

Marcion's movement was probably the most dangerous of those associated with Gnosticism. He sundered Christianity from its historic background as completely as had the more speculative Gnostic theories. He denied a real incarnation, and condemned the Old Testament. All this was the more plausible because done in the name of a protest against growing legalism. For such a protest there was much justification. His churches spread extensively, in the Orient especially, and survived into the fifth century. His own later history is wholly unknown.

Montanism

Unlike Gnosticism, Montanism was a movement distinctly of Christian origin. In most of the churches of the second century the early hope of the speedy return of Christ was growing dim. The consciousness of the constant inspiration of the Spirit, characteristic of the Apostolic Churches, had also largely faded. With this declining sense of the immediacy of the Spirit's present work came an increasing emphasis on His significance as the agent of revelation. Paul had identified the Spirit and Christ. That was not the general feeling half a century later. The Spirit had been the inspiration of prophecy in the Old Testament. He guided the New Testament writers. Christian thought at the beginning of the second century the Holy Spirit was differentiated from Christ, but was classed, like Him, with God.

This appears in the Trinitarian baptismal formula, which was displacing the older baptism in the name of Christ. Trinitarian formula were frequently in use by the close of the first and beginning of the second century.

The Johannine Gospel represented Christ as promising the coming of the Holy Spirit to the disciples: "When the Comforter is come, whom I will send unto you from the Father, even the Spirit of Truth, which proceedeth from the Father, He shall bear Witness of Me," (15 26). The second century was convinced, therefore, not only that the Holy Spirit was in peculiar association with God the Father and Christ ; but that Christ had promised the Spirit s coming in more abundant measure in the future. It was this thought of the special dispensation of the Holy Spirit, combined with a fresh outburst of the early prophetic enthusiasm, and a belief that the end of the world-age was close at hand, that were represented in Montanism.

To a considerable extent Montanism was, also, a reaction from the secular tendencies already at work in the church. Montanus, from whom the movement was named, was of

Ardabau, near the region of Asia Minor known as Phrygia long noted for its ecstatic type of religion. A tradition, recorded by Jerome, affirmed that, before conversion, he had been a priest of Cybele. About 156 Montanus proclaimed himself the passive instrument through whom the Holy Spirit spoke. In this new revelation Montanus declared the promise of Christ fulfilled, and the dispensation of the Holy Spirit begun. To him were soon joined two prophetesses, Prisca and Maximilla. They now affirmed, as mouthpieces of the Spirit, that the end of the world was at hand, and that the heavenly Jerusalem was about to be established in Phrygia, whither believers should betake themselves. In preparation for the fast-approaching consummation the most strenuous asceticism should be practiced, celibacy, fastings, and abstinence from meat. This vigorous attitude won response as a protest against the growing worldliness of the church at large, and to many was the most attractive feature of Montanism.

The movement speedily attained considerable proportions. By the bishops of Asia Minor, who felt their authority threatened, one or more synods were held soon after 160, which have the distinction of being the earliest synods of church history, and in which Montanism was condemned. Its progress was not easily checked, even by the death of the last of its original prophets, Maximilla, in 179. Soon after 179 it was represented in Rome, and for years the Roman church was more or less turmoiled by it. In Carthage it won Tertullian, about 207, attracted chiefly by its ascetic demands, who thenceforth was the most eminent Montanist. Though gradually driven out of the dominant church, Montanism continued to be represented in the Orient till long after the acceptance of Christianity by the imperial government. In Carthage the followers of Tertullian persisted till the time of Augustine. In its ascetic demands Montanism represented a wide-spread tendency, and an asceticism as strict as anything Montanism taught was later to find a place in the great church in monasticism. What made Marcion distinct from the many who sought to recover the authentic Jesus, was that he believed that while the universe was created by Yahweh, the God behind Jesus and his teachings is not the same as the universal creator. This position has led many in orthodox branches to label his teachings Gnostic, as they make use of the concept of the Demiurge and a Docetic Christ.

Williston Walker, A History of the Christian Church, 1918

PEOPLE

Ignatius of Antioch (? – c. 98/110)
Justin Martyr (100–165)
Irenaeus (c. 130–202)
Tertullian (155–230)
Origen (185–254)
Cyprian (200–258)

Ignatius of Antioch

Dates

(AD? – c. 98/110)

Famous for being

Martyr

Known as: *Ignatius Theophoros* (Greek: "God Bearer")

Important writings

Seven epistles to various churches

One of his quotations

"I am a grain of the wheat of God, and I would be ground by the teeth of wild beasts, that I may be found pure bread of God."

1. Life of Ignatius

Ignatius, surnamed Theophorus, stood at the head of the Church of Antioch at the close of the first century and the beginning of the second, and was thus contemporaneous with Clement of Rome and Simeon of Jerusalem. The church of Antioch was the mother-church of Gentile Christianity; and the city was the second city of the Roman empire. Great numbers of Christians and a host of heretical tendencies were collected there, and pushed the development of doctrine and organization with great rapidity.

As in the case of Rome, tradition differs concerning the first episcopal succession of Antioch, making Ignatius either the second or the first bishop of this church after Peter, and calling him now a disciple of Peter, now of Paul, now of John. . . .

But his peculiar glory, in the eyes of the ancient church, was his martyrdom. The minute account of it, in the various versions of the Martyrium S. Ignatii, contains many embellishments of pious fraud and fancy; but the fact itself is confirmed by general tradition. Ignatius himself says, in his Epistle to the Romans, according to the Syriac version:

> From Syria to Rome I fight with wild beasts, on water and on land, by day and by night, chained to ten leopards [soldiers], made worse by signs of kindness. Yet their wickednesses do me good as a disciple; but not on this account am I justified. Would that I might be glad of the beasts made ready for me. And I pray that they may be found ready for me. Nay, I will fawn upon them, that they may devour me quickly, and not, as they have done with some, refuse to touch me from fear. Yea, and if they will not voluntarily do it, I will bring them to it by force.

The Acts of his martyrdom relate more minutely, that Ignatius was brought before the Emperor Trajan at Antioch in the ninth year of his reign (107–108), was condemned to death as a Christian, was transported in chains to Rome, was there thrown to lions in the Coliseum for the amusement of the people, and that his remains were carried back to Antioch as an invaluable treasure. The transportation may be accounted for as designed to cool the zeal of the bishop, to terrify other Christians on the way, and to prevent an outbreak of fanaticism in the church of Antioch. . . .

2. His letters

On his journey to Rome, Bishop Ignatius, as a prisoner of Jesus Christ, wrote seven epistles to various churches, mostly in Asia Minor. Eusebius and Jerome put them in the following order:

To the Ephesians
To the Magnesians
To the Trallians
To the Romans
To the Philadelphians
To the Smyrneans
To Polycarp, bishop of Smyrna

3. His character and place in history

Ignatius stands out in history as the ideal of a catholic martyr, and as the earliest advocate of the hierarchical principle in both its good and its evil points. As a writer, he is remarkable for originality, freshness and force of ideas, and for terse, sparkling and sententious style; but in apostolic simplicity and soundness, he is inferior to Clement and Polycarp, and presents a stronger contrast to the epistles of the New Testament. Clement shows the calmness, dignity and governmental wisdom of the Roman character. Ignatius glows with the fire and impetuosity of the Greek and Syrian temper which carries him beyond the bounds of sobriety.

He was a very unusual man, and made a powerful impression upon his age. He is the incarnation, as it were, of the three closely connected ideas:

the glory of martyrdom,
the omnipotence of episcopacy,
and the hatred of heresy and schism.

Hierarchical pride and humility, Christian charity and churchly exclusiveness are typically represented in Ignatius.

As he appears personally in his epistles, his most beautiful and venerable trait is his glowing love for Christ as God incarnate, and his enthusiasm for martyrdom. If great patriots thought it sweet to die for their country, he thought it sweeter and more honorable to die for Christ, and by his blood to fertilize the soil for the growth of His Church.

"I would rather die for Christ," says he, "than rule the whole earth." "It is glorious to go down in the world, in order to go up into God." He beseeches the Romans:

> Leave me to the beasts, that I may by them be made partaker of God. I am a grain of the wheat of God, and I would be ground by the teeth of wild beasts, that I may be found pure bread of God. Rather fawn upon the beasts, that they may be to me a grave, and leave nothing of my body, that, when I sleep, I may not be burdensome to any one. Then will I truly be a disciple of Christ, when the world can no longer even see my body. Pray the Lord for me, that through these instruments I may be found a sacrifice to God.
>
> [And further on:] Fire, and cross, and exposure to beasts, scattering of the bones, hewing of the limbs, crushing of the whole body, wicked torments of the devil, may come upon me, if they only make me partaker of Jesus Christ . . . . My love is crucified, and there is no fire in me, which loves earthly stuff . . . . I rejoice not in the food of perishableness, nor in the pleasures of this life. The bread of God would I have, which is the flesh of Christ; and for drink I wish his blood, which is imperishable love.

From these and similar passages, however, we perceive also that his martyr-spirit exceeds the limits of the genuine apostolic soberness and resignation, which is equally willing to depart or to remain according to the Lord's good pleasure. It degenerates into boisterous impatience and morbid fanaticism. It resembles the lurid torch rather than the clear calm light. There mingles also in all his extravagant professions of humility and entire unworthiness a refined spiritual pride and self-commendation.

Samuel M. Jackson, Biographical Sketches of Ecclesiastical Writers, 1882

Justin Martyr

Dates
AD 100–165

Famous for being
Philosopher and martyr

Important writings
Two Apologies, against the heathen
Dialogue with the Jew Trypho

One of his quotations

"We desire nothing more than to suffer for our Lord Jesus Christ; for this gives us salvation and joyfulness before his dreadful judgment seat, at which all the world must appear."

Justin the Philosopher and Martyr

The most eminent among the Greek Apologists of the second century is Flavius Justinus, surnamed "Philosopher and Martyr." He is the typical apologist, who devoted his whole life to the defense of Christianity at a time when it was most assailed, and he sealed his testimony with his blood. He is also the first Christian philosopher or the first philosophic theologian. His writings were well known to Irenaeus, Hippolytus, Eusebius, Epiphanius, Jerome, and Photius, and the most important of them have been preserved to this day.

1. His life

Justin was born towards the close of the first century. His conversion occurred in his early manhood. Thirsting for truth as the greatest possession, he made the round of the systems of philosophy and knocked at every gate of ancient wisdom, except the Epicurean which he despised. He threw himself with great zeal into the arms of Platonism. He was overpowered by the perception of immaterial things and the contemplation of eternal ideas of truth, beauty, and goodness. He thought that he was already near the promised goal of this philosophy-the vision of God-when, in a solitary walk not far from the sea-shore, a venerable old Christian of pleasant countenance and gentle dignity, entered into a conversation with him, which changed the course of his life. The unknown friend shook his confidence in all human wisdom, and pointed him to the writings of the Hebrew prophets who were older than the philosophers and had seen and spoken the truth, not as reasoners, but as witnesses. More than this: they had foretold the coming of Christ, and their prophecies were fulfilled in his life and work.

The old man departed, and Justin saw him no more, but he took his advice and soon found in the prophets of the Old Testament as illuminated and confirmed by the Gospels, the true and infallible philosophy which rests upon the firm ground of revelation. Thus the enthusiastic Platonist became a believing Christian.

After his conversion Justin sought the society of Christians, and received from them instruction in the history and doctrine of the gospel. He now devoted himself wholly to the spread and vindication of the Christian religion. He was an itinerant evangelist or teaching missionary, with no fixed abode and no regular office in the church. There is no trace of his ordination; he was as far as we know a lay-preacher, with a commission from the Holy Spirit; yet be accomplished far more for the good of the church than any known bishop or presbyter of his day.

"Every one," says he, "who can preach the truth and does not preach it, incurs the judgment of God." Like Paul, he felt himself a debtor to all men, Jew and Gentile, that he might show them the way of salvation. And, like Aristides, Athenagoras, Tertullian, Heraclas, Gregory Thaumaturgus, he retained his philosopher's cloak, that he might the more readily discourse on the highest themes of thought; and when he appeared in early morning upon a public walk, many came to him with a "Welcome, philosopher!" He spent some time in Rome where he met and combated Marcion. In Ephesus he made an effort to gain the Jew Trypho and his friends to the Christian faith.

He labored last, for the second time, in Rome. Here, at the instigation of a Cynic philosopher, Crescens, whom he had convicted of ignorance about Christianity, Justin, with six other Christians, about the year 166, was scourged and beheaded. Fearlessly and joyfully, as in life, so also in the face of death, he bore witness to the truth before the tribunal of Rusticus, the prefect of the city, refused to sacrifice, and proved by his own example the steadfastness of which he had so often boasted as a characteristic trait of his believing brethren. When asked to explain the mystery of Christ, he replied: "I am too little to say something great of him." His last words were: "We desire nothing more than to suffer for our Lord Jesus Christ; for this gives us salvation and joyfulness before his dreadful judgment seat, at which all the world must appear."

Justin is the first among the fathers who may be called a learned theologian and Christian thinker. He had acquired considerable classical and philosophical culture before his conversion, and then made it subservient to the defense of faith. He was not a man of genius and accurate scholarship, but of respectable talent, extensive reading, and enormous memory. He had some original and profound ideas and was remarkably liberal in his judgment of the noble heathen and the milder section of the Jewish Christians. He lived in times when the profession of Christ was a crime under the Roman law against secret societies and prohibited religious. He had the courage of a confessor in life and of a martyr in death. It is impossible not to admire his fearless devotion to the cause of truth and the defense of his persecuted brethren. If not a great man, he was (what is better) an eminently good and useful man, and worthy of an honored place in "the noble army of martyrs."

2. Writings

His chief works are his two Apologies against the heathen, and his Dialogue with the Jew Trypho. The First or larger Apology (68 chapters) is addressed to the Emperor Antoninus Pius (137–161) and his adopted sons, and was probably written about 147. The Second or smaller Apology (25 chapters) is a supplement to the, former, perhaps its conclusion, and belongs to the same reign.

3. Theology

As to the sources of his religious knowledge, Justin derived it partly from the Holy Scriptures, partly from the living church tradition. He cites, most frequently, and generally from memory, hence often inaccurately, the Old Testament prophets (in the Septuagint), and the "Memoirs" of Christ, or "Memoirs by the Apostles," as he calls the canonical Gospels, without naming the authors. He says that they were publicly read in the churches with the prophets of the Old Testament. He only quotes the words and acts of the Lord. He makes most use of Matthew and Luke, but very freely, and from John's Prologue (with the aid of Philo whom he never names) he derived the inspiration of the Logos-doctrine, which is the heart of his theology.

Justin forms the transition from the apostolic fathers to the church fathers properly so called. Christianity was to Justin, theoretically, the true philosophy, and, practically, a new law of holy living and dying. The former is chiefly the position of the Apologies, the latter that of the Dialogue.

The Christian faith of Justin is faith in God the Creator, and in his Son Jesus Christ the Redeemer, and in the prophetic Spirit. All other doctrines which are revealed through the prophets and apostles, follow as a matter of course. Below the deity are good and bad angels; the former are messengers of God, the latter servants of Satan, who caricature Bible doctrines in heathen mythology, invent slanders, and stir up persecutions against Christians, but will be utterly overthrown at the second coming of Christ. The human soul is a creature, and hence perishable, but receives immortality from God, eternal happiness as a reward of piety, eternal fire as a punishment of wickedness. Man has reason and free will, and is hence responsible for all his actions; he sins by his own act, and hence deserves punishment. Christ came to break the power of sin, to secure forgiveness and regeneration to a new and holy life.

Samuel M. Jackson, Biographical Sketches of Ecclesiastical Writers, 1882

Irenaeus

Dates

c. AD 130–202

Famous for being

Champion of the Christian faith

Important writings

Refutation of Gnosticism

One of his quotations

"The glory of God is a living man; and the life of man consists in beholding God."

Almost simultaneously with the apology against false religions without arose the polemic literature against the heresies, or various forms of pseudo-Christianity, especially the Gnostic; and upon this was formed the dogmatic theology of the church. At the head of the old catholic controversialists stand Irenaeus and his disciple Hippolytus, both of Greek education, but both belonging, in their ecclesiastical relations and labors, to the West.

Asia Minor, the scene of the last labors of St. John, produced a luminous succession of divines and confessors who in the first three quarters of the second century reflected the light of the setting sun of the apostolic age, and may be called the pupils of St. John. Among them were Polycarp of Smyrna, Papias of Hierapolis, Apolinarius of Hierapolis, Melito of Sardis, and others less known but honorably mentioned in the letter of Polycrates of Ephesus to bishop Victor of Rome (190).

The last and greatest representative of this school is Irenaeus, the first among the fathers properly so called, and one of the chief architects of the Catholic system of doctrine.

1. Life and character

Little is known of Irenaeus except what we may infer from his writings. He sprang from Asia Minor, probably from Smyrna, where he spent his youth. He enjoyed the instruction of the venerable Polycarp of Smyrna, the pupil of John, and of other "Elders," who were mediate or immediate disciples of the apostles. The spirit of his preceptor passed over to him. "What I heard from him" says he, "that wrote I not on paper, but in my heart, and by the grace of God I constantly bring it afresh to mind."

After the martyrdom of Pothinus he was elected bishop of Lyons (178), and labored there with zeal and success, by tongue and pen, for the restoration of the heavily visited church, for the spread of Christianity in Gaul, and for the defense and development of its doctrines. He thus combined a vast missionary and literary activity. If we are to trust the account of Gregory of Tours, he converted almost the whole population of Lyons and sent notable missionaries to other parts of pagan France.

2. His character and position.

Irenaeus is the leading representative of catholic Christianity in the last quarter of the second century, the champion of orthodoxy against Gnostic heresy, and the mediator between the Eastern and Western churches. He united a learned Greek education and philosophical penetration with practical wisdom and moderation.

He is neither very original nor brilliant, but eminently sound and judicious. His individuality is not strongly marked, but almost lost in his catholicity. He modestly disclaims elegance and eloquence, and says that he had to struggle in his daily administrations with the barbarous Celtic dialect of Southern Gaul; but he nevertheless handles the Greek with great skill on the most abstruse subjects

His position gives him additional weight, for he is linked by two long lives, that of his teacher and grand-teacher, to the fountain head of Christianity. We plainly trace in him the influence of the spirit of Polycarp and John. "The true way to God," says he, in opposition to the false Gnosis, "is love. It is better to be willing to know nothing but Jesus Christ the crucified, than to fall into ungodliness through over-curious questions and paltry subtleties."

We may trace in him also the strong influence of the anthropology and soteriology of Paul. But he makes more account than either John or Paul of the outward visible church, the episcopal succession, and the sacraments; and his whole conception of Christianity is predominantly legalistic. Herein we see the catholic churchliness which so strongly set in during the second century.

Irenaeus is an enemy of all error and schism, and, on the whole, the most orthodox of the ante-Nicene fathers. Bishop Lightfoot says that Irenaeus, "On all the most important points conforms to the standard which has satisfied the Christian church ever since."

Irenaeus is the first among patristic writers who makes full use of the New Testament. The Apostolic Fathers re-echo the oral traditions; the Apologists are content with quoting the Old Testament prophets and the Lord's own words in the Gospels as proof of divine revelation; but Irenaeus showed the unity of the Old and New Testaments in opposition to the Gnostic separation, and made use of the four Gospels and nearly all Epistles in opposition to the mutilated canon of Marcion.

With all his zeal for pure and sound doctrine, Irenaeus was liberal towards subordinate differences, and remonstrated with the bishop of Rome for his unapostolic efforts to force an outward uniformity in respect to the time and manner of celebrating Easter. We may almost call him a forerunner of Gallicanism in its protest against ultramontane despotism. "The apostles have ordained," says he in the third fragment, which appears to refer to that controversy, "that we make conscience with no one of food and drink, or of particular feasts, new moons, and sabbaths. Whence, then, controversies; whence schisms? We keep feasts but with the leaven of wickedness and deceit, rending asunder the church of God, and we observe the outward, to the neglect of the higher, faith and love." He showed the same moderation in the Montanistic troubles. He was true to his name Peaceful and to his spiritual ancestry.

3. His writings

The most important work of Irenaeus is his *Refutation of Gnosticism*, in five books, usually called today, *Against Heresies*. To the ever-shifting and contradictory opinions of the heretics Irenaeus opposes the unchanging faith of the catholic church which is based on the Scriptures and tradition, and compacted together by the episcopal organization.

Samuel M. Jackson, Biographical Sketches of Ecclesiastical Writers, 1882

Tertullian

Dates
AD 155–230

Famous for being
Father of the Latin Church

Important writings
Apologeticus (The Apology)

Two of his quotations
"The blood of the martyrs is the seed [of the Church]."

"If the River Tiber reaches the walls,
if the River Nile does not rise to the fields,
if the sky does not move or the earth does,
if there is famine,
if there is plague,
the cry is at once: 'The Christians to the lion!' What, all of the to one lion?"

1. Life of Tertullian

Quintus Septimius Florens Tertullianus is the father of the Latin theology and church language, and one of the greatest men of Christian antiquity. We know little of his life but what is derived from his book and from the brief notice of Jerome in his catalogue of illustrious men. But few writers have impressed their individuality so strongly in their books as this African father. In this respect, as well as in others, he resembles St. Paul, and Martin Luther.

He was born about the year 150, at Carthage, the ancient rival of Rome, where his father was serving as captain of a Roman legion under the proconsul of Africa. He received a liberal Graeco-Roman education.

Between 199 and 203, he joined the puritanic, though orthodox, sect of the Montanists. Tertullian remained a zealous advocate of the catholic faith, and wrote, even from his schismatic position, several of his most effective works against the heretics, especially the Gnostics. Indeed, as a divine, he stood far above this fanatical sect, and gave it by his writings an importance and an influence in the church itself which it certainly would never otherwise have attained.

He labored in Carthage as a Montanist presbyter and an author, and died, as Jerome says, in decrepit old age, according to some about the year 220, according to others not till 240; for the exact time, as well as the manner of his death, are unknown.

Strange that this most powerful defender of old catholic orthodoxy and the teacher of the high-churchly Cyprian, should have been a schismatic and all antagonist of Rome.

2. Character

Tertullian was a rare genius, perfectly original and fresh, but angular, boisterous and eccentric; full of glowing fantasy, pointed wit, keen discernment, polemic dexterity, and moral earnestness, but wanting in clearness, moderation, and symmetrical development. He resembled a foaming mountain torrent rather than a calm, transparent river in the valley. His vehement temper was never fully subdued, although he struggled sincerely against it. He was a man of strong convictions, and never hesitated to express them without fear or favor.

Tertullian's theology revolves about the great Pauline antithesis of sin and grace, and breaks the road to the Latin anthropology and soteriology afterwards developed by his like-minded, but clearer, calmer, and more considerate countryman, Augustin. For his opponents, be they heathens, Jews, heretics, or Catholics, he has as little indulgence and regard as Luther. With the adroitness of a special pleader he entangles them in self-contradictions, pursues them into every nook and corner, overwhelms them with arguments, sophisms, apophthegms, and sarcasms, drives them before him with unmerciful lashings, and almost always makes them ridiculous and contemptible. His polemics everywhere leave marks of blood. It is a wonder that he was not killed by the heathens, or excommunicated by the Catholics.

In short, we see in this remarkable man both intellectually and morally, the fermenting of a new creation, but not yet quite set free from the bonds of chaotic darkness and brought into clear and beautiful order.

3. The writings of Tertullian.

Tertullian developed an extraordinary literary activity in two languages between about 190 and 220. His earlier books in the Greek language, and some in the Latin, are lost. Those which remain are mostly short; but they are numerous, and touch nearly all departments of religious life. They present a graphic picture of the church of his day. Most of his works, according to internal evidence, fill in the first quarter of the third century, in the Montanistic period of his life, and among these many of his ablest writings against the heretics; while, on the other hand, the gloomy moral austerity, which predisposed him to Montanism, comes out quite strongly even in his earliest productions.

His works may be grouped in three classes:

apologetic;
polemic or anti-heretical; and
ethic or practical;

to which may be added as a fourth class the expressly Montanistic tracts against the Catholics.

1. In the Apologetic works against heathens and Jews, he pleads the cause of all Christendom, and deserves the thanks of all Christendom. Pre-eminent among them is the Apologeticus (or Apologeticum). It was composed in the reign of Septimius Severus, between 197 and 200. It is unquestionably one of the most beautiful monuments of the heroic age of the church. In this work, Tertullian enthusiastically and triumphantly repels the attacks of the heathens upon the new religion, and demands for it legal toleration and equal rights with the other sects of the Roman empire. It is the first plea for religious liberty, as an inalienable right which God has given to every man, and which the civil government in its own interest should not only tolerate but respect and protect. He claims no support, no favor, but simply justice. The church was in the first three centuries a self-supporting and self-governing society (as it ought always to be), and no burden, but a blessing to the state, and furnished to it the most peaceful and useful citizens. The cause of truth and justice never found a more eloquent and fearless defender in the very face of despotic power, and the blazing fires of persecution, than the author of this book. It breathes from first to last the assurance of victory in apparent defeat.

2. His polemic works are occupied chiefly with the refutation of the Gnostics. Here belongs first of all his thoroughly catholic tract." On the Prescription of Heretics." It is of a general character and lays down the fundamental principle of the church in dealing with heresy. Tertullian cuts off all errors and neologies at the outset from the right of legal contest and appeal to the holy Scriptures, because these belong only to the catholic church as the legitimate heir and guardian of Christianity. Irenaeus had used the same argument, but Tertullian gave it a legal or forensic form. The same argument, however, turns also against his own secession; for the difference between heretics and schismatics is really only relative, at least in Cyprian's view. Tertullian afterwards asserted, in contradiction with this book, that in religious matters not custom nor long possession, but truth alone, was to be consulted.

Among the heretics, he attacked chiefly the Valentinian Gnostics, and Marcion.

3. His numerous Practical or Ascetic treatises throw much light on the moral life of the early church, as contrasted with the immorality of the heathen world. Among these belong the books "On Prayer" "On Penance" "On Patience."

4. His strictly Montanistic or anti-catholic writings, in which the peculiarities of this sect are not only incidentally touched, as in many of the works named above, but vindicated expressly and at large, are likewise of a practical nature, and contend, in fanatical rigor, against the restoration of the lapsed (De Pudicitia), flight in persecutions, and second marriage (De Monogamia).

Samuel M. Jackson, Biographical Sketches of Ecclesiastical Writers, 1882

Origen

Dates
AD 185–254

Famous for being
Theologian and biblical scholar

Important writings
de Principiis
Hexapla

One of his quotations
"Conscience is the chamber of justice."

1. Life and character

Origenes, surnamed "Adamantius" on account of his industry and purity of character is one of the most remarkable men in history for genius and learning, for the influence he exerted on his age, and for the controversies and discussions to which his opinions gave rise. He was born of Christian parents at Alexandria, in the year 185, and probably baptized in childhood, according to Egyptian custom which be traced to apostolic origin.

In the year 203, though then only eighteen years of age, he was nominated by the bishop Demetrius, afterwards his opponent, president of the catechetical school of Alexandria, left vacant by the flight of Clement. To fill this important office, he made himself acquainted with the various heresies, especially the Gnostic, and with the Grecian philosophy; he was not even ashamed to study under the heathen Ammonius Saccas, the celebrated founder of Neo-Platonism. He learned also the Hebrew language, and made journeys to Rome (211), Arabia, Palestine (215), and Greece.

In the Decian persecution he was cast into prison, cruelly tortured, and condemned to the stake; and though he regained his liberty by the death of the emperor, yet he died some time after, at the age of sixty-nine, in the year 253 or 254, at Tyre, probably in consequence of that violence. He belongs, therefore, at least among the confessors, if not among the martyrs. He was buried at Tyre.

It is impossible to deny a respectful sympathy, veneration and gratitude to this extraordinary man, who, with all his brilliant talents and a best of enthusiastic friends and admirers, was driven from his country, stripped of his sacred office, excommunicated from a part of the church, then thrown into a dungeon, loaded with chains, racked by torture, doomed to drag his aged frame and dislocated limbs in pain and poverty, and long after his death to have his memory branded, his name anathematized, and his salvation denied; but who nevertheless did more than all his enemies combined to advance the cause of sacred learning, to refute and convert heathens and heretics, and to make the church respected in the eyes of the world.

2. His theology

Origen was the greatest scholar of his age, and the most gifted, most industrious, and most cultivated of all the ante-Nicene fathers. Even heathens and heretics admired or feared his brilliant talent and vast learning. His knowledge embraced all departments of the philology, philosophy, and theology of his day. With this he united profound and fertile thought, keen penetration, and glowing imagination. As a true divine, he consecrated all his studies by prayer, and turned them, according to his best convictions, to the service of truth and piety.

He may be called in many respects the Schleiermacher of the Greek church. He was a guide from the heathen philosophy and the heretical Gnosis to the Christian faith. He exerted an immeasurable influence in stimulating the development of the catholic theology and forming the great Nicene fathers, Athanasius, Basil, the two Gregories, Hilary, and Ambrose, who consequently, in spite of all his deviations, set great value on his services. But his best disciples proved unfaithful to many of his most peculiar views, and adhered far more to the reigning faith of the church. For—and in this too he is like Schleiermacher—he can by no means be called orthodox, either in the Catholic or in the Protestant sense. His leaning to idealism, his predilection for Plato, and his noble effort to reconcile Christianity with reason, and to commend it even to educated heathens and Gnostics, led him into many grand and fascinating errors. Among these are his extremely ascetic and almost docetistic conception of corporeity, his denial of a material resurrection, his doctrine of the pre-existence and the pre-temporal fall of souls (including the pre-existence of the human soul of Christ), of eternal creation, of the extension of the work of redemption to the inhabitants of the stars and to all rational creatures, and of the final restoration of all men and fallen angels.

Origen's greatest service was in exegesis. He is father of the critical investigation of Scripture, and his commentaries are still useful to scholars for their suggestiveness. Gregory Thaumaturgus says, he had "received from God the greatest gift, to be an interpreter of the word of God to men." For that age this judgment is perfectly just. Origen remained the exegetical oracle until Chrysostom far surpassed him, not indeed in originality and vigor of mind and extent of learning, but in sound, sober tact, in simple, natural analysis, and in practical application of the text. His great defect is the neglect of the grammatical and historical sense and his constant desire to find a hidden mystic meaning. He even goes further in this direction than the Gnostics, who everywhere saw transcendental, unfathomable mysteries. His hermeneutical principle assumes a threefold sense—somatic, psychic, and pneumatic; or literal, moral, and spiritual. His allegorical interpretation is ingenious, but often runs far away from the text and degenerates into the merest caprice;

while at times it gives way to the opposite extreme of a carnal literalism, by which he justifies his ascetic extravagance.

3. The writings of Origen

Origen was an uncommonly prolific author, but by no means an idle bookmaker. Jerome says, he wrote more than other men can read. His books extend to all branches of the theology of that day.

1. His biblical works were the most numerous, and may be divided into critical, exegetical, and hortatory.

Critical

Among the critical were the *Hexapla* (the *Sixfold Bible*) and the shorter *Tetrapla* (the *Fourfold*), on which he spent eight-and-twenty years of the most unwearied labor. The *Hexapla* was the first polyglott Bible.

Exegetical

His commentaries covered almost all the books of the Old and New Testaments, and contained a vast wealth of original and profound suggestions, with the most arbitrary allegorical and mystical fancies.

Hortatory

The refutation of Celsus's attack upon Christianity, in eight books, written in the last years of his life, about 248, is preserved complete in the original, and is one of the ripest and most valuable productions of Origen, and of the whole ancient apologetic literature.

Among his practical works may be mentioned a treatise on prayer, with an exposition of the Lord's Prayer, and an exhortation to martyrdom, written during the persecution of Maximin (235–238), and addressed to his friend and patron Ambrosius.

Among the works of Origen is also usually inserted the Philocalia, or a collection, in twenty-seven chapters, of extracts from his writings on various exegetical questions, made by Gregory Nazianzen and Basil the Great.

Samuel M. Jackson, Biographical Sketches of Ecclesiastical Writers, 1882

Cyprian

Dates

AD 200–258

Famous for being

First bishop-martyr of Africa

Important writings
Unity of the Church

One of his quotations
"There is no salvation outside the church."

1. Life of Cyprian

Thascius Caecilius Cyprianus, bishop and martyr, and the impersonation of the catholic church of the middle of the third century, sprang from a noble and wealthy heathen family of Carthage, where he was born about the year 200, or earlier. His deacon and biographer, Pontius, considers his earlier life not worthy of notice in comparison with his subsequent greatness in the church. Jerome tells us, that he stood in high repute as a teacher of rhetoric. He was, at all events, a man of commanding literary, rhetorical, and legal culture, and of eminent administrative ability which afterwards proved of great service to him in the episcopal office. He lived in worldly splendor to mature age, nor was he free from the common vices of heathenism, as we must infer from his own confessions. But the story, that he practiced arts of magic arises perhaps from some confusion, and is at any rate unattested. Yet, after he became a Christian he believed, like Tertullian and others, in visions and dreams, and had some only a short time before his martyrdom.

He himself, in a tract soon afterwards written to a friend, gives us the following oratorical description of his conversion: While I languished in darkness and deep night, tossing upon the sea of a troubled world, ignorant of my destination, and far from truth and light, I thought it, according to my then habits, altogether a difficult and hard thing that a man could be born anew, and that, being quickened to new life by the bath of saving water, he might put off the past, and, while preserving the identity of the body, might transform the man in mind and heart. How, said I, is such a change possible? How can one at once divest himself of all that was either innate or acquired and grown upon him? . . . Whence does he learn frugality, who was accustomed to sumptuous feasts? And how shall he who shone in costly apparel, in gold and purple, come down to common and simple dress? He who has lived in honor and station, cannot bear to be private and obscure . . . . But when, by the aid of the regenerating water, the stain of my former life was washed away, a serene and pure light poured from above into my purified breast. So soon as I drank the spirit from above and was transformed by a second birth into a new man, then the wavering mind became wonderfully firm; what had been closed opened; the dark became light; strength came for that which had seemed difficult; what I had thought impossible became practicable."

Cyprian now devoted himself zealously, in ascetic retirement, to the study of the Scriptures and the church teachers, especially Tertullian, whom be called for daily with the words: "Hand me the master!"

For ten years, ending with his triumphant martyrdom, Cyprian administered the episcopal office in Carthage with exemplary energy, wisdom, and fidelity, and that in a most stormy time, amidst persecutions from without and schismatic agitations within. The persecution under Valerian brought his active labors to a close. He was sent into exile for eleven months, then tried before the Proconsul, and condemned to be beheaded. When the sentence was pronounced, he said: "Thanks be to God," knelt in prayer, tied the bandage over his eyes with his own hand, gave to the executioner a gold piece, and died with the dignity and composure of a hero. His friends removed and buried his body by night. Two chapels were erected on the spots of his death and burial. The anniversary of his death was long observed; and five sermons of Augustin still remain in memory of Cyprian's martyrdom, Sept. 14, 258.

2. Character and position

As Origen was the ablest scholar, and Tertullian the strongest writer, so Cyprian was the greatest bishop, of the third century. He was born to be a prince in the church. In executive talent, he even surpassed all the Roman bishops of his time; and he bore himself towards them, also, as "frater" and "collega," in the spirit of full equality. Augustin calls him by, eminence, "the catholic bishop and catholic martyr;" and Vincentius of Lirinum, "the light of all saints, all martyrs, and all bishops." His stamp of character was more that of Peter than either of Paul or John.

His peculiar importance falls not so much in the field of theology, where he lacks originality and depth, as in church organization and discipline. While Tertullian dealt mainly with heretics, Cyprian directed his polemics against schismatics, among whom he had to condemn, though he never does in fact, his venerated teacher, who died a Montanist.

3. His writings

As an author, Cyprian is far less original, fertile and vigorous than Tertullian, but is clearer, more moderate, and more elegant and rhetorical in his style. He wrote independently only on the doctrines of the church, the priesthood, and sacrifice.

His most important works relate to practical questions on church government and discipline. Among these is his tract on the *Unity of the Church* (251), that "magna charta" of the old catholic high-church spirit. Then eighty-one Epistles, some very long, to various bishops, to the clergy and the churches of Africa and of Rome, to the confessors, to the lapsed, &c.; comprising also some letters from others in reply, as from Cornelius of Rome and Firmilian of Caesarea. They give us a very graphic picture of his pastoral labors, and of the whole church life of that day. To the same class belongs also his treatise: De Lapsis (250) against loose penitential discipline.

Samuel M. Jackson, Biographical Sketches of Ecclesiastical Writers, 1882

Other Christian leaders in the age of expansion and persecution

Polycarp of Smyrna (c. 70 – c. 155/167)

Papias (first half of second century)

Clement of Alexandria (?185—211/216)

Polycarp of Smyrna (c. AD 70 – c. 155/167)

Polycarp, a disciple of the apostle John, a younger friend of Ignatius, and the teacher of Irenaeus (between 130 and 140), presided as presbyter-bishop over the church of Smyrna in Asia Minor in the first half of the second century; and died at the stake in the persecution under Antoninus Pius 155, at a great age, having served the Lord six and eighty years.

He was not so original and intellectually active as Clement or Ignatius, but a man of truly venerable character, and simple, patriarchal piety.

His disciple Irenaeus of Lyons in a letter to his fellow-pupil Florinus (who had fallen into the error of Gnosticism) has given us most valuable reminiscences of this "blessed and apostolic presbyter," which show how faithfully he held fast the apostolic tradition, and how he deprecated all departure from it. He remembered vividly his mode of life and personal appearance, his discourses to the people, and his communications respecting the teaching and miracles of the Lord, as he had received them from the mouth of John and other eye-witnesses, in agreement with the Holy Scriptures.

In another place, Irenaeus says of Polycarp, that he had all the time taught what he had learned from the apostles, and what the church handed down; and relates, that he once called the Gnostic Marcion in Rome, "the first-born of Satan." In the epistle of Polycarp to the Philippians, he says: "Whoever doth not confess, that Jesus Christ is come in the flesh, is antichrist, and whoever doth not confess the mystery of the cross, is of the devil; and he, who wrests the words of the Lord according to his own pleasure, and saith, there is no resurrection and judgment, is the first-born of Satan."

The epistle to the Philippians

This epistle, consisting of fourteen short chapters, is the only document that remains to us from the Johannean age. The epistle is interwoven with many reminiscences of the Synoptic Gospels and the epistles of Paul, John and First Peter, which give to it considerable importance in the history of the canon.

Samuel M. Jackson, Biographical Sketches of Ecclesiastical Writers, 1882

Papias (first half of second century)

Papias was one of the early leaders of the Christian church, canonized as a saint. Eusebius calls him "Bishop of Hierapolis" (modern Pamukkale, Turkey) which is 22km from Laodicea and near Colossae (see Col. 4:13), in the Lycus river valley in Phrygia, Asia Minor.

His *Interpretations of the Sayings of the Lord* (his word for "sayings" is *logia*) in five books, would have been a prime early authority in the exegesis of the sayings of Jesus.

The book has utterly disappeared, known only through fragments quoted in later writers, with neutral approval in Irenaeus' *Against Heresies* and later with scorn by Eusebius of Caesarea in "Ecclesiastical History".

Papias describes his way of gathering information:

> I will not hesitate to add also for you to my interpretations what I formerly learned with care from the Presbyters and have carefully stored in memory, giving assurance of its truth. For I did not take pleasure as the many do in those who speak much, but in those who teach what is true, nor in those who relate foreign precepts, but in those who relate the precepts which were given by the Lord to the faith and came down from the Truth itself. And also if any follower of the Presbyters happened to come, I would inquire for the sayings of the Presbyters, what Andrew said, or what Peter said, or what Philip or what Thomas or James or what John or Matthew or any other of the Lord's disciples, and for the things which other of the Lord's disciples, and for the things which Aristion and the Presbyter John, the disciples of the Lord, were saying. For I considered that I should not get so much advantage from matter in books as from the voice which yet lives and remains.

Thus Papias reports he heard things that came from an unwritten, oral tradition of the Presbyters, a "sayings" or *logia* tradition that had been passed from Jesus to such of the apostles and disciples as he mentions in the fragmentary quote.

About the origins of the Gospels, Papias (as quoted by Eusebius) wrote this:

> Mark having become the interpreter of Peter, wrote down accurately whatsoever he remembered. It was not, however, in exact order that he related the sayings or deeds of Christ. For he neither heard the Lord nor accompanied Him. But afterwards, as I said, he accompanied Peter, who accommodated his instructions to the necessities [of his hearers], but with no intention of giving a regular narrative of the Lord's sayings.

Wherefore Mark made no mistake in thus writing some things as he remembered them. For of one thing he took especial care, not to omit anything he had heard, and not to put anything fictitious into the statements. Matthew put together the oracles [of the Lord] in the Hebrew language, and each one interpreted them as best he could.

Clement of Alexandria (AD? 211/216)

Clement of Alexandria (Titus Flavius Clemens), was one of its most distinguished teachers of the Church of Alexandria.

The thoroughness of his education is shown by his constant quotation of the Greek poets and philosophers. He traveled in Greece, Italy, Palestine, and finally Egypt. He became the colleague of Pantaenus, the head of the Catechetical School of Alexandria, and finally succeeded him in the direction of the school. One of his most popular pupils was Origen. During the persecution of Septimius Severus (202 or 203) he sought refuge with Alexander, then bishop (possibly of Flaviada) in Cappadocia, afterward of Jerusalem, from whom he brought a letter to Antioch in 211.

Clement of Alexandria's great trilogy

The trilogy into which Clement's principal remains are connected by their purpose and mode of treatment is composed of:

the Protrepticus ("Exhortation to the Greeks")
the Paedagogus ("Instructor")
the Stromata ("Miscellanies")

Overbeck calls it the boldest literary undertaking in the history of the Church, since in it Clement for the first time attempted to set forth Christianity for the faithful in the traditional forms of secular literature.

The first book deals with the religious basis of Christian morality, the second and third with the individual cases of conduct. As with Epictetus, true virtue shows itself with him in its external evidences by a natural, simple, and moderate way of living.

Quotations about Clement of Alexandria

"[Clement and Origen were] men eminent for their information in every department of literature and science."

Socrates Scholasticus c. 380

"Clement, a presbyter of Alexandria, in my judgment the most learned of men. . . [He has produced] notable volumes full of learning and eloquence using both Scripture and secular literature."

St. Jerome

"Perhaps nothing in the whole range of early patristic literature is more stimulating to the modern reader than (Clement's) great trilogy of graduated instruction in the Christian life."

H. B. Swete

"[Clement was] the first systematic teacher of Christian doctrine, the formal champion of liberal culture in the Church."

J. Patrick

"I do not know where we shall look for a purer or truer man than this Clement of Alexandria . . . He seems to me to be one of the old Fathers whom we should all have reverenced most as a teacher, and loved most as a friend."

Frederick Denison Maurice

Quotations by Clement of Alexandria

"All things are arranged with a view to the salvation of the universe by the Lord of the universe, both generally and particularly. It is then the function of the righteousness of salvation to improve everything as far as practicable. For even minor matters are arranged with a view to the salvation of that which is better, and for an abode suitable for people's character. Now everything that is virtuous changes for the better; having as the proper cause of change the free choice of knowledge, which the soul has in its own power. But necessary corrections, through the goodness of the great overseeing Judge, both by the attendant angels, and by various acts of anticipative judgment, and by the perfect judgment, compel egregious sinners to repent."

Clement of Alexandria, Stromata, Book 7, Chapter 2, ANF, Vol 2

"1 John 2:2. 'And not only for our sins,'—that is for those of the faithful,—is the Lord the propitiator, does he say, "but also for the whole world." He, indeed, saves all; but some [He saves], converting them by punishments; others, however, who follow voluntarily [He saves] with dignity of honor; so "that every knee should bow to Him, of things in heaven, and things on earth, and things under the earth;" that is, angels, men, and souls that before His advent have departed from this temporal life."

Clement of Alexandria, Commentary on 1 John 2.2,
Fragments from the Latin Translation of Cassiodorus, ANF, Vol 2

Christian writings from the time of expansion and persecution

The writings of the Ante-Nicene Fathers to 325

The Ante-Nicene Fathers

For an exhaustive treasure trove of early Christian writings the best place to turn to is *The Ante-Nicene Fathers* (10 Volumes)

The Ante-Nicene Fathers ranges from the Apostolic Fathers to various third and fourth century sources including the liturgies and ancient Syriac documents. It gives English translations of nearly all the works of the Fathers down to the first General Council held at Nicaea in 325

The General Editor of *The Ante-Nicene Fathers,* Phillip Schaff (1819–1893), was born in Switzerland, was educated at Tübingen, Halle, and Berlin, and later took a position as Professor of Church history at German Reformed Seminary in Mercersburg, Penn., and

Union Theological Seminary in New York. He was involved in the formation of the Evangelical Alliance, the revision of the English Bible (the Revised Version), and the Alliance of the Reformed Churches. Schaff was founder of the American Society of Church History and was the author of *The History of the Christian Church* (8 volumes).

Extracts from Christian writings from the time of expansion and persecution

Polycarp, *The Martyrdom of. Polycarpi*
The Epistle of Barnabas
The Shepherd of Hermas
Mathetes, *Epistle to Diognetus*
Justin Martyr, *The Resurrection*
Irenaeus, "The treasure hid in the Scriptures is Christ," *Against Heresies, IV, 26*
Origen, *Commentary on the Gospel of John*
Tertullian, *The Testimony of the Soul*
Cyprian, *Treatise 1: The Unity of the Church*

Polycarp
The Martyrdom of Polycarp* or *Letter of the Smyrnaeans

0:1 The Church of God which sojourned at Smyrna to the Church of God which sojourned in Philomelium and to all the brotherhoods of the holy and universal Church sojourning in every place;

0:2 mercy and peace and love from God the Father and our Lord Jesus Christ be multiplied.

1:1 We write unto you, brethren, an account of what befell those that suffered martyrdom and especially the blessed Polycarp, who stayed the persecution, having as it were set his seal upon it by his martyrdom.

1:2 For nearly all the foregoing events came to pass that the Lord might show us once more an example of martyrdom which is conformable to the Gospel. . . .

6:5 And the captain of the police, who chanced to have the very name, being called Herod, was eager to bring him into the stadium that he himself might fulfill his appointed lot, being made a partaker with Christ, while they—his betrayers—underwent the punishment of Judas himself.

7:1 So taking the lad with them, on the Friday about the supper hour, the gendarmes and horsemen went forth with their accustomed arms, hastening {as against a robber.}

7:2 And coming up in a body late in the evening, they found the man himself in bed in an upper chamber in a certain cottage;

7:3 and though he might have departed thence to another place, he would not, saying, {The will of God be done.}

7:4 So when he heard that they were come, he went down and conversed with them the bystanders marveling at his age and his constancy, and wondering how there should be so much eagerness for the apprehension of an old man like him.

7:5 Thereupon forthwith he gave orders that a table should be spread for them to eat and drink at that hour, as much as they desired.

7:6 And he persuaded them to grant him an hour that he might pray unmolested;

7:7 and on their consenting, he stood up and prayed, being so full of the grace of God, that for two hours he could not hold his peace, and those that heard were amazed, and many repented that they had come against such a venerable old man.

8:1 But when at length he brought his prayer to an end, after remembering all who at any time had come in his way, small and great, high and low, and all the universal Church throughout the world, the hour of departure being come, they seated him, on an ass and brought him into the city, it being a high Sabbath.

8:2 And he was met by Herod the captain of police and his father Nicetes, who also removed him to their carriage and tried to prevail upon him, seating themselves by his side and saying, 'Why what harm is there in saying, Caesar is Lord, and offering incense', with more to this effect, 'and saving thyself?'

8:3 But he at first gave them no answer.

8:4 When however they persisted, he said, 'I am not going to do what ye counsel me.'

8:5 Then they, failing to persuade him, uttered threatening words and made him dismount with speed, so that he bruised his shin, as he got down from the carriage.

8:6 And without even turning round, he went on his way promptly and with speed, as if nothing had happened to him, being taken to the stadium;

8:7 there being such a tumult in the stadium that no man's voice could be so much as heard.

9:1 But as Polycarp entered into the stadium, a voice came to him from heaven;

9:2 'Be strong, Polycarp, and play the man.'

9:3 And no one saw the speaker, but those of our people who were present heard the voice.

9:4 And at length, when he was brought up, there was a great tumult, for they heard that Polycarp had been apprehended.

9:5 When then he was brought before him, the proconsul enquired whether he were the man.

9:6 And on his confessing that he was, he tried to persuade him to a denial saying, 'Have respect to thine age,' and other things in accordance therewith, as it is their wont to say;

9:7 'Swear by the genius of Caesar;

9:8 repent and say, Away with the atheists.'

9:9 Then Polycarp with solemn countenance looked upon the whole multitude of lawless heathen that were in the stadium, and waved his hand to them;

9:10 and groaning and looking up to heaven he said, 'Away with the atheists.'

9:11 But when the magistrate pressed him hard and said, 'Swear the oath, and I will release thee;

9:12 revile the Christ,' Polycarp said, 'Fourscore and six years have I been His servant, and He hath done me no wrong.

9:13 How then can I blaspheme my King who saved me?'

10:1 But on his persisting again and saying, 'Swear by the genius of Caesar,' he answered, 'If thou supposest vainly that I will swear by the genius of Caesar, as thou sayest, and feignest that thou art ignorant who I am, hear thou plainly, I am a Christian.

10:2 But if thou wouldest learn the doctrine of Christianity, assign a day and give me a hearing.'

10:3 The proconsul said;

10:4 'Prevail upon the people.'

10:5 But Polycarp said;

10:6 'As for thyself, I should have held thee worthy of discourse;

10:7 for we have been taught to render, as is meet, to princes and authorities appointed by God such honor as does us no harm;

10:8 but as for these, I do not hold them worthy, that I should defend myself before them.'

11:1 Whereupon the proconsul said;

11:2 'I have wild beasts here and I will throw thee to them, except thou repent.'

11:3 But he said, 'Call for them:

11:4 for the repentance from better to worse is a change not permitted to us;

11:5 but it is a noble thing to change from untowardness to righteousness.'

11:6 Then he said to him again, 'I will cause thee to be consumed by fire, if thou despisest the wild beasts, unless thou repent.'

11:7 But Polycarp said;

11:8 'Thou threatenest that fire which burneth for a season and after a little while is quenched for thou art ignorant of the fire of the future judgment and eternal punishment, which is reserved for the ungodly.

11:9 But why delayest thou Come, do what thou wilt.'

12:1 Saying these things and more besides, he was inspired with courage and joy, and his countenance was filled with grace, so that not only did it not drop in dismay at the things which were said to him, but on the contrary the proconsul was astounded and sent his own herald to proclaim three times in the midst of the stadium, Polycarp hath confessed himself to be a Christian.'

12:2 When this was proclaimed by the herald, the whole multitude both of Gentiles and of Jews who dwelt in Smyrna cried out with ungovernable wrath and with a loud shout, 'This is the teacher of Asia, the father of the Christians, the puller down of our gods, who teacheth numbers not to sacrifice nor worship.'

12:3 Saying these things, they shouted aloud and asked the Asiarch Philip to let a lion loose upon Polycarp.

12:4 But he said that it was not lawful for him, since he had brought the sports to a close.

12:5 Then they thought fit to shout out with one accord that Polycarp should be burned alive.

12:6 For it must needs be that the matter of the vision should be fulfilled, which was shown him concerning his pillow, when he saw it on fire while praying, and turning round he said prophetically to the faithful who were with him, 'I must needs be burned alive.'

13:1 These things then happened with so great speed, quicker than words could tell, the crowds forthwith collecting from the workshops and baths timber and faggots, and the Jews more especially assisting in this with zeal, as is their wont.

13:2 But when the pile was made ready, divesting himself of all his upper garments and loosing his girdle, he endeavored also to take off his shoes, though not in the habit of doing this before, because all the faithful at all times vied eagerly who should soonest touch his flesh.

13:3 For he had been treated with all honor for his holy life even before his gray hairs came.

13:4 Forthwith then the instruments that were prepared for the pile were placed about him;

13:5 and as they were going likewise to nail him to the stake, he said;

13:6 'Leave me as I am;

13:7 for He that hath granted me to endure the fire will grant me also to remain at the pile unmoved, even without the security which ye seek from the nails.'

14:1 So they did not nail him, but tied him.

14:2 Then he, placing his hands behind him and being bound to the stake, like a noble ram out of a great flock for an offering, a burnt sacrifice made ready and acceptable to God, looking up to heaven said;

14:3 'O Lord God Almighty, the Father of Thy beloved and blessed Son Jesus Christ, through whom we have received the knowledge of Thee, the God of angels and powers and of all creation and of the whole race of the righteous, who live in Thy presence;

14:4 I bless Thee for that Thou hast granted me this day and hour, that I might receive a portion amongst the number of martyrs in the cup of [Thy] Christ unto resurrection of eternal life, both of soul and of body, in the incorruptibility of the Holy Spirit.

14:5 May I be received among these in Thy presence this day, as a rich and acceptable sacrifice, as Thou didst prepare and reveal it beforehand, and hast accomplished it, Thou that art the faithful and true God.

14:6 For this cause, yea and for all things, I praise Thee, I bless Thee, I glorify Thee, through the eternal and heavenly High-priest, Jesus Christ, Thy beloved Son, through whom with Him and the Holy Spirit be glory both now [and ever] and for the ages to come. Amen.'

15:1 When he had offered up the Amen and finished his prayer, the firemen lighted the fire.

15:2 And, a mighty flame flashing forth, we to whom it was given to see, saw a marvel, yea and we were preserved that we might relate to the rest what happened.

15:3 The fire, making the appearance of a vault, like the sail of a vessel filled by the wind, made a wall round about the body of the martyr;

15:4 and it was there in the midst, not like flesh burning, but like [a loaf in the oven or like] gold and silver refined in a furnace.

15:5 For we perceived such a fragrant smell, as if it were the wafted odor of frankincense or some other precious spice.

16:1 So at length the lawless men, seeing that his body could not be consumed by the fire, ordered an executioner to go up to him and stab him with a dagger.

16:2 And when he had done this, there came forth [a dove and] a quantity of blood, so that it extinguished the fire;

16:3 and all the multitude marveled that there should be so great a difference between the unbelievers and the elect.

16:4 In the number of these was this man, the glorious martyr Polycarp, who was found an apostolic and prophetic teacher in our own time, a bishop of the holy Church which is in Smyrna.

16:5 For every word which he uttered from his mouth was accomplished and will be accomplished.

Translated by J. B. Lightfoot

The Epistle of Barnabas

Introduction

The Epistle of Barnabas, is anonymous, and omits all allusion to the name or residence of the readers. He addresses them not as their teacher, but as one among them. Though not addressed to any particular congregation, it is intended for a particular class of Christians who were in danger of relapsing into Judaizing errors.

Barnabas proclaims thus an absolute separation of Christianity from Judaism. In this respect he goes further than any post-apostolic writer.

The Epistle of Barnabas has considerable historical, doctrinal, and apologetic value. He confirms the principal facts and doctrines of the gospel. He testifies to the general observance of Sunday on "the eighth day," as the joyful commemoration of Christ's resurrection, in strict distinction from the Jewish Sabbath on the seventh. He furnishes the first clear argument for the canonical authority of the Gospel of Matthew (without naming it) by quoting the passage: "Many are called, but few are chosen," with the solemn formula of Scripture quotation: "as it is written."

1:1 I Bid you greeting, sons and daughters, in the name of the Lord that loved us, in peace.

1:2 Seeing that the ordinances of God are great and rich unto you, I rejoice with an exceeding great and overflowing joy at your blessed and glorious spirits; so innate is the grace of the spiritual gift that ye have received.

1:3 Wherefore also I the more congratulate myself hoping to be saved, for that I truly see the Spirit poured out among you from the riches of the fount of the Lord. So greatly did the much-desired sight of you astonish me respecting you.

1:4 Being therefore persuaded of this, and being conscious with myself that having said much among you I know that the Lord journeyed with me on the way of righteousness, and am wholly constrained also myself to this, to love you more than my own soul (for great faith and love dwelleth in you through the hope of the life which is His)—considering this therefore, that,

1:5 if it shall be my care to communicate to you some portion of that which I received, it shall turn to my reward for having ministered to such spirits, I was eager to send you a trifle, that along with your faith ye might have your knowledge also perfect.

1:6 Well then, there are three ordinances of the Lord; *the hope of life, which is the beginning and end of our faith; and righteousness, which is the beginning and end of judgment; love shown in gladness and exultation, the testimony of works of righteousness.

1:7 For the Lord made known to us by His prophets things past and present, giving us likewise the firstfruits of the taste of things future. And seeing each of these things severally coming to pass, according as He spake, we ought to offer a richer and higher offering to the fear of Him. But I, not as though I were a teacher, but as one of yourselves, will show forth a few things, whereby ye shall be gladdened in the present circumstances.

2:1 Seeing then that the days are evil, and that the Active One himself has the authority, we ought to give heed to ourselves and to seek out the ordinances of the Lord.

2:2 The aids of our faith then are fear and patience, and our allies are long-suffering and self-restraint.

2:3 While these abide in a pure spirit in matters relating to the Lord, wisdom, understanding, science, knowledge rejoice with them.

2:4 For He hath made manifest to us by all the prophets that He wanteth neither sacrifices nor whole burnt offerings nor oblations, saying at one time;

2:5 What to Me is the multitude of your sacrifices, saith the Lord I am full of whole burnt-offerings, and the fat of lambs and the blood of bulls and of goats desire not, not though ye should come to be seen of Me. or who required these things at your hands? Ye shall continue no more to tread My court. If ye bring fine flour, it is in vain; incense is an abomination to Me; your new moons and your Sabbaths I cannot away with.

2:6 These things therefore He annulled, that the new law of our Lord Jesus Christ, being free from the yoke of constraint, might have its oblation not made by human hands.

2:7 And He saith again unto them; Did command your fathers when they went forth from the land of Egypt to bring Me whole burnt offerings and sacrifices?

2:8 Nay, this was My command unto them, Let none of you bear a grudge of evil against his neighbor in his heart, and love you not a false oath.

2:9 So we ought to perceive, unless we are without understanding, the mind of the goodness of our Father; for He speaketh to us, desiring us not to go astray like them but to seek how we may approach Him.

2:10 Thus then speaketh He to us; The sacrifice unto God is a broken heart, the smell of a sweet savor unto the Lord is a heart that glorifies its Maker. We ought therefore, brethren, to learn accurately concerning our salvation, lest the Evil One having effected an entrance of error in us should fling us away from our life.

3:1 He speaketh again therefore to them concerning these things; Wherefore fast ye for Me, saith the Lord, so that your voice is heard this day crying aloud? This is not the fast which have chosen, saith the Lord; not a man abasing his soul;

3:2 not though ye should bend your neck as a hoop, and put on sackcloth and make your bed of ashes, not even so shall ye call a fast that is acceptable.

3:3 But unto us He saith; Behold, this is the fast which I have chosen, saith the Lord; loosen every band of wickedness, untie the tightened cords of forcible contracts, send away the broken ones released and tear in pieces every unjust bond. Break thy bread to the hungry, and if thou seest one naked clothe him; bring the shelterless into thy house, and if thou seest a humble man, thou shalt not despise him, neither shall any one of thy household and of thine own seed.

3:4 Then shall thy light break forth in the morning, and thy healing shall arise quickly, and righteousness shall go forth before thy face, and the glory of God shall environ thee.

3:5 Then shalt thou cry out and God shall hear thee; while thou art still speaking, He shall say 'Lo, I am here'; if thou shalt take away from thee the yoke and the stretching forth of the finger and the word of murmuring, and shalt give thy bread to the hungry heartily, and shalt pity the abased soul.

3:6 To this end therefore, my brethren, He that is long-suffering, foreseeing that the people whom He had prepared in His well-beloved would believe in simplicity, manifested to us beforehand concerning all things, that we might not as novices shipwreck ourselves upon their law.

4:1 It behooves us therefore to investigate deeply concerning the present, and to search out the things which have power to save us. Let us therefore flee altogether from all the works of lawlessness, lest the works of lawlessness overpower us; and let us loathe the error of the present time, that we may be loved for that which is to come.

4:2 Let us give no relaxation to our soul that it should have liberty to consort with sinners and wicked men, lest haply we be made like unto them.

Translated by J. B. Lightfoot

The Shepherd of Hermas

Introduction

The Shepherd of Hermas (sometimes just called *The Shepherd*) is a Christian work of the second century. *The Shepherd* had great authority in the 2nd and 3rd centuries. It was cited as Scripture by Irenaeus and Tertullian and was bound with the New Testament in the Codex Sinaiticus.

The Shepherd of Hermas takes its title because the author calls himself Hermas and is instructed by the angel of repentance in the form of a shepherd. It differs from all other writings of the apostolic fathers by its literary form. It is the oldest Christian allegory, an apocalyptic book, a sort of didactic religious romance. The following extract is the opening vision in the book.

1. "He who had brought me up, sold me to a certain Rhoda at Rome. Many years after, I met her again and began to love her as a sister. Some time after this, I saw her bathing in the river Tiber, and I gave her my hand and led her out of the river. And when I beheld her beauty, I thought in my heart, saying: 'Happy should I be, if I had a wife of such beauty and goodness.' This was my only thought, and nothing more.

"After some time, as I went into the villages and glorified the creatures of God, for their greatness, and beauty, and power, I fell asleep while walking. And the Spirit seized me and carried me through a certain wilderness through which no man could travel, for the ground was rocky and impassable, on account of the water.

"And when I had crossed the river, I came to a plain; and falling upon my knees, I began to pray unto the Lord and to confess my sins. And while I was praying, the heaven opened, and I beheld the woman that I loved saluting me from heaven, and saying: 'Hail, Hermas!'

And when I beheld her, I said unto her: 'Lady, what doest thou here?'

But she answered and said: 'I was taken up, in order that I might bring to light thy sins before the Lord.'

And I said unto her: 'Hast thou become my accuser?'

'No,' said she; 'but hear the words that I shall say unto thee. God who dwells in heaven, and who made the things that are out of that which is not, and multiplied and increased them on account of his holy church, is angry with thee because thou hast sinned against me.'

I answered and said unto her: 'Have I sinned against thee? In what way? Did I ever say unto thee an unseemly word? Did I not always consider thee as a lady? Did I not always respect thee as a sister? Why doest thou utter against me, O Lady, these wicked and foul lies?'

But she smiled and said unto me: 'The desire of wickedness has entered into thy heart. Does it not seem to thee an evil thing for a just man, if an evil desire enters into his heart? Yea, it is a sin, and a great one (said she). For the just man devises just things, and by devising just things is his glory established in the heavens, and he finds the Lord merciful unto him in all his ways; but those who desire evil things in their hearts, bring upon themselves death and captivity, especially they who set their affection upon this world, and who glory in their wealth, and lay not hold of the good things to come. The souls of those that have no hope, but have cast themselves and their lives away, shall greatly regret it. But do thou pray unto God, and thy sins shall be healed, and those of thy whole house and of all the saints.'

2. "After she had spoken these words, the heavens were closed, and I remained trembling all over and was sorely troubled. And I said within myself: 'If this sin be set down against me, how can I be saved? or how can I propitiate God for the multitude of my sins? or with what words shall I ask the Lord to have mercy upon me?'

"While I was meditating on these things, and was musing on them in my heart, I beheld in front of me a great white chair made out of fleeces of wool; and there came an aged woman, clad in very shining raiment, and having a book in her hand, and she sat down by herself on the chair and saluted me, saying: 'Hail, Hermas!"

And I, sorrowing and weeping, said unto her: 'Hail, Lady!'

And she said unto me: 'Why art thou sorrowful, O Hermas, for thou wert wont to be patient, and good-tempered, and always smiling? Why is thy countenance cast down? and why art thou not cheerful?'

And I said unto her: 'O Lady, I have been reproached by a most excellent woman, who said unto me that I sinned against her.'

And she said unto me: 'Far be it from the servant of God to do this thing. But of a surety a desire after her must have come into thy heart. Such an intent as this brings a charge of sin against the servant of God; for it is an evil and horrible intent that a devout and tried spirit should lust after an evil deed; and especially that the chaste Hermas should do so-he who abstained from every evil desire, and was full of all simplicity, and of great innocence!'

3. "'But [she continued] God is not angry with thee on account of this, but in order that thou mayest convert thy house, which has done iniquity against the Lord, and against you who art their parent. But thou, in thy love for your children didst not rebuke thy house, but didst allow it to become dreadfully wicked. On this account is the Lord angry with thee; but He will heal all the evils that happened aforetime in thy house; for through the sins and iniquities of thy household thou hast been corrupted by the affairs of this life. But the mercy of the Lord had compassion upon thee, and upon thy house, and will make thee strong and establish thee in His glory. Only be not slothful, but be of good courage and strengthen thy house. For even as the smith, by smiting his work with the hammer, accomplishes the thing that he wishes, so shall the daily word of righteousness overcome all iniquity. Fail not, therefore, to rebuke thy children, for I know that if they will repent with all their heart, they will be written in the book of life, together with the saints.'

"After these words of hers were ended, she said unto me: 'Dost thou wish to hear me read?'

I said unto her: 'Yea, Lady, I do wish it.'

She said unto me: 'Be thou a hearer, and listen to the glories of God.'

Then I heard, after a great and wonderful fashion, that which my memory was unable to retain; for all the words were terrible, and beyond man's power to bear. The last words, however, I remembered; for they were profitable for us, and gentle: 'Behold the God of power, who by his invisible strength, and His great wisdom, has created the world, and by His magnificent counsel hath crowned His creation with glory, and by His mighty word has fixed the heaven, and founded the earth upon the waters, and by His own wisdom and foresight has formed His holy church, which He has also blessed! Behold, He removes the heavens from their places, and the mountains, and the hills, and the stars, and everything becomes smooth before His elect, that He may give unto them the blessing which He promised them with great glory and joy, if only they shall keep with firm faith the laws of God which they have received.'

4. "When, therefore, she had ended her reading, and had risen up from the chair, there came four young men, and took up the chair, and departed towards the east. Then she called me, and touched my breast, and said unto me: 'Hast thou been pleased with my reading?'

And I said unto her: 'Lady, these last things pleased me; but the former were hard and harsh.'

But she spake unto me, saying: 'These last are for the righteous; but the former are for the heathen and the apostates."

While she was yet speaking with me, there appeared two men, and they took her up in their arms and departed unto the east, whither also the chair had gone. And she departed joyfully; and as she departed, she said: 'Be of good courage, O Hermas!'

The Shepherd of Hermas

Epistle to Diognetus (late second century)

Introduction

The Epistle of Mathetes to Diognetus is probably the earliest example of Christian apologetics, writings defending Christianity from its accusers. The Greek writer and recipient are not otherwise known, but the language and other textual evidence dates the work to the late 2nd century; some assume an even earlier date and count it among the Apostolic Fathers. "Mathetes" is not a proper name; it simply means "a disciple." Diognetus was a tutor of the emperor Marcus Aurelius, who admired him for his freedom from superstition and sound educational advice.

The writer does not use the name "Jesus" or the expression the "Christ" but prefers the use of "the Word."

In the 11th chapter "Mathetes" presents himself as "having been a disciple of Apostles I come forward as a teacher of the Gentiles, ministering worthily to them" placing himself in a class with authoritative figures like John the Presbyter. Two chapters make up the following extract.

Chapter 6

The relation of Christians to the world

To sum up all in one word what the soul is in the body, that are Christians in the world. The soul is dispersed through all the members of the body, and Christians are scattered through all the cities of the world. The soul dwells in the body, yet is not of the body; and Christians dwell in the world, yet are not of the world. The invisible soul is guarded by the visible body, and Christians are known indeed to be in the world, but their godliness remains invisible. The flesh hates the soul, and wars against it, though itself suffering no injury, because it is prevented from enjoying pleasures; the world also hates the Christians, though in nowise injured, because they abjure pleasures. The soul loves the flesh that hates it, and loves also the members; Christians likewise love those that hate them. The soul is imprisoned in the body, yet preserves that very body; and Christians are confined in the world as in a prison, and yet they are the preservers of the world. The immortal soul dwells in a mortal tabernacle; and Christians dwell as sojourners in corruptible bodies, looking for an incorruptible dwelling in the heavens. The soul, when but illprovided with food and drink, becomes better; in like manner, the Christians, though subjected day by day to punishment, increase the more in number. God has assigned them this illustrious position, which it were unlawful for them to forsake.

Chapter 7

The manifestation of Christ

For, as I said, this was no mere earthly invention which was delivered to them, nor is it a mere human system of opinion, which they judge it right to preserve so carefully, nor has a dispensation of mere human mysteries been committed to them, but truly God Himself, who is almighty, the Creator of all things, and invisible, has sent from heaven, and placed among men, [Him who is] the truth, and the holy and incomprehensible Word, and has firmly established Him in their hearts. He did not, as one might have imagined, send to men any servant, or angel, or ruler, or any one of those who bear sway over earthly things, or one of those to whom the government of things in the heavens has been entrusted, but the very Creator and Fashioner of all things by whom He made the heavens by whom he enclosed the sea within its proper bounds whose ordinances all the stars faithfully observe from whom the sun has received the measure of his daily course to be observed whom the moon obeys, being commanded to shine in the night, and whom the stars also obey, following the moon in her course; by whom all things have been arranged, and placed within their proper limits, and to whom all are subject the heavens and the things that are therein, the earth and the things that are therein, the sea and the things that are therein fire, air, and the abyss the things which are in the heights, the things which are in the depths, and the things which lie between. This messenger He sent to them. Was it then, as one might conceive, for the purpose of exercising tyranny, or of inspiring fear and terror? By no means, but under the influence of clemency and meekness. As a king sends his son, who is also a king, so sent He Him; as God He sent Him; as to men He sent Him; as a Savior He sent Him, and as seeking to persuade, not to compel us; for violence has no place in the character of God. As calling us He sent Him, not as vengefully pursuing us; as loving us He sent Him, not as judging us. For He will yet send Him to judge us, and who shall endure His appearing? . . . Do you not see them exposed to wild beasts, that they may be persuaded to deny the Lord, and yet not overcome? Do you not see that the more of them are punished, the greater becomes the number of the rest? This does not seem to be the work of man: this is the power of God; these are the evidences of His manifestation.

Mathetes

Justin Martyr

The Resurrection

Introduction

This writing comes from fragments of the lost work of Justin on the resurrection.

Chapter 1

The self-evidencing power of truth

The word of truth is free, and carries its own authority, disdaining to fall under any skilful argument, or to endure the logical scrutiny of its hearers. But it would be believed for its own nobility, and for the confidence due to Him who sends it. Now the word of truth is sent from God; wherefore the freedom claimed by the truth is not arrogant. For being sent with authority, it were not fit that it should be required to produce proof of what is said; since neither is there any proof beyond itself, which is God. For every proof is more powerful and trustworthy than that which it proves; since what is disbelieved, until proof is produced, gets credit when such proof is produced, and is recognized as being what it was stated to be. But nothing is either more powerful or more trustworthy than the truth; so that he who requires proof of this is like one who wishes it demonstrated why the things that appear to the senses do appear.

For the test of those things which are received through the reason, is sense; but of sense itself there is no test beyond itself. As then we bring those things which reason hunts after, to sense, and by it judge what kind of things they are, whether the things spoken be true or false, and then sit in judgment no longer, giving full credit to its decision; so also we refer all that is said regarding men and the world to the truth, and by it judge whether it be worthless or no. But the utterances of truth we judge by no separate test, giving full credit to itself. And God, the Father of the universe, who is the perfect intelligence, is the truth. And the Word, being His Son, came to us, having put on flesh, revealing both Himself and the Father, giving to us in Himself resurrection from the dead, and eternal life afterwards.

And this is Jesus Christ, our Savior and Lord. He, therefore, is Himself both the faith and the proof of Himself and of all things.

Wherefore those who follow Him, and know Him, having faith in Him as their proof, shall rest in Him. But since the adversary does not cease to resist many, and uses many and divers arts to ensnare them, that he may seduce the faithful from their faith, and that he may prevent the faithless from believing, it seems to me necessary that we also, being armed with the invulnerable doctrines of the faith, do battle against him in behalf of the weak.

Chapter 2

Objections to the resurrection of the flesh

They who maintain the wrong opinion say that there is no resurrection of the flesh; giving as their reason that it is impossible that what is corrupted and dissolved should be restored to the same as it had been. And besides the impossibility, they say that the salvation of the flesh is disadvantageous; and they abuse the flesh, adducing its infirmities, and declare that it only is the cause of our sins, so that if the flesh, say they, rise again, our infirmities also rise with it. And such sophistical reasons as the following they elaborate: If the flesh rise again, it must rise either entire and possessed of all its parts, or imperfect. But its rising imperfect argues a want of power on God's part, if some parts could be saved, and others not; but if all the parts are saved, then the body will manifestly have all its members. But is it not absurd to say that these members will exist after the resurrection from the dead, since the Savior said, "They neither marry, nor are given in marriage, but shall be as the angels in heaven?" And the angels, say they, have neither flesh, nor do they eat, nor have sexual intercourse; therefore there shall be no resurrection of the flesh. By these and such like arguments, they attempt to distract men from the faith. And there are some who maintain that even Jesus Himself appeared only as spiritual, and not in flesh, but presented merely the appearance of flesh: these persons seek to rob the flesh of the promise.

First, then, let us solve those things which seem to them to be insoluble; then we will introduce in an orderly manner the demonstration concerning the flesh, proving that it partakes of salvation.

Chapter 4

Must the deformed rise deformed?

Well, they say, if then the flesh rise, it must rise the same as it falls; so that if it die with one eye, it must rise one-eyed; if lame, lame; if defective in any part of the body, in this part the man must rise deficient. How truly blinded are they in the eyes of their hearts! For they have not seen on the earth blind men seeing again, and the lame walking by His word. All things which the Savior did, He did in the first place in order that what was spoken concerning Him in the prophets might be fulfilled, "that the blind should receive sight, and the deaf hear," and so on; but also to induce the belief that in the resurrection the flesh shall rise entire. For if on earth He healed the sicknesses of the flesh, and made the body whole, much more will He do this in the resurrection, so that the flesh shall rise perfect and entire. In this manner, then, shall those dreaded difficulties of theirs be healed.

Justin Martyr, translated by M. Dods

Irenaeus

"The Treasure Hid in the Scriptures Is Christ," from ***Against Heresies***

Introduction

Irenæus was one of the leading churchmen of the second century. Around the year 178 he became bishop of the churches in Lyons. At that time Gnostic heresies were flourishing, and so shortly after his ordination as bishop, Irenæus wrote a five-part treatise against them called "The Refutation and Overthrow of the Knowledge (Gnosis) Falsely So Called." Later writers referred to this work as Irenæus' Five Books Against the Heresies (*Adversus Hæreses*).

Among the many errors of the Gnostics was their opinion that the Old Testament was not to be regarded as canonical Scripture. They contended that many things in the Old Testament did not agree with the message of the New Testament (as they understood it), and so they rejected it. But Irenæus argued that the Old Testament is a thoroughly Christian book when it is rightly understood. Below we give an excerpt from the fourth book of *Adversus Hæreses*, in which Irenæus explains the right approach to the interpretation of the Old Testament.

Chapter 26

The treasure hid in the Scriptures is Christ; the true exposition of the scriptures is to be found in the church alone.

1. If any one, therefore, reads the Scriptures with attention, he will find in them an account of Christ, and a foreshadowing of the new calling. For Christ is the treasure which was hid in the field, that is, in this world; but the treasure hid in the Scriptures is Christ, since He was pointed out by means of types and parables. Hence His human nature could not be understood, prior to the consummation of those things which had been predicted, that is, the advent of Christ. And therefore it was said to Daniel the prophet: "Shut up the words, and seal the book even to the time of consummation, until many learn, and knowledge be completed. For at that time, when the dispersion shall be accomplished, they shall know all these things."

But Jeremiah also says, "In the last days they shall understand these things." For every prophecy, before its fulfillment, is to men full of enigmas and ambiguities. But when the time has arrived, and the prediction has come to pass, then the prophecies have a clear and certain exposition. And for this reason, indeed, when at this present time the law is read to the Jews, it is like a fable; for they do not possess the explanation of all things pertaining to the advent of the Son of God, which took place in human nature; but when it is read by the Christians, it is a treasure, hid indeed in a field, but brought to light by the cross of Christ, and explained, both enriching the understanding of men, and showing forth the wisdom of God and declaring His dispensations with regard to man, and forming the kingdom of Christ beforehand, and preaching by anticipation the inheritance of the holy Jerusalem, and proclaiming beforehand that the man who loves God shall arrive at such excellency as even to see God, and hear His word, and from the hearing of His discourse be glorified to such an extent, that others cannot behold the glory of his countenance, as was said by Daniel: "Those who do understand, shall shine as the brightness of the firmament, and many of the righteous as the stars for ever and ever."

Thus, then, I have shown it to be, if any one read the Scriptures. For thus it was that the Lord discoursed with, the disciples after His resurrection from the dead, proving to them from the Scriptures themselves "that Christ must suffer, and enter into His glory, and that remission of sins should be preached in His name throughout all the world." And the disciple will be perfected, and rendered like the householder, "who bringeth forth from his treasure things new and old."

2. Wherefore it is incumbent to obey the presbyters who are in the Church,—those who, as I have shown, possess the succession from the apostles; those who, together with the succession of the episcopate, have received the certain gift of truth, according to the good pleasure of the Father. But it is also incumbent to hold in suspicion others who depart from the primitive succession, and assemble themselves together in any place whatsoever, looking upon them either as heretics of perverse minds, or as schismaries puffed up and self-pleasing, or again as hypocrites, acting thus for the sake of lucre and vainglory. For all these have fallen from the truth. And the heretics, indeed, who bring strange fire to the altar of God—namely, strange doctrines—shall be burned up by the fire from heaven, as were Nadab and Abiud. But such as rise up in opposition to the truth, and exhort others against the Church of God, shall remain among those in hell, being swallowed up by an earthquake, even as those who were with Chore, Dathan, and Abiron. But those who cleave asunder, and separate the unity of the Church, shall receive from God the same punishment as Jeroboam did.

3. Those, however, who are believed to be presbyters by many, but serve their own lusts, and, do not place the fear of God supreme in their hearts, but conduct themselves with contempt towards others, and are puffed up with the pride of holding the chief seat, and work evil deeds in secret, saying, "No man sees us," shall be convicted by the Word, who does not judge after outward appearance, nor looks upon the countenance, but the heart; and they shall hear those words, to be found in Daniel the prophet: "O thou seed of Canaan, and not of Judah, beauty hath deceived thee, and lust perverted thy heart. Thou that art waxen old in wicked days, now thy sins which thou hast committed aforetime are come to

light; for thou hast pronounced false judgments, and hast been accustomed to condemn the innocent, and to let the guilty go free, albeit the Lord saith, The innocent and the righteous shalt thou not slay." Of whom also did the Lord say: "But if the evil servant shall say in his heart, My lord delayeth his coming, and shall begin to smite the man-servants and maidens, and to eat and drink and be drunken; the lord of that servant shall come in a day that he looketh not for him, and in an hour that he is not aware of, and shall cut him asunder, and appoint him his portion with the unbelievers."

4. From all such persons, therefore, it be-bores us to keep aloof, but to adhere to those who, as I have already observed, do hold the doctrine of the apostles, and who, together with the order of priesthood, display sound speech and blameless conduct for the confirmation and correction of others. In this way, Moses, to whom such a leadership was entrusted, relying on a good conscience, cleared himself before God, saying, "I have not in covetousness taken anything belonging to one of these men, nor have I done evil to one of them." In this way, too, Samuel, who judged the people so many years, and bore rule over Israel without any pride, in the end cleared himself, saying, "I have walked before you from my childhood even unto this day: answer me in the sight of God, and before His anointed; whose ox or whose ass of yours have I taken, or over whom have I tyrannized, or whom have I oppressed? or if I have received from the hand of any a bribe or so much as a shoe, speak out against me, and I will restore it to you."

And when the people had said to him, "Thou hast not tyrannized, neither hast thou oppressed us neither hast thou taken ought of any man's hand," he called the Lord to witness, saying, "The Lord is witness, and His Anointed is witness this day, that ye have not found ought in my hand. And they said to him, He is witness." In this strain also the Apostle Paul, inasmuch as he had a good conscience, said to the Corinthians: "For we are not as many, who corrupt the Word of God: but as of sincerity, but as of God, in the sight of God speak we in Christ;" "We have injured no man, corrupted no man, circumvented no man."

5. Such presbyters does the Church nourish, of whom also the prophet says: "I will give thy rulers in peace, and thy bishops in righteousness." Of whom also did the Lord declare, "Who then shall be a faithful steward, good and wise, whom the Lord sets over His household, to give them their meat in due season? Blessed is that servant whom his Lord, when He cometh, shall find so doing." Paul then, teaching us where one may find such, says, "God hath placed in the Church, first, apostles; secondly, prophets; thirdly, teachers." Where, therefore, the gifts of the Lord have been placed, there it behoves us to learn the truth, namely, from those who possess that succession of the Church which is from the apostles? and among whom exists that which is sound and blameless in conduct, as well as that which is unadulterated and incorrupt in speech. For these also preserve this faith of ours in one God who created all things; and they increase that love which we have for the Son of God, who accomplished such marvelous dispensations for our sake: and they

expound the Scriptures to us without danger, neither blaspheming God, nor dishonoring the patriarchs, nor despising the prophets.

Irenaeus, Against Heresies, IV, 26

Origen

Commentary on the Gospel of John

Three chapters from Origen's commentary on John's Gospel follow.

Chapter 5

All Scripture is Gospel; but the Gospels are distinguished above other Scriptures

Here, however, some one may object, appealing to the notion just put forward of the unfolding of the first fruits last, and may say that the Acts and the letters of the Apostles came after the Gospels, and that this destroys our argument to the effect that the Gospel is the first fruits of all Scripture. To this we must reply that it is the conviction of men who are wise in Christ, who have profited by those epistles which are current, and who see them to be vouched for by the testimonies deposited in the law and the prophets, that the apostolic writings are to be pronounced wise and worthy of belief, and that they have great authority, but that they are not on the same level with that "Thus says the Lord Almighty." 2 Corinthians 6:18 Consider on this point the language of St. Paul. When he declares that 2 Timothy 3:16 "Every Scripture is inspired of God and profitable," does he include his own writings? Or does he not include his dictum, 1 Corinthians 7:12 "I say, and not the Lord," and 1 Corinthians 7:17 "So I ordain in all the churches," and 2 Timothy 3:11 "What things I suffered at Antioch, at Iconium, at Lystra," and similar things which he writes in virtue of his own authority, and which do not quite possess the character of words flowing from divine inspiration. Must we also show that the old Scripture is not Gospel, since it does not point out the Coming One, but only foretells Him and heralds His coming at a future time; but that all the new Scripture is the Gospel. It not only says as in the beginning of the Gospel, John 1:29 "Behold the Lamb of God, which takes away the sin of the world;" it also contains many praises of Him, and many of His teachings, on whose account the Gospel is a Gospel. Again, if God set in the Church Ephesians 4:11 apostles and prophets and evangelists (gospellers), pastors and teachers, we must first enquire what was the office of the evangelist, and mark that it is not only to narrate how the Savior cured a man who was blind from his birth, John 9:1 or raised up a dead man who was already stinking, John 11:39 or to state what extraordinary works he wrought; and the office of the evangelist being thus defined, we shall not hesitate to find Gospel in such discourse also as is not narrative but hortatory and intended to strengthen belief in the mission of Jesus; and thus we shall arrive at the position that whatever was written by the Apostles is Gospel. As to this second definition, it might be objected that the Epistles are not entitled "Gospel," and that we are wrong in applying the name of Gospel to the whole of the New Testament. But to this we answer that it happens not infrequently in Scripture when two or more persons or things are named by the same name, the name attaches itself most significantly to one of those things or persons. Thus the Savior says, Matthew 23:8–9 "Call no man Master upon the earth;" while the Apostle says that Masters have been appointed in the Church. These latter accordingly will not be Masters in the strict sense of the dictum of the Gospel. In the same way the Gospel in the Epistles will not extend to every word of them, when it is compared with the narrative of Jesus' actions and sufferings and discourses. No: the Gospel is the first fruits of all Scripture, and to these first fruits of the Scriptures we devote the first fruits of all those actions of ours which we trust to see turn out as we desire.

Chapter 6

The Fourfold Gospel. John's the first fruits of the four. qualifications necessary for interpreting it

Now the Gospels are four. These four are, as it were, the elements of the faith of the Church, out of which elements the whole world which is reconciled to God in Christ is put together; as Paul says, 2 Corinthians 5:19 "God was in Christ, reconciling the world to Himself;" of which world Jesus bore the sin; for it is of the world of the Church that the word is written, John 1:29 "Behold the Lamb of God which takes away the sin of the world." The Gospels then being four, I deem the first fruits of the Gospels to be that which you have enjoined me to search into according to my powers, the Gospel of John, that which speaks of him whose genealogy had already been set forth, but which begins to speak of him at a point before he had any genealogy.

For Matthew, writing for the Hebrews who looked for Him who was to come of the line of Abraham and of David, says: Matthew 1:1 "The book of the generation of Jesus Christ, the son of David, the son of Abraham."

And Mark, knowing what he writes, narrates the beginning of the Gospel; we may perhaps find what he aims at in John; in the beginning the Word, God the Word.

But Luke, though he says at the beginning of Acts, "The former treatise did I make about all that Jesus began to do and to teach," yet leaves to him who lay on Jesus' breast the greatest and completest discourses about Jesus.

For none of these plainly declared His Godhead, as John does when he makes Him say, "I am the light of the world," "I am the way and the truth and the life," "I am the resurrection," "I am the door," "I am the good shepherd;" and in the Apocalypse, "I am the Alpha and the Omega, the beginning and the end, the first and the last."

We may therefore make bold to say that the Gospels are the first fruits of all the Scriptures, but that of the Gospels that of John is the first fruits. No one can apprehend the meaning of it except he have lain on Jesus' breast and received from Jesus Mary to be his mother also. Such an one must he become who is to be another John, and to have shown to him, like John, by Jesus Himself Jesus as He is. For if Mary, as those declare who with sound mind extol her, had no other son but Jesus, and yet Jesus says to His mother, "Woman, behold your son," John 19:26 and not "Behold you have this son also," then He virtually said to her, "Lo, this is Jesus, whom you bore."

Is it not the case that every one who is perfect lives himself no longer, Galatians 2:20 but Christ lives in him; and if Christ lives in him, then it is said of him to Mary, "Behold your son Christ." What a mind, then, must we have to enable us to interpret in a worthy manner this work, though it be committed to the earthly treasure-house of common speech, of writing which any passer-by can read, and which can be heard when read aloud by any one who lends to it his bodily ears? What shall we say of this work? He who is accurately to apprehend what it contains should be able to say with truth, "We have the mind of Christ, that we may know those things which are bestowed on us by God."

It is possible to quote one of Paul's sayings in support of the contention that the whole of the New Testament is Gospel. He writes in a certain place: Romans 2:16 "According to my Gospel." Now we have no written work of Paul which is commonly called a Gospel. But all that he preached and said was the Gospel; and what he preached and said he was also in the habit of writing, and what he wrote was therefore Gospel. But if what Paul wrote was Gospel, it follows that what Peter wrote was also Gospel, and in a word all that was said or written to perpetuate the knowledge of Christ's sojourn on earth, and to prepare for His second coming, or to bring it about as a present reality in those souls which were willing to receive the Word of God as He stood at the door and knocked and sought to come into them.

Chapter 7

What good things are announced in the Gospels.

But it is time we should inquire what is the meaning of the designation "Gospel," and why these books have this title. Now the Gospel is a discourse containing a promise of things which naturally, and on account of the benefits they bring, rejoice the hearer as soon as the promise is heard and believed. Nor is such a discourse any the less a Gospel that we define it with reference to the position of the hearer. A Gospel is either a word which implies the actual presence to the believer of something that is good, or a word promising the arrival of a good which is expected. Now all these definitions apply to those books which are named Gospels.

For each of the Gospels is a collection of announcements which are useful to him who believes them and does not misinterpret them; it brings him a benefit and naturally makes him glad because it tells of the sojourn with men, on account of men, and for their salvation, of the first-born of all creation, Colossians 1:15 Christ Jesus. And again each Gospel tells of the sojourn of the good Father in the Son with those minded to receive Him, as is plain to every believer; and moreover by these books a good is announced which had been formerly expected, as is by no means hard to see.

For John the Baptist spoke in the name almost of the whole people when he sent to Jesus and asked, Matthew 11:3 "Are you He that should come or do we look for another?" For to the people the Messiah was an expected good, which the prophets had foretold, and they all alike, though under the law and the prophets, fixed their hopes on Him, as the Samaritan woman bears witness when she says: John 4:25 "I know that the Messiah comes, who is called Christ; when He comes He will tell us all things." Simon and Cleopas too, when talking to each other about all that had happened to Jesus Christ Himself, then risen, though they did not know that He had risen from the dead, speak thus, Luke 24:18–21 "Do you sojourn alone in Jerusalem, and know not the things which have taken place there in these days? And when he said what things? they answered, The things concerning Jesus of Nazareth, which was a prophet, mighty in deed and in word before God and all the people, and how the chief priests and our rulers delivered Him up to be sentenced to death and crucified Him. But we hoped that it was He which should redeem Israel."

Again, Andrew the brother of Simon Peter found his own brother Simon and said to him, John 1:42 "We have found the Messiah, which is, being interpreted, Christ." And a little further on Philip finds Nathanael and says to him, John 1:46 "We have found Him of whom Moses in the law, and the prophets, wrote, Jesus the son of Joseph, from Nazareth."

Origen

Tertullian
The Testimony of the Soul

Chapter 1

If, with the object of convicting the rivals and persecutors of Christian truth, from their own authorities, of the crime of at once being untrue to themselves and doing injustice to us, one is bent on gathering testimonies in its favor from the writings of the philosophers, or the poets, or other masters of this world's learning and wisdom, he has need of a most inquisitive spirit, and a still greater memory to carry out the research. Indeed, some of our people, who still continued their inquisitive labors in ancient literature, and still occupied memory with it, have published works we have in our hands of this very sort; works in which they relate and attest the nature and origin of their traditions, and the grounds on which opinions rest, and from which it may be seen at once that we have embraced nothing new or monstrous-nothing for which we cannot claim the support of ordinary and well-known writings, whether in ejecting error from our creed, or admitting truth into it.

But the unbelieving hardness of the human heart leads them to slight even their own teachers, otherwise approved and in high renown, whenever they touch upon arguments which are used in defense of Christianity. Then the poets are fools, when they describe the gods with human passions and stories; then the philosophers are without reason, when they knock at the gates of truth. He will thus far be reckoned a wise and sagacious man who has gone the length of uttering sentiments that are almost Christian; while if, in a mere affectation of judgment and wisdom, he sets himself to reject their ceremonies, or to convicting the world of its sin, he is sure to be branded as a Christian. We will have nothing, then, to do with the literature and the teaching, perverted in its best results, which is believed in its errors rather than its truth. We shall lay no stress on it, if some of their authors have declared that there is one God, and one God only. Nay, let it be granted that there is nothing in heathen writers which a Christian approves, that it may be put out of his power to utter a single word of reproach.

For all are not familiar with their teachings; and those who are, have no assurance in regard to their truth. Far less do men assent to our writings, to which no one comes for guidance unless he is already a Christian. I call in a new testimony, yea, one which is better known than all literature, more discussed than all doctrine, more public than all publications, greater than the whole man—I mean all which is man's.

Stand forth, O soul, whether thou art a divine and eternal substance, as most philosophers believe if it be so, thou wilt be the less likely to lie—or whether thou art the very opposite of divine, because indeed a mortal thing, as Epicurus alone thinks—in that case there will be the less temptation for thee to speak falsely in this case: whether thou art received from heaven, or sprung from earth; whether thou art formed of numbers, or of atoms; whether thine existence begins with that of the body, or thou art put into it at a later stage; from whatever source, and in whatever way, thou makest man a rational being, in the highest degree capable of thought and knowledge—stand forth and give thy witness. But I call thee not as when, fashioned in schools, trained in libraries, fed in Attic academies and porticoes, thou belchest wisdom. I address thee simple, rude, uncultured and untaught, such as they have thee who have thee only; that very thing of the road, the street, the workshop, wholly. I want thine inexperience, since in thy small experience no one feels any confidence. I demand of thee the things thou bringest with thee into man, which thou knowest either from thyself, or from thine author, whoever he may be. Thou art not, as I well know, Christian; for a man becomes a Christian, he is not born one. Yet Christians earnestly press thee for a testimony; they press thee, though an alien, to bear witness against thy friends, that they may be put to shame before thee, for hating and mocking us on account of things which convict thee as an accessory.

Chapter 2.

We give offence by proclaiming that there is one God, to whom the name of God alone belongs, from whom all things come, and who is Lord of the whole universe. Bear thy testimony, if thou knowest this to be the truth; for openly and with a perfect liberty, such as we do not possess, we hear thee both in private and in public exclaim, 'Which may God grant', and, 'If God so will'. By expressions such as these thou declarest that there is one who is distinctively God, and thou confessest that all power belongs to him to whose will, as

Sovereign, thou dost look. At the same time, too, thou deniest any others to be truly gods, in calling them by their own names of Saturn, Jupiter, Mars, Minerva; for thou affirmest him to be God alone to whom thou givest no other name than God; and though thou sometimes callest these others gods, thou plainly usest the designation as one which does not really belong to them, but is, so to speak, a borrowed one. Nor is the nature of the God we declare unknown to thee: 'God is good, God does good', thou art wont to say; plainly suggesting further, 'But man is evil'.

In asserting an antithetic proposition, thou, in a sort of indirect and figurative way, reproachest man with his wickedness in departing from a God so good. So, again, as among us, as belonging to the God of benignity and goodness, 'Blessing' is a most sacred act in our religion and our life, thou too sayest as readily as a Christian needs, 'God bless thee'; and when thou turnest the blessing of God into a curse, in like manner thy very words confess with us that his power over us is absolute and entire. There are some who, though they do not deny the existence of God, hold withal that he is neither Searcher, nor Ruler, nor Judge; treating with especial disdain those of us who go over to Christ out of fear of a coming judgment, as they think, honoring God in freeing him from the cares of keeping watch, and the trouble of taking note,-not even regarding him as capable of anger. For if God, they say, gets angry, then he is susceptible of corruption and passion; but that of which passion and corruption can be affirmed may also perish, which God cannot do. But these very persons elsewhere, confessing that the soul is divine, and bestowed on us by God, stumble against a testimony of the soul itself, which affords an answer to these views. For if either divine or God-given, it doubtless knows its giver; and if it knows him, it undoubtedly fears him too, and especially as having been by him endowed so amply. Has it no fear of him whose favor it is so desirous to possess, and whose anger it is so anxious to avoid? Whence, then, the soul's natural fear of God, if God cannot be angry? How is there any dread of him whom nothing offends? What is feared but anger? Whence comes anger, but from observing what is done? What leads to watchful oversight, but judgment in prospect? Whence is judgment, but from power? To whom does supreme authority and power belong, but to God alone?

So thou art always ready, O soul, from thine own knowledge, nobody casting scorn upon thee, and no one preventing, to exclaim, 'God sees all', and 'I commend thee to God', and 'May God repay', and 'God shall judge between us'. How happens this, since thou art not Christian? How is it that, even with the garland of Ceres on the brow, wrapped in the purple cloak of Saturn, wearing the white robe of the goddess Isis, thou invokest God as judge? Standing under the statue of Sculapius, adorning the brazen image of Juno, arraying the helmet of Minerva with dusky figures, thou never thinkest of appealing to any of these deities. In thine own forum thou appealest to a God who is elsewhere; thou permittest honor to be rendered in thy temples to a foreign god. Oh, striking testimony to truth, which in the very midst of demons obtains a witness for us Christians!

Chapter 3

But when we say that there are demons-as though, in the simple fact that we alone expel them from the men's bodies, we did not also prove their existence-some disciple of Chrysippus begins to curl the lip. Yet thy curses sufficiently attest that there are such beings, and that they are objects of thy strong dislike. As what comes to thee as a fit expression of thy strong hatred of him, thou callest the man a demon who annoys thee with his filthiness, or malice, or insolence, or any other vice which we ascribe to evil spirits. In expressing vexation, contempt, or abhorrence, thou hast Satan constantly upon thy lips ; the very same we hold to be the angel of evil, the source of error, the corrupter of the whole world, by whom in the beginning man was entrapped into breaking the commandment of God. And (the man) being given over to death on account of his sin, the entire human race, tainted in their descent from him, were made a channel for transmitting his condemnation. Thou seest, then, thy destroyer; and though he is fully known only to Christians, or to whatever sect confesses the Lord, yet, even thou hast some acquaintance with him while yet thou abhorrest him!

Chapter 4

Even now, as the matter refers to thy opinion on a point the more closely belonging to thee, in so far as it bears on thy personal well-being, we maintain that after life has passed away thou still remainest in existence, and lookest forward to a day of judgment, and according to thy deserts art assigned to misery or bliss, in either way of it for ever; that, to be capable of this, thy former substance must needs return to thee, the matter and the memory of the very same human being: for neither good nor evil couldst thou feel if thou wert not endowed again with that sensitive bodily organization, and there would be no grounds for judgment without the presentation of the very person to whom the sufferings of judgment were due. That Christian view, though much nobler than the Pythagorean, as it does not transfer thee into beasts; though more complete than the Platonic, since it endows thee again with a body; though more worthy of honor than the Epicurean, as it preserves thee from annihilation,-yet, because of the name connected with it, it is held to be nothing but vanity and folly, and, as it is called, a mere presumption. But we are not ashamed of ourselves if our presumption is found to have thy support.

Well, in the first place, when thou speakest of one who is dead, thou sayest of him, 'Poor man'-poor, surely, not because he has been taken from the good of life, but because he has been given over to punishment and condemnation. But at another time thou speakest of the dead as free from trouble; thou professest to think life a burden, and death a blessing. Thou art wont, too, to speak of the dead as in repose, when, returning to their graves beyond the city gates with food and dainties, thou art wont to present offerings to thyself rather than to them; or when, coming from the graves again, thou art staggering under the effects of wine. But I want thy sober opinion. Thou callest the dead poor when thou speakest thine own thoughts, when thou art at a distance from them. For at their feast, where in a sense they are present and recline along with thee, it would never do to cast reproach upon their lot. Thou canst not but adulate those for whose sake thou art feasting it so sumptuously. Dost thou then speak of him as poor who feels not? How happens it that thou cursest, as one capable of suffering from thy curse, the man whose memory comes back on thee with the sting in it of some old injury? It is thine imprecation that 'the earth may lie heavy on him', and that there may be trouble 'to his ashes in the realm of the dead'. In like manner, in thy kindly feeling to him to whom thou art indebted for favors, thou entreatest 'repose to his bones and ashes', and thy desire is that among the dead he may 'have pleasant rest'. If thou hast no power of suffering after death, if no feeling remains,-if, in a word, severance from the body is the annihilation of thee, what makes thee lie against thyself, as if thou couldst suffer in another state? Nay, why dost thou fear death at all? There is nothing after death to be feared, if there is nothing to be felt. For though it may be said that death is dreadful not for anything it threatens afterwards, but because it deprives us of the good of life; yet, on the other hand, as it puts an end to life's discomforts, which are far more numerous, death's terrors are mitigated by a gain that more than outweighs the loss. And there is no occasion to be troubled about a loss of good things, which is amply made up for by so great a blessing as relief from every trouble.

There is nothing dreadful in that which delivers from all that is to be dreaded. If thou shrinkest from giving up life because thy experience of it has been sweet, at any rate there is no need to be in any alarm about death if thou hast no knowledge that it is evil. Thy dread of it is the proof that thou art aware of its evil. Thou wouldst never think it evil—thou wouldst have no fear of it at all—if thou weft not sure that after it there is something to make it evil, and so a thing of terror. Let us leave unnoted at this time that natural way of fearing death. It is a poor thing for any one to fear what is inevitable. I take up the other side, and argue on the ground of a joyful hope beyond our term of earthly life; for desire of posthumous fame is with almost every class an inborn thing. I have not time to speak of the Curtii, and the Reguli, or the brave men of Greece, who afford us innumerable cases of death despised for after renown. Who at this day is without the desire that he may be often remembered when he is dead? Who does not give all endeavor to preserve his name by works of literature, or by the simple glory of his virtues, or by the splendor even of his tomb? How is it the nature of the soul to have these posthumous ambitions and with such amazing effort to prepare the things it can only use after decease? It would care nothing about the future, if the future were quite unknown to it. But perhaps thou thinkest thyself surer, after thy exit from the body, of continuing still to feel, than of any future resurrection, which is a doctrine laid at our door as one of our presumptuous suppositions. But it is also the doctrine of the soul; for if any one inquires about a person lately dead as though he were alive, it occurs at once to say, 'He has gone'. He is expected to return, then.

Tertullian, Translated by S. Thelwall

Cyprian

On the Unity of the Church

1. Since the Lord warns us, saying, "Ye are the salt of the earth," and since He bids us to be simple to harmlessness, and yet with our simplicity to be prudent, what else, beloved brethren, befits us, than to use foresight and watching with an anxious heart, both to perceive and to beware of the wiles of the crafty foe, that we, who have put on Christ the wisdom of God the Father, may not seem to be wanting in wisdom in the matter of providing for our salvation? For it is not persecution alone that is to be feared; nor those things which advance by open attack to overwhelm and cast down the servants of God. Caution is more easy where danger is manifest, and the mind is prepared beforehand for the contest when the adversary avows himself.

The enemy is more to be feared and to be guarded against, when he creeps on us secretly; when, deceiving by the appearance of peace, he steals forward by hidden approaches, whence also he has received the name of the Serpent. That is always his subtlety; that is his dark and stealthy artifice for circumventing man. Thus from (he very beginning of the world he deceived; and flattering with lying words, he misled inexperienced souls by an incautious credulity. Thus he endeavored to tempt the Lord Himself: he secretly approached Him, as if he would creep on Him again, and deceive; yet he was understood, and beaten back, and therefore prostrated, because he was recognized and detected.

2. From which an example is given us to avoid the way of the old man, to stand in the footsteps of a conquering Christ, that we may not again be incautiously turned back into the nets of death, but, foreseeing our danger, may possess the immortality that we have received. But how can we possess immortality, unless we keep those commands of Christ whereby death is driven out and overcome, when He Himself warns us, and says, "If thou wilt enter into life, keep the commandments?" And again: "If ye do the things that I command you, henceforth I call you not servants, but friends." Finally, these persons He calls strong and steadfast; these He declares to be founded in robust security upon the rock, established with immoveable and unshaken firmness, in opposition to all the tempests and hurricanes of the world. "Whosoever," says He, "heareth my words, and doeth them, I will liken him unto a wise man, that built his house upon a rock: the rain descended, the floods came, the winds blew, and beat upon that house; and it fell not: for it was founded upon a rock." We ought therefore to stand fast on His words, to learn and do whatever He both taught and did. But how can a man say that he believes in Christ, who does not do what Christ commanded him to do? Or whence shall he attain to the reward of faith, who will not keep the faith of the commandment? He must of necessity waver and wander, and, caught away by a spirit of error, like dust which is shaken by the wind, be blown about; and he will make no advance in his walk towards salvation, because he does not keep the truth of the way of salvation.

3. But, beloved brethren, not only must we beware of what is open and manifest, but also of what deceives by the craft of subtle fraud. And what can be more crafty, or what

more subtle, than for this enemy, detected and cast down by the advent of Christ, after light has come to the nations, and saving rays have shone for the preservation of men, that the deaf might receive the hearing of spiritual grace, the blind might open their eyes to God, the weak might grow strong again with eternal health, the lame might run to the church, the dumb might pray with clear voices and prayers-seeing his idols forsaken, and his lanes and his temples deserted by the numerous concourse of believers-to devise a new fraud, and under the very title of the Christian name to deceive the incautious? He has invented heresies and schisms, whereby he might subvert the faith, might corrupt the truth, might divide the unity. Those whom he cannot keep in the darkness of the old way, he circumvents and deceives by the error of a new way. He snatches men from the Church itself; and while they seem to themselves to have already approached to the light, and to have escaped the night of the world, he pours over them again, in their unconsciousness, new darkness; so that, although they do not stand firm with the Gospel of Christ, and with the observation and law of Christ, they still call themselves Christians, and, walking in darkness, they think that they have the light, while the adversary is flattering and deceiving, who, according to the apostle's word, transforms himself into an angel of light, and equips his ministers as if they were the ministers of righteousness, who maintain night instead of day, death for salvation, despair under the offer of hope, perfidy under the pretext of faith, antichrist under the name of Christ; so that, while they feign things like the truth, they make void the truth by their subtlety. This happens, beloved brethren, so long as we do not return to the source of truth, as we do not seek the head nor keep the teaching of the heavenly Master.

4. If any one consider and examine these things, there is no need for lengthened discussion and arguments. There is easy proof for faith in a short summary of the truth. The Lord speaks to Peter, saying, "I say unto thee, that thou art Peter; and upon this rock I will build my Church, and the gates of hell shall not prevail against it. And I will give unto thee the keys of the kingdom of heaven; and whatsoever thou shalt bind on earth shall be bound also in heaven, and whatsoever thou shalt loose on earth shall be loosed in heaven." And again to the same He says, after His resurrection, "Feed nay sheep." And although to all the apostles, after His resurrection, He gives an equal power, and says, "As the Father hath sent me, even so send I you: Receive ye the Holy Ghost: Whose soever sins ye remit, they shall be remitted unto him; and whose soever sins ye retain, they shall be retained;" yet, that He might set forth unity, He arranged by His authority the origin of that unity, as beginning from one. Assuredly the rest of the apostles were also the same as was Peter, endowed with a like partnership both of honor and power; but the beginning proceeds from unity. Which one Church, also, the Holy Spirit in the Song of Songs designated in the person of our Lord, and says, "My dove, my spotless one, is but one. She is the only one of her mother, elect of her that bare her." Does he who does not hold this unity of the Church think that he holds the faith? Does he who strives against and resists the Church trust that he is in the Church, when moreover the blessed Apostle Paul teaches the same thing, and sets forth the

sacrament of unity, saying, "There is one body and one spirit, one hope of your calling, one Lord, one faith, one baptism, one God?" . . .

Cyprian

History of Bible translations

Number of languages Bible had been translated into during this period

AD 10–200

6–7 languages

AD 300–400

10–11 languages

CHAPTER 3

THE CHRISTIAN CHURCH AND THE ROMAN EMPIRE

From Clement of Alexandria to Columba
AD 311–590

Important dates in the time of the Christian Church and the Roman Empire

311 Separation of the Donatists from the Church
312 Constantine is converted after seeing a vision of the cross
313 Edict of Milan; ends persecution of Christians
314 Council of Arles, about the Donatists
319 Arius begins to publish his heresy
325 The First General Council held at Nicaea
325 Arius condemned
325 The Nicene Creed formulated
326 Athanasius, bishop of Alexandria
337 Death of Constantine
343 Persecution in Persia
347 Revolt, defeat, and banishment of the Donatists
348 Ulfilas, apostle to the Goths
356 Death of Antony the hermit
361 Julian emperor; paganism restored
362 The Donatists recalled
363 Death of Julian
370 Basil, bishop of Caesarea, in Cappadocia
373 Death of Athanasius
374 Ambrose, bishop of Milan
379 Theodosius, emperor
380 Gregory, bishop of Constantinople
380 Death of Basil
385 Execution of Priscillian
386/7 Augustine converted
390 Massacre at Thessalonica, repentance of Theodosius
391 Destruction of the Temple of Serapis

395 Death of Theodosius
395 Augustine becomes bishop of Hippo
397 Death of Ambrose
397 Chrysostom, bishop of Constantinople

5th Century

400 Pelagius teaches his heresy at Rome
403 Death of Telemachus at Rome
404 Chrysostom banished to Cucusus
405 Jerome completes the Latin Vulgate version of the Bible that becomes the standard for the next one thousand years
407 Death of Chrysostom
409 The Romans withdraw from Britain
410 Rome taken by Alaric
410 Pelagius and Celestius in Africa
411 Conference with the Donatists at Carthage
412 Ninian bishop of Whithorn
430 Death of Augustine
431 Condemnation of Nestorius
432 Death of Ninian
432 Patrick goes to Ireland as missionary
440 Leo I the Great becomes Pope
447 Council of Toledo added *Filioque* clause to Nicene Creed of 381
449 "Robber Council" meets at Ephesus
476 Fall of Rome and end of the Western Empire
484–519 Schism between Rome and Constantinople
493 Death of Patrick
496 Conversion of Frankish King Clovis; conquers half of France and paves the way for Charlemagne's "Holy Roman Empire"

6th Century

527 Justinian, emperor
529 Benedict of Nursia draws up his Rule for monks
565 Columba settles at Iona
589 Third Council of Toledo
590 Gregory the Great, bishop of Rome

Introduction

The period of the history of the Church in the time of the Roman Empire extends from the emperor Constantine to the pope Gregory I.; from the beginning of the fourth century to the close of the sixth.

During this period Christianity still moves, as in the first three centuries, upon the geographical scene of the Graeco-Roman empire and the ancient classical culture, the countries around the Mediterranean Sea. But its field and its operation are materially enlarged, and even touch the barbarians on the limit of the empire. Above all, its relation to the temporal power, and its social and political position and import, undergo an entire and permanent change. We have here to do with the church of the Graeco-Roman empire, and with the beginning of Christianity among the Germanic barbarians.

Philip Schaff, History of the Christian Church, 1890

EVENTS

Important events in the time of the Christian Church and the Roman Empire

Council of Nicea, AD 325
The growth of the desert father movement
Jerome's Vulgate Bible

PEOPLE

Christian leaders in the time of the Christian Church and the Roman Empire

Athanasius (AD 297–373)
Basil the Great (AD 330–375)
Ambrose (AD 340–397)
Jerome (AD 340–420)
Chrysostom (AD 347–407)
Augustine (AD 354–430)
Patrick (AD ?390–461)
Leo the Great AD ?400–461)
Columba (AD 521–597)

An historian's overview of the Christian Church and the Roman Empire

From the Christianity of the Apostles and Martyrs we proceed to the Christianity of the Patriarchs and Emperors.

The reign of Constantine the Great marks the transition of the Christian religion from under persecution by the secular government to union with the same; the beginning of the state-church system. The Graeco-Roman heathenism, the most cultivated and powerful form of idolatry, which history knows, surrenders, after three hundred years' struggle, to Christianity, and dies of incurable consumption, with the confession: Galilean, thou hast conquered!

The ruler of the civilized world lays his crown at the feet of the crucified Jesus of Nazareth. The successor of Nero, Domitian, and Diocletian appears in the imperial purple at the council of Nice as protector of the church, and takes his golden throne at the nod of bishops, who still bear the scars of persecution. The despised sect, which, like its Founder in the days of His humiliation, had not where to lay its head, is raised to sovereign authority in the state, enters into the prerogatives of the pagan priesthood, grows rich and powerful, builds countless churches out of the stones of idol temples to the honor of Christ and his martyrs, employs the wisdom of Greece and Rome to vindicate the foolishness of the cross, exerts a molding power upon civil legislation, rules the national life, and leads off the history of the world. But at the same time the church, embracing the mass of the population of the empire, from the Caesar to the meanest slave, and living amidst all its institutions, received into her bosom vast deposits of foreign material from the world and from heathenism, exposing herself to new dangers and imposing upon herself new and heavy labors.

The union of church and state extends its influence, now healthful, now baneful, into every department of our history.

The Christian life of the Nicene and post-Nicene age reveals a mass of worldliness within the church; an entire abatement of chiliasm with its longing after the return of Christ and his glorious reign, and in its steady an easy repose in the present order of things; with a sublime enthusiasm, on the other hand, for the renunciation of self and the world, particularly in the hermitage and the cloister, and with some of the noblest heroes of Christian holiness.

Monasticism, in pursuance of the ascetic tendencies of the previous period, and in opposition to the prevailing secularization of Christianity, sought to save the virgin purity of the church and the glory of martyrdom by retreat from the world into the wilderness; and it carried the ascetic principle to the summit of moral heroism, though not rarely to the borders of fanaticism and brutish stupefaction. It spread with incredible rapidity and irresistible fascination from Egypt over the whole church, east and west, and received the sanction of the greatest church teachers, of an Athanasius, a Basil, a Chrysostom, an Augustine, a Jerome, as the surest and shortest way to heaven.

It soon became a powerful rival of the priesthood, and formed a third order, between the priesthood and the laity. The more extraordinary and eccentric the religion of the anchorets and monks, the more they were venerated among the people. The whole conception of the Christian life from the fourth to the sixteenth century is pervaded with the ascetic and monastic spirit, and pays the highest admiration to the voluntary celibacy, poverty, absolute obedience, and excessive self-punishments of the pillar-saints and the martyrs of the desert; while in the same degree the modest virtues of every-day household and social life are looked upon as an inferior degree of morality.

In this point the old Catholic ethical ideas essentially differ from those of evangelical Protestantism and modern civilization. But, to understand and appreciate them, we must consider them in connection with the corrupt social condition of the rapidly decaying empire of Rome. The Christian spirit in that age, in just its most earnest and vigorous forms, felt compelled to assume in some measure an anti-social, seclusive character, and to prepare itself in the school of privation and solitude for the work of transforming the world and founding a new Christian order of society upon the ruins of the ancient heathenism.

In the development of doctrine the Nicene and post-Nicene age is second in productiveness and importance only to those of the apostles and of the reformation. It is the classical period for the objective fundamental dogmas, which constitute the ecumenical or old Catholic confession of faith. The Greek church produced the symbolical definition of the orthodox view of the holy Trinity and the person of Christ, while the Latin church made considerable advance with the anthropological and soteriological doctrines of sin and grace. The fourth and fifth centuries produced the greatest church fathers, Athanasius and Chrysostom in the East, Jerome and Augustine in the West.

All learning and science now came into the service of the church, and all classes of society, from the emperor to the artisan, took the liveliest, even a passionate interest, in the theological controversies. Now, too, for the first time, could ecumenical councils be held, in which the church of the whole Roman empire was represented, and fixed its articles of faith in an authoritative way.

Now also, however, the lines of orthodoxy were more and more strictly drawn; freedom of inquiry was restricted; and all as departure from the state-church system was met not only, as formerly, with spiritual weapons, but also with civil punishments. So early as the fourth century the dominant party, the orthodox as well as the heterodox, with help of the imperial authority practiced deposition, confiscation, and banishment upon its opponents. It was but one step thence to the penalties of torture and death, which were ordained in the middle age, and even so lately as the middle of the seventeenth century, by state-church authority, both Protestant and Roman Catholic, and continue in many countries to this day, against religious dissenters of every kind as enemies to the prevailing order of things. Absolute freedom of religion and of worship is in fact logically impossible on the state-church system. It requires the separation of the spiritual and temporal powers. Yet, from the very beginning of political persecution, loud voices rise against it and in behalf of ecclesiastico-religious toleration; though the plea always comes from the oppressed party, which, as soon as it gains the power, is generally found, in lamentable inconsistency, imitating the violence of its former oppressors. The protest springs rather from the sense of personal injury, than from horror of the principle of persecution, or from any clear apprehension of the nature of the gospel and its significant words: "Put up thy sword into the sheath;" "My kingdom is not of this world."

The organization of the church adapts itself to the political and geographical divisions of the empire. The powers of the hierarchy are enlarged, the bishops become leading officers of the state and acquire a controlling influence in civil and political affairs, though more or less at the expense of their spiritual dignity and independence, especially at the Byzantine court. The episcopal system passes on into the metropolitan and patriarchal. In the fifth century the patriarchs of Rome, Constantinople, Antioch, Alexandria, and Jerusalem stand at the head of Christendom. Among these Rome and Constantinople are the most powerful rivals, and the Roman patriarch already puts forth a claim to universal spiritual supremacy, which subsequently culminates in the medieval papacy, though limited to the West and resisted by the constant protest of the Greek church and of all non-Catholic sects. In addition to provincial synods we have now also general synods, but called by the emperors and more or less affected, though not controlled, by political influence.

From the time of Constantine church discipline declines; the whole Roman world having become nominally Christian, and the host of hypocritical professors multiplying beyond all control. Yet the firmness of Ambrose with the emperor Theodosius shows, that noble instances of discipline are not altogether wanting.

Worship appears greatly enriched and adorned; for art now comes into the service of the church. A Christian architecture, a Christian sculpture, a Christian painting, music, and poetry arise, favoring at once devotion and solemnity, and all sorts of superstition and empty display. The introduction of religious images succeeds only after long and violent opposition. The element of priesthood and of mystery is developed, but in connection with a superstitious reliance upon a certain magical operation of outward rites. Church festivals are multiplied and celebrated with great pomp; and not exclusively in honor of Christ, but in connection with an extravagant veneration of martyrs and saints, which borders on idolatry, and often reminds us of the heathen hero-worship not yet uprooted from the general mind. The multiplication and accumulation of religious ceremonies impressed the senses and the imagination, but prejudiced simplicity, spirituality, and fervor in the worship of God. Hence also the beginnings of reaction against ceremonialism and formalism.

Notwithstanding the complete and sudden change of the social and political circumstances of the church, which meets us on the threshold of this period, we have still before us the natural, necessary continuation of the pre-Constantine church in its light and shade, and the gradual transition of the old Graeco-Roman Catholicism into the Germano-Roman Catholicism of the middle age.

Our attention will now for the first time be turned in earnest, not only to Christianity in the Roman empire, but also to Christianity among the Germanic barbarians, who from East and North threaten the empire and the entire civilization of classic antiquity. The church prolonged, indeed, the existence of the Roman empire, gave it a new splendor and elevation, new strength and unity, as well as comfort in misfortune; but could not prevent its final dissolution, first in the West (476), afterwards (1453) in the East. But she herself survived the storms of the great migration, brought the pagan invaders under the influence of Christianity, taught the barbarians the arts of peace, planted a higher civilization upon the ruins of the ancient world, and thus gave new proof of the indestructible, all-subduing energy of her life.

In the history of the fourth, fifth, and sixth centuries we should mark the following subdivisions:

1. The Constantinian and Athanasian, or the Nicene and Trinitarian age, from 311 to the second general council in 381, distinguished by the conversion of Constantine, the alliance of the empire with the church, and the great Arian and semi-Arian controversy concerning the Divinity of Christ and the Holy Spirit.
2. The post-Nicene, or Christological and Augustinian age, extending to the fourth general council in 451, and including the Nestorian and Eutychian disputes on the person of Christ, and the Pelagian controversy on sin and grace.
3. The age of Leo the Great (440–461), or the rise of the papal supremacy in the West, amidst the barbarian devastations which made an end to the western Roman empire in 476.
4. The Justinian age (527–565), which exhibits the Byzantine state-church despotism at the height of its power, and at the beginning of its decline.
5. The Gregorian age (590–604) forms the transition from the ancient Graeco-Roman to the medieval Romano-Germanic Christianity, and will be more properly included in the church history of the middle ages.

Philip Schaff, History of the Christian Church, 1890

Nestorianism

Nestorianism is basically the doctrine that Jesus existed as two persons, the man Jesus and the divine Son of God, rather than as a unified person. This doctrine is identified with Nestorius (c. 386–451), Patriarch of Constantinople, although he himself denied holding this belief. This view of Christ was condemned at the Council of Ephesus in 431, and the conflict over this view led to the Nestorian schism, separating the Assyrian Church of the East from the Byzantine Church.

The motivation for this view was an aversion to the idea that "God" suffered and died on the cross, be it the divinity itself, the Trinity, or one of the persons of the Trinity. Thus, they would say, Jesus the perfect man suffered and died, not the divine second person of the Trinity, for such is an impossible thought—hence the inference that two "persons" essentially inhabited the one body of Jesus. Nestorius himself argued against calling Mary the "Mother of God" (*Theotokos*) as the church was beginning to do. He held that Mary was the mother of Christ only in respect to His humanity. The council at Ephesus (431) accused Nestorius of the heresy of teaching "two persons" in Christ and insisted that Theotokos was an appropriate title for Mary.

The problem with Nestorianism is that it threatens the atonement. If Jesus is two persons, then which one died on the cross? If it was the "human person" then the atonement is not of divine quality and thereby insufficient to cleanse us of our sins.

Theopedia

Christianity under Emperor Constantine

Introduction

Christianity, a persecuted minority faith at Constantine's conversion in AD 312, had become the religion of the Empire by the end of the fourth century.

Constantine I: Emperor of the Roman Empire (272–337)

Gaius Flavius Valerius Aurelius Constantinus (27 February 272–22 May 337), commonly known as Constantine I, Constantine the Great, or (among Eastern Christians of Byzantine tradition) Saint Constantine, was a Roman Emperor, proclaimed Augustus by his troops on July 25, 306 and who ruled an ever-growing portion of the Roman Empire until his death.

Constantine is best remembered in modern times for the Edict of Milan in 313, which bestowed imperial favor on Christianity in the Empire, for the first time. He was not, however, the first to legalize the practice of Christianity in the Empire. Galerius was the first emperor to issue an edict of toleration for all religious creeds including Christianity in April of 311.

Constantine is also remembered for the Council of Nicaea in 325; these actions are considered major factors in the spreading of the Christian religion. His reputation as the "first Christian Emperor" has been promulgated by historians from Lactantius and Eusebius of Caesarea to the present day, although there has been debate over the veracity of his faith. This debate stems from his continued support for pagan deities and the fact that he was only baptized very close to his death.

Wikipedia

Constantine and Christianity

In his biography, *The Life of the Blessed Emperor Constantine* Eusebius records how Constantine came under the influence of Christianity.

It was by the Will of God that Constantine, became possessed of the Empire

Praise then the God of all, the Supreme Governor of the whole universe, who by his own will appointed Constantine, the descendant of so renowned a parent, to be prince and sovereign so that, while others have been raised to this distinction by the election of their fellow-men, he is the only one to whose elevation no mortal may boast of having contributed.

Chapter 24

Victories of Constantine over the Barbarians and the Britons

As soon, then, as he was established on the throne, he began to care for the interests of his paternal inheritance and visited with much considerate kindness all those provinces which had previously been under his father's government. Some tribes of the barbarians who dwelt on the banks of the Rhine, and the shores of the Western ocean, having ventured to revolt, he reduced them all to obedience, and brought them from their savage state to one of gentleness. He contented himself with checking the inroads of others and drove from his dominions, like untamed and savage beasts, those whom he perceived to be altogether incapable of the settled order of civilized life. Having disposed of these affairs to his satisfaction, he directed his attention to other quarters of the world and first passed over to the British nations, which lie in the very bosom of the ocean. These he reduced to submission and then proceeded to consider the state of the remaining portions of the empire, that he might be ready to tender his aid wherever circumstances might require it.

Chapter 25

How he resolved to deliver Rome from Maxentius

He regarded the entire world as one immense body, and perceived that the head of it all, the royal city of the Roman empire, was bowed down by the weight of a tyrannous oppression. At first he had left the task of liberation to those who governed the other divisions of the empire, as being his superiors in point of age. But when none of these proved able to afford relief, and those who had attempted it had experienced a disastrous termination of their enterprise, he said that life was without enjoyment to him as long as he saw the imperial city thus afflicted, and prepared himself for the overthrow of the tyranny.

Chapter 26

That after reflecting on the downfall of those who had worshipped Idols, he made choice of Christianity

Being convinced, however, that he needed some more powerful aid than his military forces could afford him, on account of the wicked and magical enchantments which were so diligently practiced by the tyrant, he sought Divine assistance, deeming the possession of arms and a numerous soldiery of secondary importance, but believing the cooperating power of Deity invincible and not to be shaken.

He considered, therefore, on what God he might rely for protection and assistance. While engaged in this inquiry, the thought occurred to him that, of the many emperors who had preceded him, those who had rested their hopes in a multitude of gods, and served them with sacrifices and offerings, had in the first place been deceived by flattering predictions, and oracles which promised them all prosperity, and at last had met with an unhappy end, while not one of their gods had stood by to warn them of the impending wrath of heaven. While one alone who had pursued an entirely opposite course, who had condemned their error and honored the one Supreme God during his whole life, had found him to be the Savoir and Protector of his empire, and the Giver of every good thing.

Reflecting on this, and well weighing the fact that they who had trusted in many gods had also fallen by manifold forms of death, without leaving behind them either family or offspring, stock, name, or memorial among men, while the God of his father had given to him, on the other hand, manifestations of his power and very many tokens: and considering farther that those who had already taken arms against the tyrant, and had marched to the battle-field under the protection of a multitude of gods, had met with a dishonorable end (for one of them had shamefully retreated from the contest without a blow, and the other, being slain in the midst of his own troops, became, as it were, the mere sport of death). Reviewing, I say, all these considerations, he judged it to be folly indeed to join in the idle worship of those who were no gods, and, after such convincing evidence, to err from the truth; and therefore felt it incumbent on him to honor his father's God alone.

Chapter 27

How, while he was praying, God sent him a vision of a cross of light in the heavens at mid-day, with an inscription admonishing him to conquer by that

Accordingly, he called on Him with earnest prayer and supplications that He would reveal to him who he was, and stretch forth his right hand to help him in his present difficulties. And while he was thus praying with fervent entreaty, a most marvelous sign appeared to him from heaven, the account of which it might have been hard to believe had it been related by any other person. But since the victorious emperor himself long afterwards declared it to the writer of this history, when he was honored with his acquaintance and society, and confirmed his statement by an oath, who could hesitate to accredit the relation, especially since the testimony of after-time has established its truth? He said that about noon, when the day was already beginning to decline, he saw with his own eyes the trophy of a cross of light in the heavens, above the sun, and bearing the inscription, CONQUER BY THIS. At this sight he himself was struck with amazement, and his whole army also, which followed him on this expedition, and witnessed the miracle.

Chapter 28

How the Christ of God appeared to him in his sleep and commanded him to use in his wars a standard made in the form of the cross

He said, moreover, that he doubted within himself what the import of this apparition could be. And while he continued to ponder and reason on its meaning, night suddenly came on. Then, in his sleep, the Christ of God appeared to him with the same sign which he had seen in the heavens and commanded him to make a likeness of that sign which he had seen in the heavens and to use it as a safeguard in all engagements with his enemies.

Chapter 29

The making of the Standard of the Cross

At dawn of day he arose and communicated the marvel to his friends. Then, calling together the workers in gold and precious stones, he sat in the midst of them and described to them the figure of the sign he had seen, bidding them represent it in gold and precious stones. And this representation I myself have had an opportunity of seeing.

Chapter 30

A description of the Standard of the Cross, which the Romans now call the Labarum.

Now it was made in the following manner: A long spear, overlaid with gold, formed the figure of the cross by means of a transverse bar laid over it. On the top of the whole was fixed a wreath of gold and precious stones, and within this, the symbol of the Savior's name, two letters indicating the name of Christ by means of its initial characters, the letter P being intersected by X in its center, and these letters the emperor was in the habit of wearing on his helmet at a later period. From the crossbar of the spear was suspended a cloth, a royal piece, covered with a profuse embroidery of most brilliant precious stones which, being also richly interlaced with gold, presented an indescribable degree of beauty to the beholder. This banner was of a square form, and the upright staff, whose lower section was of great length, bore a golden half-length portrait of the pious emperor and his children on its upper part, beneath the trophy of the cross, and immediately above the embroidered banner.

The emperor constantly made use of this sign of salvation as a safeguard against every adverse and hostile power and commanded that others similar to it should be carried at the head of all his armies.

Chapter 31

Eusebius, The Life of the Blessed Emperor Constantine

The Arian heresy, the Council of Nicea, and the Nicene Creed

The Arian heresy

Arius (250–336) was a presbyter, or priest, in Alexandria under bishop Alexander. His teachings began to be noticed around the year 318, and soon his bishop had him removed from office. However, he had friends and contacts all over the eastern Empire, and he began writing letters and teaching in other ways. He even composed jingles and set his doctrines to music. The essence of his teaching was that the Son of God was not eternal, was not always with God, but was made by the father before all time. The Son was the highest of the creations of God. He maintained his rank by his obedience and love for the Father, but he indeed was a creation and could, hypothetically, fall from obedience. The key phrase that characterized Arian teaching was, "there was [a time] when he was not."

Arius was not merely a wicked unbeliever, although it is commonplace for orthodox writers to treat him so. He believed that the uniqueness of God was compromised by the current doctrine of the Trinity, because as God his nature could not be divided, as it seemed to him the Trinity must require. Note that the error, the heresy, was influenced as much by philosophical considerations as by any Scriptural data.

Athanasius (293–373) was the antagonist on the other side from Arius and the Arians. He was a deacon in the church of Alexandria, and a theological advisor to the bishop, Alexander. In time he himself became bishop of Alexandria. Even though his thought matured over time, he made an early diagnosis of the problems of Arianism and opposed him from the start. Athanasius was a man like ourselves, and did have his faults (harsh treatment of his opponents among them), but his service to the church is incalculable.

The Council of Nicea, AD 325

Constantine was on a trip East to visit the Holy Land, having just secured the entire Empire for himself and looking forward to some relaxation, when he found that his newly adopted church was consumed in the East with the Arian controversy. He was not happy. He sent a letter to Alexander and Arius, glossing over the differences and exhorting them to harmony.

When this did not work, he decided to summon a general council of the church. This was a first in Christian history. An emperor summoned the church. He also addressed the council, and participated in the debates. According to some accounts, he suggested the crucial word *homoousios* be added to the statement of faith being drawn up.

An interesting sidelight to this whole story is to note that this council was meeting only 12 years after the end of the persecutions. Many of the bishops present had been exiled or tortured. Constantine kissed the face of one of the bishops who had lost an eye in the persecutions. These were not just ivory tower theologians meeting to chew the fat. These were men of integrity who had almost given their lives for the faith, a faith that now seemed in danger of being consumed by heresy.

The Council of Nicaea did not waste much time in condemning Arius, even though the outcome was doubtful at first. The Arian party was so bold in proclaiming Christ to be a created being, that it shocked the bishops into action.

The Council produced a statement of faith, not today's "Nicene Creed" but an early version of it, often called the Creed of Nicaea to distinguish it from the Nicene Creed. It contained the crucial word, *homoousios*, affirming that the Son was "consubstantial" or "of one substance" with the Father. All but two bishops signed it. Arius was condemned.

Unfortunately this almost-unanimous result didn't last long. The Arian party grew, and in years afterward influenced Constantine, and especially his son the emperor Constantius. The emperors interfered more and more in the church, deposing and exiling whichever bishops did not affirm the doctrine of those who had the emperor's ear. Athanasius himself was exiled several times, but always came back.

Arianism grew in importance for many years. It was instrumental in the "conversion" of many of the barbarian tribes. Indeed, Arianism was a more palatable form of

Christianity and could be a powerful missionary faith. It lowered the barriers between Christianity and the dominant Neoplatonist form of paganism, by emphasizing the oneness of God and representing the Son and the Spirit as high creatures. It also brought Christianity closer to the normal polytheism that the barbarian tribes were accustomed to. Many of the barbarian tribes remained Arian for centuries. Clovis, king of the Franks, was the first major barbarian king to convert to Catholic (i.e., Trinitarian) Christianity. He was baptized in 496.

For a time it was as if Arianism would be the faith of the church, at least the Eastern church. Italy itself was ruled by Arians when the barbarians took over the remnants of the western empire in the 400's. Within the church, various parties suggested compromises and new wordings to explain the mystery of the Trinity, often accusing all the rest of being Arian or Sabellian. But gradually, through the efforts of Athanasius and the Cappadocian Fathers (the two Gregories and Basil), the orthodox Nicene doctrine began to prevail. Even the orthodox statements had grown in subtlety and nuance. Some call the doctrines of the 380's "neo-Nicene" rather than simply Nicene. Terminology differences between Greek and Latin speakers had been resolved, especially at the Council of Alexandria in 362. By 381, enough had been worked out that a new Council was able to affirm Nicene orthodoxy again.

Homoiousians

One party in particular should be mentioned: the "homoiousians." Most of these were basically orthodox believers who could not agree on terminology with the Nicene orthodox. They believed that *homoousios* must inevitably lead to Sabellianism; therefore they proclaimed that Christ was like in nature to the Father. This was to preserve the distinction between persons. This distinction between *homoousios* and *homoiousios* has caused a lot of hooting among those who ridicule the Christian faith, or who ridicule distinctions in theology. But Athanasius, for one, wouldn't budge on *homoousios*, and he was in the end vindicated. He maintained that as long as we teach that Christ is like the Father, we are not giving him his full glory and worship that he deserves as God. He is co-eternal with the Father and is fully divine. Finally the majority of homoiousians were won over by the Nicene party.

At the risk of great oversimplification, one might say that an orthodox Christian believer of any century must steer a straight course between Arianism on the one hand and Sabellianism on the other. We must neither divide the substance nor confuse the persons, as the Athanasian Creed states.

The Athanasian Creed is a precise statement of the Trinity which is not a creed at all, nor is it from Athanasius. It may date from the 5th century. However, it is quite orthodox, and will continue to be studied by anybody who is interested in the knowledge of God.

Athanasian Creed

1. Whosoever will be saved, before all things it is necessary that he hold the catholic faith;
2. Which faith except every one do keep whole and undefiled, without doubt he shall perish everlastingly.
3. And the catholic faith is this: That we worship one God in Trinity, and Trinity in Unity;
4. Neither confounding the persons nor dividing the substance.
5. For there is one person of the Father, another of the Son, and another of the Holy Spirit.
6. But the Godhead of the Father, of the Son, and of the Holy Spirit is all one, the glory equal, the majesty coeternal.
7. Such as the Father is, such is the Son, and such is the Holy Spirit.
8. The Father uncreate, the Son uncreate, and the Holy Spirit uncreate.
9. The Father incomprehensible, the Son incomprehensible, and the Holy Spirit incomprehensible.
10. The Father eternal, the Son eternal, and the Holy Spirit eternal.
11. And yet they are not three eternals but one eternal.
12. As also there are not three untreated nor three incomprehensible, but one untreated and one incomprehensible.
13. So likewise the Father is almighty, the Son almighty, and the Holy Spirit almighty.
14. And yet they are not three almighties, but one almighty.
15. So the Father is God, the Son is God, and the Holy Spirit is God;
16. And yet they are not three Gods, but one God.
17. So likewise the Father is Lord, the Son Lord, and the Holy Spirit Lord;
18. And yet they are not three Lords but one Lord.
19. For like as we are compelled by the Christian verity to acknowledge every Person by himself to be God and Lord;
20. So are we forbidden by the catholic religion to say; There are three Gods or three Lords.
21. The Father is made of none, neither created nor begotten.
22. The Son is of the Father alone; not made nor created, but begotten.
23. The Holy Spirit is of the Father and of the Son; neither made, nor created, nor begotten, but proceeding.
24. So there is one Father, not three Fathers; one Son, not three Sons; one Holy Spirit, not three Holy Spirits.
25. And in this Trinity none is afore or after another; none is greater or less than another.
26. But the whole three persons are coeternal, and coequal.

27. So that in all things, as aforesaid, the Unity in Trinity and the Trinity in Unity is to be worshipped.
28. He therefore that will be saved must thus think of the Trinity.
29. Furthermore it is necessary to everlasting salvation that he also believe rightly the incarnation of our Lord Jesus Christ.
30. For the right faith is that we believe and confess that our Lord Jesus Christ, the Son of God, is God and man.
31. God of the substance of the Father, begotten before the worlds; and man of substance of His mother, born in the world.
32. Perfect God and perfect man, of a reasonable soul and human flesh subsisting.
33. Equal to the Father as touching His Godhead, and inferior to the Father as touching His manhood.
34. Who, although He is God and man, yet He is not two, but one Christ.
35. One, not by conversion of the Godhead into flesh, but by taking of that manhood into God.
36. One altogether, not by confusion of substance, but by unity of person.
37. For as the reasonable soul and flesh is one man, so God and man is one Christ;
38. Who suffered for our salvation, descended into hell, rose again the third day from the dead;
39. He ascended into heaven, He sits on the right hand of the Father, God, Almighty;
40. From thence He shall come to judge the quick and the dead.
41. At whose coming all men shall rise again with their bodies;
42. And shall give account of their own works.
43. And they that have done good shall go into life everlasting and they that have done evil into everlasting fire.
44. This is the catholic faith, which except a man believe faithfully he cannot be saved.

Nicene Creed

Theodosius I, the eastern emperor, summoned the Council of Constantinople in 381. It ratified the final form of the Nicene Creed which brought back the word ***homoousios.***

The Nicene-Constantinopolitan Creed

I believe in one God the Father Almighty,
maker of heaven and earth,
and of all things visible and invisible;
And in one Lord Jesus Christ, the only-begotten Son of God,
begotten of his Father before all worlds,
God of God, Light of Light,
very God of very God,

begotten, not made,
being of one substance with the Father;
by whom all things were made;
who for us men and for our salvation came down from heaven,
and was incarnate by the Holy Ghost of the Virgin Mary,
and was made man;
and was crucified also for us under Pontius Pilate;
he suffered and was buried;
and the third day he rose again according to the Scriptures,
and ascended into heaven,
and sitteth on the right hand of the Father;
and he shall come again, with glory, to judge both the quick and the dead;
whose kingdom shall have no end.
And I believe in the Holy Ghost, the Lord and Giver of Life,
who proceedeth from the Father*;
who with the Father and the Son together is worshiped and glorified;
who spake by the Prophets.
And I believe one holy Catholic and Apostolic Church;
I acknowledge one Baptism for the remission of sins;
and I look for the resurrection of the dead,
and the life of the world to come. Amen.

*Note: The text given here is from the Book of Common Prayer, which here inserts the words "and the Son," which is the form of the Creed favored by all Western churches. These words (actually one word in Latin, *filioque*) were added by unknown Western churchmen in early medieval times, and became an accepted part of the Creed. However, they were not in the original text, and they caused great controversy between the Western church and the Eastern, which has never accepted the addition.

The Desert Fathers

There has been no age in the history of the Church in which the idea of imitating Christ has failed to make an appeal to the souls of the faithful. Yet even this desire has had its period of special intensity, its peculiar region where it became for a while the expression of Christianity. During the fourth and fifth centuries, in, the deserts of Egypt and Palestine, the craving for perfection was more painful and more narrowly exclusive than ever elsewhere. Thousands of men and women, in response to a passionate hunger after righteousness, set themselves to become perfect, as the Father in heaven is perfect. They were not, indeed, careless about right belief and the holding fast of the faith. The accusation of heresy was a thing which seemed to them wholly intolerable. Yet to them the supreme importance of being good was so felt that it seemed of necessity to bring with it a true faith. "What is the faith?" "asked a brother once. The abbot Pimenion replied to him, "It is to live always in charity and humility, and to do good to your neighbor." Their absorption in the pursuit of holiness made speculation seem vain and impious. "Oh, Anthony," said the heavenly voice, "turn your attention to yourself. As for the judgments of God, it is not fitting that you should learn them."

First of all, it is necessary to understand that they were not chiefly theologians, or churchmen, or philanthropists, but imitators of Christ. Their desire was to be good. That they also believed rightly and did good followed—and these things, did follow—from their being good.

To us the activities of life—the getting and spending, the learning and teaching, philanthropy, intercourse, and the opportunities for influence—constitute life itself. It is as difficult for us to form a definite conception of a life apart from the world, from business, society, and the movements of human thought, as it is to realize that life of disembodied waiting which we expect in Paradise. Yet this complete isolation was what the Egyptian hermits strove to attain; and if we are to appreciate the value of their teaching we must, first of all, grasp the fact that they were real men on whom the sun shone and the winds blew, men with local habitations, and not phantoms or unsubstantial figures in a dream.

There were five distinct and widely separated regions in which Egyptian monasticism existed and flourished during the fourth century. First, Nitria, with its offshoot The Cells; second, Scete; third, the region in Upper Egypt which came under St. Antony's more immediate influence; fourth, Southern Egypt; fifth, the sea-coast of the Nile Delta. In very close connection with these, so as to be predominatingly Egyptian in the tone of their monasticism, were the hermitages and lauras of south-western Palestine and the settlements in the Sinai peninsula. Outlying from the greater centers were single hermitages and small lauras, wherever the monks hoped to find solitude.

For the most part in the deserts north of the Thebaid the monks saw very little of each other. Even the inhabitants of grouped cells led almost solitary lives. On Saturdays and Sundays they met for public worship and perhaps a common meal, but during the rest of the week they lived alone in their cells, or with a single disciple. If the monk were wise, he worked. Sometimes he wove mats or baskets. These were afterwards exchanged by the hermit himself or his disciple for the necessities of life in some neighboring village.

Besides working, the monks prayed. Hours every day were spent in prayer, which must have been more of the nature of meditation than intercession. In the intervals of prayer and work they sang or said psalms, and often repeated aloud long passages from the prophets. Books were scarce among them, and we read of monks visiting. each other for the purpose of learning off by heart fresh passages of Holy Scripture.

I am not inclined to either minimize or explain away the fact that the whole literature of early Egyptian monasticism is shot through and through with evidences of a belief in the reality, personality, and power of demons. The monks believed that every temptation which came to them was the work of a special demon. There was the demon of anger, who provoked brethren to quarrel with one another; there was the demon of despair, whose voice reminded the penitent of former sins, and urged the impossibility of his salvation; there was the demon who walked at noonday—he lured the monk into the sin of accidie; there were demons of gluttony, of pride, of vainglory, of covetousness. The demons had the power of assuming appalling or seducing forms, of becoming visible and palpable. Monks heard them clamoring and roaring, felt their blows, smelt them when they were present. Victorious fiends who had terrified their victims into submission or lured them into sin vanished amid peals of derisive laughter. Defeated, they departed with lamentable and awe-inspiring shrieks. Men who had experienced the ferocity and insistence of these powers of evil cannot be accused of being unpractical or merely speculative when they discuss their nature. To the Egyptian monk the power of devils was, except only the power of God, the most practical and pressing question which could be discussed.

One more prejudice remains to be noticed, and this is one which has most to do with alienating our sympathy from the early monks. It has been said—there is no comment on monasticism which we hear more frequently—that the hermit life was a selfish one, and therefore essentially remote from the spirit of Christ. There is a very obvious retort to this accusation which, in spite of its obviousness, is not so superficial as it seems. The charge is directed against men who gave up everything that is usually counted as desirable. Renunciation like that of the hermits is not usually a symptom of selfishness. It comes from the lips of a generation who have found the service of Christ not incompatible with the full enjoyment of all life's comforts and most of life's pleasures. Perhaps, however, this retort, like most others of its kind, misses the real true point of the charge.

The hermits are called selfish because they aimed at being good and not at being useful. The charge derives its real force from the fact that philanthropy, that is, usefulness to humanity, is our chief conception of what religion is. We appeal to the fact that Christ went about doing good, and we hold that the true imitation of Him consists in doing as He did rather than in being as He was. The hermits thought differently. Philanthropy was, in their view, an incidental result, as it were, a by-product of the religious spirit. Here, no doubt, there is a great gulf fixed between us and them. There is a difference of ideal. It is possible to aim at doing good, and snatch now and then, as opportunity offers, a space for the culture and of spirituality, for the "making" of the soul. It is possible also to shape life for the attainment of perfection, welcoming, as it may happen to offer itself, the chance of usefulness. The latter was the ideal of the hermits. Is the former ours? Surely the purest altruism will decline to accept it. We recognize, when we are at our best, that what we ought to aim at is that good should get done, and not that we ourselves should do it. The faithful soul, even when most pitiful of suffering, will still desire less to be useful than to be used in the cause of humanity. Impatience, that glorious impatience to be up and doing which we cannot but admire, rebels against delay and indirect approach.

The evil around us is so clamorous for amendment that it seems like a betrayal to spend our strength any way but in the combat with it. Yet it remains, at least for the student of history, a question whether in the end, there is not more good accomplished for humanity through the agency of those who, in the first instance, only aim at being good. The case of the Egyptian hermits is an illustration of what I mean. They did not aim at doing good. This is why we call them selfish. Yet certainly there was accomplished through them a great work for religion and for the Church. We can only guess at how great an incentive to piety their lives, viewed from far off, were for Christians, who remained "in the world." We know that many men, clergy and laity alike, visited the hermits, sought and, we cannot doubt it, received from them fresh spiritual strength, rekindled in the desert cells lamps that had gone out for want of oil. We can only guess, too, at what their share was in the great battle for the catholic faith. How much did St. Athanasius owe to them when he stood against the world? It was no small thing for him to know that there stood behind him men whom no court party had any bribes to buy, whom no emperor's frown had any power to terrify. The student of their literature will remember also that they did something for the material benefit of the Egyptian people. I do not insist upon the cures they wrought, or the devils they cast out of those possessed.

Some of these stories belong to the region of the miraculous, though others are, and more no doubt will be, recognized as natural by the scientific mind. Apart altogether from these miracles, the hermits did an immense, but now quite unrecognized, amount of charitable work. Many of them earned a great deal more than they needed to spend, and all that they could spare was given to the poor. They appointed some of their number to oversee the distribution of their alms. They not only fed the hungry and relieved the destitute with whom they came into actual contact, but they sent camel and boat-loads of food to the poor in the great Egyptian cities. They tried to alleviate the misery of the prisoners confined in jail. On at least one occasion they organized a collection and distribution of food on a large scale in a famine-stricken district. We shall, surely, not want to quarrel with a way of life which in fact proves to be very useful, even according to our own standard of usefulness, because in the first instance it aimed at something else. It is not however only, or even mainly, by their work for their own generation that the usefulness of the Egyptian hermits must be judged.

They were the spiritual fathers of the monks of the west. It was to the Egyptian fathers that all the great founders of western monasticism looked back. St. Martin of Tours, Cassia, Benedict of Nursia, all drew their inspiration from the lives of St. Anthony and his followers. The work which the western monks did for medieval Europe is written large across the pages of history. It is recognized even by writers who are out of sympathy with the monastic ideal. It is not necessary to describe the beautiful monastic charities for which our poor—laws have proved but a dismal substitute. We are ready to grant that the medieval monasteries were useful in their day. Ought not their usefulness to be reckoned for righteousness to the Egyptian hermits, who were the fathers of all monasticism? The Benedictine Rule, the parent of all the great rules down to the time of the Mendicant Orders, was nothing but the systematic adaptation of the teaching and experience of the Egyptian hermits to the needs of western life. So long as the western monks, under any rule, remained true to the old ideal of trying to be good in simple imitation of Jesus Christ, they also did good and were, as we say, useful.

It is only when they forget or turn away from this ideal, when are touched with the spirit of the world, or set themselves to the accomplishment of some policy, that their organizations tend to do mischief. From this point of view the usefulness of the hermits far outlasted their own generation. Through them was effected a great good which could not have been foreseen. It is perhaps just because they denied themselves the satisfaction of aiming at usefulness that they were so greatly used. This seems to be one of the laws of the divine government of things. The Lord Himself suggests it when He says: "Seek ye first the kingdom of God and His righteousness, and all these things shall be added unto you."

It seems quite possible then that what is called selfishness in the hermits, may be in reality the loftiest altruism. If so, the gulf between their ideal and ours is not so great that the heart cannot cross it. It is only needful that we should see clearer and think deeper than we do, that we should be less sure that only we have grasped the meaning of the Master's life. It is in the hope that the study of them may make for clearer vision, deeper thought, and most desirable humility that I offer these fragments of the wisdom of the desert to those who sincerely desire to be the friends of Jesus Christ.

James, O. Hannay, 1904

The Orthodox Church

Introduction

The Orthodox Church was founded by our Lord Jesus Christ and is the living manifestation of His presence in the history of the mankind. The most conspicuous characteristics of Orthodoxy are its rich liturgical life and its faithfulness to the apostolic tradition. It is believed by Orthodox Christians that their Church has preserved the tradition and continuity of the ancient Church in its fullness compared to other Christian denominations which have departed from the common tradition of the Church of the first 10 centuries. Today Orthodox Church numbers approximately 300 million Christians who follow the faith and practices that were defined by the first seven ecumenical councils. The word orthodox ("right belief and right glory") has traditionally been used, in the Greek-speaking Christian world, to designate communities, or individuals, who preserved the true faith (as defined by those councils), as opposed to those who were declared heretical. The official designation of the church in its liturgical and canonical texts is "the Orthodox Catholic Church" (gr. *catholicos* = universal).

The Orthodox Church is a family of "*autocephalous*" (self governing) churches, with the Ecumenical (= universal) Patriarch of Constantinople holding titular or honorary primacy as primus inter pares (the first among equals). The Orthodox Church is not a centralized organization headed by a pontiff. The unity of the Church is rather manifested in common faith and communion in the sacraments and no one but Christ himself is the real head of the Church. The number of autocephalous churches has varied in history. Today there are many: the Church of Constantinople (Istanbul), the Church of Alexandria (Egypt), the Church of Antioch (with headquarters in Damascus, Syria), and the Churches of Jerusalem, Russia, Serbia, Romania, Bulgaria, Georgia, Cyprus, Greece, Poland, Albania and America

There are also "autonomous" churches (retaining a token canonical dependence upon a mother see) in the Czech and Slovak republics, Sinai, Crete, Finland, Japan, China and Ukraine. In addition there is also a large Orthodox Diaspora scattered all over the world and administratively divided among various jurisdictions (dependencies of the above mentioned autocephalous churches). The first nine autocephalous churches are headed by patriarchs, the others by archbishops or metropolitans. These titles are strictly honorary as all bishops are completely equal in the power granted to them by the Holy Spirit.

The order of precedence in which the autocephalous churches are listed does not reflect their actual influence or numerical importance. The Patriarchates of Constantinople, Alexandria, and Antioch, for example, present only shadows of their past glory. Yet there remains a consensus that Constantinople's primacy of honor, recognized by the ancient canons because it was the capital of the ancient Byzantine empire, should remain as a symbol and tool of church unity and cooperation. Modern pan-Orthodox conferences were thus convoked by the ecumenical patriarch of Constantinople. Several of the autocephalous churches are de facto national churches, by far the largest being the Russian Church; however, it is not the criterion of nationality but rather the territorial principle that is the norm of organization in the Orthodox Church.

In the wider theological sense "Orthodoxy" is not merely a type of purely earthly organization which is headed by patriarchs, bishops and priests who hold the ministry in the Church which officially is called "Orthodox." Orthodoxy is the mystical "Body of Christ," the Head of which is Christ Himself (see Eph. 1:22–23 and Col. 1:18, 24 et seq.), and its composition includes not only priests but all who truly believe in Christ, who have entered in a lawful way through Holy Baptism into the Church He founded, those living upon the earth and those who have died in the Faith and in piety."

The Great Schism between the Eastern and the Western Church (1054) was the culmination of a gradual process of estrangement between the east and west that began in the first centuries of the Christian Era and continued through the Middle Ages. Linguistic and cultural differences, as well as political events, contributed to the estrangement. From the

4th to the 11th century, Constantinople, the center of Eastern Christianity, was also the capital of the Eastern Roman, or Byzantine, Empire, while Rome, after the barbarian invasions, fell under the influence of the Holy Roman Empire of the West, a political rival.

In the West theology remained under the influence of St. Augustine of Hippo (354–430) and gradually lost its immediate contact with the rich theological tradition of the Christian East. In the same time the Roman See was almost completely overtaken by Franks. Theological differences could have probably been settled if there were not two different concepts of church authority. The growth of Roman primacy, based on the concept of the apostolic origin of the Church of Rome which claimed not only titular but also jurisdictional authority above other churches, was incompatible with the traditional Orthodox ecclesiology. The Eastern Christians considered all churches as sister churches and understood the primacy of the Roman bishop only as primus inter pares among his brother bishops. For the East, the highest authority in settling doctrinal disputes could by no means be the authority of a single Church or a single bishop but an Ecumenical Council of all sister churches. In the course of time the Church of Rome adopted various wrong teachings which were not based in the Tradition and finally proclaimed the teaching of the Pope's infallibility when teaching ex cathedra. This widened the gap even more between the Christian East and West.

The Protestant communities which split from Rome in the course of centuries diverged even more from the teaching of the Holy Fathers and the Holy Ecumenical Councils. Due to these serious dogmatic differences the Orthodox Church is not in communion with the Roman Catholic and Protestant communities. More traditional Orthodox theologians do not recognize the ecclesial and salvific character of these Western churches at all, while the more liberal ones accept that the Holy Spirit acts to a certain degree within these communities although they do not possess the fullness of grace and spiritual gifts like the Orthodox Church. Many serious Orthodox theologians are of the opinion that between Orthodoxy and heterodox confessions, especially in the sphere of spiritual experience, the understanding of God and salvation, there exists an ontological difference which cannot be simply ascribed to cultural and intellectual estrangement of the East and West but is a direct consequence of a gradual abandonment of the sacred tradition by heterodox Christians.

At the time of the Schism of 1054 between Rome and Constantinople, the membership of the Eastern Orthodox Church was spread throughout the Middle East, the Balkans, and Russia, with its center in Constantinople, the capital of the Byzantine Empire, which was also called New Rome. The vicissitudes of history have greatly modified the internal structures of the Orthodox Church, but, even today, the bulk of its members live in the same geographic areas. Missionary expansion toward Asia and emigration toward the West, however, have helped to maintain the importance of Orthodoxy worldwide. Today, the Orthodox Church is present almost everywhere in the world and is bearing witness of true, apostolic and patristic tradition to all peoples.

The Orthodox Church is well known for its developed monasticism (see next entry). The uninterrupted monastic tradition of Orthodox Christianity can be traced from the Egyptian desert monasteries of the 3rd and 4th centuries. Soon monasticism had spread all over the Mediterranean basin and Europe: in Palestine, Syria, Cappadocia, Gaul, Ireland, Italy, Greece and Slavic countries. Monasticism has always been a beacon of Orthodoxy and has made and continues to make a strong and lasting impact on Orthodox spirituality.

The Orthodox Church today is an invaluable treasury of the rich liturgical tradition handed down from the earliest centuries of Christianity. The sense of the sacred, the beauty and grandeur of the Orthodox Divine Liturgy make the presence of heaven on earth live and intensive. Orthodox Church art and music has a very functional role in the liturgical life and helps even the bodily senses to feel the spiritual grandeur of the Lord's mysteries. Orthodox icons are not simply beautiful works of art which have certain aesthetic and didactic functions. They are primarily the means through which we experience the reality of the Heavenly Kingdom on earth. The holy icons enshrine the immeasurable depth of the mystery of Christ's incarnation in defense of which thousands of martyrs sacrificed their lives.

Monks at Decani Monastery in Kosovo

Orthodox Monasticism

Introduction

The innermost spiritual sense of Orthodox Monasticism is revealed in joyful mourning. This paradoxical phrase denotes a spiritual state in which a monk in his prayer grieves for the sins of the world world and at the same time experiences the regenerating spiritual joy of Christ's forgiveness and resurrection. A monk dies in order to live, he forgets himself in order to find his real self in God, he becomes ignorant of worldly knowledge in order to attain real spiritual wisdom which is given only to the humble ones.

With the development of monasticism in the Church there appeared a peculiar way of life, which however did not proclaim a new morality. The Church does not have one set of moral rules for the laity and another for monks, nor does it divide the faithful into classes according to their obligations towards God. The Christian life is the same for everyone. All Christians have in common that "their being and name is from Christ". This means that the true Christian must ground his life and conduct in Christ, something which is hard to achieve in the world.

What is difficult in the world is approached with dedication in the monastic life. In his spiritual life the monk simply tries to do what every Christian should try to do: to live according to God's commandments. The fundamental principles of monasticism are not different from those of the lives of all the faithful. This is especially apparent in the history of the early Church, before monasticism appeared.

In the tradition of the Church there is a clear preference for celibacy as opposed to the married state. This stance is not of course hostile to marriage, which is recognized as a profound mystery, but simply indicates the practical obstacles marriage puts in the way of the pursuit of the spiritual life. For this reason, from the earliest days of Christianity many of the faithful chose celibacy. Thus Athenagoras the Confessor in the second century wrote: "You can find many men and women who remain unmarried all their lives in the hope of coming closer to God".

From the very beginning the Christian life has been associated with self denial and sacrifice: "If any man would come after me, let him deny himself and take up his cross and follow me". Christ calls on us to give ourselves totally to him: "He who loves father or mother more than me is not worthy of me, and he who loves son or daughter more than me is not worthy of me".

Finally, fervent and unceasing prayer, obedience to the elders of the Church, brotherly love and humility, as well as all the essential virtues of the monastic life were cultivated by the members of the Church from its earliest days.

One cannot deny that the monk and the married man have different ways of life, but this does not alter their common responsibility towards God and His commandments. Every one of us has his own special gift within the one and indivisible body of Christ's Church. Every way of life, whether married or solitary, is equally subject to God's absolute will. Hence no way of life can be taken as an excuse for ignoring or selectively responding to Christ's call and His commandments. Both paths demand effort and determination.

St Chrysostom is particularly emphatic on this point:

> You greatly delude yourself and err, if you think that one thing is demanded from the layman and another from the monk; since the difference between them is in that whether one is married or not, while in everything else they have the same responsibilities . . . Because all must rise to the same height; and what has turned the world upside down is that we think only the monk must live rigorously, while the rest are allowed to live a life of indolence.

Referring to the observance of particular commandments in the Gospels, he says:

> "Whoever is angry with his brother without cause, regardless of whether he is a layman or a monk, opposes God in the same way. And whoever looks at a woman lustfully, regardless of his status, commits the same sin". In general, he observes that in giving His commandments Christ does not make distinction between people: "A man is not defined by whether he is a layman or a monk, but by the way he thinks".

Christ's commandments demand strictness of life that we often expect only from monks. The requirements of decent and sober behavior, the condemnation of wealth and adoption of frugality, the avoidance of idle talk and the call to show selfless love are not given only for monks, but for all the faithful.

Therefore, the rejection of worldly thinking is the duty not only of monks, but of all Christians. The faithful must not have a worldly mind, but sojourn as strangers and travelers with their minds fixed on God. Their home is not on earth, but in the kingdom of heaven: "For here we have no lasting city, but we seek the city which is to come". The Church can be seen as a community in exodus. The world is its temporary home but the Church is bound for the kingdom of God. Just as the Israelites, freed from bondage in Egypt, journeyed towards Jerusalem through many trials and tribulations, so Christians, freed from the bondage of sin, journey through many trials and tribulations towards the kingdom of heaven.

In the early days this exodus from the world did not involve a change of place but a change of the way of life. A man does not reject God and turns towards the world physically but spiritually, because God was and is everywhere and fulfills everything, so in the same way the rejection of the world and turning towards God was not understood in physical sense but as a change of the way of life. This is especially clear in the lives of the early Christians. Although they lived in the world they were fully aware that they did not come from it nor did they belong to it: "In the world but not of the world". And those who lived in chastity and poverty, which became later fundamental principles of the monastic life, did not abandon the world or take to the mountains.

Physical detachment from the world helps the soul to reject the worldly way of life. Experience shows that human salvation is harder to achieve in the world. As Basil the Great points out, living among men who do not care for the strict observance of God's commandments is harmful. It is extremely difficult, if not impossible, to answer Christ's call to take up one's cross and follow Him within the bounds of worldly life. Seeing the multitude of sinners, one not only fails to see his own sins but also falls into temptation to believe that he has achieved something, because we tend to compare ourselves with those who are worse than we are. Furthermore, the hustle and bustle of everyday life distracts us from the remembrance of God. It does not only prevent us from feeling the joy of intense communion with God, but leads us to contempt and forgetfulness of the divine will.

This does not mean that detachment from the world guarantees salvation, but surely does help us a lot in our spiritual life. When someone devotes himself wholly to God and His will, nothing can stop him from being saved. St. Chrysostom says: "There is no obstacle to a worker striving for virtue, but men in office, and those who have a wife and children to look after, and servants to see to, and those in positions of authority can also take care to be virtuous".

Saint Simeon the New Theologian observes: "Living in a city does not prevent us from carrying out God's commandments if we are zealous, and silence and solitude are of no benefit if we are slothful and neglectful". Elsewhere he says that it is possible for all, not only monks but laymen too, to "eternally and continuously repent and weep and pray to God, and by these actions to acquire all the other virtues".

Orthodox monasticism has always been associated with stillness or silence, which is seen primarily as an internal rather than an external state. External silence is sought in order to attain inner stillness of mind more easily. This stillness is not a kind of inertia or inaction, but awakening and activation of the spiritual life. It is intense vigilance and total devotion to God. Living in a quiet place the monk succeeds in knowing himself better, fighting his passions more deeply and purifying his heart more fully, so as to be found worthy of beholding God.

The father of St Gregory Palmas, Constantine, lived a life of stillness as a senator and member of the imperial court in Constantinople. The essence of this kind of life is detachment from worldly passions and complete devotion to God. This is why St Gregory Palmas says that salvation in Christ is possible for all: "The farmer and the leather worker and the mason and the tailor and the weaver, and in general all those who earn their living with their hands and in the sweat of their brow, who cast out of their souls the desire for wealth, fame and comfort, are indeed blessed". In the same spirit St Nicolas Avails observes that it is not necessary for someone to flee to the desert, eat unusual food, change his dress, ruin his health or attempt some other such thing in order to remain devoted to God.

The monastic life, with its physical withdrawal from the world to the desert, began about the middle of the third century. This flight of Christians to the desert was partly caused by the harsh Roman persecutions of the time. The growth of monasticism, however, which began in the time of Constantine the Great, was largely due to the refusal of many Christians to adapt to the more worldly character of the now established Church, and their desire to lead a strictly Christian life. Thus monasticism developed simultaneously in various places in the southeast Mediterranean, Egypt, Palestine, Sinai, Syria and Cyprus, and soon after reached Asia Minor and finally Europe. During the second millennium. however, Mount Ethos appeared as the center of Orthodox monasticism.

The commonest and safest form of the monastic life is the coenobitic communion. In the coenobitic monastery everything is shared: living quarters, food, work, prayer, common efforts, cares, struggles and achievements. The leader and spiritual father of the coenobium is the abbot. The exhortation to the abbot in the Charter of St Athanasius the Athonite is typical: "Take care that the brethren have everything in common. No one must own as much as a needle. Your body and soul shall be your own, and nothing else. Everything must be shared equally with love between all your spiritual children, brethren and fathers". The coenobium is the ideal Christian community, where no distinction is drawn between mine and yours, but everything is designed to cultivate a common attitude and a spirit of fraternity. In the coenobium the obedience of every monk to his abbot and his brotherhood, loving kindness, solidarity and hospitality are of the greatest importance. As St Theodore of Studium observes, the whole community of the faithful should in the final analysis be a coenobitic Church. Thus the monastic coenobium is the most consistent attempt to achieve this and an image of Church in small.

In its "fuga mundi", monasticism underlines the Church's position as an "anti-community" within the world, and by its intense spiritual asceticism cultivates its eschatological spirit. The monastic life is described as "the angelic state", in other words a state of life that while on earth follows the example of the life in heaven. Virginity and celibacy come within this framework, anticipating the condition of souls in the life to come, where "they neither marry nor are given in marriage, but are like angels in heaven" 8.

Many see celibacy as a defining characteristic of monastic life. This does not mean, however, that celibacy is the most important aspect of the monastic life: it simply gives this distinctiveness to this way of life. All the other obligations, even the other two monastic vows of obedience and poverty, essentially concern all the faithful. Needless to say, all this takes on a special form in the monastic life, but that has no bearing on the essence of the matter.

All Christians are obliged to keep the Lord's commandments, but this requires efforts. Fallen human nature, enslaved by its passions is reluctant to fulfill this obligation. It seeks pleasure and avoids the pain involved in fighting the passions and selfishness. The monastic life is so arranged as to facilitate this work. On the other hand the worldly life, particularly in our secular society, makes it harder to be an ascetic. The problem for the Christian in the world is that he is called upon to reach the same goal under adverse conditions.

The tonsure, with cutting of hair, is called a "second baptism". Baptism, however, is one and the same for all members of the Church. It is participation in the death and resurrection of Christ. The tonsure does not repeat, but renews and activates the grace of the baptism. The monastic vows are essentially not different from those taken at baptism, with the exception of the vow of celibacy. Furthermore, hair is also cut during baptism.

The monastic life points the way to perfection. However, the whole Church is called to perfection. All the faithful, both laymen and monks, are called to become perfect following the divine example: "You, therefore, must be perfect, as your heavenly Father is perfect". But while the monk affirms the radical nature of the Christian life, the layman is content to regard it conventionally. The conventional morality of the layman on the one hand and the radical morality of the monk on the other create a dialectical differentiation that takes the form of a dialectical antithesis.

St Maximus the Confessor, in contrasting the monastic with the worldly life, observes that a layman's successes are a monk's failures, and vice versa: "The achievements of the worldly are failures for monks; and the achievements of monks are failures for the worldly. When the monk is exposed to what the world sees as success—wealth, fame, power, pleasure, good health and many children, he is destroyed. And when a worldly man finds himself in the state desired by monks—poverty, humility, weakness, self restraint, mortification and suchlike, he considers it a disaster. Indeed, in such despair many may consider hanging themselves, and some have actually done so".

Of course the comparison here is between the perfect monk and the very worldly Christian. However, in more usual circumstances within the Church the same things will naturally function differently, but this difference could never reach diametrical opposition. Thus for example, wealth and fame cannot be seen as equally destructive for monks and laymen. These things are always bad for monks, because they conflict with the way of life the monks have chosen. For laymen, however, wealth and fame may be beneficial, even though they involve grave risks. The existence of the family, and of the wider secular society with its various needs and demands, not only justify but sometimes make it necessary to accumulate wealth or assume office. Those things that may unite in the world divide in the monastic life. The ultimate unifier is Christ Himself.

The Christian life does not depend only on human effort but primarily on God's grace. Ascetic exercises in all their forms and degrees aim at nothing more than preparing man to harmonies his will with that of God and receive the grace of the Holy Spirit. This harmonization attains its highest expression and perfection in prayer. "In true prayer we enter into and dwell in the Divine Being by the power of the Holy Spirit". This leads man to his archetype and makes him a true person in the likeness of his Creator.

The grace of the Christian life is not to be found in its outward forms. It is not found in ascetic exercises, fasts, vigils and mortification of the flesh. Indeed, when these exercises are practiced without discernment they become abhorrent. This repulsiveness is no longer confined to their external form but comes to characterize their inner content. They become abhorrent not only because outwardly they appear as a denial of life, contempt for material things or self-abandonment, but also because they mortify the spirit, encourage pride and cultivate self justification.

The Christian life is not a denial but an affirmation. It is not death, but life. And it is not only affirmation and life, but the only true affirmation and the only true life. It is the true affirmation because if goes beyond all possibility of denial and the only true life because it conquers death. The negative appearance of the Christian life in its outward forms is due precisely to its attempt to stand beyond all human denial. Since there is no human affirmation that does not end in denial, and no worldly life that does not end in death, the Church takes its stand and reveals its life after accepting every human denial and affirming every form of earthly death.

The power of the Christian life lies in the hope of resurrection, and the goal of ascetic striving is to partake in the resurrection. The monastic life, as the angelic and heavenly life lived in time, is the foreknowledge and foretaste of eternal life. It aim is not to cast off the human element, but clothe oneself with incorruptibility and immortality: "For while we are still in this tent, we sigh with anxiety; not that we would be unclothed, but that we would be further clothed, so that what is mortal may be swallowed up by life".

There are sighing and tears produced by the presence of sin, as well as the suffering to be free of the passions and regain a pure heart. These things demand ascetic struggles, and undoubtedly have a negative form, since they aim at humility. They are exhausting and painful, because they are concerned with states and habits that have become second nature. It is however precisely through this abasement, self purification, that man clears the way for God's grace to appear and to act within his heart. God does not manifest Himself to an impure heart.

Monks are the "guardians". They choose to constrain their bodily needs in order to attain the spiritual freedom offered by Christ. They tie themselves down in death's realm in order to experience more intensely the hope of the life to come. They reconcile themselves with space, where man is worn down and annihilated, feel it as their body, transform it into the Church and orientate it towards the kingdom of God.

The monk's journey to perfection is gradual and is connected with successive renunciations, which can be summarized in three. The first renunciation involves completely abandoning the world. This is not limited to things, but includes people and parents. The second is renunciation of the individual will, and the third is freedom from pride, which is identified with liberation from the sway of the world.

These successive renunciations have a positive, not a negative meaning. They permit a man to fully open up and be perfected "in the image and likeness" of God. When man is freed from the world and from himself, he expands without limits. He becomes a true person, which "encloses" within himself the whole of humanity as Christ himself does. That is why, on the moral plane, the Christian is called upon to love all human beings, even his enemies. Then God Himself comes and dwells within him, and the man arrives to the fullness of his theanthropic being Here we can see the greatness of the human person, and can understand the superhuman struggles needed for his perfection.

The life of monasticism is life of perpetual spiritual ascent. While the world goes on its earthbound way, and the faithful with their obligations and distractions of the world try to stay within the institutional limits of the church tradition, monasticism goes to other direction and soars. It rejects any kind of compromise and seeks the absolute. It launches itself from this world and heads for the kingdom of God. This is in essence the goal of the Church itself.

In Church tradition this path is pictured as a ladder leading to heaven. Not everyone manages to reach the top of this spiritual ladder. Many are to be found on the first rungs. Others rise higher. There are also those who fall from a higher or a lower rung. The important thing is not the height reached, but the unceasing struggle to rise ever higher. Most important of all, this ascent is achieved through ever increasing humility, that is through ever increasing descent. "Keep thy mind in hell, and despair not", was the word of

God to Saint Silouan of Mount Ethos. When man descends into the hell of his inner struggle having God within him, then he is lifted up and finds the fullness of being

At the top of this spiritual ladder are the "fools for Christ's sake", as the Apostle Paul calls himself and the other apostles, or "the fools for Christ's sake", who "play the madman for the love of Christ and mock the vanity of the world", Seeking after glory among men, says Christ, obstructs belief in God. Only when man rejects pride can he defeat the world and devote himself to God.

In the lives of monks the Christian sees examples of men who took their Christian faith seriously and committed themselves to the path which everyone is called by Christ to follow. Not all of them attained perfection, but they all tried, and all rose to a certain height. Not all possessed the same talent, but all strove as good and faithful servants. They are not held up as examples to be imitated, especially by laymen. They are however valuable signposts on the road to perfection, which is common for all and has its climax in the perfectness of God.

Monks at Decani Monastery in Kosovo

Iconography

Iconography refers to the making and liturgical use of icons, pictorial representations of Biblical scenes from the life of Jesus Christ, historical events in the life of the Church, and portraits of the saints. Icons are usually two-dimensional images and may be made of paint, mosaic, embroidery, weaving, carving, engraving, or other methods.

Images have always been a vital part of the Church, but their place was the subject of the Iconoclast Controversy in the 8th and 9th centuries, especially in the East. The use of iconography is considered one of the most distinctive elements of the Byzantine rite.

Icons are to be understood in a manner similar to Holy Scripture—that is, they are not simply artistic compositions but rather are witnesses to the truth the way Scripture is. Far from being imaginative creations of the iconographer, they are more like scribal copies of the Bible.

OrthodoxWiki

PEOPLE

Athanasius (AD 297–373)
Basil the Great (AD 330–375)
Ambrose (AD 340–397)
Jerome (AD 340–420)
Chrysostom (AD 347–407)
Augustine (AD 354–430)
Patrick (AD ?390–461)
Leo the Great (AD ?400–461)
Columba (AD 521–597)

Athanasius

Dates
AD 297–373

Famous for being
Bishop of Alexandria
Known as, "Father of orthodoxy"

Important writings
Vita S. Antoni (Life of St. Anthony)

One of his quotations
"It is not by the sword or the spear, by soldiers or by armed force that truth is to be promoted, but by counsel and gentle persuasion."

Athanasius was the bishop of Alexandria and the champion of orthodoxy at the Nicene Council. Tradition has it that the Patriarch Alexander noticed Athanasius playing at baptism at the seashore as a young boy. Upon questioning, the Bishop was satisfied that the baptisms were valid and undertook to have these boys trained for the priesthood. Passed his youth in the desert under the spiritual guidance of St. Anthony, whose biography he wrote. Athanasius was ordained deacon in 319 by the Bishop of Alexandria.

Athanasius was the rival of Arius at the Nicene Council in 325. He asserts that the Members of the Trinity are three at yet at the same time one. Father, Son and Holy Ghost are co-equals in eternity, neither one preceded the other; One God, Christ sharing in the being of God. St. Athanasius summed up the purpose of the incarnation by saying "God became man that we might be made God." The council voted by a large majority against Arius and for Athanasius but did not put an end to Arianism. From 325 to 381, thirteen church councils debated the rejected doctrine. The heresy continued to spread through missionary Ulfilas (311–383) to the barbarian Goths on the outskirts of the Roman empire. As Athanasius himself was to say, "the world is overrun with Arianism."

After the council (328) Alexander died and Athanasius succeeded him as Bishop, although not yet thirty. After becoming Bishop he became the great leader of the orthodox cause, the most formidable adversary of the enemies of the Nicaen decision. Athanasius suffered exile 5 five times but held to his conviction that communion was not given to any heretic who did not hold the divinity of Christ.

Jay Atkinson

Basil the Great

Dates

AD 329–375

Famous for being

Bishop and theologian

Important writings

Hexaemeron

One of his quotations

"The love of God is not taught. No one has taught us to enjoy the light or to be attached to life more than anything else."

Basil was born in Caesarea of Cappadocia, a province in what is now central Turkey (more or less directly north of the easternmost part of the Mediterranean, but with no seacoast). He was born in 329, after the persecution of Christians had ceased, but with parents who could remember the persecutions and had lived through them. He originally planned to become a lawyer and orator, and studied at Athens (351–356), where two of his classmates were Gregory of Nazianzus (who became a close friend) and the future Emperor Julian the Apostate. When he returned home, the influence and example of his sister Macrina led him to seek the monastic life instead, and after making a tour of the monasteries of Egypt in 357, he founded a monastic settlement near his home. He remained there only five years, but the influence of his community was enormous.

Whereas in the West there are numerous monastic orders (Benedictines, Carthusians, etc.), in the East all monks are Basilian monks. His Longer Rules and Shorter Rules for the monastic life remain the standard. Basil's Rules were strict, but not severe. Basil expresses a definite preference for the communal life of the monastery over the solitary life of the hermit, arguing that the Christian life of mutual love and service is communal by its nature. In 367–8, when Cappadocia suffered a severe and widespread famine, Basil sold his family's very extensive land holdings in order to buy food for the starving, persuading many others to follow his example, and putting on an apron to work in the soup kitchen himself. In this crisis, he absolutely refused to allow any distinction to be made between Jew and Christian, saying that the digestive systems of the two are indistinguishable. He also built a hospital for the care of the sick, housing for the poor, and a hospice for travelers.

These were the years between the First Ecumenical Council (Nicea, 325) and the Second (Constantinople, 381), years in which it was uncertain whether the Church would stand by the declaration made at Nicea that the Logos (the "Word"—see John 1:1) was fully God, equally with the Father, or seek a more flexible formula in the hope of reconciliation with the Arians, who declared themselves unalterably opposed to the Nicene wording. Basil had been ordained priest in 362 in order to assist the new Bishop of Caesarea, whom he succeeded in 370. (Since Caesarea was the capital, or metropolis, of the province of Cappadocia, its bishop was automatically the metropolitan of Cappadocia, which included about fifty dioceses (bishoprics). A metropolitan was roughly what we would call an archbishop, although in ancient terminology an "archbishop" was one step above a metropolitan.) By that time, an Arian emperor, Valens, was ruling. Basil made it his policy to try to unite the so-called semi-Arians with the Nicene party against the outright Arians, making use of the formula "three persons (*hypostases*) in one substance (*ousia*)," thus explicitly acknowledging a distinction between the Father and the Son (a distinction that the Nicene party had been accused of blurring), and at the same time insisting on their essential unity.

When the emperor Valens passed through Caesarea in 371, he demanded the theological submission of Basil, who flatly refused. The imperial prefect expressed astonishment at Basil's defiance, to which Basil replied, "Perhaps you have never met a real bishop before." Valens retaliated by dividing the province of Cappadocia into two provinces, with the result that the Arian Bishop of Tyana became metropolitan of the new province of Western Cappadocia. Basil responded by going political. He ramrodded his brother Gregory of Nyssa and his friend Gregory of Nazianzus into bishoprics that they did not want, and for which they were totally unsuited, so that he would have the votes of those bishoprics when he needed them. (Neither Gregory ever quite forgave him for this.) His interests were not exclusively theological: he denounced and excommunicated those who owned houses of prostitution, he worked to secure justice for the poor against those who oppressed them, and he severely disciplined clergy who used their office to accumulate money or to live too well at the expense of the faithful.

His most famous writings include the *Hexaemeron* ("The Six Days"), a series of nine sermons on the days of creation, in which he speaks of the beauties of the created world as revelations of the splendor of God. His *Against Eunomius* defends the deity of Christ against an Arian writer, and his *On The Holy Spirit* speaks of the deity of the Third Person of the Trinity, and the rightness of worshipping Him together with the Father and the Son. In his *Address To Young Men* (originally written for his nephews), he urges Christians to make themselves acquainted with pagan philosophy and literature, arguing that this will often lead to a deeper understanding of Christian truth.

His personality comes through most clearly in his letters, of which more than three hundred have been preserved. Some deal with points of theology or ethics, some with canon law, and many simply with everyday affairs. Ten times a year the Eastern churches use the Liturgy of St. Basil rather than the more usual Liturgy of St. John Chrysostom. It differs chiefly in having a more elaborate Anaphora (the prayer of consecration offered over the bread and wine), expressing some of his characteristic turns of thought, probably dating back to his time and used by him, and possibly composed by him personally.

Basil died in 379, shortly after the death in battle of the Arian Valens removed the chief threat to the Nicene faith to which Basil had devoted his life. He was mourned by the entire city, and the weeping crowds at his funeral included Christians, Jews, and pagans. He is counted (with the two Gregories) as one of the three Cappadocian Fathers, and (with Gregory of Nazianzus and John Chrysostom) as one of the Three Holy Hierarchs. In the West, he is reckoned (with Gregory of Nazianzus, John Chrysostom, and Athanasius) as one of the Four Greek (Eastern) Doctors of the Undivided Church. (The Four Latin (Western) Doctors are Ambrose, Jerome, Augustine, and Gregory the Great.)

James Kiefer

St Basil's Rule

In his Rule St. Basil follows a catechetical method; the disciple asks a question to which the master replies. He limits himself to laying down indisputable principles which will guide the superiors and monks in their conduct. He sends his monks to the Sacred Scriptures; in his eyes the Bible is the basis of all monastic legislation, the true Rule. The questions refer generally to the virtues which the monks should practice and the vices they should avoid. The greater number of the replies contain a verse or several verses of the Bible accompanied by a comment which defines the meaning. The most striking qualities of the Basilian Rule are its prudence and its wisdom. It leaves to the superiors the care of settling the many details of local, individual, and daily life; it does not determine the material exercise of the observance or the administrative regulations of the monastery. Poverty, obedience, renunciation, and self-abnegation are the virtues which St. Basil makes the foundation of the monastic life.

The Catholic Encyclopedia, Volume II, 1907

Ambrose of Milan

Dates

AD 340–397

Famous for being

Bishop and doctor of the Church

"Hammer of Arianism"

Important writings

Chants and hymns

One of his quotations

"True repentance is cease from sinning."

Ambrose was governor of Northern Italy, with capital at Milan. When the see of Milan fell vacant, it seemed likely that rioting would result, since the city was evenly divided between Arians and Athanasians. Ambrose went to the meeting where the election was to take place, and appealed to the crowd for order and good will on both sides. He ended up being elected bishop with the support of both sides.

He gave away his wealth, and lived in simplicity. By his preaching, he converted the diocese to the Athanasian position, except for the Goths and some members of the Imperial Household. (Note: The Arian emperor Constantius (son of Constantine the Great) had sent missionaries (Arians, of course) to convert the Gothic tribes. The Goths were the chief source of mercenary troops for the Empire. Thus for many years the Army was Arian although a majority of civilians were Athanasian.) On one occasion, the Empress ordered him to turn over a church to the Arians so that her Gothic soldiers could worship in it. Ambrose refused, and he and his people occupied the church. Ambrose composed Latin hymns in the rhythm of "Praise God from Whom all blessings flow," and taught them to the people, who sang them in the church as the soldiers surrounded it. The Goths were unwilling to attack a hymn-singing congregation, and Ambrose won that dispute.

He subsequently won another dispute, when the Emperor, enraged by a crowd who defied him, ordered them all killed by his soldiers. When he next appeared at church, Ambrose met him at the door and said, "You may not come in. There is blood on your hands." The emperor finally agreed to do public penance and to promise that thereafter he would never carry out a sentence of death without a forty-day delay after pronouncing it. Less creditable, to modern Christians, is Ambrose's dispute with the emperor when certain Christians burned a Jewish synagogue, and the emperor commanded them to make restitution. Ambrose maintained that no Christian could be compelled to provide money for the building of a non-Christian house of worship, no matter what the circumstances.

Ambrose was largely responsible for the conversion of St. Augustine. The hymn *Te Deum Laudamus* ("We praise Thee, O God") was long thought to have been composed by Ambrose in thanksgiving for that conversion. The current opinion is that Ambrose did not write it, but that he may well have written the Creed known as the Athanasian Creed. He is perhaps the first writer of Christian hymns with rhyme and (accentual) meter, and northern Italy still uses his style of plainchant, known as Ambrosian chant, rather than the more widespread Gregorian chant. On the negative side, many Christians will regret his contribution to increased preoccupation with the relics of martyrs. He died 4 April 397.

Ambrose is regarded as one of the Eight Great Doctors (=Teachers) of the Undivided Church. The list includes four Latin (Western) Doctors (Ambrose, Jerome, Augustine, and Pope Gregory the Great), and four Greek (Eastern) Doctors (Athanasius, John Chrysostom, Basil the Great, and Gregory of Nazianzus—not to be confused with Gregory of Nyssa, the brother of Basil).

James Kiefer

Ambrose's influence on Augustine

St. Augustine tells in his *Confessions* how deeply the brilliance and charm of Ambrose had moved him when attending services in Milan, even stirring him to tears. Augustine, looking back on his life, sees his links with Ambrose as entirely providential. God had led him to Milan in order to encounter Ambrose, so that he could begin his return to the true faith.

From Augustine's *Confessions*

5.13.23

When therefore they of Milan had sent to Rome to the prefect of the city, to furnish them with a rhetoric reader for their city, and sent him at the public expense, I made application (through those very persons, intoxicated with Manichaean vanities, to be freed wherefrom I was to go, neither of us however knowing it) that Symmachus, then prefect of the city, would try me by setting me some subject, and so send me.

To Milan I came, to Ambrose the Bishop, known to the whole world as among the best of men, Thy devout servant; whose eloquent discourse did then plentifully dispense unto Thy people the flour of Thy wheat, the gladness of Thy oil, and the sober inebriation of Thy wine. To him was I unknowing led by Thee, that by him I might knowingly be led to Thee.

That man of God received me as a father, and showed me an Episcopal kindness on my coming. Thenceforth I began to love him, at first indeed not as a teacher of the truth (which I utterly despaired of in Thy Church), but as a person kind towards myself. And I listened diligently to him preaching to the people, not with that intent I ought, but, as it were, trying his eloquence, whether it answered the fame thereof, or flowed fuller or lower than was reported; and I hung on his words attentively; but of the matter I was as a careless and scornful looker-on; and I was delighted with the sweetness of his discourse, more recondite, yet in manner less winning and harmonious, than that of Faustus. Of the matter, however, there was no comparison; for the one was wandering amid Manichaean delusions, the other teaching salvation most soundly. But salvation is far from sinners, such as I then stood before him; and yet was I drawing nearer by little and little, and unconsciously.

5.14.24

For though I took no pains to learn what he spake, but only to hear how he spake (for that empty care alone was left me, despairing of a way, open for man, to Thee), yet together with the words which I would choose, came also into my mind the things which I would refuse; for I could not separate them. And while I opened my heart to admit "how eloquently he spake," there also entered "how truly he spake"; but this by degrees. For first, these things also had now begun to appear to me capable of defense; and the Catholic faith, for which I had thought nothing could be said against the Manichees' objections, I now thought might be maintained without shamelessness; especially after I had heard one or two places of the Old Testament resolved, and often "in a figure," which when I understood literally, I was slain spiritually. Very many places then of those books having been explained, I now blamed my despair, in believing that no answer could be given to such as hated and scoffed at the Law and the Prophets.

Augustine, Confessions, Translated by E. B. Pusey

Jerome

Dates
AD 340–420

Famous for being
Biblical scholar

Important writings
Translation of the Bible

Two of his quotations
"A man who is well-grounded in the testimonies of the Scripture is the bulwark of the Church."
"The whole world groaned in astonishment at finding itself Arian."

Saint Jerome (Eusebius Hieronymus), magisterial biblical scholar, literary artist, and advocate of asceticism, is traditionally classed as one of the "doctors" of the Latin church. The date of his birth is disputed. He died in AD 420, which according to Prosper of Aquitaine's Chronicle was his ninety-first year; other evidence however suggests that he was born not in 331 but in the 340s, probably in AD 347.

Background
Jerome's early life is fairly obscure. He was born of Christian parents in the small city of Stridon, on Dalmatia's border with Pannonia. Both his brother, Paulinian, and his sister entered upon the monastic life. His parents were prosperous, and Jerome was sent to Rome for his education. There he passed through a standard course of studies in literature and rhetoric, and was at length baptized as a Christian. In his early twenties, he left Rome for Trier, then settled for a time in Aquileia, where he began to put into practice an emerging interest in the monastic life; with a group of his close friends, Rufinus, Chromatius, and Heliodorus, he formed a small ascetic community attached to the local bishop, Valerian. He also developed at this time his understanding of Greek. After some disagreements with his companions, Jerome moved to the East, going first to Antioch, then living as a hermit in the desert at Chalcis, south of modern Aleppo. This proved a formative period, both intellectually and spiritually.

He began to learn Hebrew, and he discovered the arduousness of the ascetic life as never before. Difficult relations with local monks forced him to move on, and he returned to Antioch, where he was ordained as a priest. He was in Constantinople during 380–81, where he was able to acquaint himself with significant contemporary Greek work on Christology as well as broaden his awareness of exegetical approaches.

In 382 he went back to Rome, where he became a de facto assistant to the aging pope Damasus, who commissioned him to undertake a revision of the existing Latin versions of the Bible and to produce a new standard version. In Rome he formed close friendships with a number of aristocratic Christian women, notably Marcella, Melania, Paula, and Paula's daughter Eustochium, to whom he became a spiritual tutor and counselor. He continued to write elegant epistles and eloquent protreptics for asceticism. The combination of his literary brilliance and the patronage of his wealthy friends seemed to promise him great things, but he increasingly annoyed the Roman clergy with his bitingly satirical attacks on their manners (cf. especially his famous Ep. 22, to Eustochium). Jerome's relations with Paula in particular seemed to sit oddly with his denunciations of clerical indulgence and his impassioned advocacy of self-denial. So long as he enjoyed the patronage of Damasus, little could be done, but the advent of pope Siricius in December 384 gave Jerome's many enemies a chance to lobby for an investigation into his behavior.

In 385, following an official enquiry, he was condemned and effectively banished from Rome by a clerical body whom he labeled a "senate of the Pharisees" (Did. Spir. Sanct., praef.; cf. Epp. 33.5; 127.9). He left the city for the East, being joined en route by Paula and Eustochium. After visiting holy sites in Antioch, Egypt, and Palestine, the party finally settled at Bethlehem in the summer of 386. A monastery and a convent were built courtesy of Paula's wealth, and Jerome presided over a fairly liberal ascetic regime for the remainder of his life, devoting his energies to the kind of intense scholarly activities and spiritual discipline to which he had always been inclined.

Jerome the scholar

Jerome stands out as one of the greatest biblical scholars in the history of the church. His most remarkable achievement was his new translation of the Scriptures. The Latin Bible of the fourth century was notoriously corrupt, with differing versions in existence in Gaul, North Africa, and Italy: Jerome famously remarks that there were almost as many textual forms as there were manuscripts (Ep. Praef. Evang., to Damasus). A new edition was sorely needed.

It is a mistake, however, to think that Jerome's work proceeded according to a uniform plan, or to imagine that he was personally responsible for every part of what we have come to think of as the editio vulgata. His initial project was to produce a new rendering of the four gospels—not so much a fresh translation of the Greek as a synthesis of various Latin versions in conformity with the Greek text. The completed work was presented to Damasus shortly before his death in 384. This was followed by a new version of the Psalter, a rather crude rendering of the Septuagint. This version is traditionally associated with the Roman Psalter, the standard Roman edition until the time of Pope Pius V in the XVI Century, but the association is unreliable. In c. 392, Jerome was able to replace it with a better translation, the so-called "Gallican Psalter" (thus named after its subsequent popularity in Gaul), which used the text of the Septuagint given in Origen's Hexapla. However, further work on other parts of the Old Testament convinced him that any translation which relied only on a Greek text was simply not good enough: it was necessary to go back to the veritas Hebraica, the "Hebrew verity" (as he would typically call it) itself.

The Vulgate Bible

Among all his contemporaries, Jerome was exceptionally well-equipped to take up the challenge, and he embarked on a completely new rendering of the Hebrew Scriptures. Pursued intermittently, the work occupied about a decade and a half of his life, from 390/1 until 405/6. It included a third recension of the Psalter, though this version never attained the liturgical popularity of its "Gallican" predecessor, which was ultimately incorporated into the Vulgate manuscripts in its place. The quality of Jerome's translations varied somewhat, and it took time for them to gain acceptance; for some while they were used alongside existing versions. In the end, however, their obvious scholarly superiority over all previous renderings in the West won them the recognition they deserved, and from the sixth century onwards they started to be collected into a new Vulgate Bible.

Jerome's return to the Hebrew was seminal. It was also controversial. He was severely criticized by Augustine and others, who argued that he was in danger of relapsing into a Judaizing position by abandoning the Greek antecedents of the Bible as it had come to be known in the West. Whatever objections were raised to the theological implications of his method, however, Jerome proved an assiduous student of his subject. By way of background research into the biblical texts, he enquired into questions of topography and etymology (cf. his Onomastica), expanding on existing reference manuals in Greek and drawing also on rabbinical wisdom. He produced a number of technical commentaries which sought to discuss textual and philological issues; the most valuable of these are on the prophets, the Psalms, and on Genesis (cf. especially his Quaestiones Hebraicae in Genesim).

Exegetically, his tastes were eclectic, reflecting a range of hermeneutical influences: a concern for the literal sense of Scripture tends to predominate in his work, but spiritual interpretation is also accommodated, as his homilies also confirm. Jerome's interest in history extended beyond his work in the fields of biblical translation and exegetical comment. He also updated the Chronicle of Eusebius, continuing its sequence from 325 up to the year 378, and in his De viris illustribus he produced a survey of distinguished writers up to 393 (the first extant example of a "patrology"). He also wrote a series of vignettes of Eastern hermits (the "Lives" of Paul, Hilarion, and Malchus), which however reveal stylized moral elaborations of his own ideals of asceticism far more than biographical accuracy.

Controversialist

Jerome's scholarly gifts and outstanding literary productivity were mediated through a personality which seemed to relish controversy and delight in polemical expression. Broken relationships with friends and colleagues were part and parcel of his career at almost every stage. For many years he was an ardent devotee of Origen, and translated several series of his homilies on both Old and New Testaments into Latin. In the fierce controversy that flared up surrounding Origen's theology in the last years of the fourth century, he changed his mind, and became a bitter and tendentious opponent. Matters were not helped when his friend from boyhood, Rufinus of Aquileia, published a new (and rather free) translation of Origen's De principiis, in a bid to demonstrate that their former mentor was indeed orthodox, and pointed out in his preface that Jerome had earlier supported him.

The friendship of Rufinus and Jerome was no more, and the ensuing years witnessed a bitter war between the two, during which Jerome released his own translation of De principiis to prove just how heretical Origen really was (this work is now lost; but cf. especially the personal attacks on Rufinus in Apologia adversus libros Rufini). Again, positive evaluation of Ambrose's contributions to the subject of virginity soon gave way to scathing denunciations of Ambrose's lack of originality, couched in barely-disguised anonymity. More predictable and impassioned salvos were fired at foes such as Helvidius, the Roman layman who denied the post partum virginity of Mary (Contra Helvidium, and Jovinian, the monk whose anti-ascetic ideology also evoked the ire of Ambrose and Augustine Adversus Iovinianum. Vigilantius, a priest from Aquitania, visited Bethlehem in 395, and his stay ended in a quarrel: years later, Jerome was accusing him of opposing sacred ideals such as clerical celibacy and the principles expressed in the cult of the martyrs (Contra Vigilantium). Other diatribes were delivered against Luciferian (extreme Nicene) opponents, against John of Jerusalem, who had had Jerome temporarily excommunicated for his anti-Origenist activities (especially his support of the particularly zealous guardian of orthodoxy, Epiphanius of Salamis), and, in later years, against the Pelagians.

In an age when Greek forms still dominated much of the intellectual landscape of Christianity, Jerome demonstrated that the greatest Christian learning could also be expressed in Latin. He did a huge amount to restore the importance of the church's Jewish inheritance, evincing an enthusiasm for Hebrew texts that would not be matched in the West until the Reformation. His angular personality, and the biting language, distorted ideas, and disrupted relations which it produced, will no doubt forever be part of his legacy to the church; but so too must be his prodigious literary talent and his outstanding philological and textual scholarship.

John Chrysostom

Dates
AD 347–407

Famous for being
Preacher

Important writings
Sermons

One of his quotations
"Do you fast? Give me proof of it by your works."

John, later to be called "golden mouth" (Chrysostom), because he was regarded by some as, "the greatest preacher in the early church," was born in Antioch in 349. His mother is variously described as a pagan or as a Christian, and his father was a high ranking military officer. John's father died soon after his birth and so he was brought up by his mother. He was baptized in 368 or 373 and tonsured a reader (one of the minor orders of the Church). As a result of his mother's connections in the city, John began his education under a Pagan teacher named Libanius. From Libanius John acquired the skills for a career in rhetoric, as well as a love of the Greek language and literature. As he grew older, however, he became more deeply committed to Christianity and went on to study theology under Diodore of Tarsus (one of the leaders of the later Antiochian school). According to one Christian writer, the historian Sozomen, Libanius was supposed to have said on his deathbed that John would have been his successor "if the Christians had not taken him from us". He started practicing extreme asceticism and became a hermit circa 375; he spent the next two years continually standing, scarcely sleeping, and learning the Bible by heart. As a consequence of these practices, his stomach and kidneys were permanently damaged and poor health forced a return to Antioch.

He was then ordained a deacon in 381 by St. Meletius of Antioch, and was ordained a presbyter/priest in 386 by Bishop Flavian I of Antioch. It seems this was the happiest period of his life. Over about twelve years, he gained much popularity for the eloquence of his public speaking. Notable are his insightful expositions of Bible passages and moral teaching. The most valuable of his works are his Homilies on various books of the Bible. He emphasized almsgiving. He was most concerned with the spiritual and temporal needs of the poor. He also spoke out against abuse of wealth and personal property:

"Do you wish to honor the body of Christ? Do not ignore him when he is naked. Do not pay him homage in the temple clad in silk, only then to neglect him outside where he is cold and ill-clad. He who said: "This is my body" is the same who said: "You saw me hungry and you gave me no food", and "Whatever you did to the least of my brothers you did also to me" . . . What good is it if the Eucharistic table is overloaded with golden chalices when your brother is dying of hunger? Start by satisfying his hunger and then with what is left you may adorn the altar as well."

In 398 he was called (somewhat against his will) to be the bishop in Constantinople. He deplored the fact that Imperial court protocol would now assign to him access to privileges greater than the highest state officials. During his time as bishop he adamantly refused to host lavish entertainments. This meant he was popular with the common people, but unpopular with the wealthy and the clergy. In a sermon soon after his arrival he said "people praise the predecessor to disparage the successor". His reforms of the clergy were also unpopular with these groups. He told visiting regional preachers to return to the churches they were meant to be serving—without any pay out.

His time there was to be far less at ease than in Antioch. Theophilus, the Patriarch of Alexandria, wanted to bring Constantinople under his sway and opposed John's appointment to Constantinople. Being an opponent of Origen's teachings, he accused John of being too partial to the teachings of that master. Theophilus had disciplined four Egyptian monks (known as "the tall brothers") over their support of Origen's teachings. They fled to and were welcomed by John.

Theophilus and others of his enemies held a synod in 403 to charge John, in which the Origen factor was used against him. It resulted in his deposition and banishment. He was called back by Arcadius almost immediately, however. The people were very angry about his departure. There was also an earth tremor which was seen as a sign of God's anger. Peace was short-lived. A silver statue of Eudoxia was erected near his cathedral. John denounced the dedication ceremonies. He spoke against her in harsh terms: "Again Herodias rages; again she is confounded; again she demands the head of John on a charger" (an allusion to the events surrounding the death of John the Baptist). Once again he was banished, this time to the Caucasus in Armenia.

Pope Innocent I protested at this banishment, but to no avail. John wrote letters which still held great influence in Constantinople. As a result of this, he was further exiled to Pitiunt (Abkhazia region of Georgia), where his tomb is the shrine for pilgrims. However, he never reached this destination, as he died during the journey. His final words were "Glory be to God for all things!"

Wikipedia

Augustine

Dates

(AD 354–430)

Famous for being
Bishop of Hippo
The most significant, post-apostolic, Christian thinker

Important writings
Confessions
The City of God
Enchiridion on Faith, Hope and Love

One of his quotations
"You have made us for yourself, and our heart is restless until it rests in you."

A. His Early life

Birth and Early Years (354–373)

Augustine was born at Thagaste in Numidia Proconsularis, on Nov. 13, 354.

His father Patricius, a jovial, sensual, passionate man, and tilluntil near the end of his life a heathen, was one of the curiales of the town, but without large means.

His mother Monnica was a Christian by parentage, conviction, and character. Augustine acknowledged that he owed his all to her; conversely we can trace to her anxious care for her son's spiritual well-being a distinct deepening of her own character. ;From his mother he received the elements of Christian teaching, and, as he tells us, a devotion to the very name of Jesus Christ which his later spiritual wanderings never wholly extinguished, and which forbade him to find satisfaction in any writings which lacked it.

He laments bitterly the company he kept and the habits into which he fell. The boyish freak of robbing a pear-tree with his companions weighed heavily on his mind in later years. He tells us, however, with shame, that in order not to be outdone by his companions he boasted of licentious acts which he had not committed. This may modify our natural inferences from the self-accusing language of the Confessions.

He was sent to Carthage to study at the age of sixteen. Augustine began his "university" life; as a student of Rhetoric. Again he speaks with an agony of remorse of his life as a student. It is certain that he contracted an irregular union, and in 372 he became the father of a son, Adeodatus. But he remained faithful to his mistress until the very eve of his conversion, and watched over his son's education and character.

Manicheism (373–383)

A baffled inquirer, he was attracted by the Manichean system, which appears to have been actively pushed in Africa at this period. From Augustine's many allusions to its tenets, it appears to have been a strange medley of dualism and materialism, asceticism and license, theosophy and rationalism, free-thought and superstition. What specially attracted

Augustine appears to have been the high moral pretensions of the sect, their criticism of Scripture difficulties, and their explanation of the origin of evil by the assumption of an independent evil principle.

For nine years (373–382) Augustine was an ardent Manichean.

Rome. Philosophy (383–386)

Mainly in disgust at the rough and disorderly students of Carthage Augustine now migrated to Rome. With bitter self-reproach he tells us of the deceit by means of which he left his mother, who had followed him to Carthage, behind. At Rome, his host was a Manichean, Alypius and other Manichean friends surrounded him, and in a severe illness he received the greatest kindness from them all. But the students of Rome disappointed Augustine.

Augustine traveled to Milan. Here he was attracted by the eloquence of Ambrose, then at the height of his fame, and soon made his acquaintance. "I began to love him, not at first as a teacher of the truth, which I despaired of finding in Thy Church, but as a fellow-creature who was kind to me." Contemptuous of the subject-matter of his sermons, Augustine listened to them as an interested professional critic. "I cared not to understand what he said, but only to hear how he said it." But it was impossible to keep form and substance wholly apart, and by degrees he began to realize that the case for Catholic Christianity was not wholly beneath discussion.

Conversion (386–387)

One day a Christian fellow-townsman, Pontitianus, who held an appointment at court, called to visit Alypius. Observing with pleasure a volume of St. Paul's Epistles, he went on to talk to his friends of the wonderful history of the hermit Anthony, whose ascetic life had begun from hearing in church a passage of the gospel (Matt. xix. 21), on which he had promptly acted; he then described the spread of the monastic movement, and informed his astonished hearers that even at Milan there was a monastery in existence. As Pontitianus told his tale, Augustine was filled with self-reproach. Conscience shamed him that after ten years of study he was still carrying a burden which men wearied by no research had already cast aside.

When Pontitianus had gone, he poured out his incoherent feelings to the astonished Alypius, and then, followed by his friend, fled into the garden. "Let it be now—let it be now," he said to himself; but the vanities of his life plucked at his clothes and whispered, "Do you think you can live without us?" Then again the continence of the monks and virgins confronted him with the question, "Can you not do as these have done?"

Alypius watched him in silence. At last he broke down and, in a torrent of tears, left his friend alone. He threw himself down under a fig-tree, crying passionately, "Lord, how long?—to-morrow and to-morrow!—why not now?"

Suddenly he heard a child's voice from the next house repeating, in a sing-song voice, "Take and read" (*tolle, lege*). He tried to think whether the words were used in any kind of children's game; but no, it must be a divine command to open the Bible and read the first verse that he should happen upon. He thought of Anthony and the lesson in church. He ran back to Alypius and opened "the Apostle" at Rom. xii. 13, 14, "Not in rioting and drunkenness, not in chambering and wantonness, not in strife and envying; but put ye on the Lord Jesus Christ, and make not provision for the flesh to fulfill the lusts thereof." "No further would I read, nor was it necessary."

The peace of God was in his heart, and the shadows of doubt melted away. He marked the passage and told Alypius, the friends exchanged confidences, and Alypius applied to himself the words, a little further on, "Him that is weak in the faith receive" (Rom. xv. 1). They went in, and filled the heart of Monnica with joy at the news

(Conf. VIII. viii.). It was now the beginning of the autumn vacation. Augustine decided to resign his chair before the next term, and meanwhile wrote to Ambrose to announce his desire for baptism. His friend Verecundus, who was himself on the eve of conversion, lent his country house at Cassiciacum, near Milan, to Augustine and his party; there they spent the vacation and the months which were to elapse before baptism (winter 386–387). At Cassiciacum he spent a restful, happy time with his mother and brother, his son Adeodatus, Alypius, and his two pupils, Licentius and Trygetius, the former a son of his old patron Romanianus. He wrote several short books here, "in a style which, though already enlisted in Thy service, still breathed, in that time of waiting, the pride of the School" (Conf. IX. iv.). These were the three books contra Academicos, two de Ordine, the de Beata Vita, and two books of Soliloquies; to this period also belong letters 1–4, of which 3 and 4 are the beginning of his correspondence with Nebridius (Conf. IX. iii.). Ambrose had, in answer to his request for advice, recommended him to read Isaiah. But he found the first chapter so hard that he put it aside till he should be more able to enter into its meaning. The Psalms, however, kindled his heart at this time. To him, as to many in most diverse conditions, they seemed to interpret the depths of his soul and the inmost experiences of his life (Conf. IX. iv.). But Augustine's main intellectual interest was still philosophical. Except when engaged upon the classics with his pupils, or on fine days in country pursuits ("in rebus rusticis ordinandis," c. Acad. I. v. 14; cf. II. iv. 10), the time was spent in discussing the philosophy of religion and life. The above-mentioned books, of which those de Ordine are perhaps the most characteristic, are, excepting of course the Soliloquies, in the form of notes of these discussions. The time to give in his name for baptism was approaching, and the party returned to Milan. Augustine was baptized by Ambrose, along with his heart's friend Alypius, and his son Adeodatus. The church music, which Milan, first of all the Western churches, had recently adopted from the East, struck deep into his soul: "The tide of devotion swelled high within me, and the tears ran down, and there was gladness in those tears."

Augustine a Presbyter of Hippo (391–395)

Augustine at the time of his ordination as presbyter was a Christian Platonist. His temper was absolutely Christian, his stock of ideas wholly Platonic. He had used the Bible devotionally rather than worked at its theology.

B. Episcopate (from 395)

The Donatist Controversy

The Donatist struggle may fairly be called the one great question of his earlier episcopate. The two principles involved were: firstly, the old Cyprianic denial of the validity of sacraments conferred by heretical (or schismatical) hands; secondly, the nullity of sacraments performed by unworthy ministers. The question at issue, then, was really that of the essential nature of the church as a holy society.

Augustine had preached, corresponded, and written actively against the Donatists, who had heard his sermons and read his tracts in great numbers. Their leaders had realized that they were now opposed by a champion of unexampled power, and endeavored to keep their publications from falling into his hands. So far as Donatism fell before argument, its fall was the work of Augustine. The baptism and orders of the Donatists were valid sacramentally, but useless spiritually. In a sense, the Holy Spirit operates in schismatical sacraments, so that a convert to the Catholic church will not be re-baptized or re-ordained. But it is only in the Catholic church that the Spirit operates, as the Spirit of peace and love.

The Pelagian Controversy (412–430)

Augustine, in his first days as a Christian, held the common view that, while the grace of God is necessary to the salvation of man, the first step, the act of faith, by which man gains access to grace, is the act of man, and not itself the gift of God. But he came to see that faith itself is the gift of God, and that the very first step to Godward must be of God's doing, not of our own.

Pelagius began at Rome (405–409) to express his disapproval on such an insistence upon Divine grace as should undermine human responsibility.

Pelagianism split upon the rock of infant baptism. Had this practice not become general by the time when Pelagius arose, Augustine would have had to combat him by arguments which churchmen at large would have found difficulty in following. As it was, to the question, "Why"—if Adam's sin directly affected himself only, and extended to his descendants *non propagine sed exemplo*—"why, then, are infants baptized?" Pelagius had no satisfactory reply. Probably neither Augustine nor the Pelagians were conscious of the full consequences of their position—the naturalism of the one and the transcendentalism of the other were alike tempered by common church teaching.

Augustine and the Constitution of the Church

Augustine has no consistent theory of the ultimate organ of church authority, whether legislative, disciplinary, or dogmatic. This authority resides in the Episcopate, its content is the *catholica veritas*, and in practical matters the *consuetudo* or *traditio*. These are to be interpreted by the bishops acting in concert—especially in councils. The "regional" council is subordinate to the "plenary," the plenary council of the province to that of the whole church; while of the latter, the earlier are subject to amendment by later councils. The church is infallible, but he cannot point to an absolutely infallible organ of her authority. By his very vagueness on this point, Augustine practically paved the way for the future centralization of infallible authority in the papacy.

Death and character

Augustine died on Aug 28, 430. Augustine was attacked by fever. For ten days, at his special request, he was left alone, except when the physician came or food was brought. He spent his whole time in prayer, and died in the presence of his praying friends, in a green old age, with hearing, sight, and all his bodily faculties unimpaired.

Without doubt Augustine is the most commanding religious personality of the early church. No Christian writer since the apostolic age has bequeathed to us so deep an insight into the working of a character penetrated with the love of God, none has struck deeper into the heart of religion in man.

Henry Wace, A Dictionary of Christian Biography, 1911

Patrick of Ireland

Dates

AD ?390–461

Famous for being

Apostle to the Irish

Important writings

Lorica or "Breastplate" poem

One of his quotations

"I was like a stone lying in the deep mire; and He that is mighty came, and in His mercy lifted me up, and verily raised me aloft and placed me on the top of the wall."

Patrick was born about 390, in south-west Britain, somewhere between the Severn and the Clyde? rivers, son of a deacon and grandson of a priest. When about sixteen years old, he was kidnapped by Irish pirates and sold into slavery in Ireland. Until this time, he had, by his own account, cared nothing for God, but now he turned to God for help. After six years, he either escaped or was freed, made his way to a port 200 miles away, and there persuaded some sailors to take him onto their ship. He returned to his family much changed, and began to prepare for the priesthood, and to study the Bible.

Around 435, Patrick was commissioned, perhaps by bishops in Gaul and perhaps by the Pope, to go to Ireland as a bishop and missionary. Four years earlier another bishop, Palladius, had gone to Ireland to preach, but he was no longer there (my sources disagree on whether he had died, or had become discouraged and left Ireland to preach in Scotland). Patrick made his headquarters at Armagh in the North, where he built a school, and had the protection of the local monarch. From this base he made extensive missionary journeys, with considerable success. To say that he single-handedly turned Ireland from a pagan to a Christian country is an exaggeration, but is not far from the truth.

Almost everything we know about him comes from his own writings. He has left us an autobiography (called the *Confession*), a *Letter to Coroticus* in which he denounces the slave trade and rebukes the British chieftain Coroticus for taking part in it, and the *Lorica* (or "Breastplate" a poem of disputed authorship traditionally attributed to Patrick), a work that has been called "part prayer, part anthem, and part incantation." The *Lorica* is a truly magnificent hymn, found today in many hymnals (usually abridged by the omission of the two stanzas bracketed below). The translation into English as given here is by Cecil Frances Alexander, whose husband was Archbishop of Armagh, and thus the direct successor of Patrick. She published nearly 400 poems and hymns of her own, including the well-known "There is a green hill far away," "Once in royal David's city," "Jesus calls us; o'er the tumult," and "All things bright and beautiful, All creatures great and small."

The Lorica, or, St. Patrick's Breastplate

I bind unto myself today
 the strong Name of the Trinity,
by invocation of the same,
 the Three in One, and One in Three.
I bind this day to me forever,
 by power of faith, Christ's Incarnation;
his baptism in the Jordan river;
 his death on cross for my salvation;
his bursting from the spiced tomb;
 his riding up he heavenly way;
his coming at the day of doom:
 I bind unto myself today.

I bind unto myself the power
 of the great love of cherubim;
the sweet "Well done" in judgment hour;
 the service of the seraphim;
confessors' faith, apostles' word,
 the patriarchs' prayers, the prophets' scrolls;
all good deeds done unto the Lord,
 and purity of virgin souls.

I bind unto myself today
 the virtues of the starlit heaven,
the glorious sun's life-giving ray,
 the whiteness of the moon at even,
the flashing of the lightning free,
 the whirling wind's tempestuous shocks,
the stable earth, the deep salt sea,
 around the old eternal rocks.

I bind unto myself today
 the power of God to hold and lead,
his eye to watch, his might to stay,
 his ear to hearken to my need;
the wisdom of my God to teach,
 his hand to guide, his shield to ward;
the word of God to give me speech,
 his heavenly host to be my guard.

[Against the demon snares of sin,
 the vice that gives temptation force,
the natural lusts that war within,
 the hostile men that mar my course;
of few or many, far or nigh,
 in every place, and in all hours
against their fierce hostility,
 I bind to me these holy powers.

Against all Satan's spells and wiles,
 against false words of heresy,
against the knowledge that defiles

against the heart's idolatry,
against the wizard's evil craft,
against the death-wound and the burning
the choking wave and poisoned shaft,
protect me, Christ, till thy returning.]

Christ be with me, Christ within me,
Christ behind me, Christ before me,
Christ beside me, Christ to win me,
Christ to comfort and restore me,
Christ beneath me, Christ above me,
Christ in quiet, Christ in danger,
Christ in hearts of all that love me,
Christ in mouth of friend and stranger.
I bind unto myself the Name,
the strong Name of the Trinity,
by invocation of the same,
the Three in One, and One in Three.
Of whom all nature hath creation,
eternal Father, Spirit, Word:
praise to the Lord of my salvation,
salvation is of Christ the Lord.

An aspect of Patrick's thought that shows very clearly through his writings is his awareness of himself as an unlearned exile, a former slave and a fugitive, who has learned the hard way to put his sole trust in God.

James Kiefer

Confession of St. Patrick

The closing paragraph of Patrick's famous *Confession* follows.

" . . . And this is my confession before I die."

But I entreat those who believe in and fear God, whoever deigns to examine or receive this document composed by the obviously unlearned sinner Patrick in Ireland, that nobody shall ever ascribe to my ignorance any trivial thing that I achieved or may have expounded that was pleasing to God, but accept and truly believe that it would have been the gift of God. And this is my confession before I die.

Patrick

Leo the Great

Dates

AD ?–46

Famous for being
Pope, sometimes called the "first Pope"

Important writings
Letters and sermons

One of his quotations
"Invisible in His own nature [God] became visible in ours. Beyond our grasp, He chose to come within our grasp."

Leo the Great, a Roman aristocrat, was Pope from 440 to 461. He is the first great Pope we know much about, and even sometimes assigned the title "first Pope". He stopped the invasion of Italy by Atilla the Hun in 452 by his moral suasion, was a great theologian in his own right, and was a leading figure in the centralization of the government of the Church.

Zeal for orthodoxy
An uncompromising foe of heresy, Leo found that in the diocese of Aquileia, Pelagians were received into church communion without formal repudiation of their errors; he wrote to rebuke this culpable negligence, and required a solemn abjuration before a synod.

Manicheans fleeing before the Vandals had come to Rome in 439 and secretly organized there; Leo learned of this around 443, and proceeded against them by holding a public debate with their representatives, burning their books, and warning the Roman Christians against them. His efforts led to the edict of Valentinian III against them (June 19, 445).

Nor was his attitude less decided against the Priscillianists. Bishop Turrubius of Astorga, astonished at the spread of this sect in Spain, had addressed the other Spanish bishops on the subject, sending a copy of his letter to Leo, who did not let slip the opportunity to exercise influence in Spain. He wrote an extended treatise (July 21, 447) against the sect, examining its false teaching in detail, and calling for a Spanish general council to investigate whether it had any adherents in the episcopate—but this was prevented by the political circumstances of Spain.

Leo enforced his authority in 445 against Dioscurus, Cyril's successor in the patriarchate of Alexandria, insisting that the ecclesiastical practice of his see should follow that of Rome; since Mark, the disciple of Peter and founder of the Alexandrian Church, could have had no other tradition than that of the prince of the apostles.

The fact that the African province of Mauretania Caesariensis had been preserved to the empire and thus to the Nicene faith in the Vandal invasion, and in its isolation was disposed to rest on outside support, gave Leo an opportunity to assert his authority there, which he did decisively in regard to a number of questions of discipline.

In a letter to the bishops of Campania, Picenum, and Tuscany (443) he required the observance of all his precepts and those of his predecessors; and he sharply rebuked the bishops of Sicily (447) for their deviation from the Roman custom as to the time of baptism, requiring them to send delegates to the Roman synod to learn the proper practice.

The assertion of Roman power over Illyria had been a strong point with previous popes. Pope Innocent I had constituted the metropolitan of Thessalonica his vicar, in order to oppose the growing power of the patriarch of Constantinople there. But now the Illyrian bishops showed a tendency to side with Constantinople, and the popes had difficulty in maintaining their authority. In 444 Leo laid down in a letter to them the principle that Peter had received the primacy and oversight of the whole Church as a requital of his faith, and that thus all important matters were to be referred to and decided by Rome. In 446 he had occasion twice to interfere in the affairs of Illyria, and in the same spirit spoke of the Roman pontiff as the apex of the hierarchy of bishops, metropolitans, and primates. However, after his death the influence of Constantinople was again predominant.

Theopedia

Columba

Dates

AD 521–597

Famous for being

Apostle to the Picts

Important writings

Prayers and poems

One of his quotations

"The wise man meditates on the end of his life."

Introduction

Saint Columba is sometimes referred to as Columba of Iona, or, Columkill (meaning "Dove of the church"). He was the outstanding figure among the Gaelic missionary monks who reintroduced Christianity to Scotland. Columba occupies in missionary history the entire generation preceding the arrival of Augustine (597).

In summary

The great missionary to Scotland was Columba (521–597), a man closely related with some of the most powerful tribal families of Ireland, and a pupil of Finian of Clonard. Distinguished already as a monk and a founder of monasteries in Ireland, he transferred his labors, in 563, to Scotland, establishing himself with twelve companions on the island of

Iona or Hy, under the protection of his fellow countryman and relative, the King of Dalriada. There Columba developed a most flourishing monastery, and thence he went forth for missionary labors among the Picts, who occupied the northern two-thirds of Scotland. By Columba and his associates the kingdom of the Picts was won for the Gospel. As in Ireland, Christian institutions were largely monastic. There were no dioceses, and even the bishops were under the authority, save in ordination, of Columba, who was a presbyter, and of his successors as abbots of Iona.

Williston Walker, 1918

St. Columba, commonly pronounced Colme, was one of the greatest patriarchs of the monastic order in Ireland, and the apostle of the Picts. To distinguish him from other saints of the same name, he was surnamed Columkille, from the great number of monastic cells, called by the Irish Killes, of which he was the founder. He was of most noble extraction from Neil, and was born at Gartan, in the county of Tyrconnel, in 521. He learned from his childhood that there is nothing great, nothing worth our esteem or pursuit, which does not advance the divine love in our souls, to which he totally devoted himself with an entire disengagement of his heart from he world, and in perfect purity of mind and body. He learned the divine scriptures and the lessons of an ascetic life under the holy bishop St. Finian, in his great school of Cluain-iraird. Being advanced to the order of priesthood in 546, he began to give admirable lessons of piety and sacred learning, and in a short time formed many disciples. He founded, about the year 550, the great monastery of Dair-Magh, now called Durrogh, which original name signifies Field of Oaks, and besides many smaller, those of Doire, or Derry, in Ulster, and of Sord, or Swords, about six miles from Dublin. St. Columba composed a rule which, as Usher, Tanner, and Sir James Ware inform us, is still extant in the old Irish. This rule he settled in the hundred monasteries which he founded in Ireland and Scotland. It was chiefly borrowed from the ancient oriental monastic institutes of all the old British and Irish monastic orders.

King Dermot, or Dermitius, being offended at the zeal of St. Columba in reproving public vices, the holy abbot left his native country, and passed into North-Britain, now called Scotland. He took along with him twelve disciples, and arrived there, according to Bede, in the year of Christ 565, the ninth of the reign of Bridius, the son of Meilochon, the most powerful king of the Picts; which nation the saint converted from idolatry to the faith of Christ by his preaching, virtues, and miracles.

The Picts having embraced the faith, gave St. Columba the little island of Hy or Iona, called from him Y-colm-kille, twelve miles from the land, in which he built the great monastery which was for several ages the chief seminary of North-Britain, and continued long the burying-place of the kings of Scotland, with the bodies of innumerable saints, which rested in that place. Out of this nursery St. Columba founded several other monasteries in Scotland. In the same school were educated the holy bishops Aidan Finian, and

Colman, who converted to the faith the English Northumbers. This great monastery several ages afterwards embraced the rule of St. Bennet.

St. Columba's manner of living was always most austere. He lay on the bare floor with a stone for his pillow, and never interrupted his fast. Yet his devotion was neither morose nor severe. His countenance always appeared wonderfully cheerful, and spoke to all that beheld him the constant interior serenity of his holy soul, and the unspeakable joy with which it overflowed from the presence of the Holy Spirit. Such was his fervor, that in whatever he did, he seemed to exceed the strength of man; and us much as in him lay he strove to suffer no moment of his precious time to pass without employing it for the honor of God, principally either in praying, reading, writing, or preaching. His incomparable mildness and charity towards all men, and on all occasions, won the hearts of all who conversed with him; and his virtues, miracles, and extraordinary gift of prophecy, commanded the veneration of all ranks of men.

He had such authority, that neither king nor people did any thing without his consent. When king Aedhan, or Aidanus, succeeded to his cousin Conall in the throne of British Scotland in 574, he received the royal insignia from St. Columba. Four years before he died, St. Columba was favored with a vision of angels which left him in many tears, because he learned from those heavenly messengers that God, moved by the prayers of the British and Scottish churches, would prolong his exile on earth yet four years.

Having continued his labors in Scotland thirty-four years, he clearly and openly foretold his death, and on Saturday, the ninth of June, said to his disciple Diermit: "This day is called the Sabbath, that is, the day of rest, and such will it truly be to me, for it will put an end to my labors." He was the first in the church at Matins at midnight; but knelt before the altar, received the viaticum, and having given his blessing to his spiritual children, sweetly slept in the Lord in the year 597, the seventy-seventh of his age. His body was buried in this island, but some ages after removed to Down, in Ulster, and laid in one vault with the remains of St. Patrick and St. Brigit. The great monastery of Durrogh in King's county afterwards embraced the rule of the canons regular, as did also the houses founded by St. Brendan, St. Comgal, &c He was honored both in Ireland and Scotland, among the principal patrons of those countries.

Alban Butler, The Lives or the Fathers,
Martyrs and Other Principal Saints, 1864

Prayer of St. Columba

Let me bless almighty God,
whose power extends over sea and land,
whose angels watch over all.

Let me study sacred books to calm my soul:
I pray for peace,
kneeling at heaven's gates.

Let me do my daily work,
gathering seaweed, catching fish,
giving food to the poor.

Let me say my daily prayers,
sometimes chanting, sometimes quiet,
always thanking God.

Delightful it is to live
on a peaceful isle, in a quiet cell,
serving the King of kings.

Other Christian leaders in the time of the Christian Church and the Roman Empire
Clement of Alexandria (AD ?150–211/16)
Anthony (AD c. 251–356)
Eusebius (AD 263–339)
St. Benedict (AD 480–543)

Clement of Alexandria (AD ?150–211/16)

Clement, a native of Athens, was converted to Christianity by Pantaenus, founder of the Catechetical School at Alexandria (then the intellectual capital of the Mediterranean world), and succeeded his teacher as head of the School about 180. For over 20 years he labored effectively as an apologist for the faith and catechist of the faithful. He regarded the science and philosophy of the Greeks as being, like the Torah of the Hebrews, a preparation for the Gospel, and the curriculum of his School undertook to give his students both a knowledge the Gospel of Christ and a sound liberal education. His speculative theology, his scholarly defense of the faith and his willingness to meet non-Christian scholars on their own grounds, helped to establish the good reputation of Christianity in the world of learning and prepare the way for his pupil, Origen, the most eminent theologian of Greek Christianity.

James Kiefer

Anthony (AD c. 251–356)

Introduction

Anthony was the first major Christian monk, father of Christian monasticism. He first went to the deserts in Egypt around 271 where he subjected himself to the ascetic life.

His many temptations from Satan have been immortalized in Athanasius' biography of him. Anthony became an inspiration to a thousand years of monks, as well as a favorite subject of art.

[See below: Extracts from Christian writings in the time of the Christian Church and the Roman Empire: Athanasius of Alexandria, Life of St. Anthony]

Eusebius (AD 263–339)

Introduction

Eusebius Of Caesarea was bishop, exegete, polemicist, Palestinian theologian, scholar and historian. His account of the early Christianity, in his *Ecclesiastical History*, is a landmark in Christian historiography. He is known as the "Father of ecclesiastic history."

Eusebius, known as "the father of church history," was bishop of Caesarea and a man of extensive learning.

Eusebius was a witness of the cruelties of the Diocletian persecution. With his literary industry Eusebius saved for us the invaluable monuments of the first three centuries down to the Nicene Council. Eusebius was also Constantine the Great's friend and eulogist.

Eusebius studied under Pamphilius (c. 240–309). a Christian scholar and presbyter in the church at Caesarea. Pamphilius was an ardent disciple of Origen and Eusebius became deeply influenced by the Origenist tradition. His major work was his *History of the Church*, a massive piece of research that preserves quotations from many older writers that would otherwise have been lost.

Quotation of Eusebius

"He that will deserve the name of a Christian must be such a man as excelleth through the knowledge of Christ and His doctrine; in modesty and righteousness of mind, in constancy of life, in virtuous fortitude, and in maintaining sincere piety toward the one and the only God, who is all in all."

Eusebius

Benedict (AD 480–543)

Benedict was born at Nursia (Norcia) in Umbria, Italy, around 480 AD. He was sent to Rome for his studies, but was repelled by the dissolute life of most of the populace, and withdrew to a solitary life at Subiaco. A group of monks asked him to be their abbot, but some of them found his rule too strict, and he returned alone to Subiaco. Again, other monks called him to be their abbot, and he agreed, founding twelve communities over an interval of some years. His chief founding was Monte Cassino, an abbey which stands to this day as the mother house of the world-wide Benedictine order.

Totila the Goth visited Benedict, and was so awed by his presence that he fell on his face before him. Benedict raised him from the ground and rebuked him for his cruelty, telling him that it was time that his iniquities should cease. Totila asked Benedict to remember him in his prayers and departed, to exhibit from that time an astonishing clemency and chivalry in his treatment of conquered peoples.

Benedict drew up a rule of life for monastics, a rule which he calls "a school of the Lord's service, in which we hope to order nothing harsh or rigorous." The Rule gives instructions for how the monastic community is to be organized, and how the monks are to spend their time. An average day includes about four hours to be spent in liturgical prayer (called the Divinum Officium—the Divine Office), five hours in spiritual reading and study, six hours of labor, one hour for eating, and about eight hours for sleep. The Book of Psalms is to be recited in its entirety every week as a part of the Office.

A Benedictine monk takes vows of "obedience, stability, and conversion of life." That is, he vows to live in accordance with the Benedictine Rule, not to leave his community without grave cause, and to seek to follow the teaching and example of Christ in all things. Normal procedure today for a prospective monk is to spend a week or more at the monastery as a visitor. He then applies as a postulant, and agrees not to leave for six months without the consent of the Abbot. (During that time, he may suspect that he has made a mistake, and the abbot may say, "Yes, I think you have. Go in peace." Alternately, he may say, "It is normal to have jitters at this stage. I urge you to stick it out a while longer and see whether they go away." Many postulants leave before the six months are up.) After six months, he may leave or become a novice, with vows for one year. After the year, he may leave or take vows for three more years. After three years, he may leave, take life vows, or take vows for a second three years. After that, a third three years. After that, he must leave or take life vows (fish or cut bait). Thus, he takes life vows after four and a half to ten and a half years in the monastery. At any point in the proceedings at which he has the option of leaving, the community has the option of dismissing him.

The effect of the monastic movement, both of the Benedictine order and of similar orders that grew out of it, has been enormous. We owe the preservation of the Holy Scriptures and other ancient writings in large measure to the patience and diligence of monastic scribes. In purely secular terms, their contribution was considerable. In Benedict's time, the chief source of power was muscle, whether human or animal. Ancient scholars apparently did not worry about labor-saving devices. The labor could always be done by oxen or slaves. But monks were both scholars and workers. A monk, after spending a few hours doing some laborious task by hand, was likely to think, "There must be a better way of doing this." The result was the systematic development of windmills and water wheels for grinding grain, sawing wood, pumping water, and so on. The rotation of crops (including legumes) and other agricultural advances were also originated or promoted by monastic farms. The monks, by their example, taught the dignity of labor and the importance of order and planning.

James Kiefer

The Rule of Benedict

Introduction

These excerpts illustrate the concept and practice of prayerful, devotional reading, known traditionally as, *Lectio Divina.*

"[The Rule of Benedict is] an epitome of Christianity, a learned and mysterious abridgement of all the doctrines of the Gospel, all the institutions of the Fathers, and all the counsels of perfection."

Bossuet, 1627–1704, Bishop of Meaux

Idleness is the enemy of the soul. Therefore, the brothers should have specified periods for manual labor as well as for prayerful reading (*lectione divina*).

Rule of Benedict, 48:1

From Easter to the first of October, . . . [f]rom the fourth hour until the time of Sext, they will devote themselves to reading. But after Sext and their meal, they may rest on their beds in complete silence; should a brother wish to read privately, let him do so, but without disturbing the others.

Rule of Benedict, 48:3–5

From the first of October to the beginning of Lent, the brothers ought to devote themselves to reading until the end of the second hour. . . . [After their meal they will devote themselves to their reading or to the psalms.

Rule of Benedict, 48:10, 13

During the days of Lent, they should be free in the morning to read until the third hour. . . . During this time of Lent each one is to receive a book from the library, and is to read the whole of it straight through. These books are to be distributed at the beginning of Lent.

Rule of Benedict, 48:14–16

Above all, one or two seniors must surely be deputed to make the rounds of the monastery while the brothers are reading. Their duty is to see that no brother is so apathetic as to waste time or engage in idle talk to the neglect of his reading, and so not only harm himself but also distract others.

Rule of Benedict, 48: 17–18

On Sunday all are to be engaged in reading except those who have been assigned various duties. If anyone is so remiss and indolent that he is unwilling or unable to study or to read, he is to be given some work in order that he may not be idle.

Rule of Benedict, 48:22–23

For anyone hastening on to the perfection of the monastic life, there are the teachings of the holy Fathers, the observance of which will lead him to the very heights of perfection. What page, what passage of the inspired books of the Old and New Testaments is not the truest of guides for human life? Or what book of the holy catholic Fathers does not resoundingly summon us along the true way to reach the Creator? Then, besides the Conferences of the Fathers, their Institutes and their Lives, there is also the rule of our holy father Basil. For observant and obedient monks, all these are nothing less than tools for the cultivation of virtues.

Rule of Benedict, 73:2–6

Classic Christian devotional books in the time of the Christian Church and the Roman Empire

Anthony (c. 251–356), Ascetic sermons

Eusebius (263–339), *Church History or Ecclesiastical History (Historia Ecclesiastica), Life of Constantine (Vita Constantini), Martyrs of Palestine*

Athanasius (297–373), *Against the Heathen, On the Incarnation of the Word*

Basil the Great (330–375), *De Spiritu Sancto (On the Holy Spirit), Nine Homilies of Hexaemeron*

Jerome (340–420), Bible commentaries

Chrysostom (347–407), Old Testament Homilies, New Testament Homilies, *The Divine Liturgy of St. John Chrysostom*

Augustine (354–430), *Confessions, Letters, The City of God, Homilies on the Gospels, Expositions on the Psalms*

Patrick (?390–461), *The Confession, an autobiography*

Leo the Great (?400–461), Sermons, Letters

St. Benedict (480–543), *Rule*

Columba (521–597), Poems, Prayers

John Climacus (c. 525–606), *Scale (Ladder) of Divine Ascent*

Extracts from Christian writings in the time of the Christian Church and the Roman Empire

Eusebius, *Martyrs of Palestine*

Athanasius of Alexandria, *Life of St. Anthony*

Basil the Great, *On the Holy Spirit*

John Chrysostom, *Homily on the Resurrection*

Augustine

"Augustine's Conversion," *Confessions,* 29. 12

Handbook on Faith, Hope, and Love, Predestination and the justice of God

Leo the Great, Sermon 85, On the Feast of St. Laurence the Martyr

Eusebius

Martyrs of Palestine

Introduction

Eusebius of Caesarea in Palestine (the Roman empire offered many cities with the name), sometimes known as 'Pamphilus' or the 'son of Pamphilus,' was born a little after 260, became bishop of Caesarea about 313 and lived there until his death in 339. Eusebius seems to have taken quite an interest in martyrs; his history offers many examples treated at length

Chapter 1

The first of the martyrs of Palestine was Procopius, who, before he had received the trial of imprisonment, immediately on his first appearance before the governor's tribunal, having been ordered to sacrifice to the so-called gods, declared that he knew only one to whom it was proper to sacrifice, as he himself wills. But when he was commanded to offer libations to the four emperors, having quoted a sentence which displeased them, he was immediately beheaded.

The quotation was from the poet: "The rule of many is not good; let there be one ruler and one king." It was the seventh day of the month Desius, the seventh before the ides of June, as the Romans reckon, and the fourth day of the week, when this first example was given at Caesura in Palestine. Afterwards, in the same city, many rulers of the country churches readily endured terrible sufferings, and furnished to the beholders an example of noble conflicts. But others, benumbed in spirit by terror, were easily weakened at the first onset.

Of the rest, each one endured different forms of torture, as scourgings without number, and rackings, and tearings of their sides, and insupportable fetters, by which the hands of some were dislocated. Yet they endured what came upon them, as in accordance with the inscrutable purposes of God. For the hands of one were seized, and he was led to the altar, while they thrust into his right hand the polluted and abominable offering, and he was dismissed as if he had sacrificed. Another had not even touched it, yet when others said that he had sacrificed, he went away in silence. Another, being taken up half dead, was cast aside as if already dead, and released from his bonds, and counted among the sacrificers. When another cried out, and testified that he would not obey, he was struck in the mouth, and silenced by a large band of those who were drawn up for this purpose, and driven away by force, even though he had not sacrificed. Of such consequence did they consider it, to seem by any means to have accomplished their purpose.

Therefore, of all this number, the only ones who were honored with the crown of the holy martyrs were Alphaeus and Zacchaeus. After stripes and scrapings and severe bonds and additional tortures and various other trials, and after having their feet stretched for a night and day over four holes in the stocks, on the seventeenth day of the month Dius,—

that is, according to the Romans, the fifteenth before the Kalends of December,—having confessed one only God and Christ Jesus as king, as if they had uttered some blasphemy, they were beheaded like the former martyr.

Chapter 2

What occurred to Romanus on the same day at Antioch, is also worthy of record. For he was a native of Palestine, a deacon and exorcist in the parish of Caesarea; and being present at the destruction of the churches, he beheld many men, with women and children, going up in crowds to the idols and sacrificing. But, through his great zeal for religion, he could not endure the sight, and rebuked them with a loud voice. Being arrested for his boldness, he proved a most noble witness of the truth, if there ever was one.

For when the judge informed him that he was to die by fire, he received the sentence with cheerful countenance and most ready mind, and was led away. When he was bound to the stake, and the wood piled up around him, as they were awaiting the arrival of the emperor before lighting the fire, he cried, "Where is the fire for me?"

Having said this, he was summoned again before the emperor, and subjected to the unusual torture of having his tongue cut out. But he endured this with fortitude and showed to all by his deeds that the Divine Power is present with those who endure any hardship whatever for the sake of religion, lightening their sufferings and strengthening their zeal. When he learned of this strange mode of punishment, the noble man was not terrified, but put out his tongue readily, and offered it with the greatest alacrity to those who cut it off. After this punishment he was thrown into prison, and suffered there for a very long time.

At last the twentieth anniversary of the emperor being near, when, according to an established gracious custom, liberty was proclaimed everywhere to all who were in bonds, he alone had both his feet stretched over five holes in the stocks, and while he lay there was strangled, and was thus honored with martyrdom, as he desired. Although he was outside of his country, yet, as he was a native of Palestine, it is proper to count him among the Palestinian martyrs. These things occurred in this manner during the first year, when the persecution was directed only against the rulers of the Church.

Eusebius

Athanasius of Alexandria
Life of St. Anthony

His early ascetic life.

3. And again as he went into the church, hearing the Lord say in the Gospel Matthew 6:34, 'be not anxious for the morrow,' he could stay no longer, but went out and gave those things also to the poor. Having committed his sister to known and faithful virgins, and put

her into a convent to be brought up, he henceforth devoted himself outside his house to discipline, taking heed to himself and training himself with patience. For there were not yet so many monasteries in Egypt, and no monk at all knew of the distant desert; but all who wished to give heed to themselves practiced the discipline in solitude near their own village.

Now there was then in the next village an old man who had lived the life of a hermit from his youth up. Anthony, after he had seen this man, imitated him in piety. And at first he began to abide in places outside the village: then if he heard of a good man anywhere, like the prudent bee, he went forth and sought him, nor turned back to his own palace until he had seen him; and he returned, having got from the good man as it were supplies for his journey in the way of virtue. So dwelling there at first, he confirmed his purpose not to return to the abode of his fathers nor to the remembrance of his kinsfolk; but to keep all his desire and energy for perfecting his discipline.

He worked, however, with his hands, having heard, 'he who is idle let him not eat,' and part he spent on bread and part he gave to the needy. And he was constant in prayer, knowing that a man ought to pray in secret unceasingly. For he had given such heed to what was read that none of the things that were written fell from him to the ground, but he remembered all, and afterwards his memory served him for books. . . .

Early conflicts with the devil.

5. But the devil, who hates and envies what is good, could not endure to see such a resolution in a youth, but endeavored to carry out against him what he had been wont to effect against others.

First of all he tried to lead him away from the discipline, whispering to him the remembrance of his wealth, care for his sister, claims of kindred, love of money, love of glory, the various pleasures of the table and the other relaxations of life, and at last the difficulty of virtue and the labor of it; he suggested also the infirmity of the body and the length of the time. In a word he raised in his mind a great dust of debate, wishing to debar him from his settled purpose. But when the enemy saw himself to be too weak for Anthony's determination, and that he rather was conquered by the other's firmness, overthrown by his great faith and falling through his constant prayers, then at length putting his trust in the weapons which are 'in the navel of his belly' and boasting in them—for they are his first snare for the young—he attacked the young man, disturbing him by night and harassing him by day, so that even the onlookers saw the struggle which was going on between them. The one would suggest foul thoughts and the other counter them with prayers: the one fire him with lust, the other, as one who seemed to blush, fortify his body with faith, prayers, and fasting. And the devil one night even took upon him the shape of a woman and imitated all her acts simply to beguile Anthony. But he, his mind filled with Christ and the nobility inspired by Him, and considering the spirituality of the soul, quenched the coal of the other's deceit.

Again the enemy suggested the ease of pleasure. But he like a man filled with rage and grief turned his thoughts to the threatened fire and the gnawing worm, and setting these in array against his adversary, passed through the temptation unscathed. All this was a source of shame to his foe. For he, deeming himself like God, was now mocked by a young man; and he who boasted himself against flesh and blood was being put to flight by a man in the flesh. For the Lord was working with Anthony—the Lord who for our sake took flesh and gave the body victory over the devil, so that all who truly fight can say 1 Corinthians 15:10, 'not I but the grace of God which was with me.' . . .

Details of his life at this time (271–285?)

7. This was Anthony's first struggle against the devil, or rather this victory was the Savior's work in Anthony, 'Who condemned sin in the flesh that the ordinance of the law might be fulfilled in us who walk not after the flesh but after the spirit.' But neither did Anthony, although the evil one had fallen, henceforth relax his care and despise him; nor did the enemy as though conquered cease to lay snares for him. For again he went round as a lion seeking some occasion against him. But Anthony having learned from the Scriptures that the devices Ephesians 6:11 of the devil are many, zealously continued the discipline, reckoning that though the devil had not been able to deceive his heart by bodily pleasure, he would endeavor to ensnare him by other means. For the demon loves sin. Wherefore more and more he repressed the body and kept it in subjection, lest haply having conquered on one side, he should be dragged down on the other. He therefore planned to accustom himself to a severer mode of life. And many marveled, but he himself used to bear the labor easily; for the eagerness of soul, through the length of time it had abode in him, had wrought a good habit in him, so that taking but little initiation from others he showed great zeal in this matter.

He kept vigil to such an extent that he often continued the whole night without sleep; and this not once but often, to the marvel of others. He ate once a day, after sunset, sometimes once in two days, and often even in four. His food was bread and salt, his drink, water only. Of flesh and wine it is superfluous even to speak, since no such thing was found with the other earnest men. A rush mat served him to sleep upon, but for the most part he lay upon the bare ground. He would not anoint himself with oil, saying it behoved young men to be earnest in training and not to seek what would enervate the body; but they must accustom it to labor, mindful of the Apostle's words 2 Corinthians 12:10, 'when I am weak, then am I strong.' 'For,' said he, 'the fiber of the soul is then sound when the pleasures of the body are diminished.' And he had come to this truly wonderful conclusion, 'that progress in virtue, and retirement from the world for the sake of it, ought not to be measured by time, but by desire and fixity of purpose.' He at least gave no thought to the past, but day by day, as if he were at the beginning of his discipline, applied greater pains for advancement, often repeating to himself the saying of Paul Philippians 3:14: 'Forgetting the things which are behind and stretching forward to the things which are before.' He was also mindful of the words spoken by the prophet in 1 Kings 18:15, 'the Lord lives before whose presence I stand today.' For he observed that in saying 'today' the prophet did not compute the time that had gone by: but daily as though ever commencing he eagerly endeavored to make himself fit to appear before God, being pure in heart and ever ready to submit to His counsel, and to Him alone. And he used to say to himself that from the life of the great Elias the hermit ought to see his own as in a mirror. . . .

His address to monks, rendered from Coptic, exhorting them to perseverance, and encouraging them against the wiles of Satan.

16. One day when he had gone forth because all the monks had assembled to him and asked to hear words from him, he spoke to them in the Egyptian tongue as follows:

The Scriptures are enough for instruction, but it is a good thing to encourage one another in the faith, and to stir up with words. Wherefore you, as children, carry that which you know to your father; and I as the elder share my knowledge and what experience has taught me with you. Let this especially be the common aim of all, neither to give way having once begun, nor to faint in trouble, nor to say: We have lived in the discipline a long time: but rather as though making a beginning daily let us increase our earnestness. For the whole life of man is very short, measured by the ages to come, wherefore all our time is nothing compared with eternal life. And in the world everything is sold at its price, and a man exchanges one equivalent for another; but the promise of eternal life is bought for a trifle. For it is written, "The days of our life in them are threescore years and ten, but if they are in strength, fourscore years, and what is more than these is labor and sorrow." Whenever, therefore, we live full fourscore years, or even a hundred in the discipline, not for a hundred years only shall we reign, but instead of a hundred we shall reign for ever and ever. And though we fought on earth, we shall not receive our inheritance on earth, but we have the promises in heaven; and having put off the body which is corrupt, we shall receive it incorrupt. . . .

35. 'When, therefore, they come by night to you and wish to tell the future, or say, "we are the angels," give no heed, for they lie. Yea even if they praise your discipline and call you blessed, hear them not, and have no dealings with them; but rather sign yourselves and your houses, and pray, and you shall see them vanish. For they are cowards, and greatly fear the sign of the Lord's Cross, since of a truth in it the Savior stripped them, and made an example of them Colossians 2:15. But if they shamelessly stand their ground, capering and changing their forms of appearance, fear them not, nor shrink, nor heed them as though they were good spirits. For the presence either of the good or evil by the help of God can easily be distinguished. The vision of the holy ones is not fraught with distraction: "For they will not strive, nor cry, nor shall any one hear their voice." But it comes so quietly and gently that immediately joy, gladness and courage arise in the soul. For the Lord who is our joy is

with them, and the power of God the Father. And the thoughts of the soul remain unruffled and undisturbed, so that it, enlightened as it were with rays, beholds by itself those who appear. For the love of what is divine and of the things to come possesses it, and willingly it would be wholly joined with them if it could depart along with them. But if, being men, some fear the vision of the good, those who appear immediately take fear away; as Gabriel Luke 1:13 did in the case of Zacharias, and as the angel Matthew 28:5 did who appeared to the women at the holy sepulcher, and as He did who said to the shepherds in the Gospel, "Fear not." For their fear arose not from timidity, but from the recognition of the presence of superior beings. Such then is the nature of the visions of the holy ones.'

36. 'But the inroad and the display of the evil spirits is fraught with confusion, with din, with sounds and cryings such as the disturbance of boorish youths or robbers would occasion. From which arise fear in the heart, tumult and confusion of thought, dejection, hatred towards them who live a life of discipline, indifference, grief, remembrance of kinsfolk and fear of death, and finally desire of evil things, disregard of virtue and unsettled habits. Whenever, therefore, you have seen ought and are afraid, if your fear is immediately taken away and in place of it comes joy unspeakable, cheerfulness, courage, renewed strength, calmness of thought and all those I named before, boldness and love toward God,—take courage and pray. For joy and a settled state of soul show the holiness of him who is present. Thus Abraham beholding the Lord rejoiced John 8:56; so also John Luke 1:41 at the voice of Mary, the God-bearer, leaped for gladness. But if at the appearance of any there is confusion, knocking without, worldly display, threats of death and the other things which I have already mentioned, know that it is an onslaught of evil spirits.'

37. 'And let this also be a token for you: whenever the soul remains fearful there is a presence of the enemies. For the demons do not take away the fear of their presence as the great archangel Gabriel did for Mary and Zacharias, and as he did who appeared to the women at the tomb; but rather whenever they see men afraid they increase their delusions that men may be terrified the more; and at last attacking they mock them, saying, "fall down and worship." Thus they deceived the Greeks, and thus by them they were considered gods, falsely so called. But the Lord did not suffer us to be deceived by the devil, for He rebuked him whenever he framed such delusions against Him, saying: "Get behind me, Satan: for it is written, You shall worship the Lord your God, and Him only shall you serve Matthew 4:10." More and more, therefore, let the deceiver be despised by us; for what the Lord has said, this for our sakes He has done: that the demons hearing like words from us may be put to flight through the Lord who rebuked them in those words.'

38. 'And it is not fitting to boast at the casting forth of the demons, nor to be uplifted by the healing of diseases: nor is it fitting that he who casts out devils should alone be highly esteemed, while he who casts them not out should be considered naught. But let a man learn the discipline of each one and either imitate, rival, or correct it. For the working of signs is not ours but the Savior's work: and so He said to His disciples: "Rejoice not that the

demons are subject to you, but that your names are written in the heavens Luke 10:20." For the fact that our names are written in heaven is a proof of our virtuous life, but to cast out demons is a favor of the Savior who granted it. Wherefore to those who boasted in signs but not in virtue, and said: "Lord, in Your name did we not cast out demons, and in Your name did many mighty works Matthew 7:22?" He answered, "Verily I say unto you, I know you not;" for the Lord knows not the ways of the wicked. But we ought always to pray, as I said above, that we may receive the gift of discerning spirits; that, as it is written 1 John 4:1, we may not believe every spirit.'

39. 'I should have liked to speak no further and to say nothing from my own promptings, satisfied with what I have said: but lest you should think that I speak at random and believe that I detail these things without experience or truth; for this cause even though I should become as a fool, yet the Lord who hears knows the clearness of my conscience, and that it is not for my own sake, but on account of your affection towards me and at your petition that I again tell what I saw of the practices of evil spirits. How often have they called me blessed and I have cursed them in the name of the Lord! How often have they predicted the rising of the river, and I answered them, "What have you to do with it?" Once they came threatening and surrounded me like soldiers in full armor. At another time they filled the house with horses, wild beasts and creeping things, and I sang: "Some in chariots and some in horses, but we will boast in the name of the Lord our God;" and at the prayers they were turned to flight by the Lord. Once they came in darkness, bearing the appearance of a light, and said, "We are come to give you a light, Anthony." But I closed my eyes and prayed, and immediately the light of the wicked ones was quenched. And a few months after they came as though singing psalms and babbling the words of Scripture, "But I like a deaf man, heard not." Once they shook the cell with an earthquake, but I continued praying with unshaken heart. And after this they came again making noises, whistling and dancing. But as I prayed and lay singing psalms to myself they forthwith began to lament and weep, as if their strength had failed them. But I gave glory to the Lord who had brought down and made an example of their daring and madness.'

40. 'Once a demon exceeding high appeared with pomp, and dared to say, "I am the power of God and I am Providence, what do you wish that I shall give you?" But I then so much the more breathed upon him, and spoke the name of Christ, and set about to smite him. And I seemed to have smitten him, and forthwith he, big as he was, together with all his demons, disappeared at the name of Christ. At another time, while I was fasting, he came full of craft, under the semblance of a monk, with what seemed to be loaves, and gave me counsel, saying, "Eat and cease from your many labors. Thou also art a man and art like to fall sick." But I, perceiving his device, rose up to pray; and he endured it not, for he departed, and through the door there seemed to go out as it were smoke. How often in the desert has he displayed what resembled gold, that I should only touch it and look on it. But I sang psalms against him, and he vanished away. Often they would beat me with stripes,

and I repeated again and again, "Nothing shall separate me from the love of Christ Romans 8:35," and at this they rather fell to beating one another. Nor was it I that stayed them and destroyed their power, but it was the Lord, who said, "I beheld Satan as lightning fall from Heaven; Luke 10:18" but I, children, mindful of the Apostle's words, transferred 1 Corinthians 4:6 this to myself, that you might learn not to faint in discipline, nor to fear the devil nor the delusions of the demons.'

41. 'And since I have become a fool in detailing these things, receive this also as an aid to your safety and fearlessness; and believe me for I do not lie. Once some one knocked at the door of my cell, and going forth I saw one who seemed of great size and tall. Then when I enquired, "Who are you?" he said, "I am Satan." Then when I said, "Why are you here?" he answered, "Why do the monks and all other Christians blame me undeservedly? Why do they curse me hourly?" Then I answered, "Wherefore do you trouble them?" He said, "I am not he who troubles them, but they trouble themselves, for I am become weak. Have they not read," "The swords of the enemy have come to an end, and you have destroyed the cities?" "I have no longer a place, a weapon, a city. The Christians are spread everywhere, and at length even the desert is filled with monks. Let them take heed to themselves, and let them not curse me undeservedly." Then I marveled at the grace of the Lord, and said to him: "You who art ever a liar and never speakest the truth, this at length, even against your will, you have truly spoken. For the coming of Christ has made you weak, and He has cast you down and stripped you." But he having heard the Savior's name, and not being able to bear the burning from it, vanished.'

42. 'If, therefore, the devil himself confesses that his power is gone, we ought utterly to despise both him and his demons; and since the enemy with his hounds has but devices of this sort, we, having got to know their weakness, are able to despise them. Wherefore let us not despond after this fashion, nor let us have a thought of cowardice in our heart, nor frame fears for ourselves, saying, I am afraid lest a demon should come and overthrow me; lest he should lift me up and cast me down; or lest rising against me on a sudden he confound me. Such thoughts let us not have in mind at all, nor let us be sorrowful as though we were perishing; but rather let us be courageous and rejoice always, believing that we are safe. Let us consider in our soul that the Lord is with us, who put the evil spirits to flight and broke their power. Let us consider and lay to heart that while the Lord is with us, our foes can do us no hurt. For when they come they approach us in a form corresponding to the state in which they discover us, and adapt their delusions to the condition of mind in which they find us. If, therefore, they find us timid and confused, they forthwith beset the place, like robbers, having found it unguarded; and what we of ourselves are thinking, they do, and more also. For if they find us faint-hearted and cowardly, they mightily increase our terror, by their delusions and threats; and with these the unhappy soul is thenceforth tormented. But if they see us rejoicing in the Lord, contemplating the bliss of the future, mindful of the Lord, deeming all things in His hand, and that no evil spirit has any strength

against the Christian, nor any power at all over any one—when they behold the soul fortified with these thoughts—they are discomfited and turned backwards. Thus the enemy, seeing Job fenced round with them, withdrew from him; but finding Judas unguarded, him he took captive. Thus if we are wishful to despise the enemy, let us ever ponder over the things of the Lord, and let the soul ever rejoice in hope. And we shall see the snares of the demon are like smoke, and the evil ones themselves flee rather than pursue. For they are, as I said before, exceeding fearful, ever looking forward to the fire prepared for them.'

43. 'And for your fearlessness against them hold this sure sign—whenever there is any apparition, be not prostrate with fear, but whatsoever it be, first boldly ask, Who are you? And from whence do you come? And if it should be a vision of holy ones they will assure you, and change your fear into joy. But if the vision should be from the devil, immediately it becomes feeble, beholding your firm purpose of mind. For merely to ask, Who are you Joshua 5:13? and whence do you come? is a proof of coolness. By thus asking, the son of Nun learned who his helper was; nor did the enemy escape the questioning of Daniel.' . . .

Of his sickness and his last will.

91. But he, knowing the custom, and fearing that his body would be treated this way, hastened, and having bidden farewell to the monks in the outer mountain entered the inner mountain, where he was accustomed to abide. And after a few months he fell sick. Having summoned those who were there—they were two in number who had remained in the mountain fifteen years, practicing the discipline and attending on Anthony on account of his age—he said to them,

'I, as it is written Joshua 23:14, go the way of the fathers, for I perceive that I am called by the Lord. And do you be watchful and destroy not your long discipline, but as though now making a beginning, zealously preserve your determination. For you know the treachery of the demons, how fierce they are, but how little power they have. Wherefore fear them not, but rather ever breathe Christ, and trust Him. Live as though dying daily. Give heed to yourselves, and remember the admonition you have heard from me. Have no fellowship with the schismatics, nor any dealings at all with the heretical Arians. For you know how I shunned them on account of their hostility to Christ, and the strange doctrines of their heresy. Therefore be the more earnest always to be followers first of God and then of the Saints; that after death they also may receive you as well-known friends into the eternal habitations. Ponder over these things and think of them, and if you have any care for me and are mindful of me as of a father, suffer no one to take my body into Egypt, lest haply they place me in the houses, for to avoid this I entered into the mountain and came here. Moreover you know how I always put to rebuke those who had this custom, and exhorted them to cease from it. Bury my body, therefore, and hide it underground yourselves, and let my words be observed by you that no one may know the place but you alone. For at the resurrection of the dead I shall receive it incorruptible from the Savior. And divide my garments. To Athanasius the bishop give one sheepskin and the garment whereon I am laid, which he himself gave me new, but which with me has grown old. To Serapion the bishop give the other sheepskin, and keep the hair garment yourselves. For the rest fare ye well, my children, for Anthony is departing, and is with you no more.'

Athanasius, Select Works and Letters

Basil the Great

On the Holy Spirit

Chapter 11

That they who deny the Spirit are transgressors

"Who hath woe? Who bath sorrow?" For whom is distress and darkness? For whom eternal doom? Is it not for the transgressors? For them that deny the faith? And what is the proof of their denial? Is it not that they have set at naught their own confessions? And when and what did they confess? Belief in the Father and in the Son and in the Holy Ghost, when they renounced the devil and his angels, and uttered those saving words. What fit title then for them has been discovered, for the children of light to use? Are they not addressed as transgressors, as having violated the covenant of their salvation? What am I to call the denial of God? What the denial of Christ? What but transgressions? And to him who denies the Spirit, what title do you wish me to apply? Must it not be the same, inasmuch as he has broken his covenant with God? And when the confession of faith in Him secures the blessing of true religion. and its denial subjects men to the doom of godlessness, is it not a fearful thing for them to set the confession at naught, not through fear of fire, or sword, or cross, or scourge, or wheel, or rack, but merely led astray by the sophistry and seductions of the *pneumatomachi*? I testify to every man who is confessing Christ and denying God, that Christ will profit him nothing; to every man that calls upon God but rejects the Son, that his faith is vain; to every man that sets aside the Spirit, that his faith in the Father and the Son will be useless, for he cannot even hold it without the presence of the Spirit. For he who does not believe the Spirit does not believe in the Son, and he who has not believed in the Son does not believe in the Father. For none "can say that Jesus is the Lord but by the Holy Ghost," and "No man hath seen God at any time, but the only begotten God which is in the bosom of the Father, he hath declared him."

Such an one hath neither part nor lot in the true worship; for it is impossible to worship the Son, save by the Holy Ghost; impossible to call upon the Father, save by the Spirit of adoption.

Basil the Great

John Chrysostom
Homily on the Resurrection

Introduction

John Chrysostom's Homily on the Resurrection, also known as, The Paschal Homily of St. John Chrysostom, is read each Pascha (Easter) in Orthodox churches.

Is there anyone who is a devout lover of God? Let them enjoy this beautiful bright festival! Is there anyone who is a grateful servant? Let them rejoice and enter into the joy of their Lord!

Are there any weary with fasting? Let them now receive their wages! If any have toiled from the first hour, let them receive their due reward; If any have come after the third hour, let him with gratitude join in the Feast! And he that arrived after the sixth hour, let him not doubt; for he too shall sustain no loss. And if any delayed until the ninth hour, let him not hesitate; but let him come too. And he who arrived only at the eleventh hour, let him not be afraid by reason of his delay.

For the Lord is gracious and receives the last even as the first. He gives rest to him that comes at the eleventh hour, as well as to him that toiled from the first. To this one He gives, and upon another He bestows. He accepts the works as He greets the endeavor. The deed He honors and the intention He commends.

Let us all enter into the joy of the Lord! First and last alike receive your reward; rich and poor, rejoice together! Sober and slothful, celebrate the day!

You that have kept the fast, and you that have not, rejoice today for the Table is richly laden! Feast royally on it, the calf is a fatted one. Let no one go away hungry. Partake, all, of the cup of faith. Enjoy all the riches of His goodness!

Let no one grieve at his poverty, for the universal kingdom has been revealed. Let no one mourn that he has fallen again and again; for forgiveness has risen from the grave. Let no one fear death, for the Death of our Savior has set us free.

He has destroyed it by enduring it.

He destroyed Hades when He descended into it. He put it into an uproar even as it tasted of His flesh. Isaiah foretold this when he said, "You, O Hell, have been troubled by encountering Him below."

Hell was in an uproar because it was done away with. It was in an uproar because it is mocked. It was in an uproar, for it is destroyed. It is in an uproar, for it is annihilated. It is in an uproar, for it is now made captive. Hell took a body, and discovered God. It took earth, and encountered Heaven. It took what it saw, and was overcome by what it did not see.

O death, where is thy sting? O Hades, where is thy victory?

Christ is Risen, and you, O death, are annihilated! Christ is Risen, and the evil ones are cast down! Christ is Risen, and the angels rejoice! Christ is Risen, and life is liberated! Christ is Risen, and the tomb is emptied of its dead; for Christ having risen from the dead, is become the first-fruits of those who have fallen asleep.

To Him be Glory and Power forever and ever. Amen!

John Chrysostom

Augustine

Augustine's Conversion

[Augustine, who became bishop of Hippo and a leading Christian theologian, recalls his own conversion experience in the first autobiography in Western literature, *The Confessions.*]

I was . . . weeping in the most bitter contrition of my heart, when suddenly I heard the voice of a boy or a girl I know not which—coming from the neighboring house, chanting over and over again, "Pick it up, read it; pick it up, read it." ["*tolle lege, tolle lege*"] Immediately I ceased weeping and began most earnestly to think whether it was usual for children in some kind of game to sing such a song, but I could not remember ever having heard the like. So, damming the torrent of my tears, I got to my feet, for I could not but think that this was a divine command to open the Bible and read the first passage I should light upon. For I had heard how Anthony, accidentally coming into church while the gospel was being read, received the admonition as if what was read had been addressed to him: "Go and sell what you have and give it to the poor, and you shall have treasure in heaven; and come and follow me." By such an oracle he was forthwith converted to thee.

So I quickly returned to the bench where Alypius was sitting, for there I had put down the apostle's book when I had left there. I snatched it up, opened it, and in silence read the paragraph on which my eyes first fell: "Not in rioting and drunkenness, not in chambering and wantonness, not in strife and envying, but put on the Lord Jesus Christ, and make no provision for the flesh to fulfill the lusts thereof." I wanted to read no further, nor did I need to. For instantly, as the sentence ended, there was infused in my heart something like the light of full certainty and all the gloom of doubt vanished away.

Augustine, Confessions 29.12

Handbook on Faith, Hope, and Love

Chapter 15

Predestination and the justice of God

Who would be so impiously foolish as to say that God cannot turn the evil wills of men—as he willeth, when he willeth, and where he willeth—toward the good? But, when he acteth, he acteth through mercy; when he doth not act, it is through justice. For, "he hath mercy on whom he willeth; and whom he willeth, he hardeneth." Rom. 9:18.

Now when the apostle said this, he was commending grace, of which he had just spoken in connection with the twin children in Rebecca's womb: "Before they had yet been born, or had done anything good or bad, in order that the electing purpose of God might continue—not through works but through the divine calling—it was said of them, 'The elder shall serve the younger.'" Rom. 9:11, 12. Accordingly, he refers to another prophetic witness, where it is written, "Jacob I loved, but Esau have I hated." Cf. Mal. 1:2, 3 and Rom. 9:13. Then, realizing how what he said could disturb those whose understanding could not penetrate to this depth of grace, he adds: "What therefore shall we say to this? Is there unrighteousness in God? God forbid!" Rom. 9:14. Yet it does seem unfair that, without any merit derived from good works or bad, God should love the one and hate the other. Now, if the apostle had wished us to understand that there were future good deeds of the one, and evil deeds of the other—which God, of course, foreknew—he would never have said "not of good works" but rather "of future works." Thus he would have solved the difficulty; or, rather, he would have left no difficulty to be solved. As it is, however, when he went on to exclaim, "God forbid!"—that is, "God forbid that there should be unfairness in God"—he proceeds immediately to add (to prove that no unfairness in God is involved here), "For he says to Moses, 'I will have mercy on whom I will have mercy, and I will show pity to whom I will show pity.'" Rom. 9:15. Now, who but a fool would think God unfair either when he imposes penal judgment on the deserving or when he shows mercy to the undeserving? Finally, the apostle concludes and says, "Therefore, it is not a question of him who wills nor of him who runs but of God's showing mercy." Rom. 9:15.

Thus, both the twins were "by nature children of wrath," Eph. 2:3. not because of any works of their own, but because they were both bound in the fetters of damnation originally forged by Adam. But He who said, "I will have mercy on whom I will have mercy," loved Jacob in unmerited mercy, yet hated Esau with merited justice. Since this judgment [of wrath] was due them both, the former learned from what happened to the other that the fact that he had not, with equal merit, incurred the same penalty gave him no ground to boast of his own distinctive merits—but, instead, that he should glory in the abundance of divine grace, because "it is not a question of him who wills nor of him who runs, but of God's showing mercy." Rom. 9:16. And, indeed, the whole visage of Scripture and, if I may speak so, the lineaments of its countenance, are found to exhibit a mystery, most profound and salutary, to admonish all who carefully look thereupon "that he who glories, should glory in the Lord." I Cor. 1 :31; cf. Jer. 9:24. The religious intention of Augustine's emphasis upon divine sovereignty and predestination is never so much to account for the doom of the wicked as to underscore the sheer and wonderful gratuity of salvation.

Now, after the apostle had commended God's mercy in saying, "So then, there is no question of him who wills nor of him who runs, but of God's showing mercy," next in order he intends to speak also of his judgment—for where his mercy is not shown, it is not unfairness but justice. For with God there is no injustice. Thus, he immediately added, "For the Scripture says to Pharaoh, 'For this very purpose I raised you up, that I may show through you my power, and that my name may be proclaimed in all the earth." Rom. 9:17; cf. Ex. 9:16. Then, having said this, he draws a conclusion that looks both ways, that is, toward mercy and toward judgment: "Therefore," he says, "he hath mercy on whom he willeth, and whom he willeth he hardeneth." He showeth mercy out of his great goodness; he hardeneth out of no unfairness at all. In this way, neither does he who is saved have a basis for glorying in any merit of his own; nor does the man who is damned have a basis for complaining of anything except what he has fully merited.

For grace alone separates the redeemed from the lost, all having been mingled together in the one mass of perdition, arising from a common cause which leads back to their common origin. But if any man hears this in such a way as to say: "Why then does he find fault? For who resists his will?" Rom. 9:19.—as if to make it seem that man should not therefore be blamed for being evil because God "hath mercy on whom he willeth and whom he willeth he hardeneth"—God forbid that we should be ashamed to give the same reply as we see the apostle giving: "O man, who are you to reply to God? Does the molded object say to the molder, 'Why have you made me like this?' Or is not the potter master of his clay, to make from the same mass one vessel for honorable, another for ignoble, use?" Rom. 9:20, 21.

There are some stupid men who think that in this part of the argument the apostle had no answer to give; and, for lack of a reasonable rejoinder, simply rebuked the audacity of his gainsayer. But what he said—"O man, who are you?"—has actually great weight and in an argument like this recalls man, in a single word, to consider the limits of his capacity and, at the same time, supplies an important explanation.

For if one does not understand these matters, who is he to talk back to God? And if one does understand, he finds no better ground even then for talking back. For if he understands, he sees that the whole human race was condemned in its apostate head by a divine judgment so just that not even if a single member of the race were ever saved from it, no one could rail against God's justice. And he also sees that those who are saved had to be saved on such terms that it would show—by contrast with the greater number of those not saved but simply abandoned to their wholly just damnation—what the whole mass deserved and to what end God's merited judgment would have brought them, had not his undeserved mercy interposed. Thus every mouth of those disposed to glory in their own merits should be stopped, so that "he that glories may glory in the Lord." I Cor. 1:31.

Augustine, Handbook on Faith, Hope, and Love

Leo the Great

Sermon 85

On the Feast of St. Laurence the Martyr

1. The example of the martyrs is most valuable
2. The saint's martyrdom described

3. The description of his sufferings continued
4. Laurentius has conquered his persecutor

1. *The example of the martyrs is most valuable*

Whilst the height of all virtues, dearly-beloved, and the fullness of all righteousness is born of that love, wherewith God and one's neighbor is loved, surely in none is this love found more conspicuous and brighter than in the blessed martyrs; who are as near to our Lord Jesus, Who died for all men, in the imitation of His love, as in the likeness of their suffering. For, although that Love, wherewith the Lord has redeemed us, cannot be equaled by any man's kindness, because it is one thing that a man who is doomed to die one day should die for a righteous man, and another that One Who is free from the debt of sin should lay down His life for the wicked : yet the martyrs also have done great service to all men, in that the Lord Who gave them boldness, has used it to show that the penalty of death and the pain of the cross need not be terrible to any of His followers, but might be imitated by many of them. If therefore no good man is good for himself alone, and no wise man's wisdom befriends himself only, and the nature of true virtue is such that it leads many away from the dark error on which its light is shed, no model is more useful in teaching God's people than that of the martyrs. Eloquence may make intercession easy, reasoning may effectually persuade; but yet examples are stronger than words, and there is more teaching in practice than in precept.

2. *The saint's martyrdom described*

And how gloriously strong in this most excellent manner of doctrine the blessed martyr Laurentius is, by whose sufferings to-day is marked, even his persecutors were able to feel, when they found that his wondrous courage, born principally of love for Christ, not only did not yield itself, but also strengthened others by the example of his endurance. For when the fury of the gentile potentates was raging against Christ's most chosen members, and attacked those especially who were of priestly rank, the wicked persecutor's wrath was vented on Laurentius the deacon, who was pre-eminent not only in the performance of the sacred rites, but also in the management of the church's property, promising himself double spoil from one man's capture: for if he forced him to surrender the sacred treasures, he would also drive him out of the pale of true religion. And so this man, so greedy of money and such a foe to the truth, arms himself with double weapon: with avarice to plunder the gold; with impiety to carry off Christ. He demands of the guileless guardian of the sanctuary that the church wealth on which his greedy mind was set should be brought to him. But the holy deacon showed him where he had them stored, by pointing to the many troops of poor saints, in the feeding and clothing of whom he had a store of riches which he could hot lose, and which were the more entirely safe that the money had been spent on so holy a cause.

3. *The description of his sufferings continued*

The baffled plunderer, therefore, frets, and blazing out into hatred of a religion, which had put riches to such a use, determines to pillage a still greater treasure by carrying off that sacred deposit, wherewith he was enriched, as he could find no solid hoard of money in his possession. He orders Laurentius to renounce Christ, and prepares to ply the deacon's stout courage with frightful tortures: and, when the first elicit nothing, fiercer follow. His limbs, torn and mangled by many cutting blows, are commanded to be broiled upon the fire in an iron framework, which was of itself already hot enough to burn him, and on which his limbs were turned from time to time, to make the torment fiercer, and the death more lingering.

4. *Laurentius has conquered his persecutor*

Thou gainest nothing, thou prevailest nothing, O savage cruelty. His mortal frame is released from thy devices, and, when Laurentius departs to heaven, thou art vanquished. The flame of Christ's love could not be overcome by thy flames, and the fire which burnt outside was less keen than that which blazed within. Thou didst but serve the martyr in thy rage, O persecutor: thou didst but swell the reward in adding to the pain. For what did thy cunning devise, which did not redound to the conqueror's glory, when even the instruments of torture were counted as part of the triumph?

Let us rejoice, then, dearly-beloved, with spiritual joy, and make our boast over the happy end of this illustrious man in the Lord, Who is "wonderful in His saints," in whom He has given us a support and an example, and has so spread abroad his glory throughout the world, that, from the rising of the sun to its going down, the brightness of his deacon's light doth shine, and Rome is become as famous in Laurentius as Jerusalem was ennobled by Stephen. By his prayer and intercession we trust at all times to be assisted; that, because all, as the Apostle says, "who wish to live holily in Christ, suffer persecution," we may be strengthened with the spirit of love, and be fortified to overcome all temptations by the perseverance of steadfast faith. Through our Lord Jesus Christ, &c.

Leo the Great

History of Bible translations

Number of languages Bible had been translated into during this period

AD 300–400

10–11 languages

AD 500

13 languages

Bible translations from this period

Jerome's Latin Vulgate (405)

The intention of St Jerome, translating into Latin the Hebrew of the Old Testament and the Greek of the New Testament, was that ordinary Christians of the Roman empire should be able to read the word of God. 'Ignorance of the scriptures', he wrote, 'is ignorance of Christ'. 1518—1648

The Gothic Bible translation

Wulfila (311–383), also known as Ulfilas, was a Western Gothic bishop who translated the bible from Greek for the benefit of his converted Goths. Only part of this bible translation has survived, comprising three quarters of the New Testament and part of Nehemiah from the Old Testament, both in manuscripts from the sixth century. The most important and attractive of these manuscripts is the *Codex Argenteus*.

CHAPTER 4

MEDIEVAL CHRISTIANITY

From Gregory the Great to John Huss [Jan Hus]
AD 591–1517

Important dates in the time of Medieval Christianity

589–615 Missionary work of St Columba
597 Landing of Augustine in Kent

7th Century

604 Deaths of Gregory and Augustine of Canterbury
607 Pope Boniface III, first Bishop of Rome to be called "Pope" and "Universal Bishop"
616 Conversion of King Ethelbert
627 Jerusalem taken by the Muslins
632 Death of Mohammed.
635 Settlement of Scottish missionaries in Holy Island
664 Council of Whitby, unites Celtic Christianity of British Isles with Roman Catholic Church

8th Century

704 Spain is invaded by the Moors
714 Boniface of England, the "Apostle of Germany," is a missionary to the Germans for forty years
734(?) Death of the Venerable Bede
752 Pipin becomes king of the Franks
787 Second Council of Nicaea, condemned iconoclasm

9th Century

800 Charles the Great crowned first Holy Roman Emperor
826–865 Missionary work of Anskar (Ansgar), Archbishop of Bremen, "Apostle of the North," who evangelizes North Germany, Denmark, and Sweden
840 St. Cyril and St. Methodius, the "Apostles of the Slavs" evangelize the Serbs
860 870 Conversion of Bulgarians, Moravians, Bohemians

10th Century

909 Abbey of Cluny, Benedictine monastery in France established

962 Otto I, emperor

966 Mieszko I, duke of Poland, baptized, Poland becomes a Christian country

997–998 First Papal Schism with 3 popes

994–1030 Conversion of Norwegians.

11th Century

1045 Sigfrid of Sweden, Benedictine evangelist

1046 Council of Sutri

1054 The Great Schism: Split between Eastern Orthodox-Western Roman Catholic churches

1065 Dedication of Westminster Abbey

1073 Hildebrand elected pope (Gregory VII)

1074 Founding of the Carthusian Order

1085 Death of Gregeory VII

1093–1109 Anselm, Archbishop of Canterbury, writes his important book on the atonement, *Cur Deus Homo (Why God Became Man)*

1098 Founding of reforming monastery of Citeaux, leading to the growth of the Cistercian Order

1099 Jerusalem taken in the First Crusade

12th Century

1104 Acre taken by the Crusaders, fell to Moslems again in 1191

1113 Order of St John (or Hospitalers) founded

1115 St Bernard establishes monastery at Clairvaux

1118 Order of the Temple (Knights Templar) founded

1123 First Lateran Council. Agreement between pope and emperor at Worms

1147–1149 The Second Crusade

1150 Peter Lombard writes his *Libri Quattuor Sententiarum The Four Books of Sentences*

1154 Nicolas Breakspeare, an Englishman, chosen pope (Adrian IV)

1155 Carmelite Order founded

1170 Murder of Archbishop Thomas Becket

1170 Pope Alexander III established rules for the canonization of saints

1173 Waldensian movement begins in Lyons

1182 Notre Dame Cathedral consecrated

1187 Loss of Jerusalem to muslim general Saladin

1189 The Third Crusade

1190 German Hospitalers founded (later becoming the Teutonic Order)
1194 Rebuilding of Chartres Cathedral begins
1198 Innocent III elected pope

13th Century

1203 Constantinople taken by Crusaders
1205 Francis of Assisi becomes a hermit and founds Franciscan order of friars, 1209
1212 The Children's Crusade
1215 Fourth Council of the Lateran: medieval doctrines reinforced
1215 Innocent sanctions the Dominican and Franciscan Orders of Mendicant (preaching) Friars
1220 Dominican Friars established as a teaching order, later entrusted by the Pope with the Inquisition. Some became missionaries to Central Asia, Persian Gulf, India, and China.
1231 Institution of the Medieval Inquisition by Pope Gregory IX
1240 First Crusade of St. Louis
1270 Second Crusade and death of St. Louis
1274 Thomas Aquinas summarizes Scholastic Theology in his *Summa Theologica*

14th Century

1300 Boniface celebrates the first jubilee
1302 Papal bull *Unam sanctum* pronounces the highest papal claims to supremacy
1303 Death of Boniface
1309–1377 "Babylonian Captivity" of papacy. Pope resides in Avignon, France
1312 Council of Vienne disbands Knights Templar
1377 Gregory XI moves the papacy from Avignon to Rome
1378 Beginning of the Great Schism of the West in Roman Catholicism
1384 Death of John Wycliffe

15th Century

1414–1417 Council of Constance
1415 Pope John XXIII deposed
1415 John Huss burnt by order of the Council
1417 Election of Pope Martin V and end of the dual papacy (France and Italy)
1418 Religious war of Bohemia breaks out
1431 Council of Basel opened
1431 French peasant woman Joan of Arc is burned at Rouen as a witch
1438 Council of Ferrara and Florence
1453 Constantinople taken by the Turks. St Sophia Basilica turned into a mosque

1453 Johann Gutenburg develops his printing press and prints the first Bible
1479 The Inquisition against heresy in Spain set up by Ferdinand and Isabella with papal approval
1492 Columbus' voyage and a new age of exploration and Christian expansion begin
1498 Savonarola burned
1498 The Vatican Library is founded by Nicholas V

16th Century
1503 Death of Pope Alexander VI
1514 Publication of first volume of Ximenez's *Complutension Polyglot*, combining the Hebrew OT, the Septuagint, and the Vulgate

Introduction

The Middle Ages stretch from the time after the fall of the Roman Empire until the arrival of the scientific revolution in the beginning of the sixteenth century.

Some historians have divided this nine hundred year span into the following three smaller periods, the Early Middle Ages, the High Middle Ages, and the Late Middle Ages.

Early Middle Age: Mohammed and Charlemagne
High Middle Age: East-West Schism and the Crusades
Late Middle Age: The Western Schism with 3 popes

Alternatively, the history of the Medieval Church may be divided into three periods as follows.

1. The missionary period

The missionary period covers the time from Gregory I. to Hildebrand or Gregory VII., 590–1073. It includes:

The conversion of the northern barbarians
The dawn of a new civilization
The origin and progress of Islam
The papal exile and the papal schism
The great schism between the Orthodox and Catholic Churches

2. The period of papal theocracy

The time of papal theocracy stretches from Gregory VII. to Boniface VIII., 1073–1294. It includes:

The height of the papacy
Monasticism and scholasticism
The Crusades
The conflict between the Pope and the Emperor

3. The decline of medieval Catholicism

The decline of medieval Catholicism and the time of preparation for modern Christianity starts with Boniface VIII and concludes with the Reformation, 1294–1517. It includes:

The reformatory councils
The decay of scholasticism
The growth of mysticism
The revival of letters
The art of printing
The discovery of America
The forerunners of Protestantism
The dawn of the Reformation.

EVENTS

Important events during the time of Medieval Christianity

Crusades
Great schism (*Filioque* clause)
Scholasticism

PEOPLE

Christian leaders during the time of Medieval Christianity

Gregory the Great (540–604)
Alcuin (735–804)
Anselm (1033–1109)
Francis of Assisi (1182–1226
Thomas Aquinas (1225–1274)
John Wycliffe (1320–1384)
John Huss (1369–1415)

An historian's overview of medieval Church History

1. The Middle Age. Limits and General Character

The Middle Age, as the term implies, is the period which intervenes between ancient and modern times, and connects them, by continuing the one, and preparing for the other. It forms the transition from the Graeco-Roman civilization to the Romano-Germanic, civilization, which gradually arose out of the intervening chaos of barbarism. The connecting link is Christianity, which saved the best elements of the old, and directed and molded the new order of things.

Gregory the Great to the Reformation

Politically, the middle age dates from the great migration of nations and the downfall of the western Roman Empire in the fifth century; but for ecclesiastical history it begins with Gregory the Great, the last of the fathers and the first of the popes, at the close of the sixth century. Its termination, both for secular and ecclesiastical history, is the Reformation of the sixteenth century (1517), which introduces the modern age of the Christian era.

Europe

The theatre of medieval Christianity is mainly Europe. In Western Asia and North Africa, the Cross was supplanted by the Crescent; and America, which opened a new field for the ever-expanding energies of history, was not discovered until the close of the fifteenth century.

Heathen barbarians

Europe was peopled by a warlike emigration of heathen barbarians from Asia.

Migration of nations

The great migration of nations marks a turning point in the history of religion and civilization. It was destructive in its first effects, and appeared like the doom of the judgment-day; but it proved the harbinger of a new creation, the chaos preceding the cosmos. The change was brought about gradually. The forces of the old Greek and Roman world continued to work for centuries alongside of the new elements. The barbarian irruption came not like a single torrent which passes by, but as the tide which advances and retires, returns and at last becomes master of the flooded soil. The savages of the north swept down the valley of the Danube to the borders of the Greek Empire, and southward over the Rhine and the Vosges into Gaul, across the Alps into Italy, and across the Pyrenees into Spain.

They were not a single people, but many independent tribes; not an organized army of a conqueror, but irregular hordes of wild warriors ruled by intrepid kings; not directed by the ambition of one controlling genius, like Alexander or Caesar, but prompted by the irresistible impulse of an historical instinct, and unconsciously bearing in their rear the future destinies of Europe and America. They brought with them fire and sword, destruction and desolation, but also life and vigor, respect for woman, sense of honor, love of liberty—noble instincts, which, being purified and developed by Christianity, became the governing principles of a higher civilization than that of Greece and Rome.

The Christian monk Salvian, who lived in the midst of the barbarian flood, in the middle of the fifth century, draws a most gloomy and appalling picture of the vices of the orthodox Romans of his time, and does not hesitate to give preference to the heretical (Arian) and heathen barbarians, "whose chastity purifies the deep stained with the Roman debauches." St. Augustin (d. 430), who took a more sober and comprehensive view, intimates, in his great work on the *City of God*, the possibility of the rise of a new and better civilization from the ruins of the old Roman empire; and his pupil, Orosius, clearly expresses this hopeful view. He says,

> Men assert that the barbarians are enemies of the State. I reply that all the East thought the same of the great Alexander; the Romans also seemed no better than the enemies of all society to the nations afar off, whose repose they troubled. But the Greeks, you say, established empires; the Germans overthrow them. Well, the Macedonians began by subduing the nations which afterwards they civilized. The Germans are now upsetting all this world; but if, which Heaven avert, they, finish by continuing to be its masters, peradventure some day posterity will salute with the title of great princes those in whom we at this day can see nothing but enemies.

2. The Nations of Medieval Christianity

The Kelt, the Teuton, and the Slav

The new national forces which now enter upon the arena of church history may be divided into four groups:

A. Romanic or Latin nations

The Romanic or Latin nations of Southern Europe, including the Italians, Spaniards, Portuguese and French. They are the natural descendants and heirs of the old Roman nationality and Latin Christianity, yet mixed with the new Keltic and Germanic forces. Their languages are all derived from the Latin; they inherited Roman laws and customs, and adhered to the Roman See as the center of their ecclesiastical organization; they carried Christianity to the advancing barbarians, and by their superior civilization gave laws to the conquerors. They still adhere, with their descendants in Central and South America, to the Roman Catholic Church.

B. The Keltic race

The Keltic race, embracing the Gauls, old Britons, the Picts and Scots, the Welsh and Irish with their numerous emigrants in all the large cities of Great Britain and the United States, appear in history several hundred years before Christ, as the first light wave of the vast Aryan migration from the mysterious bowels of Asia, which swept to the borders of the extreme West.

The Gauls were conquered by Caesar, but afterwards commingled with the Teutonic Francs, who founded the French monarchy. The Britons were likewise subdued by the Romans, and afterwards driven to Wales and Cornwall by the Anglo-Saxons. The Scotch in the highlands (Gaels) remained Keltic, while in the lowlands they mixed with Saxons and Normans.

The mental characteristics of the Kelts remain unchanged for two thousand years: quick wit, fluent speech, vivacity, sprightliness, impressibility, personal bravery and daring, loyalty to the chief or the clan, but also levity, fickleness, quarrelsomeness and incapacity for self-government. "They shook all empires, but founded none."

The elder Cato says of them: "To two things are the Kelts most attent: to fighting, and to adroitness of speech." Caesar censures their love of levity and change. The apostle Paul complains of the same weakness. Thierry, their historian, well describes them thus:

> Their prominent attributes are personal valor, in which they excel all nations; a frank, impetuous spirit open to every impression; great intelligence, but joined with extreme mobility, deficient perseverance, restlessness under discipline and order, boastfulness and eternal discord, resulting from boundless vanity.

Mommsen quotes this passage, and adds that the Kelts make good soldiers, but bad citizens; that the only order to which they submit is the military, because the severe general discipline relieves them of the heavy burden of individual self-control.

Keltic Christianity was at first independent of Rome, and even antagonistic to it in certain subordinate rites; but after the Saxon and Norman conquests, it was brought into conformity, and since the Reformation, the Irish have been more attached to the Roman Church than even the Latin races. The French formerly inclined likewise to a liberal Catholicism (called Gallicanism); but they sacrificed the Gallican liberties to the Ultramontanism of the Vatican Council.

The Welsh and Scots, on the contrary, with the exception of a portion of the Highlanders in the North of Scotland, embraced the Protestant Reformation in its Calvinistic rigor, and are among its sternest and most vigorous advocates. The course of the Keltic nations had been anticipated by the Galatians, who first embraced with great readiness and heartiness the independent gospel of St. Paul, but were soon turned away to a Judaizing legalism by false teachers, and then brought back again by Paul to the right path.

C. The Germanic or Teutonic nations

The Germanic or Teutonic nations followed the Keltic migration in successive westward and southward waves, before and after Christ, and spread over Germany, Switzerland, Holland, Scandinavia, the Baltic provinces of Russia, and, since the Anglo-Saxon invasion, also over England and Scotland and the northern (non-Keltic) part of Ireland. In modern times their descendants peacefully settled the British Provinces and the greater part of North America.

The Germanic nations are the fresh, vigorous, promising and advancing races of the middle age and modern times. Their Christianization began in the fourth century, and went on in wholesale style till it was completed in the tenth. The Germans, under their leader Odoacer in 476, deposed Romulus Augustulus—the shadow of old Romulus and Augustus—and overthrew the West Roman Empire, thus fulfilling the old augury of the twelve birds of fate, that Rome was to grow six centuries and to decline six centuries. Wherever they went, they brought destruction to decaying institutions. But with few exceptions, they readily embraced the religion of the conquered Latin provinces, and with childlike docility submitted to its educational power.

They were predestinated for Christianity, and Christianity for them. It curbed their warlike passions, regulated their wild force, and developed their nobler instincts, their devotion and fidelity, their respect for woman, their reverence for all family-relations, their love of personal liberty and independence. The Latin church was to them only a school of discipline to prepare them for an age of Christian manhood and independence, which dawned in the sixteenth century. The Protestant Reformation was the emancipation of the Germanic races from the pupilage of medieval and legalistic Catholicism.

Tacitus, the great heathen historian, no doubt idealized the barbarous Germans in contrast with the degenerate Romans of his day (as Montaigne and Rousseau painted the savages "in a fit of ill humor against their country"); but he unconsciously prophesied their future greatness, and his prophecy has been more than fulfilled.

D. The Slavs

The Slavonic or Slavic or Slavs in the East and North of Europe, including the Bulgarians, Bohemians (Czechs), Moravians, Slovaks, Servians, Croatians, Wends, Poles, and Russians, were mainly converted through Eastern missionaries since the ninth and tenth century. The Eastern Slavs, who are the vast majority, were incorporated with the Greek Church, which became the national religion of Russia, and through this empire acquired a territory almost equal to that of the Roman Church. The western Slavs, the Bohemians and Poles, became subject to the Papacy.

The Slavs, who number in all nearly 80,000,000, occupy a very subordinate position in the history of the middle ages, and are isolated from the main current; but recently, they have begun to develop their resources, and seem to have a great future before them through the commanding political power of Russia in Europe and in Asia. Russia is the bearer of the destinies of Panslavism and of the, Eastern Church.

E. Greeks

The Greek nationality, which figured so conspicuously in ancient Christianity, maintained its independence down to the fall of the Byzantine Empire in 1453; but it was mixed with Slavonic elements. The Greek Church was much weakened by the inroads of Mohammedanism and lost the possession of the territories of primitive Christianity, but secured a new and vast missionary field in Russia.

3. Genius of Medieval Christianity

Medieval Christianity is, on the one hand, a legitimate continuation and further development of ancient Catholicism; on the other hand, a preparation for Protestantism.

Its leading form are the papacy, monasticism, and scholasticism, which were developed to their height, and then assailed by growing opposition from within.

Christianity, at its first introduction, had to do with highly civilized nations; but now it had to lay the foundation of a new civilization among barbarians. The apostles planted churches in the cities of the Jews, Greeks, and Romans, and the word "pagan" i.e., villager, backwoodsman, gradually came to denote an idolater. They spoke and wrote in a language which had already a large and immortal literature; their progress was paved by the high roads of the Roman legions; they found everywhere an established order of society, and government; and their mission was to infuse into the ancient civilization a new spiritual life and to make it subservient to higher moral ends. But the missionaries of the dark ages had to visit wild woods and untilled fields, to teach rude nations the alphabet, and to lay the foundation for society, literature and art.

Hence Christianity assumed the character of a strong disciplinary institution, a training school for nations in their infancy, which had to be treated as children. Hence the legalistic, hierarchical, ritualistic and romantic character of medieval Catholicism. Yet in proportion as the nations were trained in the school of the church, they began to assert their independence of the hierarchy and to develop a national literature in their own language. Compared with our times, in which thought and reflection have become the highest arbiter of human life, the middle age was an age of passion. The written law, such as it was developed in Roman society, the barbarian could not understand and would not obey. But he was easily impressed by the spoken law, the living word, and found a kind of charm in bending his will absolutely before another will. Thus the teaching church became the law in the land, and formed the very foundation of all social and political organization.

"The dark ages"

The middle ages are often called "the dark ages:" truly, if we compare them with ancient Christianity, which preceded, and with modern Christianity, which followed; falsely and unjustly, if the church is made responsible for the darkness. Christianity was the light that shone in the darkness of surrounding barbarism and heathenism, and gradually dispelled it. Industrious priests and monks saved from the wreck of the Roman Empire the treasures of classical literature, together with the Holy Scriptures and patristic writings, and transmitted them to better times.

The medieval light was indeed the borrowed star and moon-light of ecclesiastical tradition, rather than the clear sun-light from the inspired pages of the New Testament; but it was such light as the eyes of nations in their ignorance could bear, and it never ceased to shine till it disappeared in the day-light of the great Reformation. Christ had his witnesses in all ages and countries, and those shine all the brighter who were surrounded by midnight darkness.

Pause where we may upon the desert-road,
Some shelter is in sight, some sacred safe abode.

"The ages of faith"

On the other hand, the middle ages are often called, especially by Roman Catholic writers, "the ages of faith." They abound in legends of saints, which had the charm of religious novels. All men believed in the supernatural and miraculous as readily as children do now. Heaven and hell were as real to the mind as the kingdom of France and the, republic of Venice. Skepticism and infidelity were almost unknown, or at least suppressed and concealed. But with faith was connected a vast deal of superstition and an entire absence of critical investigation and judgment. Faith was blind and unreasoning, like the faith of children. The most incredible and absurd legends were accepted without a question. And yet the morality was not a whit better, but in many respects ruder, coarser and more passionate, than in modern times.

The church's monopoly

The church as a visible organization never had greater power over the minds of men. She controlled all departments of life from the cradle to the grave. She monopolized all the learning and made sciences and arts tributary to her. She took the lead in every progressive movement. She founded universities, built lofty cathedrals, stirred up the crusades, made and unmade kings, dispensed blessings and curses to whole nations. The medieval hierarchy centering in Rome re-enacted the Jewish theocracy on a more comprehensive scale. It was a carnal anticipation of the millennial reign of Christ. It took centuries to rear up this imposing structure, and centuries to take it down again.

Opposition

The opposition came partly from the anti-Catholic sects, which, in spite of cruel persecution, never ceased to protest against the corruptions and tyranny of the papacy; partly from the spirit of nationality which arose in opposition to an all-absorbing hierarchical centralization; partly from the revival of classical and biblical learning, which undermined the reign of superstition and tradition; and partly from the inner and deeper life of the Catholic Church itself, which loudly called for a reformation, and struggled through the severe discipline of the law to the light and freedom of the gospel. The medieval Church was a schoolmaster to lead men to Christ. The Reformation was an emancipation of Western Christendom from the bondage of the law, and a re-conquest of that liberty "wherewith Christ hath made us free" (Gal. v. 1).

Philip Schaff, History of the Christian Church, 1890

The conversion of barbarians

Charlemagne

Charlemagne becomes sole King of the Franks in 771. Charlemagne (Charles the Great, c. 742–814) is crowned the first "Holy Roman Emperor" by Pope St. Leo III at St. Peters in Rome on Christmas day of the year 800.

The Pope, St. Leo III, by crowning him "Emperor of Rome in the West" was setting himself up as the spiritual master of Europe, who could make kings and emperors; it was taken by some as a tacit declaration of the Church's primacy over secular authority.

Evangelism

During the Middle Ages the church in the West continued its evangelizing work:

Boniface of England went to the Germans as a missionary for forty years before being murdered by pagans in 754.

Augustine of Canterbury went to England to re-establish the church.

Anskar converted Germany, and the Scandinavian countries.

Cyril and Methodius among the Slavs (863)

After the Slavs were baptized along with their prince Rastislav Sviatopolk and Kotsel (members of the prince's family), they sent a request to Emperor Michael (of Constantinople, 842–867, asking: "Our country has been baptized, but we have no master to preach to us, instruct us and explain the holy books to us. We understand neither Greek nor Latin: some teach us one thing and some another, and we do not understand the meaning of the sacred books and their power. So send us masters who are capable of explaining to us the letter of the holy books and their spirit."

On hearing this, the Emperor Michael assembled all his philosophers and told them all that the Slav princes had said.

The philosophers replied: "At Thessalonica there is a man called Leo: he has sons who know Slavonic well, two trained in the sciences, and philosophers."

As soon as they arrived, Constantine (Cyril) and Methodius established the letters of the Slavonic alphabet and translated the Acts of the Apostles and the Gospel. The Slavs rejoiced at hearing the mighty works of God in their own tongue . . . Now some people began to find fault with the Slavonic books, saying, "No people has the right to its alphabet save the Hebrews the Greeks and the Latins, as is shown by what Pilate wrote on the Savior's cross."

The Pope of Rome (John VIII), on hearing that, found fault with those who murmured against the Slavonic books, saying: "Let the words of Holy Scripture be fulfilled: that all tongues should praise God."

Nestorian Chronicle XX an eleventh-century text

The origin and progress of Islam

The coming of Mohammed was a catastrophe for Christianity. Mohammed (c. 570–629) founds the religion of Islam, which begins to supplant Christianity across the Middle East and North Africa.

In 622, with the establishment of Islam, the five hundred bishops of Africa and the Middle East became only 8eight.

Jerusalem was taken by the Muslims in 637.

Even Egypt, the pride of Christianity, became a Muslim country in 641 when the Arabs conquered Egypt, including Alexandria.

The Moors were Muslims from North Africa. They occupied Spain and Portugal from 711. The Muslims stayed in Spain 800 years, in Portugal 600 years, in Greece 500 years, in Sicily 300 years, in Serbia 400 years, in Bulgaria 500 years, in Rumania 400 years, and in Hungary 150 years.

The Great schism between the Orthodox and Catholic churches

The break between the Latin and the Greek churches, also known as "The Great Schism" came to a head in 1054.

Growing apart

Over the centuries, going back as far as the fifth century the Western and Eastern churches drifted away from each other. The Eastern church tended to ruled by the emperor of Constantinople, while the Western church was focused on supporting the empire in the West.

Additionally, the Eastern church did not know Latin and the Western church no longer understood Greek and so they tended to despise one another. To the Byzantines, the Latin people were from the dark ages, wild and uncultured with huge appetites. The Latin people thought that the Greeks were degenerates, effeminate hairsplitters. Byzantine became a foul word.

The following extract from a contemporary document explains how the Great Schism took place. This sentence of excommunication delivered by Cardinal Humbert against Michael Cerularius drove the Eastern Church away from the Western Church.

Sentence of excommunication delivered by Cardinal Humbert against Michael Cerularius

As for Michael, who has improperly been given the title patriarch, and those who share in his folly, they sow an abundance of heresies each day in their midst (in the city of Constantinople). Like the Simonians, they sell the gift of God; like the Valesians, they make their hosts eunuchs and then elevate them up not to the priesthood but also to the episcopate. Like the Nicolaitans, they allow ministers of the holy altar to be contracted in marriage . . . Like the Pneumatomachi (those who fought against the Spirit) they have suppressed the procession of the Holy Spirit a *filio* in the creed. Like the Manichaeans, they declare that fermented bread is alive . . . Moreover, allowing beard and hair to grow, they refuse communion with those who, following the custom of the Roman church, cut their hair and shave their beard . . .

That is why, being unable to bear these unprecedented injuries and these outrages directed against the chief apostolic see . . . we sign against Michael and his supporters the anathema that our most reverend pope has pronounced against them if they do not return to their senses . . .

May Michael, the neophyte, who improperly bears the title of patriarch . . . and all those who follow him in the above mentioned errors, may they all fall under the anathema, Maranatha, with the Simonians, and all the heretics, and indeed with the devil and his angels, unless they return to their senses. Amen, Amen, Amen!

Monasteries

Introduction

Monastery, a term derived from the Greek word (*monasterion*), denotes the habitation and workplace of a community of monks or nuns.

Order of Cluny

The founding of the Order of Cluny, a Benedictine monastery established 909 at Cluny, kick-started a reform movement in the church. It set its face against the increasing tide of secularization in its institutions and practices.

The first Medieval monks adhered to the Benedictine Rule which was established by St. Benedict in 529 AD. Different orders of Medieval monks were also established during the Middle Ages.

Orders of medieval monks and friars

The two main categories of monks and friars were those belonging to the Monastic orders, and those who spend most of their time outside monasteries, the Mendicant (Preaching) friars

Monastic monks
Benedictines
Carthusians
Cistercians
Mendicant friars
Franciscans
Dominicans
Carmelites

Christian monastic orders

Augustinians, founded in 1256, which evolved from the canons who would normally work with the Bishop: they lived with him as monks under St. Augustine's rule

Benedictines, founded in 529 by St. Benedict at Monte Cassino, stresses manual labor in a self-subsistent monastery. They are less of a unified order than most other orders.

Bridgettines, founded c. 1350

Camaldolese, founded c. 1000

Carmelites, founded between 1206 and 1214, a Contemplative Order

Carthusians

Celestines

Cistercians, founded in 1098 by St. Bernard of Clairvaux

Conventuals

Cluniacs

Discalced Carmelites

Dominicans, founded in 1215

Franciscans, founded in 1209 by St. Francis of Assisi

Jesuits

Melanesian Brotherhood

Olivetans

Premonstratensians, also known as Norbertines.

Silvesterines

Trappists, began c. 1664

Vallombrosans

Visitation Sisters

Major orders of medieval monks were:

The Benedictine Monks—the Black Monk

The Cistercian Monks—the White Monk

The Carthusian Monks—the Silent Monks

Carthusians and Cistercians

In the eleventh century these two great mystical orders, both of which went on to initiate reforms in the church, came into being.

Carthusians

The Carthusians were founded in 1074 by St. Bruno. Although Carthusians are part of their own monastic community, most of their days were spent alone in there cells, where they prayed, had their meals and slept.

Carthusians attended three services every day:

the Night Office,

the morning Eucharist and
Vespers towards the night.

Cistercians

The Cistercians, founded in 1098 at Citeaux (Cisterce), sought to live a life in strict conformity to the Rule of St. Benedict.

By 1150 they had 350 abbeys, but a century later they had 647 abbeys which stretched from Ireland and Scotland to Poland, and from northern Norway to Sicily. They had 20,000 monks. Bernard of Clairvaux (1090–1153) was a Cistercian.

The daily life of medieval monks

The daily life of Medieval monks in the Middle Ages were based on the three main vows:
The Vow of Poverty
The Vow of Chastity
The Vow of Obedience

Medieval Monks chose to renounce all worldly life and goods and spend their lives working under the strict routine and discipline of life in a monastery.

The daily life of Medieval monks was dedicated to worship, reading, and manual labor. In addition to their attendance at church, the monks spent several hours in reading from the Bible, private prayer, and meditation. During the day the Medieval monks worked hard in the monastery and on its lands.

The life of medieval monks were filled with the following work:

Washing and cooking for the monastery
Planting vegetables and grain
Reaping, Sowing, Ploughing, Binding and Thatching, Haymaking and Threshing
Producing wine, ale and honey
Providing medical care for the community
Providing education for boys and novices
Copying the manuscripts of classical authors
Providing hospitality for pilgrims

The daily routine

The daily life of a Medieval monk centered around the hours. The Book of Hours was the main prayer book and was divided into eight sections, or hours, that were meant to be read at specific times of the day. Each section contained prayers, psalms, hymns, and other readings intended to help the monks secure salvation for himself. Each day was divided into these eight sacred offices, beginning and ending with prayer services in the monastery church.

This tradition is supposed to be based on Psalm 119:164, which stated: "Seven times a day do I praise thee because of thy righteous judgments." These "seven times" were the times specified for the recitation of divine office which was the term used to describe the cycle of daily devotions. The times of these prayers were called by the following names:

Lauds : the early morning service of divine office approx 5am
Matins : the night office; the service recited at 2 am in the divine office
Prime : The 6am service
Sext : Recited at the sixth hour (noon)
Nones : Recited at the ninth hour (3 pm)
Terce : Recited at the third hour (9 am)
Vespers : the evening service of divine office, recited before dark (4–5pm)
Compline : the last of the day services of divine office, recited before retiring (6pm)

(The Devotions of the 3rd Hour Terce)

INTRODUCTION TO EVERY HOUR

In the name of the Father, and the Son, and the Holy Spirit, one God. Amen.

Kyrie eleison. Lord have mercy, Lord have mercy, Lord bless us. Amen.

Glory to the Father, and to the Son, and to the Holy Spirit, now and forever and unto the ages of all ages. Amen.

THE LORD'S PRAYER

Make us worthy to pray thankfully:

Our Father Who art in heaven; hallowed be Thy name. Thy kingdom come. Thy will be done on earth as it is in heaven. Give us this day our daily bread. And forgive us our trespasses, as we forgive those who trespass against us. And lead us not into temptation, but deliver us from evil, in Christ Jesus our Lord. For Thine is the kingdom, the power and the glory, forever. Amen.

THE PRAYER OF THANKSGIVING

Let us give thanks to the beneficent and merciful God, the Father of our Lord, God and Savior, Jesus Christ, for He has covered us, helped us, guarded us, accepted us unto Him, spared us, supported us, and brought us to this hour. Let us also ask Him, the Lord our God, the Almighty, to guard us in all peace this holy day and all the days of our life.

O Master, Lord, God the Almighty, the Father of our Lord, God and Savior, Jesus Christ, we thank You for every condition, concerning every condition, and in every condition, for You have covered us, helped us, guarded us, accepted us unto You, spared us, supported us, and brought us to this hour.

Therefore, we ask and entreat Your goodness, O Lover of mankind, to grant us to complete this holy day, and all the days of our life, in all peace with Your fear. All envy, all temptation, all the work of Satan, the counsel of wicked men, and the rising up of enemies, hidden and manifest, take them away from us, and from all Your people, and from this holy place that is Yours.

But those things which are good and profitable do provide for us; for it is You Who have given us the authority to tread on serpents and scorpions, and upon all the power of the enemy.

And lead us not into temptation, but deliver us from evil, by the grace, compassion and love of mankind, of Your Only-Begotten Son, our Lord, God and Savior, Jesus Christ, through Whom the glory, the honor, the dominion, and the adoration are due unto You, with Him, and the Holy Spirit, the Life-Giver, Who is of one essence with You, now and at all times, and unto the ages of all ages. Amen.

PSALM 19
PSALM 22
PSALM 23
PSALM 25
PSALM 28
PSALM 29
PSALM 33
PSALM 40
PSALM 42
PSALM 44
PSALM 45
PSALM 46
PSALM 50

THE HOLY GOSPEL ACCORDING TO ST. JOHN (CH. 14:26–31 & CH. 15:1–4)

Glory to God forever. Amen.

We worship You O Christ with Your Good Father and the Holy Spirit, for You have come and saved us.

Your Holy Spirit, O Lord Whom You sent forth upon Your holy disciples and honored apostles in the third hour, do not take away from us, O Good One, but renew Him within us. Create in me a clean heart, O God, and renew a steadfast spirit within me. Do not cast me away from Your presence. And do not take Your Holy Spirit away from me.

Glory to the Father, and the Son, and the Holy Spirit.

O Lord who sent down Your Holy Spirit upon Your holy disciples and Your honored apostles in the third hour, do not take Him away from us, O Good One, but we ask You to renew Him within us, O Lord Jesus Christ, Son of God, the Word; a steadfast and life giving spirit, a spirit of prophecy and chastity, a spirit of holiness, justice and authority, O the Almighty One, for You are the light of our souls. O Who shines upon every man that comes into the world, have mercy on me.

Now and forever and unto the ages of all ages, Amen.

O Theotokos, you are the true vine who bore the Cluster of Life, we ask you, O full of grace, with the apostles, for the salvation of our souls. Blessed is the Lord our God. Blessed is the Lord day by day. He prepares our way, for He is God of our salvation.

Now and forever and unto the ages of all ages, Amen.

O Heavenly King, the Comforter, the Spirit of truth, who is present in all places and fills all, the treasury of good things and the Life-Giver, graciously come, and dwell in us and purify us from all defilement, O Good One, and save our souls.

Glory to the Father, and the Son, and the Holy Spirit.

Just as You were with Your disciples, O Savior, and gave them peace, graciously come also and be with us, and grant us Your peace, and save us, and deliver our souls.

Now and forever and unto the ages of all ages, Amen.

Whenever we stand in Your holy sanctuary, we are considered standing in heaven. O Theotokos, you are the gate of heaven, open for us the gate of mercy.

Lord, hear us and have mercy on us and forgive us our sins. Amen.

(Lord have mercy) 41 times

HOLY HOLY HOLY

Holy Holy Holy. Lord of hosts. Heaven and earth are full of Your glory and honor. Have mercy on us, O God the Father, the Almighty O Holy Trinity, have mercy on us. O Lord, God of hosts, be with us. For we have no helper in our hardships and tribulations but You. Absolve, forgive, and remit, O God, our transgressions; those which we have committed willingly and those we have committed unwillingly, those which we have committed knowingly and those which we have committed unknowingly, the hidden and manifest, O Lord forgive us, for the sake of Your Holy name which is called upon us.

Let it be according to Your mercy, O Lord, and not according to our sins.

Make us worthy to pray thankfully:

Our Father Who art in heaven . . .

ABSOLUTION

O God of all compassion, and Lord of all comfort, who comforted us at all times with the comfort of Your Holy Spirit, we thank You for You raised us for prayer in this holy hour, in which You abundantly poured the grace of Your Holy Spirit upon Your holy disciples and honorable and blessed apostles, like tongues of fire.

We ask and entreat You, O lover of mankind, to accept our prayers, and forgive our sins, and send forth upon us the grace of Your Holy Spirit, and purify us from all defilement of body and spirit.

Change us into a spiritual manner of life, that we may walk in the Spirit and not fulfill the lusts of the flesh. And make us worthy to serve You with purity and righteousness all the days of our life. For unto You is due glory, honor, and dominion, with Your good Father and the Holy Spirit, now and forever and unto the ages of all ages. Amen.

THE CONCLUSION OF EVERY HOUR

Have mercy on us, O God, and have mercy on us, who, at all times and in every hour, in heaven and on earth, is worshipped and glorified, Christ our God, the good, the long suffering, the abundant in mercy, and the great in compassion, who loves the righteous and has mercy on the sinners of whom I am chief; who does not wish the death of the sinner but rather that he returns and lives, who calls all to salvation for the promise of the blessings to come.

Lord receive from us our prayers in this hour and in every hour. Ease our life and guide us to fulfill Your commandments. Sanctify our spirits. Cleanse our bodies. Conduct our thoughts. Purify our intentions. Heal our diseases. Forgive our sins. Deliver us from every evil grief and distress of heart. Surround us by Your holy angels, that, by their camp, we may be guarded and guided, and attain the unity of faith, and the knowledge of Your imperceptible and infinite glory. For You are blessed forever. Amen.

Any work immediately ceased at these times of daily prayer.

Importance of monasteries

Throughout the greater part of the Middle Ages monasteries were virtually the only centers of scholarship and learning in Europe. Many monasteries contained huge libraries which contained important ancient texts. Many monks spent their days in libraries involved in copying religious and other texts. Much of our knowledge of the ancient world has only survived because of the existence of monks and monasteries.

A Description of Clairvaux, c. 1143

At the first glance as you entered Clairvaux by descending the hill you could see that it was a temple of God; and the still, silent valley bespoke, in the modest simplicity of its buildings, the unfeigned humility of Christ's poor. Moreover, in this valley full of men, where no one was permitted to be idle, where one and all were occupied with their allotted tasks, a silence deep as that of night prevailed. The sounds of labor, or the chants of the brethren in the choral service, were the only exceptions. The orderliness of this silence, and the report that went forth concerning it struck such a reverence even into secular persons that they dreaded breaking it—I will not say by idle or wicked conversation, but even by proper remarks. The solitude, also, of the place—between dense forests in a narrow gorge of neighboring hills—in a certain sense recalled the cave of our father St. Benedict, so that while they strove to imitate his life, they also had some similarity to him in their habitation and loneliness . . . .

Although the monastery is situated in a valley, it has its foundations on the holy hills, whose gates the Lord loves more than all the dwellings of Jacob. Glorious things are spoken of it, because the glorious and wonderful God therein works great marvels. There the insane recover their reason, and although their outward man is worn away, inwardly they are born again. There the proud are humbled, the rich are made poor, and the poor have the Gospel preached to them, and the darkness of sinners is changed into light. A large multitude of blessed poor from the ends of the earth have there assembled, yet have they one heart and one mind; justly, therefore, do all who dwell there rejoice with no empty joy. They have the certain hope of perennial joy, of their ascension heavenward already commenced. In Clairvaux, they have found Jacob's ladder, with angels upon it; some descending, who so provide for their bodies that they faint not on the way; others ascending, who so rule their souls that their bodies hereafter may be glorified with them.

For my part, the more attentively I watch them day by day, the more do I believe that they are perfect followers of Christ in all things. When they pray and speak to God in spirit and in truth, by their friendly and quiet speech to Him, as well as by their humbleness of demeanor, they are plainly seen to be God's companions and friends.

When, on the other hand, they openly praise God with psalms, how pure and fervent are their minds, is shown by their posture of body in holy fear and reverence, while by their careful pronunciation and modulation of the psalms, is shown how sweet to their lips are the words of God—sweeter than honey to their mouths. As I watch them, therefore, singing without fatigue from before midnight to the dawn of day, with only a brief interval, they appear a little less than the angels, but much more than men . . . .

As regards their manual labor, so patiently and placidly, with such quiet countenances, in such sweet and holy order, do they perform all things, that although they exercise themselves at many works, they never seem moved or burdened in anything, whatever the labor may be. Whence it is manifest that that Holy Spirit works in them who disposes of all things with sweetness, in whom they are refreshed, so that they rest even in their toil.

Many of them, I hear, are bishops and earls, and many illustrious through their birth or knowledge; but now, by God's grace, all distinction of persons being dead among them, the greater anyone thought himself in the world, the more in this flock does he regard himself as less than the least. I see them in the garden with hoes, in the meadows with forks or rakes, in the fields with scythes, in the forest with axes. To judge from their outward appearance, their tools, their bad and disordered clothes, they appear a race of fools, without speech or sense. But a true thought in my mind tells me that their life in Christ is hidden in the heavens. Among them I see Godfrey of Peronne, Raynald of Picardy, William of St. Omer,

Walter de Lisle, all of whom I knew formerly in the old man, whereof I now see no trace, by God's favor. I knew them proud and puffed up; I see them walking humbly under the merciful hand of God.

William of St. Thierry, Frederic Austin Ogg, ed., A Source Book of Medieval History: Documents Illustrative of European Life and Institutions from the German Invasions to the Renaissance (New York, 1907)

Scholasticism

Introduction

Scholasticism comes from the Latin word *scholasticus* which means "that [which] belongs to the school", and is the school of philosophy taught by the academics (or schoolmen) of medieval universities circa 1100–1500. Scholasticism attempted to reconcile the philosophy of the ancient classical philosophers with medieval Christian theology.

The primary purpose of scholasticism was to find the answer to a question or resolve a contradiction. It is most well known in its application in medieval theology but was applied to classical philosophy and other fields of study. It is not a philosophy or theology on its own, but a tool and method for learning which puts emphasis on dialectical reasoning.

John Scotus Erigena (c. 810–877), one of greatest theologians of early middle ages, helped to pave the way for scholasticism. He was involved in eucharistic controversy with Radbertus and maintained that in the Lord's Supper we partake of the Lord "mentally not dentally."

Strictly speaking scholasticism may be said to have begun with the *Sentences* of Peter Lombard, and the *Decretum* of Gratian, at the beginning of the 12th century. To this may be added many new Latin translations of classical philosophers such as Aristotle. This new learning was assimilated by the Dominicans Albertus Magnus and his famous pupil Thomas Aquinas. Aquinas' *Summa Theologicae* is recognized as the pinnacle of scholastic theology.

Scholastic method

The scholastics would choose a book by a renowned scholar (called *auctor*) as a subject of investigation. By reading the book thoroughly and critically, the disciples learned to appreciate the theories of the *auctor*. Other documents related to the source document would be referenced, such as Church councils, papal letters, or anything written on the subject, be it ancient text or contemporary. The points of disagreement and contention between these multiple sources would be written down. For example, the Bible's apparent contradictions have been written about by scholars both ancient and contemporary, and so scholastics would gather all arguments concerning each contradiction, viewing them from all sides with an open mind.

Once the sources and points of disagreement were laid out through a series of dialectics, the two sides of an argument would be made whole so that they would be found to be in agreement and avoid contradictions. This was accomplished in two ways:

Through the use of *philological analysis* words were examined and it was argued that these words could have more than one meaning. That is, the author could have intended the word to mean something else. Ambiguity in words could be used to find common ground between two otherwise contradictory statements.

Through *logical analysis* they sought to show that contradictions in fact did not exist, but were subjective to the reader.

Famous Scholastics

Early scholastics (1000–1250):

- Anselm of Canterbury
- Pierre Abélard
- Solomon Ibn Gabirol
- Peter Lombard
- Gilbert de la Porrée

High scholastics (1250–1350):

- Robert Grosseteste
- Roger Bacon
- Albertus Magnus
- Thomas Aquinas
- Boëthius de Dacia
- Duns Scotus
- Radulphus Brito
- William of Ockham
- Jean Buridan

Late scholastics (1350–1500):

- Marsilius of Padua
- Francisco de Vitoria

Important anti-Scholastics

- Bernard of Clairvaux

  During his lifetime Bernard was the fiercest opponent to scholasticism

Theopedia, The Encyclopedia of Biblical Christianity

The Crusades

Introduction

The Crusades were a series of wars initiated by Christians to win back their holy lands from Muslims, with a total of 8 Crusades in almost 200 years.

In the 10th and 11th centuries, the expansion of Islam threatened both Christian thought and Christian activities. In 1009 Muslims sacked the Holy Sepulcher in Jerusalem. In 1095 Pope Urban II proclaims the First Crusade to reclaim Jerusalem from the Muslims. In 1099 the Crusaders take Jerusalem.

At the Council of Clermont (1095) Pope Blessed Urban II preached a sermon that started the First Crusade.

The pilgrimage to Jerusalem

The origins of crusades began in Jerusalem. This place was first and foremost a place of ritual of purification and penitence. Christians believed that to share in the life and death of Christ on the same ground would assure them a place in heaven. In Spain it was claimed that those who died fighting the infidels, Moslems, were assured of salvation. The Turks threatened Constantinople and the emperor of Greece called to the West for help.

The Crusades were a series of several military campaigns—usually sanctioned by the Papacy—that took place during the 11th through 13th centuries. Originally, they were Roman Catholic endeavors to capture the Holy Land from the Muslims, but some were directed against other Europeans, such as the Fourth Crusade against Constantinople, the Albigensian Crusade against the Cathars of southern France and the Northern Crusades.

The major Crusades

A traditional numbering scheme for the crusades gives us nine during the 11th to 13th centuries, as well as other smaller crusades that are mostly contemporaneous and unnumbered. There were frequent "minor" crusades throughout this period, not only in Palestine but also in Spain and central Europe, against not only Muslims, but also Christian heretics and personal enemies of the Papacy or other powerful monarchs. Such "crusades" continued into the 16th century, until the Renaissance and Reformation when the political and religious climate of Europe was significantly different than that of the Middle Ages. The following is a listing of the "major" crusades.

First Crusade

After Byzantine emperor Alexius I called for help with defending his empire against the Seljuk Turks, in 1095 Pope Urban II called upon all Christians to join a war against the Turks. In this call to the crusade—at the Council of Clermont (1095)—Pope Urban II asked the knights of the West to go to the East and win back the holy places. The pope granted plenary indulgences and dispensation from all penances to those who took up the sword in the name of the church.

Crusader armies marched to Jerusalem, sacking several cities on their way. In 1099, they took Jerusalem and massacred the population. As a result of the First Crusade, several small Crusader states were created, notably the Kingdom of Jerusalem.

The Council of Clermont (1095)

Pope Urban II gave a moving description, with many details, of the desolation of Christianity in the East and expounded the atrocious suffering and oppression which Saracens were inflicting on the Christians. In his pious allocution the orator, who was moved almost to tears, equally stressed the way in which Jerusalem and the Holy Places where the Son of God had lived in the flesh, with his most holy companions, were trampled underfoot. He also reduced many of his audience to tears; they shared his deep emotion and his pious compassion for their brothers. With the eloquence of the one who sows the word of truth, he delivered to the assembly a long and very persuasive discourse.

He called on the great men of the West and their companions-at-arms to respect the peace scrupulously in all their dealings, to hang the sign of the saving cross from their right shoulder and to prove themselves the elite and famous soldiers that they were by military valor against the pagans.

There was a prodigious desire among rich and poor, women, monks and clergy, country dwellers and city folk, to go to Jerusalem or to help those who were going. The husbands decided to leave their dear wives at home; however, these, with tears, wanted to follow their husbands on pilgrimage and abandon their children and all their riches.

Lands which hitherto had been costly were now sold cheaply, and arms were bought so that divine vengeance should be exacted on the friends of Allah. Thieves, pirates and other criminals rose from the depths of wickedness; touched by the Spirit of God, they confessed their crimes and, repudiating them, took pail in the crusade to make satisfaction to God for their sins.

However the pope, a prudent man, summoned to war against the enemy of God all those who were capable of bearing arms and, by virtue of the authority which he holds from God, absolved from all their sins all the penitents from the moment that they took up the cross of Christ, mercifully also dispensing them from all the troubles that arise from fasts and other macerations of the flesh.

Ordericus Vitalis, a Norman monk, History of the Church. (1135)

The capture of Jerusalem at the time of the first Crusade, 15 July 1099

On the Friday (15 July) very early in the morning, we launched a general assault on the city without being able to harm it, and we were stupefied and struck with great fear. Then when the hour approached at which Our Lord Jesus Christ consented to suffer for us the torment of the cross, our knights posted on the siege engine fought fiercely among others Duke Godfrey and Count Eustace his brother. At that moment one of our knights, called Lietaud, scaled the wall of the city. As soon as he reached the top all the defenders of the city fled from the walls across the city. Our men pursued them and smiting them with their swords, as far as the temple of Solomon where there was such carnage that our men walked in blood up to their ankles . . .

Having broken through the pagans, our soldiers seized a large number of men and women in the temple, and they killed them or spared them depending on what seemed good to them. A large group of pagans of both sexes to whom Tancred and Gaston of Bearn had given their banners as safe conduct had taken refuge on top of the temple of Solomon.

The crusaders soon ran through the city, seizing gold, silver, horses, and mules, and pillaging the houses, which were bulging with riches. Then, happy and weeping for joy, our men went to adore the sepulcher of our Savior Jesus and paid their debt to him (their vow to go on crusade). The next morning, our men climbed on to the roof of the temple, attacked the Saracens, men and women and, having drawn sword, beheaded them. Some threw themselves down from the temple. When he saw this, Tancred was filled with indignation.

Anonymous History of the First Crusade,
written by a knight who took part in the crusade

Second Crusade

After a period of relative peace, in which Christians and Muslims co-existed in the Holy Land, Bernard of Clairvaux called for a new crusade when the town of Edessa was conquered by the Turks. French and German armies marched to Asia Minor in 1147, but failed to accomplish any major successes, and indeed endangered the survival of the Crusader states with a foolish attack on Damascus. In 1149, both leaders had returned to their countries without any result.

Third Crusade

In 1187, Saladin recaptured Jerusalem. Pope Gregory VIII preached a crusade, which was led by several of Europe's most important leaders: Philip II of France, Richard I of England and Frederick I, Holy Roman Emperor. Frederick drowned in Cilicia in 1190, leaving an unstable alliance between the English and the French. Philip left in 1191 after the Crusaders had recaptured Acre from the Muslims.

The Crusader army headed down the coast of the Mediterranean Sea. They defeated the Muslims near Arsuf and were in sight of Jerusalem. However, an inability for Crusaders to thrive in the locale due to inadequate food and water resulted in an empty victory. Richard left the following year after establishing a truce with Saladin. On Richard's way home his ship was wrecked leading him to Austria. In Austria his enemy Duke Leopold captured him and Richard was held for a king's ransom.

Fourth Crusade

The Fourth Crusade was initiated by Pope Innocent III in 1202, with the intention of invading the Holy Land through Egypt. The Venetians gained control of this crusade and diverted it to Constantinople where they attempted to place a Byzantine exile on the throne. After a series of misunderstandings and outbreaks of violence, the city was sacked in 1204. The popular spirit of the movement was now dead, and the succeeding crusades are to be explained rather as arising from the Papacy's struggle to divert the military energies of the European nations toward Syria.

Albigensian Crusade

The Albigensian Crusade was launched in 1209 to eliminate the "heretical" Cathars of southern France. It was a decades-long struggle that had as much to do with the concerns of northern France to extend its control southwards as it did with heresy. In the end, both the Cathars and the independence of southern France were exterminated.

Children's Crusade

The Children's Crusade is a possibly fictitious or misinterpreted crusade of 1212. The story is that an outburst of the old popular enthusiasm led a gathering of children in France and Germany, which Pope Innocent III interpreted as a reproof from heaven to their unworthy elders. None of the children actually reached the Holy Land, being sold as slaves or dying of hunger during the journey.

Fifth Crusade

By processions, prayers, and preaching, the Church attempted to set another crusade on foot, and the Fourth Council of the Lateran (1215) formulated a plan for the recovery of the Holy Land. A crusading force from Hungary, Austria, and Bavaria achieved a remarkable feat in the capture of Damietta in Egypt in 1219, but under the urgent insistence of the papal legate, Pelagius, they proceeded to a foolhardy attack on Cairo, and an inundation of the Nile compelled them to choose between surrender and destruction.

Innocent III: Summons to A Crusade, 1215

Aspiring with ardent desire to liberate the Holy Land from the hands of the ungodly, by the counsel of prudent men who fully know the circumstances of times and places the holy council approving: we decree that the crusaders shall so prepare themselves that, at the Calends of the June following the next one, all who have arranged to cross by sea shall come together in the kingdom of Sicily; some, as shall be convenient and fitting, at Brindisi, and others at Messina and the places adjoining on both sides where we also have arranged then to be present in person if God wills it, in order that by our counsel and aid the Christian army may be healthfully arranged, about to start with the divine and apostolic benediction.

1. Against the same term, also, those who have decided to go by land shall endeavor to make themselves ready; announcing to us, in the meantime, this determination, so that we may grant them, for counsel and aid, a suitable legate from our side.

2. Priests, moreover, and other clergy who shall be in the Christian army, subordinates as well as prelates, shall diligently insist with prayer and exhortation, reaching the crusaders by word and example alike that they should always have the divine fear and love before their eves, and that they should not say or do anything which might offend the divine majesty. Although at times they may lapse into sin, through true penitence they shall soon arise again; showing humility of heart and body, and observing moderation as well in their living as in their apparel; altogether avoiding dissensions and emulations; rancor and spleen being entirely removed from them. So that, thus armed with spiritual and material weapons, they may fight the more securely against the enemies of the faith; not presuming in their own power, but hoping in the divine virtue. . . .

9. We, also, and our brothers the cardinals of the holy Roman Church, shall pay fully one tenth; and they shall all know that they are all bound to faithfully observe this under penalty of excommunication; so that those who in this matter shall knowingly commit fraud shall incur sentence of excommunication. . . .

13. Moreover we excommunicate and anathematize those false and impious Christians who, against Christ Himself and the Christian people, carry arms, iron, and wood for ships to the Saracens. Those also who sell to them galleys or ships and who, in the pirate ships of the Saracens, keep watch or do the steering, or give them any aid, counsel or favor with regard to their war machines or to anything else, to the harm of the Holy Land; we decree shall be punished with the loss of their own possessions and shall be the slaves of those who capture them. And we command that on Sundays and feast days, throughout all the maritime cities, this sentence shall be renewed; and to such the lap of the church shall not be opened unless they shall send all that they have received from such damnable gains, and as much more of their own as aid to the afore. said Land; so that. they may be punished with a penalty equal to the amount of their original fault.

But if by chance they be insolvent, those guilty of such things shall be otherwise punished; that through their punishment others may be prevented from having the audacity to presume to act similarly. . . .

17. We therefore, trusting in the mercy of almighty God and in the authority of the blessed apostles Peter and Paul, from that power of binding and loosing which God conferred on us, although unworthy, do grant to all who shall undergo this labor in their

own persons and at their own expense, full pardon of their sins of which in their heart they shall have freely repented, and which they shall have confessed; and, at the retribution of the just, we promise them an increase of eternal salvation. To those, moreover, who do not go hither in their own persons, but who only at their own expense, according to their wealth quality, send suitable men; and to those likewise, although at another's expense, go, nevertheless, in own persons: we grant full pardon of their sins. Of this remission, we will and grant that, according to the quality of their aid and the depth of their devotion, all shall be partakers, who shall suitably minister from their goods towards the aid of that same Land, or who shall give timely counsel and aid. To all, moreover, who piously proceed in this work the general synod imparts in common the aid of all its benefits, that it may help them to salvation.

Given at the Lateran, on the nineteenth day before the Calends of January (Dec 14th) in the eighteenth year of our pontificate.

In Ernest F. Henderson, Select Historical Documents of the Middle Ages, (London: George Bell and Sons, 1910), pp. 337–344

Sixth Crusade

In 1228, Emperor Frederick II set sail from Brindisi for Syria, though laden with the papal excommunication. Through diplomacy he achieved unexpected success, Jerusalem, Nazareth, and Bethlehem being delivered to the Crusaders for a period of ten years. This was the first major crusade not initiated by the Papacy, a trend that was to continue for the rest of the century.

Seventh Crusade

The papal interests represented by the Templars brought on a conflict with Egypt in 1243, and in the following year a Khwarezmian force summoned by the latter stormed Jerusalem. Although this provoked no widespread outrage in Europe as the fall of Jerusalem in 1187 had done, Louis IX of France organized a crusade against Egypt from 1248 to 1254, leaving from the newly constructed port of Aigues-Mortes in southern France. It was a failure and Louis spent much of the crusade living at the court of the Crusader kingdom in Acre. In the midst of this crusade was the first Shepherds' Crusade in 1251.

Eighth Crusade

The eighth Crusade was organized by Louis IX in 1270, again sailing from Aigues-Mortes, initially to come to the aid of the remnants of the Crusader states in Syria. However, the crusade was diverted to Tunis, where Louis spent only two months before dying.

Ninth Crusade

The future Edward I of England undertook another expedition in 1271, after having accompanied Louis on the Eighth Crusade. He accomplished very little in Syria and retired the following year after a truce. With the fall of Antioch (1268), Tripoli (1289), and Acre (1291) the last traces of the Christian occupation of Syria disappeared.

Crusades in Baltic and Central Europe

The Crusades in the Baltic Sea area and in Central Europe were efforts by (mostly German) Christians to subjugate and convert the peoples of these areas to Christianity. These Crusades ranged from the 12th century, contemporaneous with the Second Crusade, to the 16th century

Theopedia, The Encyclopedia of Biblical Christianity

Pilgrimages

Pilgrimages were first made to sites connected with the birth, life, crucifixion and resurrection of Jesus. Surviving descriptions of Christian pilgrimages to the Holy Land date from the 4th century, when pilgrimage was encouraged by church fathers like Saint Jerome. Pilgrimages also began to be made to Rome and other sites associated with the Apostles, Saints and Christian martyrs, as well as to places where there have been apparitions of the Virgin Mary. The crusades to the holy land are also considered to be mass armed pilgrimages.

The second largest single pilgrimage in the history of Christendom was to the Funeral of Pope John Paul II after his death on April 2, 2005. An estimated four million people travelled to Vatican City, in addition to the almost three million people already living in Rome, to see the body of Pope John Paul II lie in state.

World Youth Day is a major Catholic Pilgrimage, specifically for people aged 16–35. It is held internationally every 2–3 years. In 2005, young Catholics visited Cologne, Germany. In 1995, the largest gathering of all time was to World Youth Day in Manila, Philippines, where four million people from all over the world attended.

The major Christian pilgrimages are to:

Jerusalem. Site of the crucifixion and resurrection of Jesus.

Rome on roads such as the Via Francigena. Site of the deaths of Saint Peter, Saint Paul and other early martyrs. Location of sacred relics of various saints, relics of the Passion, important churches and headquarters of the Catholic Church.

Constantinople (today Istanbul, Turkey). Former capital of the Byzantine Empire and the see of one of the five ancient Patriarchates and spiritual see of the Eastern Orthodox Church. Hagia Sophia, former cathedral and burial place of many

Ecumenical Patriarchs.

Lourdes, France. Apparition of the Virgin Mary. The second most visited Christian pilgrimage site after Rome.

Santiago de Compostela in Spain on the Way of St James (Spanish: El Camino de Santiago).

The Inquisition

The Inquisition—came into being in 1220–1230 and the death stake became the norm for dissenters. Death was not the only punishment though, people were imprisoned, fined or sent on pilgrimages.

Three kinds of inquisitions came into being:
The secular Inquisition of Frederic II (1224) and Louis IX in (1229);
The Episcopal Inquisition in Toulouse (1229)
The papal inquisition (1229).

Pope Gregory IX made the inquisition a special tribunal responsible directly to him. He enlisted Franciscans and Dominicans. A special procedure for torture was developed. The church took direct responsibility for conducting the punishments in the name of God. It was convinced that its very existence was in danger and took these extreme measures to ensure its continued existence.

Theological justification for the repression of heretics

With regard to heretics, two considerations are to be kept in mind:
1. On their side.
2. On the side of the church.

1. There is the sin, whereby they deserve not only to be separated from the church by excommunication, but also to be shut off from the world by death. For it is a much more serious matter to corrupt faith, through which comes the soul's life, than to forge money, through which temporal life is supported. Hence if forgers of money or other malefactors are straightway justly put to death by secular princes, with much more justice can heretics, immediately upon conviction, be not only excommunicated but also put to death.

2. But on the side of the church there is mercy, with a view to the conversion of them that are in error; and therefore the church does not straightway condemn, but after a first and second admonition, as the apostle tells us. After that, if he be found still stubborn, the church gives up hope of his conversion and takes thought for the safety of others, by

separating him from the church by sentence of excommunication, and further, leaves him to the secular court, to be exterminated from the world by death.

Thomas Aquinas, Summa Theologica, IIa, IIae, 11, art.3.

The Waldensians

According to a description of them dating from 1179, the Waldensians "go about in twos, barefoot, in woolen garments, owning nothing, holding all things in common like the apostles."

The Waldensians, Waldenses or Vaudois are a Christian denomination believing in poverty and austerity, founded around 1173, promoting true poverty, public preaching and the literal interpretation of the scriptures. Declared heretical, the movement was brutally persecuted during the 12th and 13th centuries and nearly totally destroyed, but the Waldensian Church survives to this day.

Wikipedia

It is little wonder that the Waldensians became the target of the Inquisition with accusations against them like those found in *Reinerius Saccho, Of the Sects of the Modern Heretics 1254*

First, they say that the Romish Church, is not the Church of Jesus Christ, but a church of malignants and that it apostatized under Sylvester, when the poison of temporalities was infused into the h. And they say, that they are the church of Christ, because they observe both in word, and deed, the doctrine of Christ, of the Gospel, and of the Apostles.

Their second error is that all vices and sins are in the church, and that they alone live righteously.

That scarcely anyone in the church, but themselves, preserves the evangelical doctrine.

That they are the true poor in spirit, and suffer persecution for righteousness and faith.

That they are the Church of Jesus Christ.

That the Church of Rome is the Harlot in the Apocalypse, on account of its superfluous decoration which the Eastern Church does not regard.

That they despise all the statutes of the Church, because they are heavy and numerous.

That the Pope is the head of all errors.

That the Prelates are Scribes; and the Monks, Pharisees.

That the Pope and all Bishops, are homicides on account of wars.

That we are not to obey Prelates; but only God.

That no one is greater than another in the church.

That no one ought to bow the knee before a priest.

That tithes are not to be given, because first fruits were not given to the church.

That the clergy ought not to have possessions.

That it is a bad thing to found and endow churches and monasteries.

Also, they condemn the sacrament of Marriage.

The sacrament of Unction, they reprobate, because it is only given to the rich; and because several priests are required for it-also, they say that the sacrament of Orders is nothing-also, they say that every good layman is a priest, as the Apostles were laymen-also, that the prayer of an evil priest does not profit-also, they deride the clerical tonsure.

Also, they say that the doctrine of Christ and the Apostles is sufficient for salvation without the statutes of the church-that the tradition of the church is the tradition of the Pharisees; and that there is more made of the transgression of a human tradition than of a divine law.

Reinerius Saccho, Of the Sects of Modern Heretics (1254)

Papal Great Schism: 1378–1414

Introduction

There are two events which are both referred to as the "Great Schism".

One is the separation of the Roman Catholic Church and the Eastern Orthodoxy.

The second one is the presence of three popes in the 14th century.

Two popes

The papal Great Schism is also called the "Western Schism" and the "Great Schism". It started immediately after the death of Pope Gregory XI. The Cardinals in Rome elected Urban VI to replace him, but another council in France elected a different man, who took the name Clement VII and who took up residence in Avignon. For several decades, the competing colleges elected competing Popes. Since then, the Popes elected in Rome have been deemed the "properly-elected" ones, the Avignon-elected popes are remembered as "anti-popes."

Three popes

At one point (1409) the issue became even more clouded, as a council held at Pisa elected a third Pope, when the Avignon-elected anti-pope at that time (Benedict XIII) had turned out to be corrupt.

To resolve this situation the Avignon- and Pisa-elected anti-popes abdicated and the remaining Pope, Benedict IX, convened a council to decide the issue.

The Council of Constance in 1414 resolved the controversy by dismantling the last vestiges of the Avignon papacy. By 1417, the Papal Schism ended, with the election of Pope Martin V.

The Inquisition of Spain

Introduction

The Inquisition in Spain is set up by Ferdinand and Isabella in 1479 with Pope Sixtus IV approval. Their goal was to combat Jews and Muslims who had converted to Catholicism then apostatized, as well as heretics. Under the grand inquisitor Torquemada Jews are given 3 months to become Christians or leave the country. Roughly 2000 people were burned at the stake during his tenure.

Torture

To the modern mind the judicial use of torture, as a means of ascertaining truth, is so repellant and illogical that we are apt to forget that it has, from the most ancient times, been practiced by nearly all civilized nations. With us the device of the jury has relieved the judge of the responsibility resting upon him in other systems of jurisprudence. That responsibility had to be met; a decision had to be reached, even in the most doubtful cases and, where evidence was defective and conflicting, the use of torture as an expedient to obtain a confession, or, by its endurance, to indicate innocence, has seemed, until modern times, after the disuse of compurgation and the judgments of God, to be the only means of relieving the judicial conscience.

It was admitted to be dangerous and fallacious, to be employed only with circumspection, but there was nothing to take its place.

That it should be used by the Inquisition was a matter of course, for the crime of heresy was often one peculiarly difficult to prove; confession was sought in all cases and, from the middle of the thirteenth century, the habitual employment of torture by the Holy Office had been the most efficient factor in spreading its use throughout Christendom, at the expense of the obsolescent Barbarian customs.

Harsher Penalties

The scourge

Scourging was a favorite penalty which was lavishly and often mercilessly employed. In the Saragossa auto of June 6, 1585, out of a total of seventy-nine penitents, twenty-two were scourged; in that of Valencia, in 1607, of forty-seven penitents, twenty-four received the lash.

This, however, exceeds the average. The Toledo reports, from 1575 to 1610, present a hundred and thirty-three cases of scourging which, allowing for a break in the record, give about four per annum. On the other hand, a collection of autos de fe celebrated between 1721 and 1727, embracing in all nine hundred and sixty-two cases, affords two hundred and ninety-seven sentences of scourging, or about thirty per cent. When we recall that, in the list of officials reported by Murcia, in 1746, there figures Joseph García Bentura as *notario de acotaciones*—a notary of scourgings—to keep record of the stripes, with a salary of about 2500 *reales*, we realize how prominent a feature it was in inquisitorial penology. The brutalizing effect on the populace of these wholesale exhibitions of flogging, especially of women, can readily be estimated.

The stake

The condemnation of a human being to a death by fire, as the penalty of spiritual error, is so abhorrent to the moral sense and so oppugnant to the teachings of Christ, that modern apologists have naturally sought to relieve the Church from responsibility for such atrocity. On the surface a tolerably plausible argument can be made. The ministers of religion, the spiritual courts, the Inquisition itself rendered no judgments of blood. Any ecclesiastic who might be concerned in them incurred "irregularity" requiring a dispensation before he could validly perform his functions or obtain preferment. The execution of heretics was a matter purely of secular law and burning them alive is not prescribed in canon.

The Inquisition, through whose agency heretics were consigned to the stake, did not itself condemn them to it, but merely pronounced them to be heretics of whose conversion no hope was entertained.

The *Auto De Fe*

The Act of Faith—the *Auto de Fe*—was the name by which the Spanish Holy Office dignified the Sermo of the Old Inquisition. In its full development it was an elaborate public solemnity, carefully devised to inspire awe for the mysterious authority of the Inquisition, and to impress the population with a wholesome abhorrence of heresy, by representing in so far as it could the tremendous drama of the Day of Judgment.

At the height of its power the Inquisition spared no labor or expense to lend impressiveness to the *auto publico* general, as a demonstration of its authority and of the success with which it performed its functions. . . .

The procession starts with the soldiers of the Zarza at its head; then the cross of the parish church, shrouded in black, with an acolyte who tolls a bell mournfully at intervals. Then come the penitents, one by one, each with a familiar on either side; first are the impostors, then personators of officials of the Inquisition, followed in order by blasphemers, bigamists, Judaizers, Protestants, the effigies and chests of bones and finally those to be relaxed, each with two frailes. Mounted officials follow, then familiars in pairs, the standard of the Inquisition, and finally the inquisitors bring up the rear. Thus the procession moves through the designated streets, filled with a densely packed crowd, kept off by railings, to the plaza, where the culprits are seated in the same order, the lightest offenders on the lowest benches. . . .

Then the sentences are read from the alternate pulpits, the alguazil mayor producing each culprit to hear his sentence. . . .

The place of burning—the *quemadero* or *brasero*—as a rule was outside of the city. In an auto held in Madrid in 1632 the city had constructed the brasero beyond the Puerta de Alcalá; as there were seven to be burnt, it was made fifty feet square, and had the requisite stakes with garrotes. The confusion and crowd were great, and so also was the fire, which lasted until eleven o'clock at night, by which time the bodies were reduced to ashes, so that the memory of the impious might vanish from the earth. The scattering of the ashes over the fields, or into running water, was a prescription of old standing, to prevent disciples of heresiarchs from preserving fragments to be venerated as relics.

Henry Charles Lea, A History of the Inquisition of Spain, 1905

PEOPLE

Gregory the Great (540–604)
Alcuin (735–804)
Anselm (1033–1109)
The Ontological Argument
Francis of Assisi (1182–1226
Thomas Aquinas (1225–1274)
Summa Theologica
John Wycliffe (1320–1384)
John Huss (1369–1415)

Gregory the Great

Dates
AD 540–604

Famous for being
Pope, Teacher, Doctor of the Church

Important writings
Sermons and Papal *Register* of Letters

One of his quotations
"All that which our blessed Savior wrought in his mortal body, he did it for our example and instruction, to the end that, following his steps, according to our poor ability, we might without offense pass over this present life."

Introduction

Pope Gregory I the Great (590–604), a Benedictine, was the first monk elected pope. He sent St. Augustine of Canterbury and a company of monks to evangelize England, and other missionaries to France, Spain, and Africa.

Gregory also collected the melodies and plain chant now known as Gregorian Chants. Organs begin to be used in churches. Church bells are used to call people to worship and to give the hours to the monks in the monasteries.

As one of the four great Doctors of the Latin Church (with Augustine, Ambrose and Jerome) Gregory wrote seminal works on the Mass and Office. He gave the Mass much of the shape it has today.

1. From birth to 574

Gregory loved to meditate on the Scriptures and to listen attentively to the conversations of his elders, so that he was "devoted to God from his youth up". His rank and prospects pointed him out naturally for a public career, and he doubtless held some of the subordinate offices wherein a young patrician embarked on public life. That he acquitted himself well in these appears certain, since we find him about the year 573, when little more than thirty years old, filling the important office of prefect of the city of Rome. But, after long prayer and inward struggle that Gregory decided to abandon everything and become a monk. This event took place most probably in 574. His decision once taken, he devoted himself to the work and austerities of his new life with all the natural energy of his character. He took the cowl, so that "he who had been wont to go about the city clad in the trabea and aglow with silk and jewels, now clad in a worthless garment served the altar of the Lord" (Greg. Tur., X, i).

2. As monk and abbot (c. 574–590)

. . . In the year 586 he was recalled to Rome, and with the greatest joy returned to St. Andrew's, of which he became abbot soon afterwards. The monastery grew famous under his energetic rule, producing many monks who won renown later, and many vivid pictures of this period may be found in the "Dialogues". Gregory gave much of his time to lecturing on the Holy Scriptures.

3. As pope (590–604)

Fourteen years of life remained to Gregory, and into these he crowded work enough to have exhausted the energies of a lifetime. What makes his achievement more wonderful is his constant ill-health. He suffered almost continually from indigestion and, at intervals, from attacks of slow fever, while for the last half of his pontificate he was a martyr to gout. In spite of these infirmities, which increased steadily, his biographer, Paul the Deacon, tells us "he never rested" (Vita, XV).

(1) Life and Work in Rome

As pope Gregory still lived with monastic simplicity. One of his first acts was to banish all the lay attendants, pages, etc., from the Lateran palace, and substitute clerics in their place. There was now no *magister militum* living in Rome, so the control even of military matters fell to the pope.

Gregory's sermons, which drew immense crowds, are mostly simple, popular expositions of Scripture. Chiefly remarkable is the preacher's mastery of the Bible, which he quotes unceasingly, and his regular use of anecdote to illustrate the point in hand, in which respect he paves the way for the popular preachers of the Middle Ages. In July, 595, Gregory held his first synod in St. Peter's, which consisted almost wholly of the bishops of the suburbicarian sees and the priests of the Roman titular churches. Six decrees dealing with ecclesiastical discipline were passed, some of them merely confirming changes already made by the pope on his own authority.

As bishop, he is the trustee of God and St. Peter, and his agents must show that they realize this by their conduct. Consequently, under his able management the estates of the Church increased steadily in value, the tenants were contented, and the revenues paid in with unprecedented regularity. The only fault ever laid at his door in this matter is that, by his boundless charities, he emptied his treasury. But this, if a fault at all, was a natural consequence of his view that he was the administrator of the property of the poor, for whom he could never do enough.

(2) Relations with the Lombards

Two points stand out for special notice in Gregory's dealings with the Lombards: first, his determination that, in spite of the apathy of the imperial authorities, Rome should not pass into the hands of some half-civilized Lombard duke and so sink into insignificance and decay; second, his independent action in appointing governors to cities, providing munitions of war, giving instructions to generals, sending ambassadors to the Lombard king, and even negotiating a peace without the exarch's aid. Whatever the theory may have been, there is no doubt about the fact that, besides his spiritual jurisdiction, Gregory actually exercised no small amount of temporal power.

(3) *Missionary Work*

Gregory's zeal for the conversion of the heathen, it must be said that he lost no opportunity for the exercise of his missionary zeal, making every effort to root out paganism in Gaul, Donatism in Africa, and the Schism of the Three Chapters in North Italy and Istria. In his treatment of heretics, schismatics, and pagans his method was to try every means—persuasions, exhortations, threats—before resorting to force; but, if gentler treatment failed, he had no hesitation in accordance with the ideas of his age, in resorting to compulsion, and invoking the aid of the secular arm therein.

(4) Gregory and Monasticism

Although the first monk to become pope, Gregory was in no sense an original contributor to monastic ideals or practice. He took monasticism as he found it established by St. Benedict, and his efforts and influence were given to strengthening and enforcing the prescriptions of that greatest of monastic legislators. . . .

(65) Death

The last years of Gregory's life were filled with every kind of suffering. His mind, naturally serious, was filled with despondent forebodings, and his continued bodily pains were increased and intensified. His "sole consolation was the hope that death would come quickly" (Epp., XIII, xxvi). The end came on 12 March, 604, and on the same day his body was laid to rest in front of the sacristy in the portico of St. Peter's Basilica.

Conclusion

In the history of dogmatic development he is important as summing up the teaching of the earlier Fathers and consolidating it into a harmonious whole, rather than as introducing new developments, new methods, new solutions of difficult questions. It was precisely because of this that his writings became to a great extent the compendium theologiae or textbook of the Middle Ages, a position for which his work in popularizing his great predecessors fitted him well. Achievements so varied have won for Gregory the title of "the Great".

G. Roger Huddleston, The Catholic Encyclopedia, Volume VI. Published 1909

Angles or angels?

In those days slavery was common throughout all the known world, and, although the gospel had wrought a great improvement in the treatment of slaves, by making the masters feel that they and their slaves were brethren in Christ, it yet had not forbidden slavery.

Gregory, then, while he was yet a monk, went one day into the market at Rome, just after the arrival of some merchants with a large cargo of slaves for sale. Some of these poor creatures, perhaps, had been taken in war; others had probably been sold by their own parents for the sake of the price which they fetched; for we are told that this shocking practice was not uncommon among some of the ruder nations. As Gregory looked at them, his eyes fell on some boys with whose appearance he was greatly struck. Their skin was fair, unlike the dark complexions of the Italians and other southern nations whom he had been used to see, their features were beautiful, and they had long light flowing hair.

He asked the merchants from what land these boys had been brought. "From Britain," they said; and they told him that the bright complexion which he admired so much was common among the people of that island. Perhaps Gregory had never thought of Britain before. It was nearly two hundred years since the Roman troops had been withdrawn from it, and its habitants had been left to themselves. And since that time the pagan Saxons had overrun it; the Romans had lost the countries which lay between them and it; and Britain had quite disappeared from their knowledge. Gregory, therefore, was obliged to ask whether the people were Christians or heathens, and he was told that they were still heathens.

The good monk sighed deeply. "Alas, and woe!" said he, "that people with such faces of light should belong to the author of darkness, and that so goodly an outward favor should be void of inward grace."

He asked what was the name of their nation, and was told that they were "Angles".

"It is well," he said, "for they have angels' faces, and such as they ought to be joint-heirs with the angels in heaven.—What is the name of the province from which they come?"

He was told that it was Deira (a Saxon kingdom, which stretched along the eastern side of Britain, from the Humber to the Tyne). The name of Deira sounded to Gregory's ears like two Latin words, which mean "from wrath." "Well, again," he said, "they are delivered from the wrath of God, and are called to the mercy of Christ.—What is the name of the king of that country?"

"Aella," was the answer.

"Alleluiah!" ("Praise to God!") exclaimed Gregory, "the praises of God their maker ought to be sung in that kingdom."

He went at once to the pope, and asked leave to go as a missionary to the heathens of Britain. But, although the pope consented, the people of Rome were so much attached to Gregory that they would not allow him to set out, and he was obliged to give up the plan. Yet he did not forget the heathens of Britain, and when he became pope, although he could not himself go to them, he was able to send others for the work of their conversion.

In the year 596 Gregory sent off a party of monks as missionaries to the English Saxons. The head of them was Augustine, who had been provost of the monastery to which the pope himself had formerly belonged.

J. C. Robertson, Sketches of Church History, Chapter 31

Alcuin

Dates
AD 735–804

Famous for being
Deacon, Scholar, and Abbot of Tours

Important achievement
Invention of cursive script

One of his quotations
"*Vox Populi, Vox Dei.*" "The voice of the people is the voice of God."

Flaccus Albinus, or, as he is commonly called in the Old English form, Alcuin ("friend of the temple"), the ecclesiastical prime minister of Charlemagne, was born in Yorkshire about 735. He sprang from a noble Northumbrian family, the one to which Willibrord, apostle of the Frisians, belonged, and inherited considerable property, including the income of a monastic society on the Yorkshire coast.

At tender age he was taken to the famous cathedral school at York, and there was educated by his loving and admiring friends, Egbert, archbishop of York (732–766) and founder of the school, and Ethelbert, its master. With the latter he made several literary journeys on the continent, once as far as Rome, and each time returned laden with MS. treasures, secured, by a liberal expenditure of money, from different monasteries. Thus they greatly enlarged the library which Egbert had founded.

In 766 Ethelbert succeeded Egbert in the archbishopric of York, and appointed Alcuin, who had previously been a teacher, master of the cathedral school, ordained him a deacon, Feb. 2, 767, and made him one of the secular canons of York Minster. In 767 he had Liudger for a pupil. Some time between the latter year and 780, Ethelbert sent him to Italy on a commission to Charlemagne, whom he met, probably at Pavia. In 780 Ethelbert retired from his see and gave over to Alcuin the care of the library, which now was without a rival in England. Alcuin gives a catalogue of it, thus throwing welcome light upon the state of learning at the time.

In 780 Alcuin again visited Rome to fetch the pallium for Eanbald, Ethelbert's successor. On his return he met Charlemagne at Parma (Easter, 781), and was invited by him to become master of the School of the Palace. This school was designed for noble youth, was attached to the court, and held whenever the court was. Charlemagne and his family and courtiers frequently attended its sessions, although they could not be said to be regular scholars. The invitation to teach this school was a striking recognition of the learning and ability of Alcuin, and as he perceived the possibilities of the future thus unexpectedly opened to him he accepted it, although the step involved a virtual abnegation of his just claim upon the archiepiscopate of York. In the next year (782), having received the necessary permission to go from his king and archbishop, he began his work. The providential design in this event is unmistakable. Just at the time when the dissensions of the English kings practically put a stop to educational advance in England, Alcuin, the greatest teacher of the day, was transferred to the continent in order that under the fostering and stimulating care of Charlemagne he might rescue it from the bondage of ignorance. But the effort taxed his strength. Charlemagne, although he attended his instruction and styles him "his dear teacher," at the same time abused his industry and patience, and laid many very heavy burdens upon him.

Alcuin had not only to teach the Palatine school, which necessitated his moving about with the migratory court to the serious interruption of his studies, but to prepare and revise books for educational and ecclesiastical uses, and in general to superintend the grand reformatory schemes of Charlemagne. How admirably he fulfilled his multifarious duties, history attests. The famous capitulary of 787 which Charlemagne issued and which did so much to advance learning, was of his composition. The Caroline books, which were quite as remarkable in the sphere of church life, were his work, at least in large measure. For his pecuniary support and as a mark of esteem Charlemagne gave him the monasteries of St. Lupus at Troyes and Bethlehem at Ferrières, and the cell of St. Judecus on the coast of Picardy (St. Josse sur mer). But the care of these only added to his burdens. In 789 he went to England on commission from Charlemagne to King Offa of Mercia, and apparently desired to remain there.

Thence in 792 he sent in the name of the English bishops a refutation of image-worship. But in 793 Charlemagne summoned him to his side to defend the church against the heresy of Adoptionism and image-worship, and he came. In 794 he took a prominent part, although simply a deacon, in the council of Frankfort, which spoke out so strongly against both, and in 799, at the council of Aachen, he had a six days' debate with Felix, the leader of the Adoptionists, which resulted in the latter's recantation. In his negotiations with the Adoptionists he had the invaluable aid of the indefatigable monk, Benedict, of Nursia. In 796, Charlemagne gave him in addition to the monasteries already mentioned that of St. Martin at Tours and in 800 those of Cormery and Flavigny. The monastery of Tours owned twenty thousand serfs and its revenue was regal. To it Alcuin retired, although he would have preferred to go to Fulda.

There he did good work in reforming the monks, regulating the school and enlarging the library. His most famous pupil during this period of his life was Rabanus Maurus. In the year of his death he established a hospice at Duodecim Pontes near Troyes; and just prior to this event he gave over the monastery of Tours to his pupil Fredegis, and that of Ferrières to another pupil, Sigulf. It is remarkable that he died upon the anniversary on which he had desired to die, the Festival of Pentecost, May 19, 804.

He was buried in the church of St. Martin, although in his humility he had requested to be buried outside of it. One of his important services to religion was his revision of the Vulgate (about 802) by order of Charlemagne, on the basis of old and correct manuscripts, for he probably knew little Greek and no Hebrew. This preserved a good Vulgate text for some time.

Alcuin was of a gentle disposition, willing, patient and humble, and an unwearied student. He had amassed all the treasures of learning then accessible. He led his age, yet did not transcend it, as Scotus Erigena did his. He was not a deep thinker, rather he brought out from his memory the thoughts of others. He was also mechanical in his methods. Yet he was more than a great scholar and teacher, he was a leader in church affairs, not only on the continent, but, as his letters show, also in England. Charlemagne consulted him continually, and would have done better had he more frequently followed his advice. Particularly is this true respecting missions. Alcuin saw with regret that force had been applied to induce the

Saxons to submit to baptism. He warned Charlemagne that the result would be disastrous. True Christians can not be made by violence, but by plain preaching of the gospel in the spirit of love. He would have the gospel precepts gradually unfolded to the pagan Saxons, and then as they grew in knowledge would require from them stricter compliance.

Alcuin gave similar council in regard to the Huns. His opinions upon other practical points are worthy of mention. Thus, he objected to the employment of bishops in military affairs, to capital punishment, to the giving up of persons who had taken refuge in a church, and to priests following a secular calling. He was zealous for the revival of preaching and for the study of the Bible. On the other hand he placed a low estimate upon pilgrimages, and preferred that the money so spent should be given to the poor.

Samuel M. Jackson, Biographical Sketches of Ecclesiastical Writers, 1882

Anselm

Dates

1033–1109

Famous for being

Monk, Archbishop of Canterbury, Theologian, "Father of Scholasticism", Doctor of the Church

Important writings

Proslogium

Why Did God Become Man?

One of his quotations

"For I do not seek to understand that I may believe, but I believe in order to understand. For this I believe—that unless I believe, I should not understand."

Anselm is the most important Christian theologian in the West between Augustine and Thomas Aquinas. His two great accomplishments are his *Proslogium* (in which he undertakes to show that Reason requires that men should believe in God), and his Cur Deus Homo? (in which he undertakes to show that Divine Love responding to human rebelliousness requires that God should become a man).

He was born in Italy about 1033, and in 1060 he entered the monastery of Bec in Normandy to study under Stephen Lanfranc, whom he succeeded in office, first as prior of Bec, and later as Archbishop of Canterbury.

In 1078 he was elected abbot of Bec. The previous year, he completed a work called the Monologium, in which he argues for the existence of God from the existence of degrees of perfection (Aquinas's Fourth Way is a variation of this argument).

In 1087, while still at Bec, he produced his *Proslogium*, an outline of his "ontological argument" for the existence of God. Taking as his text the opening of Psalm 14 ("The fool hath said in his heart: There is no God."), Anselm undertakes to show that the fool is contradicting himself—that the concept of God is unique in that anyone who understands what is meant by the question, "Does God exist?" will see that the answer must be "Yes." . . .

King William II of England had no fondness for the Church, and at the death of Lanfranc he kept the See of Canterbury vacant until he was gravely ill, whereon he promised to let Anselm be made Archbishop. Anselm was made Archbishop (4 December 1093), the King recovered, and the two began to dispute the extent of the King's right to intervene in Church matters. Anselm went into exile in 1097 and remained in Italy for three years until the King died in 1100.

From the Preface to the *Proslogion*:

I have written the little work that follows . . . in the role of one who strives to raise his mind to the contemplation of God and one who seeks to understand what he believes.

I acknowledge, Lord, and I give thanks that you have created your image in me, so that I may remember you, think of you, love you. But this image is so obliterated and worn away by wickedness, it is so obscured by the smoke of sins, that it cannot do what it was created to do, unless you renew and reform it. I am not attempting, O Lord, to penetrate your loftiness, for I cannot begin to match my understanding with it, but I desire in some measure to understand your truth, which my heart believes and loves. For I do not seek to understand in order that I may believe, but I believe in order to understand. For this too I believe, that "unless I believe, I shall not understand." (Isa. 7:9)

A Song of Anselm

Jesus, as a mother you gather your people to you:
You are gentle with us as a mother with her children;
Often you weep over our sins and our pride:
tenderly you draw us from hatred and judgment.
You comfort us in sorrow and bind up our wounds:
in sickness you nurse us,
and with pure milk you feed us.
Jesus, by your dying we are born to new life:
by your anguish and labor we come forth in joy.
Despair turns to hope through your sweet goodness:
through your gentleness we find comfort in fear.
Your warmth gives life to the dead:

your touch makes sinners righteous.
Lord Jesus, in your mercy heal us:
in your love and tenderness remake us.
In your compassion bring grace and forgiveness:
for the beauty of heaven may your love prepare us.

James E. Kiefer

The Ontological Argument

The ontological argument for the existence of God was first proposed by Anselm in Chapter 2 of his *Proslogion*. While Anselm did not propose an ontological system, he was very much concerned with the nature of being. He argued that there are necessary beings – things that cannot not exist – and contingent beings – things that may exist but whose existence is not necessary.

Anselm presents the ontological argument as part of a prayer directed to God. He starts with a definition of God, or a necessary assumption about the nature of God.

"Now we believe that [the Lord] is something than which nothing greater can be imagined."

Then Anselm asks: does God exist?

"Then is there no such nature, since the fool has said in his heart: God is not?"

To answer this, first he tries to show that God exist "in the understanding":

"But certainly this same fool, when he hears this very thing that I am saying – something than which nothing greater can be imagined – understands what he hears; and what he understands is in his understanding, even if he does not understand that it is. For it is one thing for a thing to be in the understanding and another to understand that a thing is."

Anselm goes on to justify his assumption, using the analogy of a painter:

"For when a painter imagines beforehand what he is going to make, he has in his understanding what he has not yet made but he does not yet understand that it is. But when he has already painted it, he both has in his understanding what he has already painted and understands that it is.

"Therefore even the fool is bound to agree that there is at least in the understanding something than which nothing greater can be imagined, because when he hears this he understands it, and whatever is understood is in the understanding."

Now Anselm introduces another assumption.

"And certainly that than which a greater cannot be imagined cannot be in the understanding alone. For if it is at least in the understanding alone, it can be imagined to be in reality too, which is greater."

"Therefore if that than which a greater cannot be imagined is in the understanding alone, that very thing than which a greater cannot be imagined is something than which a greater can be imagined. But certainly this cannot be."

Anselm has thus found a contradiction, and from that contradiction, he draws his conclusion:

"There exists, therefore, beyond doubt something than which a greater cannot be imagined, both in the understanding and in reality."

The following seven steps follow Anselm's line of reasoning

1. God is the entity than which no greater entity can be conceived.
2. The concept of God exists in human understanding.
3. God does not exist in reality (assumed in order to refute).
4. The concept of God existing in reality exists in human understanding.
5. If an entity exists in reality and in human understanding, this entity is greater than it would have been if it existed only in human understanding (a statement of existence as a perfection).
6. From 1, 2, 3, 4, and 5 An entity can be conceived which is greater than God, the entity than which no greater entity can be conceived (logical self-contradiction).
7. Assumption 3 is wrong, therefore God exists in reality (assuming 1, 2, 4, and 5 are accepted as true).

Francis of Assisi

Dates

1182–1226

Famous for being

Friar

Founded the Franciscan Order or "Friars Minor"

Important writings

Canticle to Brother Sun

One of his quotations

"Preach the Gospel at all times and when necessary use words."

Introduction

Francesco Bernardone was born in Assisi in 1181. His father Pietro was a successful merchant and hoped his son would succeed him in that role. However, in 1205 Francis had returned from an abortive attempt to win military glory in southern Italy, Francis has been aware that something important is going on within him.

Now perfectly changed in heart and soon to be changed in body, Francis was strolling one day near the old church of St. Damian, which was nearly destroyed and abandoned by all. The spirit led him to enter the church and pray. Devoutly lying prostrate before the crucifix, stirred by unusual visitations, he found he was different than when he had entered.

While he was in this affected state, something absolutely unheard-of occurred. The crucifix moved its lips and began to speak. "Francis," it said, calling him by name, "go and repair my house, which, as you see, is completely destroyed."

Francis was stupefied and nearly deranged by this speech. He prepared to obey, surrendering himself completely to the project. From then on compassion for the crucified one was imprinted in his holy soul and, one may devoutly suspect, the stigmata of the holy passion were deeply imprinted in his heart, though not yet in his flesh.

Behold, the blessed servant of the most high was so disposed and strengthened by the Holy Spirit that the time had come for him to follow the blessed impulse of his soul, progressing to higher things and trampling worldly interests underfoot. It was unwise to delay any longer, for a deadly illness was spreading everywhere. It seized the joints and, if the physician delayed even for a bit, it shut off the vital spirit and snatched away life.

Francis rose, fortifying himself with the sign of the cross, and when his horse was ready he mounted. Taking some fine cloth with him, he rode to the city of Foligno. There, being a successful merchant, he sold all his cloth as usual and even left behind the horse he was riding, having received a good price for it. Then, having left all his baggage behind, he started back, wondering as he traveled what he should do with the money.

Soon, converted to God's work in a marvelous way, he felt it would be burdensome to carry the money for even an hour and, treating it as if it were sand, he decided to get rid of it as fast as possible. As he approached the city of Assisi, he passed the church built in honor of St. Damian long ago, but now about to collapse with age.

When the new soldier of Christ arrived at the church, he was stirred with pity for its condition and entered with fear and reverence. Finding a poor priest inside, Francis kissed his sacred hands and offered him the money he was carrying, telling the priest what he intended to do. The priest was stunned. Astonished by such an incredibly sudden conversion, he refused to believe what he heard. Since he thought he was being deceived, he refused to keep the money that had been offered him. He had seen Francis just the other day, so to speak, living riotously among his relations and acquaintances, acting even more stupidly than the rest.

Francis, stubbornly insistent, tried to prove he was sincere. He begged the priest to let him stay there for the sake of the Lord. Finally the priest agreed that he could stay but, fearing Francis' parents, he would not accept the money. Francis, genuinely contemptuous of money, threw it on a windowsill, treating it as if it were dust. He wanted to possess wisdom, which is better than gold, and prudence, which is more precious than silver.

[Francis' father locked his son up at home, but Francis' mother let him out while Pietro was away on a business trip. Finally, despairing of private solutions, early in 1206 Pietro brought his son before the bishop of Assisi.]

When he had been led before the bishop, Francis neither delayed nor explained himself, but simply stripped off his clothes and threw them aside, giving them back to his father. He did not even keep his trousers, but stood there in front of everyone completely naked. The bishop, sensing his intention and admiring his constancy, rose and wrapped his arms around Francis, covering him with his own robe. He saw clearly that Francis was divinely inspired and that his action contained a mystery. Thus he became Francis' helper, cherishing and comforting him.

[Celano now portrays Francis traveling around Umbria, living among lepers, and rebuilding the church of St. Damian.]

Meanwhile this holy man, having changed his attire and repaired the aforesaid church, went to another place near Assisi and began to rebuild a certain dilapidated and nearly ruined church, ceasing only when the task was finished. Then he went to still another place called the Portiuncula, the site of a church. This church, built long ago, was now deserted and cared for by no one. When the holy man of God saw how destroyed the church was, he was moved with pity and began to spend a great deal of time there. It was in the third year of his conversion that he began to repair this church. At that time he wore a sort of hermit's attire, a leather belt around his waist and a staff in his hands, and he went about wearing shoes.

One day, however, when the gospel story of Christ sending his disciples to preach was read in the church, the holy man of God was present and more or less understood the words of the gospel. After mass he humbly asked the priest to explain the gospel to him. He heard that Christ's disciples were supposed to possess neither gold, nor silver, nor money; were to have neither bread nor staff; were to have neither shoes nor two tunics; but were to preach the kingdom of God and penance. When the priest had finished, Francis, rejoicing in the spirit of God, said, "This is what I want! This is what I'm looking for! This is what I want to do from the bottom of my heart!"

Thus the holy father, overflowing with joy, hurried to fulfill those healing words, nor did he suffer any delay in carrying out what he had heard. He took off his shoes, tossed away his staff, was satisfied with a single tunic, and exchanged his leather belt for a cord. He made himself a tunic that looked like the cross so that he could beat off the temptations of the devil. It was rough in order to crucify the vices and sins of the flesh. It was poor and mean so that the world would not covet it. With the greatest diligence and reverence he tried to do everything else that he had heard, for he was not a deaf hearer of the gospel but, laudably committing all that he had heard to memory, he diligently attempted to fulfill them to the letter. . . .

Seeing that the Lord God daily increased their number, Francis wrote simply and in a few words a form of life and rule for himself and his brothers both present and to come. It mainly used the words of the gospel, for the perfection of which alone he yearned. Nevertheless, he did insert a few other things necessary for the pursuit of a holy life.

He came to Rome with all his brothers, hoping that Pope Innocent III would confirm what he had written. At that time the venerable bishop of Assisi, Guido, who honored Francis and the brothers and prized them with a special love, also happened to be in Rome. When he saw Francis and his brothers there and did not know the cause, he was very upset, since he feared they were planning to desert their native city, in which God was now doing great things through his servants. He was pleased to have such men in his diocese and relied greatly on their life and manners. Having heard the cause of their visit and understood their plan, he was relieved and promised to give them advice and aid.

Saint Francis also went to the bishop of Sabina, John of Saint Paul, one of the great members of the Roman court who seemed to despise earthly things and love heavenly ones. Receiving Francis with kindness and love, the bishop praised him highly for his request and intent ion.

Since he was a prudent and discreet man, the bishop began to question Francis about many things and tried to convince him that he should try the life of a monk or hermit. Saint Francis humbly refused his advice as well as he could, not because he despised what the bishop suggested but because, impelled by a higher desire, he devoutly wished for something else. The lord bishop marveled at his fervor and, fearing that he might eventually slip back from such high intentions, tried to show him a path that would be easier to follow. Finally, won over by Francis' constancy, the bishop agreed to his petition and attempted to further his plan before the pope.

At that time the church was led by Innocent III, who was famous, very learned, gifted in speech, and burning with zeal for what ever would further the cause of the Christian faith. When he had discovered what these men of God wanted and thought the matter over, he assented to their request and did what had to be done. Exhorting and admonishing them about m any things, he blessed Saint Francis and his brothers, saying to them, "Go with the Lord, brothers, and preach penance to all as the Lord will inspire you. Then, when the Lord increases you in number and in grace, return joyously to me. At that time I will concede more to you and commit greater things to you more confidently."

Like other holy men of the time, Francis and his followers practiced mortification of the flesh, not because the body was considered evil—it, too, was created by God—but because in a fallen world it could distract one from higher pursuits. In Francis' case, such mortification was related not only to the cultivation of spiritual experience, or what was known as the contemplative life, but also to the Franciscan emphasis on humility and the equally Franciscan desire to imitate Christ.

The virtue of patience so enfolded them that they sought to be where they could suffer bodily persecution rather than where, their sanctity being known and praised, they might be exalted by the world. Many times when they were insulted, ridiculed, stripped naked, beaten, bound or imprisoned, they trusted in no one's patronage but rather bore all so manfully that only praise and thanksgiving echoed in their mouths. Scarcely or never did they cease their prayers and praise of God. Instead, continually discussing what they had done, they thanked God for what they had done well and shed tears over what they had neglected to do or done carelessly.

They thought themselves abandoned by God if in their worship they did not find themselves constantly visited by their accustomed fervor. When they wanted to throw themselves into prayer, they developed certain techniques to keep from being snatched off by sleep. Some held themselves up by suspended ropes in order to make sure their worship would not be disturbed by sleep creeping up on them. Others encased their bodies in iron instruments. Still others encased themselves in wooden girdles. If, as usually occurs, their sobriety was disturbed by abundance of food or drink, or if they exceeded the limits of necessity by even a little because they were tired from a journey, they harshly tormented themselves by abstinence for many days. They tried to repress the promptings of the flesh by such great mortification that they did not hesitate to strip naked in the coldest ice or inundate their bodies with a flow of blood by piercing themselves all over with thorns. . . .

In the thirteenth year of his conversion, Francis proceeded to Syria, for great and deadly battles between Christians and pagans were going on there every day. Francis, who was traveling with a companion, was not afraid to present himself before the sultan of the Saracens. But who can say with what constancy of mind he stood before him, with what strength of spirit he spoke, with what eloquence and assurance he answered those who insulted the Christian law? Before he was brought before the sultan he was captured by soldiers, insulted, and beaten with a lash; yet he was not afraid, was not terrified by the threats of torture, and did not grow pale when threatened with death. And though he was reproached by many who were opposed in mind and hostile in spirit, he was very honorably received by the sultan. He was moved by Francis' words and listened to him willingly. In all these things the Lord did not fulfill Francis' desire for martyrdom, since he was reserving for him the prerogative of a singular grace. . . .

His highest intention, greatest desire, and supreme purpose was to observe the holy gospel in and through all things. He wanted to follow the doctrine and walk in the footsteps of our Lord Jesus Christ, and to do so perfectly, with all vigilance, all zeal, complete desire of the mind, complete fervor of the heart. He remembered Christ's words through constant meditation and recalled his actions through wise consideration. The humility of the incarnation and the love of the passion so occupied his memory that he scarcely wished to think of anything else. Hence what he did in the third year before the day of his glorious death, in the town called Greccio, on the birthday of our Lord Jesus Christ, should be reverently remembered.

There was in that place a certain man named John, of good reputation and even better life, whom the blessed Francis particularly loved. Noble and honorable in his own land, he had trodden on nobility of the flesh and pursued that of the mind. Around fifteen days before the birthday of Christ Francis sent for this man, as he often did, and said to him, "If you wish to celebrate the approaching feast of the Lord at Greccio, hurry and do what I tell you. I want to do something that will recall the memory of that child who was born in Bethlehem, to see with bodily eyes the inconveniences of his infancy, how he lay in the manger, and how the ox and ass stood by." Upon hearing this, the good and faithful man hurried to prepare all that the holy man had requested.

The day of joy drew near, the time of exultation approached. The brothers were called from their various places. With glad hearts, the men and women of that place prepared, according to their means, candles and torches to light up that night which has illuminated all the days and years with its glittering star. Finally the holy man of God arrived and, finding everything prepared, saw it and rejoiced.

The manger is ready, hay is brought, the ox and ass are led in. Simplicity is honored there, poverty is exalted, humility is commended and a new Bethlehem, as it were, is made from Greccio. Night is illuminated like the day, delighting men and beasts. The people come and joyfully celebrate the new mystery. The forest resounds with voices and the rocks respond to their rejoicing. The brothers sing, discharging their debt of praise to the Lord, and the whole night echoes with jubilation. The holy man of God stands before the manger full of sighs, consumed by devotion and filled with a marvelous joy. The solemnities of the mass are performed over the manger and the priest experiences a new consolation.

The holy man of God wears a deacon's vestments, for he was indeed a deacon, and he sings the holy gospel with a sonorous voice. And his voice, a sweet voice, a vehement voice, a clear voice, a sonorous voice, invites all to the highest rewards. Then he preaches to the people standing about, telling them about the birth of the poor king and the little city of Bethlehem. Often, too, when he wished to mention Jesus Christ, burning with love he called him "the child of Bethlehem," and speaking the word "Bethlehem" or "Jesus," he licked his lips with his tongue, seeming to taste the sweetness of these words.

The gifts of the Almighty are multiplied here and a marvelous vision is seen by a certain virtuous man. For he saw a little child lying lifeless in the manger, and he saw the holy man of God approach and arouse the child as if from a deep sleep. Nor was this an unfitting vision, for in the hearts of many the child Jesus really had been forgotten, but now, by his grace and through his servant Francis, he had been brought back to life and impressed here by loving recollect ion. Finally the celebration ended and each returned joyfully home.

Francis' hands and feet seemed to be pierced by nails, with the heads of the nails appearing in the palms of his hands and on the upper sides of his feet, the points appearing on the other side. The marks were round on the palm of each hand but elongated on the other side, and small pieces of flesh jutting out from the rest took on the appearance of the nail-ends, bent and driven back. In the same way the marks of nails were impressed on his feet and projected beyond the rest of the flesh. Moreover, his right side had a large wound as if it had been pierced with a spear, and it often bled so that his tunic and trousers were soaked with his sacred blood. . . .

During this period Francis' body began to be beset by more serious illnesses than previously. He suffered frequent illnesses because for many years he had castigated his body perfectly, reducing it to servitude. For during the preceding eighteen years his flesh had scarcely or never found rest, but traveled constantly throughout various wide areas so that the prompt, devout and fervent spirit within him could scatter God's word everywhere.

Thomas of Celano, First and Second Lives of Saint Francis, translated by David Burr

Thomas Aquinas

Dates
1225–1274

Famous for being
Priest, Friar, Philosopher, Theologian, "Angelic Doctor"

Important writings
Summa Theologica

Two of his quotations
"*Intelligo ut credam.*" "I understand, in order that I may believe."

"To one who has faith, no explanation is necessary. To one without faith, no explanation is possible."

Introduction

Thomas Aquinas summarizes Scholastic Theology in his *Summa Theologica*, 1271, writing, *intelligo ut credam* "I understand, in order that I may believe."

Aquinas came from noble blood, born in Aquino, Italy in 1225. His family sent him to Monte Cassino at age 5 and he remained there until age 14. He then went to study at the University of Naples. After his study there he entered the Dominican order. His decision to take monastic vows angered his family who tried to dissuade him tempting him with a prostitute, kidnapping him and then offering to purchase the see of the Archbishop of Naples for him. He successfully rejected all these offers.

Aquinas attempted to harmonize human reason with divine revelation. He sought to separate the two emphasizing that all human knowledge comes from the senses. He argued that this fact in no way detracted from the reality of revelation. He stated that men base philosophy on data available to all men. Men base theology, on the other hand, on revelation linked with logical deduction. His two most famous writings, *Summa Theologiae* (A Summary of Theology) and *Summa Contra Gentiles*, demonstrated his approach. He based the former on revelation—Scripture. He designed the latter to support Christian belief from human reason alone. Aquinas developed his famous "five ways," essentially a rational use of human reason, to prove God's existence.

In many respects, Aquinas's methodology sounds normal today. He began with the statement of a problem. He then quoted his authority which included Scripture and early Christian writers. Then he moved on to consider all relevant data and only then drew his conclusion. Even though we consider this a rational way to arrive at conclusions, others rejected his work. The University of Paris condemned, in part, his works in 1277. Other Medieval scholastics criticized his efforts because they believed reason and revelation incompatible. In 1879, the Pope declared Aquinas's work valid and it became the basis for modern Roman Catholic theology.

Michael Hines

St. Thomas Aquinas' Five Ways

Introduction

Aquinas wrote: "The truth of the Christian faith . . . surpasses the capacity of reason, nevertheless that truth that the human reason is naturally endowed to know can not be opposed to the truth of the Christian faith."

First Way: The argument from motion

St. Thomas Aquinas, studying the works of the Greek philosopher Aristotle, concluded from common observation that an object that is in motion (e.g. the planets, a rolling stone) is put in motion by some other object or force. From this, Aquinas believes that ultimately there must have been an *Unmoved Mover (God)* who first put things in motion. Aquinas argued:

1) Nothing can move itself.

2) If every object in motion had a mover, then the first object in motion needed a mover.

3) This first mover is the Unmoved Mover, called God.

Second Way: Causation of existence

This way deals with the issue of existence. Aquinas concluded that common sense observation tells us that no object creates itself. So some previous object had to create it.

Aquinas believed that ultimately there must have been an *Uncaused First Cause (God)* who began the chain of existence for all things. Aquinas argued:

1) There exists things that are caused (created) by other things.
2) Nothing can be the cause of itself (nothing can create itself.)
3) There can not be an endless string of objects causing other objects to exist.
4) Therefore, there must be an uncaused first cause called God.

Third Way: Contingent and necessary objects

This Way defines two types of objects in the universe: contingent beings and necessary beings. A contingent being is an object that can not exist without a necessary being causing its existence. Aquinas believed that the existence of contingent beings would ultimately necessitate a being which must exist for all of the contingent beings to exist. This being, called a necessary being, is what we call God. Aquinas argued:

1) Contingent beings are caused.
2) Not every being can be contingent.
3) There must exist a being which is necessary to cause contingent beings.
4) This necessary being is God.

Fourth Way: The argument from degrees and perfection

St. Thomas formulated this Way from a very interesting observation about the qualities of things. For example one may say that of two marble sculptures one is more beautiful than the other. So for these two objects, one has a greater degree of beauty than the next. This is referred to as degrees or gradation of a quality. From this fact Aquinas concluded that for any given quality (e.g. goodness, beauty, knowledge) there must be an perfect standard by which all such qualities are measured. These perfections are contained in God.

Fifth Way: The argument from intelligent design

The final Way that St. Thomas Aquinas speaks of has to do with the observable universe and the order of nature. Aquinas states that common sense tells us that the universe works in such a way, that one can conclude that is was designed by an intelligent designer, God. In other words, all physical laws and the order of nature and life were designed and ordered by God, the intelligent designer.

Summa Theologica

This work immortalized St. Thomas. The author himself modestly considered it simply a manual of Christian doctrine for the use of students. In reality it is a complete scientifically arranged exposition of theology and at the same time a summary of Christian philosophy. In the brief prologue St. Thomas first calls attention to the difficulties experienced by students of sacred doctrine in his day, the causes assigned being: the multiplication of useless questions, articles, and arguments; the lack of scientific order; frequent repetitions, "which beget disgust and confusion in the minds of learners". Then he adds: "Wishing to avoid these and similar drawbacks, we shall endeavor, confiding in the Divine assistance, to treat of these things that pertain to sacred doctrine with brevity and clearness, in so far as the subject to he treated will permit."

In the introductory question, "On Sacred Doctrine", he proves that, besides the knowledge which reason affords, Revelation also is necessary for salvation first, because without it men could not know the supernatural end to which they must tend by their voluntary acts; secondly, because, without Revelation, even the truths concerning God which could be proved by reason would be known "only by a few, after a long time, and with the admixture of many errors". When revealed truths have been accepted, the mind of man proceeds to explain them and to draw conclusions from them.

Hence results theology, which is a science, because it proceeds from principles that are certain (Answer 2). The object, or subject, of this science is God; other things are treated in it only in so far as they relate to God (Answer 7). Reason is used in theology not to prove the truths of faith, which are accepted on the authority of God, but to defend, explain, and develop the doctrines revealed (Answer 8). He thus announces the division of the "Summa": "Since the chief aim of this sacred science is to give the knowledge of God, not only as He is in Himself, but also as He is the Beginning of all things, and the End of all, especially of rational creatures, we shall treat first of God; secondly, of the rational creature's advance towards God; thirdly, of Christ, Who, as Man, is the way by which we tend to God."

God in Himself, and as He is the Creator; God as the End of all things, especially of man; God as the Redeemer—these are the leading ideas, the great headings, under which all that pertains to theology is contained.

Uniform plan

The entire "Summa" contains 38 Treatises, 612 Questions, subdivided into 3120 articles, in which about 10,000 objections are proposed and answered. So admirably is the promised order preserved that, by reference to the beginning of the Tracts and Questions, one can see at a glance what place it occupies in the general plan, which embraces all that can be known through theology of God, of man, and of their mutual relations . . .

"The whole Summa is arranged on a uniform plan. Every subject is introduced as a question, and divided into articles. . . . Each article has also a uniform disposition of parts. The topic is introduced as an inquiry for discussion, under the term Utrum, whether—e.g. Utrum Deus sit? The objections against the proposed thesis are then stated. These are generally three or four in number, but sometimes extend to seven or more. The conclusion adopted is then introduced by the words, Respondeo dicendum. At the end of the thesis expounded the objections are answered, under the forms, ad primum, ad secundum, etc." . . .

The "Summa" is Christian doctrine in scientific form; it is human reason rendering its highest service in defense and explanation of the truths of the Christian religion. It is the answer of the matured and saintly doctor to the question of his youth: What is God? Revelation, made known in the Scriptures and by tradition; reason and its best results; soundness and fullness of doctrine, order, conciseness and clearness of expression, effacement of self, the love of truth alone, hence a remarkable fairness towards adversaries and calmness in combating their errors; soberness and soundness of judgment, together with a charmingly tender and enlightened piety—these are all found in this "Summa" more than in his other writings, more than in the writings of his contemporaries, for "among the Scholastic doctors, the chief and master of all, towers Thomas Aquinas, who, as Cajetan observes (In 2am 2ae, Q. 148, a. 4) 'because he most venerated the ancient doctors of the Church in a certain way seems to have inherited the intellect of all'" (Encyclical, "Aeterni Patris", of Leo XIII).

Written by D. J. Kennedy. Transcribed by Kevin Cawley. The Catholic Encyclopedia, *Volume XIV. Published 1912*

John Wycliffe

Dates

1320–1384

Famous for being

Theologian, Bible Translator

Known as: "The Morning Star of the Reformation"

Important writings

His English translation of the Bible

One of his quotations

[Speaking of the Christian Gospel] "O, marvelous power of the Divine seed, which overpowers the strong man armed, softens obdurate hearts, and changes into divine men those who were brutalized in sin, and removed to an infinite distance from God."

An Account of the Life and Persecutions of John Wycliffe

This celebrated reformer, denominated the "Morning Star of the Reformation," was born about the year 1324, in the reign of Edward II. Of his extraction we have no certain account. His parents designing him for the Church, sent him to Queen's College, Oxford, about that period founded by Robert Eaglesfield, confessor to Queen Philippi. But not meeting with the advantages for study in that newly established house which he expected, he removed to Merton College, which was then esteemed one of the most learned societies in Europe.

Wycliffe inveighed, in his lectures, against the pope-his usurpation-his infallibility-his pride—his avarice—and his tyranny. He was the first who termed the pope Antichrist. From the pope, he would turn to the pomp, the luxury, and trappings of the bishops, and compared them with the simplicity of primitive bishops. Their superstitions and deceptions were topics that he urged with energy of mind and logical precision.

From the patronage of the duke of Lancaster, Wycliffe received a good benefice; but he was no sooner settled in his parish, than his enemies and the bishops began to persecute him with renewed vigor. The duke of Lancaster was his friend in this persecution, and by his presence and that of Lord Percy, earl marshal of England, he so overawed the trial, that the whole ended in disorder.

In 1378 Wycliffe was seized with a violent disorder, which it was feared might prove fatal. The begging friars, accompanied by four of the most eminent citizens of Oxford, gained admittance to his bed chamber, and begged of him to retract, for his soul's sake, the unjust things he had asserted of their order. Wycliffe, surprised at the solemn message, raised himself in his bed, and with a stern countenance replied, "I shall not die, but live to declare the evil deeds of the friars."

When Wycliffe recovered, he set about a most important work, the translation of the Bible into English. Before this work appeared, he published a tract, wherein he showed the necessity of it. The zeal of the bishops to suppress the Scriptures greatly promoted its sale, and they who were not able to purchase copies, procured transcripts of particular Gospels or Epistles. Afterward, when Lollardy increased, and the flames kindled, it was a common practice to fasten about the neck of the condemned heretic such of these scraps of Scripture as were found in his possession, which generally shared his fate.

At this period, the disputes between the two popes continued. Urban published a bull, in which he earnestly called upon all who had any regard for religion, to exert themselves in its cause; and to take up arms against Clement and his adherents in defense of the holy see.

A war, in which the name of religion was so vilely prostituted, roused Wycliffe's inclination, even in his declining years. He took up his pen once more, and wrote against it with the greatest acrimony. He expostulated with the pope in a very free manner, and asks him boldly: 'How he durst make the token of Christ on the cross (which is the token of peace, mercy and charity) a banner to lead us to slay Christian men, for the love of two false priests, and to oppress Christendom worse than Christ and his apostles were oppressed by the Jews? 'When,' said he, 'will the proud priest of Rome grant indulgences to mankind to live in peace and charity, as he now does to fight and slay one another?'

This severe piece drew upon him the resentment of Urban, and was likely to have involved him in greater troubles than he had before experienced, but providentially he was delivered out of their hands. He was struck with the palsy, and though he lived some time, yet it was in such a way that his enemies considered him as a person below their resentment.

Wycliffe returning within short space, either from his banishment, or from some other place where he was secretly kept, repaired to his parish of Lutterworth, where he was parson; and there, quietly departing this mortal life, slept in peace in the Lord, in the end of the year 1384, upon Silvester's day. It appeared that he was well aged before he departed, "and that the same thing pleased him in his old age, which did please him being young."

Wycliffe had some cause to give them thanks, that they would at least spare him until he was dead, and also give him so long respite after his death, forty-one years to rest in his sepulcher before they engraved him, and turned him from earth to ashes; which ashes they also took and threw into the river. And so was he resolved into three elements, earth, fire, and water, thinking thereby utterly to extinguish and abolish both the name and doctrine of Wycliffe forever.

Not much unlike the example of the old Pharisees and sepulcher knights, who, when they had brought the Lord unto the grave, thought to make him sure never to rise again. But these and all others must know that, as there is no counsel against the Lord, so there is no keeping down of verity, but it will spring up and come out of dust and ashes, as appeared right well in this man; for though they dug up his body, burned his bones, and drowned his ashes, yet the Word of God and the truth of his doctrine, with the fruit and success thereof, they could not burn.

John Foxe, Book of Martyrs

John Huss

Dates

1369–1415

Famous for being

Priest, Philosopher, Reformer and Martyr

Important writings

Sermons

One of his quotations

[As a chain was passed round his neck in preparation for his burning]."It is thus that you silence the goose, but a hundred years hence there will arise a swan whose singing you shall not be able to silence."

Born into a peasant family, Jan Hus became a leader in a movement that sought to reform the church and to lessen foreign influence in Bohemia.

He was educated at a Latin school and entered the University of Prague c. 1390, from which he graduated with an M.A. about six years later. He earned money as a choirboy until his election in 1401 to the philosophy faculty. He lectured on the philosophy of Aristotle and of John Wycliffe, whose theological works were not yet known in Bohemia. Hus became, the following year, the rector of Bethlehem Chapel, where he preached in the vernacular and which became a center for the nationalist movement. About this time, Jerome of Prague introduced Wycliffe's theology into Bohemia; some say this was made possible by the marriage of Richard II of England with Anne, sister of Wenceslaus IV of Bohemia.

In 1403, Hus was appointed preacher of the synod, and the university condemned 45 of Wycliffe's theological statements, especially those that concerned remanence, a belief that the bread and wine of the Eucharist remain bread and wine. Although Hus did not accept this position, he did accept many of Wycliffe's propositions, including a belief that one's conduct made one worthy or unworthy of grace. Hus agreed that the Bible alone is the basis of all faith, doctrine, and teaching; he was sympathetic to predestination. Hus attacked clerical immorality, such as the sale of indulgences. He also attacked the church for owning so much property.

Summoned to Rome to defend his ideas, Hus sent representatives and was excommunicated for failure to appear. However, after he criticized John XXIII's crusade against Ladislas of Naples, John placed Prague under interdict, and Hus left the city. In 1413, he published *De ecclesia*, the first ten chapters of which are taken from Wycliffe's writings. The Council of Constance summoned him to defend his theology. Promised safe passage by the emperor Sigismund, Hus traveled to Germany, where he was imprisoned and tried for heresy. He was burned at the stake; the University of Prague declared him a martyr. He is a national hero, and his writings in Czech are considered literary classics.

Other Christian leaders in the Middle Ages

Venerable Bede (c. 672–735)
St Symeon the New Theologian (949–1022)
Boniface (c. 672–754)
Bernard of Clairvaux (1090–1153)
Peter Abelard (1079–1142)
Thomas Becket (1117–1170)
Innocent III (1160–1216)
Catherine of Siena (c. 1347–1380)

Venerable Bede (c. 672–735)

Introduction

Bede was the most outstanding Christian writer, teacher and scholar of the early Middle Ages.

The Venerable Bede is never spoken of without affectionate interest, and yet so uneventful was his useful life that very little can be said about him personally. He was born in 673, probably in the village of Jarrow, on the south bank of the Tyne, Northumbria, near the Scottish border.

At the age of seven, being probably an orphan, he was placed in the monastery of St. Peter, at Wearmouth, on the north bank of the Wear, which had been founded by Benedict Biscop in 674. In 682 he was transferred to the newly-founded sister monastery of St. Paul, five miles off, at Jarrow. He is not known ever to have gone away from it farther than to the sister monastery and to visit friends in contiguous places, such as York. The stories of his visit to Rome and professorship at Cambridge scarcely deserve mention.

His first teacher was Benedict Biscop, a nobleman who at twenty-five became a monk and freely put his property and his learning at the public service. Biscop traveled five times to Rome and each time returned, like Ethelbert and Alcuin subsequently, laden with rich literary spoils and also with pictures and relics. Thus the library at Wearmouth became the largest and best appointed in England at the time. It was Biscop's enterprise and liberality which rendered it possible that Bede's natural taste for learning should receive such careful culture. So amid the wealth of books he acquired Latin, Greek and Hebrew, and laid up a rich store of multifarious knowledge.

Such was his character and attainments that at nineteen, six years before the then canonical age, he was ordained deacon, and at thirty a priest. He thus describes his mode of life:

> All the remaining time of my life [i.e., after leaving Wearmouth] I spent in that, monastery [of Jarrow], wholly applying myself to the study of Scripture, and amidst observance of regular discipline and the daily care of singing in the church. I always took delight in learning, teaching and writing.

It appears that he published nothing before he was thirty years old, for he says himself: "From which time [i.e., of his taking priest's orders] till the fifty-ninth year of my age, I have made it my business, for the use of me and mine, to compile out of the works of the venerable Fathers, and to interpret and explain according to their meaning these following pieces." Then follows his list of his works. The result of such study and writing was that Bede became the most learned man of his time, and also the greatest of its authors. Yet he was also one of the humblest and simplest of men.

His death

He died on Wednesday, May 26, 735, of a complaint accompanied with asthma, from which he had long suffered. The circumstances of his death are related by his pupil Cuthbert. During Lent of the year 735 Bede carried on the translation of the Gospel of John and "some collections out of the Book of Notes" of Archbishop Isidore of Seville.

The day before he died he spent in dictating his translations, saying now and then, "Go on quickly, I know not how long I shall hold out, and whether my Maker will not soon take me away." He progressed so far with his rendering of John's Gospel that at the third hour on Wednesday morning only one chapter remained to be done. On being told this he said, "Take your pen, and make ready, and write fast." The scribe did so, but at the ninth hour Bede said to Cuthbert:

> I have some little articles of value in my chest, such as pepper, napkins and incense: run quickly, and bring the priests of our monastery to me, that I may distribute among them the gifts which God has bestowed on me. The rich in this world are bent on giving gold and silver and other precious things. But I, in charity, will joyfully give my brothers what God has given unto me.

He spoke to every one of them, admonishing and entreating them that they would carefully say masses and prayers for him, which they readily promised; but they all mourned and wept, especially because he said, "they should no more see his face in this world."

They rejoiced for that he said, "It is time that I return to Him who formed me out of nothing: I have lived long; my merciful Judge well foresaw my life for me; the time of my dissolution draws nigh; for I desire to die and to be with Christ."

Having said much more, he passed the day joyfully till the evening, and the boy [i.e., his scribe] said, "Dear master, there is yet one sentence not written."

He answered, "Write quickly."

Soon after the boy said, "It is ended."

He replied, "It is well, you have said the truth. It is ended. Receive my head into your hands, for it is a great satisfaction to me to sit facing my holy place, where I was wont to pray, that I may also sitting call upon my Father."

And thus on the pavement of his little cell, singing, "Glory be to the Father, and to the Son, and to the Holy Ghost," when he had named the Holy Ghost, he breathed his last, and so departed to the heavenly kingdom."

Burial

Bede's body was buried in the church at Jarrow, but between 1021 and 1042 it was stolen and removed to Durham by Elfred, a priest of its cathedral, who put it in the same chest with the body of St. Cuthbert. In 1104 the bodies were separated, and in 1154 the relics of Bede were placed in a shrine of gold and silver, adorned with jewels. This shrine was destroyed by an ignorant mob in Henry VIII's time (1541), and only a monkish inscription remains to chronicle the fact that Bede was ever buried there.

Venerable

The epithet, "Venerable," now so commonly applied to Bede, is used by him to denote a holy man who had not been canonized, and had no more reference to age than the same name applied today to an archdeacon in the Church of England. By his contemporaries he was called either Presbyter or Dominus. He is first called the Venerable in the middle of the tenth century.

Bede's Writings are very numerous, and attest the width and profundity of his learning, and also the independence and soundness of his judgment. His fame, if we may judge from the demand for his works immediately after his death, extended wherever the English missionaries or negotiators found their way."

Ecclesiastical History of England

This is Bede's great work. Begun at the request of King Ceolwulf, it was his occupation for many years, and was only finished a short time before his death. It consists of five books and tells in a simple, clear style the history of England from the earliest times down to 731. The first twenty-two chapters of the first book are compiled from Orosius and Gildas, but from the mission of Augustin in the 23d chapter (596) it rests upon original investigation. Bede took great pains to ensure accuracy, and he gives the names of all persons who were helpful to him.

The History is thus the chief and in many respects the only source for the church history of England down to the eighth century. In it as in his other books Bede relates a great many strange things; but he is careful to give his authorities for each statement. It is quite evident, however, that he believed in these "miracles," many of which are susceptible of rational explanation. It is from this modest, simple, conscientious History that multitudes have learned to love the Venerable Bede.

Samuel M. Jackson, Biographical Sketches of Ecclesiastical Writers, 1882

St. Symeon the New Theologian (949–1022)

One of the most beloved Holy Fathers is St. Symeon the New Theologian, who was the abbot of St. Mamas in Constantinople. He is one of three great Fathers whom the Orthodox Church has granted the title of "Theologian", because he is one of a few, in the history of Christianity, to 'know' God. The other two Theologians are St. John the Evangelist, and St. Gregory of Nazianzus (AD 390).

St. Symeon was born in Galatia in Paphlagonia (Asia Minor) in AD 949. His parents, Basal and Theophana, were Byzantine provincial nobles. St. Symeon received only the basics of a primary Greek school education until he was about eleven years old. He finished his secondary education at the age of 14 in the court of the two brother emperors Basil and Constantine Porphyrogenetes. At 14, he met St. Symeon the Studite, who became his spiritual father and who led him into the life of asceticism and prayer. Although he wanted to enter the famous monastery of the Stoudion at the age of 14, his spiritual father had him wait until he turned 27. During this period of preparation, St. Symeon's elder continued to counsel and guide him, preparing him gradually for the monastic life even in the midst of worldly cares. St. Symeon occupied himself with the management of a patrician's household and possibly entered the service of his emperor as a diplomat and a senator. While 'busy in the world' he also strove to live a monk's life in the evenings, spending his time in night vigils and reading the spiritual works of Mark the Hermit and Diadochus of Photike. One of his elder's advice was, "if you desire to have always a soul-saving guidance, pay heed to your conscience and without fail do what it will instill in you"

St. Symeon's words still speak to us today, even though he lived a thousand years ago. Of special note is his emphasizes to return to the essence or spirit of the early Orthodox Church, and not merely depend on or shelter under the outward forms of Church life. His burning conviction is that the Christian life must be more than just a routine or habit, but rather it should be a personal experience of the living Christ. St. Symeon urges both monks and baptized laity back to a living spiritual experience of the Triune, calling himself the "enthusiastic zealot" who has personal, mystical experiences. His spiritual emphases is, however, misused by many 'charismatic Christians' and others today who claim to have "gifts of the Holy Spirit", which are probably emotional or 'scholastic' rather than spiritual. The following is a quote from St. Symeon on Spirituality,

> Do not say that it is impossible to receive the Spirit of God.
> Do not say that it is possible to be made whole without Him.
> Do not say that one can possess Him without knowing it.
> Do not say that God does not manifest Himself to man.
> Do not say that men cannot perceive the divine light, or that it is impossible in this age!
> Never is it found to be impossible, my friends.
> On the contrary, it is entirely possible when one desires it.
> *(Hymn 27, 125–132).*

Boniface (c. 672–754)

Apostle of Germany

Although the Church of Ireland was in a somewhat rough state at home, many of its clergy undertook missionary work on the Continent; and by them and others much was done for the conversion of various tribes in Germany and in the Netherlands. But the most famous missionary of those times was an Englishman named Winfrid, who is styled the Apostle of Germany.

Winfrid to Boniface

Winfrid was born near Crediton, in Devonshire, about the year 680. He became a monk at an early age, and perhaps it was then that he took the name of Boniface, by which he is best known. He might probably have risen to a high place in the church of his own country if he had wished to do so; but he was filled with a glowing desire to preach the Gospel to the heathen. He therefore refused all the tempting offers which were made to him at home, crossed the sea, and began to labor in Friesland and about the lower part of the Rhine. For three years he assisted another famous English missionary, Willibrord, bishop of Utrecht, who wished to make Boniface his successor; but Boniface thought that he was bound rather to labor in some country where his work was more needed; so, leaving Willibrord, he went into Hessia, where he made and baptized many thousands of converts. The pope, Gregory the Second, on hearing of this success, invited him to Rome, consecrated him as a bishop, and sent him back with letters recommending him to the princes and peoples of the countries in which his work was to lie.

Heathen superstitions

In some places Boniface found a strange mixture of heathen superstitions with Christianity, and he did all that he could to root them out. He had also much trouble with missionaries from Ireland, whose notions of Christian doctrine and practice differed in some things from his; and perhaps he did not always treat them with so much of wisdom and gentleness as might have been wished. But after all he was right in thinking that the sight of more than one kind of Christian religion, different from each other and opposed to each other; must puzzle the heathen and hinder their conversion; so that we can understand his jealousy of these Irish missionaries, even if we cannot wholly approve of it.

Archbishop of Mentz

In reward of his labors and success, Boniface was made an archbishop by Pope Gregory III in 732; and, although at first he was not fixed in any one place, he soon brought the German Church into such a state of order that it seemed to be time for choosing some city as the seat of its chief bishop, just as the chief bishop of England was settled at Canterbury.

Boniface himself wished to fix himself at Cologne; but at that very time the bishop of Mentz got into trouble by killing a Saxon, who, in a former war, had killed the bishop's father. Although it had been quite a common thing in those rough days for bishops to take a part in fighting, Boniface and his councils had made rules forbidding such things, as unbecoming the ministers of peace; and the case of the bishop of Mentz, coming just after those rules had been made, could not well be passed over. The bishop, therefore, was obliged to give up his see; and Mentz was chosen to be the place where Boniface should be fixed as archbishop and primate of Germany, having under him five bishops, and all the nations which had received the Gospel through his preaching.

Martyrdom

When Boniface had grown old, he felt himself again drawn to Frisia, where, as we have seen, he had labored in his early life; and at the age of seventy-five he left his archbishopric, with all that invited him to spend his last days there in quiet and honor, that he might once more go forth as a missionary to the barbarous Frieslanders. Among them he preached with much success; but on Whitsun Eve, 755, while he was expecting a great number of his converts to meet, that they might receive confirmation from him, he and his companions were attacked by an armed party of heathens, and the whole of the missionaries, fifty-two in number, were martyred. But although Boniface thus ended his active and useful life by martyrdom at the hands of those whom he wished to bring into the way of salvation, his work was carried on by other missionaries, and the conversion of the Frisians was completed within no long time. Boniface's body was carried up the Rhine, and was buried at Fulda, a monastery which he had founded amidst the loneliness of a vast forest, and there the tomb of the "Apostle of the Germans" was visited with reverence for centuries.

J. C. Robertson, Sketches of Church History, from AD 33 to the Reformation

Bernard of Clairvaux (1090–1153)

Abbot, Theologian, and Poet

Bernard, third son of a Burgundian nobleman, was born in 1090. His brothers were trained as soldiers, but Bernard from youth was destined for scholarship. One Christmas Eve as a child he had a dream about the infant Christ in the manger; and the memory of it, and consequent devotion to the mystery of the Word made flesh, remained with him throughout his life.

Bernard had good prospects of success as a secular scholar, but he began to believe that he was called to the monastic life, and after a period of prayer for guidance, he decided at age 22 to enter the monastery of Citeaux, an offshoot of the Benedictines which had adopted a much stricter rule than theirs, and became the founding house of the Cistercian order. He persuaded four of his brothers, one uncle, and 26 other men to join him. They were the first novices that Citeaux had had for several years. After three years, the abbot ordered Bernard to take twelve monks and found a new house at La Ferte. The first year was one of great hardship. They had no stores and lived chiefly on roots and barley bread. Bernard imposed such severe discipline that his monks became discouraged, but he realized his error and became more lenient. The reputation of the monastery, known as Clairvaux, spread across Europe. Many new monks joined it, and many persons wrote letters or came in person to seek spiritual advice. By the time of his death, 60 new monasteries of the Cistercian order were established under his direction.

For four years after 1130 Bernard was deeply involved with a disputed papal election, championing the claims of Innocent II against his rival Anacletus II. He traveled throughout France, Germany, and Italy mustering support for his candidate (and, it should be added, preaching sermons denouncing injustices done to Jews), and returned from one of these journeys with Peter Bernard of Paganelli as a postulant for the monastery. The future Pope Eugenius III spent the next year stoking the monastery fires. Years later, Bernard wrote a major treatise of advice to Eugenius on the spiritual temptations of spiritual power.

The papal election was not the only dispute in which Bernard became involved. He was highly critical of Peter Abelard, one of the most brilliant theologians of the day. Bernard believed that Abelard was too rationalistic in his approach, and failed to allow sufficiently for the element of mystery in the faith. When Abelard rejected some of the ways of stating Christian doctrines to which Bernard was accustomed, Bernard concluded, perhaps too hastily, that this was equivalent to rejecting the doctrine itself. A conference was scheduled at Sens, where Abelard's views were to be examined, but soon after it began Abelard decided that he was not about to get a fair hearing, announced that he was appealing to Rome, and left. He set out for Rome and got as far as Cluny, where he stopped. Peter the Venerable, the abbot, was a friend of both Abelard and Bernard, and managed to reconcile them before they died.

One of Bernard's most influential acts, for better or worse, was his preaching of the Second Crusade. The First Crusade had given the Christian forces control of a few areas in Palestine, including the city of Edessa. When Moslem forces captured Edessa in 1144, King Louis VII of France was eager to launch a crusade to retake Edessa and prevent a Moslem recapture of Jerusalem. He asked Bernard for help, and Bernard refused. He then asked the Pope to order Bernard to preach a Crusade. The pope gave the order, and Bernard preached, with spectacular results. Whole villages were emptied of able-bodied males as Bernard preached and his listeners vowed on the spot to head for Palestine and defend the Sacred Shrines with their lives.

The preaching of the Crusade had an ugly side-effect. In the Rhineland, a monk named Raoul wandered about telling crowds that if they were going to fight for the faith, the logical first step was to kill the Jews who were near at hand. There were anti-Jewish riots in Mainz, where the archbishop sheltered the Jews, or many of them, in his palace, and sent an urgent message to Bernard to come before both he and they were killed. Bernard came. He called Raoul arrogant and without authority, a preacher of mad and heretical doctrines, a liar and a murderer. Then he got nasty. Raoul sneaked off the scene, and the riots were over. From that day to this, Bernard has been remembered among Rhineland Jews and their descendants as an outstanding example of a "righteous Gentile," and many of them (e.g. Bernard Baruch) bear his name.

As for the Crusade, things went wrong from the start. The various rulers leading the movement were distrustful of one another and not disposed to work together. Of the soldiers who set out (contemporary estimates vary from 100,000 to 1,500,000), most died of disease and starvation before reaching their goal, and most of the remainder were killed or captured soon after their arrival. The impact on Bernard was devastating, and so was the impact on Europe.

In 1153, Bernard journeyed to reconcile the warring provinces Metz and Lorraine. He persuaded them to peace and to an agreement drawn up under his mediation, and then, in failing health, returned home to die.

If Bernard in controversy was fierce and not always fair, it is partly because he was a man of intense feeling and dedication, quick to respond to any real or supposed threat to what he held sacred. It is his devotional writings, not his polemical ones, that are still read today. Among the hymns attributed to him are the Latin originals of "O Sacred Head, sore wounded," "Jesus, the very thought of Thee," and "O Jesus, thou joy of loving hearts." His sermons on the Song of Songs, treated as an allegory of the love of Christ, are his best-known long work.

James Kiefer

A Cistercian Hymn

O Sacred Head, Now Wounded

1. O sacred Head, now wounded,
With grief and shame weighed down,
Now scornfully surrounded
With thorns, Thine only crown.
O sacred Head, what glory,
What bliss, till now was Thine!
Yet, though despised and gory,
I joy to call Thee mine.

2. Men mock and taunt and jeer Thee,
Thou noble countenance,
Though mighty worlds shall fear Thee
And flee before Thy glance.
How art thou pale with anguish,
With sore abuse and scorn!
How doth Thy visage languish
That once was bright as morn!

3. Now from Thy cheeks has vanished
Their color, once so fair;
From Thy red lips is banished
The splendor that was there.
Grim Death, with cruel rigor,
Hath robbed Thee of Thy life;
Thus Thou has lost Thy vigor,
Thy strength, in this sad strife.

4. My burden in Thy Passion,
Lord, Thou hast borne for me,
For it was my transgression
Which brought this woe on thee.
I cast me down before Thee,
Wrath were my rightful lot;
Have mercy, I implore Thee;
Redeemer, spurn me not!

5. My Shepherd, now receive me;
My Guardian, own me Thine.
Great blessings Thou didst give me,
O Source of gifts divine!
Thy lips have often fed me
With words of truth and love,
Thy Spirit oft hath led me
To heavenly joys above.

6. Here I will stand beside Thee,
From Thee I will not part;
O Savior, do not chide me!
When breaks Thy loving heart,
When soul and body languish
In death's cold, cruel grasp,
Then, in Thy deepest anguish,
Thee in mine arms I'll clasp.

7. The joy can ne'er be spoken,
Above all joys beside,
When in Thy body broken
I thus with safety hide.
O Lord of life, desiring
Thy glory now to see,
Beside Thy cross expiring,
I'd breathe my soul to Thee.

8. What language shall I borrow
To thank Thee, dearest Friend,
For this, Thy dying sorrow,
Thy pity without end?
Oh, make me thine forever!
And should I fainting be,
Lord, let me never, never,
Outlive my love for Thee.

9. My Savior, be Thou near me
When death is at my door;
Then let Thy presence cheer me,
Forsake me nevermore!
When soul and body languish,
Oh, leave me not alone,
But take away mine anguish
By virtue of Thine own!

10. Be Thou my Consolation,
My Shield when I must die;
Remind me of Thy Passion
When my last hour draws nigh.
Mine eyes shall then behold Thee,
Upon Thy cross shall dwell,
My heart by faith enfold Thee.
Who dieth thus dies well!

Translated by Paul Gerhardt, 1656, and James W. Alexander, 1830

Peter Abelard (1079–1142)

Best-known now for his romance with Héloïse, Peter Abelard was a gifted teacher and scholar whose resolution of the debate between the realists and the nominalists prefigured that of Aquinas.

Abelard was born in 1079 into a knightly family in Pallet, near Nantes. He abandoned his military heritage to study philosophy under Roscelin, William of Champeaux, and Anselm of Laon, all of whom he eventually debated. Abelard lectured in Paris from c. 1108 until 1118, when he and the pregnant Héloïse left Paris so she could bear their child (Astrolabe) in the security of his sister's house. Although the lovers were later married, Héloïse's uncle avenged her supposed wrong. She became a nun at Argenteuil, where she had been educated, and he became a monk. His book on the Trinity was condemned in 1121 at the Council of Soissons, after which the book was burned. While a monk at St.-Denis, Abelard established that St. Denis of Paris was not Dionysios the Areopagite; the monks were critical of his reasoning, and since he considered them barbarians, he left to become a hermit at the Paraclete in Troyes, which he later left to Héloïse and a community of nuns, for whom he wrote a monastic rule and gave spiritual guidance.

Around 1136, he began to teach in Paris, and he is said to have founded the University of Paris, which grew up around the site of his school. Several of his students went on to become respected and now-forgotten churchmen; John of Salisbury is his most famous student. Some scholars believe that Arnold of Brescia was Abelard's student, but it is not clear if Arnold was a student or an associate. At the instigation of Bernard of Clairvaux, Abelard and Arnold were condemned at the Council of Sens (1140/41). Each was confined to a separate monastery in Paris. Through the efforts of Peter of Cluny, Abelard was reconciled to Bernard and to Innocent II, who had confirmed the decision of Sens. When Abelard died in 1142, he was buried at the Paraclete. In the XIX Century, Abelard and Héloïse were reburied together in Paris.

Abelard put forth the idea that universals exist a thoughts based on the particulars of things, in contrast to the idea that only things exist and the idea that only classes exist. Abelard also suggested in Ethica that intent is the criterion by which one ought to judge sin because a deed by itself is neutral. Abelard wrote, in addition to his ethics and book on the Trinity, an *Introduction to Theology, A Dialogue among Philosophers*, and *The History of Calamaties* (his autobiography). He and Héloïse compiled and published their letters in the 1130's.

Thomas Becket (1117–1170)

St. Thomas, son of Gilbert Becket, was born in Southwark, England, in 1117. When a youth he was attached to the household of Theobald, Archbishop of Canterbury, who sent him to Paris and Bologna to study law. He became Archdeacon of Canterbury, then Lord High Chancellor of England; and in 1160, when Archbishop Theobald died, the king insisted on the consecration of St. Thomas in his stead. St. Thomas refused, warning the king that from that hour their friendship would be broken. In the end he yielded, and was consecrated. The conflict at once broke out; St. Thomas resisted the royal customs, which violated the liberties of the Church and the laws of the realm. After six years of contention, partly spent in exile, St. Thomas, with full foresight of martyrdom before him, returned as a good shepherd to his Church. On the 29th of December, 1170, just as vespers were beginning, four knights broke into the cathedral, crying: "Where is the archbishop? where is the traitor?" The monks fled, and St. Thomas might easily have escaped. But he advanced, saying: "Here I am—no traitor, but archbishop. What seek you?" "Your life," they cried. "Gladly do I give it," was the reply; and bowing his head, the invincible martyr was hacked and hewn till his soul went to God. Six months later Henry II. submitted to be publicly scourged at the Saint's Shrine, and restored to the Church her full rights. "Learn from St. Thomas," says Father Faber, "to fight the good fight, even to the shedding of blood, or, to what men find harder, the shedding of their good name by pouring it out to waste on the earth."

Lives of the Saints compiled by Rev. Alban Butler, 1894

Innocent III (1160–1216)

Innocent III was born into a Roman family as Lothair of Segni. He attended school in Paris and Bologna where he studied theology and law respectively. He became Cardinal Deacon of St. Sergius and St. Bacchus in 1190, and in January of 1198 was elected Pope. He was ordained in February and came to office as Fredrick II of Sicily, Otto of Brunswick, and Philip of Hohenstaufen were vying for leadership of the Holy Roman Empire. Innocent used this struggle to strengthen the role of papal intervention in political decisions. He believed in a system of papal monarchy in which the Pope acted as the Vicar of Jesus Christ and in which bishops were under his direct authority. Innocent's two main interests were heresy and crusade. He declared the church a state in order to make heresy a crime against the state and called crusades with the goal of reuniting the Greek and Latin churches. In 1215 Innocent III held the most widely attended council of the Middle Ages, the Fourth Lateran Council, which dealt with over 70 decrees written by Innocent III himself.

Copyright © 1995, April S. Blazevic

Catherine of Siena (c. 1347–1380)

Catherine Benincasa was the youngest of twenty-five children of a wealthy dyer of Sienna (or Siena). At the age of six, she had a vision of Christ in glory, surrounded by His saints. From that time on, she spent most of her time in prayer and meditation, over the opposition of her parents, who wanted her to be more like the average girl of her social class. Eventually they gave in, and at the age of sixteen she joined the Third Order of St. Dominic (First Order = friars, Second Order = nuns, Third Order = laypersons), where she became a nurse, caring for patients with leprosy and advanced cancer whom other nurses disliked to treat.

She began to acquire a reputation as a person of insight and sound judgment, and many persons from all walks of life sought her spiritual advice, both in person and by letter. She persuaded many priests who were living in luxury to give away their goods and to live simply.

In her day, the popes, officially Bishops of Rome, had been living for about seventy years, not at Rome but at Avignon in France, where they were under the political control of the King of France (the Avignon Papacy, sometimes called the Babylonian Captivity of the Papacy, began when Philip the Fair, King of France, captured Rome and the Pope in 1303). Catherine visited Avignon in 1376 and told Pope Gregory XI that he had no business to live away from Rome. He heeded her advice, and moved to Rome. She then acted as his ambassador to Florence, and was able to reconcile a quarrel between the Pope and the leaders of that city. She then retired to Sienna, where she wrote a book called the Dialog, an account of her visions and other spiritual experiences, with advice on cultivating a life of prayer.

After Gregory's death in 1378, the Cardinals, mostly French, elected an Italian Pope, Urban VI, who on attaining office turned out to be arrogant and abrasive and tyrannical, and perhaps to have other faults as well. The Cardinals met again elsewhere, declared that the first election had been under duress from the Roman mob and therefore invalid, and elected a new Pope, Clement VII, who established his residence at Avignon. Catherine worked tirelessly, both to persuade Urban to mend his ways (her letters to him are respectful but severe and uncompromising—as one historian has said, she perfected the art of kissing the Pope's feet while simultaneously twisting his arm), and to persuade others that the peace and unity of the Church required the recognition of Urban as lawful Pope. Despite her efforts, the Papal Schism continued until 1417. It greatly weakened the prestige of the Bishops of Rome, and thus helped to pave the way for the Protestant Reformation a century later.

Catherine is known:

as a mystic, a contemplative who devoted herself to prayer

as a humanitarian, a nurse who undertook to alleviate the suffering of the poor and the sick

as an activist, a renewer of Church and society, who took a strong stand on the issues affecting society in her day, and who never hesitated (in the old Quaker phrase) "to speak truth to power"

as an adviser and counselor, with a wide range of interests, who always made time for troubled and uncertain persons who told her their problems—large and trivial, religious and secular.

James Kiefer

Classic Christian devotional books from Medieval Christianity

Boethius, Anicius Manlius Torquatus Severinus (480–524), *Consolation of Philosophy*

Gregory I (c. 540–604), *Life of Our most Holy Father S. Benedict*

St. Bede ("The Venerable," c. 673–735), *Ecclesiastical History of England*

Saint Symeon the New Theologian (949–1022), *Symeon the New Theologian, the Discourses*

William of St. Thierry (1084–1148), *On the Contemplation of God*

Bernard of Clairvaux (1090–1153), *On Loving God*

Hildegard of Bingen (1098–1179), *Book of Divine Works Letters and Songs*

Francis of Assisi (1182–1226), *Canticum Fratris Solis, the Canticle to Brother Sun; Prayer before the Crucifix, 1205; The Earlier Rule, 1221; The Later Rule, 1223; Testament, 1226; Admonitions The Little Flowers of St. Francis of Assisi*

Saint Albert the Great (1193?–1280), *On Cleaving to God*
Mechtild of Magdeburg (1212–1282), *Beguine Spirituality: Mystical Writings of Mechtild of Magdeburg, Beatrice of Nazareth, and Hadewijch of Brabant*
Nicephorus the Solitary (second half of thirteenth century), *The Jesus Prayer*
Bonaventure (1221–1274), *Office of the Passion*
St. Gertrude the Great (1256–1302), *The Herald of God's Loving Kindness*
St. Dominic (1260–1288), *The Nine Ways of Prayer*
Meister Eckhart (1260–1327), Sermons
Richard Rolle of Hampole (c. 1290–c. 1349), *Incendium Amoris (Fire of Love)*
St. John of Ruysbroeck (1293–1381), *Adornment of the Spiritual Marriage*
Theologia Germanica, author unknown (mid 1300's)
Hadewijch (13th Century), *Beguine Spirituality: Mystical Writings of Mechtild of Magdeburg, Beatrice of Nazareth, and Hadewijch of Brabant*
Henry Suso (c. 1295–1366), *A Little Book of Eternal Wisdom*
Johannes Tauler (1300–1365), *The Inner Way*
St. Bridget (1303–1373), *Life and Selected Revelations*
Julian of Norwich (1343–1443), *Revelations of Divine Love*
Catherine of Siena (1347–1380), *Dialog of Catherine of Siena*
Walter Hilton (d. 1396), *The Scale of Perfection*
Margery Kempe (1373–1438), *The Book of Margery Kempe*
Thomas a Kempis (1380–1471), *The Imitation of Christ*
Catherine of Genoa (1447–1510), *Life of St Catherine of Genoa*

Extracts from Classic Christian devotional books from Medieval Christianity

Bernard of Clairvaux (1090–1153), *On Loving God*
Nicephorus the Solitary (2d half of 13C), *The Jesus Prayer*
Theologia Germanica, author unknown (mid 1300's)
Julian of Norwich (1343–1443), *Revelations of Divine Love*
Walter Hilton (d. 1396), *The Scale of Perfection*
Thomas a Kempis (1380–1471) *The Imitation of Christ*
Catherine of Genoa (1447–1510), *Life of St Catherine of Genoa*

Bernard of Clairvaux

On Loving God

[In 1115 Bernard established the Clairvaux and became the "greatest churchman of the 12th century."]

Chapter 6

Admit that God deserves to be loved very much, yea, boundlessly, because He loved us first, He infinite and we nothing, loved us, miserable sinners, with a love so great and so free. This is why I said at the beginning that the measure of our love to God is to love immeasurably. For since our love is toward God, who is infinite and immeasurable, how can we bound or limit the love we owe Him? Besides, our love is not a gift but a debt. And since it is the Godhead who loves us, Himself boundless, eternal, supreme love, of whose greatness there is no end, yea, and His wisdom is infinite, whose peace passeth all understanding; since it is He who loves us, I say, can we think of repaying Him grudgingly? 'I will love Thee, O Lord, my strength. The Lord is my rock and my fortress and my deliverer, my God, my strength, in whom I will trust' (Ps. 18.1f). He is all that I need, all that I long for. My God and my help, I will love Thee for Thy great goodness; not so much as I might, surely, but as much as I can. I cannot love Thee as Thou deservest to be loved, for I cannot love Thee more than my own feebleness permits. I will love Thee more when Thou deemest me worthy to receive greater capacity for loving; yet never so perfectly as Thou hast deserved of me. 'Thine eyes did see my substance, yet being unperfect; and in Thy book all my members were written' (PS. 139.16). Yet Thou recordest in that book all who do what they can, even though they cannot do what they ought. Surely I have said enough to show how God should be loved and why. But who has felt, who can know, who express, how much we should love him.

Bernard of Clairvaux, On Loving God

Nicephorus the Solitary

The Jesus Prayer

[Nicephorus the Solitary (second half of the thirteenth century), who came from Calabria, was a monk at Constantinople and then on Mount Athos. He composed a treatise *On Keeping the Heart.* He put forward the following method of prayer.]

First of all let your life be tranquil, free from all care, and at peace with all. Then enter your room, shut yourself in, and, sitting in a corner, say what I shall tell you:

You know that breathing brings air into the heart. And so sit quietly and take your mind and lead it by the path of breathing into the very heart and hold it there; do not give it freedom to escape as it would wish to.

While holding it there do not leave your mind idle but give it the following holy words to say: "Lord Jesus Christ, Son of God, have mercy on me!" And let the mind repeat them day and night.

Try to get accustomed to this inner dwelling with the assigned prayer and do not allow your mind to leave the heart too soon, because at the beginning it will get very tired and lonely in such interior confinement.

Then when it gets used to it, the mind will be happy and joyful to be there and it will want of itself to stay there. just as a man who returns home from a foreign country is beside himself with joy at seeing his wife and children, in like manner the mind, when it is united with the heart, is full of unspeakable joy and delight.

When you are successful in entering the heart by this means which I have shown you, give thanks to God and continue with this activity unceasingly, for it will teach you what you cannot learn in any other way.

Nicephorus the Solitary, Philokalia of the Prayer of the Heart. The Philokalia *('love of beauty) is a collection of Eastern spiritual texts published in the eighteenth century.*

Theologia Germanica

[Sub-title] Which setteth forth many fair lineaments of divine truth, and saith very lofty and lovely things touching a perfect life

[After the Bible, Martin Luther said that Theologia Germanica was his favorite book.]

Chapter 12

Touching that true inward Peace, which Christ left to His Disciples at the last.

Any say they have no peace nor rest, but so many crosses and trials, afflictions and sorrows, that they know not how they shall ever get through them. Now he who in truth will perceive and take note, perceiveth clearly, that true peace and rest lie not in outward things; for if it were so, the Evil Spirit also would have peace when things go according to his will [which is nowise the case; for the prophet declareth, "There is no peace, saith my God, to the wicked."] And therefore we must consider and see what is that peace which Christ left to His disciples at the last, when He said: "My peace I leave with you, My peace I give unto you." [We may perceive that in these words Christ did not mean a bodily and outward peace; for His beloved disciples, with all His friends and followers, have ever suffered, from the beginning, great affliction, persecution, nay, often martyrdom, as Christ Himself said: "In this world ye shall have tribulation." But Christ meant that true, inward peace of the heart, which beginneth here, and endureth for ever hereafter. Therefore He said:] "Not as the world giveth," for the world is false, and deceiveth in her gifts [she promiseth much, and performeth little. Moreover there liveth no man on earth who may always have rest and peace without troubles and crosses, with whom things always go according to his will; there is always something to be suffered here, turn which way you will. And as soon as you are quit of one assault, perhaps two come in its place. Wherefore yield thyself willingly to them, and seek only that true peace of the heart, which none can take away from thee, that thou mayest overcome all assaults].

Thus then, Christ meant that inward peace which can break through all assaults and crosses of oppression, suffering, misery, humiliation and what more there may be of the like, so that a man may be joyful and patient therein, like the beloved disciples and followers of Christ. Now he who will in love give his whole diligence and might thereto, will verily come to know that true eternal peace which is God Himself, as far as it is possible to a creature; [insomuch that what was bitter to him before, shall become sweet, and his heart shall remain unmoved under all changes, at all times, and after this life, he shall attain unto everlasting peace].

Author unknown, Translated by Susanna Winkworth, 1901

Julian of Norwich

Revelations of Divine Love

"Love was our Lord's Meaning"

This book is begun by God's gift and His grace, but it is not yet performed, as to my sight.

For Charity pray we all; [together] with God's working, thanking, trusting, enjoying. For thus will our good Lord be prayed to, as by the understanding that I took of all His own meaning and of the sweet words where He saith full merrily: I am the Ground of thy beseeching. For truly I saw and understood in our Lord's meaning that He shewed it for that He willeth to have it known more than it is: in which knowing He will give us grace to love Him and cleave to Him. For He beholdeth His heavenly treasure with so great love on earth that He willeth to give us more light and solace in heavenly joy, in drawing to Him of our hearts, for sorrow and darkness which we are in.

And from that time that it was shewed I desired oftentimes to learn what was our Lord's meaning. And fifteen years after, and more, I was answered in ghostly understanding, saying thus: Wouldst thou see clearly thy Lord's meaning in this thing? Learn it well: Love was His meaning. Who shewed it thee? Love. What shewed He thee? Love. Wherefore shewed it He? For Love. Hold thee therein and thou shalt learn and know more in the same. But thou shalt never know nor learn therein other thing without end Thus was I learned that Love was our Lord's meaning.

And I saw full surely that ere God made us He loved us; which love was never slacked, nor ever shall be. And in this love He hath done all His works; and in this love He hath made all things profitable to us; and in this love our life is everlasting. In our making we had beginning; but the love wherein He made us was in Him from without beginning: in which love we have our beginning. And all this shall we see in God, without end.

Julian of Norwich, Revelations of Divine Love, Chapter 86

Walter Hilton

The Scale (Ladder) of Perfection

Of Covetousness and how a Man may know how much of it is hid in his Heart

Heave up this image, and look well about it, and into it, and then shalt thou see covetousness and love of earthly things possess a great part of this image, though it seem little of it. Thou hast forsaken riches and the having much of this world, and art shut up in a cell, but hast thou cleanly forsaken the love of all this? I fear not yet, for it is less mastery to forsake worldly goods than to forsake the love of them. Peradventure thou hast not forsaken thy covetousness, but only hast changed it from great things unto small; from a pound unto a penny, and from a silver dish unto a dish of a halfpenny. This is but a simple change; thou art no good merchant. These examples are childish, nevertheless they signify much more. If thou believe not what I say, put thyself upon the trial. If thou have love and delight in the having and holding of anything that thou hast, how mean soever it may be, with the which love thou feedest thy heart for a time, or if thou have a desire and yearning for to have something that thou hast not, with the which desire thy heart is disquieted and stumbled through unreasonable thinking of the thing, that the pure desire of virtue and of God cannot rest therein; this is a sign that there is covetousness in this image. And if thou wilt put thyself further to the trial, look if anything that thou hast be taken away from thee by violence, or by borrowing, or any other way, so that thou canst not get it again, and for this thou art disquieted, angered, and troubled in thine heart, both for the loss of that thing which thou wouldst have again, and canst not; and also art stirred against him that hath it, to strive and chide with him that may restore it, and will not, this is a token that thou lovest worldly goods. For thus do worldly men when their goods and riches are taken from them; they are heavy, sorry and angry, chiding and striving with them that have them, openly, both by word and deed. But thou dost all this in thy heart privily, where God seeth, and therein thou art in more default than a worldly man; for thou hast forsaken in appearance the love of worldly things, but a worldly man hath not so, and therefore he is excused, though he strive and pursue for his goods by lawful means, for to have them again.

But now sayest thou, that it behoveth thee to have thy necessaries of such things as belong unto thee, as well as a worldly man. I grant well thereto; but thou shouldst not love it for itself, nor have liking in the holding nor in the keeping, nor feel sorrow and heaviness in the losing, or in the withdrawing of it. For as St Gregory saith: As much sorrow as thou hast in losing of a thing, so much love hast thou in the keeping of it. And therefore if so be thy heart made whole, and thou hadst truly felt a desire of spiritual things, and therewith hadst a true sight of the least spiritual thing that is, thou wouldst set at nought all the love and liking of any earthly thing, it would not cleave to thee.

For to love and have more than thou reasonably needest, only for lust and liking, is a great fault. Also, to fix thy love upon the thing which thou needest, for the thing itself, is a fault also, but not so great. But to have and use that thing that thou needest without love of it, more than nature and need requireth, without which the thing cannot be used, is no fault.

Soothly in this point I fear that many who have taken upon them the state and likeness of poverty are much letted and hindered in their pursuit of the love of God; I accuse no man, nor reprove any state, for in each state there be some good, and some otherwise; but one thing I say to every man or woman that hath taken the state of voluntary poverty, whether he be religious or secular, or what degree he be in, as long as his love and his affection is bounden and fastened, and as it were glued with the love of any earthly thing, which he hath, or would have, he cannot have nor feel soothfastly the clean love, and the clear sight of spiritual things. For St Austin said to our Lord thus: Lord, he loveth Thee but little, that loveth anything with Thee, which he loveth not for Thee. For the more love and covetousness of any earthly thing is with thee, the less is the love of God in thy heart. For though it be so, that this love of earthly things putteth them not out of charity; but if it be so much that it strangleth the love of God and of their neighbor, verily it hindereth and letteth them from the fervor of charity, and also from that special reward which they should have in the bliss of heaven for perfect poverty, and that is a great loss if thou couldst see it. For who so could understand the spiritual reward, how good, how precious and how worthy it is (for it is everlasting), he would not for the love of all earthly joy, or having all earthly things (though he might have them without sin) hinder, no, nor lessen the least reward of the bliss of heaven, which he might have if that he would; but God knows I speak more than I do myself. But I pray thee do thus as I say, by the grace of God, if thou canst, or any other man that will, for it would be a comfort to my heart (though I have it not in myself that which I say) that I might have it in thee, or in any other creature, which hath received more plenty of His grace than I.

But see, now then, since covetousness, in the naked ground of it, letteth a man or woman so much from the spiritual feeling of the love of God, how much more, then, doth it let and cumber worldly men and women, who by all their wits and bodily business night and day, study and travail how they may get riches and plenty of worldly goods? They can have no other delight but in worldly things; nay, they will not, for they seek it not. I say no more of them at this time; for in this writing I spake not to them. But this I say, that if they would see, or could see what they do, they would not do so.

Walter Hilton, The Scale (Ladder) of Perfection, Chapter 7

Thomas a Kempis

The Imitation of Christ

Whoever desires to understand and take delight in the words of Christ must strive to conform his whole life to him. Of what use is it to discourse learnedly on the Trinity, if you lack humility and therefore displease the Trinity? Lofty words do not make a man just or holy; but a good life makes him dear to God.

If you knew the whole Bible by heart, and all the teachings of the philosophers, how would this help you without the grace and love of God? 'Vanity of vanities, and all is vanity, except to love God and serve him alone. And this is supreme wisdom to despise the world, and draw daily nearer to the kingdom of heaven (I.1).

A humble countryman who serves God is more pleasing to him than a conceited intellectual who knows the course of the stars, but neglects his own soul . . . Restrain an inordinate desire for knowledge, in which is found much anxiety and deception . . . If it seems to you that you know a great deal and have wide experience in many fields, yet remember that there are many matters of which you are ignorant. A true understanding and humble estimate of oneself is the highest and most valuable of all lessons (1.2).

No motive, even that of affection for anyone, can justify the doing of evil. But to help someone in need, a good word may sometimes be left, or a better undertaken in its place (I.15).

'The kingdom of God is within you', says Our Lord. Turn to the Lord with all your heart, forsake this sorry "world, and your soul shall find rest. Learn to turn from worldly things, and give yourself to spiritual things, and you will see the kingdom of God come within you (II.1).

My son, you cannot always burn with zeal for virtue, nor remain constantly in high contemplation; the weakness of sinful human nature "ill at times compel you to descend to lesser things, and bear with sorrow dens of this present life. (III.51)

Thomas a Kempis, The Imitation of Christ

Catherine of Genoa

Life of St Catherine of Genoa

Chapter 16

So great was the humility of this holy soul that she saw her own nothingness most clearly, and would never speak of herself, neither well nor ill. She said:

"As to the evil, I know well that is all my own, the good I could not possibly do of myself, for nothing cannot produce something." Nor would she speak, as is customary, of being wicked, lest her lower nature might grow confident and presume upon the knowledge of its incapacity for good: and having such an opinion of herself, instead of desiring the esteem of others, she cut away even the root of presumption, saying:

"I will never say anything about myself, either good or bad, lest I should come to esteem myself of some importance: and when I have sometimes heard myself spoken of by others, especially if I were praised, I have said inwardly: 'If you knew what I am within, you would not speak thus.' And then, turning to myself, I say: 'When thou hearest thyself named, or listenest to words which perhaps may seem to praise thee, know that they are not spoken of what is thine; for the only virtue and glory thou hast belong to God, and thou hast at least in thine earthly and carnal nature no more conformity with good than has the demon; but when evil is spoken of thee, remember that all could not be said which is in reality true; thou art unworthy even to be called worthless, because to speak of thee at all lends thee a fictitious value.'"

Hence, knowing herself, all the confidence of this great soul was in God, in whom she was so grounded and established that it was hardly to be called faith, for she saw herself more secure in the hands of God, her Love, than if she were actually in possession of all the goods and felicities which it is possible to desire or to think of having in this world; and having placed all her trust in God, and given him full control of her, she covered herself under the mantle of his providential care.

Catherine of Genoa

History of Bible translations

Number of languages Bible had been translated into during this period.

600–700

14 languages

800–1100

15–19 languages

1200

22 languages

1300

26 languages

1400

30 languages

1500

34 languages

Examples of Bible translations from the Middle Ages

An Anglo-Saxon manuscript of 995

"God lufode middan-eard swa, dat he seade his an-cennedan sunu, dat nan ne forweorde de on hine gely ac habbe dat ece lif."

John 3:16

Wycliffe

The first hand-written English language Bible manuscripts were produced in the 1380's AD by John Wycliffe, an Oxford professor, scholar, and theologian.

Matthew 5:1–16

1 And Jhesus, seynge the puple, wente vp in to an hil; and whanne he was set, hise disciplis camen to hym.

2 And he openyde his mouth, and tauyte hem, and seide,

3 Blessed ben pore men in spirit, for the kyngdom of heuenes is herne.

4 Blessid ben mylde men, for thei schulen welde the erthe.

5 Blessid ben thei that mornen, for thei schulen be coumfortid.

6 Blessid ben thei that hungren and thristen riytwisnesse, for thei schulen be fulfillid.

7 Blessid ben merciful men, for thei schulen gete merci.

8 Blessid ben thei that ben of clene herte, for thei schulen se God.

9 Blessid ben pesible men, for thei schulen be clepid Goddis children.

10 Blessid ben thei that suffren persecusioun for riytfulnesse, for the kingdam of heuenes is herne.

11 `Ye schulen be blessid, whanne men schulen curse you, and schulen pursue you, and shulen seie al yuel ayens you liynge, for me.

12 Ioie ye, and be ye glad, for youre meede is plenteuouse in heuenes; for so thei han pursued `also profetis that weren bifor you.

13 Ye ben salt of the erthe; that if the salt vanysche awey, whereynne schal it be saltid? To no thing it is worth ouere, no but that it be cast out, and be defoulid of men.

14 Ye ben liyt of the world; a citee set on an hil may not be hid;

15 ne me teendith not a lanterne, and puttith it vndur a busschel, but on a candilstike, that it yyue liyt to alle that ben in the hous.

16 So schyne youre liyt befor men, that thei se youre goode werkis, and glorifie youre fadir that is in heuenes.

The first "Wycliffe" edition of the Bible

CHAPTER 5

THE REFORMATION AND THE COUNTER-REFORMATION

From Desiderius Erasmus to Francis de Sales
AD 1518–1648

Important dates in the time of the Reformation and the Counter Reformation

16th Century

[1516–17 Erasmus publishes his edition of Greek-Latin New Testament, *Novum Instrumentum*; this translation powerfully demonstrated the corruption of the Latin Vulgate's text; Erasmus promotes the translation of the Bible into vernacular tongues for reading by the plowboy and the "simplest woman"]

1517 Martin Luther posts his 95 theses at Wittenberg

1517 Pope Leo X commissions Prierias to respond to Luther's 95 thesis Prierias' *Dialogus* is sent to Luther who responds with *Responsio*

1518 Ulrich Zwingli becomes priest at the Great Minster in Zurich

1518 Melanchthon begins teaching Greek at Wittenberg

1519 Anabaptists: Grebel (after Ulrich Zwingli)

1520 Papal bull "Exsurge Domine" gives Luther 60 days to recant or be excommunicated; writes 3 seminal documents: *To the Christian Nobility, On the Babylonian Captivity of the Church*, and *The Freedom of a Christian*; burns papal bull and canon law

1520 Pope Leo X issues *Exsurge Domine*, condemning Martin Luther as a heretic

1521 Edict of Worms issued by Charles V declares Luther an outlaw

1521 Luther is "kidnapped" and taken to Wartburg Castle

1521 Pope Leo X calls King Henry VIII "Defender of the Faith" for his publication of an anti-Luther tract

1522 Luther translates New Testament into German

1525 Eck publishes *Arguments against Luther and Other Enemies of the Church*

1525 Anabaptist movement begins in Zürich, spreads to Germany

1527 Johann Eck publishes *On the Sacrifice of the Mass* to refute Zwingli's rejection of the mass

1529 The term "Protestant" was first used at the Diet of Speyer when supporters of Luther formally protested against the imperial efforts to limit the spread of Lutheranism

1530 Augsburg Confession. Luther founds Lutheran Church

1532 Calvin starts Protestant movement in France; publishes his first work—a commentary on Seneca's De Clementia

1534 Ignatius of Loyola founds the Jesuits

1534 Luther completes translation of Bible into German

1534 Act of Supremacy Henry VIII establishes himself as Supreme Head of Church and clergy of England

1535 Calvin moves to Geneva

1536 William Tyndale burned at stake

1536 Calvin publishes the first edition of his *Institutes of the Christian Religion*

1536 Menno Simons breaks with Rome; becomes Anabaptist leader in Netherlands

1537 Johann Eck publishes a German translation of the Bible

1538 Pope Paul III excommunicates King Henry VIII of England.

1539 Menno Simons publishes *Christian Baptism*

1540 The Society of Jesus founded by Ignatius Loyola, the Jesuit order works for the pope

1541 John Calvin establishes theocracy in Geneva

1541 John Knox establishes Calvinist Reformation in Scotland

1542 Pope Paul III establishes the Congregation of the Inquisition

1545–1563 Council of Trent as part of the Counter-Reformation

1545 The Council of Trent adopts Jerome's Latin Vulgate as the official Bible of the Roman Catholic Church

1545 Martin Luther wrote *Against the Papacy at Rome, an Institution of the Devil*

1546 Luther dies in Eisleben

1546 Francis Xavier and companions sail for Goa, the first modern Christian missionaries to travel to India

1548 Ignatius Loyola's *Spiritual Exercises* first published in its entirety

1549 Cranmer's *The Book of Common Prayer* (Episcopal Church) was adopted in England, establishing a liturgy for the Church of England

1555 Nicholas Ridley and Hugh Latimer burned at the stake

1556 Ignatius Loyola dies

1560 Publication of complete Geneva Bible

1561 Menno Simons founds Mennonites

1564 The term "Puritan" first used

1564 John Calvin dies

1572 John Knox founds Presbyterian Church in Scotland

1572 August 24, St Bartholomew's Day Massacre, over 100,000 Protestant Huguenots slaughtered

1582 Congregationalism: R. Brown

1582 Douay Version of the New Testament (English translation) was completed. After the Old Testament translation was completed in 1610, this became the first English translation of the Bible authorized by and for Roman Catholics
1587 Christians were persecuted in Japan for the first time
1593 Diet of Uppsala in Sweden upheld Martin Luther's doctrines
1596 Ukranian Catholic Church formed when Ukranian subjects of the king of Poland were reunited with Rome, thus creating the largest Byzantine Catholic Church

17th Century

1605 Baptists, John Smith baptizes the first "Baptists" in England, establishes Baptist Church in 1608
1607 Jamestown begins in USA
1611 King James Version of the English Bible released
1618 Synod of Dort
1620 Episcopalians: S. Seabury (Henry VIII)
1620 Separatists ("Pilgrims") land at Plymouth Rock on Cape Cod, Massachusetts, in the "Mayflower"; found New Plymouth
1622–1625 Execution of Christian missionaries to Japan reached its high point
1628 Jan Amos Comenius is driven from Moravia and spends the rest of his life spreading educational reform and Christian reconciliation
1633 Galileo forced by the Inquisition to abjure Copernicus' theories
1634 The first Oberammergau Passion Play
1636 Roger Williams founds Rhode Island
1640 Root and Branch petition presented to British Parliament
1646 Presbyterianism was established as the national religion in England by the Long Parliament. This lasted through English Civil War and, afterward, during interregnum
1646 Westminster Confession drafted at Westminster Abbey
1648 George Fox enters the public ministry

Introduction

The history of the Reformation is the history of one of the greatest outpourings of the life that cometh from God.

J. H. Merle D'Aubigne

The Reformation of the sixteenth century is, next to the introduction of Christianity, the greatest event in history. It marks the end of the Middle Ages and the beginning of modern times. Starting from religion, it gave, directly or indirectly, a mighty impulse to every forward movement, and made Protestantism the chief propelling force in the history of modern civilization.

Philip Schaff

EVENTS

Important events during the time of the Reformation and the Counter-Reformation

Martin Luther posting his 95 theses at Wittenberg
The Council of Trent
Formation of the Jesuits

PEOPLE

Christian leaders of during the time of the Reformation and the Counter-Reformation

Martin Luther (1483–1546)
Ulrich [Huldrych] Zwingli (1484–1531)
Thomas Cranmer (1489–1556)
Ignatius of Loyola (1491–1556)
William Tyndale (1494–1536)
Menno Simons (1496–1561)
Francis Xavier (1506–1552)
John Calvin (1509–1564)
Teresa of Avila (1515–1582)

Historian's overview of the Reformation and the Counter-Reformation

1. The turning point of modern history

The age of the Reformation bears a strong resemblance to the first century. Both are rich beyond any other period in great and good men, important facts, and permanent results. Both contain the ripe fruits of preceding, and the fruitful germs of succeeding ages.

They are turning points in the history of mankind.

They are felt in their effects to this day, and will be felt to the end of time.

They refashioned the world from the innermost depths of the human soul in its contact, with the infinite Being.

They were ushered in by a providential concurrence of events and tendencies of thought.

The way for Christianity was prepared by Moses and the Prophets, the dispersion of the Jews, the conquests of Alexander the Great, the language and literature of Greece, the arms and laws of Rome, the decay of idolatry, the spread of skepticism, the aspirations after a new revelation, the hopes of a coming Messiah.

The Reformation was preceded and necessitated by
the corruptions of the papacy,
the decline of monasticism and scholastic theology,
the growth of mysticism,
the revival of letters,
the resurrection of the Greek and Roman classics,
the invention of the printing press,
the discovery of a new world,
the publication of the Greek Testament,
the general spirit of enquiry,
the striving after national independence and personal freedom.

In both centuries we hear the creative voice of the Almighty calling light out of darkness.

The sixteenth century is the age of the renaissance in religion, literature, and art. The air was stirred by the spirit of progress and freedom. The snows of a long winter were fast, melting before the rays of the vernal sun. The world seemed to be renewing its youth; old things were passing away, all things were becoming new. Pessimists and timid conservatives took alarm at the threatened overthrow of cherished notions and institutions, and were complaining, fault-finding and desponding. A very useless business. Intelligent observers of the signs of the times looked hopefully and cheerfully to the future. "O century!" exclaimed Ulrich von Hutten, "the studies flourish, the spirits are awake, it is a luxury to live." And Luther wrote in 1522: "If you read all the annals of the past, you will find no century like this since the birth of Christ. Such building and planting, such good living and dressing, such enterprise in commerce, such a stir in all the arts, has not been since Christ came into the world. And how numerous are the sharp and intelligent people who leave nothing hidden and unturned: even a boy of twenty years knows more nowadays than was known formerly by twenty doctors of divinity."

The Protestant Reformation assumed the helm of the liberal tendencies and movements of the renaissance, directed them into the channel of Christian life, and saved the world from a disastrous revolution. For the Reformation was neither a revolution nor a restoration, though including elements of both. It was negative and destructive towards error, positive and constructive towards truth; it was conservative as well as progressive; it built up new institutions in the place of those which it pulled down; and for this reason and to this extent it has succeeded.

Under the motherly care of the Latin Church, Europe had been Christianized and civilized, and united into a family of nations under the spiritual government of the Pope and the secular government of the Emperor, with one creed, one ritual, one discipline, and one sacred language. The state of heathenism and barbarism at the beginning of the sixth century contrasts with the state of Christian Europe at the beginning of the sixteenth century as midnight darkness compared with the dawn of the morning. But the sun of the day had not yet arisen.

All honor to the Catholic Church and her inestimable services to humanity. But Christianity is far broader and deeper than any ecclesiastical organization. It burst the shell of medieval forms, struck out new paths, and elevated Europe to a higher plane of intellectual, moral and spiritual culture than it had ever attained before.

2. Protestantism and Romanism

Protestantism represents the most enlightened and active of modern church history, but not the whole of it.

We must distinguish between Catholicism and Romanism. The former embraces the ancient Oriental church, the medieval church, and we may say, in a wider sense, all the modern evangelical churches. Romanism is the Latin church turned against the Reformation, consolidated by the Council of Trent and completed by the Vatican Council of 1870 with its dogma of papal absolutism and papal infallibility. Medieval Catholicism is pre-evangelical, looking to the Reformation; modern Romanism is anti-evangelical, condemning the Reformation, yet holding with unyielding tenacity the oecumenical doctrines once sanctioned, and doing this all the more by virtue of its claim to infallibility.

Catholicism and Protestantism represent two distinct types of Christianity which sprang from the same root, but differ in the branches.

Catholicism is legal Christianity which served to the barbarian nations of the Middle Ages as a necessary school of discipline; Protestantism is evangelical Christianity which answers the age of independent manhood. Catholicism is traditional, hierarchical, ritualistic, conservative; Protestantism is biblical, democratic, spiritual, progressive. The former is ruled by the principle of authority, the latter by the principle of freedom. But the law, by awakening a sense of sin and exciting a desire for redemption, leads to the gospel; parental authority is a school of freedom; filial obedience looks to manly self-government.

Romanism and orthodox Protestantism believe in one God, Father, Son, and Holy Spirit, and in one divine-human Lord and Savior of the race. They accept in common the Holy Scriptures and the oecumenical faith. They agree in every article of the Apostles' Creed. What unites them is far deeper, stronger and more important than what divides them.

But Romanism holds also a large number of "traditions of the elders," which Protestantism rejects as extra-scriptural or anti-scriptural; such are the papacy, the worship of saints and relics, transubstantiation, the sacrifice of the mass, prayers and masses for the dead, works of supererogation, purgatory, indulgences, the system of monasticism with its perpetual vows and ascetic practices, besides many superstitious rites and ceremonies.

Protestantism, on the other hand, revived and developed the Augustinian doctrines of sin and grace; it proclaimed the sovereignty of divine mercy in man's salvation, the sufficiency of the Scriptures as a rule of faith, and the sufficiency of Christ's merit as a source of justification; it asserted the right of direct access to the Word of God and the throne of grace, without human mediators; it secured Christian freedom from bondage; it substituted social morality for monkish asceticism, and a simple, spiritual worship for an imposing ceremonialism that addresses the senses and imagination rather than the intellect and the heart.

The Reformation began simultaneously in Germany and Switzerland, and swept with astonishing rapidity over France, Holland, Scandinavia, Bohemia, Hungary, England and Scotland; since the seventeenth century it has spread by emigration to North America, and by commercial and missionary enterprises to every Dutch and English colony, and every heathen land. It carried away the majority of the Teutonic and a part of the Latin nations, and for a while threatened to overthrow the papal church.

But towards the close of the sixteenth century the triumphant march of the Reformation was suddenly arrested. Romanism rose like a wounded giant, and made the most vigorous efforts to reconquer the lost territory in Europe, and to extend its dominion in Asia and South America. Since that time the numerical relation of the two churches has undergone little change. But the progress of secular and ecclesiastical history has run chiefly in Protestant channels.

3. Necessity of a reformation

The corruption and abuses of the Latin church had long been the complaint of the best men, and even of general councils.

The papacy was secularized, and changed into a selfish tyranny whose yoke became more and more unbearable. The scandal of the papal schism had indeed been removed, but papal morals, after a temporary improvement, became worse than ever during the years 1492 to 1521. Alexander VI. was a monster of iniquity; Julius II. was a politician and warrior rather than a chief shepherd of souls; and Leo X. took far more interest in the revival of heathen literature and art than in religion, and is said to have even doubted the truth of the gospel history.

Discipline was nearly ruined. Whole monastic establishments and orders had become nurseries of ignorance and superstition, idleness and dissipation.

Theology was a maze of scholastic subtleties, Aristotelian dialectics and idle speculations, but ignored the great doctrines of the gospel. Carlstadt, the older colleague of Luther, confessed that he had been doctor of divinity before he had seen a complete copy of the Bible. Education was confined to priests and nobles. The mass of the laity could neither read nor write, and had no access to the word of God except the Scripture lessons from the pulpit.

The priest's chief duty was to perform, by his magic words, the miracle of transubstantiation, and to offer the sacrifice of the mass for the living and the dead in a foreign tongue. Many did it mechanically, or with a skeptical reservation, especially in Italy. Preaching was neglected, and had reference, mostly, to indulgences, alms, pilgrimages and processions.

The churches were overloaded with good and bad pictures, with real and fictitious relics. Saint-worship and image-worship, superstitious rites and ceremonies obstructed the direct worship of God in spirit and in truth.

It was evidently the design of Providence to develop a new type of Christianity outside of the restraints of the papacy, and the history of three centuries is the best explanation and vindication of that design. Every movement in history must be judged by its fruits.

The elements of such an advance movement were all at work before Luther and Zwingli protested against papal indulgences.

4. The preparations for the Reformation.

The Reformers, it should not be forgotten, were all born, baptized, confirmed, and educated in the Roman Catholic Church, and most of them had served as priests at her altars with the solemn vow of obedience to the pope on their conscience. They stood as closely related to the papal church, as the Apostles and Evangelists to the Synagogue and the Temple; and for reasons of similar urgency, they were justified to leave the communion of their fathers; or rather, they did not leave it, but were cast out by the ruling hierarchy.

The Reformation went back to first principles in order to go forward. It struck its roots deep in the past and bore rich fruits for the future. It sprang forth almost simultaneously from different parts of Europe and was enthusiastically hailed by the leading minds of the age in church and state. No great movement in history—except Christianity itself—was so widely and thoroughly prepared as the Protestant Reformation.

The reformatory Councils of Pisa, Constance, and Basel;
the conflict of the Emperors with the Popes;
the contemplative piety of the mystics with their thirst after direct communion with God;
the revival of classical literature;
the general intellectual awakening;
the biblical studies of Reuchlin, and Erasmus;
the rising spirit of national independence;
Wycliffe, and the Lollards in England;
Hus, and the Hussites in Bohemia;
John von Goch, John von Wesel, and Johann Wessel in Germany and the Netherlands;
Savonarola in Italy;
the Brethren of the Common Life,
the Waldenses,
the Friends of God,

—contributed their share towards the great change and paved the way for a new era of Christianity. The innermost life of the church was pressing forward to a new era. There is scarcely a principle or doctrine of the Reformation which was not anticipated and advocated in the fourteenth and fifteenth centuries. Luther made the remark that his opponents might charge him with having borrowed everything from John Wessel if he had known his writings earlier. The fuel was abundant all over Europe, but it required the spark which would set it ablaze.

5. The genius and aim of the Reformation

The Reformation was at first a purely religious movement, and furnishes a striking illustration of the all-pervading power of religion in history. It started from the question: What must a man do to be saved? How shall a sinner be justified before God, and attain peace of his troubled conscience? The Reformers were supremely concerned for the salvation of the soul, for the glory of Christ and the triumph of his gospel. They thought much more of the future world than of the present, and made all political, national, and literary interests subordinate and subservient to religion. The Reformation removed the obstructions which the papal church had interposed between Christ and the believer.

There are three fundamental principles of the Reformation:

the supremacy of the Scriptures over tradition,

the supremacy of faith over works,

and the supremacy of the Christian people over an exclusive priesthood.

6. The authority of the Scriptures

The objective principle of Protestantism maintains that the Bible, as the inspired record of revelation, is the only infallible rule of faith and practice; in opposition to the Roman Catholic coordination of Scripture and ecclesiastical tradition, as the joint rules of faith.

The teaching of the living church is by no means rejected, but subordinated to the Word of God. The achievement of the Reformation was a source of incalculable blessings for all time to come. In a few years Luther's version had more readers among the laity than ever the Latin Vulgate had among priests; and the Protestant Bible societies circulate more Bibles in one year than were copied during the fifteen centuries before the Reformation.

We must remember, however, that this wonderful progress was only made possible by the previous invention of the art of printing and by the subsequent education of the people. The Catholic Church had preserved the sacred Scriptures through ages of ignorance and barbarism; the Latin Bible was the first gift of the printing press to the world; fourteen or more editions of a German version were printed before 1518; the first two editions of the Greek Testament we owe to the liberality of a Spanish cardinal (Ximenes), and the enterprise of a Dutch scholar in Basel (Erasmus); and the latter furnished the text from which, with the aid of Jerome's Vulgate, the translations of Luther and Tyndale were made.

7. Justification by faith

The subjective principle of Protestantism is the doctrine of justification and salvation by faith in Christ; as distinct from the doctrine of justification by faith and works or salvation by grace and human merit. Luther's formula is *sola fide* (by faith alone). Calvin goes further back to God's eternal election, as the ultimate ground of salvation and comfort in life and in death. But Luther and Calvin meant substantially the same thing, and agree in the more general proposition of salvation by free grace through living faith in Christ (Acts 4:12), in opposition to any Pelagian or Semi-pelagian compromise which divides the work and merit between God and man. And this is the very soul of evangelical Protestantism.

Protestantism does by no means despise or neglect good works or favor antinomian license; it only subordinates them to faith, and measures their value by quality rather than quantity.

8. The priesthood of the laity

The social or ecclesiastical principle of Protestantism is the general priesthood of believers, in distinction from the special priesthood which stands mediating between Christ and the laity.

The Roman church is an exclusive hierarchy, and assigns to the laity the position of passive obedience. The bishops are the teaching and ruling church; they alone constitute a council or synod, and have the exclusive power of legislation and administration. Laymen have no voice in spiritual matters, they can not even read the Bible without the permission of the priest, who holds the keys of heaven and hell.

In the New Testament every believer is called a saint, a priest, and a king. "All Christians," says Luther, "are truly of the spiritual estate, and there is no difference among them, save of office alone. As St. Paul says, we are all one body, though each member does its own work, to serve the others. This is because we have one baptism, alike; one gospel, one faith, and are all Christians for baptism, gospel and faith, these alone make spiritual and Christian people."

Philip Schaff, History of the Christian Church, 1890

Indulgences

Introduction

John Tetzel (1465–1519) was a German Dominican friar remembered for selling indulgences using the catchy line, "As soon a coin in coffer rings, the soul from purgatory springs."

Tetzel even went as far as creating a chart that listed a price for each type of sin. In 1517, Tetzel was trying to raise money for the ongoing construction of St. Peter's Basilica and it is believed that Martin Luther was inspired to write his 95 Theses, in part, due to Tetzel's actions during this period of time.

An indulgence, 1517

An indulgence bearing the signature of Johann Tetzel translates as follows:

With the Authority of all Saints and with mercy for you, I free you of all
and excuse you from all punishments for ten days – *Johann Tetzel.*

Luther issued his challenge to the theological world from religious motives only, so happened that it fully coincided with the political views of the Elector; but, to the cr of both Prince and monk, it should be remembered that there was no mutual understanding between them. They had never seen each other before the publication of the 95 Theses; nor did they correspond on the subject, although they were of one accord about it. Frederick always viewed it with disfavor, and begrudged that such large amounts of money should be sent to Rome under the cloak of Indulgences, and we have seen how he had employed the proceeds resulting from their former sale. Now, however, he must have objected still more to the attempt to drain his poor country, because the object of the sale was not a holy war—if ever a war can be so called—but the alleged erection of St. Peter's Church. If such was really the case, it might be truly said that Leo X. undermined the Chair of St. Peter for the sake of the Church of St. Peter. But people were incredulous. It was whispered, that the Pope required the money for the benefit of his family.

Another disagreeable element in the whole transaction was the then commonly known fact, that the Archbishop of Mentz had actually "farmed" the sale of the Indulgences in his own episcopal territory on condition that one half of the proceeds should fall to his share. He had promised to bear the expenses of obtaining the Pall himself, and having borrowed a considerable amount of money from the celebrated house of Fugger, he allowed their agents to travel about in company with the notorious Tetzel, as commercial controllers, and to take possession of half of the proceeds as they came in. Through this and other circumstances the affair assumed the ugly aspect of a very worldly and mercenary transaction, carried on in the meanest spirit. There was, besides, a tension between Frederick and the Prince Elector of Mentz; it was, therefore, natural that the step which Luther had taken should meet with his tacit approval. More than this Luther did not expect, for he well knew the lethargic character of Frederick; but under the circumstances that was quite sufficient, for the latter granted him shelter and protection, in spite of the urgent entreaties of zealots to deliver up the bold Augustinian monk at once to Rome.

C. A. Buchheim, The Political Course of the Reformation in Germany (1517–1546)

Luther's 95 Theses

Introductory letter

. . . Papal indulgences are being carried about, under your most distinguished authority, for the building of St. Peter's. In respect of these I do not so much accuse the extravagant sayings of the preachers, which I have not heard, but I grieve at the very false ideas which the people conceive from them, and which are spread abroad in common talk on every ls believe that, if they buy letters of indulgences, they are as soon as they have thrown their contribution into the rgatory; and furthermore, that so great is the grace thus at—even, as they say, if, by an impossibility, any one had at it may be pardoned; and again, that by these indulment and guilt.

souls committed to your care, most excellent Father, death, and a most severe account, which you will have to render them, is growing and increasing. Hence I have not been able to keep silence any longer on this subject, for by no function of a bishop's office can a man become sure of salvation, since he does not even become sure through the grace of God infused into him, but the Apostle bids us to be ever working out our salvation in fear and trembling. (Phil. ii. 12.) Even the righteous man—says Peter—shall scarcely be saved. (1 Pet. iv. 18.) In fine, so narrow is the way which leads unto life, that the Lord, speaking by the prophets Amos and Zachariah, calls those who are to be saved brands snatched from the burning, and our Lord everywhere declares the difficulty of salvation.

Why then, by these false stories and promises of pardon, do the preachers of them make the people to feel secure and without fear? Since indulgences confer absolutely no good on souls as regards salvation or holiness, but only take away the outward penalty which was wont of old to be canonically imposed. . . .

This faithful discharge of my humble duty I entreat that your most illustrious Grace will deign to receive in a princely and bishoplike spirit—that is, with all clemency—even as I offer it with a most faithful heart, and one most devoted to your most reverend Fatherhood, since I too am part of your flock. May the Lord Jesus keep your most reverend Fatherhood for ever and ever. Amen.

Martin Luther, from Wittemberg, on the eve of All Saints, in the year 1517

1. Our Lord and Master Jesus Christ in saying: "Repent ye," In the Latin, from the Vulgate, "agite pœnitentiam," sometimes translated "Do penance." The effect of the following theses depends to some extent on the double meaning of "pœnitentia"—penitence and penance. etc., intended that the whole life of believers should be penitence.

2. This word cannot be understood of sacramental penance, that is, of the confession and satisfaction which are performed under the ministry of priests.

3. It does not, however, refer solely to inward penitence; nay such inward penitence is naught, unless it outwardly produces various mortifications of the flesh.

4. The penalty. "Pœna," the connection between "pœna" and "pœnitentia" being again suggestive. thus continues as long as the hatred of self—that is, true inward penitence—continues; namely, till our entrance into the kingdom of heaven.

5. The Pope has neither the will nor the power to remit any penalties, except those which he has imposed by his own authority, or by that of the canons.

6. The Pope has no power to remit any guilt, except by declaring and warranting it to have been remitted by God; or at most by remitting cases reserved for himself; in which cases, if his power were despised, guilt would certainly remain.

7. God never remits any man's guilt, without at the same 7time subjecting him, humbled in all things, to the authority of his representative the priest.

8. The penitential canons are imposed only on the living, and no burden ought to be imposed on the dying, according to them.

9. Hence the Holy Spirit acting in the Pope does well for us, in that, in his decrees, he always makes exception of the article of death and of necessity.

10. Those priests act wrongly and unlearnedly, who, in the case of the dying, reserve the canonical penances for purgatory.

11. Those tares about changing of the canonical penalty into the penalty of purgatory seem surely to have been sown while the bishops were asleep.

12. Formerly the canonical penalties were imposed not after, but before absolution, as tests of true contrition.

13. The dying pay all penalties by death, and are already dead to the canon laws, and are by right relieved from them.

14. The imperfect soundness or charity of a dying person necessarily brings with it great fear, and the less it is, the greater the fear it brings.

15. This fear and horror is sufficient by itself, to say nothing of other things, to constitute the pains of purgatory, since it is very near to the horror of despair.

16. Hell, purgatory, and heaven appear to differ as despair, almost despair, and peace of mind differ.

17. With souls in purgatory it seems that it must needs be that, as horror diminishes, so charity increases.

18. Nor does it seem to be proved by any reasoning or any scriptures, that they are outside of the state of merit or of the increase of charity.

19. Nor does this appear to be proved, that they are sure and confident of their own blessedness, at least all of them, though we may be very sure of it.

20. Therefore the Pope, when he speaks of the plenary remission of all penalties, does not mean simply of all, but only of those imposed by himself.

21. Thus those preachers of indulgences are in error who say that, by the indulgences of the Pope, a man is loosed and saved from all punishment.

22. For in fact he remits to souls in purgatory no penalty which they would have had to pay in this life according to the canons.

23. If any entire remission of all penalties can be granted to any one, it is certain that it is granted to none but the most perfect, that is, to very few.

24. Hence the greater part of the people must needs be deceived by this indiscriminate and high-sounding promise of release from penalties.

25. Such power as the Pope has over purgatory in general, such has every bishop in his own diocese, and every curate in his own parish, in particular.

26. The Pope acts most rightly in granting remission to souls, not by the power of the keys (which is of no avail in this case) but by the way of suffrage.

27. They preach man, who say that the soul flies out of purgatory as soon as the money thrown into the chest rattles.

28. It is certain that, when the money rattles in the chest, avarice and gain may be increased, but the suffrage of the Church depends on the will of God alone.

29. Who knows whether all the souls in purgatory desire to be redeemed from it, according to the story told of Saints Severinus and Paschal.

30. No man is sure of the reality of his own contrition, much less of the attainment of plenary remission.

31. Rare as is a true penitent, so rare is one who truly buys indulgences—that is to say, most rare.

32. Those who believe that, through letters of pardon, they are made sure of their own salvation, will be eternally damned along with their teachers.

33. We must especially beware of those who say that these pardons from the Pope are that inestimable gift of God by which man is reconciled to God.

34. For the grace conveyed by these pardons has respect only to the penalties of sacramental satisfaction, which are of human appointment.

35. They preach no Christian doctrine, who teach that contrition is not necessary for those who buy souls out of purgatory or buy confessional licences.

36. Every Christian who feels true compunction has of right plenary remission of pain and guilt, even without letters of pardon.

37. Every true Christian, whether living or dead, has a share in all the benefits of Christ and of the Church, given him by God, even without letters of pardon.

38. The remission, however, imparted by the Pope is by no means to be despised, since it is, as I have said, a declaration of the Divine remission.

39. It is a most difficult thing, even for the most learned theologians, to exalt at the same time in the eyes of the people the ample effect of pardons and the necessity of true contrition.

40. True contrition seeks and loves punishment; while the ampleness of pardons relaxes it, and causes men to hate it, or at least gives occasion for them to do so.

41. Apostolical pardons ought to be proclaimed with caution, lest the people should falsely suppose that they are placed before other good works of charity.

42. Christians should be taught that it is not the mind of the Pope that the buying of pardons is to be in any way compared to works of mercy.

43. Christians should be taught that he who gives to a poor man, or lends to a needy man, does better than if he bought pardons.

44. Because, by a work of charity, charity increases, and the man becomes better; while, by means of pardons, he does not become better, but only freer from punishment.

45. Christians should be taught that he who sees any one in need, and, passing him by, gives money for pardons, is not purchasing for himself the indulgences of the Pope, but the anger of God.

46. Christians should be taught that, unless they have superfluous wealth, they are bound to keep what is necessary for the use of their own households, and by no means to lavish it on pardons.

47. Christians should be taught that, while they are free to buy pardons, they are not commanded to do so.

48. Christians should be taught that the Pope, in granting pardons, has both more need and more desire that devout prayer should be made for him, than that money should be readily paid.

49. Christians should be taught that the Pope's pardons are useful, if they do not put their trust in them, but most hurtful, if through them they lose the fear of God.

50. Christians should be taught that, if the Pope were acquainted with the exactions of the preachers of pardons, he would prefer that the Basilica of St. Peter should be burnt to ashes, than that it should be built up with the skin, flesh, and bones of his sheep.

51. Christians should be taught that, as it would be the duty, so it would be the wish of the Pope, even to sell, if necessary, the Basilica of St. Peter, and to give of his own money to very many of those from whom the preachers of pardons extract money.

52. Vain is the hope of salvation through letters of pardon, even if a commissary—nay, the Pope himself—were to pledge his own soul for them.

53. They are enemies of Christ and of the Pope, who, in order that pardons may be preached, condemn the word of God to utter silence in other churches.

54. Wrong is done to the word of God when, in the same sermon, an equal or longer time is spent on pardons than on it.

55. The mind of the Pope necessarily is that, if pardons, which are a very small matter, are celebrated with single bells, single processions, and single ceremonies, the Gospel, which is a very great matter, should be preached with a hundred bells, a hundred processions, and a hundred ceremonies.

56. The treasures of the Church, whence the Pope grants indulgences, are neither sufficiently named nor known among the people of Christ.

57. It is clear that they are at least not temporal treasures, for these are not so readily lavished, but only accumulated, by many of the preachers.

58. Nor are they the merits of Christ and of the saints, for these, independently of the Pope, are always working grace to the inner man, and the cross, death, and hell to the outer man.

59. St. Lawrence said that the treasures of the Church are the poor of the Church, but he spoke according to the use of the word in his time.

60. We are not speaking rashly when we say that the keys of the Church, bestowed through the merits of Christ, are that treasure.

61. For it is clear that the power of the Pope is alone sufficient for the remission of penalties and of reserved cases.

62. The true treasure of the Church is the Holy Gospel of the glory and grace of God.

63. This treasure, however, is deservedly most hateful, because it makes the first to be last.

64. While the treasure of indulgences is deservedly most acceptable, because it makes the last to be first.

65. Hence the treasures of the Gospel are nets, wherewith of old they fished for the men of riches.

66. The treasures of indulgences are nets, wherewith they now fish for the riches of men.

67. Those indulgences, which the preachers loudly proclaim to be the greatest graces, are seen to be truly such as regards the promotion of gain.

68. Yet they are in reality in no degree to be compared to the grace of God and the piety of the cross.

69. Bishops and curates are bound to receive the commissaries of apostolical pardons with all reverence.

70. But they are still more bound to see to it with all their eyes, and take heed with all their ears, that these men do not preach their own dreams in place of the Pope's commission.

71. He who speaks against the truth of apostolical pardons, let him be anathema and accursed.

72. But he, on the other hand, who exerts himself against the wantonness and licence of speech of the preachers of pardons, let him be blessed.

73. As the Pope justly thunders against those who use any kind of contrivance to the injury of the traffic in pardons,

74. Much more is it his intention to thunder against those who, under the pretext of pardons, use contrivances to the injury of holy charity and of truth.

75. To think that Papal pardons have such power that they could absolve a man even if—by an impossibility—he had violated the Mother of God, is madness.

76. We affirm on the contrary that Papal pardons cannot take away even the least of venial sins, as regards its guilt.

77. The saying that, even if St. Peter were now Pope, he could grant no greater graces, is blasphemy against St. Peter and the Pope.

78. We affirm on the contrary that both he and any other Pope has greater graces to grant, namely, the Gospel, powers, gifts of healing, etc. (1 Cor. xii. 9.)

79. To say that the cross set up among the insignia of the Papal arms is of equal power with the cross of Christ, is blasphemy.

80. Those bishops, curates, and theologians who allow such discourses to have currency among the people, will have to render an account.

81. This licence in the preaching of pardons makes it no easy thing, even for learned men, to protect the reverence due to the Pope against the calumnies, or, at all events, the keen questionings of the laity.

82. As for instance:—Why does not the Pope empty purgatory for the sake of most holy charity and of the supreme necessity of souls—this being the most just of all reasons—if he redeems an infinite number of souls for the sake of that most fatal thing money, to be spent on building a basilica—this being a very slight reason?

83. Again; why do funeral masses and anniversary masses for the deceased continue, and why does not the Pope return, or permit the withdrawal of the funds bequeathed for this purpose, since it is a wrong to pray for those who are already redeemed?

84. Again; what is this new kindness of God and the Pope, in that, for money's sake, they permit an impious man and an enemy of God to redeem a pious soul which loves God, and yet do not redeem that same pious and beloved soul, out of free charity, on account of its own need?

85. Again; why is it that the penitential canons, long since abrogated and dead in themselves in very fact and not only by usage, are yet still redeemed with money, through the granting of indulgences, as if they were full of life?

86. Again; why does not the Pope, whose riches are at this day more ample than those of the wealthiest of the wealthy, build the one Basilica of St. Peter with his own money, rather than with that of poor believers?

87. Again; what does the Pope remit or impart to those who, through perfect contrition, have a right to plenary remission and participation?

88. Again; what greater good would the Church receive if the Pope, instead of once, as he does now, were to bestow these remissions and participations a hundred times a day on any one of the faithful?

89. Since it is the salvation of souls, rather than money, that the Pope seeks by his pardons, why does he suspend the letters and pardons granted long ago, since they are equally efficacious.

90. To repress these scruples and arguments of the laity by force alone, and not to solve them by giving reasons, is to expose the Church and the Pope to the ridicule of their enemies, and to make Christian men unhappy.

91. If then pardons were preached according to the spirit and mind of the Pope, all these questions would be resolved with ease; nay, would not exist.

92. Away then with all those prophets who say to the people of Christ: "Peace, peace," and there is no peace.

93. Blessed be all those prophets, who say to the people of Christ: "The cross, the cross," and there is no cross.

94. Christians should be exhorted to strive to follow Christ their head through pains, deaths, and hells.

95. And thus trust to enter heaven through many tribulations, rather than in the security of peace.

Protestation

I, Martin Luther, Doctor, of the Order of Monks at Wittemberg, desire to testify publicly that certain propositions against pontifical indulgences, as they call them, have been put forth by me. Now although, up to the present time, neither this most celebrated and renowned school of ours, nor any civil or ecclesiastical power has condemned me, yet there are, as I hear, some men of headlong and audacious spirit, who dare to pronounce me a heretic, as though the matter had been thoroughly looked into and studied. But on my part, as I have often done before, so now too I implore all men, by the faith of Christ, either to point out to me a better way, if such a way has been divinely revealed to any, or at least to submit their opinion to the judgment of God and of the Church. For I am neither so rash as to wish that my sole opinion should be preferred to that of all other men, nor so senseless as to be willing that the word of God should be made to give place to fables, devised by human reason.

Martin Luther

Condemnation of Luther

Papal Bull of Pope Leo X issued June 15, 1520

In virtue of our pastoral office committed to us by the divine favor we can under no circumstances tolerate or overlook any longer the pernicious poison of the above errors without disgrace to the Christian religion and injury to orthodox faith. Some of these errors we have decided to include in the present document; their substance is as follows:

It is a heretical opinion, but a common one, that the sacraments of the New Law give pardoning grace to those who do not set up an obstacle.

To deny that in a child after baptism sin remains is to treat with contempt both Paul and Christ.

The inflammable sources of sin, even if there be no actual sin, delay a soul departing from the body from entrance into heaven.

To one on the point of death imperfect charity necessarily brings with it great fear, which in itself alone is enough to produce the punishment of purgatory, and impedes entrance into the kingdom.

That there are three parts to penance: contrition, confession, and satisfaction, has no foundation in Sacred Scripture nor in the ancient sacred Christian doctors.

Contrition, which is acquired through discussion, collection, and detestation of sins, by which one reflects upon his years in the bitterness of his soul, by pondering over the gravity of sins, their number, their baseness, the loss of eternal beatitude, and the acquisition of eternal damnation, this contrition makes him a hypocrite, indeed more a sinner.

It is a most truthful proverb and the doctrine concerning the contritions given thus far is the more remarkable: "Not to do so in the future is the highest penance; the best penance, a new life."

By no means may you presume to confess venial sins, nor even all mortal sins, because it is impossible that you know all mortal sins. Hence in the primitive Church only manifest mortal sins were confessed.

As long as we wish to confess all sins without exception, we are doing nothing else than to wish to leave nothing to God's mercy for pardon.

Sins are not forgiven to anyone, unless when the priest forgives them he believes they are forgiven; on the contrary the sin would remain unless he believed it was forgiven; for indeed the remission of sin and the granting of grace does not suffice, but it is necessary also to believe that there has been forgiveness.

By no means can you have reassurance of being absolved because of your contrition, but because of the word of Christ: "Whatsoever you shall loose, etc." Hence, I say, trust confidently, if you have obtained the absolution of the priest, and firmly believe yourself to have been absolved, and you will truly be absolved, whatever there may be of contrition.

If through an impossibility he who confessed was not contrite, or the priest did not absolve seriously, but in a jocose manner, if nevertheless he believes that he has been absolved, he is most truly absolved.

In the sacrament of penance and the remission of sin the pope or the bishop does no more than the lowest priest; indeed, where there is no priest, any Christian, even if a woman or child, may equally do as much.

No one ought to answer a priest that he is contrite, nor should the priest inquire.

Great is the error of those who approach the sacrament of the Eucharist relying on this, that they have confessed, that they are not conscious of any mortal sin, that they have sent their prayers on ahead and made preparations; all these eat and drink judgment to themselves. But if they believe and trust that they will attain grace, then this faith alone makes them pure and worthy.

It seems to have been decided that the Church in common Council established that the laity should communicate under both species; the Bohemians who communicate under both species are not heretics, but schismatics.

The treasures of the Church, from which the pope grants indulgences, are not the merits of Christ and of the saints.

Indulgences are pious frauds of the faithful, and remissions of good works; and they are among the number of those things which are allowed, and not of the number of those which are advantageous.

Indulgences are of no avail to those who truly gain them, for the remission of the penalty due to actual sin in the sight of divine justice.

They are seduced who believe that indulgences are salutary and useful for the fruit of the spirit.

Indulgences are necessary only for public crimes, and are properly conceded only to the harsh and impatient.

For six kinds of men indulgences are neither necessary nor useful; namely, for the dead and those about to die, the infirm, those legitimately hindered, and those who have not committed crimes, and those who have committed crimes, but not public ones, and those who devote themselves to better things.

Excommunications are only external penalties and they do not deprive man of the common spiritual prayers of the Church.

Christians must be taught to cherish excommunications rather than to fear them.

The Roman Pontiff, the successor of Peter, is not the vicar of Christ over all the churches of the entire world, instituted by Christ Himself in blessed Peter.

The word of Christ to Peter: "Whatsoever you shall loose on earth," etc., is extended merely to those things bound by Peter himself.

It is certain that it is not in the power of the Church or the pope to decide upon the articles of faith, and much less concerning the laws for morals or for good works.

If the pope with a great part of the Church thought so and so, he would not err; still it is not a sin or heresy to think the contrary, especially in a matter not necessary for salvation, until one alternative is condemned and another approved by a general Council.

A way has been made for us for weakening the authority of councils, and for freely contradicting their actions, and judging their decrees, and boldly confessing whatever seems true, whether it has been approved or disapproved by any council whatsoever.

Some articles of John Hus, condemned in the Council of Constance, are most Christian, wholly true and evangelical; these the universal Church could not condemn.

In every good work the just man sins.

A good work done very well is a venial sin.

That heretics be burned is against the will of the Spirit.

To go to war against the Turks is to resist God who punishes our iniquities through them.

No one is certain that he is not always sinning mortally, because of the most hidden vice of pride.

Free will after sin is a matter of title only; and as long as one does what is in him, one sins mortally.

Purgatory cannot be proved from Sacred Scripture which is in the canon.

The souls in purgatory are not sure of their salvation, at least not all; nor is it proved by any arguments or by the Scriptures that they are beyond the state of meriting or of increasing in charity.

The souls in purgatory sin without intermission, as long as they seek rest and abhor punishment.

The souls freed from purgatory by the suffrages of the living are less happy than if they had made satisfactions by themselves.

Ecclesiastical prelates and secular princes would not act badly if they destroyed all of the money bags of beggary.

. . . Therefore let Martin himself and all those adhering to him, and those who shelter and support him, through the merciful heart of our God and the sprinkling of the blood of our Lord Jesus Christ by which and through whom the redemption of the human race and the upbuilding of holy mother Church was accomplished, know that from our heart we exhort and beseech that he cease to disturb the peace, unity, and truth of the Church for which the Savior prayed so earnestly to the Father. Let him abstain from his pernicious errors that he may come back to us. If they really will obey, and certify to us by legal documents that they have obeyed, they will find in us the affection of a father's love, the opening of the font of the effects of paternal charity, and opening of the font of mercy and clemency.

We enjoin, however, on Martin that in the meantime he cease from all preaching or the office of preacher . . .

The Diet of Worms

The Diet of Worms was the first diet called by Charles V. It lasted from January 27, 1520 to May 25, 1521. At the diet, Martin Luther was ordered to recant his "heretical" teachings.

At the Diet of Worms Luther defended his writings before the Emperor Charles and all the dignitaries of the Empire. Here he made his timeless reply, on 18 April 1521, when asked if he would recant his writings:

I cannot submit my faith either to the Pope or to the Councils, because it is clear as day they have frequently erred and contradicted each other. Unless therefore, I am convinced by the testimony of Scripture . . . I can and will not retract . . . Here I stand . . . I can do no other. So help me God, Amen!!

The Edict of Worms, signed on May 25, 1521 by Charles V declared Luther a heretic and an outlaw.

Council of Trent

The Council of Trent was called by pope Pope Paul III to address the issues raised by the Protestant Reformation.

The council held three sessions (1545–1547, 1551–1552, 1562–1563).

The first session addressed doctrinal issues. It affirmed the Latin Vulgate as the official Scripture of the Church. It also affirmed the authority of tradition along with Scripture (Thus rejecting *sola scriptura.*). Also addressed were justification and original sin.

The second session affirmed all seven sacraments and was attended by a few protestant clergy.

The third session enacted measures to halt abuses of indulgences. It also set standards to enact moral and educational reforms for the clergy.

Decree on justification

Introduction

Whereas there is, at this time, not without the shipwreck of many souls, and grievous detriment to the unity of the Church, a certain erroneous doctrine disseminated touching Justification; the sacred and holy, oecumenical and general Synod of Trent, lawfully assembled in the Holy Ghost,—the most reverend lords, Giammaria del Monte, bishop of Palaestrina, and Marcellus of the title of the Holy Cross in Jerusalem, priest, cardinals of the holy Roman Church, and legates apostolic a latere, presiding therein, in the name of our most holy father and lord in Christ, Paul III., by the providence of God, Pope,-purposes, unto the praise and glory of Almighty God, the tranquillizing of the Church, and the salvation of souls, to expound to all the faithful of Christ the true and sound doctrine touching the said Justification; which (doctrine) the sun of justice, Christ Jesus, the author and finisher of our faith, taught, which the apostles transmitted, and which the Catholic Church, the Holy Ghost reminding her thereof, has always retained; most strictly forbidding that any henceforth presume to believe, preach, or teach, otherwise than as by this present decree is defined and declared.

Canons on justification

CANON I.-If any one saith, that man may be justified before God by his own works, whether done through the teaching of human nature, or that of the law, without the grace of God through Jesus Christ; let him be anathema.

CANON II.-If any one saith, that the grace of God, through Jesus Christ, is given only for this, that man may be able more easily to live justly, and to merit eternal life, as if, by free will without grace, he were able to do both, though hardly indeed and with difficulty; let him be anathema.

CANON III.-If any one saith, that without the prevenient inspiration of the Holy Ghost, and without his help, man can believe, hope, love, or be penitent as he ought, so as that the grace of Justification may be bestowed upon him; let him be anathema.

CANON IV.-If any one saith, that man's free will moved and excited by God, by assenting to God exciting and calling, nowise co-operates towards disposing and preparing itself for obtaining the grace of Justification; that it cannot refuse its consent, if it would, but that, as something inanimate, it does nothing whatever and is merely passive; let him be anathema.

CANON V.-If any one saith, that, since Adam's sin, the free will of man is lost and extinguished; or, that it is a thing with only a name, yea a name without a reality, a figment, in fine, introduced into the Church by Satan; let him be anathema.

CANON VI.-If any one saith, that it is not in man's power to make his ways evil, but that the works that are evil God worketh as well as those that are good, not permissively only, but properly, and of Himself, in such wise that the treason of Judas is no less His own proper work than the vocation of Paul; let him be anathema.

CANON VII.-If any one saith, that all works done before Justification, in whatsoever way they be done, are truly sins, or merit the hatred of God; or that the more earnestly one strives to dispose himself for grace, the more grievously he sins: let him be anathema.

CANON VIII.-If any one saith, that the fear of hell,-whereby, by grieving for our sins, we flee unto the mercy of God, or refrain from sinning,-is a sin, or makes sinners worse; let him be anathema.

CANON IX.-If any one saith, that by faith alone the impious is justified; in such wise as to mean, that nothing else is required to co-operate in order to the obtaining the grace of Justification, and that it is not in any way necessary, that he be prepared and disposed by the movement of his own will; let him be anathema.

CANON X.-If any one saith, that men are just without the justice of Christ, whereby He merited for us to be justified; or that it is by that justice itself that they are formally just; let him be anathema.

CANON XI.-If any one saith, that men are justified, either by the sole imputation of the justice of Christ, or by the sole remission of sins, to the exclusion of the grace and the charity which is poured forth in their hearts by the Holy Ghost, and is inherent in them; or even that the grace, whereby we are justified, is only the favor of God; let him be anathema.

CANON XII.-If any one saith, that justifying faith is nothing else but confidence in the divine mercy which remits sins for Christ's sake; or, that this confidence alone is that whereby we are justified; let him be anathema.

CANON XIII.-If any one saith, that it is necessary for every one, for the obtaining the remission of sins, that he believe for certain, and without any wavering arising from his own infirmity and disposition, that his sins are forgiven him; let him be anathema.

CANON XIV.-If any one saith, that man is truly absolved from his sins and justified, because that he assuredly believed himself absolved and justified; or, that no one is truly justified but he who believes himself justified; and that, by this faith alone, absolution and justification are effected; let him be anathema.

CANON XV.-If any one saith, that a man, who is born again and justified, is bound of faith to believe that he is assuredly in the number of the predestinate; let him be anathema.

CANON XVI.-If any one saith, that he will for certain, of an absolute and infallible certainty, have that great gift of perseverance unto the end,-unless he have learned this by special revelation; let him be anathema.

CANON XVII.-If any one saith, that the grace of Justification is only attained to by those who are predestined unto life; but that all others who are called, are called indeed, but receive not grace, as being, by the divine power, predestined unto evil; let him be anathema.

CANON XVIII.-If any one saith, that the commandments of God are, even for one that is justified and constituted in grace, impossible to keep; let him be anathema.

CANON XIX.-If any one saith, that nothing besides faith is commanded in the Gospel; that other things are indifferent, neither commanded nor prohibited, but free; or, that the ten commandments nowise appertain to Christians; let him be anathema.

CANON XX.-If any one saith, that the man who is justified and how perfect soever, is not bound to observe the commandments of God and of the Church, but only to believe; as if indeed the Gospel were a bare and absolute promise of eternal life, without the condition of observing the commandments ; let him be anathema.

CANON XXI.-If any one saith, that Christ Jesus was given of God to men, as a redeemer in whom to trust, and not also as a legislator whom to obey; let him be anathema.

CANON XXII.-If any one saith, that the justified, either is able to persevere, without the special help of God, in the justice received; or that, with that help, he is not able; let him be anathema.

CANON XXIII.-If any one saith, that a man once justified can sin no more, nor lose grace, and that therefore he that falls and sins was never truly justified; or, on the other hand, that he is able, during his whole life, to avoid all sins, even those that are venial,-except by a special privilege from God, as the Church holds in regard of the Blessed Virgin; let him be anathema.

CANON XXIV.-If any one saith, that the justice received is not preserved and also increased before God through good works; but that the said works are merely the fruits and signs of Justification obtained, but not a cause of the increase thereof; let him be anathema.

CANON XXV.-If any one saith, that, in every good work, the just sins venially at least, or-which is more intolerable still-mortally, and consequently deserves eternal punishments; and that for this cause only he is not damned, that God does not impute those works unto damnation; let him be anathema.

CANON XXVI.-If any one saith, that the just ought not, for their good works done in God, to expect and hope for an eternal recompense from God, through His mercy and the merit of Jesus Christ, if so be that they persevere to the end in well doing and in keeping the divine commandments; let him be anathema.

CANON XXVII.-If any one saith, that there is no mortal sin but that of infidelity; or, that grace once received is not lost by any other sin, however grievous and enormous, save by that of infidelity ; let him be anathema.

CANON XXVIII.-If any one saith, that, grace being lost through sin, faith also is always lost with it; or, that the faith which remains, though it be not a lively faith, is not a true faith; or, that he, who has faith without charity, is not as Christ taught; let him be anathema.

CANON XXIX.-If any one saith, that he, who has fallen after baptism, is not able by the grace of God to rise again; or, that he is able indeed to recover the justice which he has lost, but by faith alone without the sacrament of Penance, contrary to what the holy Roman and universal Church-instructed by Christ and his Apostles-has hitherto professed, observed, and taught; let him be anathema.

CANON XXX.-If any one saith, that, after the grace of Justification has been received, to every penitent sinner the guilt is remitted, and the debt of eternal punishment is blotted out in such wise, that there remains not any debt of temporal punishment to be discharged either in this world, or in the next in Purgatory, before the entrance to the kingdom of heaven can be opened (to him); let him be anathema.

CANON XXXI.-If any one saith, that the justified sins when he performs good works with a view to an eternal recompense; let him be anathema.

CANON XXXII.-If any one saith, that the good works of one that is justified are in such manner the gifts of God, as that they are not also the good merits of him that is justified; or, that the said justified, by the good works which he performs through the grace of God and the merit of Jesus Christ, whose living member he is, does not truly merit increase of grace, eternal life, and the attainment of that eternal life,-if so be, however, that he depart in grace,-and also an increase of glory; let him be anathema.

CANON XXXIII.-If any one saith, that, by the Catholic doctrine touching Justification, by this holy Synod inset forth in this present decree, the glory of God, or the merits of our Lord Jesus Christ are in any way derogated from, and not rather that the truth of our faith, and the glory in fine of God and of Jesus Christ are rendered (more) illustrious; let him be anathema.

The Canons and Decrees of the Council of Trent : with a supplement, containing the condemnations of the early reformers, and other matters relating to the council, translated Theodore Alois Buckley, 1851

Council of Trent on Predestination

That a rash presumptuousness in the matter of Predestination is to be avoided:

No one, moreover, so long as he is in this mortal life, ought so far to presume as regards the secret mystery of divine predestination, as to determine for certain that he is assuredly in the number of the predestinate; as if it were true, that he that is justified, either cannot sin any more, or, if he do sin, that he ought to promise himself an assured repentance; for except by special revelation, it cannot be known whom God hath chosen unto Himself.

Index Librorum Prohibitorum

The principle of a list of forbidden books was adopted at the Fifth Lateran Council in 1515, then confirmed by the Council of Trent in 1546. The first edition of the *Index Librorum Prohibitorum*, dated 1557 was published by Pope Paul IV. The 32nd edition, published in 1948 included 4000 titles. The Index was suppressed in 1966.

The first official censorship had come in 1559 with the publication of the Index *auctorum et librorum prohibitorum* under the direction of Pope Paul IV. The Pauline index, as it became known, was the first in a long succession of papal indexes, forty-two in all. The purpose of these indexes was to guide censors in their decisions of what publications to authorize and which to disallow, for printers were not free to publish books without official permission.

In January of 1562 the Council of Trent took up the issue of the Index and was deeply divided. The Pauline index had been seen by many as too controversial and excessively restrictive. After the opening speeches, the council appointed a commission to draft a new index. Although the council closed before the task of the commission was completed, the new Tridentine index was taken up by Pope Pius IV and published in 1564 by Paulus Manutius in Rome. This index constituted the most authoritative guide the church had yet published; its lists formed the basis of all subsequent indexes, while its rules were accepted as the guide for future censors and compilers.

The Five Solas of the Reformation

Sola Fide—Faith Alone
Sola Scriptura—Scripture Alone
Sola Gratia—Grace Alone
Solus Christus—Christ Alone
Soli Deo Gloria—To the Glory of God Alone

Church organization

Following the history of the earliest church recounted in the New Testament book, The Acts of the Apostles, Calvin divided church organization into four levels:

Pastors: These were five men who exercised authority over religious matters in Geneva.

Teachers: This was a larger group whose job it was to teach doctrine to the population.

Elders: The Elders were twelve men (after the twelve Apostles) who were chosen by the municipal council; their job was to oversee everything that everybody did in the city.

Deacons: Modeled after the Seven in Acts 6–8, the deacons were appointed to care for the sick, the elderly, the widowed and the poor.

Calvin shaped the thought and motivated the ideals of Protestantism in France, the Netherlands, Poland, Hungry, Scotland, and the English Puritans; many of whom settled in America.

The great American historian George Bancroft stated, "He that will not honor the memory, and respect the influence of Calvin, knows but little of the origin of American liberty."

The famous German historian, Leopold von Ranke, wrote, "John Calvin was the virtual founder of America."

John Adams, the second president of the United States, wrote: "Let not Geneva be forgotten or despised. Religious liberty owes it most respect."

American Vision's Biblical Worldview

Martin Luther and Christian freedom

Luther believed that God had laid down the laws which were essential to the due guidance of human nature, that he had prescribed sufficiently the limits within which that nature might range, and had indicated the trees of which it could not safely eat. To erect any rules beyond these as of general obligation, to restrict the free play of nature by any other limitations, he treated as an unjust violation of liberty, which would provoke a dangerous reaction. But let men be brought face to face with God, and with His reasonable and merciful laws, let them be taught that He is their Father, that all His restrictions are for their benefit, all His punishments for their reformation, all His restraints on liberty for their ultimate good, and you have then established an authority which cannot be shaken, and under which human nature may be safely left to develop. In this faith, but in this alone, he let loose men's natural instincts, he taught men that married life, and lay life, and all lawful occupations, were holy and divine, provided they were carried on in faith and in obedience to God's will.

The result was a burst of new life wherever the Reformation was adopted, alike in national energies, in literature, in all social developments, and in natural science. But while we prize and celebrate the liberty thus won, let us beware of forgetting, or allowing others to forget, that it is essentially a Christian Liberty, and that no other Liberty is really free. Luther's whole work, and his whole power, lay in his recognition of our personal relation to God, and of a direct revelation, promise, and command, given to us by God. Any influences, under whatever color, which tend to obscure the reality of that revelation, which would substitute for it any mere natural laws or forces, are undoing Luther's work, and contradicting his most essential principles. If he was a great Reformer, it was because he was a great divine; if he was a friend of the people, it was because he was the friend of God.

C. A. Buchheim, First Principles of the Reformation

Martin Luther on faith and good deeds

"That is why both these affirmations are true: 'Good works do not make a man good, but a good man does good works. Evil works do not make a man evil, but an evil man does evil works. 'So it is necessary for the substance itself, or the person, to be good before any good work. It is as Christ says: 'A bad tree does not produce good fruits; a good tree does not produce evil fruits."

Martin Luther, The Freedom of a Christian, 1520

The Augsburg Confession

The Augsburg Confession, also known as the "Augustana" from its Latin name, *Confessio Augustana*, is the primary confession of faith of the Lutheran Church and one of the most important documents of the Lutheran reformation. It was written in both German and Latin, and was presented by a number of German rulers and free-cities at the Diet of Augsburg on June 25, 1530. The Holy Roman Emperor Charles V had called on the Princes and Free Territories in Germany to explain their religious convictions in an attempt to restore religious and political unity in the Holy Roman Empire, and rally support against the Turkish invasion. It is the fourth document contained in the Lutheran Book of Concord.

Wikipedia

Article II: Of Original Sin.

Also they teach that since the fall of Adam all men begotten in the natural way are born with sin, that is, without the fear of God, without trust in God, and with concupiscence; and that this disease, or vice of origin, is truly sin, even now condemning and bringing eternal death upon those not born again through Baptism and the Holy Ghost.

They Condemn the Pelagians and others who deny that original depravity is sin, and who, to obscure the glory of Christ's merit and benefits, argue that man can be justified before God by his own strength and reason.

Article IV: Of Justification.

Also they teach that men cannot be justified before God by their own strength, merits, or works, but are freely justified for Christ's sake, through faith, when they believe that they are received into favor, and that their sins are forgiven for Christ's sake, who, by His death, has made satisfaction for our sins. This faith God imputes for righteousness in His sight. Rom. 3 and 4.

Article IX: Of Baptism

Of Baptism they teach that it is necessary to salvation, and that through Baptism is offered the grace of God, and that children are to be baptized who, being offered to God through Baptism are received into God's grace.

They condemn the Anabaptists, who reject the baptism of children, and say that children are saved without Baptism.

Article X

Of the Lord's Supper

Of the Supper of the Lord they teach that the Body and Blood of Christ are truly present, and are distributed to those who eat the Supper of the Lord; and they reject those that teach otherwise.

The Augsburg Confession

The Westminster Confession of Faith

The Westminster Confession of Faith is a Reformed confession of faith in the Calvinist theological tradition. Its most controversial statements are those relating to Calvinistic predestination.

Chapter III

Of God's Eternal Decree

I. God from all eternity, did, by the most wise and holy counsel of His own will, freely, and unchangeably ordain whatsoever comes to pass;[1] yet so, as thereby neither is God the author of sin,[2] nor is violence offered to the will of the creatures; nor is the liberty or contingency of second causes taken away, but rather established.[3]

II. Although God knows whatsoever may or can come to pass upon all supposed conditions;[4] yet has He not decreed anything because He foresaw it as future, or as that which would come to pass upon such conditions.[5]

III. By the decree of God, for the manifestation of His glory, some men and angels[6] are predestinated unto everlasting life; and others foreordained to everlasting death.[7]

IV. These angels and men, thus predestinated, and foreordained, are particularly and unchangeably designed, and their number so certain and definite, that it cannot be either increased or diminished.[8]

V. Those of mankind that are predestinated unto life, God, before the foundation of the world was laid, according to His eternal and immutable purpose, and the secret counsel and good pleasure of His will, has chosen, in Christ, unto everlasting glory,[9] out of His mere free grace and love, without any foresight of faith, or good works, or perseverance in either of them, or any other thing in the creature, as conditions, or causes moving Him thereunto;[10] and all to the praise of His glorious grace.[11]

VI. As God has appointed the elect unto glory, so has He, by the eternal and most free purpose of His will, foreordained all the means thereunto.[12] Wherefore, they who are elected, being fallen in Adam, are redeemed by Christ,[13] are effectually called unto faith in Christ by His Spirit working in due season, are justified, adopted, sanctified,[14] and kept by His power, through faith, unto salvation.[15] Neither are any other redeemed by Christ, effectually called, justified, adopted, sanctified, and saved, but the elect only.[16]

VII. The rest of mankind God was pleased, according to the unsearchable counsel of His own will, whereby He extends or withholds mercy, as He pleases, for the glory of His sovereign power over His creatures, to pass by; and to ordain them to dishonor and wrath for their sin, to the praised of His glorious justice.[17]

VIII. The doctrine of this high mystery of predestination is to be handled with special prudence and care,[18] that men, attending the will of God revealed in His Word, and yielding obedience thereunto, may, from the certainty of their effectual vocation, be assured of their eternal election.[19] So shall this doctrine afford matter of praise, reverence, and admiration of God;[20] and of humility, diligence, and abundant consolation to all that sincerely obey the Gospel.[21]

[1] EPH 1:11 In whom also we have obtained an inheritance, being predestinated according to the purpose of him who worketh all things after the counsel of his own will. ROM 11:33 O the depth of the riches both of the wisdom and knowledge of God! how unsearchable are his judgments, and his ways past finding out! HEB 6:17 Wherein God, willing more abundantly to shew unto the heirs of promise the immutability of his counsel, confirmed it by an oath. ROM 9:15 For he saith to Moses, I will have mercy on whom I will have mercy, and I will have compassion on whom I will have compassion. 18 Therefore hath he mercy on whom he will have mercy, and whom he will he hardeneth.

[2] JAM 1:13 Let no man say when he is tempted, I am tempted of God: for God cannot be tempted with evil, neither tempteth he any man. 17 Every good gift and every perfect gift is from above, and cometh down from the Father of lights, with whom is no variableness, neither shadow of turning. 1JO 1:5 This then is the message which we have heard of him, and declare unto you, that God is light, and in him is no darkness at all.

[3] ACT 2:23 Him, being delivered by the determinate counsel and foreknowledge of God, ye have taken, and by wicked hands have crucified and slain. MAT 17:12 But I say unto you, That Elias is come already, and they knew him not, but have done unto him whatsoever they listed. Likewise shall also the Son of man suffer of them. ACT 4:27 For of a truth against thy holy child Jesus, whom thou hast anointed, both Herod, and Pontius Pilate, with the Gentiles, and the people of Israel, were gathered together, 28 For to do whatsoever thy hand and thy counsel determined before to be done. JOH 19:11 Jesus answered, Thou couldest have no power at all against me, except it were given thee from above: therefore he that delivered me unto thee hath the greater sin. PRO 16:33 The lot is cast into the lap; but the whole disposing thereof is of the Lord.

[4] ACT 15:18 Known unto God are all his works from the beginning of the world. 1SA 23:11 Will the men of Keilah deliver me up into his hand? will Saul come down, as thy servant hath heard? O Lord God of Israel, I beseech thee, tell thy servant. And the Lord said, He will come down. 12 Then said David, Will the men of Keilah deliver me and my men into the hand of Saul? And the Lord said, They will deliver thee up. MAT 11:21 Woe unto thee, Chorazin! woe unto thee, Bethsaida! for if the mighty works, which were done in you, had been done in Tyre and Sidon, they would have repented long ago in sackcloth and ashes. 23 And

thou, Capernaum, which art exalted unto heaven, shalt be brought down to hell: for if the mighty works, which have been done in thee, had been done in Sodom, it would have remained until this day.

[5] ROM 9:11 (For the children being not yet born, neither having done any good or evil, that the purpose of God according to election might stand, not of works, but of him that calleth;) 13 As it is written, Jacob have I loved, but Esau have I hated. 16 So then it is not of him that willeth, nor of him that runneth, but of God that sheweth mercy. 18 Therefore hath he mercy on whom he will have mercy, and whom he will he hardeneth.

[6] 1TI 5:21 I charge thee before God, and the Lord Jesus Christ, and the elect angels, that thou observe these things without preferring one before another, doing nothing by partiality. MAT 25:41 Then shall he say also unto them on the left hand, Depart from me, ye cursed, into everlasting fire, prepared for the devil and his angels.

[7] ROM 9:22 What if God, willing to shew his wrath, and to make his power known, endured with much longsuffering the vessels of wrath fitted to destruction: 23 And that he might make known the riches of his glory on the vessels of mercy, which he had afore prepared unto glory. EPH 1:5 Having predestinated us unto the adoption of children by Jesus Christ to himself, according to the good pleasure of his will, 6 To the praise of the glory of his grace, wherein he hath made us accepted in the beloved. PRO 16:4 The Lord hath made all things for himself: yea, even the wicked for the day of evil.

[8] 2TI 2:19 Nevertheless the foundation of God standeth sure, having this seal, The Lord knoweth them that are his. And, Let every one that nameth the name of Christ depart from iniquity. JOH 13:18 I speak not of you all: I know whom I have chosen: but that the scripture may be fulfilled, He that eateth bread with me hath lifted up his heel against me.

[9] EPH 1:4 According as he hath chosen us in him before the foundation of the world, that we should be holy and without blame before him in love: 9 Having made known unto us the mystery of his will, according to his good pleasure which he hath purposed in himself: 11 In whom also we have obtained an inheritance, being predestinated according to the purpose of him who worketh all things after the counsel of his own will. ROM 8:30 Moreover whom he did predestinate, them he also called: and whom he called, them he also justified: and whom he justified, them he also glorified. 2TI 1:9 Who hath saved us, and called us with an holy calling, not according to our works, but according to his own purpose and grace, which was given us in Christ Jesus before the world began. 1TH 5:9 For God hath not appointed us to wrath, but to obtain salvation by our Lord Jesus Christ.

[10] ROM 9:11 (For the children being not yet born, neither having done any good or evil, that the purpose of God according to election might stand, not of works, but of him that calleth;) 13 As it is written, Jacob have I loved, but Esau have I hated. 16 So then it is not of him that willeth, nor of him that runneth, but of God that sheweth mercy. EPH 1:4 According as he hath chosen us in him before the foundation of the world, that we should be holy and without blame before him in love. 9 Having made known unto us the mystery of his will, according to his good pleasure which he hath purposed in himself.

[11]EPH. 1:6,12.

[12] 1PE 1:2 Elect according to the foreknowledge of God the Father, through sanctification of the Spirit, unto obedience and sprinkling of the blood of Jesus Christ: Grace unto you, and peace, be multiplied.

EPH 1:4 According as he hath chosen us in him before the foundation of the world, that we should be holy and without blame before him in love: 5 Having predestinated us unto the adoption of children by Jesus Christ to himself, according to the good pleasure of his will. 2:10 For we are his workmanship, created in Christ Jesus unto good works, which God hath before ordained that we should walk in them. 2TH 2:13 But we are bound to give thanks alway to God for you, brethren beloved of the Lord, because God hath from the beginning chosen you to salvation through sanctification of the Spirit and belief of the truth.

[13] 1TH 5:9 For God hath not appointed us to wrath, but to obtain salvation by our Lord Jesus Christ, 10 Who died for us, that, whether we wake or sleep, we should live together with him. TIT 2:14 Who gave himself for us, that he might redeem us from all iniquity, and purify unto himself a peculiar people, zealous of good works.

[14] ROM 8:30 Moreover whom he did predestinate, them he also called: and whom he called, them he also justified: and whom he justified, them he also glorified. EPH 1:5 Having predestinated us unto the adoption of children by Jesus Christ to himself, according to the good pleasure of his will. 2TH 2:13 But we are bound to give thanks alway to God for you, brethren beloved of the Lord, because God hath from the beginning chosen you to salvation through sanctification of the Spirit and belief of the truth.

[15] 1PE 1:5 Who are kept by the power of God through faith unto salvation ready to be revealed in the last time.

[16] JOH 17:9 I pray for them: I pray not for the world, but for them which thou hast given me; for they are thine. ROM 8:28 And we know that all things work together for good to them that love God, to them who are the called according to his purpose. JOH 6:64 But there are some of you that believe not. For Jesus knew from the beginning who they were that believed not, and who should betray him. 65 And he said, Therefore said I unto you, that no man can come unto me, except it were given unto him of my Father. 10:26 But ye believe not, because ye are not of my sheep, as I said unto you. 8:47 He that is of God heareth God's words: ye therefore hear them not, because ye are not of God. 1JO 2:19 They went out from us, but they were not of us; for if they had been of us, they would no doubt have continued with us: but they went out, that they might be made manifest that they were not all of us.

[17] MAT 11:25 At that time Jesus answered and said, I thank thee, O Father, Lord of heaven and earth, because thou hast hid these things from the wise and prudent, and hast revealed them unto babes. 26 Even so, Father: for so it seemed good in thy sight. ROM 9:17 For the scripture saith unto Pharaoh, Even for this same purpose have I raised thee up, that I might shew my power in thee, and that my name might be declared throughout all the earth. 18 Therefore hath he mercy on whom he will have mercy, and whom he will he hardeneth. 21 Hath not the potter power over the clay, of the same lump to make one vessel unto honor, and another unto dishonor? 22 What if God, willing to shew his wrath, and to make his power known, endured with much longsuffering the vessels of wrath fitted to destruction. 2TI 2:19 Nevertheless the foundation of God standeth sure, having this seal, The Lord knoweth them that are his. And, Let every one that nameth the name of Christ depart from iniquity. 20 But in a great house there are not only vessels of gold and of silver, but also of wood and of earth; and some to honor, and some to dishonor. JUD 4 For there are certain men crept in unawares, who were before of old ordained to this condemnation, ungodly men, turning the grace of our God into lasciviousness, and denying the only Lord God, and our Lord Jesus Christ. 1PE 2:8 And a

stone of stumbling, and a rock of offence, even to them which stumble at the word, being disobedient: whereunto also they were appointed.

[18] ROM 9:20 Nay but, O man, who art thou that repliest against God? Shall the thing formed say to him that formed it, Why hast thou made me thus? 11:33 O the depth of the riches both of the wisdom and knowledge of God! how unsearchable are his judgments, and his ways past finding out! DEU 29:29 The secret things belong unto the Lord our God: but those things which are revealed belong unto us and to our children for ever, that we may do all the words of this law.

[19] 2PE 1:10 Wherefore the rather, brethren, give diligence to make your calling and election sure: for if ye do these things, ye shall never fall.

[20] EPH 1:6 To the praise of the glory of his grace, wherein he hath made us accepted in the beloved. ROM 11:33 O the depth of the riches both of the wisdom and knowledge of God! how unsearchable are his judgments, and his ways past finding out!

[21] ROM 11:5 Even so then at this present time also there is a remnant according to the election of grace. 6 And if by grace, then is it no more of works: otherwise grace is no more grace. But if it be of works, then is it no more grace: otherwise work is no more work. 20 For when ye were the servants of sin, ye were free from righteousness. 2PE 1:10 Wherefore the rather, brethren, give diligence to make your calling and election sure: for if ye do these things, ye shall never fall. ROM 8:33 Who shall lay any thing to the charge of God's elect? It is God that justifieth. LUK 10:20 Notwithstanding in this rejoice not, that the spirits are subject unto you; but rather rejoice, because your names are written in heaven.

Protestant Denominations

Introduction

A denomination, in the Christian sense of the word, is an identifiable religious body under a common name, structure, and/or doctrine. Once the Reformation took hold in Europe Christians who left the Roman Catholic church formed or joined a Christian denomination.

Founders of Christian denominations

1457 United Brethren (Moravians): Huss

1517 Lutherans: Martin Luther

1519 Anabaptists: Grebel (after Ulrich Zwingli).

1534 Church of England: Henry VIII

1536 Calvinism: John Calvin

1560 Presbyterians: J. Knox (Calvin)

1570 Puritans: T. Cartwright

1582 Congregationalism: R. Brown

1605 Baptists: John Smith (Zwingli)

1620 Episcopalians: S. Seabury (Henry VIII)

1654 Quakers: Fox

Moravians: United Brethren, after Huss

In 1457, some followers of Huss, founded the "Church of the Brotherhood". This is considered to be the pioneer and the earliest independent Protestant body, long before Martin Luther.

Later, in 1727, it became the "United Brethren, or Moravian Church".

Their influence has been enormous, and they are accredited with being the first to light the torch of Protestant missionary zeal.

Lutherans

Founded by Martin Luther, in Wittenberg, Germany, 1517; the key figure in the Reformation. He rejected the authority of the Catholic Pope; retained the bishops, but named by the kings, instead of the Pope.

The Bible was the ultimate authority for all matters of religious belief and practice. Every Christian is a priest, he should read the Bible.

Salvation is by grace, by faith alone in Jesus Christ; faith that involves not merely intellectual assent but an act of confidence by the will.

He retained the sacraments of baptism, penance and Holy Communion. He held that in the Holy Communion the consecrated bread and wine are the Body and Blood of Christ.

He rejected purgatory, indulgences, invocation of the Saints, and prayers for the dead.

Membership

Today, it is the largest Protestant denomination in the world, with 75 million. In the USA, it is the fourth largest denomination with 8.4 million. Many of the five hundred million Protestant Christians trace their history back to Luther's reforming work.

Authority: Scripture alone

The "Book of Concord" (1580), has the statements of faith which have shaped the confessional life of Lutheranism. It includes the 3 "creeds": Apostles', Nicene, and Athanasian; Luther's large and small catechisms; the Augsburg Confession of 1530; the Treatise on the Power and Primacy of the Pope of 1537; and the Formula of Concord of 1577.

Zwingli: Anabaptists

"Ana-Baptist", means "re-baptism". Anabaptists (Greek ανα (again) βαπτιξω (baptize), thus, "re-baptizers") are Christians of the Radical Reformation.

The term "anabaptist" comes from the practice of baptizing individuals who had been baptized previously, often as infants. Anabaptists believe infant baptism is not valid, because a child cannot commit to a religious faith, and they instead support what's called believer's baptism.

Today Anabaptists refer to the descendants of this 16th century European movement, particularly the Baptists, Amish, Hutterites, Mennonites, Church of the Brethren, and Brethren in Christ.

Anabaptists have been called the "left wing of Reformation", and they developed in Zurich, the German-speaking Switzerland, where Zwingli was working as the second great Reformer. It was Zwingli who coined the word "Anabaptist" for a radical group who preferred to be called "Brethren in Christ".

Ulrich Zwingli believed that the Lord's Supper was only a memorial, and a symbol.

Many Anabaptist groups who adopted many of the beliefs of Zwingli, but later opposed him and favored Calvin's theology. Zwingli proposed that the government of the church should be placed in the hands of the congregation rather than under the control of the clergy.

The "born-again" experience, is one distinguishing mark of the Anabaptists.

A complete separation of church and state to protect the liberty of the church, is another feature of the Anabaptists.

Anabaptists are of the "congregational" type of church government, where each local church is autonomous. There is no Pope.

Mennonites

Menno Simons, an Anabaptist leader in the Netherlands, founded the "Mennonites" (after Menno) in Holland, who later went to Pennsylvania in 1653.

Church of England

The Anglican Church regards itself derived not from Reformation influences but from the renunciation of Papal jurisdiction by King Henry VIII in 1534. With the Act of Supremacy, the King was declared the supreme head of the English Church.

They rejected the authority of the Pope.

Anglicans are the second largest Protestant denomination, after the Lutherans.

Its basic tenets of beliefs, are stated in the "Book of Common Prayer", specifically in its Thirty-Nine Articles.

Calvinists

John Calvin established the Reformation in the French-speaking area of Switzerland. He rejected the Pope.

In 1536 he established a theocratic government in Geneva in which the affairs of the city were controlled by Calvin's new church. Geneva became a model of Puritan sobriety.

Calvin taught that the body and blood of Christ are received in Holy Communion, but in a spiritual manner.

Calvin opened the way for more radical forms of Protestantism which exist today as worldwide churches:

Presbyterians of Scotland,

Congregational, Separatists, Puritans of England

Dutch Reformed Churches

The Huguenots in France.

Presbyterian

John Knox, founded the basically Calvinistic Scotch Presbyterian Church, in 1560, in Scotland. It is called "Presbyterian" because church policy centers around assemblies of presbyters or elders.

They practice infant baptism and the Lord's Supper is celebrated at intervals. The services are simple and dignified, and the sermon is central.

The government of the church, is placed in the hands of a small body of presbyters, or elders, elected by the congregation, plus pastors and administrative aids called deacons. However the governing board of the church, the synod or presbytery, is subject to the civil government.

Puritans

In 1560, T. Cartwright, and some other "Puritans" or "Precisians", thought the Anglicans were too Catholic, and the Church should be "purified" of the old leaven of Catholicism, and reformed along Calvinist lines in severe simplicity.

They wanted the government of the Church of England to be reformed, as well as some of its worship, and teachings. They did not want clerical dress to be worn any more or for people to kneel at the Lord's Supper, or for the sign of the cross to be made.

They wanted ministers to be chosen by the people, and for the office of the bishop abolished. This amounted to a demand for the Presbyterian form of church, as in Calvinism, to replace the Episcopalian way of Anglicanism.

Puritans in the U.S.

1. Types of English Puritanism

Puritanism essentially wanted to replace Anglicanism and its ecclesiastical system with the system proposed by John Calvin. Calvin, of course, perfected his system in Geneva. Followers transplanted it to Scotland and then into England. Many Puritans did not repudiate the king's authority or the principle of uniformity. They simply wanted to establish a Presbyterian order. It was the question of what constituted a "true church" that gave rise to Puritan congregationalism.

In 1581, Robert Browne taught that only those who could prove they were among God's elect could be the true church. A believer knew they were among the elect when they exhibited Christian character along with a conversion experience, an experience others could evaluate. "Proved saints" who chose to associate together voluntarily made up congregations. Such people confessed their faith to one another then bound themselves together by a covenant. The idea of covenant was central to their whole concept.

Over the years Puritanism developed two distinct schools of thought. There were separatists and the non-separatists.

Separatist Puritans considered every church a distinct unit independent of all outside control. This meant they considered outside bodies such as synods, presbyteries, and the hierarchical clergy as unscriptural and unnecessary. Separatists refused to recognize congregations subservient to outside organizations as "true churches." Anglicanism could not be a form of the "true church." Therefore, genuine Christians should withdraw from Anglicans at all costs.

Nonseparatist Puritans agreed with Separatists on the necessity of restricting church membership to proven saints. However, they did not condemn the Church of England. They contended that true Christians could and did remain in the Church of England in spite of its unscriptural practices. Furthermore, they believed Christians always existed within the church regardless of the form it took. Nonseparatists hoped to bring about change from within the established church. Separating from the Anglicans would frustrate that goal.

The essentials of Congregational Puritanism:

The visible church is a particular congregation, never an outside body.
The church is formally gathered through covenanting.
The church is composed of holy or regenerate members
The only head of the church is Jesus.

Puritanism also developed a unique social theory. The theory's backbone is "The Law of Relatives." They tied this "law" to a medieval philosophy held by Peter Ramus, a strict Augustinian. Ramus envisioned society as a series of one-to-one relationships. This idea did not see people as individuals, rather each person was identifiable only in their peculiar set of relationships. The "Law of Relatives" set up a complex set of chain-of-command structures of superiors to inferiors. Puritans considered anyone outside these structures alienated from society. Puritans forced singles, widows, widowers, orphans and others into family structures so they would be in a relationship. The father had absolute authority in each family. Puritans believed that in ideal situations, Superiors didn't abuse inferiors in the relationship structure.

Puritans valued the family as the basic and permanent human institution. They permitted no divorce except for abandonment although they would allow an annulment because of infertility. They saw marriage as a civil rather than religious custom. Puritans arranged marriages for their children and no one could marry outside the church. A girl could veto a choice but no one expected her to use the right. Love meant physically caring for someone so romance was unnecessary for marriage. In spite of popular mythology, the Puritans respected a healthy sexuality and saw human sexual relationships as normal unless they became obsessive. They punished illegitimacy albeit gently. When a girl conceived out of wedlock, Puritans generally tried to establish a family. Pregnancies often resulted from the Puritans' curious custom of "bundling." Bundling allowed a courting couple to sleep together in the girl's home provided they were individually bundled. While the Puritans appeared to take a loose position on fornication they severely punished adultery and they executed homosexuals.

2. The Settlement of Separatist Puritans

Separatist Puritans were a serious source of irritation to the crown. James I directed most of his ire to them. Puritans who settled in Holland under the leadership of John Robinson were Separatists. In time, these Puritans raised sufficient funds to allow a group of these Separatists to escape to America where they became known as the Pilgrims.

On August 5, 1620, the Speedwell and the Mayflower set sail for Virginia. The sailors soon discovered the Speedwell was not seaworthy, so after they put into England for supplies they left her behind. One hundred forty-nine Puritans crowded onto the Mayflower for the trip. Of these, 48 were officers and crew, the rest colonists. Most, but certainly not all, passengers were Separatists. John Alden, a cooper, and Miles Standish, the colony's military adviser, were not Separatists. Alden went to America to care for and make beer barrels while Standish went as a typical soldier of fortune. Alden, however, became a church member after his marriage to Priscilla Mullins. That relationship also kept him in the colony long after he intended to return home.

Separatist Puritans came to America hoping to preserve their church structure. After all, Scripture approved it and none other. They wanted to establish a colony where they could apply biblical principles without interference. They dreamed of establishing a "city on a hill" which would clearly show England their superiority. The Pilgrims expected to remain here only temporarily. Once England saw how well their ideas worked they would be called home to implement them there. These colonists had no permanent commitment to America.

The colonists experienced some unrest before landing in Massachusetts (they were blown off course during their voyage). To settle all issues before landing, the group met to form a typical Puritan covenant. This covenant, The Mayflower Compact, set the colony's tone.

For many years the Plymouth Separatists had no ministerial guidance. A London group partially underwrote the trip expecting a profitable return on their investment. Some of their financial backers came from successful English merchants. Other Pilgrims remained in Leyden but the colony's backers had no interest in sending more settlers to Massachusetts. Instead, they sent young men to the colony; young men who would reap windfalls trapping and trading furs.

In 1624, the Anglican church sent John Lyford to Massachusetts. The Puritans thought Lyford a Puritan so they accepted him. During their almost four years the colony's proven saints had not taken the Lord's Supper nor seen a single baptism. When they discovered Lyford's true colors and realized he was sent under the auspices of their financial backers, the Puritans "bought out" the London partners and dismissed Lyford. In 1629 they secured Ralph Smith who proved satisfactory.

3. The Great Migration

The Plymouth Colony survived a first hard winter then expanded. That expansion opened the door to other New England colonial efforts. On March 4, 1628/29, the Massachusetts Bay Company received its charter in England. The company then became New England's chief colonizing agency.

Puritans settled Salem, near Boston, in 1626 (note that it was before the company received it's charter). The Massachusetts Bay Company chose to establish it's colony of Non-Separatist Puritans in the Salem vicinity. When their effort began, they had a complete strategy for development. Jamestown's failures taught them to carefully plan things out. Puritans arrived in America as complete family units. Each group contained men with a wide variety of skills. Quite often, entire English congregations moved as a unit. By colonizing Massachusetts, the colonists repopulated an area where smallpox epidemics had eliminated whole Indian tribes which meant they had little Indian resistance. In 1630, Puritans began arriving in America en masse. In a very short time some 30,000 moved to seven platted towns prepared for them.

When the towns became large, the Puritans followed a formal expansion plan. New England, therefore, expanded in an orderly fashion. Southern expansion tended to be unplanned and disorganized.

New Englanders did not utilize Virginia's headright plan. Instead, the Massachusetts Bay Company chartered new towns. When Puritans decided to establish a new town, three to five prominent men requested a charter from the colony's governor. The governor, who acted on the company's behalf, granted the charter only if these men could prove they could successfully establish such a community. Before issuing the charter, the representatives had to show the governor they had families with essential skills and a minister. When the group had the new town's charter in hand it moved en masse. When the group moved, they moved as a covenanted group with an agreed upon government, a method of land distribution, a church, criteria for future town citizenship, and an elected leadership. They usually distributed land according to status and once they settled the area they made a second distribution again based on status and ability.

Francis Higginson and Samuel Skelton, both Nonseparatists, arrived in 1629 to form a church. This new church was independent and congregational. Like their Separatist kin, these Massachusetts Bay settlers hoped to demonstrate the viability of the congregational system. They, too, expected to return home in style when England saw their example.

Eleven vessels sailed for Massachusetts from England on March 29, 1630. Before the year ended 17 other vessels landed with 1,000 of what became a total of 30,000 colonists. By 1645, the Puritans had established 23 churches and between 1630–1641 some 65 ministers arrived in the colony.

4. Puritan Theology

Puritanism followed John Calvin's teachings. They believed in the Bible as God's inspired Word. They emphasized Calvin's teachings as shaped by Peter Ramus, William Ames, and others. Puritans believed God cleansed man making it possible for man to respond to God's call. After that cleansing, Puritans searched for evidence of salvation although they never came to certainty. As a result, Puritans saw conversion as a process involving complete humility. To the Puritan mind, success accompanied one's salvation. They had such confidence in God's ultimate sovereignty that they had confidence to pursue their course even when facing momentary setbacks. An individual Puritan might doubt God's election, but none doubted God's call and election of the whole group.

Puritanism was not ascetic. Puritans believed God created the universe good and intended man to enjoy it in moderation. The average Puritan dressed flashily for the day but they emphasized utility over enjoyment. Enjoyment came as a byproduct. Even though Puritans rejected Christmas observances and the theater on the Sabbath (some rejected the theater altogether because of the immorality associated with it), they still observed holidays with feasting and merriment.

Historians used to think Puritan preachers proclaimed hairsplitting dogmatism in three hour diatribes. In reality, Puritan services rarely lasted longer than an hour and their preaching tended towards practicality.

Michael Hines, Christian Chronicler

Congregationalists

In 1582, R. Brown, and some Puritans saw that to reform the Episcopalian Church of England from within was hopeless. Therefore, they separated from the Church, and they were called Separatists, Dissenters, Independents, and Congregationalists, because they believed that each congregation should be independent, autonomous, a complete church in itself, and also that no church should have anything to say about any other church. They were Calvinists.

Those American colonists who established the Plymouth Colony in 1620 were "Separatists", and were called Pilgrims. Those who came 9 years later and established the Massachusetts Colony were "Puritans".

Baptists

Baptists comprise the largest of all American Protestant denominations, and are made up of thirty bodies.

They were founded by John Smith in 1605 in England. In America, Roger Williams founded the first Baptist church in Providence in 1639.

They are called "Baptists" because of their doctrine concerning baptism. It is called an "ordinance". They reject "infant baptism", and consider only baptism by immersion as valid, to persons who can decide to receive it, and can feel the personal experience of being "born again".

Separation of church and state is an important feature of the Baptists.

Baptists do not have a formal creed, but subscribe to two professions of faith formulated in 1689 and 1832, and they are in general agreement with classical Protestantism theology regarding Scripture as the sole rule of faith, original sin, justification through faith in Christ, and the nature of the Church.

The organization is congregational; each local church is autonomous.

Baptists have had and continue to have well known Christian leaders in their ranks, such as Martin Luther King Jr., Billy Graham, and Jesse Jackson.

Episcopalians

Founded by S. Seabury in 1620, Episcopalians are part of the Anglican Communion. They regard the Archbishop of Canterbury as the "First among Equals", though not under his authority, and use the same "Book of Common Prayer", adopted at a General Convention held in 1789, when it became independent of the jurisdiction of England.

It is called "Episcopal" ("bishop"), because the church is organized under an Episcopal system, like the Church of England; but presbyters (priests), deacons, and lay persons have an active voice in church affairs. At the parish level, the congregation has the right to select its own rector, with the consent of the bishop.

Quakers: Society of Friends

The Quakers were founded in England, 1654, by a shoemaker, George Fox.

They are called "Quakers", because in the first days of enthusiasm they "trembled" in their assemblies, but they resent that name. Their organization is not called a church but the "Society of Friends".

For them the Bible remains a closed book unless the mind is illuminated by the Holy Spirit. Fox called this illumination the "Inner Light", so, their first name was "Children of Truth", and later, "Children of Light".

In their "meetings", there is no pulpit nor songs, they just sit down and wait in silence for the Spirit to move them. If no one is moved by the Spirit, they leave without a word having been spoken. But if the Spirit moves one of the Friends, he or she gets up and gives his massage. Between massages, a painful silence may elapse . . . this "divine guidance" applies to all their life.

PEOPLE
Martin Luther (AD 1483–1546)
Ulrich [Huldrych] Zwingli (AD 1484–1531)
Thomas Cranmer (AD 1489–1556)
Ignatius of Loyola (AD 1491–1556)
William Tyndale (AD 1494–1536)
Francis Xavier (AD 1506–1552)
John Calvin (AD 1509–1564)
Teresa of Avila (AD 1515–1582)

Martin Luther

Dates
AD 1483–1546

Famous for being
German theologian. Leader of the Protestant Reformation

Important writings
The 95 Theses
The Large Catechism
Table Talk
The Smalcald Articles
An Open Letter to The Christian Nobility
Die Bibel, Martin Luther translation

One of his quotations

"Unless I am convinced by Scripture and plain reason—I do not accept the authority of the Popes and councils, for they have contradicted each other—my conscience is captive to the Word of God. I cannot and I will not recant anything for to go against conscience is neither right nor safe. God help me. Amen."

Chronology of Martin Luther
1463 Frederick the Wise, elector of Saxony is born.
1465 Johann Tetzel probably born in this year.
1480 Andreas Rudolf Bodenstein von Karlstadt is born.
1483 Luther is born in Eisleben.

1502 University of Wittenberg established by Frederick, Elector of Saxony.

1510 Luther visits Rome.

1517 October 31 Luther posts the *95 These*s to the door of the Wittenberg Castle church.

1517 Pope Leo X commissions *Prierias* to respond to Luther's 95 thesis. *Prierias' Dialogus* is sent to Luther who responds with *Responsio*

1519 Leipzig Disputation between Luther and Eck. Karlstadt also debates Eck. Leipzig Disputation

1520 Luther Writes: *To the Christian Nobility, On the Babylonian Captivity of the Church,* and *The Freedom of a Christian*

1521 Edict of Worms issued by Charles V declares Luther an outlaw.

1521 Pope Leo X calls King Henry VIII "Defender of the Faith" for his publication of an anti-Luther tract.

1521 Diet of Worms

1521 May. Luther is "kidnapped" and taken to Wartburg Castle

1524 August 21 Luther and Karlstadt meet at the Black Bear Inn in Jena.

1525 Eck publishes, *Arguments against Luther and Other Enemies of the Church*

1525 Luther marries Katherine von Bora

1525 Schwenckfeld visits Wittenberg and debates Martin Luther concerning the Eucharist.

1525 Luther allows Karlstadt to seek refuge in Wittenberg.

1529 Luther and Zwingli debate at Marburg

1546 Luther dies in Eisleben

Introduction

Martin Luther was a Christian theologian and Augustinian monk whose teachings inspired the Lutheran and Protestant Reformations and deeply influenced the doctrines of Protestant and other Christian traditions (a broad movement composed of many congregations and church bodies). His call to the Church to return to the teachings of the Bible resulted in the formation of new traditions within Christianity and the Counter-Reformation in the Roman Catholic Church, culminating at the Council of Trent.

On October 31, 1517 Luther preached a sermon against indulgences and posted the 95 Theses to the door of the castle's Church of All Saints in Wittenberg (the University's customary notice board) as an open invitation to debate them. The Theses condemn the Church's greed and worldliness (especially the selling of indulgences) as an abuse and ask for a theological disputation. Soon they were widely copied and printed; within two weeks they spread throughout Germany, and within two months throughout Europe.

Life of Luther

Martin Luther was a German monk, priest, professor, theologian, and church reformer. His teachings inspired the Reformation and deeply influenced the doctrines and culture of the Lutheran and Protestant traditions, as well as the course of Western civilization.

Martin Luther's life and work are closely connected to the end of the Middle Ages and the beginning of the Modern Era in the West. His translation of the Bible furthered the development of a standard version of the German language and added several principles to the art of translation. His translation significantly influenced the English King James Version of the Bible. Due to the recently developed printing press, his writings were widely read, influencing many subsequent Reformers and thinkers, giving rise to diversifying Protestant traditions in Europe and elsewhere.

Luther's hymns, including his best-known "A Mighty Fortress is Our God", inspired the development of congregational singing within Christianity.

His marriage on June 13, 1525, to Katharina von Bora reintroduced the practice of clerical marriage within many Christian traditions.

Today, nearly seventy million Christians belong to Lutheran churches worldwide, with some four hundred million Protestant Christians tracing their history back to Luther's reforming work.

Wikipedia

Martin Luther's last words

Luther died on the morning of February 18, 1546. These are his last words:

On the 17th he was so ill that the Counts entreated him not to quit his house. At supper, on the same day, he spoke a great deal about his approaching death; and some one having asked him whether we should recognize one another in the next world, he said he thought we should.

"I feel very weak," he exclaimed, "and my pains are worse than ever. If I could manage to sleep for half an hour, I think it would do me good."

He did fall asleep, and remained in gentle slumber for an hour and a half. On awaking about eleven he asked, "What! are you still there? Will you not go and rest yourselves?" On their replying that they would remain, he began to cry with fervor, "'Into Thy hands I commend my spirit: Thou hast redeemed me, O Lord God of truth' Pray, all of you, dear friends, for the Gospel of our Lord; pray that its reign may extend, for the Council of Trent and the Pope menace it round about." He then slumbered about an hour.

When he awoke, he remarked, "I feel very ill. I think I shall remain here at Eisleben, here—where I was born."

He walked almost the room, and then lay down, and had a number of clothes and cushions placed over him to produce perspiration; but they had not the desired effect.

"O my Father!" he went on to pray, "Thou, the God of our Lord Jesus Christ; Thou, the source of all consolation, I thank Thee for having revealed unto me Thy well-beloved Son, in whom I believe; whom I have preached and acknowledged, and made known; whom I have loved and celebrated, and whom the Pope and the impious persecute. I commend my soul to Thee, O my Lord Jesus Christ I am about to quit this terrestrial body, I am about to be removed from this life; but I know that I shall abide eternally with Thee. 'Into thy hands I commend my spirit: Thou hast redeemed me, O Lord God of truth.'"

His eyes closed, and he fell back in a swoon.

When he revived, Jonas said to him, "Reverend father, do you die firm in the faith you have taught?"

He opened his eyes, looked fixedly, and replied, "Yes."

Soon after, those nearest saw him grow paler and paler; he became cold; his breathing seemed more and more faint; at length, heaving one deep sigh, Martin Luther expired.

Ulrich [Huldrych] Zwingli

Dates

1484–1531

Famous for being

Swiss Reformer

Important writings

Exposition of the Christian faith

One of his quotations

"Superfluity of wine is something which the young man must avoid like poison."

Chronology of Ulrich Zwingli

1484 Born at Wildhaus, Switzerland, January 1. His education began with training in Latin by his Uncle, Bartholomew Zwingli

1498 After attending Schools in Basle and Berne, Zwingli attended the University of Vienna

1504 Zwingli received his Bachelor's Degree then went to Basle for his Master's Degree in 1506. During Zwingli's education, he was trained as a humanist scholar—with much training in the Classics. Lectures by Thomas Wyttenbach at Basle pointed him towards the Gospel. An accomplished musician, he could play almost any instrument.

1506 Becomes Pastor at Glarus.

1512–16 Receiving a Papal pension, he made at least two trips to Italy accompanying Swiss mercenary soldiers as a chaplain.

1514 Zwingli was present at the Battle of Marigano, September13 & 14, between Frances 1 of France and the Kingdom of Milan. In this 28 hour battle, thousands of close packed phalanxes of Swiss Pikemen were slaughtered by French cannon—the first modern battle whose outcome was decided by artillery.

1516 Following a "situation" involving a barber's daughter, Zwingli became a Pastor at Einsieden—where his preaching was popular. Zwingli moved to an evangelical interpretation of the Scriptures. He engaged in a controversy over indulgences with Bernardo Sampson. Also while at Einsieden, he entered into correspondence with Erasmus, and copied and memorized much of Erasmus' Greek New Testament. He also began a study of Hebrew.

1519 Zwingli became the People's Priest at The Great Minster Church in Zurich. He abandoned the liturgical calendar and started preaching through the Bible book by book. He began to challenge unscriptural practices.

1519 Plague struck Zurich killing one quarter of the population and Zwingli stayed to minister to the sick and dying. Stricken himself, he recovered with a greater commitment to the Lord. Zwingli worked to bring the an end to the practice of hiring out Swiss soldiers as mercenaries. Zwingli was present at another defeat at Bicocca, but through his efforts, that practice was first curbed and finally stopped in Zurich (1522) and other nearby cantons.

1522 Following the arrest of some printers for eating sausages during Lent, Zwingli rose to their defense, beginning the reforms in Zurich. Challenging also the practice of clerical celibacy, Zwingli was secretly married to Anna Meyer in 1522, and then publically in 1524, a widow with three children, who would bear him four more.

1523 Zwingli publishes his Sixty Seven Articles on January 19th. At a disputation on the 29th, attended by over 600 people, the Papal representative Johann Faber was unable to support Celibacy and other matters from Scripture alone—the principle now adopted by the Council. Zwingli debated with John Eck in April at Baden. Two more disputations followed—bringing thorough reform to Christian practices and rejecting the authority of the Bishop in Constance.

1524 Zurich was "cleansed" of organs, images, relics and religious houses by zealous citizens.

1525 The yearly Mass is abolished and replaced by a quarterly communion. Baptism is also changed. Zwingli's work "True and False Religion" is published. Worship is now a Preaching and Prayer service, without music.

1526 The City council took over Church disciplinary matters and excommunication. Zurich is now a Christian Commonwealth ruled by Magistrates. Roman Catholics are tolerated, but restricted in their activities and civic position.

1528 As the Reformation spread in Switzerland through neighboring cantons, increasing opposition by Catholic Cantons motivates the formation of a Christian Civic

League uniting Zurich, Berne, Basel, Schaffhausen, and St. Gall and the free Imperial city of Constance. Zwingli wrote the 12 Theses of Berne for this conference attended by Oecolampadius, Haller, Bucer, Kolb and Capito with some vigorous preaching by each of them. A war between the cantons was avoided as national spirit over came differences as the opposing troops made peace with a tub of butter, bread and a common meal. The Peace of Kappel encouraged the Protestants to continue evangelical efforts in the Catholic cantons, but such efforts only increase tensions.

1529 Zwingli attended the Colloquy at Marburg called by Philip of Hesse in an attempt to bring together the German and Swiss Reformations. Agreeing on almost every point, Martin Luther was unwilling to accept Zwingli's view on the Lord's Supper as a Memorial. Efforts at unity fail.

1530 A confession written by Zwingli was presented to Charles the V at the Diet of Augsburg in July of 1530, but was not read and treated with contempt, the only response being a slanderous refutation by Eck.

1531 Returning to Zurich, Zwingli set about defending the faith. He wrote a Exposition of the Christian faith and sent the manuscript to Frances 1 of France, warning of the lies and slanders being circulated against the Protestants, it also remained unread. In October, Zwingli mustered the citizenry to prepare for defense against the Catholic Cantons. A Catholic army of 8,000 men advanced against Zurich's 1500 defenders. Zwingli accompanying the troops with a sword was slain along with 26 members of the Town council and 24 other pastors among the 500 Protestant dead. The following treaty of peace left religious boundaries as they were, but prevented any further Protestant expansion in Switzerland. Zwingli's work was continued by Bullinger.

Thomas Cranmer

Dates

1489–1556

Famous for being

Archbishop of Canterbury and martyr

Important writings

Writing material for the Book of Common Prayer

One of his quotations

[As he was being burnt at the stake] "This was the hand that wrote it (his recantation), therefore it shall suffer first punishment."

Thomas Cranmer was Archbishop of Canterbury in the days of Henry, and defended the position that Henry's marriage to Katharine of Aragon (Spain) was null and void.

When Edward came to the throne, Cranmer was foremost in translating the worship of the Church into English (his friends and enemies agree that he was an extraordinarily gifted translator) and securing the use of the new forms of worship. When Mary came to the throne, Cranmer was in a quandary. He had believed, with a fervor that many people today will find hard to understand, that it is the duty of every Christian to obey the monarch, and that "the powers that be are ordained of God" (Romans 13). As long as the monarch was ordering things that Cranmer thought good, it was easy for Cranmer to believe that the king was sent by God's providence to guide the people in the path of true religion, and that disobedience to the king was disobedience to God.

Now Mary was Queen, and commanding him to return to the Roman obedience. Cranmer five times wrote a letter of submission to the Pope and to Roman Catholic doctrines, and four times he tore it up. In the end, he submitted. However, Mary was unwilling to believe that the submission was sincere, and he was ordered to be burned at Oxford on 21 March 1556. At the very end, he repudiated his final letter of submission, and announced that he died a Protestant. He said, "I have sinned, in that I signed with my hand what I did not believe with my heart. When the flames are lit, this hand shall be the first to burn." And when the fire was lit around his feet, he leaned forward and held his right hand in the fire until it was charred to a stump. Aside from this, he did not speak or move, except that once he raised his left hand to wipe the sweat from his forehead.

James Kiefer

Ignatius of Loyola

Dates

1491–1556

Famous for being

Founder of the Society of Jesus (Jesuits)

Important writings

The Spiritual Exercises of St. Ignatius of Loyola

One of his quotations

"Ad majorem Dei gloriam"—"for the greater glory of God." The Jesuit motto

A real soldier from Guipuzcua, Spain, becomes a soldier of Christ after reading the lives of the Saints, mystic of the Eucharist, founded the Jesuits and the Spiritual Exercises and worked the Counter-Reform with a special forth vow of obedience to the Pope.

The crying saint

One of his greatest achievements is the foundation of the Jesuits who today have over 500 universities and colleges, 30,000 members, and teach over 200,000 students each year.

In Loyola's *Spiritual Autobiography* he recounts his experiences in the Holy Mass of each day: For example how on Pentecost, "I cried for 3 hours before Mass, during the Mass I was crying all the time with love and thanksgiving, and after the Mass I was also having tears all over for 2 or 3 hours."

Early history

Loyola was wounded in the leg by a cannonball at the siege of Pampeluna on 20 May 1521, an injury that left him partially crippled for life. During his recuperation the only books he had access to were *The Golden Legend*, a collection of lives of the saints, and the *Life of Christ* by Ludolph the Carthusian. These books, and the time spent in contemplation, changed him.

On his recovery he took a vow of chastity, hung his sword before the altar of the Virgin of Montserrat in Barcelona, and donned a pilgrim's robes.

Lived in a cave from 1522 to 1523

It was during this year of conversion that he began to write down material that later became his greatest work, the *Spiritual Exercises.*

Then Loyola traveled to Rome and the Holy Land where he worked to convert Muslims.

He went on to study theology at Alcala and Paris, receiving his degree on 14 March 1534. His meditations, prayers, visions and insights led to forming the Constitutions of the Society of Jesus (Jesuits) on 15 August 1534.

He traveled Europe and the Holy Lands, then settled in Rome to direct the Jesuits. His health suffered in later years, and he was nearly blind at death.

Ignatius was a true mystic. He centered his spiritual life on the essential foundations of Christianity—the Trinity, Christ, the Eucharist. His spirituality is expressed in the Jesuit motto, *ad majorem Dei gloriam*—"for the greater glory of God." In his concept, obedience was to be the prominent virtue, to assure the effectiveness and mobility of his men. All activity was to be guided by a true love of the Church and unconditional obedience to the Holy Father, for which reason all professed members took a fourth vow to go wherever the pope should send them for the salvation of souls.

The Counter-Reformation:

Luther nailed his theses to the church door at Wittenberg in 1517. Seventeen years later, Ignatius founded the Society that was to play so prominent a part in the Counter-Reformation. He was an implacable foe of Protestantism. Yet the seeds of ecumenism may be found in his words: "Great care must be taken to show forth orthodox truth in such a way that if any heretics happen to be present they may have an example of charity and Christian moderation. No hard words should be used nor any sort of contempt for their errors be shown."

J. Dominguez, M.D.

Soul of Christ (*Anima Christi*)

Soul of Christ, sanctify me.
Body of Christ, save me.
Blood of Christ, inebriate me.
Water from the side of Christ, wash me.
Passion of Christ, strengthen me.
O good Jesus, hear me.
Within Thy wounds hide me.
Separated from Thee let me never be.
From the malignant enemy, defend me.
At the hour of death, call me.
And close to Thee bid me.
That with Thy saints I may be
Praising Thee, forever and ever. Amen.

Ignatius of Loyola

Teach us, Good Lord

Teach us, Good Lord, to serve Thee as Thou deservest:
To give, and not to count the cost;
to fight, and not to heed the wounds;
to toil and not to seek for rest;
to labor and not to ask for any reward,
save that of knowing that we do Thy will.
Through Jesus Christ Our Lord.

Ignatius of Loyola

William Tyndale

Dates

1494–1536

Famous for being

Bible translator and martyr

Important writings
Translating Bible

One of his quotations
"I perceived how that it was impossible to establish the lay people in any truth except the Scripture were plainly laid before their eyes in their mother tongue."

Introduction

William Tyndale is believed to have been born near Dursley, Gloucestershire, UK in 1494.

The Tyndales were also known by the surname 'Hychyns'. It was as William Hychyns that Tyndale went to Magdalen Hall, Oxford, now part of Hertford College. He was admitted to the Degree of Bachelor of Arts on 4 July 1512 and to Master of Arts on 2 July 1515.

Fluent in at least 7 languages, he translated much of the Bible into English from the original Greek and Hebrew sources. (Earlier, John Wycliffe had worked from Jerome's Latin 'Vulgate'.) In doing so he gave the English language many of its best known phrases. Much of his work appears, unchanged but unacknowledged in the 'Authorized' (or 'King James') version of the Bible.

At that time, translating the Bible was considered heretical. Tyndale fled to Germany in 1524, later to Belgium. He continued his work, translating the New Testament in 1526 and again in 1534. Eventually, he was betrayed to the authorities. He was strangled, and his dead body was burnt, on 6 October 1536.

The Life and Story of the True Servant and Martyr of God

William Tyndale, the faithful minister of Christ, was born about the borders of Wales, and brought up from a child in the University of Oxford, where he, by long continuance, increased as well in the knowledge of tongues, and other liberal arts, as especially in the knowledge of the Scriptures, whereunto his mind was singularly addicted; insomuch that he, lying then in Magdalen Hall, read privily to certain students and fellows of Magdalen College some parcel of divinity; instructing them in the knowledge and truth of the Scriptures. His manners and conversation being correspondent to the same, were such that all they that knew him reputed him to be a man of most virtuous disposition, and of life unspotted.

Thus he, in the University of Oxford, increasing more and more in learning, and proceeding in degrees of the schools, spying his time, removed from thence to the University of Cambridge, where he likewise made his abode a certain space. Being now further ripened in the knowledge of God's Word, leaving that university, he resorted to one Master Welch, a knight of Gloucestershire, and was there schoolmaster to his children, and in good favor with his master. As this gentleman kept a good ordinary commonly at his table, there resorted to him many times sundry abbots, deans, archdeacons, with divers other doctors, and great beneficed men; who there, together with Master Tyndale sitting at the same table, did use many times to enter communication, and talk of learned men, as of Luther and of Erasmus; also of divers other controversies and questions upon the Scripture. . . .

Master Tyndale happened to be in the company of a certain divine, recounted for a learned man, and, in communing and disputing with him, he drove him to that issue, that the said great doctor burst out into these blasphemous words, "We were better to be without God's laws than the pope's." Master Tyndale, hearing this, full of godly zeal, and not bearing that blasphemous saying, replied, "I defy the pope and all his laws;" and added, "If God spare my life, ere many years I will cause a boy that driveth the plough to know more of the Scripture than thou dost." . . .

Master Tyndale considered this only, or most chiefly, to be the cause of all mischief in the Church, that the Scriptures of God were hidden from the people's eyes; for so long the abominable doings and idolatries maintained by the pharisaical clergy could not be espied; and therefore all their labor was with might and main to keep it down, so that either it should not be read at all, or if it were, they would darken the right sense with the mist of their sophistry, and so entangle those who rebuked or despised their abominations; wresting the Scripture unto their own purpose, contrary unto the meaning of the text, they would so delude the unlearned lay people, that though thou felt in thy heart, and wert sure that all were false that they said, yet couldst thou not solve their subtle riddles. . . .

The godly books of Tyndale, and especially the New Testament of his translation, after that they began to come into men's hands, and to spread abroad, wrought great and singular profit to the godly; but the ungodly (envying and disdaining that the people should be anything wiser than they and, fearing lest by the shining beams of truth, their works of darkness should be discerned) began to sir with no small ado. . . .

At last, after much reasoning, when no reason would serve, although he deserved no death, he was condemned by virtue of the emperor's decree, made in the assembly at Augsburg. Brought forth to the place of execution, he was tied to the stake, strangled by the hangman, and afterwards consumed with fire, at the town of Vilvorde, 1536; crying at the stake with a fervent zeal, and a loud voice, "Lord! open the king of England's eyes."

Such was the power of his doctrine, and the sincerity of his life, that during the time of his imprisonment (which endured a year and a half), he converted, it is said, his keeper, the keeper's daughter, and others of his household.

As touching his translation of the New Testament, because his enemies did so much carp at it, pretending it to be full of heresies, he wrote to John Frith, as followeth, "I call God to record against the day we shall appear before our Lord Jesus, that I never altered one syllable of God's Word against my conscience, nor would do this day, if all that is in earth, whether it be honor, pleasure, or riches, might be given me."

John Foxe, Book of Martyrs, edited by William Byron Forbush, 1868–1927

Menno Simons

Dates

1496–1561

Famous for being

Anabaptist leader

Important writings

Foundation of Christian Doctrine

One of his quotations

"Spears and swords of iron we leave to those who, alas, consider human blood and swine's blood of well-nigh equal value"

Although he was not the founder of the Anabaptist movement, he certainly was its most important leader in the Netherlands during the sixteenth century. He assumed leadership during a crucial period in which the Anabaptist movement was in danger of losing its original identity. His prolific writings and moderate leadership were essential in unifying the Anabaptists and maintaining their peaceful beliefs.

Menno took his motto from 1 Corinthians 3:11 – "For no one can lay any foundation other than the one already laid, which is Jesus Christ." (NIV)

Menno's followers became known as Mennonites, a name that was later adopted by the Swiss Anabaptists who emigrated to America. Today there are about 1.3 million Mennonites in 65 countries.

Menno Simons' writings

Much of Menno's influence is due to his writings. His first writing was *The Blasphemy of Jan van Leyden*. He wrote this pamphlet around 1535 but it was not printed until 1627. In the pamphlet Menno criticized Jan van Leyden, who had assumed the role of a second David of the New Jerusalem at Münster.

Other important writings were *The Spiritual Resurrection (Van de Geestlijke Verrijsenisse*, ca. 1536), *The New Birth (De nieuwe Creatuere*, ca. 1537) and the *Meditation on the Twenty-Fifth Psalm (Christelycke leringhen op den* 25. Psalm, ca. 1538).

Menno's magnum opus was *Foundation of Christian Doctrine (Dat Fundament des Christelycken leers*, 1539–40). The title of the book is taken from 1 Corinthians 3:11: The

Foundation Book was almost immediately accepted by Menno's followers as a guide book for the life of faith.

Francis Xavier

Dates
1506–1552

Famous for being
Missionary: apostle to India

Important writings
Letters and sermons

One of his quotations
"Give me the children until they are seven and anyone may have them afterwards."

Francis Xavier, was a Basque. (The Basques are a people from the region of Biscay in northern Spain, whose language is unrelated to any other known language.) He was born in 1506 and studied at the University of Paris, where he met Ignatius Loyola and joined together with him and five others in dedicating their lives to the will and service of God, and forming the Society of Jesus (the Jesuits) in 1534.

In 1541 Francis sailed with two companions from Portugal to the Portuguese colony of Goa on the west coast of India (arriving in May 1542), where he set about learning the language and writing a catechism for the instruction of converts.

He visited the prisons and the hospitals, conducted worship services among the lepers, and walked the streets ringing a bell to call the children for religious instruction. His chief method of instructing the people was to write verses in their language setting forth the truths of the Christian faith, and set them to music. Both words and tunes tended to be "catchy," and his doggerel instructions were extremely popular and were sung everywhere. He preached tirelessly, both to the native peoples and to the Europeans living there.

Francis found to his dismay that the Portuguese settlers and soldiers of the colony were brutal in their treatment of the natives, and that, even aside from this, their manner of life did not commend their nominal faith to the native observer. He wrote boldly to the King of Portugal to complain: "It is possible that when our Lord God calls your Highness to his Judgment that your Highness may hear angry words from him: "Why did you not punish those who were your subjects and owned your authority, and were enemies to me in India?'"

After five months in Goa, Francis went to the east coast of India, near Sri Lanka (Ceylon), where he preached to a people called the Paravas, with considerable success until the ruler of Jaffna in northern Ceylon became alarmed and suppressed his mission by force.

Throughout most of 1545 to 1547, Francis preached in Malacca (another Portuguese possession) and other places on or near the Malay Peninsula. Here he encountered a Japanese expatriate (Anjiro, later baptized as Paul), and became interested in the possibility of a Japanese mission. After a brief return to Goa, he set out for Japan with another Jesuit priest and three Japanese converts. Here he learned the language, wrote a catechism, and preached. The authorities welcomed him in some towns and prevented him from teaching in others. Altogether Francis, the first to preach the Gospel in Japan, made perhaps 2000 converts there.

He then determined to carry the Gospel to China, at that time closed to outsiders. He bribed a ship's captain to smuggle him into the country, but had barely arrived there when he was stricken with fever and died on 3 December 1552. His body was brought back to Goa and buried there.

By all accounts, he was a man who preached the Gospel with tireless energy, and with great power and effectiveness. Estimates of the number of converts that he personally baptized vary, but some of them are in the six-digit range. One biographer says that he preached to more persons than anyone else since New Testament times.

Francis wrote as follows in a letter to Ignatius:

Many, many people hereabouts are not becoming Christians for one reason only: there is nobody to make them Christians. Again and again I have thought of going around the universities of Europe, especially Paris, and crying out to the scholars: "What a tragedy: how many souls are being shut out of heaven, thanks to you!"

This thought would certainly stir most of them to listen actively to what God is saying to them. They would forget their own desires and give themselves over entirely to God's will and his choice. They would cry out with all their heart: "Lord, here am I! Send me. Send me anywhere you like—even to India!"

James Kiefer

John Calvin

Dates

1509–1564

Famous for being

Leading reformer

Important writings

Institutes of the Christian Religion

Commentaries on the Bible

One of his quotations

"Christ is the most perfect image of God, into which we are so renewed as to bear the image of God, in knowledge, purity, righteousness, and true holiness."

Introduction

John Calvin was a prominent French theologian during the Protestant Reformation and the father of the theological system known as Calvinism. Martin Luther and Calvin are arguably the most significant architects of the Reformation.

Biographical summary

As a student in Paris, he studied the liberal arts before continuing his studies in theology at his father's request. Later, when his father had a falling-out with the local bishop, he instructed John to pursue an education in civil law, which he did in Orleans. After graduating as a Doctor of Law in 1531, he returned to Paris.

During his time in Paris, Calvin converted from Roman Catholicism to evangelicalism, and subsequently became an informal leader to other Paris evangelicals. All that is known about the occasion is what he himself says in the preface to his commentary on the Psalms:

> To this pursuit I endeavored faithfully to apply myself in obedience to the will of my father; but God, by the secret guidance of his providence, at length gave a different direction to my course. And first, since I was too obstinately devoted to the superstitions of Popery to be easily extricated from so profound an abyss of mire, God by a sudden conversion subdued and brought my mind to a teachable frame, which was more hardened in such matters than might have been expected from one at my early period of life.

On his way to Basel in 1536, he passed through Geneva where reformer William Farel persuaded him to stay and help the cause of the church, which he did for nearly two years. As a result of government resistance, Farel and Calvin left Geneva and Calvin moved to Strasbourg where he pastored from 1538 until 1541. When Calvin's supporters won election to the Geneva city council, he was invited back to the city in 1541 where he remained until his death in 1564.

Calvin's writings

John Calvin was a prolific writer of theology. His most notable work was the *Institutes of the Christian Religion*, the first edition of which was published in 1536, when he was 26 years old. Calvin revised the Institutes thoroughly several times. The first edition was a small, compact work, but the final edition published in 1559 was a thorough systematic theology comprising four volumes. Calvin also published commentaries on most of the Bible. These commentaries have proved to be of lasting value to students of the Bible and are still in print after over 400 years.

Sacraments

Calvin taught two sacraments: baptism and the Lord's supper. He differed from sacramentalists who believed that the sacraments were a means of receiving justifying grace. Rather, they are the badges, or marks, of Christian profession, testifying to God's grace.

Infant baptism

Calvin was a paedobaptist, believing that infants were the proper objects of baptism. He differed from Catholic and Lutheran paedobaptists in arguing that baptism did not regenerate infants. Rather, it symbolized entrance into the New Covenant, just as circumcision did for the Old Covenant. His argument for infant baptism draws many parallels between the two signs.

The Lord's Supper

Whereas Luther and the Catholic church believed that Christ's body was literally present in the Eucharist, and Zwingli taught that the Lord's Supper was a mere memorial, Calvin took a middle ground between the two positions. The elements were a symbol and therefore could not be the thing they signified; the doctrines of transubstantiation and consubstantiation confused the symbol and the substance. On the other hand, Zwingli's memorialism divorced symbol and substance completely. Calvin taught that when one receives the bread and wine, which are literal food and drink, in a spiritual sense he receives the spiritual food and drink of the Christian. Christ is spiritually present when the Eucharist is received by faith.

Church government

Calvin is the founder of the Presbyterian system of church government.

The Protestant work ethic

Calvin repudiated the distinction between "sacred" and "secular" duty and the prevailing notion that work is a necessary evil. Rather, he taught, work is a calling from God. Therefore, one glorifies God in his work by working diligently and joyfully.

Calvin did not invent capitalism, but he did teach that one of the rewards of hard work is wealth. His philosophy of work allowed capitalism to flourish where it was practiced.

Theopedia

Timeline of Calvin

1509 John Calvin is born

1532 John Calvin publishes his first work—a commentary on Seneca's *De Clementia*

1535 Calvin moves to Geneva

1536 Calvin publishes the first edition of his *Institutes of the Christian Religion*

1537 January 16, The Little Council and the Council of Two Hundred adopt Calvin's *21 Articles*

1538 Calvin and William Farel are banished from Geneva

1538 April 21, Calvin and Farel refuse to serve communion in Geneva

1540 Calvin publishes his commentary on Romans

1540 Calvin attends Diet of Hagenau

1540 August Calvin marries Idelette de Bures

1541 Calvin attends Diet of Regensburg

1541 November 20, Geneva city councils approve Calvin's *Ecclesiastical Ordinances* as the church constitution.

1541 September 13, Calvin returns to Geneva

1553 Michael Servetus arrested in Geneva and burned at the stake

1564 John Calvin dies

Teresa of Avila

Dates

1515–1582

Famous for being

First woman Doctor of the Church

Important writings

Autobiography

One of her quotations

"It is love alone that gives worth to all things."

Teresa of Avila, also known as The Roving Nun, was a great mystical visionary and writer, the first woman Doctor of the Church who reformed the Carmelites, the Church and the world. She also founded several monasteries and traveled all over Spain.

Early history

Teresa Sanchez of Avila learned to read by reading the lives of the saints. When she was seven, therefore, she talked her little brother, Rodrigo, into running off to Africa with her to be martyred by the Moslems. Fortunately, the runaways encountered their uncle, who promptly brought them back home.

After she had been a nun for twenty-five years St. Teresa' started her work as a reformer. Having first reformed herself, she was now ready to help others to become holier.

Visions

She began receiving visions, and was examined by Dominicans and Jesuits, including Saint Francis Borgia and the Franciscan St. Peter of Alcantara who pronounced the visions to be holy and true.

Teresa established a stricter life in her own Carmelite monastery in Avila. Then she set up about a further dozen convents. She also established two reformed monasteries of Carmelite men. This more austere branch of the Carmelites, men and women alike, was called the "Discalced Carmelites" because the members wore open sandals rather than shoes.

J. Dominguez, M.D.

Other Christian leaders in the Reformation and the Counter-Reformation

Desiderius Erasmus (1466–1536)
Philipp Melanchthon (1497–1560)
Theodore Beza (1519–1605)
John of the Cross (1542–1559)
Francis de Sales (1567–1622)

Desiderius Erasmus (1466–1536)

Desiderius Erasmus was a Dutch humanist and Roman Catholic theologian.

A native of the Low Countries, Erasmus was the leading northern European humanist in the late fifteenth and early sixteenth centuries and a luminary throughout Europe. He revered antiquity and learning in both church and culture. A severe critic of abuse and corruption in the church, he advocated simplicity in both faith and life for the church. As one contribution to reform he published a critical edition of the Greek New Testament that served as the basis for scholarly interpretation for centuries to come. His other scholarly and polemical works were read throughout Europe. Although sympathetic to reform, Erasmus eventually broke with Martin Luther whom Erasmus thought extreme and fractious, especially in his views on the human will and predestination. Erasmus was a classical scholar who wrote in a "pure" Latin style. Although he remained a Roman Catholic throughout his lifetime, he harshly criticized what he considered the excesses of the Roman Catholic Church.

He prepared new Latin and Greek editions of the New Testament. "Today we would call Erasmus's work a "study Bible." It had three parts: the Greek text, which Erasmus edited; his new Latin translation, a more elegant and accurate alternative to the traditional Vulgate; and brief scholarly comments on exegetical issues. Erasmus prefaced this monumental work of scholarship with an exhortation to Bible study. The New Testament, he proclaimed, contains the 'philosophy of Christ,' a simple and accessible teaching with the power to transform lives."

Philipp Melanchthon (1497–1560)

Philipp Melanchthon was a German professor and theologian, a key leader of the Lutheran Reformation, and a friend and associate of Martin Luther.

Melanchthon distinguished himself from his contemporaries not only through his works as a humanist and his extraordinary gift for Greek, Latin, and Hebrew, but also through his outstanding achievements as a reformer, politician, and educator.

Augsburg confession

Although based on the Marburg and Schwabach articles of Luther, the Augsburg confession, which was laid before the Diet of Augsburg in 1530, was mainly the work of Melanchthon. It is true, Luther did not conceal the fact that the irenical attitude of the confession was not what he had wished, but neither he nor Melanchthon was conscious of any difference in doctrine, and so the most important Protestant symbol is a monument of the harmony of the two Reformers on Gospel teachings.

Wikipedia

Theodore Beza (1519–1605)

Theodore Beza was a French Protestant Christian theologian and scholar who played an important role in the early Reformation.

Theodore Beza was born in Vezelay, France, his father the bailiff of the county. Adopted by his uncle after the death of his mother, tutored by Melchior Wolmar and attended the University of Orleans and received the degree of licentiate of the law. After a serious illness, he realized he held to Protestant beliefs, and he remembered the teachings of Wolmer. Embracing the Protestant cause, he left France with his wife and left for Switzerland.

He associated with the Reformed church and became a lifelong friend of John Calvin. From 1549 to 1558 he was professor of Greek at Lausanne. In 1558 he became professor of Greek at Geneva and succeeded Calvin in the chair of theology at Geneva. He was considered the leader of the French Reformed and Huguenot adherents. he made many trips to France and attempted to reconcile the differences between the Catholic leadership and the Reformed congregations.

Examples of Beza's writings

A Brief Declaration Of The Table Of Predestination

Also saith moreover: As he that hath received the gift, can better exhort and preach: so he that hath received this gift, doth hear the Preacher more obediently, & with greater reverence, &c. We do therefore exhort and preach, but they only which have ears to hear do hear us quietly, & to their comfort: and in those that have them not, this sentence is fulfilled, that hearing with their ears they do not hear, for they hear with the outward sense, but not with the inward consent. Now why some men have these ears, and others not, it is, because it is given to some to come, and to others not. Who knew God's counsel? must that be denied which is plain and evident, because that cannot be known which is hid and secret?

Theodore Beza

The Holy Spirit and faith

The Holy Spirit makes us partakers of Jesus Christ by Faith Alone

The Holy Spirit is therefore the One through whom the Rather places and maintains His elect in possession of Jesus Christ, His Son; and, consequently, of all the graces which are necessary to their salvation.

But it is necessary, in the first place, that the Holy Spirit makes us suitable and ready to receive Jesus Christ. This is what He does in creating in us, by His pure goodness and Divine mercy, that which we call 'faith' (Eph. 1: 17; Phil 1: 29; 2 'Mess 3:2), the sole instrument by which we take hold of Jesus Christ when He is offered to us, the sole vessel to receive Him (John 3:1–13, 33–36).

The means which the Holy Spirit uses to create and preserve faith in us

In order to create in us this instrument of faith, and also to feed and strengthen it more and more, the Holy Spirit uses two ordinary means (without however communicating to them His power, but working by them): the preaching of the Word of God, and His Sacraments (Matt 29:19–20; Acts 6:4; Rom 10:17; James 1:18; 1 Pet 1:23–25).

Theodore Beza

That Which We Call The Word Of God: Its Two Parts—Law And Gospel

The majority of men, blinded by the just judgment of God, have indeed never seriously considered what curse the Law subjects us to, nor why it has been ordained by God. And, as for the Gospel, they have nearly always thought that it was nothing other than a second Law, more perfect than the first. From this has come the erroneous distinction between precept and advice; there has followed, little by little, the total ruin of the benefit of Jesus Christ.

Theodore Beza

John of the Cross (1542–1559)

Juan de Ypres y Alvarez was born in 1542. His father died soon after, and Juan was brought up in an orphanage. (His father was probably Jewish. It is remarkable how many of the most memorable Spanish Christians have been of Jewish background.) At seventeen, he enrolled as a student in a Jesuit college, and at twenty-one, he joined the Carmelite Friars. He was ordained in 1567, and almost immediately met Teresa of Avila, a Carmelite Nun who was undertaking to return the Order to its original strict rule, which had been gradually relaxed to the detriment, as she believed, of the spiritual lives of the members of the Order. Those who followed the strict rule as promulgated by Teresa went barefoot or wore sandals instead of shoes, and so became known as Discalced (unshod) Carmelites, or Carmelites of the Strict Observance. John undertook to adopt the stricter rule and encourage others to do so.

Not all members of the order welcomed the change. In 1577 a group of Calced Carmelites, or Carmelites of the Ancient Observance, kidnapped John and demanded that he renounce the reform. When he refused, he was imprisoned in complete darkness and solitude in a Calced monastery in Toledo for about nine months. He then escaped and fled to a Calced monastery. While imprisoned at Toledo, he had begun to compose some poems, and now he wrote them down, with commentaries on their spiritual significance.

He was given various positions of leadership among the reformed friars, but then dissension broke out among the reformers between "moderates" and "extremists." John supported the moderate party, and when the extremists gained control, they denounced him as a traitor to the reform. He was sent to a remote friary, and fell ill, and finally died at Ubeda during the night preceding 14 December 1591.

His poems include:

The Dark Night of the Soul (about the experience of spiritual desolation, of feeling abandoned and rejected by God, and why this is for some Christians a means by which God increases our faith in Him; about the Christian walk, the life of prayer and contemplation, and growing in love and grace)

The Ascent of Mount Carmel (same poem as the preceding, but with a different commentary attached)

The Spiritual Canticle (about the love between the Christian and Christ as symbolized by the love between bride and groom; draws heavily upon the imagery of the Song of Solomon)

The Living Flame of Love (about the soul transformed by grace)

James Kiefer

John of the Cross and "The Dark Night"

John of the Cross' axiom is that the soul must empty itself of self in order to be filled with God, that it must be purified of the last traces of earthly dross before it is fit to become united with God. In the application of this simple maxim he shows the most uncompromising logic. Supposing the soul with which he deals to be habitually in the state of grace and pushing forward to better things, he overtakes it on the very road leading it, in its opinion to God, and lays open before its eyes a number of sores of which it was altogether ignorant, viz. what he terms the spiritual capital sins. Not until these are removed (a most formidable task) is it fit to be admitted to what he calls the "Dark Night", which consists in the passive purgation, where God by heavy trials, particularly interior ones, perfects and completes what the soul had begun of its own accord. It is now passive, but not inert, for by submitting to the Divine operation it co-operates in the measure of its power. Here lies one of the essential differences between St. John's mysticism and a false quietism.

Benedict Zimmerman, The Catholic Encyclopedia, Volume VIII, 1910

Francis de Sales (1567–1622)

Francis de Sales was born in the Savoy district of France in 1567 and ordained a priest in 1593. At that time the religious and political struggles of the time had placed under the control of Roman Catholic rulers several regions in which the people were mostly Protestants. Francis was sent to preach in one such region near his birthplace, attempting to persuade his hearers to become Roman Catholics. Since he was seen to be persuasive, he was appointed in 1602 to be Roman Catholic bishop of Geneva, a Calvinist stronghold which had been captured by the Roman Catholic Duke of Savoy. Here again, he brought many to his way of thinking. His motto was, "He who preaches with love, preaches effectively." His numerous controversial tracts are unfailingly courteous to his opponents. Many Christians who are not at all convinced of the truth of the Romanist position by his arguments nevertheless read him with delight because of his obvious love for God and his neighbor.

By no means all of his writings were concerned with disputation. His best known and best loved treatises were concerned with the life of prayer, and were written to advise those who wish to become more aware of the presence of God in their lives. His *Introduction To the Devout Life* was highly praised by John Wesley. C.S. Lewis has referred to the "dewy freshness" that permeates the book.

James Kiefer

Classic Christian devotional books from the Reformation and the Counter Reformation

John Calvin

On the Christian Life

Institutes of the Christian Religion

Calvin's commentaries on individual books of the Bible

John Foxe, *Book of Martyrs*

Martin Luther

The 95 Theses

The Large Catechism

Preface to Romans

Commentary on Romans

Commentary on Galatians

Table Talk

Thomas Cranmer, *Book of Common Prayer*

Ignatius of Loyola (1491–1556), *Spiritual Exercises of Ignatius of Loyola*

Teresa of Avila

Autobiography

The Interior Castle

John of the Cross (1542–1591)

Spiritual Canticle

Dark Night of the Soul

Ascent of Mount Carmel

Sayings of Love and Peace

Francis de Sales (1567–1622)

Introduction To The Devout Life

Treatise on the Love of God

Jeremiah Burroughs (1599–1646) *The Rare Jewel of Christian Contentment*

Extracts from Classic Christian devotional books from the Reformation and the Counter Reformation

Martin Luther (1483–1546)

A mighty fortress is our God

Selected Passages of Martin Luther

Preface to the letter of St. Paul to the Romans

John Calvin (1509–1564), *Institutes of the Christian Religion*

Teresa of Avila (1515–1582), *Life*

Francis de Sales (1567–1622), *Meditations of St Francis De Sales*

Martin Luther

A Mighty Fortress Is Our God

A mighty fortress is our God,
A bulwark never failing;
Our helper He, amid the flood
Of mortal ills prevailing.

For still our ancient foe
Doth seek to work us woe;
His craft and pow'r are great,
And, armed with cruel hate,
On earth is not his equal.

Did we in our own strength confide,
Our striving would be losing,
Were not the right Man on our side,
The Man of God's own choosing.
Dost ask who that may be?
Christ Jesus, it is He;
Lord Sabaoth His name,
From age to age the same,
And He must win the battle.

And though this world, with devils filled,
Should threaten to undo us,
We will not fear, for God hath willed
His truth to triumph through us.
The prince of darkness grim -
We tremble not for him;
His rage we can endure,
For lo! his doom is sure;
One little word shall fell him.

That word above all earthly pow'rs -
No thanks to them—abideth;
The Spirit and the gifts are ours
Through Him Who with us sideth.
Let goods and kindred go,
This mortal life also;
The body they may kill;
God's truth abideth still,
His kingdom is for ever.

Martin Luther, translated by
Frederick H. Hedge,1529

Selected Passages of Martin Luther

A definition of faith

Faith is not what some people think it is. Their human dream is a delusion. Because they observe that faith is not followed by good works or a better life, they fall into error, even though they speak and hear much about faith.

"Faith is not enough," they say, "You must do good works, you must be pious to be saved."

They think that, when you hear the gospel, you start working, creating by your own strength a thankful heart which says, "I believe." That is what they think true faith is. But, because this is a human idea, a dream, the heart never learns anything from it, so it does nothing and reform doesn't come from this `faith,' either.

Instead, faith is God's work in us, that changes us and gives new birth from God. (John 1:13). It kills the Old Adam and makes us completely different people. It changes our hearts, our spirits, our thoughts and all our powers. It brings the Holy Spirit with it. Yes, it is a living, creative, active and powerful thing, this faith. Faith cannot help doing good works constantly. It doesn't stop to ask if good works ought to be done, but before anyone asks, it already has done them and continues to do them without ceasing. Anyone who does not do good works in this manner is an unbeliever. He stumbles around and looks for faith and good works, even though he does not know what faith or good works are. Yet he gossips and chatters about faith and good works with many words.

Faith is a living, bold trust in God's grace, so certain of God's favor that it would risk death a thousand times trusting in it. Such confidence and knowledge of God's grace makes you happy, joyful and bold in your relationship to God and all creatures. The Holy Spirit makes this happen through faith. Because of it, you freely, willingly and joyfully do good to everyone, serve everyone, suffer all kinds of things, love and praise the God who has shown you such grace. Thus, it is just as impossible to separate faith and works as it is to separate heat and light from fire! Therefore, watch out for your own false ideas and guard against good-for-nothing gossips, who think they're smart enough to define faith and works, but really are the greatest of fools. Ask God to work faith in you, or you will remain forever without faith, no matter what you wish, say or can do.

Martin Luther, An Introduction to St. Paul's Letter to the Romans, Luther's German Bible of 1522

Martin Luther on quoting Martin Luther

Because I see that the mobs are always growing, the number of errors are always increasing and Satan's rage and ruin have no end, I wish to confess with this work my faith before God and the whole world, point by point. I am doing this, lest certain people cite me or my writings, while I am alive or after I am dead, to support their errors, as those fanatics, the Sacramentarians and the Anabaptists, have begun to do. I will remain in this confession until my death (God help me!), will depart from this world in it, and appear before the Judgment Seat of our Lord Jesus Christ.

So that no one will say after my death, ``If Luther was alive, he would teach and believe this article differently, because he did not think it through sufficiently," I state the following, once and for all: I, by God's grace, I have diligently examined these articles in the light of passages throughout the Scriptures. I have worked on them repeatedly and you can be sure that I want to defend them, in the same way that I have just defended the Sacrament of the Altar.

No, I'm not drunk or impulsive. I know what I am saying and understand fully what this will mean for me as I stand before the Lord Jesus Christ on the Last Day. No one should think that I am joking or rambling. I'm serious! By God's grace, I know Satan very well. If Satan can turn God's Word upside down and pervert the Scriptures, what will he do with my words—or the words of others?

Martin Luther, Spiritual Last Will & Testament

What is your God?

The First Commandment

You must not have other gods.

That is, I must be your only God.

Question: What does this saying mean? How should we understand it? What does it mean to have a god? What is God?

Answer: To have a god means this: You expect to receive all good things from it and turn to it in every time of trouble. Yes, to have a god means to trust and to believe in Him with your whole heart. I have often said that only the trust and faith of the heart can make God or an idol. If your faith and trust are true, you have the true God, too. On the other hand, where trust is false, is evil, there you will not have the true God either. Faith and God live together. I tell you, whatever you set your heart on and rely on is really your god.

Martin Luther, Large Catechism

Discovering the Gospel: The Tower experience

Meanwhile in that same year, 1519, I had begun interpreting the Psalms once again. I felt confident that I was now more experienced, since I had dealt in university courses with St. Paul's Letters to the Romans, to the Galatians, and the Letter to the Hebrews. I had conceived a burning desire to understand what Paul meant in his Letter to the Romans, but thus far there had stood in my way, not the cold blood around my heart, but that one word which is in chapter one: "The justice of God is revealed in it." I hated that word, "justice of God," which, by the use and custom of all my teachers, I had been taught to understand philosophically as referring to formal or active justice, as they call it, i.e., that justice by which God is just and by which he punishes sinners and the unjust.

But I, blameless monk that I was, felt that before God I was a sinner with an extremely troubled conscience. I couldn't be sure that God was appeased by my satisfaction. I did not love, no, rather I hated the just God who punishes sinners. In silence, if I did not blaspheme, then certainly I grumbled vehemently and got angry at God. I said, "Isn't it enough that we miserable sinners, lost for all eternity because of original sin, are oppressed by every kind of calamity through the Ten Commandments? Why does God heap sorrow upon sorrow through the Gospel and through the Gospel threaten us with his justice and his wrath?" This was how I was raging with wild and disturbed conscience. I constantly badgered St. Paul about that spot in Romans 1 and anxiously wanted to know what he meant.

I meditated night and day on those words until at last, by the mercy of God, I paid attention to their context: "The justice of God is revealed in it, as it is written: 'The just person lives by faith.'" I began to understand that in this verse the justice of God is that by which the just person lives by a gift of God, that is by faith. I began to understand that this verse means that the justice of God is revealed through the Gospel, but it is a passive justice, i.e. that by which the merciful God justifies us by faith, as it is written: "The just person lives by faith." All at once I felt that I had been born again and entered into paradise itself through open gates. Immediately I saw the whole of Scripture in a different light. I ran through the Scriptures from memory and found that other terms had analogous meanings, e.g., the work of God, that is, what God works in us; the power of God, by which he makes us powerful; the wisdom of God, by which he makes us wise; the strength of God, the salvation of God, the glory of God.

I exalted this sweetest word of mine, "the justice of God," with as much love as before I had hated it with hate. This phrase of Paul was for me the very gate of paradise. Afterward I read Augustine's "On the Spirit and the Letter," in which I found what I had not dared hope for. I discovered that he too interpreted "the justice of God" in a similar way, namely, as that with which God clothes us when he justifies us. Although Augustine had said it imperfectly and did not explain in detail how God imputes justice to us, still it pleased me that he taught the justice of God by which we are justified.

Martin Luther, Preface to the Complete Edition of Luther's Latin Works (1545)

On faith and love

Furthermore, here is the example of love for the one learned in Christ toward the leper. Because there you see how love made Him a servant, that He might help the poor freely and without any return; he sought neither profit nor honor from it, but only the benefit of the poor and the honor of God the Father. That is why He also commanded him, that he should tell it to no one, so that it would be a truly pure work of free and good love. That is, as I have often said, In the way that faith makes us lords, love makes us servants, even that through faith we become Gods and partakers of the Divine nature and name, as Psalm 81 says, "I have said, you are Gods, and all children of the most high." Yet through love we all become like the poorest one. Through faith we lack nothing and have abundance. Through love we serve everyone. Through faith we receive good things from God above. Through love we distribute them to a neighbor. Just as Christ lacked nothing according to Divinity, but according to humanity served everyone, according to their need.

We have spoken of this often enough, that we also then through faith must be born to be God's children and gods, lords and kings, just as Christ was born of the Father in eternity, a true God. And furthermore, through love we reach out to abundantly help those nearby, just as Christ became man to help us all. And Christ is God in the same way, not through merit of work done before, nor through what He earned as a man; but He was the same from birth, without any work, and earlier, before He was man. Thus we also have the divine sonship, that is the forgiving of our sins and that death and hell cannot harm, not earned through work or love, but without work and before love, through the faith in the gospel received out of grace. And as Christ first of all, being eternal God, became man to serve us, so we should likewise do good and love our neighbor, if we are already devout, without sin, enlivened, blessed and children of God. That is from the first example of the leper.

Martin Luther, Fastenpostille 1525, Matt. 8:1ff

On the Word became flesh

Just as the Word of God became flesh, it is also certainly necessary to say that the flesh became Word. For the Word became flesh in order that the flesh might become Word. That is, God becomes man in order that man might become God. Likewise strength becomes weakness in order that weakness might become strength. He put on our form and figure and image and likeness in order that He might clothe us with His image, form and likeness. For wisdom becomes foolishness in order that foolishness might become wisdom; and likewise in all other things pertaining to God and to us, in all of them He took on what is ours in order to give us what is His.

Martin Luther, Sermo Lutheri in natali Christi, [December 25, 1514]

If Christ had come with trumpets sounding

A Wonderful thing happened [when the angel announced this birth to the shepherds].

All of this occurred, to present this birth to us with tender, loving care and to attract hearts to it, so that these hearts might love Christ.

If this birth had been proclaimed to the nobles of this world; If the shepherds had measured themselves against the standard of these important fellows; If the shepherds had compared to royal wisdom and wealth, they would have been afraid, because power frightens and wisdom intimidates people.

If Christ had come with trumpets sounding; If he had a cradle of gold, His birth would have been a stately thing. But it wouldn't comfort me. So, He had to lay in a poor girl's lap and be scarcely noticed by the world. In that lap I can come to see Him; In this way He now reveals Himself to the distressed.

Yes, He would've had greater fame, if He'd have come in great power, splendor, wisdom and high class. Yet, He will come some day, in another way, when He comes to oppose the great nobles. But now He comes to the poor, who need a Savior. Then He will come as judge to oppose those who oppress the poor now.

Martin Luther, Sermon on Luke 2:1–14,
preached at noon on Christmas Day 1530

Preface to the Letter of St. Paul to the Romans

[Luther's preface to the book of Romans was instrumental in John Wesley's conversion. In Wesley's Journal of May 24, 1738, he wrote:

In the evening I went very unwillingly to a society in Aldersgate Street, where one was reading Luther's preface to the Epistle to the Romans. About a quarter before nine, while he was describing the change which God works in the heart through faith in Christ, I felt my heart strangely warmed. I felt I did trust in Christ, Christ alone, for salvation; and an assurance was given me that he had taken away my sins, even mine, and saved me from the law of sin and death.]

This letter is truly the most important piece in the New Testament. It is purest Gospel. It is well worth a Christian's while not only to memorize it word for word but also to occupy himself with it daily, as though it were the daily bread of the soul. It is impossible to read or to meditate on this letter too much or too well. The more one deals with it, the more precious it becomes and the better it tastes. Therefore I want to carry out my service and, with this preface, provide an introduction to the letter, insofar as God gives me the ability, so that every one can gain the fullest possible understanding of it. Up to now it has been darkened by glosses and by many a useless comment, but it is in itself a bright light, almost bright enough to illumine the entire Scripture.

To begin with, we have to become familiar with the vocabulary of the letter and know what St. Paul means by the words law, sin, grace, faith, justice, flesh, spirit, etc. Otherwise there is no use in reading it.

You must not understand the word law here in human fashion, i.e., a regulation about what sort of works must be done or must not be done. That's the way it is with human laws: you satisfy the demands of the law with works, whether your heart is in it or not. God judges what is in the depths of the heart. Therefore his law also makes demands on the depths of the heart and doesn't let the heart rest content in works; rather it punishes as hypocrisy and lies all works done apart from the depths of the heart. All human beings are called liars (Psalm 116), since none of them keeps or can keep God's law from the depths of the heart. Everyone finds inside himself an aversion to good and a craving for evil. Where there is no free desire for good, there the heart has not set itself on God's law. There also sin is surely to be found and the deserved wrath of God, whether a lot of good works and an honorable life appear outwardly or not.

Therefore in chapter 2, St. Paul adds that the Jews are all sinners and says that only the doers of the law are justified in the sight of God. What he is saying is that no one is a doer of the law by works. On the contrary, he says to them, "You teach that one should not commit adultery, and you commit adultery. You judge another in a certain matter and condemn yourselves in that same matter, because you do the very same thing that you judged in another." It is as if he were saying, "Outwardly you live quite properly in the works of the law and judge those who do not live the same way; you know how to teach everybody. You see the speck in another's eye but do not notice the beam in your own."

Outwardly you keep the law with works out of fear of punishment or love of gain. Likewise you do everything without free desire and love of the law; you act out of aversion and force. You'd rather act otherwise if the law didn't exist. It follows, then, that you, in the depths of your heart, are an enemy of the law. What do you mean, therefore, by teaching another not to steal, when you, in the depths of your heart, are a thief and would be one outwardly too, if you dared. (Of course, outward work doesn't last long with such hypocrites.) So then, you teach others but not yourself; you don't even know what you are teaching. You've never understood the law rightly. Furthermore, the law increases sin, as St. Paul says in chapter 5. That is because a person becomes more and more an enemy of the law the more it demands of him what he can't possibly do.

In chapter 7, St. Paul says, "The law is spiritual." What does that mean? If the law were physical, then it could be satisfied by works, but since it is spiritual, no one can satisfy it unless everything he does springs from the depths of the heart. But no one can give such a heart except the Spirit of God, who makes the person be like the law, so that he actually conceives a heartfelt longing for the law and henceforward does everything, not through fear or coercion, but from a free heart. Such a law is spiritual since it can only be loved and fulfilled by such a heart and such a spirit. If the Spirit is not in the heart, then there remain sin, aversion and enmity against the law, which in itself is good, just and holy.

You must get used to the idea that it is one thing to do the works of the law and quite another to fulfill it. The works of the law are every thing that a person does or can do of his own free will and by his own powers to obey the law. But because in doing such works the heart abhors the law and yet is forced to obey it, the works are a total loss and are completely useless. That is what St. Paul means in chapter 3 when he says, "No human being is justified before God through the works of the law." From this you can see that the schoolmasters [i.e., the scholastic theologians] and sophists are seducers when they teach that you can prepare yourself for grace by means of works. How can anybody prepare himself for good by means of works if he does no good work except with aversion and constraint in his heart? How can such a work please God, if it proceeds from an averse and unwilling heart?

But to fulfill the law means to do its work eagerly, lovingly and freely, without the constraint of the law; it means to live well and in a manner pleasing to God, as though there were no law or punishment. It is the Holy Spirit, however, who puts such eagerness of unconstained love into the heart, as Paul says in chapter 5. But the Spirit is given only in, with, and through faith in Jesus Christ, as Paul says in his introduction. So, too, faith comes only through the word of God, the Gospel, that preaches Christ: how he is both Son of God and man, how he died and rose for our sake. Paul says all this in chapters 3, 4 and 10.

That is why faith alone makes someone just and fulfills the law; faith it is that brings the Holy Spirit through the merits of Christ. The Spirit, in turn, renders the heart glad and free, as the law demands. Then good works proceed from faith itself. That is what Paul means in chapter 3 when, after he has thrown out the works of the law, he sounds as though the wants to abolish the law by faith. No, he says, we uphold the law through faith, i.e. we fulfill it through faith.

Sin in the Scriptures means not only external works of the body but also all those movements within us which bestir themselves and move us to do the external works, namely, the depth of the heart with all its powers. Therefore the word "do" should refer to a person's completely falling into sin. No external work of sin happens, after all, unless a person commit himself to it completely, body and soul. In particular, the Scriptures see into the heart, to the root and main source of al sin: unbelief in the depth of the heart. Thus, even as faith alone makes just and brings the Spirit and the desire to do good external works, so it is only unbelief which sins and exalts the flesh and brings desire to do evil external works. That's what happened to Adam and Eve in Paradise (cf. Genesis 3).

That is why only unbelief is called sin by Christ, as he says in John, chapter 16, "The Spirit will punish the world because of sin, because it does not believe in me." Furthermore, before good or bad works happen, which are the good or bad fruits of the heart, there has to be present in the heart either faith or unbelief, the root, sap and chief power of all sin. That is why, in the Scriptures, unbelief is called the head of the serpent and of the ancient dragon which the offspring of the woman, i.e. Christ, must crush, as was promised to Adam (cf. Genesis 3). "Grace" and "gift" differ in that grace actually denotes God's kindness or favor which he has toward us and by which he is disposed to pour Christ and the Spirit with his gifts into us, as becomes clear from chapter 5, where Paul says, "Grace and gift are in

Christ, etc." The gifts and the Spirit increase daily in us, yet they are not complete, since evil desires and sins remain in us which war against the Spirit, as Paul says in chapter 7, and in Galatians, chapter 5. And Genesis, chapter 3, proclaims the enmity between the offspring of the woman and that of the serpent. But grace does do this much: that we are accounted completely just before God. God's grace is not divided into bits and pieces, as are the gifts, but grace takes us up completely into God's favor for the sake of Christ, our intercessor and mediator, so that the gifts may begin their work in us.

In this way, then, you should understand chapter 7, where St. Paul portrays himself as still a sinner, while in chapter 8 he says that, because of the incomplete gifts and because of the Spirit, there is nothing damnable in those who are in Christ. Because our flesh has not been killed, we are still sinners, but because we believe in Christ and have the beginnings of the Spirit, God so shows us his favor and mercy, that he neither notices nor judges such sins. Rather he deals with us according to our belief in Christ until sin is killed.

Faith is not that human illusion and dream that some people think it is. When they hear and talk a lot about faith and yet see that no moral improvement and no good works result from it, they fall into error and say, "Faith is not enough. You must do works if you want to be virtuous and get to heaven." The result is that, when they hear the Gospel, they stumble and make for themselves with their own powers a concept in their hearts which says, "I believe." This concept they hold to be true faith. But since it is a human fabrication and thought and not an experience of the heart, it accomplishes nothing, and there follows no improvement.

Faith is a work of God in us, which changes us and brings us to birth anew from God (cf. John 1). It kills the old Adam, makes us completely different people in heart, mind, senses, and all our powers, and brings the Holy Spirit with it. What a living, creative, active powerful thing is faith! It is impossible that faith ever stop doing good. Faith doesn't ask whether good works are to be done, but, before it is asked, it has done them. It is always active. Whoever doesn't do such works is without faith; he gropes and searches about him for faith and good works but doesn't know what faith or good works are. Even so, he chatters on with a great many words about faith and good works.

Faith is a living, unshakeable confidence in God's grace; it is so certain, that someone would die a thousand times for it. This kind of trust in and knowledge of God's grace makes a person joyful, confident, and happy with regard to God and all creatures. This is what the Holy Spirit does by faith. Through faith, a person will do good to everyone without coercion, willingly and happily; he will serve everyone, suffer everything for the love and praise of God, who has shown him such grace. It is as impossible to separate works from faith as burning and shining from fire. Therefore be on guard against your own false ideas and against the chatterers who think they are clever enough to make judgments about faith and good works but who are in reality the biggest fools. Ask God to work faith in you; otherwise you will remain eternally without faith, no matter what you try to do or fabricate.

Now "justice" is just such a faith. It is called God's justice or that justice which is valid in God's sight, because it is God who gives it and reckons it as justice for the sake of Christ our Mediator. It influences a person to give to everyone what he owes him. Through faith a person becomes sinless and eager for God's commands. Thus he gives God the honor due him and pays him what he owes him. He serves people willingly with the means available to him. In this way he pays everyone his due. Neither nature nor free will nor our own powers can bring about such a justice, for even as no one can give himself faith, so too he cannot remove unbelief. How can he then take away even the smallest sin? Therefore everything which takes place outside faith or in unbelief is lie, hypocrisy and sin (Romans 14), no matter how smoothly it may seem to go.

You must not understand flesh here as denoting only unchastity or spirit as denoting only the inner heart. Here St. Paul calls flesh (as does Christ in John 3) everything born of flesh, i.e. the whole human being with body and soul, reason and senses, since everything in him tends toward the flesh. That is why you should know enough to call that per son "fleshly" who, without grace, fabricates, teaches and chatters about high spiritual matters. You can learn the same thing from Galatians, chapter 5, where St. Paul calls heresy and hatred works of the flesh. And in Romans, chapter 8, he says that, through the flesh, the law is weakened. He says this, not of unchastity, but of all sins, most of all of unbelief, which is the most spiritual of vices.

On the other hand, you should know enough to call that person "spiritual" who is occupied with the most outward of works as was Christ, when he washed the feet of the disciples, and Peter, when he steered his boat and fished. So then, a person is "flesh" who, inwardly and outwardly, lives only to do those things which are of use to the flesh and to temporal existence. A person is "spirit" who, inwardly and outwardly, lives only to do those things which are of use to the spirit and to the life to come.

Unless you understand these words in this way, you will never understand either this letter of St. Paul or any book of the Scriptures. Be on guard, therefore against any teacher who uses these words differently, no matter who he be, whether Jerome, Augustine, Ambrose, Origen or anyone else as great as or greater than they. . . .

Martin Luther

John Calvin
Institutes of the Christian Religion

In all acts of life we must consider our vocation

Finally, this point is to be noted; the Lord bids each one of us all life's actions to look to his calling. For he knows with what great restlessness human nature flames, with what fickleness it is borne hither and thither, how its ambition longs to embrace various things at once.

Therefore lest through our stupidity and rashness everything be turned topsy-turvy, he has appointed duties for everyman in this particular way of life. And that no one may thoughtlessly transgress his limits, he has named these various kinds of living 'callings'. Therefore each individual has his own kind of living assigned to him by the Lord as a kind of sentry post so that he may not heedlessly wander about through life.

John Calvin: Institutes of the Christian Religion, Book 3, Chapter 10

The distinction between the invisible church and the visible church

I have observed that the Scriptures speak of the Church in two ways. Sometimes when they speak of the Church they mean the Church as it really is before God—the Church into which none are admitted but those who by the gift of adoption are sons of God, and by the sanctification of the Spirit true members of Christ. In this case it not only comprehends the saints who dwell on the earth, but all the elect who have existed from the beginning of the world.

Often, too, by the name of Church is designated the whole body of mankind scattered throughout the world, who profess to worship one God and Christ, who by baptism are initiated into the faith; by partaking of the Lord's Supper profess unity in true doctrine and charity, agree in holding the word of the Lord, and observe the ministry which Christ has appointed for the preaching of it.

In this Church there is a very large mixture of hypocrites, who have nothing of Christ but the name and outward appearance: of ambitious, avaricious, envious, evil-speaking men, some also impurer lives, who are tolerated for a time, either because their guilt cannot be legally established, or because due strictness of discipline is not always observed.

Hence, as it is necessary to believe the invisible Church, which is manifest to the eye of God only, so we are also enjoined to regard this Church which is so-called with reference to man, and to cultivate its communion.

John Calvin: Institutes of the Christian Religion, Book 4, Chapter 1

The marks of the visible church

From this the face of the church comes forth and becomes visible to our eyes. "Wherever we see the Word of God purely preached and heard, and the sacraments administered according to Christ's institution, there, it is not to be doubted, a church of God exists (cf. Eph. 2.20). For his promise cannot fail: 'Wherever two or three are gathered in my name, there I am in the midst of them (Matt.18.20).

The church universal is a multitude gathered from all nations; it is divided and dispersed in separate places, but agrees on the one truth of divine doctrine, and is bound by the bond of the same religion.

Under it are thus included individual churches, disposed in towns and villages according human need, so that each rightly has the name and authority of the church.

John Calvin, Institutes of the Christian Religion, Book 4, Chapters 1, 7 and 9

Teresa of Avila

The Beauty of Christ

After a vision of Christ there remained with me an impression of his exceeding great beauty, which I have preserved to this very day. And if one single vision sufficed to effect this, how much greater would be the power of all those which of his favor the Lord has granted me!

One very great benefit which I received was this. I had a very serious fault, which led me into great trouble. It was that, if I began to realize that a person liked me, and I took to him myself, I would grow so fond of him that my memory would feel compelled to revert to him and I would always be thinking of him without intentionally giving any offence to God, I would delight in seeing him and think about him and his good qualities. This was such a harmful thing that it was ruining my soul. But once I had seen the great beauty of the Lord, I saw no one who by comparison with him seemed acceptable to me or on whom my thoughts wished to dwell. For if I merely turn the eyes of my mind to the image of him which I have in my soul, I feel I have such freedom that from that time forward everything I see appears nauseating to me by comparison with the excellences and glories which I have seen in the Lord. Nor is there any knowledge of any kind of consolation to which I can attach the slightest esteem by comparison with that which it causes me to hear a single word coming from that divine mouth—and more wonderful still is it when I hear many. And unless for my sins the Lord allows this memory to fade, I consider it impossible for me to lie so deeply absorbed in anything that I do not regain freedom when I run once more in thought, even for a moment, to this Lord.

Teresa of Avila, Life, Chapter 37

Francis de Sales

Meditations of St Francis De Sales

Second Meditation: Why We Were Created Preparation

Place yourself in the Presence of God and ask Him to inspire you.

Considerations

1. God has not placed you in the world because He needs you, for you are useless to Him, but simply to manifest His goodness in you by giving you His grace and glory; and to this end, He has given you an intellect to know Him, a memory to remember Him, a will to love Him, an imagination to represent to yourself His benefits, eyes to look upon the wonder of His works, a tongue to speak His praise . . . and so of your other faculties.

2. Since you were created and put in the world for this end, you must reject and avoid any actions which lead you away from it, and count as vain and useless those which lead you no nearer.

3. Consider the wretchedness of worldly people who never think of their true purpose, but live as though they were created only to build houses, plant trees, amass riches and amuse themselves.

Spiritual acts and resolutions

1. Reproach yourself humbly for your wretchedness in never having thought of these things before. What was I thinking about, my God, when not of Thee? What was I remembering when I was forgetful of Thee? Where was my heart when not set upon Thee? Truth should have been my food and yet I gorged myself with vanity, serving the world created to serve me.

2. Detest your past life. Vain thoughts and useless reasonings, I turn from you. Hateful and empty memories, I renounce you. Faithless and false friendships, harmful and wretched habits, selfish pleasure and unhappy indulgence, I will have no part with you.

3. Turn to God. My God and my Savior, from now on I will think only of Thee; no more of things which may displease Thee. My memories shall be ever of Thy greatness and Thy Mercy so tenderly exercised on me. My heart shall find all its delight in Thee and Thou shalt be the object of its love. From now on I will detest the useless follies which have occupied my days and all the useless objects of my love, and accordingly, amend my life.

Conclusion

1. Thanksgiving. Thank God for having created you for so high a destiny. Thou hast made me for Thyself, O Lord, that I may rejoice for ever in the immensity of Thy glory. Thy glory! When shall I be worthy of it? When shall I bless Thee as I ought?

2. Offering. I offer Thee, my Creator, these spiritual acts and resolutions with all my heart and soul.

3. Petition. Accept, O God, these desires and aspirations and give me Thy blessing that I may put them into practice through the merits of Thy Son, Who shed His Precious Blood for me upon the Cross.

Meditations of St Francis De Sales

History of Bible translations

Number of languages Bible had been translated into during this period.

1500

34 languages

1600

36 languages

1700

52 languages

Examples of Bible translations from the Reformation and the Counter-Reformation

1516 Erasmus Produces a Greek/Latin Parallel New Testament.

1522 Martin Luther's German New Testament.

1526 William Tyndale's New Testament; The First New Testament to be printed in the English Language. (Worms edition)

1530 Tyndale's translation of the Pentateuch is printed.

1531 Tyndale's translation of the Book of Jonah is printed.

1534 Tyndale's revised New Testament is printed.

1535 Myles Coverdale's Bible is printed.

1537 Matthews Bible.

1539 The "Great Bible" is printed; The First English Language Bible to be authorized for public use.

1560 The Geneva Bible printed; The first English language Bible to include verses and chapters.

1568 The Bishops Bible printed; The Bible of which the King James was a revision.

1609 The Douay Old Testament is added to the Rheimes New Testament (of 1582) making the first complete English Catholic Bible; translated from the Latin Vulgate.

1611 The King James Bible printed.

John 3:16 as translated in the following famous printings of the English Bible:

First edition, King James (1611)

"For God so loued the world, that he gaue his only begotten Sonne: that whosoeuer beleeueth in him, should not perish, but haue euerlasting life."

Rheims (1582)

"For so God loued the vvorld, that he gaue his only-begotten sonne: that euery one that beleeueth in him, perish not, but may haue life euerlasting"

Geneva (1557)

"For God so loueth the world, that he hath geuen his only begotten Sonne: that none that beleue in him, should peryshe, but haue euerlasting lyfe."

Great Bible (1539)

"For God so loued the worlde, that he gaue his only begotten sonne, that whosoeuer beleueth in him, shulde not perisshe, but haue euerlasting lyfe."

Tyndale (1534)

"For God so loveth the worlde, that he hath geven his only sonne, that none that beleve in him, shuld perisshe: but shuld have everlastinge lyfe."

Wycliffe (1380)

"for god loued so the world; that he gaf his oon bigetun sone, that eche man that bileueth in him perisch not: but haue euerlastynge liif,"

Martin Luther's translation of the Bible

Introduction

While Luther perhaps cannot be said to have created the modern German language, Bluhm (an authority on Luther's Bible) states, "He enriched and endowed it more impressively and shaped it more significantly than any other author."

Luther's translation brought to life one of the fundamental doctrines of the Protestant Reformation: the "Open Bible," through which God could speak directly to the people without the intermediary services of the established Church. Remarkably, Luther completed his translation of the New Testament in just three months, basing his text in large part on Erasmus' 1518–19 Greek New Testament (2nd edition), and it was published in 1522. Luther's complete Old Testament was not published until 1534, along with the first complete Luther Bible.

CHAPTER 6

THE AGE OF REASON AND REVIVAL

From Blaise Pascal to John Newton
AD 1649–1799

Important dates in the time of the Age of Reason and Revival

17th Century

1653 Quakers founded by George Fox
1654 Death of St. Peter Claver, Colombia
1667 John Milton's *Paradise Lost*
1670 Blaise Pascal's *Pensées*
1670 William Penn and William Mead arrested for preaching in public
1672 The Eastern Orthodox council of Jerusalem
1675 John Owen publishes *Pneumatologia*, a theological discourse on the Holy Spirit
1675 Philipp Jakob Spener publishes *Pia Desideria*, a manifesto for pietism
1678 John Bunyan's *Pilgrim's Progress*
1692 Nineteen executed for witchcraft in Salem, Massachusetts

18th Century

1730–1749 First Great Awakening in U.S.
1738 John Wesley's conversion
1741 Shakers: Ann Lee
1744 Methodists and John and Charles Wesley
1748 John Newton's conversion
1757 Pope Benedict XIV permits nations to have the Bible in their native language
1774 Unitarians: T. Lindsay.
1772 Emanuel Swedenborg founds Swedenborgianism
1789 John Carroll becomes first Roman Catholic bishop in the United States
1789–1801 French Revolution and dechristianization of France
1791 First Amendment of the United States Constitution

Introduction

The Enlightenment, also known as the Age of Reason, was a time when man began to use his reason to discover the world, casting off the superstition and fear of the medieval world. The effort to discover the natural laws which governed the universe led to scientific, political and social advances. Enlightenment thinkers examined the rational basis of all beliefs and in the process rejected the authority of church and state. Immanuel Kant expressed the motto of the Enlightenment well—"Aude Sapere" (Dare to Think!).

Theopedia

EVENTS

Important events in the Age of Reason and Revival

Methodist movement

First Great Awakening

Bunyan writing *Pilgrim's Progress*

PEOPLE

Christian leaders during the Age of Reason and Revival

Blaise Pascal (1623–1662)

John Owen (1616–1683)

John Bunyan (1628–1688)

George Fox (1624–1691)

Philipp Jakob Spener (1635–1705)

Jonathan Edwards (1703–1758)

John Wesley (1703–1791)

Charles Wesley (1707–1788)

George Whitefield (1714–1770)

American church history

Introduction

. . . Let it not be thought, as some of us might be prone to think, that the timeliness of the discovery of the western hemisphere, in its relation to church history, is summed up in this, that it coincided with the Protestant Reformation, so that the New World might be planted with a Protestant Christianity. For a hundred years the colonization and evangelization of America were, in the narrowest sense of that large word, Catholic, not Protestant. But the Catholicism brought hither was that of the sixteenth century, not of the fifteenth. It is a most one-sided reading of the history of that illustrious age which fails to recognize that the great Reformation was a reformation of the church as well as a reformation from the church. It was in Spain itself, in which the corruption of the church had been foulest, but from which all symptoms of "heretical pravity" were purged away with the fiercest zeal as fast as they appeared,—in Spain under the reign of Ferdinand and Isabella the Catholic,—that the demand for a Catholic reformation made itself earliest and most effectually felt. The highest ecclesiastical dignitary of the realm, Ximenes, confessor to the queen, Archbishop of Toledo, and cardinal, was himself the leader of reform. No changes in the rest of Christendom were destined for many years to have so great an influence on the course of evangelization in North America as those which affected the church of Spain; and of these by far the most important in their bearing on the early course of Christianity in America were, first, the purifying and quickening of the miserably decayed and corrupted mendicant orders,—ever the most effective arm in the missionary service of the Latin Church,—and, a little later, the founding of the Society of Jesus, with its immense potency for good and for evil. At the same time the court of Rome sobered in some measure, by the perilous crisis that confronted it, from its long orgy of simony, nepotism, and sensuality, began to find time and thought for spiritual duties.

The establishment of the "congregations" or administrative boards, and especially of the Congregatio de Propaganda Fide, or board of missions, dates chiefly from the sixteenth century. The revived interest in theological study incident to the general spiritual quickening gave the church, as the result of the labors of the Council of Trent, well-defined body of doctrine, which nevertheless was not so narrowly defined as to preclude differences and debates among the diverse sects of the clergy, by whose competitions and antagonisms the progress of missions both in Christian and in heathen lands was destined to be so seriously affected. . . .

The earlier pages of American church history will not be intelligently read unless it is well understood that the Christianity first to be transplanted to the soil of the New World was the Christianity of Spain—the Spain of Isabella and Ximenes, of Loyola and Francis Xavier and St. Theresa, the Spain also of Torquemada and St. Peter Arbues and the zealous and orthodox Duke of Alva.

Chapter 10

The American Church On The Eve Of The Great Awakening—A General View

By the end of one hundred years from the settlement of Massachusetts important changes had come upon the chain of colonies along the Atlantic seaboard in America. In the older colonies the people had been born on the soil at two or three generations' remove from the original colonists, or belonged to a later stratum of migration superimposed upon the first. The exhausting toil and privations of the pioneer had been succeeded by a good measure of thrift and comfort. There were yet bloody campaigns to be fought out against the ferocity and craft of savage enemies wielded by the strategy of Christian neighbors; but the severest stress of the Indian wars was passed. In different degrees and according to curiously diverse types, the institutions of a Christian civilization were becoming settled.

The Massachusetts theocracy, so called, fell with the revocation of the charter by James II. It had stood for nearly fifty years—long enough to accomplish the main end of that Nationalist principle which the Puritans, notwithstanding their fraternizing with the Pilgrim Separatists, had never let go. The organization of the church throughout New

England, excepting Rhode Island, had gone forward in even step with the advance of population. Two rules had with these colonists the force of axioms: first, that it was the duty of every town, as a Christian community, to sustain the town church; secondly, that it was the duty of every citizen of the town to contribute to this end according to his ability. The breaking up of the town church by schisms and the shirking of individual duty on the ground of dissent were alike discountenanced, sometimes by severely intolerant measures. The ultimate 129collision of these principles with the sturdy individualism that had been accepted from the Separatists of Plymouth was inevitable. It came when the "standing order" encountered the Baptist and the Quaker conscience. It came again when the missionaries of the English established church, with singular unconsciousness of the humor of the situation, pleaded the sacred right of dissenting and the essential injustice of compelling dissenters to support the parish church.

The tendency toward Baptist principles early disclosed itself among the colonists. In the year 1718 the Baptist church of Boston received fraternal recognition from the foremost representatives of the Congregational clergy of Boston, with a public confession of the wrong that they had done.

The English church, enjoying "the prestige of royal favor and princely munificence," suffered also the drawbacks incidental to these advantages—the odium attending the unjust and despotic measures resorted to for its advancement, the vile character of royal officials, who condoned their private vices by a more ostentatious zeal for their official church, and the well-founded popular suspicion of its pervading disloyalty to the interests and the liberties of the colonies in their antagonism to the encroachments of the British government.

A third element in the early Christianity of New York was the Presbyterians. These were represented, at the opening of the eighteenth century, by that forerunner of the Scotch-Irish immigration, Francis Makemie. The arrest and imprisonment of Makemie in 1706, under the authority of Lord Cornbury, for the offense of preaching the gospel without a license from the government, his sturdy defense and his acquittal, make an epoch in the history of religious liberty in America, and a perceptible step in the direction of American political liberty and independence.

Chapter 11

The Great Awakening

It was not wholly dark in American Christendom before the dawn of the Great Awakening. The censoriousness which was the besetting sin of the evangelists in that great religious movement, the rhetorical temptation to glorify the revival by intensifying the contrast with the antecedent condition, and the exaggerated revivalism ever since so prevalent in the American church,—the tendency to consider religion as consisting mainly in, scenes and periods of special fervor, and the intervals between as so much void space and waste time,—all these have combined to deepen the dark tints in which the former state is set before us in history.

The power of godliness was manifest in the earlier days by many infallible signs, not excluding those "times of refreshing" in which the simultaneous earnestness of many souls compels the general attention. Even in Northampton, where the doctrine of the venerable Stoddard as to the conditions of communion has been thought to be the low-water mark of church vitality, not less than five such "harvest seasons" were within recent memory. It was to this parish in a country town on the frontier of civilization, but the most important in Massachusetts outside of Boston, that there came, in the year 1727, to serve as colleague to his aged grandfather, Pastor Stoddard, a young man whose wonderful intellectual and spiritual gifts had from his childhood awakened the pious hopes of all who had known him, and who was destined in his future career to be recognized as the most illustrious of the saints and doctors of the American church. The authentic facts of the boyhood of Jonathan Edwards read like the myths that adorn the legendary Lives of the Saints. As an undergraduate of Yale College, before the age of seventeen, his reflections on the mysteries of God, and the universe, and the human mind, were such as even yet command the attention and respect of students of philosophy. He remained at New Haven two years after graduation, for the further study of theology, and then spent eight months in charge of the newly organized Presbyterian church in New York. Of how little relative importance was this charge may be judged from the fact that a quarter-century later, when the famous Joseph Bellamy was invited to it from his tiny parish of Bethlem, Conn., the council called to advise in the case judged that the interests of Bethlem were too important to be sacrificed to the demands of New York. After this he spent two years as tutor at Yale,—"one of the pillar tutors, and the glory of the college,"—at the critical period after the defection of Rector Cutler to the Church of England.

From this position he was called in 1726, at the age of twenty-three, to the church at Northampton. There he was ordained February 15, 1727, and thither a few months later he brought his "espoused saint," Sarah Pierpont, consummate flower of Puritan womanhood, thenceforth the companion not only of his pastoral cares and sorrows, but of his seraphic contemplations of divine things.

The intensely earnest sermons, the holy life, and the loving prayers of one of the greatest preachers in the history of the church were not long in bearing abundant fruit. In a time of spiritual and moral depression, when the world, the flesh, and the devil seemed to be gaining against the gospel, sometime in the year 1733 signs began to be visible of yielding to the power of God's Word. The frivolous or wanton frolics of the youth began to be exchanged for meetings for religious conference. The pastor was encouraged to renewed tenderness and solemnity in his preaching. His themes were justification by faith, the awfulness of God's justice, the excellency of Christ, the duty of pressing into the kingdom of God. Presently a young woman, a leader in the village gayeties, became "serious, giving evidence," even to the severe judgment of Edwards, "of a heart truly broken and sanctified." A general seriousness began to spread over the whole town. Hardly a single person, old or young, but felt concerned about eternal things. According to Edwards's "Narrative":

> The work of God, as it was carried on, and the number of true saints multiplied, soon made a glorious alteration in the town, so that in the spring and summer, anno 1735, the town seemed to be full of the presence of God. It was never so full of love, nor so full of joy, and yet so full of distress, as it was then. There were remarkable tokens of God's presence in almost every house. It was a time of joy in families on the account of salvation's being brought unto them; parents rejoicing over their children as being new-born, and husbands over their wives, and wives over their husbands. The goings of God were then seen in his sanctuary. God's day was a delight, and his tabernacles were amiable. Our public assemblies were then beautiful; the congregation was alive in God's service, every one intent on the public worship, every hearer eager to drink in the words of the minister as they came from his mouth; the assembly in general were from time to time in tears while the Word was preached, some weeping with sorrow and distress, others with joy and love, others with pity and concern for the souls of their neighbors. Our public praises were then greatly enlivened; God was then served in our psalmody in some measure in the beauty of holiness.

The crucial test of the divineness of the work was given when the people presented themselves before the Lord with a solemn act of thanksgiving for his great goodness and his gracious presence in the town of Northampton, with publicly recorded vows to renounce their evil ways and put away their abominations from before his eyes. They solemnly promise thenceforth, in all dealings with their neighbor, to be governed by the rules of honesty, justice, and uprightness; not to overreach or defraud him, nor anywise to injure him, whether willfully or through want of care; to regard not only their own interest, but his; particularly, to be faithful in the payment of just debts; in the case of past wrongs against any, never to rest till they have made full reparation; to refrain from evil speaking, and from everything that feeds a spirit of bitterness; to do nothing in a spirit of revenge; not to be led by private or partisan interest into any course hurtful to the interests of Christ's kingdom; particularly, in public affairs, not to allow ambition or partisanship to lead them counter to the interest of true religion. Those who are young promise to allow themselves in no diversions that would hinder a devout spirit, and to avoid everything that tends to lasciviousness, and which will not be approved by the infinitely pure and holy eye of God. Finally, they consecrate themselves watchfully to perform the relative duties of parents and children, husbands and wives, brothers and sisters, masters, mistresses, and servants.

So great a work as this could not be hid. The whole region of the Connecticut Valley, in Massachusetts and Connecticut, and neighboring regions felt the influence of it. The fame of it went abroad. A letter of Edwards's in reply to inquiries from his friend, Dr. Colman, of Boston, was forwarded to Dr. Watts and Dr. Guise, of London, and by them published under the title of "Narrative of Surprising Conversions." A copy of the little book was carried in his pocket for wayside reading on a walk from London to Oxford by John Wesley, in the year 1738. Not yet in the course of his work had he "seen it on this fashion," and he writes in his journal: "Surely this is the Lord's doing, and it is marvelous in our eyes."

Both in this narrative and in a later work on "The Distinguishing Marks of a Work of the Spirit of God," one cannot but admire the divine gift of a calm wisdom with which Edwards had been endowed as if for this exigency. He is never dazzled by the incidents of the work, nor distracted by them from the essence of it. His argument for the divineness of the work is not founded on the unusual or extraordinary character of it, nor on the impressive bodily effects sometimes attending it, such as tears, groans, outcries, convulsions, or faintings, nor on visions or ecstasies or "impressions." What he claims is that the work may be divine, notwithstanding the presence of these incidents. It was doubtless owing to the firm and judicious guidance of such a pastor that the intense religious fervor of this first awakening at Northampton was marked by so much of sobriety and order. In later years, in other regions, and under the influence of preachers not of greater earnestness, but of less wisdom and discretion, there were habitual scenes of extravagant and senseless enthusiasm, which make the closing pages of this chapter of church history painfully instructive.

It was in that year (1735) in which the town of Northampton was all ablaze with the glory of its first revival under Edwards that George Whitefield, first among the members of Wesley's "Holy Club" at Oxford, attained to that "sense of the divine love" from which he was wont to date his conversion. In May, 1738, when the last reflections from the Northampton revival had faded out from all around the horizon, the young clergyman, whose first efforts as a preacher in pulpits of the Church of England had astonished all hearers by the power of his eloquence, arrived at Savannah, urged by the importunity of the Wesleys to take up the work in Georgia in which they had so conspicuously failed. He entered eagerly into the sanguine schemes for the advantage of the young colony, and especially into the scheme for building and endowing an orphan-house in just that corner of the earth where there was less need of such an institution than anywhere else. After three months' stay he started on his return to England to seek priest's orders for himself, and funds for the orphans that might be expected sometime in Georgia. He was successful in both his errands. He was ordained; he collected more than one thousand pounds for the orphan-house; and being detained in the kingdom by an embargo, he began that course of evangelistic preaching which continued on either side of the ocean until his death, and which is without a parallel in church history. His incomparable eloquence thronged the parish churches, until the churches were closed against him, and the Bishop of London warned the people against him in a pastoral letter. Then he went out into the open fields, in the service, as he said, of him "who had a mountain for his pulpit, and the heavens for his sounding-board, and who, when his gospel was refused by the Jews, sent his servants into the highways and hedges." Multitudes of every rank thronged him; but especially the heathenized and embruted colliers near Bristol listened to the unknown gospel, and their awakened feelings were revealed to the preacher by his observing the white gutters made by the tears that ran down their grimy faces. At last the embargo was raised, and committing his work to Wesley, whom he had drawn into field-preaching, he sailed in August, 1739, for Philadelphia, on his way to Georgia. His fame had gone before him, and the desire to hear him was universal. The churches would not contain the throngs. It was long remembered how, on those summer evenings, he would take his stand in the balcony of the old court-house in Market Street, and how every syllable from his wonderful voice would be heard aboard the river-craft moored at the foot of the street, four hundred feet away.

Seeing the solemn eagerness of the people everywhere to hear him, he determined to make the journey to Savannah by land, and again he turned the long journey into a campaign of preaching. Arriving at Savannah in January, 1740, he laid the foundation of his orphan-house, "Bethesda," and in March was again on his way northward on a tour of preaching and solicitation of funds. Touching at Charleston, where the bishop's commissary, Dr. Garden, was at open controversy with him, he preached five times and received seventy pounds for his charitable work. Landing at New Castle on a Sunday morning, he preached morning and evening. Monday morning he preached at Wilmington to a vast assemblage. Tuesday evening he preached on Society Hill, in Philadelphia, "to about eight thousand," and at the same place Wednesday morning and evening. Then once more he made the tour to New York and back, preaching at every halting-place. A contemporary newspaper contains the following item:

> New Castle, May 15th. This evening Mr. Whitefield went on board his sloop here in order to sail for Georgia. On Sunday he preached twice in Philadelphia, and in the evening, when he preached his farewell sermon, it is supposed he had twenty thousand hearers. On Monday he preached at Darby and Chester; on Tuesday at Wilmington and Whiteclay Creek; on Wednesday, twice at Nottingham; on Thursday at Fog's Manor and New Castle. The congregations were much increased since his being here last. The presence of God was much seen in the assemblies, especially at Nottingham and Fog's Manor, where the people were under such deep soul-distress that their cries almost drowned his voice. He has collected in this and the neighboring provinces about four hundred and fifty pounds sterling for his orphans in Georgia.

It is needless further to follow in detail the amazing career of Whitefield, "posting o'er land and ocean without rest," and attended at every movement by such storms of religious agitation as have been already described. In August, 1740, he made his first visit to New

England. He met with a cordial welcome. At Boston all pulpits were opened to him, and churches were thronged with eager and excited hearers. The critical historian has the unusual satisfaction, at this point, of finding a gauge by which to discount the large round numbers given in Whitefield's journal. He speaks of preaching in the Old South Church to six thousand persons. The now venerable building had at that time a seating capacity of about twelve hundred. Making the largest allowance for standing-room, we may estimate his actual audience at two thousand. Whitefield was an honest man, but sixty-six per cent. is not too large a discount to make from his figures; his estimates of spiritual effect from his labor are liable to a similar deduction. He preached on the common in the open air, and the crowds were doubled. All the surrounding towns, and the coast eastward to Maine, and the interior as far as Northampton, and the Connecticut towns along the road to New York, were wonderfully aroused by the preaching, which, according to the testimony of two nations and all grades of society, must have been of unequaled power over the feelings. Not only the clergy, including the few Church of England missionaries, but the colleges and the magistrates delighted to honor him. Belcher, the royal governor at Boston, fairly slobbered over him, with tears and embraces and kisses; and the devout Governor Talcott, at New Haven, gave God thanks, after listening to the great preacher, "for such refreshings on the way to our rest." So he was sped on his way back to the South.

There followed what became a prevailing characteristic of American Christianity, a large diversity of organization. Not only that men disagreeing in their convictions of truth would be enrolled in different bodies, but that men holding the same views, in the same statement of them, would feel free to go apart from one another, and stay apart. There was not even to be any one generally predominating organization from which minor ones should be reckoned as dissenting. One after another the organizations which should be tempted by some period of exceptional growth and prosperity to pretend to a hegemony among the churches—Catholic, Episcopalian, Presbyterian, Baptist, Methodist—would meet with some set-back as inexorable as "the law of nature that prevents the trees from growing up into the sky."

Whether for good or for evil, the few years from 1740 to 1750 were destined to impress upon the American church in its various orders, for a hundred years to come, the character of Methodism. "The Great Awakening . . . terminated the Puritan and inaugurated the Pietist or Methodist age of American church history" (Thompson, "Presbyterian Churches in the United States," p. 34). It is not unnecessary to remark that the word "Methodist" is not used in the narrow sense of "Wesleyan."

In New England, the idea, into which the first pastors had been trained by their experience as parish ministers in the English established church, of the parochial church holding correlative rights and duties toward the community in all its families, succumbed at last, after a hundred years of more or less conscious antagonism, to the incompatible principle, adopted from the Separatists of Plymouth, of the church formed according to elective affinity by the "social compact" of persons of the age of discretion who could give account to themselves and to one another of the conscious act and experience of conversion. This view, subject to important mitigations or aggravations in actual administration, held almost unquestioned dominance in the New England churches until boldly challenged by Horace Bushnell, in his "epoch-making" volume on "Christian Nurture" (1846), as a departure from the orthodoxy of the fathers.

Among the first trophies of the revival at Norwich was a Mohegan boy named Samson Occum. Wheelock, pastor at Lebanon, one of the most ardent of the revival preachers, took him into his family as a student. This was the beginning of that school for the training of Indian preachers which, endowed in part with funds gathered by Occum in England, grew at last into Dartmouth College. The choicest spiritual gifts at the disposal of the church were freely spent on the missions. Whitefield visited the school and the field, and sped Kirkland on his way to the Oneidas. Edwards, leaving Northampton in sorrow of heart, gave 180his incomparable powers to the work of the gospel among the Stockbridge Indians until summoned thence to the presidency of Princeton College. When Brainerd fainted under his burden, it was William Tennent who went out into the wilderness to carry on the work of harvest. But the great gift of the American church to the cause of missions was the gift of David Brainerd himself. His life was the typical missionary's life—the scattering of precious seed with tears, the heart-sickness of hope deferred, at last the rejoicing of the harvest-home. His early death enrolled him in the canon of the saints of modern Christendom. The story of his life and death, written by Jonathan Edwards out of that fatherly love with which he had tended the young man's latest days and hours, may not have been an unmixed blessing to the church. The long-protracted introspections, the cherished forebodings and misgivings, as if doubt was to be cultivated as a Christian virtue, may not have been an altogether wholesome example for general imitation. But think what the story of that short life has wrought! To how many hearts it has been an inspiration to self-sacrifice and devotion to the service of God in the service of man, we cannot know. Along one line its influence can be partly traced. The "Life of David Brainerd" made Henry Martyn a missionary to the heathen. As spiritual father to Henry Martyn, Brainerd may be reckoned, in no unimportant sense, to be the father of modern missions to the heathen.

Philip Schaff, *A History of American Christianity*, 1897

Denominations

Methodists

The Methodists were founded in England, in 1744, by John and Charles Wesley. Today, the Methodists are the second largest Protestant denomination in the USA.

The Wesleys formed a prayer group, the "Holy Club", which became known by the nickname, "Methodists", because they were so faithful and disciplined in the performance of their religion studies and moral lifestyle.

Methodism or the Methodist movement is a group of historically related denominations of Protestant Christianity. Through vigorous missionary activity, spread throughout the British Empire, the United States, and beyond. Originally it appealed especially to workers, agricultural workers, and slaves. Theologically Methodists are Arminian, emphasizing that all people can be saved, and low church in liturgy, although there are also Calvinist Methodists in Wales. There are now over 75 million members worldwide.

Methodists in America

Between 1776 and 1850 the Methodists in America achieved a virtual miracle of growth, rising from less than 3% of all church members in 1776 to more than 34% by 1850, making them far and away the largest religious body in the nation and the most extensive national institution other than the Federal government. Methodist growth terrified other more-established denominations.

Timeline of the United Methodist Church and its American heritage

1703 John Wesley is born

1707 Charles Wesley is born

1725 Martin Boehm is born

1726 Philip William Otterbein is born

1729 Charles Wesley forms the "Holy Club" at Oxford

1735 John Wesley serves as chaplain to Georgia Colony

1736 John Wesley learns Spanish in order to preach to the Native Americans in Georgia who were taught by Spanish Catholic missionaries.

1738 John Wesley's conversion in London

1739 Formation of Methodist Societies in and around London

John Wesley's first conference of preachers

1745 Francis Asbury is born

1747 Thomas Coke is born

1752 Otterbein arrives in America

1754 Otterbein's conversion, Lancaster, Pennsylvania

1758 John Wesley baptizes two African-American slaves which breaks the color barrier for Methodist societies.

1759 Jacob Albright is born

Methodist colonists arrive in America.

1760 Richard Allen is born

1763 Robert Strawbridge organizes a Methodist class.

Barbara Heck helps to establish a Methodist congregation in New York City which is a forerunner to the John Street Church.

1766 United Ministers, a non-sectarian group, developed. This group was a forerunner of the United Brethren Church.

1768 John Street Church in New York City is built.

1769 Richard Boardman and Joseph Pilmore arrive in America.

George Whitefield dies at Newburyport, Massachusetts on his seventh visit to America.

1770 Mary Evans Thorne is appointed class leader by Joseph Pilmore in Philadelphia. Thorne is probably the first woman in the Colonies to be appointed as such.

1771 Francis Asbury arrives in America.

1773 First conference of American Methodist preachers. George Shadford and Thomas Rankin sail for America

1774 Lovely Lane Chapel built in Baltimore

1776 Thomas Coke named by Wesley as the first superintendent for America.

Christmas Conference. Ordination of preachers.

1784 Richard Allen and Absalom Jones are the first African Americans licensed to preach

Formation of black congregations.

Cokesbury College opens in Abingdon, Maryland.

1787 Wesley writes to Asbury deploring the genocide of Native Americans.

1788 Charles Wesley dies

1789 Bishops Francis Asbury and Thomas Coke visit President Washington. Methodist Book Concern is established in Philadelphia

Jacob Albright's conversion.

Methodist Episcopal Church recognizes Sunday School as a valid ministry.

1790 African-Americans make up twenty percent of American Methodists.

The first successful American Sunday School is established in Philadelphia.

1791 John Wesley dies

1792 First quadrennial General Conference of American Methodists

1794 Beginning of the camp meeting movement at Rehoboth, North Carolina

1796 Albright began his first preaching tour

Otterbein and Boehm found the Church of the United Brethren in Christ (a.k.a. United Brethren Church).

1800 Founding of the Evangelical Association

The Shakers

Historical Background

The origins of the Shakers, like many other religious sects that splintered off mainstream Protestantism, are found in the 17th century. The Protestant Revolution, which began in Europe in 1517, along with the discoveries of new technologies and trade routes, altered the political, spiritual, and economic life of Europe and the world. The discoveries of the Americas, the uses of the vernacular tongues in writing, and the ancient earth-centered universe disproved by Tycho Brahe and other astronomers, along with the opening of new trade routes and newer technologies for warfare altered the earlier medieval conception of the universe. With new scientific and religious interpretations opening up (the publishing of the Bible in various vernacular languages helped speed the process), the creation of new Christian Churches outside the Catholic Church and the mainstream Protestant denominations (the Lutheran Church, the Calvinists and Church of England) continued in the 17th and 18th centuries. Already in Elizabethan England the Puritans were becoming separate from the Church of England. Following came the Baptist Church, the Quakers, the French Camisards, the Community of True Inspiration, the first Unitarian tract, various Anabaptist and millenarian groups, the Methodists and others. Often the congregations that created these new churches believed that the mainstream Protestant Churches were becoming too legalistic in interpretation of the Bible. Two of these newer sects, the French Camisards and the Quakers, lead the way to the Shakers.

During the 1740s, the Quakers changed their process of worship where their violent tremblings and quakings, from which they derived their name, predominated. One group in Manchester, England, retained this form of worship, and it was during the 1740s that the "Shaking Quakers," or Shakers, came under the influence of some exiled French Camisards. This group split off from mainstream Quakerism in 1747, and developed along their own lines, forming into a society with Jane and James Wardley as their leaders. Ann Lee, the founder and later leader of the American Shakers, and her parents were members of this society.

Mother Ann Lee and the Early Shakers

Ann Lee, who became the charismatic leader of the Shakers, was born the daughter of a blacksmith in the English city of Manchester in 1736. Growing up illiterate, Shaker tradition has it that Ann worked in a cotton factory, marrying a blacksmith named Abraham Standerin in 1762. The couple had four children, all of whom died in childhood. At age 22, Ann joined the Shakers and after being a member for about 12 years, she experienced "a special manifestation of Divine light." After this experience the small society of believers acknowledged her as "Mother in Christ" and Mother Ann became the leader of the Shakers. In 1774, according to Evans, "Mother Ann received a revelation, directing her to repair to America; also that the second Christian Church would be established in America . . ." With her husband and seven members of the society Ann Lee set sail for America on May 10, 1774. By late 1776 she and some followers were located in an area northwest of Albany, New York, by which point her husband had left her to marry another woman.

Shaker Beliefs

The Shakers in America lived a communal life based on common ownership of property and goods, celibate purity, and confession of sins. The Shakers did not believe in procreation and therefore had to adopt children or allow converts into their community. The adopted children were given a choice at age 21 whether to remain with the Shaker community or go their way into the world. The Shakers eventually created 19 official communities in the Northeast, Ohio, and Kentucky. From these communities came agricultural advances and quality manufactured goods. In addition, the Shakers had advanced notions of equality between the sexes and the races. The Shakers had prosperous communities and grew to be respected by people who had scorned them for their unorthodox religious practices. The Shakers, like the Quakers, were pacifists in outlook, citing the example of Jesus Christ. The Shakers believed in opportunities for intellectual and artistic development within the Society. Good sanitation, simplicity in dress, speech, and manner were encouraged, as was living in rural colonies away from the corrupting influences of the cities. Like other Utopian societies founded in the18th and19th centuries, the Shakers believed it was possible to form a more perfect society upon earth.

The Shaker belief in the equality of the sexes is symbolized by the special place their founder, Ann Lee, holds in the community. Spiritually, Shaker theology, which held that God created all things in a "dual" order, stated that the female element of Christ, manifested in Ann Lee, heralded the second Christian Church, as Christ heralded the first Christian Church. Evans states that Ann Lee became a spiritual woman, who could reveal and manifest "the Mother Spirit in Christ and in Deity," as Jesus, "being a male, could only reveal and manifest the Father in Christ and God." The belief that God is both mother and father is the theological basis for the Shaker belief in the basic equality of the sexes and has important implications for Shaker organizational structure, which required male and female representatives in key roles.

The Eastern Orthodox council of Jerusalem, 1672

By far the most important of the many synods held at Jerusalem is that of 1672, which refuted article by article the confession of Cyril Lucaris, which appeared in Latin at Geneva in 1629, and in Greek, with the addition of four questions, in 1633. Lucaris, who died in 1638 as patriarch of Constantinople, had corresponded with Western scholars and had imbibed Calvinistic views.

The great opposition which arose during Lucaris' lifetime continued after his death, and found classic expression in the highly venerated confession of Petro Mohyla, metropolitan of Kiev (1643). Though this was intended as a barrier against Calvinistic influences, certain Protestant writers, and not only Roman Catholics, persisted in claiming the support of the Greek Church for sundry of their own positions.

Against the Calvinists the synod of 1672 therefore aimed its rejection of unconditional predestination and of justification by faith alone, and its advocacy of what are substantially the Roman Catholic doctrines of transubstantiation and of purgatory. Protestant writers say that this eastern hostility to Calvinism had been fanned by the Jesuits.

Against the Roman Catholic Church, however, there was directed the affirmation that the Holy Ghost proceeds from God the Father and not from both Father and Son, that is the rejection of the *Filioque* clause in the Creed.

Importance

The 1911 Encyclopædia Britannica called the Synod of Jerusalem "the most vital statement of faith made in the Greek Church during the past thousand years." And the Protestant scholar Philip Schaff wrote in his Creeds of Christendom: "This Synod is the most important in the modern history of the Eastern Church, and may be compared to the Council of Trent."

The Confession of Dositheus

In chapter 6 of *The Acts and Decrees of the Synod of Jerusalem* the Orthodox faith is set out in eighteen decrees and four questions, commonly known as *The Confession of Dositheus.*

Decree 17

We believe the All-holy Mystery of the Sacred Eucharist, which we have enumerated above, fourth in order, to be that which our Lord delivered in the night wherein He gave Himself up for the life of the world. For taking bread, and blessing, He gave to His Holy Disciples and Apostles, saying: "Take, eat ye; This is My Body." {Matthew 26:26} And taking the chalice, and giving thanks, He said: "Drink ye all of It; This is My Blood, which for you is being poured out, for the remission of sins." {Matthew 26:28} In the celebration whereof we believe the Lord Jesus Christ to be present, not typically, nor figuratively, nor by superabundant grace, as in the other Mysteries, nor by a bare presence, as some of the Fathers have said concerning Baptism, or by impanation, so that the Divinity of the Word is united to the set forth bread of the Eucharist hypostatically, as the followers of Luther most ignorantly and wretchedly suppose, but truly and really, so that after the consecration of the bread and of the wine, the bread is transmuted, transubstantiated, converted and transformed into the true Body Itself of the Lord, Which was born in Bethlehem of the ever-Virgin, was baptized in the Jordan, suffered, was buried, rose again, was received up, sitteth at the right hand of the God and Father, and is to come again in the clouds of Heaven; and the wine is converted and transubstantiated into the true Blood Itself of the Lord, Which as He hung upon the Cross, was poured out for the life of the world. {John 6:51}

Further [we believe] that after the consecration of the bread and of the wine, there no longer remaineth the substance of the bread and of the wine, but the Body Itself and the Blood of the Lord, under the species and form of bread and wine; that is to say, under the accidents of the bread.

Further, that the all-pure Body Itself, and Blood of the Lord is imparted, and entereth into the mouths and stomachs of the communicants, whether pious or impious. Nevertheless, they convey to the pious and worthy remission of sins and life eternal; but to the impious and unworthy involve condemnation and eternal punishment.

Further, that the Body and Blood of the Lord are severed and divided by the hands and teeth, though in accident only, that is, in the accidents of the bread and of the wine, under which they are visible and tangible, we do acknowledge; but in themselves to remain entirely unsevered and undivided. Wherefore the Catholic Church also saith: "Broken and distributed is He That is broken, yet not severed; Which is ever eaten, yet never consumed, but sanctifying those that partake," that is worthily.

Further, that in every part, or the smallest division of the transmuted bread and wine there is not a part of the Body and Blood of the Lord—for to say so were blasphemous and wicked—but the entire whole Lord Christ substantially, that is, with His Soul and Divinity, or perfect God and perfect man. So that though there may be many celebrations in the world at one and the same hour, there are not many Christs, or Bodies of Christ, but it is one and the same Christ that is truly and really present; and His one Body and His Blood is in all the several Churches of the Faithful; and this not because the Body of the Lord that is in the Heavens descendeth upon the Altars; but because the bread of the Prothesis set forth in all the several Churches, being changed and transubstantiated, becometh, and is, after consecration, one and the same with That in the Heavens. For it is one Body of the Lord in many places, and not many; and therefore this Mystery is the greatest, and is spoken of as wonderful, and comprehensible by faith only, and not by the sophistries of man's wisdom; whose vain and foolish curiosity in divine things our pious and God-delivered religion rejecteth.

Further, that the Body Itself of the Lord and the Blood That are in the Mystery of the Eucharist ought to be honored in the highest manner, and adored with latria. For one is the adoration of the Holy Trinity, and of the Body and Blood of the Lord. Further, that it is a true and propitiatory Sacrifice offered for all Orthodox, living and dead; and for the benefit of all, as is set forth expressly in the prayers of the Mystery delivered to the Church by the Apostles, in accordance with the command they received of the Lord. . . .

The Confession of Dositheus

Unitarians

The formation of a distinct Unitarian denomination dates from the secession (1773) of Theophilus Lindsey (1723–1808) from the Anglican Church, on the failure of the Feathers petition to parliament (1772) for relief from subscription. Lindsey's secession had been preceded in Ireland by that of William Robertson, D.D. (1705–1783), who has been called "the father of Unitarian nonconformity".

They denied the Trinity, and proclaimed that Jesus was not God. They also taught that the atonement of Jesus is invalid, and salvation is only by works.

In the United States and Canada most Unitarians are Unitarian Universalist or UU, reflecting an institutional consolidation between Unitarianism and Universalism. Today, most Unitarian Universalists do not consider themselves Christians, even if they share some beliefs quite similar to those of mainstream Christians.

Swedenborgianism

The founder of Swedenborgianism, Emanuel Swedenborg, was born in Stockholm, Sweden in 1688 and he died in 1772.

It is based on the 35 volumes of writings by Swedenborg.

Swedenborg sought truth by way of meditations and "systematically opened his consciousness to inner influences." Through opening himself up in this manner, Swedenborg was contacted by a being who claimed to be Jesus Christ. He claims to have learned much about the spirit world through such spiritual encounters, laying the basis for Swedenborgian theology.

Swedenborgianism has been condemned as a dangerous mystical non-Christian religion on account of its denial of the Trinity and the Holy Spirit, the vicarious atonement, and rejection of Acts and the Pauline epistles.

A New Age

According to official Swedenborg teaching we are now living in: "A New Age. One of Swedenborg's premises is that the Second Coming has taken place—and in fact still is taking place. The Second Coming is not an actual physical appearance of the Lord, but rather His return in spirit and truth that is being effected as a present reality—in today's terms, the Age of Aquarius, or in Swedenborg's terms, the New Church. The information revealed to Swedenborg, he felt, is a continually-occurring Second Coming in that the new information enables a new perception of the Word of God."

History of Swedenborgianism

Fifteen years after Swedenborg's death in 1772, the first sect of his followers were organized in England by a British printer named Robert Hindmarsh. In 1789 a conference met in the London church, and has met almost every year since. Swedenborg's teachings reached the United States in the 1780's.

The first American society was organized in Baltimore in 1792, and the first American ministers were ordained in 1798. The General Convention of the New Jerusalem in the U.S.A. was founded in 1817 in Philadelphia.

Salem witch trials

Background

In 1692, Salem Village was torn by internal disputes between neighbors who disagreed about the choice of Samuel Parris as their first ordained minister. In January 1692, York, at the "Eastward" frontier of Maine, was attacked by the Abenaki Indians, and many of its citizens were massacred or taken captive, echoing the brutality of King Philip's War of 1675–76.

Increasing family size fueled disputes over land between neighbors and within families, especially on the frontier where the economy was based on farming. Changes in the weather or blights could easily wipe out a year's crop. A farm that could support an average-sized family could not support the many families of the next generation, prompting farmers to push further into the wilderness to find farmland—and encroach upon the indigenous people who already lived there. As the Puritans had vowed to create a theocracy in this new land, religious fervor added another tension to the mix: losses of crops, of livestock, and of children, as well as earthquakes and bad weather were typically attributed to the wrath of God. Within the Puritan faith, one's soul was considered predestined from birth as to whether they had been chosen for Heaven or condemned for Hell, and they constantly searched for hints, assuming God's pleasure and displeasure could be read in such signs given in the visible world. The invisible world was inhabited by God and the angels—including the Devil, a fallen angel, and to Puritans this invisible world was as real to them as the visible one around them.

The patriarchal beliefs that Puritans held in the community further stressed the atmosphere: women should be totally subservient to men, that by nature a woman was more likely to enlist in the Devil's service than a man was, and that women were naturally lustful.

The Salem witch trials, which began in 1692 (also known as the Salem witch hunt and the Salem witchcraft episode), resulted in a number of convictions and executions for witchcraft in both Salem Village and Salem Town, Massachusetts. Some have argued that it was the result of a period of factional infighting and Puritan witch hysteria which led to the executions of 20 people (14 women, 6 men) and the imprisonment of between 175 and 200 people. In addition to those executed at least five people died in prison.

PEOPLE

Blaise Pascal (1623–1662)
John Owen (1616–1683)
John Bunyan (1628–1688)
George Fox (1624–1691)
Philipp Jakob Spener (1635–1705)
Jonathan Edwards (1703–1758)
John Wesley (1703–1791)
Charles Wesley (1707–1788)
George Whitefield (1714–1770)

Blaise Pascal

Dates
1623–1662

Famous for being
Physicist, mathematician, theologian

Important writings
Pensées

One of his quotations
"It is the heart which perceives God and not the reason."

The short life of Blaise Pascal (1623–1662) was one of intense intellectual brilliance, physical anguish, and mystical vision. The son of a French bureaucrat, Pascal exhibited extraordinary mathematical and scientific abilities at an early age.

By the time he was twelve he was working on problems in geometry on his own, and he had invented a mechanical calculator before reaching his mid–20s. He would produce key works in the study of atmospheric pressure and vacuum, resulting in the complete outline of a system of hydrostatics, the science of how liquids exert and transmit pressure. Other studies addressed issues such as projective geometry and theories of probability.

But Pascal was not just a mathematical genius; he was a Catholic whose faith grew in fits and starts before finally emerging in full maturity on November 23, 1654. It was on that evening that he had a "definite conversion," the result of a mystical vision that lasted two hours and which he called a "night of fire." In this powerful event, known as the "Memorial," Pascal experienced "Fire. The God of Abraham, the God of Isaac, The God of Jacob. Not of the philosophers and intellectuals. . . . The God of Jesus Christ." Not long after this mysterious encounter with God, Pascal began writing notes for what he planned to be a thorough apologetic for Christianity. However, he started to experience serious physical ailments and was often unable to sleep for long periods of time or consume much food or drink. He died at the age of thirty-nine, his body ravaged by illness.

The notes, many of them just short phrases or paragraphs, that Pascal had been putting together for his work of apologetics were collected and published as the Pensées. Despite its fragmented nature—or perhaps partially due to it—Pensées forms one of the most unique and powerful defenses of the Christian faith ever written. It does not reflect a systematic or scientific approach to apologetics, but "owes its force to the wealth of psychological perception which it embodies." (Oxford Dictionary of the Christian Church). Instead of using Thomistic proofs, which were oriented to readers who accepted—at least generally—a common worldview and approach to knowledge, Pascal addresses the condition of mankind without God: wretched, lonely, corrupt, and lost. He recognized that people of his time were turning their backs on objective truth and could not be approached on the basis of shared cultural beliefs or naked logic alone. This is why Peter Kreeft explains in Christianity for Modern Pagans (Ignatius, 1993), his excellent guide to the Pensées, that "Pascal is the first postmedieval apologist. He is 'for today' because he speaks to modern pagans, not to medieval Christians . . . He is the first to realize the new dechristianized, desacramentalized world and to address it."

Just as the twentieth century novelist Walker Percy perceived that humanity is immersed in a "modern malaise," Pascal clearly saw that people without God must either stare into the dark, cold hole of meaninglessness, or turn to distraction and false happiness for comfort: "We desire truth and find in ourselves nothing but uncertainty. We seek happiness and find only wretchedness and death. We are incapable of not desiring truth and happiness and incapable of either certainty or happiness." (Pensées, 401). Man must desire the truth in order to seek it; without an inner hunger for truth, no amount of logic or argument will suffice: "Truth is so obscured nowadays and lies [are] so well established that unless we love the truth we shall never recognize it." (Pensées, 739).

It is this sort of apologetic approach to non-Christians, especially those who can accurately be called secularists or materialists, that needs to be embraced. While some people live without God out of simple blindness or lack of knowledge, there is most often a conscious decision to avoid or reject God underneath the layers of apathy and indifference. As Kreeft, himself a philosopher, admits: "One of the things that delay our finding God is ignorance. That can indeed be addressed by purely rational apologetics. But the primary obstacle is an attitude of the will, and this must be addressed by a different kind of apologetics: Pascal's kind." And this "kind" of apologetics is absolutely personal and logical, for it is both rooted in and oriented towards a Person who is both divine love and logic: Jesus Christ.

Four hundred years after Pascal's death, the fathers of the Second Vatican Council penned Gaudium et Spes, the Pastoral Constitution on the Church in the Modern World.

At the heart of this great document is a simple phrase—"Christ fully reveals man to himself" (GS 22)—repeated often in the years since by one of the architects of the document. Undoubtedly that man, Pope John Paul II, has long been aware of these words of Pascal: "Not only do we only know God through Jesus Christ, but we only know ourselves through Jesus Christ; we only know life and death through Jesus Christ. Apart from Jesus Christ we cannot know the meaning of our life or of our death, of God, or of ourselves." (Pensées, 417)

Carl E. Olson, © CatholicExchange.com

John Owen

Dates

1616–1683

Famous for being

The leading Puritan theologian: "The theologian's theologian"

Important writings

The Death of Death in the Death of Christ

One of his quotations

"A man may take the measure of his growth and decay in grace according to his thoughts and meditations upon the person of Christ."

John Owen was an English theologian and "was without doubt not only the greatest theologian of the English Puritan movement but also one of the greatest European Reformed theologians of his day, and quite possibly possessed the finest theological mind that England ever produced" ("Owen, John", in *Biographical Dictionary of Evangelicals*, p. 494)

Owen entered Queen's College, Oxford, at the age of twelve and received a B.A. in 1632 and an M.A. in 1635 at the age of nineteen. In 1637 Owen became a pastor; in the 1640s he was chaplain to Oliver Cromwell, and in 1651 he was made Dean of Christ Church, Oxford's largest college. In 1652 he was given the additional post of Vice-Chancellor of the University. After 1660 he led the Independents through the bitter years of persecution until his death in 1683.

Owen's first publication was *A Display of Arminianism* (1642), a severe critique of the Arminian theology becoming prevalent in his day. Later works included *Of the Mortification of Sin in Believers* (1656) and *Of Temptation: The Nature and Power of It* (1658), which reflect Owen's more pastoral nature.

His most influential work, The Death of Death in the Death of Christ (1647), when Owen was 31 years old, is an exhaustive treatment and defense of the doctrine of limited atonement. More specifically, it is an extended reflection on "the inner-trinitarian life of God for the incarnation and atonement, and an attempt to draw out the implications of the Old Testament sacrificial context for understanding the events of Calvary . . . Owen's concern was to ask the simple question of whether Christ's death made salvation possible or actual. He affirmed the latter. . . ." Regarding this work, J. I. Packer notes, "Nobody has a right to dismiss the doctrine of the limitedness, or particularity, of atonement as a monstrosity of Calvinistic logic until he has refuted Owen's proof that it is part of the uniform biblical presentation of redemption, clearly taught in plain text after plain text. And nobody has done that yet." ("Owen, John", in *Biographical Dictionary of Evangelicals*, p. 494)

In 1662 the Act of Uniformity established various rules and requirements which were to be followed in the Church. Owen did not ascribe to this, and thus was known as a nonconformist.

Later works of Owen involved massive works on the Holy Spirit and Hebrews.

Theopedia

John Bunyan

Dates

1628–1688

Famous for being

Author and preacher

Important writings

Pilgrim's Progress

One of his quotations

"When you pray, rather let your heart be without words than your words without heart."

John Bunyan, author of the "Pilgrim's Progress," "Holy War," "Grace abounding," &c., was born at the village of Elstow, Bedfordshire [England], a little more than a mile south of the town of Bedford, in November 1628. His baptism is recorded in the parish register of Elstow on the 30th of that month.

John Bunyan's father, Thomas Bunyan, was what we should now call a whitesmith, a maker and mender of pots and kettles. In his will he designates himself a "brasier;" his son, who carried on the same trade and adopted the same designation when describing himself, is more usually styled a "tinker."

Bunyan's parents sent their son to school, either to the recently founded Bedford grammar school, or, which is more probable, to some humbler school at Elstow. He learned reading and writing "according to the rate of other poor men's children." "I never went to school," he writes, "to Aristotle or Plato, but was brought up at my father's house in a very mean condition, among a company of poor countrymen." And what little he learned, he confesses with shame, when he was called from his primer and copy-book to help his father at his trade, was soon lost, "even almost utterly."

In his sixteenth year (June 1644) Bunyan suffered the irreparable misfortune of the loss of his mother, which was aggravated by his father marrying a second wife within two months of her decease. The arrival of a stepmother seems to have estranged Bunyan from his home, and to have led to his enlisting as a soldier. The civil war was then drawing near the end of its first stage. Bedfordshire was distinctly parliamentarian in its sympathies.

When the forces were disbanded, Bunyan must have returned to his native village and resumed his paternal trade. He "presently afterwards changed his condition into a married state." With characteristic reticence Bunyan gives neither the name of his wife nor the date of his marriage; but it seems to have occurred at the end of 1648 or the beginning of 1649, when he was not much more than twenty. He and his wife were "as poor as poor might be," without "so much household stuff as a dish or spoon between them." But his wife came of godly parents, and brought two pious books of her father's to her new home, the reading of which awakened the slumbering sense of religion in Bunyan's heart, and produced an external change of habits.

For a time he was well content with himself. "I thought no man in England could please God better than I." But his self-satisfaction did not last long. The insufficiency of such a merely outward change was borne in upon him by the spiritual conversation of a few poor women whom he overheard one day when pursuing his tinker's craft at Bedford, "I sitting at a door in the sun and talking about the things of God." Though by this time somewhat of "a brisk talker on religion," he found himself a complete stranger to their inner experience. This conversation was the beginning of the tremendous spiritual conflict described by him with such graphic power in his "Grace abounding." It lasted some three or four years, at the end of which, in 1653, he joined the nonconformist body, to which these poor godly women belonged. This body met for worship in St. John's Church, Bedford, of which the "holy Mr. Gifford," once a loose young officer in the royal army, had been appointed rector in the same year. His temptations ceased, his spiritual conflict was over, and he entered on a peace which was rendered all the more precious by the previous mental agony. The sudden alternations of hope and fear, the fierce temptations, the torturing illusions, the strange perversions of isolated texts, the harassing doubts of the truth of Christianity, the depths of despair and the elevations of joy through which he passed are fully described "as with a pen of fire" in that marvelous piece of religious autobiography, unrivalled saved by the "Confessions" of St. Augustine, his "Grace abounding to the Chief of Sinners."

Bunyan was at this time still resident at Elstow, where his blind child Mary and his second daughter Elizabeth were born. It was probably in 1655 that Banyan removed to Bedford. Here he soon lost the wife to whose piety he had owed so much, and about the same time his pastor and friend the "holy Mr. Gifford."

In 1655 Bunyan, who had been chosen one of the deacons, began to exercise his gift of exhortation, at first privately, and as he gained courage and his ministry proved acceptable "in a more public way." In 1657 his calling as a preacher was formally recognized, and he was set apart to that office, "after solemn prayer and fasting," another member being appointed deacon in his room, "brother Bunyan being taken off by preaching the gospel." His fame as a preacher soon spread, When it was known that the once blaspheming tinker had turned preacher, they flocked "by hundreds, and that from all parts," to hear him, though, as he says, "upon sundry and divers accounts"—some to marvel, some to mock, but some with an earnest desire to profit by his words. After his ordination Bunyan continued to pursue his trade as a brasier, combining with it the exercise of his preaching gifts as occasion served in the various villages visited by him, "in woods, in barns, on village greens, or in town chapels." Opposition was naturally aroused among the settled ministry by such remarkable popularity.

On the Restoration the old acts against nonconformists were speedily revived. The meeting-houses were closed. All persons were required under severe penalties to attend their parish church. The ejected clergy were reinstated. It became an illegal act to conduct divine service except in accordance with the ritual of the church, or for one not in episcopal orders to address a congregation. Bunyan continued his ministrations in barns, in private houses, under the trees, wherever he found brethren ready to pray and hear. So daring and notorious an offender was not likely to go long unpunished. Within six months of Charles's landing he was arrested, on 12 Nov. 1660, at the little hamlet of Lower Samsell by Harlington, about thirteen miles from Bedford to the south, where he was going to hold a religious service in a private house. The issuing of the warrant had become known, and Bunyan might have escaped if he had been so minded, but be was not the man to play the coward. If he fled, it would "make an ill-savor in the county" and dishearten the weaker brethren. If he ran before a warrant, others might run before "great words." While he was conducting the service he was arrested and taken before Mr. Justice Wingate, who, though really desirous to release him, was compelled by his obstinate refusal to forbear preaching to commit him for trial to the county gaol, which, with perhaps a brief interval of enlargement in 1666, was to be his "close and uncomfortable" place of abode for the next twelve years.

Bunyan's twelve years imprisonment came to an end in 1672. With the covert intent of setting up the Roman catholic religion in England, Charles II had suspended all penal statutes against nonconformists and popish recusants. Bunyan was one of those who profited by this infamous subterfuge. His pardon under the great seal bears date 13 Sept

1672. This, however, was no more than official sanction of what had been already virtually granted and acted on. For Bunyan had received one of the first licenses to preach given by the royal authority, dated 9 May of that year, and had been called to the pastorate of the nonconformist congregation at Bedford, of which he had been so long a member, on the 21st of the preceding January. The church of St. John, which had been occupied by this congregation during the Protectorate, had, on the Restoration, returned to its rightful owners, and the place licensed for the exercise of Bunyan's ministry was a barn in the orchard belonging to a member of the body. This continued to be the place of meeting of the congregation until 1707, when a new chapel was erected on its site. Though Bunyan made Bedford the center of his work, he extended his ministrations through the whole county, and even beyond its limits. One of his first acts after his liberation was to apply to the government for licenses for preachers and preaching places in the country round. Among these he made stated circuits, being playfully known as "Bishop Bunyan," his diocese being a large one, and, in spite of strenuous efforts at repression by the ecclesiastical authorities, steadily increasing in magnitude and importance. It is interesting to notice that Bunyan's father, the tinker of Elstow, lived on till 1676, being buried at Elstow on 7 Feb. of that year. In his will, while leaving a shilling apiece to his famous son and his three other children, he bequeathed all be had to his third wife, Ann, who survived him four years, and was buried in the same churchyard as her husband on 25 Sept. 1680.

There is little more to notice in Bunyan's life. His activity was ceaseless, but "the only glimpses we get of him during this time are from the church records, and these were but scantily kept," and are quite devoid of public interest, chiefly dealing with the internal discipline of the body. Troublous times fell upon nonconformists. The Declaration of Indulgence was withdrawn the same year it was issued. The Test Act became law the next year (1673). In 1675 the acts against nonconformists were put in force. Bunyan's preaching journeys were not always free from risk. There is a tradition that he visited Reading disguised as a wagoner, with a long whip in his hand, to escape detection. But he continued free from active molestation, with the exception of the somewhat hazy imprisonment placed by Mr. Brown in 1675. In Mr. Froude's words, "he abstained, as he had done steadily throughout his life, from all interference with politics, and the government in turn never meddled with him." He frequently visited London to preach, always getting large congregations. Twelve hundred would come together to hear him at seven o'clock on a weekday morning in winter. When he preached on a Sunday, the meetinghouse would not contain the throng, half being obliged to go away. A sermon delivered by him at Pinners' Hall in Old Broad Street was the basis of one of his theological works. He was on intimate terms with Dr. John Owen, who, when Charles II expressed his astonishment that so learned a divine could listen to an illiterate tinker, is recorded to have replied that he would gladly give up all his learning for the tinker's power of reaching the heart. In the year of his death he was chaplain, though perhaps unofficially, to Sir John Shorter, then lord mayor of London.

Bunyan did not live to see the revolution. His death took place in 1688, four months after the acquittal of the seven bishops. In the spring of that year he had been enfeebled by an attack of "sweating sickness." He caught a severe cold on a ride through heavy rain to London from Reading, whither he had gone to effect a reconciliation between a father and a son. A fever ensued, and he died on 31 Aug. at the house of his friend John Strudwick, who kept a grocer's and chandler's shop at the sign of the Star, Holborn Bridge, two months before he had completed his sixtieth year. He continued his literary activity to the last. Four books from his pen had been published in the first half of the year, and he partly revised the sheets of a short treatise entitled "The Acceptable Sacrifice" on his deathbed. He was buried in Mr. Stradwick's vault in the burial-ground in Bunhill Fields, Finsbury. His personal estate was sworn under 100£.

Dictionary of National Biography, 1886

George Fox

Dates
1624–1691

Famous for being
Founder of the Society of Friends (The Quakers)

Important writings
Journal

One of his quotations
"The Lord showed me, so that I did see clearly, that he did not dwell in these temples which men had commanded and set up, but in people's hearts . . . his people were his temple, and he dwelt in them."

George Fox was a 17th-century Christian leader who rejected the formal trappings of religion, encouraged believers to follow their "inner light," and became the leader of the Society of Friends, known as the Quakers. Reared in the faith of the Church of England, Fox began an itinerant public ministry in 1647 after experiencing visions and voices as messages from God. Convinced that all people possess light granted by Jesus Christ, Fox assumed leadership of a worshiping community of "friends" about 1652. Eventually dubbed "Quakers" by those who ridiculed their emotional exuberance, they had no professional ministers, refused to take oaths, opposed slavery and war, emphasized mutual respect and equality before God, and sought lives transformed by inward spiritual experience. Many Quakers were punished and some were executed for their public critiques of political violence and of established churches; Fox was imprisoned eight times. The movement grew nonetheless. The American Quaker colony of Pennsylvania, known for its religious freedom, was founded by Fox associate William Penn.

Philipp Jakob Spener

Dates
1635–1705

Famous for being
Leader of pietism movement, known as, "Father of pietism"

Important writings
Pia Desideria (Pious Wishes)

One of his quotations
"No little damage is done when one tries to be smart and clever without the Scriptures or beyond them."

Pietism
Originally a German Lutheran religious movement of the 17th and 18th centuries, pietism emphasized heartfelt religious devotion, ethical purity, charitable activity, and pastoral theology rather than sacramental or dogmatic precision. The term now refers to all religious expressions that emphasize inward devotion and moral purity. With roots in Dutch precisionism and mysticism, pietism emerged in reaction to the formality of Lutheran orthodoxy.

In his *Pia Desideria* (1675), Philipp Jakob Spener proposed a "heart religion" to replace the dominant "head religion." Beginning with religious meetings in Spener's home, the movement grew rapidly, especially after August Hermann Francke (1663—1727) made the new University of Halle a Pietist center. Nikolaus Ludwig, Graf von Zinzendorf, a student of Francke's and godson of Spener, helped spread the movement. His Moravian Church promoted evangelical awakenings throughout Europe and in North America in the 18th and 19th centuries. John Wesley and Methodism were profoundly influenced by pietism.

James D Nelson

Philip Jacob Spener was born in Alsace and educated at Strasbourg. He had completed his doctoral dissertation and was prepared to teach, but instead served as a pastor in Frankfurt. The deadness and moral laxity of the congregation moved him to offer a specific program for change, spelled out in Pia Desideria, or "Pious Desires," first published in 1675. This controversial writing marks the birth of Pietism as a renewal movement within Lutheranism and beyond it. Pia Desideria's five proposals were:

greater use of Scripture;

lay participation in the life of the church through small groups for prayer and Bible study;

balance of doing and believing in the Christian life;

ministerial training in piety as well as academics;

sermons which encourage a living, active faith.

Spener prized the theology of Martin Luther; at the same time he charged scholasticism with codifying Lutheran theology and neglecting the Christian life. Among those influenced by Spener was John Wesley (1703–1791), whose Methodist movement also used small groups and lay leadership. Spener was a forerunner of the modern small group movement.

Summary

The term Pietism connotes a movement in behalf of practical religion within the Lutheran Church of the seventeenth and eighteenth centuries. Established at Halle by Philipp Jakob Spener, and following distinct and individual courses of development in Halle, Württemberg, and Herrnhut, it received a bond of union in its conviction that the type of Christianity then prevailing in Lutheranism stood in urgent need of reform, and that this could be brought about by "piety," or living faith made active and manifest in upright conduct.

The Pia Desideria

The event that formed an epoch in Spener's life and attracted wide attention was the publication of his little *Pia desideria* (Frankfort, 1675). In this work Spener first depicted the Christianity of his period, which left much to be desired in every rank and station. Nevertheless, God had promised better times for the Church militant, which were to begin when Israel should have become converted and papal Rome should have fallen. Meanwhile he proposed the following helpful measures: the word of God must be more widely diffused among the people, this end being furthered by discussions on the Bible under the pastor's guidance; the establishment and maintenance of the spiritual priesthood, which is not possessed by the clergy alone, but is rather constituted by the right and duty of all Christians to instruct others, to punish, to exhort, to edify, and to care for their salvation; the fact must be emphasized that mere knowledge is in sufficient in Christianity, which is expressed rather in action; more gentleness and love between denominations are needed in polemics; the university training of the clergy must be changed so as to include personal piety and the reading of books of edification, as well as intellectual knowledge and dogmatic controversies; and, finally, sermons should be prepared on a more edifying plan, with less emphasis on rhetorical art and homiletic erudition.

Spener did not stand entirely alone among his contemporaries. He had his forerunners and colaborers. He was not the "Father of Pietism" in the sense that it emanated exclusively from him. He was met half-way, as it were, by a widely diffused sentiment in the Lutheran Church of Germany, and he was aided in many phases of the situation by the change which took place in the general spirit of the age. There were also cooperative influences proceeding from England, Holland, and Switzerland. For the Lutheran Church of Germany, however, Spener was the acknowledged and honorable protagonist; he was the most eminent advocate and the spiritual center of all those forces which so vigorously sought to reform the Lutheran Church in the last quarter of the seventeenth century.

Paul Grüberg, Schaff-Herzog Encyclopedia of Religious Knowledge, Vol. IX

Jonathan Edwards

Dates
1703–1758

Famous for being
Instrumental in bringing about the Great Awakening

Important writings
The Life and Diary of David Brainerd, and, Freedom of the Will

One of his quotations
"Grace is but glory begun and glory is but grace perfected"

Jonathan Edwards, considered by many to be one of the greatest preachers and churchmen in American history, was born in East Windsor, Connecticut into a family with a long tradition of ministry. Entering Yale as one of its earliest students at the age of thirteen, Edwards graduated at the head of his class four years later and began a two-year course of theological study in New Haven. Having completed his education in 1722, he took up a pastorate in a Presbyterian church in New York, but left there to take a position as tutor at Yale in 1724, a position that he held for two years.

From 1725 he served as an assistant to his maternal grandfather, Solomon Stoddard, who was the Congregationalist pastor of Northampton, Massachusetts. Upon Stoddard's death in 1729, Edwards succeeded to the pulpit. His preaching during this period was received with mixed results. On the positive side, the power of his message is credited with bringing about the first Great Awakening of American history, beginning in 1734, when six sudden conversions in Edwards' parish turned into a flood of thirty per week, drawing people from up to a hundred miles away.

"The parish was visited with most remarkable seasons of revival, and Edwards himself was unjustly expelled from the pastoral office. A preacher of rare power, Edwards was the foremost American leader of the Great Awakening. A man of passion, integrity and honor, he labored quietly among the Indians following his removal from Northampton. A giant of intellect and a theologian of great precision, Edwards was called to the Presidency of Princeton, but sudden death claimed him soon thereafter. No one before or since has written as wisely and thoroughly on the subject of revival as this saintly man." *Richard Owen Roberts*

Despite this success, however, Edwards alienated many in his congregation by insisting on more stringent membership requirements than were customary at the time. His first inclination was to insist on visible evidence of conversion and regeneration, but he eventually settled for a public profession of faith. His move to exclude from the Communion those who did not meet these standards led to a two-year battle within the congregation. In 1750, Edwards was dismissed from his pastorate.

Much of Edwards' most celebrated work comes from his Northampton period. These works include his *Treatise Concerning Religious Affections*, his *Treatise on Grace*, and many of his most important sermons.

The ensuing years were difficult for the family as they struggled with debt and loss of income. Edwards settled Stockbridge, Massachusetts, then a frontier settlement, where he ministered to a small congregation and served as missionary to the Indians. It was here that he completed his fine work, The Freedom of the Will.

After several years on the frontier, Edwards yielded to considerable pressure and assumed the presidency of Princeton in the fall of 1757. He held the position for less than a year, dying in March 1758 of a fever in reaction to a smallpox innoculation.

More than two centuries after his death, Edwards is remembered as a fine preacher and an adamant defender of Calvinist theology.

John Wesley

Dates
AD 1703–1791

Famous for being
Founder of Methodism

Important writings
Christian Perfection

One of his quotations

"That execrable sum of all villanies commonly called a Slave Trade."

Summary

It has been estimated that John Wesley preached 42,000 sermons; at the age of 87 he still preached three times a day, in different places. During his life he traveled over 250,000 miles on horseback.

Organization

Wesley organized those who became Christians as a result of his preaching into small cells called "societies". A supervisor who would report to Wesley any member who strayed from the path of righteousness. Later, such military discipline was abolished.

John Wesley was the "head of his Church" in England, and in the colonies he appointed subordinate agents called superintendents, later designated as bishops. The system was modeled upon the Episcopal or form of church government as practiced by the Church of England.

Theology

While Wesley had a strong leaning towards Calvinism, he rejected absolute predestination, and maintained that Christ offers grace freely to all men, not just to a select elite.

John Wesley's life

John Wesley evangelist and leader of Methodism, fifteenth child and second surviving son of Samuel Wesley (1662–1735, was born at Epworth Rectory, Lincolnshire, on 17 June 1703. His early education from the age of five was under his mother, whose methods were exacting; a single day was allowed for learning the alphabet. His rescue from a devastating house fire on 9 February 1708 at Epworth Rectory fixed itself in his mind as a work of divine providence.

On 24 June 1720 John Wesley was elected scholar of Christ Church, Oxford; he matriculated on 18 July. He graduated B.A. in 1724. Till the following year he had apparently no thought of taking orders. On 19 Sept. 1725 he was ordained deacon by John Potter, then bishop of Oxford. His first sermon was preached (16 Oct.) at South Leigh, near Whitney, Oxfordshire.

In August 1727 he became his father's curate, living and officiating mainly at Wroot, paying visits to Oxford, where he was ordained priest (22 Sept. 1728) by Bishop Potter.

A kindly letter from Morley (21 Oct. 1729) recalled him from his curacy to fulfill the statutory obligations of his fellowship. He returned to residence at Lincoln College on 22 Nov., and found his brother Charles and two of his friends already labeled as "Methodists" from their strict rules of study and religious observance, including the practice of weekly communion. On joining these young Methodists John Wesley naturally became their head, and directed their plans, getting the nickname of 'curator of the holy club.'

They relieved the poor, and looked after the clothing and training of school children; they daily visited the prisoners in the castle, read prayers there on Wednesdays and Fridays, preached there on Sundays, and administered the communion once a month.

The Wesleys embarked for Georgia in the Simmonds at Gravesend on 14 Oct. On board were twenty-six German Moravians. Wesley's Georgia mission lasted less than two years, the latter part broken by squabbles. Wesley's preaching was regarded as too personal, and his pastoral visitation as censorious.

On his return to England, he met Peter Böhler. From Böhler the Wesleys imbibed their doctrine of 'saving faith.' He dates his 'conversion,' following that of Charles, on 24 May (at a society meeting in Aldersgate Street).

Wesley's Conversion

Nettleton Court, off Aldersgate Street, London, May 24, 1738

Monday, Tuesday, and Wednesday I had continual sorrow and heaviness in my heart; something of which I had described, in the broken manner I was able, in the following letter to a friend:

O why is it, that so great, so wise, so holy a God will use such an instrument as me? Lord, 'let the dead bury their dead!' But wilt thou send the dead to raise the dead? Yea, thou sendest whom thou wilt send, and showest mercy by whom thou wilt show mercy! Amen! Be it then according to thy will! If thou speak the word, Judas shall cast out devils.

I feel what you say, (though not enough,) for I am under the same condemnation. I see that the whole law of God is holy, just, and good. I know every thought, every temper of my soul, ought to bear God's image and superscription. But how am I fallen from the glory of God! I feel that 'I am sold under sin.' I know that I, too, deserve nothing but wrath, being full of all abominations; and having no good thing in me, to atone for them, or to remove the wrath of God. All my works, my righteousness, my prayers, need an atonement for themselves. So that my mouth is stopped. I have nothing to plead. God is holy; I am unholy. God is a consuming fire; I am altogether a sinner, meet to be consumed.

Yet I hear a voice (and is it not the voice of God?) saying, "Believe, and thou shalt be saved. He that believeth is passed from death unto life." God so loved the world that he gave his only-begotten Son, that whosoever believeth in him should not perish, but have everlasting life.

O let no one deceive us by vain words, as if we had already obtained this faith! By its fruits we shall know. Do we already feel peace with God, and joy in the Holy Ghost? Does his Spirit bear witness with our spirit, that we are the children of God? Alas! With mine he does not. Nor, I fear, with yours.

O thou Savior of men, save us from trusting in any thing but thee! Draw us after thee! Let us be emptied of ourselves, and then fill us with all peace and joy in believing, and let nothing separate us from thy love, in time or in eternity!

What occurred on Wednesday, the 24th, I think best to relate at large, after premising what may make it the better understood. Let him that cannot receive it ask the Father of lights that he would give more light to him and me.

I believe, till I was about ten years old, I had not sinned away that "washing of the Holy Ghost" which was given me in baptism, having been strictly educated, and carefully taught that I could only be saved "by universal obedience, by keeping all the commandments of God;" in the of which I was diligently instructed. And those instructions, so far as they respected outward duties and sins, I gladly received and often thought of. But all that was said to me of inward obedience or holiness I neither understood nor remembered. So that I was, indeed, as ignorant of the true meaning of the law as I was of the gospel of Christ.

The next six or seven years were spent at school; where, outward restraints being removed, I was much more negligent than before, even of outward duties, and almost continually guilty of outward sins, which I knew to be such, though they were not scandalous in the eye of the world. However, I still read the Scriptures, and said my prayers, morning and evening. And what I now hoped to be saved by was,

Not being so bad as other people.
Having still a kindness for religion. And,
Reading the Bible, going to church, and saying my prayers.

Being removed to the university, for five years, I still said my prayers, both in public and private, and read, with the Scriptures, several other books of religion, especially comments on the New Testament. Yet I had not all this while so much as a notion of inward holiness; nay, went on habitually and, for the most part, very contentedly, in some or other known sin; indeed, with some intermission and short struggles, especially before and after the holy communion, which I was obliged to receive thrice a year. I cannot well tell what I hoped to be saved by now, when I was continually sinning against that little light I had, unless by those transient fits of what many divines taught me to call "repentance."

When I was about twenty-two, my father pressed me to enter into holy orders. At the same time the providence of God directing me to Kempis's "Christian Pattern," I began to see that true religion was seated in the heart, and that God's law extended to all our thoughts, as well as words and actions. I was, however, very angry at Kempis for being too strict, though I read him only in Dean Stanhope's translation. Yet I had frequently much sensible comfort in reading him, such as I was an utter stranger to before; and meeting likewise with a religious friend, which I never had until now, I began to alter the whole form of my conversation, and to set in earnest upon a new life. I set apart an hour or two a day for religious retirement. I communicated every week. I watched against all sin, whether in word or deed. I began to aim at, and pray for, inward holiness. So that now, "doing so much, and living so good a life," I doubted not but I was a good Christian.

Removing soon after to another college, I executed a resolution which I was before convinced was of the utmost importance, shaking off at once all my trifling acquaintance. I began to see more and more the value of time. I applied myself closer to study. I watched more carefully against actual sins. I advised others to be religious, according to that scheme of religion by which I modeled my own life. But meeting now with Mr. Law's "Christian Perfection," and "Serious Call," (although I was much offended at many parts of both, yet) they convinced me more than ever of the exceeding height, and breadth, and depth of the law of God. The light flowed in so mightily upon my soul that every thing appeared in a new view. I cried to God for help, and resolved not to prolong the time of obeying him as I never had done before. And by my continued "endeavor to keep his whole law," inward and outward, "to the utmost of my power," I was persuaded that I should be accepted of him, and that I was even then in a state of salvation.

In 1730 I began visiting the prisons, assisting the poor and sick in town, and doing what other good I could, by my presence or my little fortune, to the bodies and souls of all men. To this end I abridged myself of all superfluities, and many that are called necessaries of life. I soon became a by-word for so doing, and I rejoiced that "my name was cast out as evil." The next spring I began observing the Wednesday and Friday fasts, commonly observed in the ancient church, tasting no food till three in the afternoon. And now I knew not how to go any farther. I diligently strove against all sin. I omitted no sort of self-denial which I thought lawful; I carefully used, both in public and in private, all the means of grace at all opportunities. I omitted no occasion of doing good: I for that reason suffered evil. And all this I knew to be nothing, unless as it was directed toward inward holiness. Accordingly this, the image of God, was what I aimed at in all, by doing his will, not my own. Yet when, after continuing some years in this course, I apprehended myself to be near death, I could not find that all this gave me any comfort, or any assurance of acceptance with God. At this I was then not a little surprised, not imagining I had been all this time building on the sand, nor considering that "other foundation can no man lay than that which is laid by God, even Christ Jesus."

Soon after, a contemplative man convinced me, still more than I was convinced before, that outward works are nothing, being alone; and in several conversations instructed me how to pursue inward holiness, or a union of the soul with God. But even of his instructions, (though I then received them as the words of God,) I cannot but now observe, that he spoke so incautiously [imprudently] against trusting in outward works, that he discouraged me from doing them at all; and that he recommended (as it were, to supply what was wanting in them) mental prayer and the like exercises, as the most effectual means of purifying the soul, and uniting it with God.

Now these were, in truth, as much my own works as visiting the sick or clothing the naked; and the union with God thus pursued was as really my own righteousness as any I had before pursued under another name.

In this refined way of trusting to my own works, and my own righteousness, (so zealously inculcated by the mystic writers,) I dragged on heavily, finding no comfort or heal therein till the time of my leaving England. On shipboard, however, I was again active in outward works; where it pleased God, of his free mercy, to give me twenty-six of the Moravian brethren for companions, who endeavored to show me a more excellent way. But I understood it not at first. I was too learned and too wise: so that it seemed foolishness unto me. And I continued preaching and following after and trusting in that righteousness whereby no flesh can be justified.

All the time I was at Savannah I was thus beating the air. Being ignorant of the righteousness of Christ, which by a living faith in him bringeth salvation "to every one that believeth," I sought to establish my own righteousness, and so labored in the fire all my days. I was now properly under the law; I knew that the law of God was spiritual; I consented to it, that it was good. Yea, I delighted in it, after the inner man. Yet was I carnal, sold under sin. Every day was I constrained to cry out, "What I do, I allow not; for what I would, I do not; but what I hate, that I do. To will is 'indeed' present with me; but how to perform that which is good, I find not. For the good which I would, I do not; but the evil which I would not, that I do. I find a law, that when I would do good, evil is present with me; even the law in my members, warring against the law of my mind, and still bringing me into captivity to the law of sin."

In this vile, abject state of bondage to sin I was indeed fighting continually, but not conquering. Before, I had willingly served sin; now, it was unwillingly; but still I served it. I fell and rose, and fell again. Sometimes I was overcome, and in heaviness; sometimes I overcame, and was in joy. For as in the former state I had some foretastes of the terrors of the law, so had I in this, of the comforts of the gospel. During this whole struggle between nature and grace (which had now continued above ten years) I had many remarkable returns to prayer, especially when I was in trouble. I had many sensible comforts, which are indeed no other than short anticipations of the life of faith. But I was still under the law, not under grace: the state most who are called Christians are content to live and die in. For I was only striving with, not freed from sin; neither had I the witness of the Spirit with my spirit, and indeed could not, for I sought it not by faith, but (as it were) by the works of the law.

In my return to England, January, 1738, being in imminent danger of death, and very uneasy on that account, I was strongly convinced that the cause of that uneasiness was unbelief, and that the gaining a true, living faith was the one thing needful for me. But still I fixed not this faith on its right object: I meant only faith in God, not faith in or through Christ. Again, I knew not that I was wholly void of this faith; but only thought I had not enough of it. So that when Peter Bohler, whom God prepared for me as soon as I came to London, affirmed of true faith in Christ, (which is but one,) that it had those two fruits inseparably attending it, "dominion over sin, and constant peace from a sense of forgiveness," I was quite amazed, and looked upon it as a new gospel. If this was so, it was clear I had not faith. But I was not willing to be convinced of this. Therefore I disputed with all my might, and labored to prove that faith might be where these were not; especially where the sense of forgiveness was not: for all the scriptures relating to this, I had been long since taught to construe away, and to call all Presbyterians who spoke otherwise. Besides, I well saw no one could (in the nature of things) have such a sense of forgiveness, and not feel it. But I felt it not. If then there was no faith without this, all my pretensions to faith dropped at once.

When I met Peter Bohler again, he consented to put the dispute upon the issue which I desired, viz., Scripture and experience. I first consulted the Scripture. But when I set aside the glosses of men, and simply considered the words of God, comparing them together, endeavoring to illustrate the obscure by the plainer passages, I found they all made against me, and was forced to retreat to my last hold, "that experience would never agree with the literal interpretation of those scriptures. Nor could I, therefore, allow it to be true till I found some living witnesses of it." He replied, "He could show me such at any time; if I desired it, the next day." And accordingly the next day he came with three others, all of whom testified of their own personal experience that a true living faith in Christ is inseparable from a sense of pardon for all past, and freedom from all present sins. They added with one mouth, that this faith was the gift, the free gift of God, and that he would surely bestow it upon every soul who earnestly and perseveringly sought it. I was not thoroughly convinced, and by the grace of God I resolved to seek it unto the end:

> by absolutely renouncing all dependence, in whole or in part, upon my own works or righteousness, on which I had really grounded my hope of salvation, though I knew it not, from my youth up;
>
> by adding to the constant use of all the other means of grace continual prayer for this very thing—justifying, saving faith; a full reliance on the blood of Christ shed for me; a trust in him as my Christ, as my sole justification, sanctification, and redemption.
>
> I continued thus to seek it (though with strange indifference, dullness, and coldness, and unusually frequent relapses into sin) till Wednesday, May 24th [1738]. I think it was about five this morning that I opened my Testament on those words
>
> "There are given unto us exceeding great and precious promises, even that ye should be partakers of the divine nature . . ."
>
> 2 Pet. i, 4. Just as I went out, I opened it again on those words: "Thou art not far from the kingdom of God." [Mark 12:34]

In the afternoon I was asked to go to St. Paul's. The anthem was,

Out of the deep have I called unto thee, O Lord: Lord, hear my voice. O let thine ears consider well the voice of my complaint. If thou, Lord, wilt be extreme to mark what is done amiss, O Lord, who may abide it? But there is mercy with thee; therefore thou shalt be feared. O Israel, trust in the Lord: for with the Lord there is mercy, and with him is plenteous redemption. And he shall redeem Israel from all his sins. [Psalm 130:1–7]

In the evening I went very unwillingly to a society in Aldersgate Street, where one was reading Luther's preface to the Epistle to the Romans. About a quarter before nine, while he was describing the change which God works in the heart through faith in Christ, I felt my heart strangely warmed. I felt I did trust in Christ, Christ alone, for salvation; and an assurance was given me that he had taken away my sins, even mine, and saved me from the law of sin and death.

I began to pray with all my might for those who had in a more especial manner despitefully used me and persecuted me. I then testified openly to all there what I now first felt in my heart. But it was not long before the enemy suggested, "This cannot be faith; for where is thy joy?" Then was I taught that peace and victory over sin are essential to faith in the Captain of our salvation; but that, as to the transports of joy that usually attend the beginning of it, especially in those who have mourned deeply, God sometimes giveth, sometimes withholdeth them, according to the counsels of his own will.

After my return home, I was much buffeted with temptations; but cried out, and they fled away. They returned again and again. I as often lifted up my eyes, and he sent me help from his holy place. And herein I found the difference between this and my former state chiefly consisted. I was striving, yea, fighting with all my might under the law, as well as under grace; but then I was sometimes, if not often, conquered: now I was always conqueror.

Thursday, May 25th. The moment I awaked, "Jesus, Master," was in my heart and in my mouth; and I found all my strength lay in keeping my eye fixed upon him, and my soul waiting on him continually. Being again at St. Paul's in the afternoon, I could taste the good word of God in the anthem, which began, "My song shall be always of the loving kindness of the Lord: with my mouth will I ever be showing forth thy truth from one generation to another." Yet the enemy injected a fear, "If thou dost believe, why is there not a more sensible change?" I answered, (yet not I,) "That I know not. But this I know, I have now peace with God. And I sin not to-day, and Jesus my Master has forbid me to take thought for the morrow."

"But is not any sort of fear," continued the tempter, "a proof that thou dost not believe?" I desired my Master to answer for me, and opened his book upon those words of St. Paul: "Without were fightings, within were fears." Then, inferred I, well may fears be within me; but I must go on, and tread them under my feet.

John Wesley, Journal

The example of Whitefield's open-air preaching was repulsive at first to his sense of decency and order; but after expounding at Bristol the Sermon on the Mount, a "pretty remarkable precedent of field-preaching, though I suppose there were churches at that time also," the next afternoon he (Monday, 2 April 1739) preached "from a little eminence in a ground adjoining to the city, to about three thousand people" (*Journal*).

John Wesley's journal of missionary travel would serve as a guide-book to the British Isles, and is replete with romantic incidents and graphic pictures of life. Forty-two times he crossed the Irish Sea. Secker admirably describes Wesley's aim as "laboring to bring all the world to solid, inward, vital religion." Throughout his work he was the educator and the social reformer as well as the evangelist.

By 1763 Wesley was practically the only itinerating clergyman, and the need of clerical provision for his societies began to be acutely felt. His lay preachers were ready for separation as early as the conference of 1755. The celebration of the eucharist by lay preachers had already begun at Norwich in 1760, while Wesley was in Ireland. Earlier than this he said to Charles (19 Oct. 1754) "We have in effect ordained already," and "was inclined to lay on hands."

He is said to have preached forty thousand sermons and traveled 250,000 miles. He suffered from various ailments, including hereditary gout, had undergone a surgical operation (1774), and was attacked by diabetes in 1789.

His last entry in his account-book is dated 16 July 1790; his last sermon (at Leatherhead) was preached on 23 Feb. 1791; his last letter (to Wilberforce) was written the following day. Dr. John Whitehead attended him from 25 Feb.; he declined further medical advice. On 2 March 1791 he died at the chapel-house in City Road.

Dictionary of National Biography, Eclectic Ethereal Encyclopedia

Charles Wesley

Dates

1707–1788

Famous for being

"The Sweet singer of Methodism"

Important writings

Hymns

One of his quotations

"God buries his workmen but carries on his work."

Charles Wesley, divine and hymn-writer, eighteenth child, youngest and third surviving son of Samuel Wesley (1662–1735), was born at Epworth Rectory, Lincolnshire, on 18 Dec. 1707. In 1716 he entered Westminster school, under the care and at the cost of his brother Samuel, till he was elected king's scholar in 1721.

In 1726 Charles entered Christ Church, Oxford, as a Westminster student, matriculating on 13 June. Study brought 'serious thinking' in its train. He began to attend the weekly sacrament. By the spring of 1729 (six months before John's return to Oxford, in November) he had 'persuaded two or three young scholars to accompany me, and to observe the method of study prescribed by the statutes of the university. This gained me the harmless nickname of methodist'.

In 1730 Charles graduated B.A. and began to take pupils. His plan of associated study and religious exercises assumed new proportions under his brother's lead. He threw himself into the movement with conspicuous zeal. It was to Charles Wesley that George Whitefield first turned (1732) when he felt drawn to the Methodist movement. Yet he looked forward to no career beyond that of a tutor, and 'exceedingly dreaded entering into holy orders.' This dread was partly due to introspective views of religion derived from mystical writers, whose influence he never entirely shook off.

He graduated M.A. on 12 March 1732–3. In face of the opposition of his brother Samuel, who thought him unfit for the work, he joined John in the mission to Georgia, going as secretary to James Edward Oglethorpe, the governor. He was ordained deacon by John Potter, then bishop of Oxford, and priest by Edmund Gibson, bishop of London, in October 1735, just before starting.

Leaving his brother at Savannah, Wesley reached (9 March 1736) Frederica, St. Simon's Island. But he did not stay here for long. On he return to Oxford Wesley came under the influence of Peter Böhler, who learned English from him. The perusal of Luther on Galatians, which he met with in May, gave clearness to his religious ideas. Whit-Sunday (21 May 1738) he fixes as the date of his conversion; a similar experience reached his brother John on the following Wednesday. Full of new zeal, he resumed preaching on 2 July. On 24 July he became unlicensed curate to George Stonehouse of St. Mary's, Islington; he read daily prayers, preached constantly in London churches, visited Newgate Prison, and held private meetings for exposition and devotion.

He entered upon the itinerant ministry on 16 Aug. 1739, riding to the west of England. Taking his brother's place at Bristol, he made this his headquarters, entering on his ministry at Weavers' Hall on 31 Aug. For the next seventeen years he pursued his evangelistic journeys, finding hearers up and down England and Wales, from the 'keelmen' of Newcastle-on-Tyne to the 'tinners' of Cornwall.

At the beginning of 1788 his strength entirely failed; by March he was unable to write. He died on 29 March 1788. On 5 April he was buried, at his own express desire, in the churchyard of St. Marylebone, immediately behind the old church.

Yet among the many services rendered by Charles Wesley to the cause of religion, his work as a hymn-writer stands pre-eminent. Exercising an hereditary gift, he had early written verses both in Latin and English, but the opening of the vein of his spiritual genius was a consequence of the inward crisis of Whit-Sunday 1738. Two days later his hymn upon his conversion was written. He doubted at first whether he had done right in even showing it to a friend. The first collection of hymns issued by John Wesley (1737) contains nothing by Charles. From 1739 to 1746 the brothers issued eight collections in their joint names. Charles Wesley is said to have written 6,500 hymns; about five hundred are in constant use. Dealing with every topic from the point of view of spiritual experience, they rarely subside into the meditative mood. Rich in melody, they invite to singing, and in the best of them there is a lyrical swing and an undertone of mystical fervor which both vitalize and mellow the substratum of doctrine. Much attention has been directed to his sacramental hymns (1745), in which the 'real presence' is expressly taught.

John Wesley writes of his brother: 'His least praise was his talent for poetry; although Dr. Watts did not scruple to say that that single poem, "Wrestling Jacob," was worth all the verses he himself had written'.

Dictionary of National Biography, Eclectic Ethereal Encyclopedia

George Whitefield

Dates

1714–1770

Famous for being

Early Methodist leader

Important writings

Writings and Sermons

One of his quotations

"Mere heathen morality, and not Jesus Christ, is preached in most of our churches."

George Whitefield (pronounced wit-field) was a minister in the Church of England and one of the leaders of the Methodist movement.

Early life

He was born on December 16, 1714 at the Bell Inn, Gloucester, England, and died in Newburyport, Massachusetts on September 30, 1770. In contemporary accounts, he, not John Wesley, is spoken of as the supreme figure and even as the founder of Methodism. He was famous for his preaching in America which was a significant part of the Great Awakening movement of Christian revivals. He has been called by some historians "the first modern celebrity."

George Whitefield was the son of a widow who kept an inn at Gloucester. At an early age, he found that he had a passion and talent for acting and the theatre, a passion that he would carry on through the very theatrical re-enactments of Bible stories that he told during his sermons. He was educated at the Crypt School, Gloucester, and Pembroke College, Oxford. Because Whitefield came from a poor background, he did not have the means to pay for his tuition. He therefore entered Oxford as a servitor, the lowest rank of students at Oxford. In return for free tuition, he was assigned as a servant to a number of higher ranked students. His duties would include waking them in the morning, polishing their shoes, carrying their books and even doing their coursework. He was a part of the Holy Club at Oxford University with the brothers, John Wesley and Charles Wesley. His genuine piety led the Bishop of Gloucester to ordain him before the canonical age.

Travels and evangelism

Whitefield preached his first sermon in the Crypt Church in his home town of Gloucester. In 1738, he went to America, becoming parish priest of Savannah, Georgia. Returning home in the following year, he resumed his evangelistic activities, with open-air homilies when other denominations' churches refused to admit him.

He parted company with Wesley over the doctrine of predestination; Whitefield was a follower of Calvin in this respect. Three churches were established in England in his name: one in Bristol and two others, the "Moorfields Tabernacle" and the "Tottenham Court Road Chapel", in London. Later the society meeting at the second Kingswood School at Kingswood, a town on the eastern edge of Bristol, was also called Whitefield's Tabernacle. Whitefield acted as chaplain to Selina, Countess of Huntingdon and some of his followers joined the Countess of Huntingdon's Connexion, whose chapels were paid for at her sole expense and where a form of Calvinistic Methodism similar to Whitefield's could be spread. Many of these chapels were built in the English counties and Wales, and one was erected in London – the Spa Fields Chapel.

Whitefield's legacy is still felt in America, where he is remembered as one of the first to preach to the enslaved. The Old South Presbyterian Church in Newburyport, Massachusetts was built for the evangelist's use, and before dying Whitefield requested to be buried under the pulpit of this church, where his tomb remains to this day. In an age when crossing the Atlantic Ocean was a long and hazardous adventure, he visited America seven times, making 13 trans-Atlantic crossings in total. It is estimated that throughout his life, he preached more than 18,000 formal sermons and if less formal occasions are included, that number might rise to more than 30,000.[citation needed] In addition to his work in America and England, he made 15 journeys to Scotland, (most famously to the "Preaching Braes" of Cambuslang in 1742), 2 to Ireland, and one each to Bermuda, Gibraltar, and The Netherlands.

In 1738 Whitefield preached a series of revivals in Georgia. Here he established the Bethesda Orphanage, which still exists to this day. When he returned to America in 1740 he preached nearly every day for months to large crowds of sometimes several thousand people as he traveled throughout the colonies, especially New England.

Like his contemporary and acquaintance, Jonathan Edwards, Whitefield preached with a Calvinist theology. He was known for his powerful voice and his ability to appeal to the emotions of a crowd, and unlike most preachers of his time spoke extemporaneously, rather than reading his sermon from notes.

Revival meetings

He first took to preaching in the open air with remarkable results at Bristol, which at that time was a center of vice in all its worst forms, and he was the first to provide spiritual privileges for the colliers who lived like heathens near that city. 20,000 of these poor workers crowded to hear him, and the white gutters caused by the tears which ran down their black cheeks showed how visibly they were affected, strong men being moved to hysterical convulsions by his wondrous power. John Wesley joining him there was not a little perplexed at these "bodily symptoms"; he saw them as evident "signs of grace", notwithstanding that Whitefield considered them to be "doubtful indications". Indeed, modern psychologists would call it symptoms of mass hysteria if there were 'persons that screamed out, and put their bodies into violent agitations and distortions' during a sermon. William Hogarth satirized such effects of Methodist preaching in his print, Credulity, Superstition, and Fanaticism (1762). Even larger crowds—Whitefield himself estimated 30,000—met him, with the same dramatic (and contentious) effects in Cambuslang in 1742.

Whitefield's more democratic speaking style was greatly appealing to the American audience. Benjamin Franklin once attended a revival meeting in Philadelphia and was greatly impressed with his ability to deliver a message to such a large audience. He was also known to be able to use the newspaper media for beneficial publicity. His revolutionary preaching style shaped the way in which sermons were delivered. He was one of the fathers of Evangelicalism. He was certainly the best-known preacher in America in the 18th century, and because he traveled through all of the American colonies and drew great crowds and media coverage, he was one of the most widely recognized public figures in America before George Washington.

Wikipedia

Other Christian leaders in the Age of Reason and Revival

Sir Isaac Newton (1643–1727)
Matthew Henry (1662–1714)
Isaac Watts (1674–1748)
Count von Zinzendorf (1700–1760)
David Brainerd (1718–1747)
John Newton (1725–1807)

Sir Isaac Newton (1643–1727)

Sir Isaac Newton, was an English physicist, mathematician, astronomer, alchemist, and natural philosopher, regarded by many as the greatest figure in the history of science. His treatise *Philosophiae Naturalis Principia Mathematica*, published in 1687, described universal gravitation and the three laws of motion, laying the groundwork for classical mechanics. By deriving Kepler's laws of planetary motion from this system, he was the first to show that the motion of objects on Earth and of celestial bodies are governed by the same set of natural laws. The unifying and predictive power of his laws was integral to the scientific revolution, the advancement of heliocentrism, and the broader acceptance of the notion that rational investigation can reveal the inner workings of nature.

Newton saw God as the master creator whose existence could not be denied in the face of the grandeur of all creation.

Wikipedia

It is revealing how Newton viewed his accomplishments in light of his belief in God? Shortly before his death, he wrote, "I do not know what I may appear to the world, but to myself I seem to have been only like a boy, playing on the seashore and diverting myself in now and then finding a smoother pebble or prettier seashell than ordinary, while the great ocean of truth lay all undiscovered before me."

Matthew Henry (1662–1714)

Matthew Henry, non-conformist divine and commentator, second son of Philip Henry, was born prematurely on 18 October 1662 at Broad Oak, in the chapelry of Iscoyd, Flintshire, [Wales]. As a child he was sickly, but somewhat precocious in learning. His first tutor was William Turner; but he owed most of' his early education to his father. On 21 July 1680 he entered the academy of Thomas Doolittle, then at Islington, and remained there till 1682. On 30 October 1683, shortly after his coming of age he entered on the estate of Bronington, Flintshire, inherited from Daniel Matthews, his maternal grandfather. On the advice of Rowland Hunt of Boreatton, Shropshire, he began to study law, and was admitted at Gray's Inn on 6 May 1685. In June 1686 he began to preach in his father's neighborhood. Business took him to Chester in January 1687. While there he preached in private houses, and was asked to settle as a minister. He gave a conditional assent, and returned to Gray's Inn.

On 9 May 1687 he was privately ordained in London by six ministers at the house of Richard Steel. Henry began his ministry at Chester on 2 June 1687. In a few years his communicants numbered 250. In September 1687 James II visited Chester, when the nonconformists presented an address of thanks 'for the ease and liberty they then enjoyed under his protection.' A new charter was granted to the city (the old one having been surrendered in 1684), giving power to the crown to displace and appoint magistrates. About August 1688 Henry was applied to by the king's messenger to nominate magistrates. He declined to do so. The new charter was cancelled by another, in which the names of all the prominent nonconformists were placed upon the corporation. They refused to serve, and demanded the restoration of the original charter, which was at length obtained.

A meeting-house was erected for Henry in Crook Lane (now called Crook Street). It was begun in September 1699, and opened on 8 August 1700. In 1706 a gallery was erected for the accommodation of another congregation which united with Henry's. The communicants now rose to 350. In addition to his congregational work (including a weekly lecture) he held monthly services at five neighboring villages, and regularly preached to the prisoners in the castle. He was an energetic member of the Cheshire meeting of united ministers, founded at Macclesfeld in March 1691, on the basis of the London 'happy union.' He found time also for his labors as a commentator, which originated in his system of expository preaching. His study was a two-storeyed summerhouse, still standing, to the rear of his residence in Bolland Court, White Friars, Chester. He declined overtures from London congregations at Hackney and Salters' Hall in 1699 and 1702 respectively, from Manchester in 1705, and from Silver Street and Old Jewry, London, in 1708. In 1710 he was again invited to Hackney, and agreed to remove, though not at once. On 3 June 1711 he was in London, being the first sacrament day on which he had been absent from Chester for twenty-four years. Daniel Williams, D.D., whose will is dated 26 June 1711, named him as one of the original trustees of his educational foundations, but he did not survive to enter on the trust. He preached his farewell sermon at Chester on 11 May 1712. His ministry at Mare Street, Hackney, began on 18 May 1712. In May 1714 he revisited Cheshire. He died of apoplexy at Nantwich, in the house of the nonconformist minister, Joseph Mottershead, on 22 June 1714, and was buried in the chancel of Trinity Church, Chester, the funeral being attended by eight of the city clergy.

Henry's 'Exposition of the Old and New Testament,' which for practical uses has not been superseded, was begun in November 1704.

Dictionary of National Biography, 1891

Isaac Watts (1674–1748)

Isaac Watts' hymns are sung in every professed Christian body. When advanced in years he is described as a "little feeble old man, shy in manner yet rich in speech. . . . Wherever he goes he is regarded with veneration and love, for his mind is stored with knowledge and his heart is alive with tender sympathies."

The date of his birth was July 17th, 1674, and thus he came into the world in the stormiest days of Nonconformity. His father kept a boarding-school at Southampton, but being a steadfast Dissenter and a deacon at a chapel in the seaport town he was often called upon to suffer. On more than one occasion he was placed in a prison-cell whilst his property was sequestrated. The sorrowing mother of Isaac often took her little child and sat on a cold stone by the prison walls, and one cannot wonder that the principles of Dissent soon became very dear to the future poet. His father was never a time-server, but stood firmly amidst sore tribulations, counting it a joy to suffer for righteousness' sake, and scorning the respectability and social standing which a connection with the Established Church would have brought him.

It is recorded that almost as soon as Isaac could lisp a word his oft-repeated request was for "A book! a book! Buy a book!" His early years must be passed over with a few words. The school which he attended was one where he was well instructed, and had he been willing to forsake the conventicle he would have been sent to one of the Universities, as several wealthy people were anxious to find the necessary money for this purpose. While quite a child Watts showed much skill in writing rhymes, and when this gift was developed and sanctified he penned the hymns which are so valued by the Church of God. To complete his education he was placed under the care of Thomas Rowe, who in addition to his duties as pastor of the Independent Church in Girdlers Hall, London, kept an academy in which he trained many who became famous in their day and generation. On the return of Watts to his home his abilities were put to good use. It appears that the hymns sung at his father's chapel, whilst sound in doctrine, were very poor from a poetical point of view, and often gave offence to at least one member of the congregation. The young man was at last constrained to mention the matter to his preacher-father, who very sensibly invited him to try his own hand and endeavor to produce more pleasing lyrics. Isaac was not slow in acting upon this suggestion, and before long there were enough hymns to fill a volume.

Watts died trusting alone in the merits, righteousness and blood of Christ, of which he had so often written. One sentence from his death-bed was:

> I remember an aged minister say that the most learned and knowing Christians when they come to die have only the same plain promises of the Gospel for their support as the common and unlearned of the people of God; and so I find it. They are the plain promises which do not require labor or pains to understand them; for I

can do nothing now but look into my Bible for some promise to support me, and live upon that.

Bunhill Fields: written in honor and to the memory of the many saints of God whose bodies rest in this old London cemetery, Alfred W. Light, 1915

Count von Zinzendorf (1700–1760)

Nicholas Ludwig, Count von Zinzendorf, was born in Dresden in 1700. He was very much a part of the Pietist movement in Germany, which emphasized personal piety and an emotional component to the religious life. This was in contrast to the state Lutheran Church of the day, which had grown to symbolize a largely intellectual faith centered on belief in specific doctrines. He believed in "heart religion," a personal salvation built on the individual's spiritual relationship with Christ.

As a teenager at Halle Academy, he and several other young nobles formed a secret society, The Order of the Grain of Mustard Seed. The stated purpose of this order was that the members would use their position and influence to spread the Gospel. As an adult, Zinzendorf later reactivated this adolescent society, and many influential leaders of Europe ended up joining the group. A few included the King of Denmark, the Archbishop of Canterbury, and the Archbishop of Paris.

During his Grand Tour (a rite of passage for young aristocrats) Nicolas visited an art museum in Dusseldorf where he saw a Domenico Feti painting titled Ecce Homo, "Behold the Man." It portrayed the crucified Christ with the legend, "This have I done for you—Now what will you do for me?" The young count as profoundly moved and appears to have had an almost mystical experience while looking at the painting, feeling as if Christ himself was speaking those word to his heart. He vowed that day to dedicate his life to service to Christ.

In 1731, while attending the coronation of Christian VI in Copenhagen, the young Count met a converted slave from the West Indies, Anthony Ulrich. Anthony's tale of his people's plight moved Zinzendorf, who brought him back to Herrnhut. As a result, two young men, Leonard Dober and David Nitchmann, were sent to St. Thomas to live among the slaves and preach the Gospel. This was the first organized Protestant mission work, and grew rapidly to Africa, America, Russia, and other parts of the world. By the end of Zinzendorf's life there were active missions from Greenland to South Africa, literally from one end of the earth to the other. Though the Baptist missionary William Carey is often referred to as the "Father of Modern Missions," he himself would credit Zinzendorf with that role, for he often referred to the model of the earlier Moravians in his journal.

Zinzendorf himself visited St. Thomas, and later visited America. There he sought to unify the German Protestants of Pennsylvania, even proposing a sort of "council of churches" where all would preserve their unique denominational practices, but would work in cooperation rather than competition. He founded the town of Bethlehem, where his daughter Benigna organized the school which would become Moravian College. His overwhelming interest in the colonies involved evangelizing the native Americans, and he traveled into the wilderness with Indian agent Conrad Weiser to meet with the chieftains of several tribes and clans. As far as we have been able to identify, he is the only European noble to have gone out to meet the native American leaders in this manner.

Zinzendorf's theology was extraordinarily Christ-centered and innovative. It focused intensely on the personal experience of a relationship with Christ, and an emotional experience of salvation rather than simply an intellectual assent to certain principles. Dr David Schattschneider, Dean of Moravian Theological Seminary in Bethlehem, PA, says that it is probably the fact that Zinzendorf did not attend seminary that allowed his thinking could be so creative. Zinzendorf cast the Trinity and the believers in terms of a family, referring often to the Holy Spirit as "mother." He accorded women a much more substantial role in church life than was normal for the eighteenth century, and suffered great criticism as a result. He allowed women to preach, to hold office, and to be ordained. Anna Nitschmann, the leader of the Single Sisters and later Zinzendorf's second wife, seems to have functioned as a bishop among the women.

But all Zinzendorf's thinking also focused on missionary outreach and renewal. He envisioned the Moravians not as a separate denomination, but as a dynamic renewal society which would serve to revitalize existing denominations and help create new work in mission areas. There are numerous churches in Pennsylvania where Moravians would start a church and school for the settlers and native Americans, and then turn it over to the Lutheran Church, the Reformed Church, or whatever denomination they perceived to be the strongest in that area.

Zinzendorf came to know John and Charles Wesley, who had been converted through their contact with the Moravians. The Wesleys later had a split with Zinzendorf, and founded the Methodist Church; both retained warm affection for the Moravians throughout their lives.

Zinzendorf died in 1760 at Herrnhut. By the time of his death the Moravians (which themselves only numbered in the hundreds) had sent out 226 missionaries around the world.

John Jackman

David Brainerd (1718–1747)

Summary

Missionary to the American Indians; born at Haddam, Connecticut, April 20, 1718; died at the home of Jonathan Edwards (to whose daughter [Jerusha] he was engaged), Northampton, Massachusetts, October 9, 1747.

Brainerd entered Yale College in 1739 and was expelled in his junior year; it was the time of the Great Awakening and Brainerd, who was "sober and inclined to melancholy" from childhood, sympathized with the "New Lights" (Whitefield, Tennent, and their followers); he attended their meetings when forbidden to do so, and criticized one of the tutors as having "no more grace than a chair"; as a consequence he was expelled.

He was licensed at Danbury, Connecticut, July 29, 1742; was approved as a missionary by the New York correspondents of the Society in Scotland for Propagating Christian Knowledge, November. 25, 1742, and labored among the Indians at Kaunaumeek (Brainerd, Rensselaer County, New York, 18 miles southeast of Albany) April 1743-March 1744; was ordained as a missionary at Newark, New Jersey, June 12, 1744; ten days later began work at what was intended to be his permanent station, at the forks of the Delaware, near Easton, Pennsylvania; in October he visited the Indians on the Susquehanna, and June 19, 1745, began to preach at Crossweeksung (Crosswick, 9 miles southeast of Trenton), the scene of his greatest success.

His life among the Indians was one of hardship and suffering borne with heroic fortitude and self-devotion; his health gave way under the strain and he relinquished the work, March 20, 1747, dying from consumption. The portions of his diary dealing with his work at Crossweeksung (June 19-November 4, 1745, and November 24, 1745-June 19, 1746) were published before his death, by the commissioners of the Society (Mirabilia ddi inter Indicos: or the rise and progress of a remarkable work of grace among a number of the Indians in the provinces of New Jersey and Pennsylvania; and Divine Grace Displayed: or the continuance and progress of a remarkable work of grace, etc., both published at Philadelphia, 1746, and commonly known as "Brainerd's Journal"). All of his papers, including an account of his early life and the original copy of his diary, were left with Jonathan Edwards, who prepared An Account of the Life of the Late Rev. David Brainerd (Boston, 1749), omitting the parts of the diary already published. The life and diary entire, with his letters and other writings, were edited by S. E. Dwight (New Haven, 1822) and by J. M. Sherwood (New York, 1884).

Philip Schaff, The New Schaff-Herzog Encyclopedia of Religious Knowledge, 1908

John Newton (1725–1807)

John Newton who was born in London, July 24, 1725, and died there Dec. 21, 1807, occupied an unique position among the founders of the Evangelical School, due as much to the romance of his young life and the striking history of his conversion, as to his force of character. His mother a pious Dissenter, stored his childish mind with Scripture, but died when he was seven years old. At the age of eleven, after two years' schooling, during which he learned the rudiments of Latin, he went to sea with his father. His life at sea teems with wonderful escapes, vivid dreams and sailor recklessness. He grew into an abandoned and godless sailor. The religious fits of his boyhood changed into settled infidelity, through the study of' Shaftesbury and the instruction of one of his comrades.

Disappointing repeatedly the plans of his father, he was flogged as a deserter from the navy, and for fifteen months lived, half-starved and ill-treated, in abject degradation under a slave-dealer in Africa. The one restraining influence of his life was his faithful love for his future wife, Mary Catlett, formed when he was seventeen, and she only in her fourteenth year. A chance reading of Thomas à Kempis sowed the seed of his conversion; which quickened under the awful contemplations of a night spent in steering a water-logged vessel in the face of apparent death (1748). He was then twenty-three. The six following years, during which he commanded a slave ship, matured his Christian belief. Nine years more, spent chiefly at Liverpool, in intercourse with Whitefield, Wesley, and Nonconformists, in the study of Hebrew and Greek, in exercises of devotion and occasional preaching among the Dissenters, elapsed before his ordination to the curacy of Olney, Bucks (1764). The Olney period was the most fruitful of his life. His zeal in pastoral visiting, preaching and prayer-meetings was unwearied. He formed his lifelong friendship with [William] Cowper, and became the spiritual father of [Thomas] Scott the commentator.

At Olney his best works—Omicron's Letters (1774); Olney Hymns (1779): Cardiphonia, written from Olney, though published 1781—were composed. As rector of St. Mary Woolnoth, London, in the center of the Evangelical movement (1780–1807) his zeal was as ardent as before. In 1805, when no longer able to read his text, his reply when pressed to discontinue preaching, was, "What, shall the old African blasphemer stop while he can speak!" The story of his sins and his conversion, published by himself, and the subject of lifelong allusion, was the base of' his influence; but it would have been little but for the vigor of his mind (shown even in Africa by his reading Euclid drawing its figures on the sand), his warm heart, candor, tolerance, and piety. These qualities gained him the friendship of Hannah More, Cecil, Wilberforce, and others; and his renown as a guide in experimental religion made him the center of a host of inquirers, with whom he maintained patient, loving, and generally judicious correspondence, of which a monument remains in the often beautiful letters of Cardiphonia.

The most characteristic hymns are those which depict in the language of intense humiliation his mourning for the abiding sins of his regenerate life, and the sense of the withdrawal of God's face, coincident with the never-failing conviction of acceptance in The Beloved. The feeling may be seen in the speeches, writings, and diaries of his whole life.

A Dictionary of Hymnology, edited by John Julian, 1892

How sweet the name of Jesus sounds

How sweet the Name of Jesus sounds
In a believer's ear!
It soothes his sorrows, heals his wounds,
And drives away his fear.

It makes the wounded spirit whole,
And calms the troubled breast;

'Tis manna to the hungry soul,
And to the weary, rest.
Dear Name, the Rock on which I build,
My Shield and Hiding Place,
My never failing treasury, filled
With boundless stores of grace!

By Thee my prayers acceptance gain,
Although with sin defiled;
Satan accuses me in vain,
And I am owned a child.

Jesus! my Shepherd, Husband, Friend,
O Prophet, Priest and King,
My Lord, my Life, my Way, my End,
Accept the praise I bring.

Weak is the effort of my heart,
And cold my warmest thought;
But when I see Thee as Thou art,
I'll praise Thee as I ought.

Till then I would Thy love proclaim
With every fleeting breath,
And may the music of Thy Name
Refresh my soul in death!

John Newton

Amazing Grace!

Amazing grace! How sweet the sound
That saved a wretch like me!
I once was lost, but now am found;
Was blind, but now I see.

'Twas grace that taught my heart to fear,
And grace my fears relieved;
How precious did that grace appear
The hour I first believed!

Through many dangers, toils and snares,
I have already come;
'Tis grace hath brought me safe thus far,
And grace will lead me home.

The Lord has promised good to me,
His Word my hope secures;
He will my Shield and Portion be,
As long as life endures.

Yea, when this flesh and heart shall fail,
And mortal life shall cease,
I shall possess, within the veil,
A life of joy and peace.

The earth shall soon dissolve like snow,
The sun forbear to shine;
But God, Who called me here below,
Will be forever mine.

When we've been there ten thousand years,
Bright shining as the sun,
We've no less days to sing God's praise
Than when we'd first begun.

John Newton

Classic Christian devotional books from the age of reason and revival

John Milton (1608–1674), *Paradise Lost*

Blaise Pascal (1623–1662), *Pensées*

John Owen (1616–1683)

The Death of Death in the Death of Christ

Brief Declaration and Vindication of The Doctrine of the Trinity

Brief Instruction in the Worship of God

Christologia

Dissertation on Divine Justice

Doctrine of Justification by Faith

Doctrine of the Saints' Perseverance Explained and Confirmed

Gospel Grounds and Evidences of the Faith of God's Elect

Meditations and Discourses on the Glory of Christ
Of Communion with God the Father, Son and Holy Ghost
Of Temptation
Of the Mortification of Sin in Believers
Sacramental Discourses

John Bunyan (1628–1688)

Pilgrim's Progress
Grace Abounding to the Chief of Sinners
The Holy War
Christ—A Complete Savior
A Discourse Upon the Pharisee and Publican
A Defence of the Doctrine of Justification by Faith in Jesus Christ
A Holy Life-The Beauty of Christianity
Christian Behavior
The Life and Death of Mr. Badman

George Fox (1624–1691), *Journal*
Philipp Jakob Spener (1635–1705), *Pia Desideria*
Jonathan Edwards (1703–1758)

The Life and Diary of David Brainerd
Freedom of the Will
Sermons

John Wesley (1703–1791)

Sermons
Bible commentary
Journals
A Short History of Methodism
Christian Perfection

Charles Wesley (1707–1788), Hymns
George Whitefield (1714–1770), Sermons

Extracts from Classic Christian devotional books from the age of reason and revival

John Milton (1608–1674), *Paradise Lost*
Sir Isaac Newton (1643–1727), *Daniel and Revelation*
Blaise Pascal (1623–1662), *Pensées, Section 12, Proofs of Jesus Christ*
John Owen (1616–1683), *The Death of Death in the Death of Christ*
John Bunyan (1628–1688), Pilgrim's Progress
George Fox (1624–1691), *Journal*
Madame Guyon (1647 –1717), *Autobiography*
Jonathan Edwards (1703–1758), *Sinners in the hands of an angry God*

John Wesley (1703–1791), *A Short History of Methodism,* see also his entry under "People" for an account of his conversion

Charles Wesley (1707–1788), *Hymn collection*

George Whitefield (1714–1770), *The Almost Christian*

David Brainerd (1718–1747), *Journal*

John Milton (1608–1674), *Paradise Lost* and text of sections 3.2, 3.3, and 12.13 of that work

Sir Isaac Newton (1643–1727)
Daniel and Revelation
Introduction

This prophecy is called the Revelation, with respect to the Scripture of Truth, which Daniel was commanded to shut up and seal, till the time of the end. Daniel sealed it until the time of the end, and until that time comes, the Lamb is opening the seals: and afterward the two Witnesses prophesy out of it a long time in sackcloth, before they ascend up to heaven in a cloud. All of which is as much as to say, that the prophecies of Daniel and John should not be understood till the time of the end: but that some should prophesy out of it in an afflicted and mournful state for a long time, and that but darkly, so as to convert but few. But in the very end, the Prophecy should be so far interpreted so as to convince many. Then saith Daniel, many shall run to and fro, and knowledge shall be increased. For the Gospel must first be preached in all nations before the great tribulation, and end of the world. The palm-bearing multitude, which came out of this great tribulation, cannot be innumerable out of all nations unless they be made so by the preaching of the Gospel before it comes. There must be a stone cut of the mountain without hands, before it can fall on the toes of the Image, and become a great mountain and fill the earth. An Angel must fly through the midst of heaven with the everlasting Gospel to preach to all nations, before Babylon falls, and the Son of man reaps his harvest. The two prophets must ascend up to heaven in a cloud, before the kingdoms of this world become the kingdoms of Christ.

'Tis therefore a part of this Prophecy, that it should not be understood before the last age of the world; and therefore it makes for the credit of the Prophecy, that it is not yet understood. But if the last age, the age of opening these things, be now approaching, as by the great success of late Interpreters it seems to be, we have more encouragement than ever to look into these things. If the general preaching of the Gospel be approaching, it is for us and our posterity that these words mainly belong: In the time of the end the wise shall understand, but none of the wicked shall understand. Blessed is he that readeth, and they that hear the words of this Prophecy, and keep those things that are written therein (Daniel 12:4,10)

Sir Isaac Newton, Daniel and Revelation

Blaise Pascal (1623–1662)

Pensées

779. If men knew themselves, God would heal and pardon them. Ne convertantur et sanem eos, et dimittantur eis peccata. [Mark 4. 12. "Lest they should be converted, and their sins should be forgiven them."]

780. Jesus Christ never condemned without hearing. To Judas: Amice, ad guid venisti? [Matt. 26. 50. "Friend, wherefore art thou come?"] To him that had not on the wedding garment, the same.

781. The types of the completeness of the Redemption, as that the sun gives light to all, indicate only completeness; but the types of exclusions, as of the Jews elected to the exclusion of the Gentiles, indicate exclusion.

"Jesus Christ the Redeemer of all." Yes, for He has offered, like a man who has ransomed all those who were willing to come to Him. If any die on the way, it is their misfortune; but, so far as He was concerned, He offered them redemption. That holds good in this example, where he who ransoms and he who prevents death are two persons, but not of Jesus Christ, who does both these things. No, for Jesus Christ, in the quality of Redeemer, is not perhaps Master of all; and thus, in so far as it is in Him, He is the Redeemer of all.

When it is said that Jesus Christ did not die for all, you take undue advantage of a fault in men who at once apply this exception to themselves; and is to favor despair, instead of turning them from it to favor hope. For men thus accustom themselves in inward virtues by outward customs.

782. The victory over death. "What is a man advantaged if he gain the whole world and lose his own soul? Whosoever will save his soul, shall lose it."

"I am not come to destroy the law, but to fulfill."

"Lambs took not away the sins of the world, but I am the lamb which taketh away the sins."

"Moses hath not led you out of captivity, and made you truly free."

783. . . . Then Jesus Christ comes to tell men that they have no other enemies but themselves; that it is their passions which keep them apart from God; that He comes to destroy these, and give them His grace, so as to make of them all one Holy Church; that He comes to bring back into this Church the heathen and Jews; that He comes to destroy the idols of the former and the superstition of the latter. To this all men are opposed, not only from the natural opposition of lust; but, above all, the kings of the earth, as had been foretold, join together to destroy this religion at its birth. [Ps. 2. 1, 2. "Why do the heathen rage . . . and the rulers of the earth . . . against the Lord."]

All that is great on earth is united together; the learned, the wise, the kings. The first write; the second condemn; the last kill. And notwithstanding all these oppositions, these men, simple and weak, resist all these powers, subdue even these kings, these learned men and these sages, and remove idolatry from all the earth. And all this is done by the power which had foretold it.

784. Jesus Christ would not have the testimony of devils, nor of those who were not called, but of God and John the Baptist.

785. I consider Jesus Christ in all persons and in ourselves: Jesus Christ as a Father in His Father, Jesus Christ as a Brother in His Brethren, Jesus Christ as poor in the poor, Jesus Christ as rich in the rich, Jesus Christ as Doctor and Priest in priests, Jesus Christ as Sovereign in princes, etc. For by His glory He is all that is great, being God; and by His mortal life He is all that is poor and abject. Therefore He has taken this unhappy condition, so that He could be in all persons and the model of all conditions.

786. Jesus Christ is an obscurity (according to what the world calls obscurity), such that historians, writing only of important matters of states, have hardly noticed Him.

787. On the fact that neither Josephus, nor Tacitus, nor other historians have spoken of Jesus Christ. So far is this from telling against Christianity that, on the contrary, it tells for it. For it is certain that Jesus Christ has existed; that His religion has made a great talk; and that these persons were not ignorant of it. Thus it is plain that they purposely concealed it, or that, if they did speak of it, their account has been suppressed or changed.

788. "I have reserved me seven thousand." I love the worshippers unknown to the world and to the very prophets.

789. As Jesus Christ remained unknown among men, so His truth remains among common opinions without external difference. Thus the Eucharist among ordinary bread.

790. Jesus would not be slain without the forms of justice; for it is far more ignominious to die by justice than by an unjust sedition.

791. The false justice of Pilate only serves to make Jesus Christ suffer; for he causes Him to be scourged by his false justice, and afterwards puts Him to death. It would have been better to have put Him to death at once. Thus it is with the falsely just. They do good and evil works to please the world, and to show that they are not altogether of Jesus Christ; for they are ashamed of Him. And at last, under great temptation and on great occasions, they kill Him.

792. What man ever had more renown? The whole Jewish people foretell Him before His coming. The Gentile people worship Him after His coming. The two peoples, Gentile and Jewish, regard Him as their center.

And yet what man enjoys this renown less? Of thirty-three years, He lives thirty without appearing. For three years He passes as an impostor; the priests and the chief people reject Him; His friends and His nearest relatives despise Him. Finally, He dies, betrayed by one of His own disciples, denied by another, and abandoned by all.

What part, then, has He in this renown? Never had man so much renown; never had man more ignominy. All that renown has served only for us, to render us capable of recognizing Him; and He had none of it for Himself.

Blaise Pascal, Pensées, Section 12, Proofs of Jesus Christ, translated by W. F. Trotter

John Owen (1616–1683)
The Death of Death in the Death of Christ

Introduction

The Death of Death in the Death of Christ is John Owen's definitive work on the extent of the atonement. It is a polemical work, designed to show among other things that the doctrine of universal redemption is unscriptural and destructive of the gospel.

Chapter 1

In general of the end of the death of Christ, as it is in the Scripture proposed.

By the end of the death of Christ, we mean in general, both,—first, that which his Father and himself intended in it; and, secondly, that which was effectually fulfilled and accomplished by it. Concerning either we may take a brief view of the expressions used by the Holy Ghost:—

I. For the first. Will you know the end wherefore, and the intention wherewith, Christ came into the world? Let us ask himself (who knew his own mind, as also all the secrets of his Father's bosom), and he will tell us that the "Son of man came to save that which was lost," Matt. xviii. 11,—to recover and save poor lost sinners; that was his intent and design, as is again asserted, Luke xix. 10. Ask also his apostles, who know his mind, and they will tell you the same. So Paul, 1 Tim. i. 15, "This is a faithful saying, and worthy of all acceptation, that Christ Jesus came into the world to save sinners." Now, if you will ask who these sinners are towards whom he hath this gracious intent and purpose, himself tells you, Matt. xx. 28, that he came to "give his life a ransom for many;" in other places called us, believers, distinguished from the world: for be "gave himself for our sins, that he might deliver us from this present evil world, according to the will of God and our Father," Gal. i. 4. That was the will and intention of God, that he should give himself for us, that we might be saved, being separated from the world. They are his church: Eph. v. 25–27, "He loved the church, and gave himself for it; that he might sanctify and cleanse it with the washing of water by the word, that he might present it to himself a glorious church, not having spot, or wrinkle, or any such thing; but that it should be holy and without blemish:" which last words express also the very aim and end of Christ in giving himself for any, even that they may be made fit for God, and brought nigh unto him;—the like whereof is also asserted, Tit. ii. 14, "He gave himself for us, that he might redeem us from all iniquity, and purify unto himself a peculiar people, zealous of good works." Thus clear, then, and apparent, is the intention and design of Christ and his Father in this great work, even what it was, and towards whom,—namely, to save us, to deliver us from the evil world, to purge and wash us, to make us holy, zealous, fruitful in good works, to render us acceptable, and to bring us unto God; for through him "we have access into the grace wherein we stand" Rom. v. 2.

II. The effect, also, and actual product of the work itself, or what is accomplished and fulfilled by the death, blood-shedding, or oblation of Jesus Christ, is no less clearly manifested, but is as fully, and very often more distinctly, expressed;—as, first, Reconciliation with God, by removing and slaying the enmity that was between him and us; for "when we were enemies we were reconciled to God by the death of his Son," Rom. v. 10. "God was in him reconciling the world unto himself, not imputing their trespasses unto them," 2 Cor. v. 19; yea, he hath "reconciled us to himself by Jesus Christ," verse 18. And if you would know how this reconciliation was effected, the apostle will tell you that "he abolished in his flesh the enmity, the law of commandments consisting in ordinances; for to make in himself of twain one new man, so making peace; and that he might reconcile both unto God in one body by the cross, having slain the enmity thereby," Eph. ii. 15, 16: so that "he is our peace," verse 14. Secondly, Justification, by taking away the guilt of sins, procuring remission and pardon of them, redeeming us from their power, with the curse and wrath due unto us for them; for "by his own blood he entered into the holy place, having obtained eternal redemption for us" Heb. ix. 12. "He redeemed us from the curse, being made a curse for us," Gal. iii. 13; "his own self bearing our sins in his own body on the tree," 1 Pet. ii. 24. We have "all sinned, and come short of the glory of God;" but are "justified freely by his grace through the redemption that is in Christ Jesus, whom God hath set forth to be a propitiation through faith in his blood, to declare his righteousness for the remission of sins" Rom. iii. 23–25: for "in him we have redemption through his blood, even the forgiveness of sins," Col. i. 14. Thirdly, Sanctification, by the purging away of the uncleanness and pollution of our sins, renewing in us the image of God, and supplying us with the graces of the Spirit of holiness: for "the blood of Christ, who through the eternal Spirit offered himself to God, purgeth our consciences from dead works that we may serve the living God," Heb. ix. 14; yea, "the blood of Jesus Christ cleanseth us from all sin," 1 John i. 7. "By himself he purged our sins," Heb. i. 3. To "sanctify the people with his own blood, he suffered without the gate," chap. xiii. 12. "He gave himself for the church to sanctify and cleanse it, that it should be holy and without blemish," Eph. v. 25–27. Peculiarly amongst the graces of the Spirit, "it is given to us, for Christ's sake, to believe on him," Phil. i. 29; God "blessing us in him with all spiritual blessings in heavenly places," Eph. i. 3. Fourthly, Adoption, with that evangelical liberty and all those glorious privileges which appertain to the sons of God; for "God sent forth his Son, made of a woman, made under the law, to redeem them that were under the law, that we might receive the adoption of sons," Gal. iv. 4, 5. Fifthly, Neither do the effects of the death of Christ rest here; they leave us not until we are settled in heaven, in glory and immortality for ever. Our inheritance is a "purchased possession," Eph. i. 14: "And for this cause he is the mediator of the new testament, that by means of death, for the redemption of the transgressions that were under the first testament, they which are called might receive the promise of eternal inheritance," Heb. ix. 15. The sum of all is,—The death and blood-shedding of Jesus Christ hath wrought, and doth effectually procure, for all those that are concerned in it, eternal redemption, consisting in grace here and glory hereafter.

III. Thus full, clear, and evident are the expressions in the Scripture concerning the ends and effects of the death of Christ, that a man would think every one might run and read. But we must stay: among all things in Christian religion, there is scarce any thing more questioned than this, which seems to be a most fundamental principle. A spreading persuasion there is of a general ransom to be paid by Christ for all; that he died to redeem all and every one,—not only for many, his church, the elect of God, but for every one also of the posterity of Adam. Now, the masters of this opinion do see full well and easily, that if that be the end of the death of Christ which we have from the Scripture asserted, if those before recounted be the immediate fruits and products thereof, then one of these two things will necessarily follow:—that either, first, God and Christ failed of their end proposed, and did not accomplish that which they intended, the death of Christ being not a fitly-proportioned means for the attaining of that end (for any cause of failing cannot be assigned); which to assert seems to us blasphemously injurious to the wisdom, power, and perfection of God, as likewise derogatory to the worth and value of the death of Christ;—or else, that all men, all the posterity of Adam, must be saved, purged, sanctified, and glorified; which surely they will not maintain, at least the Scripture and the woeful experience of millions will not allow. Wherefore, to cast a tolerable color upon their persuasion, they must and do deny that God or his Son had any such absolute aim or end in the death or blood-shedding of Jesus Christ, or that any such thing was immediately procured and purchased by it, as we before recounted; but that God intended nothing, neither was any thing effected by Christ,—that no benefit ariseth to any immediately by his death but what is common to all and every soul, though never so cursedly unbelieving here and eternally damned hereafter, until an act of some, not procured for them by Christ, (for if it were, why have they it not all alike?) to wit, faith, do distinguish them from others. Now, this seeming to me to enervate the virtue, value, fruits and effects of the satisfaction and death of Christ,—serving, besides, for a basis and foundation to a dangerous, uncomfortable, erroneous persuasion—I shall, by the Lord's assistance, declare what the Scripture holds out in both these things, both that assertion which is intended to be proved, and that which is brought for the proof thereof; desiring the Lord by his Spirit to lead us into all truth, to give us understanding in all things, and if any one be otherwise minded, to reveal that also unto him.

John Owen, The Death of Death in the Death of Christ

John Bunyan (1628–1688)
"Pilgrim's Burden"

We all, like sheep, have gone astray,
 each of us has turned to his own way;
 and the LORD has laid on him
 the iniquity of us all.
Isaiah 53:6

[John Bunyan pictures, in his classic allegory *The Pilgrim's Progress*, the moment Christian has his burden of sin removed.]

Now I saw in my dream, that the highway up which Christian was to go, was fenced on either side with a wall, and that wall was called Salvation. Isaiah 26:1. Up this way, therefore, did burdened Christian run, but not without great difficulty, because of the load on his back.

He ran thus till he came at a place somewhat ascending; and upon that place stood a cross, and a little below, in the bottom, a sepulcher. So I saw in my dream, that just as Christian came up with the cross, his burden loosed from off his shoulders, and fell from off his back, and began to tumble, and so continued to do till it came to the mouth of the sepulcher, where it fell in, and I saw it no more.

Then was Christian glad and lightsome, and said with a merry heart, "He hath given me rest by his sorrow, and life by his death." Then he stood still a while, to look and wonder; for it was very surprising to him that the sight of the cross should thus ease him of his burden. He looked, therefore, and looked again, even till the springs that were in his head sent the waters down his cheeks. Zech. 12:10. Now as he stood looking and weeping, behold, three Shining Ones came to him, and saluted him with, "Peace be to thee." So the first said to him, "Thy sins be forgiven thee," Mark 2:5; the second stripped him of his rags, and clothed him with change of raiment, Zech. 3:4; the third also set a mark on his forehead, Eph. 1:13, and gave him a roll with a seal upon it, which he bid him look on as he ran, and that he should give it in at the celestial gate: so they went their way. Then Christian gave three leaps for joy, . . .

John Bunyan, The Pilgrim's Progress

George Fox (1624–1691)
***Journal* (His autobiography)**

Chapter 5

One man may shake the country for ten miles

Being again at liberty, I went on, as before, in the work of the Lord, passing through the country into Leicestershire, having meetings as I went; and the Lord's Spirit and power accompanied me.

As I was walking with several Friends, I lifted up my head and saw three steeple-house spires, and they struck at my life. I asked them what place that was. They said, "Lichfield." Immediately the Word of the Lord came to me that I must go thither. Being come to the house we were going to, I wished the Friends to walk into the house, saying nothing to them of whither I was to go. As soon as they were gone I stepped away, and went by my eye over hedge and ditch till I came within a mile of Lichfield, where, in a great field, shepherds were keeping their sheep.

Then was I commanded by the Lord to pull off my shoes. I stood still, for it was winter; and the Word of the Lord was like a fire in me. So I put off my shoes, and left them with the shepherds; and the poor shepherds trembled, and were astonished. Then I walked on about a mile, and as soon as I was got within the city, the Word of the Lord came to me again, saying, "Cry, 'Woe to the bloody city of Lichfield!'" So I went up and down the streets, crying with a loud voice, "Woe to the bloody city of Lichfield!" It being market-day, I went into the market-place, and to and fro in the several parts of it, and made stands, crying as before, "Woe to the bloody city of Lichfield!" And no one laid hands on me.

As I went thus crying through the streets, there seemed to me to be a channel of blood running down the streets, and the market-place appeared like a pool of blood.

When I had declared what was upon me, and felt myself clear, I went out of the town in peace, and, returning to the shepherds, I gave them some money, and took my shoes of them again. But the fire of the Lord was so in my feet, and all over me, that I did not matter to put on my shoes again, and was at a stand whether I should or no, till I felt freedom from the Lord so to do; then, after I had washed my feet, I put on my shoes again.

After this a deep consideration came upon me, for what reason I should be sent to cry against that city, and call it the bloody city! For, though the Parliament had had the minister one while, and the King another, and much blood had been shed in the town during the wars between them, yet that was no more than had befallen many other places. But afterwards I came to understand, that in the Emperor Diocletian's time a thousand Christians were martyred in Lichfield.

Passing on, I was moved of the Lord to go to Beverley steeple-house, which was then a place of high profession; and being very wet with rain, I went first to an inn. As soon as I came to the door, a young woman of the house came to the door, and said, "What, is it you? come in," as if she had known me before; for the Lord's power bowed their hearts. So I refreshed myself and went to bed; and in the morning, my clothes being still wet, I got ready, and having paid for what I had had in the inn, I went up to the steeple-house, where was a man preaching. When he had done, I was moved to speak to him, and to the people, in the mighty power of God, and to turn them to their teacher, Christ Jesus. The power of the Lord was so strong, that it struck a mighty dread amongst the people. The mayor came and spoke a few words to me; but none of them had any power to meddle with me.

So I passed away out of the town, and in the afternoon went to another steeple-house about two miles off. When the priest had done, I was moved to speak to him, and to the people very largely, showing them the way of life and truth, and the ground of election and reprobation. The priest said he was but a child, and could not dispute with me. I told him I did not come to dispute, but to hold forth the Word of life and truth unto them, that they might all know the one Seed, to which the promise of God was given, both in the male and in the female. Here the people were very loving, and would have had me come again on a week-day, and preach among them; but I directed them to their teacher, Christ Jesus, and so passed away.

George Fox, Journal

Madame Guyon (1647 –1717)

Autobiography

Introduction

To its opponents, Quietism was the doctrine of abandonment to God and passivity verging on pantheism, indifference to prayer, the sacraments, good works and even morality.

Jeanne-Marie Bouvier de la Motte-Guyon. Jeanne was a French mystic and one of the key advocates of Quietism. This doctrine was considered heretical by the Roman Catholic Church, and as a result, Madame Guyon was imprisoned from 1695 to 1703.

About this time I fell into a state of total privation which lasted nearly seven years. I seemed to myself cast down like Nebuchadnezzar, to live among beasts; a deplorable state, yet of the greatest advantage to me, by the use which divine wisdom made of it. This state of emptiness, darkness, and impotency, went far beyond any trials I had ever yet met. I have since experienced, that the prayer of the heart when it appears most dry and barren, nevertheless is not ineffectual nor offered in vain. God gives what is best for us, though not what we most relish or wish for. Were people but convinced of this truth, they would be far from complaining all their lives. By causing us death He would procure us life; for all our happiness, spiritual, temporal and eternal, consists in resigning ourselves to God, leaving it to Him to do in us and with us as He pleases, and with so much the more submission; as things please us less. By this pure dependence on His Spirit, everything is given us admirably. Our very weaknesses, in His hand, prove a source of humiliation. If the soul were faithful to leave itself in the hand of God, sustaining all His operations whether gratifying or mortifying, suffering itself to be conducted, from moment to moment, by His hand, and annihilated by the strokes of His Providence, without complaining, or desiring anything but what it has; it would soon arrive at the experience of the eternal truth, though it might not at once know the ways and methods by which God conducted it there.

People want to direct God instead of resigning themselves to be directed by Him. They want to show Him a way, instead of passively following that wherein He leads them. Hence many souls, called to enjoy God Himself, and not barely His gifts, spend all their lives in running after little consolations, and feeding on them—resting there only, making all their happiness to consist therein.

If my chains and my imprisonment in any way afflict you, I pray that they may serve to engage you to seek nothing but God for Himself alone, and never to desire to possess Him but by the death of your whole selves, never to seek to be something in the ways of the Spirit, but choose to enter into the most profound nothingness.

I had an internal strife, which continually racked me—two powers which appeared equally strong seemed equally to struggle for the mastery within me. On the one hand, a desire of pleasing Thee, O my God, a fear of offending, and a continual tendency of all my powers to Thee—on the other side, the view of all my inward corruptions, the depravity of my heart, and the continual stirring and rising of self. What torrents of tears, what desolations have these cost me? "Is it possible," I cried, "that I have received so many graces and favors from God only to lose them;—that I have loved Him with so much ardor, but to be eternally deprived of Him; that His benefits have only produced ingratitude; His fidelity been repaid with infidelity; that my heart has been emptied of all creatures, and created objects, and filled with His blessed presence and love, in order now to be wholly void of divine power, and only filled with wanderings and created objects!"

I could now no longer pray as formerly. Heaven seemed shut to me, and I thought justly. I could get no consolation or make any complaint; nor had I any creature on earth to apply to. I found myself banished from all beings without finding a support of refuge in anything. I could no more practice any virtue with facility. "Alas!" said I, "is it possible that this heart, formerly all on fire, should now become like ice!" I often thought all creatures combined against me. Laden with a weight of past sins, and a multitude of new ones, I could not think God would ever pardon me, but looked on myself as a victim designed for Hell. I would have been glad to do penances, to make use of prayers, pilgrimages, and vows. But still, whatever I tried for a remedy seemed only to increase the malady. I may say that tears were my drink, and sorrow my food. I felt in myself such a pain as I never could bring any to comprehend, but such as have experienced it. I had within myself an executioner who tortured me without respite. Even when I went to church, I was not easy there. To sermons I could give no attention; they were now of no service or refreshment to me. I scarcely conceived or understood anything in them, or about them.

Madame Guyon, Autobiography, Chapter 21

Jonathan Edwards (1703–1758)

Introduction

This is an extract from Edwards' most famous sermon, preached during the time of the Great Awakening.

Sinners in the hands of an angry God

"Their foot shall slide in due time." Deut. xxxii. 35

In this verse is threatened the vengeance of God on the wicked unbelieving Israelites, who were God's visible people, and who lived under the means of grace; but who, notwithstanding all God's wonderful works towards them, remained (as ver. 28.) void of counsel, having no understanding in them. Under all the cultivations of heaven, they brought forth bitter and poisonous fruit; as in the two verses next preceding the text. The expression I have chosen for my text, Their foot shall slide in due time, seems to imply the following doings, relating to the punishment and destruction to which these wicked Israelites were exposed. The truth of this observation may appear by the following considerations.

1. There is no want of power in God to cast wicked men into hell at any moment. Men's hands cannot be strong when God rises up. The strongest have no power to resist him, nor can any deliver out of his hands.-He is not only able to cast wicked men into hell, but he can most easily do it. Sometimes an earthly prince meets with a great deal of difficulty to subdue a rebel, who has found means to fortify himself, and has made himself strong by the numbers of his followers. But it is not so with God. There is no fortress that is any defense from the power of God. Though hand join in hand, and vast multitudes of God's enemies combine and associate themselves, they are easily broken in pieces. They are as great heaps of light chaff before the whirlwind; or large quantities of dry stubble before devouring flames. We find it easy to tread on and crush a worm that we see crawling on the earth; so it is easy for us to cut or singe a slender thread that any thing hangs by: thus easy is it for God, when he pleases, to cast his enemies down to hell. What are we, that we should think to stand before him, at whose rebuke the earth trembles, and before whom the rocks are thrown down?

2. They deserve to be cast into hell; so that divine justice never stands in the way, it makes no objection against God's using his power at any moment to destroy them. Yea, on the contrary, justice calls aloud for an infinite punishment of their sins. Divine justice says of the tree that brings forth such grapes of Sodom, "Cut it down, why cumbereth it the ground?" Luke xiii. 7. The sword of divine justice is every moment brandished over their heads, and it is nothing but the hand of arbitrary mercy, and God's mere will, that holds it back.

3. They are already under a sentence of condemnation to hell. They do not only justly deserve to be cast down thither, but the sentence of the law of God, that eternal and immutable rule of righteousness that God has fixed between him and mankind, is gone out against them, and stands against them; so that they are bound over already to hell. John iii. 18. "He that believeth not is condemned already." So that every unconverted man properly belongs to hell; that is his place; from thence he is, John viii. 23. "Ye are from beneath." And thither be is bound; it is the place that justice, and God's word, and the sentence of his unchangeable law assign to him.

4. They are now the objects of that very same anger and wrath of God, that is expressed in the torments of hell. And the reason why they do not go down to hell at each moment, is not because God, in whose power they are, is not then very angry with them; as he is with many miserable creatures now tormented in hell, who there feel and bear the fierceness of his wrath. Yea, God is a great deal more angry with great numbers that are now on earth:

yea, doubtless, with many that are now in this congregation, who it may be are at ease, than he is with many of those who are now in the flames of hell.

So that it is not because God is unmindful of their wickedness, and does not resent it, that he does not let loose his hand and cut them off. God is not altogether such an one as themselves, though they may imagine him to be so. The wrath of God burns against them, their damnation does not slumber; the pit is prepared, the fire is made ready, the furnace is now hot, ready to receive them; the flames do now rage and glow. The glittering sword is whet, and held over them, and the pit hath opened its mouth under them.

5. The devil stands ready to fall upon them, and seize them as his own, at what moment God shall permit him. They belong to him; he has their souls in his possession, and under his dominion. The scripture represents them as his goods, Luke xi. 12. The devils watch them; they are ever by them at their right hand; they stand waiting for them, like greedy hungry lions that see their prey, and expect to have it, but are for the present kept back. If God should withdraw his hand, by which they are restrained, they would in one moment fly upon their poor souls. The old serpent is gaping for them; hell opens its mouth wide to receive them; and if God should permit it, they would be hastily swallowed up and lost.

6. There are in the souls of wicked men those hellish principles reigning, that would presently kindle and flame out into hell fire, if it were not for God's restraints. There is laid in the very nature of carnal men, a foundation for the torments of hell. There are those corrupt principles, in reigning power in them, and in full possession of them, that are seeds of hell fire. These principles are active and powerful, exceeding violent in their nature, and if it were not for the restraining hand of God upon them, they would soon break out, they would flame out after the same manner as the same corruptions, the same enmity does in the hearts of damned souls, and would beget the same torments as they do in them. The souls of the wicked are in scripture compared to the troubled sea, Isa. lvii. 20. For the present, God restrains their wickedness by his mighty power, as he does the raging waves of the troubled sea, saying, "Hitherto shalt thou come, but no further;" but if God should withdraw that restraining power, it would soon carry all before it. Sin is the ruin and misery of the soul; it is destructive in its nature; and if God should leave it without restraint, there would need nothing else to make the soul perfectly miserable. The corruption of the heart of man is immoderate and boundless in its fury; and while wicked men live here, it is like fire pent up by God's restraints, whereas if it were let loose, it would set on fire the course of nature; and as the heart is now a sink of sin, so if sin was not restrained, it would immediately turn the soul into a fiery oven, or a furnace of fire and brimstone.

7. It is no security to wicked men for one moment, that there are no visible means of death at hand. It is no security to a natural man, that he is now in health, and that he does not see which way he should now immediately go out of the world by any accident, and that there is no visible danger in any respect in his circumstances. The manifold and continual experience of the world in all ages, shows this is no evidence, that a man is not on the very

brink of eternity, and that the next step will not be into another world. The unseen, unthought-of ways and means of persons going suddenly out of the world are innumerable and inconceivable. Unconverted men walk over the pit of hell on a rotten covering, and there are innumerable places in this covering so weak that they will not bear their weight, and these places are not seen. The arrows of death fly unseen at noon-day; the sharpest sight cannot discern them. God has so many different unsearchable ways of taking wicked men out of the world and sending them to hell, that there is nothing to make it appear, that God had need to be at the expense of a miracle, or go out of the ordinary course of his providence, to destroy any wicked man, at any moment. All the means that there are of sinners going out of the world, are so in God's hands, and so universally and absolutely subject to his power and determination, that it does not depend at all the less on the mere will of God, whether sinners shall at any moment go to hell, than if means were never made use of, or at all concerned in the case.

8. Natural men's prudence and care to preserve their own lives, or the care of others to preserve them, do not secure them a moment. To this, divine providence and universal experience do also bear testimony. There is this clear evidence that men's own wisdom is no security to them from death; that if it were otherwise we should see some difference between the wise and politic men of the world, and others, with regard to their liableness to early and unexpected death: but how is it in fact? Eccles. ii. 16. "How dieth the wise man? even as the fool."

9. All wicked men's pains and contrivance which they use to escape hell, while they continue to reject Christ, and so remain wicked men, do not secure them from hell one moment. Almost every natural man that hears of hell, flatters himself that he shall escape it; he depends upon himself for his own security; he flatters himself in what he has done, in what he is now doing, or what he intends to do. Every one lays out matters in his own mind how he shall avoid damnation, and flatters himself that he contrives well for himself, and that his schemes will not fail. They hear indeed that there are but few saved, and that the greater part of men that have died heretofore are gone to hell; but each one imagines that he lays out matters better for his own escape than others have done. . . .

And let every one that is yet out of Christ, and hanging over the pit of hell, whether they be old men and women, or middle aged, or young people, or little children, now harken to the loud calls of God's word and providence. This acceptable year of the Lord, a day of such great favors to some, will doubtless be a day of as remarkable vengeance to others. Men's hearts harden, and their guilt increases apace at such a day as this, if they neglect their souls; and never was there so great danger of such persons being given up to hardness of heart and blindness of mind. God seems now to be hastily gathering in his elect in all parts of the land; and probably the greater part of adult persons that ever shall be saved, will be brought in now in a little time, and that it will be as it was on the great out-pouring of the Spirit upon the Jews in the apostles' days; the election will obtain, and the rest will be blinded. If this should be the case with you, you will eternally curse this day, and will curse the day that ever you was born, to see such a season of the pouring out of God's Spirit, and will wish that you had died and gone to hell before you had seen it. Now undoubtedly it is, as it was in the days of John the Baptist, the axe is in an extraordinary manner laid at the root of the trees, that every tree which brings not forth good fruit, may be hewn down and cast into the fire.

Therefore, let every one that is out of Christ, now awake and fly from the wrath to come. The wrath of Almighty God is now undoubtedly hanging over a great part of this congregation: Let every one fly out of Sodom: "Haste and escape for your lives, look not behind you, escape to the mountain, lest you be consumed."

Jonathan Edwards

John Wesley (1703–1791)
A Short History of Methodism

1. It is not easy to reckon up the various accounts which have been given of the people called Methodists; very many of them as far remote from truth as that given by the good gentleman in Ireland: "Methodists! Ay, they are the people who place all religion in wearing long beards."

2. Abundance of the mistakes which are current concerning them have undoubtedly sprung from this: Men lump together, under this general name, many who have no manner of connection with each other; and then whatever any of these speaks or does is of course imputed to all.

3. The following short account may prevent persons of a calm and candid disposition from doing this; although men of a warm or prejudiced spirit will do just as they did before. But let it be observed, this is not designed for a defense of the Methodists, (so called,) or any part of them. It is a bare relation of a series of naked facts, which alone may remove abundance of misunderstandings.

4. In November, 1729, four young gentlemen of Oxford,—Mr. John Wesley, Fellow of Lincoln College; Mr. Charles Wesley, Student of Christ Church; Mr. Morgan, Commoner of Christ Church; and Mr. Kirkham, of Merton College,—began to spend some evenings in a week together, in reading, chiefly, the Greek Testament. The next year two or three of Mr. John Wesley's pupils desired the liberty of meeting with them; and afterwards one of Mr. Charles Wesley's pupils. It was in 1732, that Mr. Ingham, of Queen's College, and Mr. Broughton, of Exeter, were added to their number. To these, in April, was joined Mr. Clayton, of Brazen-nose, with two or three of his pupils. About the same time Mr. James Hervey was permitted to meet with them; and in 1735, Mr. Whitfield.

5. The exact regularity of their lives, as well as studies, occasioned a young gentleman of Christ Church to say, "Here is a new set of Methodists sprung up;" alluding to some ancient Physicians who were so called. The name was new and quaint; so it took immediately, and the Methodists were known all over the University.

6. They were all zealous members of the Church of England; not only tenacious of all her doctrines, so far as they knew them, but of all her discipline, to the minutest circumstance. They were likewise zealous observers of all the University Statutes, and that for conscience' sake. But they observed neither these nor anything else any further than they conceived it was bound upon them by their one book, the Bible; it being their one desire and design to be downright Bible-Christians; taking the Bible, as interpreted by the primitive Church and our own, for their whole and sole rule.

7. The one charge then advanced against them was, that they were "righteous overmuch;" that they were abundantly too scrupulous, and too strict, carrying things to great extremes: In particular, that they laid too much stress upon the Rubrics and Canons of the Church; that they insisted too much on observing the Statutes of the University; and that they took the Scriptures in too strict and literal a sense; so that if they were right, few indeed would be saved.

8. In October, 1735, Mr. John and Charles Wesley, and Mr. Ingham, left England, with a design to go and preach to the Indians in Georgia: But the rest of the gentlemen continued to meet, till one and another was ordained and left the University. By which means, in about two years' time, scarce any of them were left.

9. In February, 1738, Mr. Whitefield went over to Georgia with a design to assist Mr. John Wesley; but Mr. Wesley just then returned to England. Soon after he had a meeting with Messrs. Ingham, Stonehouse, Hall, Hutchings, Kinchin, and a few other Clergymen, who all appeared to be of one heart, as well as of one judgment, resolved to be Bible-Christians at all events; and, wherever they were, to preach with all their might plain, old, Bible Christianity.

10. They were hitherto perfectly regular in all things, and zealously attached to the Church of England. Meantime, they began to be convinced, that "by grace we are saved through faith;" that justification by faith was the doctrine of the Church, as well as of the Bible. As soon as they believed, they spake; salvation by faith being now their standing topic. Indeed this implied three things:

(1.) That men are all, by nature, "dead in sin," and, consequently, "children of wrath."

(2.) That they are "justified by faith alone."

(3.) That faith produces inward and outward holiness: And these points they insisted on day and night. In a short time they became popular Preachers. The congregations were large wherever they preached. The former name was then revived; and all these gentlemen, with their followers, were entitled Methodists.

11. In March, 1741, Mr. Whitefield, being returned to England, entirely separated from Mr. Wesley and his friends, because he did not hold the decrees. Here was the first breach, which warm men persuaded Mr. Whitefield to make merely for a difference of opinion. Those, indeed, who believed universal redemption had no desire at all to separate; but those who held particular redemption would not hear of any accommodation, being

determined to have no fellowship with men that "were in so dangerous errors." So there were now two sorts of Methodists, so called; those for particular, and those for general, redemption.

12. Not many years passed, before William Cudworth and James Relly separated from Mr. Whitefield. These were properly Antinomians; absolute, avowed enemies to the law of God, which they never preached or professed to preach, but termed all legalists who did. With them, "preaching the law" was an abomination. They had "nothing to do" with the law. They would "preach Christ," as they called it, but without one word either of holiness or good works. Yet these were still denominated Methodists, although differing from Mr. Whitefield, both in judgment and practice, abundantly more than Mr. Whitefield did from Mr. Wesley.

13. In the mean time, Mr. Venn and Mr. Romaine began to be spoken of; and not long after Mr. Madan and Mr. Berridge, with a few other Clergymen, who, although they had no Bridge with each other, yet preaching salvation by faith, and endeavoring to live accordingly, to be Bible-Christians, were soon included in the general name of Methodists. And so indeed were all others who preached salvation by faith, and appeared more serious than their neighbors. Some of these were quite regular in their manner of preaching; some were quite irregular; (though not by choice; but necessity was laid upon them; they must preach irregularly, or not at all;) and others were between both, regular in most, though not in all, particulars.

14. In 1762, George Bell, and a few other persons, began to speak great words. In the latter end of the year, they foretold that the world would be at an end on the 28th of February. Mr. Wesley, with whom they were then connected, withstood them both in public and private. This they would not endure; so, in January and February, 1763, they separated from him. Soon after, Mr. Maxfield, one of Mr. Wesley's Preachers, and several of the people, left Mr. Wesley; but still Mr. Maxfield and his adherents go under the general name of Methodists.

15. At present, those who remain with Mr. Wesley are mostly Church-of-England men, though they do not love their opinions. Yea, they love the Antinomians themselves; but it is with a love of compassion only: For they hate their doctrines with a perfect hatred; they abhor them as they do hell-fire; being convinced nothing can so effectually destroy all faith, all holiness, and all good works.

16. With regard to these, Mr. Relly and his adherents, it would not he strange if they should grow into reputation. For they will never shock the world, either by the harshness of their doctrine, or the singularity of their behavior. But let those who determine both to preach and to live the Gospel expect that men will say "all manner of evil of them." "The servant is not above his Master, nor the disciple above his Lord. If, then, they have called the master of the house Beelzebub, how much more them of his household?" It is their duty, indeed, "as much as lieth in them, to live peaceably with all men." But when they

labor after peace, the world will "make themselves ready for battle." It is their constant endeavor to "please all men, for their good, to edification." But yet they know it cannot be done: They remember the word of the Apostle, "If I yet please men, I am not the servant of Christ." They go on, therefore, "through honor and dishonor, through evil report and good report;" desiring only, that their Master may say in that day, "Servants of God, well done!"

John Wesley

Charles Wesley (1707–1788)
A collection of some of Charles Wesley's well known hymns

And Can It Be that I Should Gain
And can it be that I should gain
An interest in the Savior's blood?
Died He for me, who caused His pain—
For me, who Him to death pursued?
Amazing love! How can it be,
That Thou, my God, shouldst die for me?
Amazing love! How can it be,
That Thou, my God, shouldst die for me?

'Tis mystery all: th'Immortal dies:
Who can explore His strange design?
In vain the firstborn seraph tries
To sound the depths of love divine.
'Tis mercy all! Let earth adore,
Let angel minds inquire no more.
'Tis mercy all! Let earth adore;
Let angel minds inquire no more.

He left His Father's throne above
So free, so infinite His grace—
Emptied Himself of all but love,
And bled for Adam's helpless race:
'Tis mercy all, immense and free,
For O my God, it found out me!
'Tis mercy all, immense and free,
For O my God, it found out me!

Long my imprisoned spirit lay,
Fast bound in sin and nature's night;
Thine eye diffused a quickening ray—
I woke, the dungeon flamed with light;
My chains fell off, my heart was free,
I rose, went forth, and followed Thee.
My chains fell off, my heart was free,
I rose, went forth, and followed Thee.

Still the small inward voice I hear,
That whispers all my sins forgiven;
Still the atoning blood is near,
That quenched the wrath of hostile Heaven.
I feel the life His wounds impart;
I feel the Savior in my heart.
I feel the life His wounds impart;
I feel the Savior in my heart.

No condemnation now I dread;
Jesus, and all in Him, is mine;
Alive in Him, my living Head,
And clothed in righteousness divine,
Bold I approach th'eternal throne,
And claim the crown, through Christ my own.
Bold I approach th'eternal throne,
And claim the crown, through Christ my own.

Gentle Jesus, Meek and Mild

Gentle Jesus, meek and mild,
Look upon a little child;
Pity my simplicity,
Suffer me to come to Thee.

Lamb of God, I look to Thee;
Thou shalt my Example be;
Thou art gentle, meek, and mild;
Thou wast once a little child.

Lord, I would be as Thou art;
Give me Thine obedient heart;
Thou art pitiful and kind,
Let me have Thy loving mind.

Let me, above all, fulfill
God my heav'nly Father's will;
Never His good Spirit grieve;
Only to His glory live.

Loving Jesus, gentle Lamb,
In Thy gracious hands I am;
Make me, Savior, what Thou art,
Live Thyself within my heart.

Hark! The herald Angels Sing
Hark! The herald angels sing,
"Glory to the newborn King;
Peace on earth, and mercy mild,
God and sinners reconciled!"
Joyful, all ye nations rise,
Join the triumph of the skies;
With th'angelic host proclaim,
"Christ is born in Bethlehem!"

Refrain

Hark! the herald angels sing,
"Glory to the newborn King!"
Christ, by highest Heav'n adored;
Christ the everlasting Lord;
Late in time, behold Him come,
Offspring of a virgin's womb.
Veiled in flesh the Godhead see;
Hail th'incarnate Deity,
Pleased with us in flesh to dwell,
Jesus our Emmanuel.

Refrain

Hail the heav'nly Prince of Peace!
Hail the Sun of Righteousness!
Light and life to all He brings,
Ris'n with healing in His wings.
Mild He lays His glory by,
Born that man no more may die.
Born to raise the sons of earth,
Born to give them second birth.

Refrain

Come, Desire of nations, come,
Fix in us Thy humble home;
Rise, the woman's conqu'ring Seed,
Bruise in us the serpent's head.
Now display Thy saving power,
Ruined nature now restore;
Now in mystic union join
Thine to ours, and ours to Thine.

Refrain

Adam's likeness, Lord, efface,
Stamp Thine image in its place:
Second Adam from above,
Reinstate us in Thy love.
Let us Thee, though lost, regain,
Thee, the Life, the inner man:
O, to all Thyself impart,
Formed in each believing heart.

Refrain

Jesus, Lover of My Soul, Let Me to Thy Bosom Fly

Jesus, lover of my soul, let me to Thy bosom fly,
While the nearer waters roll, while the tempest still is high.
Hide me, O my Savior, hide, till the storm of life is past;
Safe into the haven guide; O receive my soul at last.

Other refuge have I none, hangs my helpless soul on Thee;
Leave, ah! leave me not alone, still support and comfort me.
All my trust on Thee is stayed, all my help from Thee I bring;
Cover my defenseless head with the shadow of Thy wing.

Wilt Thou not regard my call? Wilt Thou not accept my prayer?
Lo! I sink, I faint, I fall—Lo! on Thee I cast my care;
Reach me out Thy gracious hand! While I of Thy strength receive,
Hoping against hope I stand, dying, and behold, I live.

Thou, O Christ, art all I want, more than all in Thee I find;
Raise the fallen, cheer the faint, heal the sick, and lead the blind.
Just and holy is Thy Name, I am all unrighteousness;
False and full of sin I am; Thou art full of truth and grace.
Plenteous grace with Thee is found, grace to cover all my sin;
Let the healing streams abound; make and keep me pure within.
Thou of life the fountain art, freely let me take of Thee;
Spring Thou up within my heart; rise to all eternity.

Love Divine, All Loves Excelling

Love divine, all loves excelling,
Joy of heaven to earth come down;
Fix in us thy humble dwelling;
All thy faithful mercies crown!
Jesus, Thou art all compassion,
Pure unbounded love Thou art;
Visit us with Thy salvation;
Enter every trembling heart.
Breathe, O breathe Thy loving Spirit,
Into every troubled breast!
Let us all in Thee inherit;
Let us find that second rest.
Take away our bent to sinning;
Alpha and Omega be;
End of faith, as its Beginning,
Set our hearts at liberty.

Come, Almighty to deliver,
Let us all Thy life receive;
Suddenly return and never,
Never more Thy temples leave.
Thee we would be always blessing,
Serve Thee as Thy hosts above,
Pray and praise Thee without ceasing,
Glory in Thy perfect love.

Finish, then, Thy new creation;
Pure and spotless let us be.
Let us see Thy great salvation
Perfectly restored in Thee;
Changed from glory into glory,
Till in heaven we take our place,
Till we cast our crowns before Thee,
Lost in wonder, love, and praise.

O For a Thousand Tongues to Sing

[Wesley wrote this hymn to commemorate the first anniversary of his conversion to Christ.]

O for a thousand tongues to sing
My great Redeemer's praise,
The glories of my God and King,
The triumphs of His grace!

My gracious Master and my God,
Assist me to proclaim,
To spread through all the earth abroad
The honors of Thy name.

Jesus! the name that charms our fears,
That bids our sorrows cease;
'Tis music in the sinner's ears,
'Tis life, and health, and peace.

He breaks the power of canceled sin,
He sets the prisoner free;
His blood can make the foulest clean,
His blood availed for me.
He speaks, and, listening to His voice,
New life the dead receive,
The mournful, broken hearts rejoice,
The humble poor believe.

Hear Him, ye deaf; His praise, ye dumb,
Your loosened tongues employ;
Ye blind, behold your Savior come,
And leap, ye lame, for joy.

In Christ your Head, you then shall know,
Shall feel your sins forgiven;
Anticipate your heaven below,
And own that love is heaven.

Glory to God, and praise and love
Be ever, ever given,
By saints below and saints above,
The church in earth and heaven.

On this glad day the glorious Sun
Of Righteousness arose;
On my benighted soul He shone
And filled it with repose.

Sudden expired the legal strife,
'Twas then I ceased to grieve;
My second, real, living life
I then began to live.

Then with my heart I first believed,
Believed with faith divine,
Power with the Holy Ghost received
To call the Savior mine.

I felt my Lord's atoning blood
Close to my soul applied;
Me, me He loved, the Son of God,
For me, for me He died!
I found and owned His promise true,
Ascertained of my part,
My pardon passed in heaven I knew
When written on my heart.

Look unto Him, ye nations, own
Your God, ye fallen race;
Look, and be saved through faith alone,
Be justified by grace.
See all your sins on Jesus laid:
The Lamb of God was slain,
His soul was once an offering made
For every soul of man.

Awake from guilty nature's sleep,
And Christ shall give you light,
Cast all your sins into the deep,
And wash the Æthiop white.

Harlots and publicans and thieves
In holy triumph join!
Saved is the sinner that believes
From crimes as great as mine.

Murderers and all ye hellish crew
In holy triumph join!
Believe the Savior died for you;
For me the Savior died.

With me, your chief, ye then shall know,
Shall feel your sins forgiven;
Anticipate your heaven below,
And own that love is heaven.
Charles Wesley

George Whitefield (1714–1770)

The Almost Christian

Acts 26:28, "Almost thou persuadest me to be a Christian."

From the words of the text, shall endeavor to show these three things:

FIRST, What is meant by an almost-Christian.

SECONDLY, What are the chief reasons, why so many are no more than almost Christians.

THIRDLY, I shall consider the ineffectualness, danger, absurdity, and uneasiness which attends those who are but almost Christians; and then conclude with a general exhortation, to set all upon striving not only be almost, but altogether Christians.

I. And, FIRST, I am to consider what is meant by an almost Christians.

An almost Christian, if we consider him in respect to his duty to God, is one that halts between two opinions; that wavers between Christ and the world; that would reconcile God and Mammon, light and darkness, Christ and Belial. It is true, he has an inclination to religion, but then he is very cautious how he goes too far in it: his false heart is always crying out, Spare thyself, do thyself no harm. He prays indeed, that "God's will may be done on earth, as it is in heaven." But notwithstanding, he is very partial in his obedience, and fondly hopes that God will not be extreme to mark every thing that he willfully does amiss; though an inspired apostle has told him, that "he who offends in one point is guilty of all." But chiefly, he is one that depends much on outward ordinances, and on that account looks upon himself as righteous, and despises others; though at the same time he is as great a stranger to the divine life as any other person whatsoever. In short, he is fond of the form, but never experiences the power of godliness in his heart. He goes on year after year, attending on the means of grace, but then, like Pharaoh's lean cow, he is never the better, but rather the worse for them.

But to proceed in the character of an ALMOST CHRISTIAN: If we consider him in respect of himself; as we said he was strictly honest to his neighbor, so he is likewise strictly sober in himself: but then both his honesty and sobriety proceed from the same principle of a false self-love. It is true, he runs not into the same excess of riot with other men; but then it is not out of obedience to the laws of God, but either because his constitution will not away with intemperance; or rather because he is cautious of forfeiting his reputation, or unfitting himself for temporal business. But though he is so prudent as to avoid intemperance and excess, for the reasons before-mentioned; yet he always goes to the extremity of what is lawful. It is true, he is no drunkard; but then he has no CHRISTIAN SELF-DENIAL.

He cannot think our Savior to be so austere a Master, as to deny us to indulge ourselves in some particulars: and so by this means he is destitute of a sense of true religion, as much as if he lived in debauchery, or any other crime whatever. As to settling his principles as well as practice, he is guided more by the world, than by the word of God: for his part, he cannot think the way to heaven so narrow as some would make it; and therefore considers not so much what scripture requires, as what such and such a good man does, or what will best suit his own corrupt inclinations. Upon this account, he is not only very cautious himself, but likewise very careful of young converts, whose faces are set heavenward; and therefore is always acting the devil's part, and bidding them spare themselves, though they are doing no more than what the scripture strictly requires them to do: The consequence of which is, that "he suffers not himself to enter into the kingdom of God, and those that are entering in he hinders."

II. I proceed to the second general thing proposed; to consider the reasons why so many are no more than almost Christians.

1. And the first reason I shall mention is, because so many set out with false notions of religion; though they live in a Christian country, yet they know not what Christianity is. This perhaps may be esteemed a hard saying, but experience sadly evinces the truth of it; for some place religion in being of this or that communion; more in morality; most in a round of duties, and a model of performances; and few, very few acknowledge it to be, what it really is, a thorough inward change of nature, a divine life, a vital participation of Jesus Christ, an union of the soul with God; which the apostle expresses by saying, "He that is joined to the Lord is one spirit." Hence it happens, that so many, even of the most knowing professors, when you come to converse with them concerning the essence, the life, the soul of religion, I mean our new birth in Jesus Christ, confess themselves quite ignorant of the matter, and cry out with Nicodemus, "How can this thing be?" And no wonder then, that so many are only almost Christians, when so many know not what Christianity is: no marvel, that so many take up with the form, when they are quite strangers to the power of godliness; or content themselves with the shadow, when they know so little about the substance of it. And this is one cause why so many are almost, and so few are altogether Christians.

2. A second reason that may be assigned why so many are no more than almost Christians, is a servile fear of man: multitudes there are and have been, who, though awakened to a sense of the divine life, and have tasted and felt the powers of the world to come; yet out of a base sinful fear of being counted singular, or contemned by men, have suffered all those good impressions to wear off. It is true, they have some esteem for Jesus Christ; but then, like Nicodemus, they would come to him only by night: they are willing to serve him; but then they would do it secretly, for fear of the Jews: they have a mind to see Jesus, but then they cannot come to him because of the press, and for fear of being laughed at, and ridiculed by those with whom they used to sit at meat. But well did our Savior prophesy of such persons, "How can ye love me, who receive honor one of another?" Alas! have they never read, that "the friendship of this world is enmity with God;" and that our

Lord himself has threatened, "Whosoever shall be ashamed of me or of my words, in this wicked and adulterous generation, of him shall the Son of man be ashamed, when he cometh in the glory of his Father and of his holy angels?" No wonder that so many are no more than almost Christians, since so many "love the praise of men more than the honor which cometh of God."

3. A third reason why so many are no more than almost Christians, is a reigning love of money. This was the pitiable case of that forward young man in the gospel, who came running to our blessed Lord, and kneeling before him, inquired "what he must do to inherit eternal life;" to whom our blessed Master replied, "Thou knowest the commandments, Do not kill, Do not commit adultery, Do not steal:" To which the young man replied, "All these have I kept from my youth." But when our Lord proceeded to tell him, "Yet lackest thou one thing; Go sell all that thou hast, and give to the poor; he was grieved at that saying, and went away sorrowful, for he had great possessions!" Poor youth! He had a good mind to be a Christian, and to inherit eternal life, but thought it too dear, if it could be purchased at no less an expense than of his estate! And thus many, both young and old, now-a-days, come running to worship our blessed Lord in public, and kneel before him in private, and inquire at his gospel, what they must do to inherit eternal life: but when they find they must renounce the self-enjoyment of riches, and forsake all in affection to follow him, they cry, "The Lord pardon us in this thing! We pray thee, have us excused."

But is heaven so small a trifle in men's esteem, as not to be worth a little gilded earth? Is eternal life so mean a purchase, as not to deserve the temporary renunciation of a few transitory riches? Surely it is. But however inconsistent such a behavior may be, this inordinate love of money is too evidently the common and fatal cause, why so many are no more than almost Christians.

4. Nor is the love of pleasure a less uncommon, or a less fatal cause why so many are no more than almost Christians. Thousands and ten thousands there are, who despise riches, and would willingly be true disciples of Jesus Christ, if parting with their money would make them so; but when they are told that our blessed Lord has said, "Whosoever will come after him must deny himself;" like the pitiable young man before-mentioned, "they go away sorrowful"" for they have too great a love for sensual pleasures. They will perhaps send for the ministers of Christ, as Herod did for John, and hear them gladly: but touch them in their Herodias, tell them they must part with such or such a darling pleasure; and with wicked Ahab they cry out, "Hast thou found us, O our enemy?" Tell them of the necessity of mortification and self-denial, and it is as difficult for them to hear, as if you was to bid them "cut off a right-hand, or pluck out a right-eye." They cannot think our blessed Lord requires so much at their hands, though an inspired apostle has commanded us to "mortify our members which are upon earth." And who himself, even after he had converted thousands, and was very near arrived to the end of his race, yet professed that it was his

daily practice to "keep under his body, and bring it into subjection, lest after he had preached to others, he himself should be a cast-away!"

5. The fifth and last reason I shall assign why so many are only almost Christians, is a fickleness and instability of temper.

It has been, no doubt, a misfortune that many a minister and sincere Christian has met with, to weep and wail over numbers of promising converts, who seemingly began in the Spirit, but after a while fell away, and basely ended in the flesh; and this not for want of right notions in religion, nor out of a servile fear of man, nor from the love of money, or of sensual pleasure, but through an instability and fickleness of temper. They looked upon religion merely for novelty, as something which pleased them for a while; but after their curiosity was satisfied, they laid it aside again: like the young man that came to see Jesus with a linen cloth about his naked body, they have followed him for a season, but when temptations came to take hold on them, for want of a little more resolution, they have been stripped of all their good intentions, and fled away naked. They at first, like a tree planted by the water-side, grew up and flourished for a while; but having no root in themselves, no inward principle of holiness and piety, like Jonah's gourd, they were soon dried up and withered. Their good intentions are too like the violent motions of the animal spirits of a body newly beheaded, which, though impetuous, are not lasting. In short, they set out well in their journey to heaven, but finding the way either narrower or longer than they expected, through an unsteadiness of temper, they have made an eternal halt, and so "returned like the dog to his vomit, or like the sow that was washed to her wallowing in the more!"

III. Proceed we now to the general thing proposed, namely, to consider the folly of being no more than an almost Christian.

1. And the FIRST proof I shall give of the folly of such a proceeding is, that it is ineffectual to salvation. It is true, such men are almost good; but almost to hit the mark, is really to miss it. God requires us "to love him with all our hearts, with all our souls, and with all our strength." He loves us too well to admit any rival; because, so far as our hearts are empty of God, so far must they be unhappy. The devil, indeed, like the false mother that came before Solomon, would have our hearts divided, as she would have had the child; but God, like the true mother, will have all or none. "My Son, give me thy heart," thy whole heart, is the general call to all: and if this be not done, we never can expect the divine mercy.

Persons may play the hypocrite; but God at the great day will strike them dead, (as he did Ananias and Sapphira by the mouth of his servant Peter) for pretending to offer him all their hearts, when they keep back from him the greatest part. They may perhaps impose upon their fellow-creatures for a while; but he that enabled Elijah to cry out, "Come in thou wife of Jeroboam," when she came disguised to inquire about he sick son, will also discover them through their most artful dissimulations; and if their hearts are not wholly with him, appoint them their portion with hypocrites and unbelievers.

2. But, SECONDLY, What renders an half-way-piety more inexcusable is, that it is not only insufficient to our own salvation, but also very prejudicial to that of others.

An almost Christian is one of the most hurtful creatures in the world; he is a wolf in sheep's clothing: he is one of those false prophets, our blessed Lord bids us beware of in his sermon on the mount, who would persuade men, that the way to heaven is broader than it really is; and thereby, as it was observed before, "enter not into the kingdom of God themselves, and those that are entering in they hinder." These, these are the men that turn the world into a luke-warm Laodicean spirit; that hang out false lights, and so shipwreck unthinking benighted souls in their voyage to the haven of eternity. These are they who are greater enemies to the cross of Christ, than infidels themselves: for of an unbeliever every one will be aware; but an almost Christian, through his subtle hypocrisy, draws away many after him; and therefore must expect to receive the greater damnation.

3. But, THIRDLY, As it is most prejudicial to ourselves and hurtful to others, so it is the greatest instance of ingratitude we can express towards our Lord and Master Jesus Christ. For did he come down from heaven, and shed his precious blood, to purchase these hearts of ours, and shall we only give him half of them? O how can we say we love him, when our hearts are not wholly with him? How can we call him our Savior, when we will not endeavor sincerely to approve ourselves to him, and so let him see the travail of his soul, and be satisfied!

Had any of us purchased a slave at a most expensive rate, and who was before involved in the utmost miseries and torments, and so must have continued for ever, had we shut up our bowels of compassion from him; and was this slave afterwards to grow rebellious, or deny giving us but half his service; how, how should we exclaim against his base ingratitude! And yet this base ungrateful slave thou art, O man, who acknowledgest thyself to be redeemed from infinite unavoidable misery and punishment by the death of Jesus Christ, and yet wilt not give thyself wholly to him.

Let me therefore, to conclude, exhort you, my brethren, to have always before you the unspeakable happiness of enjoying God. And think withal, that every degree of holiness you neglect, every act of piety you omit, is a jewel taken out of your crown, a degree of blessedness lost in the vision of God. O! do but always think and act thus, and you will no longer be laboring to compound matters between God and the world; but, on the contrary, be daily endeavoring to give up yourselves more and more unto him; you will be always watching, always praying, always aspiring after farther degrees of purity and love, and consequently always preparing yourselves for a fuller sight and enjoyment of that God, in whose presence there is fullness of joy, and at whose right-hand there are pleasures for ever more. Amen! Amen!

George Whitefield

David Brainerd (1718–1747)
David Brainerd's Journal

The Journal having been so much referred to in the Life and Diary, and being originally a part of the Diary itself, this work would be very imperfect without it. It was first printed not only in two parts, but with some variation in the Titles, which are here subjoined.

The First Part was,
Mirabilia Dei inter Indicos;
Or
The Rise and Progress of a remarkable Work of Grace Amongst a number of the Indians, In the Provinces of New Jersey and Pennsylvania; Justly represented in a JOURNAL kept by order of the Honorable Society (in Scotland) for Propagating Christian Knowledge; with some General Remarks;
By David Brainerd
Minister of the Gospel, and Missionary from the said Society

The Second Part was,
Divine Grace Displayed; Or
The Continuance and Progress of a remarkable Work of Grace Among some of the Indians Belonging to the Provinces of New Jersey and Pennsylvania; Justly represented in a JOURNAL kept by order of the Honorable Society (in Scotland) for Propagating Christian Knowledge; with some General Remarks; To which is subjoined an Appendix, containing some account of sundry things, especially of the Difficulties attending the Work of a Missionary among the Indians:
By David Brainerd
DAVID BRAINERD,
Minister of the Gospel, and Missionary from the said Society

Preface
The design of this publication is to give God the glory of his distinguishing grace, and gratify the pious curiosity of those who are waiting and praying for that blessed time, when the Son of God, in a more extensive sense than has yet been accomplished, shall receive the heathen for his inheritance, and the uttermost parts of the earth for a possession.

Whenever any of the guilty race of mankind are awakened to a just concern for their eternal interest, are humbled at the footstool of a sovereign God, and are persuaded and enabled to accept the offers of redeeming love, it must always be acknowledged a wonderful work of divine grace, which demands our thankful praises. But doubtless it is a more affecting evidence of almighty power, a more illustrious display of sovereign mercy, when those are enlightened with the knowledge of salvation, who have for many ages dwelt in the grossest darkness and heathenism, and are brought to a cheerful subjection to the government of our divine Redeemer, who from generation to generation had remained the voluntary slaves of the prince of darkness.

This is that delightful scene which will present itself to the reader's view, while he attentively peruses the following pages. Nothing certainly can be more agreeable to a benevolent and religious mind, than to see those that were sunk in the most degenerate state of human nature, at once, not only renounce those barbarous customs they had been inured to from their infancy, but surprisingly transformed into the character of real and devout Christians.

This mighty change was brought about by the plain and faithful preaching of the gospel, attended with an uncommon effusion of the divine Spirit, under the ministry of the Reverend David Brainerd, a Missionary employed by the Honorable Society in Scotland, for propagating CHRISTIAN KNOWLEDGE.

And surely it will administer abundant matter of praise and thanksgiving to that honorable body, to find that their generous attempt to send the gospel among the Indian nations upon the borders of New York, New Jersey, and Pennsylvania, has met with such surprising success.

It would perhaps have been more agreeable to the taste of politer readers, if the following Journal had been cast into a different method, and formed into one connected narrative. But the worthy author, amidst his continued labors, had no time to spare for such an undertaking. Besides, the pious reader will take a peculiar pleasure to see this work described in its native simplicity, and the operations of the Spirit upon the minds of these poor benighted pagans, laid down just in the method and order in which they happened. This, it must be confessed, will occasion frequent repetitions; but these, as they tend to give a fuller view of this amazing dispensation of divine grace in its rise and progress, we trust, will be easily forgiven.

When we see such numbers of the most ignorant and barbarous of mankind, in the space of a few months, turned from darkness to light, and from the power of sin and Satan unto God, it gives us encouragement to wait and pray for that blessed time, when our victorious Redeemer shall, in a more signal manner than he has yet done, display the banner of his cross, march on from conquering to conquer, till the kingdoms of this world are become the kingdoms of our Lord and of his Christ. Yea, we cannot but lift up our heads with joy, and hope that it may be the dawn of that bright and illustrious day, when the SUN OF RIGHTEOUSNESS shall arise and shine from one end of the earth to the other; when, to use the language of the inspired prophets, the Gentiles shall come to his light, and kings to the brightness of his rising; in consequence of which, the wilderness and solitary places shall be glad, and the desert rejoice and blossom as the rose.

It is doubtless the duty of all, in their different stations, and according to their respective capacities, to use their utmost endeavors to bring forward this promised, this desired day.

There is a great want of schoolmasters among these christianized Indians, to instruct their youth in the English language, and the principles of the Christian faith; for this as yet, there is no certain provision made: if any are inclined to contribute to so good a design, we are persuaded they will do an acceptable service to the kingdom of the Redeemer. And we earnestly desire the most indigent to join, at least, in their wishes and prayers, that this work may prosper more and more, till the whole earth is filled with the glory of the Lord.

The Rise and Progress of a remarkable Work of Grace Amongst a number of the Indians, In the Provinces of New Jersey and Pennsylvania

Part 1

From 1745, June 19th to November 14th, at Crossweeksung and Forks of Delaware

Crossweeksung, in New Jersey, June, 1745.

June 19

Having spent most of my time for more than a year past amongst the Indians in the Forks of Delaware in Pennsylvania; and having in that time made two journeys to Susquehannah river, far back in that province, in order to treat with the Indians there, respecting Christianity; and not having had any considerable appearance of special success in either of those places, which damped my spirits, and was not a little discouraging to me: upon hearing that there was a number of Indians in and about a place called (by the Indians) Crossweeksung in New Jersey, near fourscore miles south-eastward from the Forks of Delaware, I determined to make them a visit, and see what might be done towards the christianizing of them; and accordingly arrived among them this day.

I found very few persons at the place I visited, and perceived the Indians in these parts were very much scattered, there being not more than two or three families in a place, and these small settlements six, ten, fifteen, twenty, and thirty miles, and some more, from the place I was then at. However, I preached to those few I found, who appeared well disposed, and not inclined to object and cavil, as the Indians had frequently done elsewhere.

When I had concluded my discourse, I informed them (there being none but a few women and children) that I would willingly visit them again the next day. Whereupon they readily set out, and traveled ten or fifteen miles, in order to give notice to some of their friends at that distance. These women, like the woman of Samaria, seemed desirous that others might see the man that told them what they had done in their lives past, and the misery that attended their idolatrous ways.

June 20

Visited and preached to the Indians again as I proposed. Numbers more were gathered at the invitations of their friends, who heard me the day before. These also appeared as attentive, orderly, and well disposed as the others. And none made any objection, as Indians in other places have usually done.

June 22

Preached to the Indians again. Their number, which at first consisted of about seven or eight persons, was now increased to near thirty. There was not only a solemn attention among them, but some considerable impressions, it was apparent, were made upon their minds by divine truths. Some began to feel their misery and perishing state, and appeared concerned for a deliverance from it.

Lord's day, June 23

Preached to the Indians, and spent the day with them. Their number still increased; and all with one consent seemed to rejoice in my coming among them. Not a word of opposition was heard from any of them against Christianity, although in times past they had been as opposite to any thing of that nature, as any Indians whatsoever. And some of them not many months before, were enraged with my interpreter, because he attempted to teach them something of Christianity.

June 24

Preached to the Indians at their desire, and upon their own motion. To see poor pagans desirous of hearing the gospel of Christ, animated me to discourse to them, although I was now very weakly, and my spirits much exhausted. They attended with the greatest seriousness and diligence; and there was some concern for their souls' salvation apparent among them.

June 27

Visited and preached to the Indians again. Their number now amounted to about forty persons. Their solemnity and attention still continued; and a considerable concern for their souls became very apparent among sundry of them.

June 28

The Indians being now gathered, a considerable number of them, from their several and distant habitations, requested me to preach twice a day to them, being desirous to hear as much as they possibly could while I was with them. I cheerfully complied with their motion, and could not but admire the goodness of God, who, I was persuaded, had inclined them thus to inquire after the way of salvation.

June 29

Preached again twice to the Indians. Saw, as I thought, the hand of God very evidently, and in a manner somewhat remarkable, making provision for their subsistence together, in order to their being instructed in divine things. For this day and the day before, with only walking a little way from the place of our daily meeting, they killed three deer, which were a seasonable supply for their wants, and without which, it seems, they could not have subsisted together in order to attend the means of grace.

Lord's day, June 30

Preached twice this day also. Observed yet more concern and affection among the poor heathens than ever; so that they even constrained me to tarry yet longer with them; although my constitution was exceedingly worn out, and my health much impaired by my late fatigues and labors, and especially by my late journey to Susquehannah in May last, in which lodged on the ground for several weeks together.

July 1

Preached again twice to a very serious and attentive assembly of Indians, they having now learned to attend the worship of God with Christian decency in all respects. There were now between forty and fifty persons of them present, old and young. I spent some considerable time in discoursing with them in a more private way, inquiring of them what they remembered of the great truths that had been taught them from day to day; and may justly say, it was amazing to see how they had received and retained the instructions given them, and what a measure of knowledge some of them had acquired in a few days.

July 2

Was obliged to leave these Indians at Crossweeksung, thinking it my duty, as soon as health would admit, again to visit those at the Forks of Delaware. When I came to take leave of them, and spoke something particularly to each of them, they all earnestly inquired when I would come again, and expressed a great desire of being further instructed. And of their own accord agreed, that when I should come again, they would all meet and live together during my continuance with them; and that they would do their utmost endeavors to gather all the Indians in these parts that were yet further remote. And when I parted, one told me with many tears, She wished God would change her heart: another, that she wanted to find Christ: and an old man that had been one of their chiefs, wept bitterly with concern for his soul. I then promised them to return as speedily as my health and business elsewhere would admit, and felt not a little concerned at parting, lest the good impressions then apparent upon numbers of them, might decline and wear off, when the means came to cease; and yet could not but hope that he who, I trusted, had begun a good work among them, and who I knew did not stand in need of means to carry it on, would maintain and promote it. At the same time I must confess, that I had often seen encouraging appearances among the Indians elsewhere prove wholly abortive; and it appeared the favor would be so great, if God should now, after I had passed through so considerable a series of almost fruitless labors and fatigues, and after my rising hopes had been so often frustrated among these poor pagans, give me any special success in my labors with them. I could not believe, and scarce dared to hope, that the event would be so happy, and scarce ever found myself more suspended between hope and fear, in any affair, or at any time, than this.

This encouraging disposition and readiness to receive instruction, now apparent among these Indians, seems to have been the happy effect of the conviction that one or two of them met with some time since at the Forks of Delaware, who have since endeavored to show their friends the evil of idolatry, &c. And although the other Indians seemed but little to regard, but rather to deride them, yet this, perhaps, has put them into a thinking posture of mind, or at least, given them some thoughts about Christianity, and excited in some of them a curiosity to hear, and so made way for the present encouraging attention. An apprehension that this might be the case here, has given me encouragement that God may in such a manner bless the means I have used with Indians in other places, where there is as yet no appearance of it. If so, may his name have the glory of it; for I have learned by experience that he only can open the ear, engage the attention, and incline the heart of poor benighted, prejudiced pagans to receive instruction.

David Brainerd

History of Bible translations

Number of languages Bible had been translated into during this period.

1600
    36 languages
1700
    52 languages
1800
    67 languages

Examples of Bible translations from the age of reason and revival

The 1663 Eliot Bible: The First Bible printed in America

Many people are shocked to discover that the first Bible printed in America was not English . . . or any other European language. In fact, English and European language Bibles would not be printed in America until a century later! Eliot's Bible did much more than bring the Gospel to the pagan natives who were worshiping creation rather than the Creator . . . it gave them literacy, as they did not have a written language of their own until this Bible was printed for them.

1782 Robert Aitken's Bible; The First English Language Bible (a King James Version without Apocrypha) to be printed in America

Although the first Bible printed in America was done in the native Algonquin Indian Language by John Eliot in 1663; the first English language Bible to be printed in America by Robert Aitken in 1782 was a King James Version. Robert Aitken's 1782 Bible was also the only Bible ever authorized by the United States Congress. He was commended by President George Washington for providing Americans with Bibles during the embargo of imported English goods due to the Revolutionary War. In 1808, Robert's daughter, Jane Aitken, would become the first woman to ever print a Bible . . . and to do so in America, of course.

1791 Isaac Collins and Isaiah Thomas Respectively Produce the First Family Bible and First Illustrated Bible Printed in America. Both were King James Versions.

In 1791, Isaac Collins vastly improved upon the quality and size of the typesetting of American Bibles and produced the first "Family Bible" printed in America . . . also a King James Version. Also in 1791, Isaiah Thomas published the first Illustrated Bible printed in America . . . in the King James Version. For more information on the earliest Bibles printed in America from the 1600's through the early 1800's, you may wish to review our more detailed discussion of The Bibles of Colonial America.

CHAPTER 7

THE CHRISTIAN CHURCH IN THE NINETEENTH CENTURY

William Wilberforce to Ira Sankey
AD 1800–1899

Important dates in the time of the Christian Church in the Nineteenth-Century

1800 Friedrich Schleiermacher and beginning of Liberal Christianity movement
1801 Cane Ridge revival
1804 British and Foreign Bible Society formed
1807 Wilberforce and anti-slavery movement succeeds in abolishing slave trade
1811 The Campbells begins Disciples of Christ and sparks Restoration Movement
1812 Adoniram and Ann Judson sail for India: the first missionaries to be sent from America
1816 The former slave Richard Allen founds the first African-American denomination: African Methodist Episcopal Church
1816 American Bible Society founded
1817 Elizabeth Fry begins ministry to women in prisons and forms committee to Newgate Prison
1819 Thomas Jefferson produces Jefferson Bible
1828 Plymouth Brethren founded
1830 Charles Finney's revival meetings and the Second Great Awaking in U.S.
1830 Mormons founded by Joseph Smith
1830 John Nelson Darby helps found the Plymouth Brethren, thus spreading the dispensational view of Scriptural interpretation
1833 John Keble's sermon "National Apostasy" initiates the Oxford movement in England
1845 Southern Baptist Convention formed in Augusta
1846 Adventists: W. Miller
1852 Jehovah's Witnesses: C. Russell
1854 Hudson Taylor arrives in China
1854 Immaculate Conception defined as Catholic dogma
1854 Søren Kierkegaard, founder of Christian existentialism, publishes *Attacks on Christendom*

1854 Charles Haddon Spurgeon becomes pastor in London
1857 David Livingstone publishes *Missionary Travels*
1859 Charles Darwin publishes *Origin of the Species*
1863 Seventh-day Adventist Church officially founded
1865 Salvation Army founded by William Booth
1870 The First Vatican Council declares the Pope infallible
1872 D. L. Moody begins preaching
1879 Christian Science founded by Mary Baker Eddy
1884 Charles Taze Russell founds Bible Student movement (known today as Jehovah's Witnesses)
1886 Moody Bible Institute founded
1886 The Student Volunteer Movement begins and many young people become missionaries
1899 Gideons International founded

Introduction

The nineteenth century is sometimes called the Protestant Century. Protestants established missions throughout the world. Organizations such as the British and Foreign Bible Society, the American Bible Society, the Sunday School Union, and the American Board of Commissioners of Foreign Missions lead in the spread of the Gospel message. Reform societies form to deal with abolition, temperance, prisons, and education

EVENTS

Important events in the Christian Church in the nineteenth century

In America, many sects including Mormons, Jehovah's Witnesses, and Christian Science are established.

New philosophies such as Darwin's evolution, Marx's communism, and Freud's psychology attack the traditional Christian view of life and history. German "higher critics" attack the historical validity of the Scriptures.

Revival leader Charles Finney establishes "new measures" in his revival meetings, believing conversions can be achieved if the right approaches are made.

Dwight L. Moody and Ira Sankey hold large revival meetings on both sides of the Atlantic, while thousands hear Charles Spurgeon preach in London's Tabernacle.

Fanny Crosby, Ira Sankey, Francis Havergal, and others poured out hymns of faith and devotion.

David Livingstone and others open the African continent to missions, while workers with Hudson Taylor's China Inland Mission spread throughout China.

Pope Pius IX condemns liberalism, socialism, and rationalism; he also proclaims the Immaculate Conception of the Virgin Mary. The First Vatican Council declares the Pope infallible in the year 1870.

PEOPLE

Christian leaders in the Church in the nineteenth century

William Wilberforce (1759–1833)
William Carey (1761–1834)
Elizabeth Fry (1780–1845)
Charles Grandison Finney (1792–1875)
Søren Kierkegaard (1813 –1855)
David Livingstone (1813–1873)
C. H. Spurgeon (1834–1892)
D. L. Moody (1837–1899)

American church history

The Second Awakening

The closing years of the eighteenth century show the lowest low-water mark of the lowest ebb-tide of spiritual life in the history of the American church. The demoralization of army life, the fury of political factions, the catchpenny materialist morality of Franklin, the philosophic deism of men like Jefferson, and the popular ribaldry of Tom Paine, had wrought, together with other untoward influences, to bring about a condition of things which to the eye of little faith seemed almost desperate.

From the beginning of the reaction from the stormy excitements of the Great Awakening, nothing had seemed to arouse the New England churches from a lethargic dullness.

From the point of view of the Episcopalian of that day the prospect was even more disheartening. Even the Methodists, the fervor of whose zeal and vitality of whose organization had withstood what seemed severer tests, felt the benumbing influence of this unhappy age. For three years ending in 1796 the total membership diminished at the rate of about four thousand a year.

The people that walked in this gross darkness beheld a great light. In 1796 a Presbyterian minister, James McGready, who for more than ten years had done useful service in Pennsylvania and North Carolina, assumed charge of several Presbyterian churches in that very Logan County which we know through the reminiscences of Peter Cartwright. As he went the round of his scattered congregations his preaching was felt to have peculiar power "to arouse false professors, to awaken a dead church, and warn sinners and lead them to seek the new spiritual life which he himself had found." Three years later two brothers, William and John McGee, one a Presbyterian minister and the other a Methodist, came through the beautiful Cumberland country in Kentucky and Tennessee, speaking, as if in the spirit and power of John the Baptist, to multitudes that gathered from great distances to hear them. On one occasion, in the woods of Logan County, in July, 1800, the gathered families, many of whom came from far, tethered their teams and encamped for several days for the unaccustomed privilege of common worship and Christian preaching. This is believed to have been the first American camp-meeting—an era worth remembering in our history. Not without abundant New Testament antecedents, it naturalized itself at once on our soil as a natural expedient for scattered frontier populations unprovided with settled institutions.

We are happy in having an account of some of these meetings from one who was personally and sympathetically interested in them, Barton Warren Stone, a Presbyterian minister serving his two congregations of Concord and Cane Ridge in Bourbon County:

There, on the edge of a prairie in Logan County, Kentucky, the multitudes came together and continued a number of days and nights encamped on the ground, during which time worship was carried on in some part of the encampment. The scene was new to me and passing strange. It baffled description. Many, very many, fell down as men slain in battle, and continued for hours together in an apparently breathless and motionless state, sometimes for a few moments reviving and exhibiting symptoms of life by a deep groan or piercing shriek, or by a prayer for mercy fervently uttered. After lying there for hours they obtained deliverance. The gloomy cloud that had covered their faces seemed gradually and visibly to disappear, and hope, in smiles, brightened into joy. They would rise, shouting deliverance, and then would address the surrounding multitude in language truly eloquent and impressive. With astonishment did I hear men, women, and children declaring the wonderful works of God and the glorious mysteries of the gospel. Their appeals were solemn, heart-penetrating, bold, and free. Under such circumstances many others would fall down into the same state from which the speakers had just been delivered.

Profoundly impressed by what he had seen and heard, Pastor Stone returned to his double parish in Bourbon County and rehearsed the story of it. "The congregation was affected with awful solemnity, and many returned home weeping." This was in the early spring. Not many months afterward there was a notable springing up of this seed.

A memorable meeting was held at Cane Ridge in August, 1801. The roads were crowded with wagons, carriages, horses, and footmen moving to the solemn camp. It was judged by military men on the ground that between twenty and thirty thousand persons were assembled. Four or five preachers spoke at the same time in different parts of the encampment without confusion. The Methodist and Baptist preachers aided in the work, and all appeared cordially united in it. They were of one mind and soul: the salvation of sinners was the one object. We all engaged in singing the same songs, all united in prayer, all preached the same things. . . . The numbers converted will be known only in eternity. Many things transpired in the meeting which were so much like miracles that they had the same effect as miracles on unbelievers. By them many were convinced that Jesus was the Christ and were persuaded to submit to him. This meeting continued six or seven days and nights, and would have continued longer, but food for the sustenance of such a multitude failed.

In one most important particular the revival of 1800 was happily distinguished from the Great Awakening of 1740. It was not done and over with at the end of a few years, and then followed by a long period of reaction. It was the beginning of a long period of vigorous and "abundant life," moving forward, not, indeed, with even and unvarying flow, yet with continuous current, marked with those alternations of exaltation and subsidence which seem, whether for evil or for good, to have become a fixed characteristic of American church history.

The widespread revivals of the first decade of the nineteenth century saved the church of Christ in America from its low estate and girded it for stupendous tasks that were about to be devolved on it. In the glow of this renewed fervor, the churches of New England successfully made the difficult transition from establishment to self-support and to the costly enterprises of aggressive evangelization into which, in company with other churches to the South and West, they were about to enter. The Christianity of the country was prepared and equipped to attend with equal pace the prodigious rush of population across the breadth of the Great Valley, and to give welcome to the invading host of immigrants which before the end of a half-century was to effect its entrance into our territory at the rate of a thousand a day. It was to accommodate itself to changing social conditions, as the once agricultural population began to concentrate itself in factory villages and commercial towns. It was to carry on systematic campaigns of warfare against instituted social wrong, such as the drinking usages of society, the savage code of dueling, the public sanction of slavery. And it was to enter the "effectual door" which from the beginning of the century opened wider and wider to admit the gospel and the church to every nation under heaven.

Philip Schaff, A History of American Christianity, 1897

A decade of controversies and schisms

During the period from 1835 to 1845 the spirit of schism seemed to be in the air. In this period not one of the larger organizations of churches was free from agitating controversies, and some of the most important of them were rent asunder by explosion.

At the time when the Presbyterian Church suffered its great schism, in 1837, it was the most influential religious body in the United States. In 120 years its solitary presbytery had grown to 135 presbyteries, including 2140 ministers serving 2865 churches and 220,557 communicants. In the four years beginning with 1831 the additions to its roll of communicants "on examination" had numbered nearly one hundred thousand. But this spiritual growth was chilled and stunted by the dissensions that arose. The revivals ceased and the membership actually dwindled.

Two very great events in this period of schism may be dispatched with a brevity out of all proportion to their importance, on account of the simplicity of motive and action by which they are characterized.

In the year 1844 the slavery agitation in the Methodist Episcopal Church culminated, not in the rupture of the church, but in the well-considered, deliberate division of it between North and South.

Under the fierce tyranny then dominant at the South the southern Baptists might not fall behind their Methodist neighbors in zeal for slavery. This time it was the South that forced the issue. The Alabama Baptist Convention, without waiting for a concrete case, demanded of the national missionary boards "the distinct, explicit avowal that slave-holders are eligible and entitled equally with non-slave-holders to all the privileges and immunities of their several unions." The answer of the Foreign Mission Board was perfectly kind, but, on the main point, perfectly unequivocal: "We can never be a party to any arrangement which would imply approbation of slavery." The result had been foreseen. The great denomination was divided between North and South.

Philip Schaff, A History of American Christianity, 1897.

Protestant liberalism

Introduction

American Protestant Liberalism grows out of German scholarship of the late 1800s. German scholars came to deny Scripture's power and they undercut the church's effectiveness. Their thought permeates European culture much sooner than it does the American. Because of the Civil War many American scholars were unable to travel abroad for study.

Liberal reflects attitudes in continuity with Enlightenment thought. It reflects an attempt to incorporate modern thinking and developments, especially in the sciences, into Christianity. Liberals tend to emphasize ethics over doctrine while stressing man's freedom—humanism.

1. Darwinian science

Charles Darwin wrote *The Origin of the Species* in 1859. It did not impact America because of the Civil War. His book found acceptance in the United States after the war. Just a few years later, 1871, Darwin added his Descent of Man to his writings. The latter work traced human descent while the first work was more general.

Darwin's work circulated among the scientific community but Herbert Spencer popularized it. Spencer took Darwin's work beyond the biological realm to the social realm. He coined the phrase "Social Darwinism" to describe his ideas that even social structures evolve. Eventually this idea captures most American intellectual thought during the 1800s. It stresses the idea that you can perfect society. Man, using his own intellect and ability, can produce a perfect society—a utopia. Within a decade, by the mid–1870s, evangelical Protestantism generally accepts the idea.

Theistic evolution

James Fiske, a historian and nominal Congregationalist, next develops the concept of "theistic evolution." Theistic evolution soothes the consciences of those finding it difficult to harmonize evolution with Christianity. Fiske said evolution is God's way of doing things. Many Christians see evolution as God's providential hand in history working change and alterations over lengthy periods. Fiske insisted Genesis is poetic and contains creation's basic order with being historically accurate.

Christians find this reasoning far more acceptable than the idea of evolution guided only by blind chance. Lyman Abbott, Henry Ward Beecher's successor at Brooklyn's Plymouth Congregational Church, brings Fiske's ideas into the church. The influential Abbott's acceptance of "theistic evolution" makes it easier for other preachers to advocate the same idea. By the end of the 1880s, preachers assert that Christianity can assimilate evolutionary concepts without compromise.

2. Bible criticism

The questioning of biblical truth coincides with the growth of evolutionary thought. During the mid–1700s, Jean Astruc, a French scholar, suggests the Pentateuch should be divided by the various editors who he supposed to have compiled it. This multi-editor or multi-author concept became part of the Graf-Wellhausen Theory, or the JEPD theory. The Pentateuch lost much of its authority as this theory gained acceptance.

Some of these ideas made their way into post-Civil War America. Robert G. Ingersoll, the best known agnostic of the period, uses the results of critical studies to lambast Christianity and question the Bible. Ingersoll traveled throughout the country lecturing on the Bible. His wit and self-assurance amused his audience as he regaled them with ribald attacks on the Old Testament. When he lampooned Scripture, his rhetorical skills enabled him to make the Bible appear quite ridiculous. He particularly focused on the flood accounts. Ingersoll calculated just how much water it would take to flood the entire earth. He talked about where that much water would come from, how much pressure it would exert and so on. By the end of the lecture the whole flood account seemed quite foolish.

3. Philosophical world view

Friedrich Schleiermacher insisted on a complete reorientation of man's thought about religion. The French Revolution impacted his day and left its mark on French culture. Europeans tended to despise anti-intellectual pietism. Schleiermacher, therefore, insisted religion was neither piety nor rationalism, but a sense of dependence on the infinite.

Schleiermacher's ideas effectively reduced religion to mysticism and a reorientation towards an emphasis on subjective feelings. He turned from thinking about God to thinking about man's thought about God. Schleiermacher represents a shift from biblical authority to believer's experience.

Georg Wilhem Friedrich Hegel took the next important step when he taught that the universe is irrational and can't be understood. He taught that culture and society evolves through synthesis development. This idea provided the basis for Marxian dialectic.

Albrecht Ritschl sought to make religion practical. To him, religion exists only to create values in man.

Adolph Harnack, a disciple of Ritschl's, defines and refines Ritschl's teachings. Harnack illustrates Liberal reductionism. Harnack argues that since the Bible is unreliable and religious truth merely produces values, one must come to some conclusion about the Bible's irreducible message. His book What Is Christianity? grew out of speeches given to German non-theology students. In his speeches he reduced Christianity to three points:

the Kingdom of God and its coming,
God the Father and the infinite value of the human soul, and
the better righteousness and the commandment of love.

Harnack emphasized a basic ethical system, he stresses none of the essential Christian doctrines.

4. Summation of Liberalism

There are eleven basic characteristics of Liberalism. They are related below:

Anthropocentrism.

This is the legacy of the Enlightenment. Man is at the center. All religious knowledge finds its source within man. Reason and observation are all important.

Autonomy.

This is the opposite of heteronomy (the recognition of outside authority). Human reason passes judgment on each belief. Every statement is therefore measured and weighed on its own merit. Edward Scribner Ames said, "The Christian is free from all external authority. Not even Christ imposes any arbitrary demands upon him." (Ames, Divinity of Christ, p. 96) Autonomy simply means the freedom to decide for one's self what is right or wrong.

Continuity.

This involves a feeling for the oneness of all things. Two major factors are involved.

(1). The Unity of Truth.

Truth comes from many sources, not just the Bible. This applies to religious truth. Thus, Christian theology is to be constructed from all spheres of information (psychology, sociology, science) as well as the Bible. There is no distinction between special and general revelation. Significance: there is no real distinction between Christianity and other religions.

(2). The Unity of Being.

All existence is qualitatively the same. There is no sharp distinction between the natural and the supernatural, between God and man, between the divine and human in Jesus.

Modernism.

This is an implication of the continuity of truth. Two facts need to be noted:

Modernism is an openness to truth as discerned through modern efforts in science, philosophy and religious studies. It includes a readiness to adapt Christianity to all modern discoveries. It includes an evolutionary view of truth ("the newer the truer"): change is always good because we are "moving toward the truth."

All Liberals were Modernists, but not all modernists were Liberals.

The Immanence of God.

This is an implication of the continuity of being. Here we need to see not only its meaning but the implications.

Immanence is the idea that God dwells in the whole world and works through all of nature, and that he works only through natural processes. God's difference (transcendence) is ignored; miracle is denied. The uniformity of nature is emphasized. Note: God is immanent in his creation, but not as accepted by the Liberal.

What are the important implications?

There are implications for our view of Christ. If there is no distinction between the supernatural or the natural, then Jesus can only be human! All qualitative distinction between Jesus and other men is erased. God then is "incarnate" in all human life.

There is an implication for our view of man. All men have a "spark of divinity" in them. To say that is to say there is a bit of God in everyone. Liberals say the human conscience is the "divine spark."

There are implications for metaphysics. There is no distinction between natural and supernatural. Since God is present in all of nature, everything is supernatural, everything is a miracle.

An evolutionary view of the Bible.

The Bible originated through ordinary processes just as other religious writings and religions evolved. We are not speaking of a God who reveals himself more and more through time. We are speaking of man's improvement of their concept of God.

This is called progressive revelation. It refers to Israel's subjective growth in religious understanding, the growing sophistication of the idea of God in the people's religious experience.

An important implication is simply that if this view is accepted it means the Bible contains different degrees of truth! There are different levels of authority, unequal ethical standards.

Reduction of Christianity to its unchanging essence.

It is the attempt to boil Christianity down to its essence. It is the attempt to save Christianity by emphasizing its "timeless truths" or "essential message" while acknowledging that its details and historical framework were relative, erroneous, and discardable. What is the framework for judging what is or what is not true: the human mind!

The centrality of the man Jesus as an ethical example.

Jesus is central in Christianity over against the Bible. The life and teachings of Jesus are the "canon within the canon."

The important thing about Jesus is his ethical example. Jesus was as perfect as a man can be in his time and place. It is possible to be as good as Jesus! Not so, Christ's divinity makes it impossible to follow him in every detail.

The church as an instrument of social progress. This is the social gospel. Liberals saw the task of the church as the establishment of the "kingdom of God" on earth via social progress.

Optimism.

This is the concept of the inevitability of human progress. Man gets better and better. Based on the Liberal view of the inherent dignity and goodness of man. Liberals considered sin to be the "residue of evolution." Sin that the Liberals emphasized is social sin. The remedy for sin is education!

Illiberality.

Liberals would vehemently deny this! It is true, however, that the Liberal tends to be very close minded towards those who differ.

Liberals stress Christology—the study of Christ. They emphasize Jesus' person while denying his divinity. Religion becomes Christocentric because Jesus is our supreme example without any stress on soteriology. Liberals stress Jesus' moral teaching while rejecting the inspiration of Scripture. They make a distinction between the Christ of the cross and the Jesus of history.

For the most part, classical Liberalism is dead. Only a few die hards hold on to it as a theological system. What remains is indistinguishable from humanism. If we follow Christ's teachings we can become what Jesus was. He only came to show men how to live; he did not come to rescue from hell. Man is perfectible; society is perfectible. Everyone can potentially become a son of god. In fact, mankind possesses a "spark of divinity," a spark which relates him to God.

Scholars identify two forms of Liberalism at the end of the 1800s. They distinguish between modernistic Liberalism and evangelical Liberalism. Modernistic Liberals attack Christianity and proposed socialistic and humanistic forms. Evangelical Liberalism reduces the emphasis on biblical Christianity but still emphasizes evangelism. Such evangelism saved from "social sin"—guilty, self, ghetto, and social problems. You can't identify any biblical concept of sin as the transgression of God's law.

5. The heresy trials

Mainstream Protestantism does not accept all this easily. Liberalism made slow but sure gains. Each year more and more preachers adopted Liberal views. Soon clashes occurred. Some of the major denominations experience heresy trials beginning in the 1870s.

In 1874, David Swing, a Chicago Presbyterian minister, faces charges of heresy before his presbytery. His accusers base their charges on the Westminster Confession of Faith. The presbytery acquits him but his enemies continued to press for his removal. Because of the continuing controversy Swing left the Presbyterian Church to form Central Church in downtown Chicago.

Southern Baptists charge Crawford Howell Toy, a professor at Louisville's Southern Baptist Theological Seminary, with heresy in 1879. According to the charges, Toy denied the inerrancy of Scripture. Toy quit under pressure and moved to Harvard University where he continued his teaching as a highly respected professor.

Conservative Presbyterians bring charges of heresy against Charles A. Briggs, a professor at Union Theological Seminary, in 1891. Briggs occupied a newly endowed Bible chair at Union. In his inaugural address he openly denied verbal inspiration of Scripture. The presbytery arraigned Briggs for heresy but he was acquitted. The Presbyterian National Assembly reversed the local presbytery's decision and the Seminary withdrew from the Presbyterian Church and became independent. In an effort to get away from continued Presbyterian harassment Briggs joined the Episcopalian Church.

Two other Presbyterians face heresy trials during this period. Henry Preserved Smith at Lane Theological Seminary and A. C. McGiffert at Union. Both men left the Presbyterian Church and became Congregationalists.

It seems Presbyterians have the most trouble. By 1900, almost every northern American Seminary has gone Liberal. Southern schools remain conservative. Southern churches don't catch up to the northerners until the Depression.

Michael Hines, Christian Chronicler

The Oxford Movement

The Oxford Movement was a loose affiliation of High Church Anglicans, most of them members of the University of Oxford, who sought to demonstrate that the Church of England was a direct descendant of the Christian church established by the Apostles. It was also known as the Tractarian Movement after its series of publications, Tracts for the Times (1833–1841); the Tractarians were also called Puseyites (usually disparagingly) after one of their leaders, Edward Bouverie Pusey, Regius Professor of Hebrew at Christ Church, Oxford.

Other prominent Tractarians included:

John Henry Newman, a fellow of Oriel College, Oxford and vicar of the University Church of St Mary the Virgin
John Keble
Archdeacon Henry Edward Manning
Richard Hurrell Froude
Gerard Manley Hopkins
Robert Wilberforce
Isaac Williams and
Sir William Palmer.

Early movement

The immediate impetus for the Movement was the secularization of the Church, focused particularly on the decision by the Government to reduce by ten the number of Irish bishoprics in the Church of Ireland following the 1832 Reform Act. Keble attacked these proposals as "National Apostasy" in his Assize Sermon in Oxford in 1833. Its leaders attacked liberalism in theology, and more positively took an interest in Christian origins which led them to reconsider the relationship of the Church of England with the Roman Catholic Church. The movement postulated the Branch Theory which states that Anglicanism along with Orthodoxy and Roman Catholicism form three "branches" of the one "Catholic Church." In the ninetieth and final Tract, Newman argued that the doctrines of the Roman Catholic Church, as defined by the Council of Trent, were compatible with the Thirty-Nine Articles of the sixteenth-century Church of England. Newman's conversion to Roman Catholicism in 1845 as a result of his being taken further than he had expected by his own arguments, followed by Manning in 1851, had a profound effect upon the movement.

Criticisms

The Oxford Movement was attacked for being a mere Romanising tendency, but it began to have an influence on the theory and practice of Anglicanism. It resulted in the establishment of Anglican religious orders, both of men and women, and an emphasis on liturgy and ceremony. In particular it brought the insights of the Liturgical Movement into the life of the Church. Its effects were so widespread that the Eucharist gradually became more central to worship, vestments became common, and a huge number of Catholic practices were introduced into worship. Inevitably this led to controversy which often ended up in court. Partly because bishops refused to give livings to Tractarian priests, many of them ended up working in the slums giving rise to a critique of social policy, local and national. The establishment of the Christian Social Union which debated issues such as the just wage, the system of property renting, infant mortality and industrial conditions, and to which a number of bishops were members, was one of the results. The more radical Catholic Crusade was much smaller. Anglo-Catholicism, as this complex of ideas, styles and organizations became known, has had a massive influence on global Anglicanism which continues to this day.

Converts to Roman Catholicism

The principal writer and proponent of the Tractarian Movement was John Henry Newman, who after writing his final tract, Tract 90 became convinced that the Branch Theory was inadequate and that in conscience he had to convert to the Roman Catholic Church. His conversion set off a series of similar conversions to the Catholic Church among Anglican clergy, and intellectuals throughout the late nineteenth and early twentieth centuries which to a lesser extent continues to the present.

Other major figures who became Catholic as a result of the movement were:

Gerard Manley Hopkins, Jesuit priest and renowned poet.

Henry Edward Manning, later created a Cardinal of the Catholic Church.

John Chapman OSB, became a Benedictine scripture scholar

John Dobree Dalgairns, along with John Henry Newman, entered the Congregation of the Oratory and was ordained a Catholic priest.

Robert Hugh Benson, former Anglican priest and son of an Archbishop of Canterbury, ordained a Catholic priest.

Thomas William Allies, Church historian and former Anglican minister.

Augusta Theodosia Drane, Dominican prioress.

Frederick William Faber, former Anglican of Calvinist influence; theologian, hymn writer, Oratorian and Catholic priest.

Lady Georgiana Fullerton, English novelist.

Robert Stephen Hawker, former Anglican priest of Catholic leanings, deathbed Catholic convert.

James Hope-Scott, English lawyer, influential Tractarian, converted with Manning.

George Jackson Mivart, English biologist banned from Oxford University for entering the Catholic Church.

Henry Nutcombe Oxenham, former Anglican minister; Catholic Church historian.

Augustus Pugin, influential English architect, designer of Parliament and many English churches.

Edward Caswall, hymn writer

William George Ward

Wikipedia

John Keble and the Christian Year

If Pusey's name was given to the followers of the Oxford Movement, it was, unquestionably, Keble who gave it its first popularity. His sermon inaugurated it, and its principles were those of his book of poems, The Christian Year. It was sub-titled: "thoughts in verse for the Sundays and holydays throughout the year."

Keble's Christian Year was a book of devotional poetry with an extraordinary impact on people of all parties who had that kind of bent. As Newman put it, "Keble struck an original note and woke up in the hearts of thousands a new music, the music of a school long unknown in England"

The Seasons of the Christian Year

"The liturgical year, also known as the Christian year, consists of the cycle of liturgical seasons in some Christian churches which determines when Feasts, Memorials, Commemorations, and Solemnities are to be observed and which portions of Scripture are to be read. Distinct liturgical colors may appear in connection with different seasons of the liturgical year. The dates of the festivals vary somewhat between the Western (Roman Catholic, Anglican, and Protestant) churches and the Eastern Orthodox Churches, though the sequence and logic is the same."

Wikipedia

The main seasons in the Christian Year are:

Advent Season

The four Sundays preceding Christmas Day

Color: Purple

Christmastide

One or two Sundays between December 25 and January 6

Color: White

Epiphany Season

Four to nine Sundays between January 6 and the beginning of Lent

Color: First Sunday, White; thereafter Green

Lenton Season
Six Sundays before Easter
Color: Purple

Eastertide
Easter Day and six other Sundays
Color: White

Pentecost Season
Eleven to sixteen Sundays beginning with Pentecost Sunday and continuing through the next to the last Sunday in August
Color: Red

Kingdomtide
Thirteen or fourteen Sundays beginning the last Sunday in August and continuing until Advent
Color: Green

Bible societies

The British and Foreign Bible Society

Summary

The first Bible Society was established in 1804. The main aim of the organization was to propagate the Christian Bible. These Bible Societies expanded rapidly at the end of the 18th century as a result of the establishment of various Missionary Societies. The most important of the Bible Societies was the British and Foreign Bible Society that produced biblical texts in 700 languages and dialects. This organization also managed to distributed over 550 million copies of the Bible to people all over the world.

Bible Society began in a tavern!

The first Scripture translation was during its very first year of existence – 1804 – and was John's Gospel in the Canadian Indian Mohawk language.

Bible Society provided Scriptures to prisoners of war during the Napoleonic war.

After the Russian royal family was murdered and the Bolsheviks took control, the Bible Society's Siberian agent Walter Davidson fled the country in 1918, arriving back in England with horrific tales.

Colporteurs across Europe shared a common purpose in providing God's Word – but had to take arms against each other during the World Wars.

One supporter recruited his parrot who shrieked, 'Give a shilling to Bible Society'!

300 people attended the inaugural meeting of Bible Society.

£5,945 was raised by auxiliaries in 1809–10, their first year of existence.

The cost of its first premises in 1816 amounted to £12,000.

Following the end of the conflict with Napoleon in 1815 Bible Society agent Steinkopff set off on his second tour of the Continent. He traveled between 4,000 and 5,000 miles, drawing on a grant of £4,000 to form Bible Societies and make Scriptures available.

In the first fifty years of its existence the Bible Society had supplied nearly 28 million copies of Scriptures in 152 languages and dialects.

American Bible Society

Organization

The American Bible Society is a donor-supported non-profit ministry with a purpose of presenting the Bible in compelling ways so that people may experience life in its fullness through faith in Jesus Christ. The American Bible Society focuses on advocacy and resourcing through strong relationships with strategic partners.

A Timeline of American Bible Society History

1816

Founding of the American Bible Society in New York City. Elias Boudinot was elected its first president.

1817

The American Bible Society made its first grant, giving 300 Bibles to the Steuben County Bible Society (Bath, NY).

Bibles were distributed to the crew of the USS John Adams, thus beginning a Scripture grant program to the armed services that continues today.

The American Bible Society Library was founded.

1818

Quarterly Extracts, the predecessor to the present day publication American Bible Society Record, was issued.

The American Bible Society published the Delaware Indian/English parallel text of three Epistles of John. Translated by Christian Frederick Dencke, this work marked the first publication by ABS in another language.

The American Bible Society received its first endowment, a $250 bequest made by Seth Warner.

1823

The American Bible Society sent a gift of $1,000 to the missionary William Carey to support his Scripture translation work in India.

1833

The American Bible Society committed $3,000 to print and distribute Scriptures in China.

1835

A gift of $1,000 to the New England Institution for the Blind resulted in the first Scriptures for the visually impaired.

1846–1848

The Mexican War was fought, and the American Bible Society supplied over 7,000 Scriptures to U.S. troops.

1861–1865

The American Bible Society provided Scriptures to both the North and South during the Civil War.

1869

The transcontinental railroad was completed, thus creating new avenues of distribution for Scriptures.

1876

The American Bible Society exhibited a collection of historical Bibles at the Philadelphia Centennial.

The Gideons International

In the autumn of the year 1898, John H. Nicholson of Janesville, Wisconsin, came to the Central Hotel at Boscobel, Wisconsin, for the night. The hotel being crowded, it was suggested that he take a bed in a double room with Samuel E. Hill of Beloit, Wisconsin. The two men soon discovered that both were Christians, and that John Nicholson, as a 12-year-old boy, had promised his dying mother that he would read God's Word and pray daily. It had been his custom for many years to read the Bible before retiring for the night. They had their evening devotions together, and on their knees before God the thoughts were given which later developed into an association.

On May 31, 1899, they met at Beaver Dam, Wisconsin, concluded to band Christian commercial travelers together for mutual recognition, personal evangelism, and united service for the Lord. They decided to call a meeting in Janesville, Wisconsin on July 1, 1899, in the YMCA.

Only three men were present at that meeting: John H. Nicholson, Samuel E. Hill, and Will J. Knights. They organized with Hill as president, Knights as vice president, and

Nicholson as secretary and treasurer. Much thought was given to what the name of the association should be, and after special prayer that God might lead them to select the proper name, Mr. Knights arose from his knees and said, "We shall be called Gideons." He read the sixth and seventh chapters of Judges and showed the reason for adopting that name.

In view of the fact that almost all of the Gideons in the early years of the association were traveling men, the question quite naturally arose regarding how they might be more effective witnesses in the hotels where they were forced to spend so much of their time. One suggestion was that a Bible might be placed at the reception desk in each hotel so that the patrons would have the privilege of borrowing it if they wished. It also occurred to these men that this would be a silent witness remaining in these hotels when they were elsewhere.

This question of advanced activities, as they called them, was carefully considered in the Cabinet meeting held in Chicago, October 19, 1907. One trustee went so far as to suggest that The Gideons furnish a Bible for each bedroom of the hotels in the United States. He commented," In my opinion, this would not only stimulate the activities of the rank and file of the membership, but would be a gracious act, wholly in keeping with the divine mission of the Gideon Association." This plan was adopted by the convention at Louisville, Kentucky, in 1908.

The Origin of Sunday School

In England during the 18th century, occasional efforts were made by charitable individuals to provide some education in religious matters as well as secular instruction to children of the poor. Probably the first to be called a Sunday school was that started (1780) by Robert Raikes for factory children in Gloucester. The curriculum largely consisted of simple lessons in reading and spelling in preparation for reading the Bible, and memorizing Scripture passages and hymns.

The American Sunday-School Union, formed (1817) among various churches of the East, determined to establish Sunday schools as rapidly as possible in the pioneer communities of the Mississippi valley. This project met with wide support and considerable success.

In 1832 a national convention of American Sunday school workers was held. At the convention of 1872 a plan of uniform lessons was adopted in cooperation with the British Sunday School Union, and from that time the movement was international.

The Philadelphia schools were organized for the benefit of such persons of either sex (and of any age) as cannot afford to educate themselves, were run by the First Day Society, which paid teachers to instruct pupils in reading and copying from the Bible.

These schools had the additional purpose of controlling children's activities. Employment of children in industries had brought together youth of similar ages who worked together on weekdays and spent their Sundays playing in alleys and wharves, to the great disturbance of the families in the vicinity of such places, and the profanation of the day.

Sunday schools provided an alternative to Sunday rowdiness. The schools would also teach proper behavior, enforcing cleanliness, providing Sunday clothing, and reprimanding children for lying, swearing, talking in an indecent manner, or other misbehavior.

For the next three decades, Sunday schools were part of an informal network of free schools operated by various religious and philanthropic groups to provide rudimentary education to children of the poor. Depending on their sponsorship and frequency of meeting, these schools placed more or less emphasis on religious and moral instruction. Schools run by the New York Free School Society, for example, combined daily academic instruction with Sunday attendance at Sunday schools. In October 1811, Presbyterian missionary Robert May opened an evening Sunday school in Philadelphia in which, unlike previous free schools, he taught religious doctrine solely and without remuneration. Schools resembling May's became increasingly common during the decade 1810–1820 as young, newly converted Protestants turned Sunday teaching as a means of expressing their newfound convictions. By 1820, there were several hundred Sunday schools in the United States. All emphasized religious instruction over reading and writing, although most taught the later subjects as a means of inculcating the former. Many Sunday school organizers, in fact, began lobbying for extension of a system of free daily schools so that they would be free to teach religion alone on Sundays.

Sunday schools then aimed at teaching basic Protestantism to children of the unchurched poor. The Bible provided the text for teaching the truths of the Gospel, a knowledge of which, Protestants believed, was essential for moral living and good citizenship. Knowledge of the Bible, they felt, would teach pupils the duty required of them as social, rational and accountable beings.

American Board of Commissioners for Foreign Missions

The American Board of Commissioners for Foreign Missions (ABCFM) was the first American Christian foreign mission agency. It was proposed in 1810 by recent graduates of Williams College and officially chartered in 1812. In 1961 it merged with other societies to form the United Church Board for World Ministries. Other organizations that draw inspiration from the ABCFM include InterVarsity Christian Fellowship and the Conservative Congregational Christian Conference.

Historical overview

The founding of the ABCFM is associated with the Second Great Awakening. Congregationalist in origin, the American Board supported missions by Presbyterian (1812–1870), Dutch-Reformed (1826–1857) and other denominational members.

Early missions

The first missionaries were sent overseas in 1812. Between 1812 and 1840, representatives of the ABCFM went to the following people and places: India (the Bombay area), northern Ceylon (modern day Sri Lanka), the Sandwich Islands (Hawaii), east Asia (China, Singapore and Siam), the Middle East (Greece, Cyprus, Turkey, Syria, the Holy Land and Persia), and Africa (Western Africa—Cape Palmas—and Southern Africa—among the Zulus). It sent its first group of five missionaries in 1812. It became the leading missionary society in the United States.

Aspects of the first thirty years

Between 1810 and 1840, the ABCFM sought first and foremost to proclaim the Gospel of Jesus Christ. At home and abroad, the Board and its supporters undertook every effort to exhort the evangelical community, to train a cadre of agents, and to send forth laborers into the mission field. As a leader in the United Front and early federal American voluntary associations, the Board influenced the nineteenth-century mission movement.

Educational, social, and medical roles served by ABCFM missionaries

Printing and literacy played crucial roles in the process and efficacy of Bible translation. Similarly, the press runs and literacy presentations contributed significantly to the social involvement exhibited by the Board. To a greater or lesser extent, education, medicine, and social concern supplemented the preaching efforts by missionaries. Schools provided ready-made audiences for preachers. Free, or Lancasterian, schools provided a large number of students, while boarders in missionary homes saw the Christian life proclaimed, however imperfectly, in the intimacy of family life. Education empowered indigenous people and enabled them to develop—mostly later than 1840—their own church leaders and take a greater role in their communities. Board missionaries established some form of education at every station. A number of Board missionaries received a little medical training before leaving for the field. Some, like Ida Scudder, were trained as physicians but ordained as missionaries and concentrated on the task of preaching. Others, such as Peter Parker, sought to hold in tension the callings of missionary and medical practicioner.

ABCFM in China

The Americans were the next to venture into the mission field of China after the London Missionary Society and the Netherlands Missionary Society. The Board of Commissioners for Foreign Missions, representing the Congregational Churches of the United States, sent out Revs. David Abeel and Elijah Coleman Bridgman in 1829, and who were received in February 1830 by Dr. Robert Morrison. These men labored among the

Chinese and Malays of the Straits Settlements, but from 1842, up to his death in 1846, Mr. Abeel devoted himself to establishing a mission in Amoy.

Wikipedia

The Salvation Army

Mission Statement

The Salvation Army, an international movement, is an evangelical part of the universal Christian church. Its message is based on the Bible. Its ministry is motivated by the love of God. Its mission is to preach the gospel of Jesus Christ and to meet human needs in His name without discrimination.

The History of the Salvation Army

William Booth embarked upon his ministerial career in 1852. His crusade was to win the lost multitudes of London to Christ. He went into the streets of London to preach the gospel of Jesus Christ to the poor, the homeless, the hungry and the destitute.

Booth abandoned the conventional concept of a church and a pulpit and took his message to the people. His fervor led to disagreement with the leaders of the church in London. They preferred traditional measures. As a result, he withdrew from the church and traveled throughout England conducting evangelistic meetings. His wife, Catherine, was a major force in The Salvation Army movement.

In 1865, William Booth was invited to hold a series of evangelistic meetings in the east end of London. He set up a tent in a Quaker graveyard and his services became an instant success. This proved to be the end of his wanderings as an independent traveling evangelist. His renown as a religious leader spread throughout London. His followers were a vigorous group dedicated to fight for the souls of men and women.

Thieves, prostitutes, gamblers and drunkards were among Booth's first converts to Christianity. His congregations were desperately poor. He preached hope and salvation. His aim was to lead them to Christ and to link them to a church for further spiritual guidance. Even though they were converted, churches did not accept Booth's followers because of what they had been. Booth gave their lives direction in a spiritual manner and put them to work to save others who were like themselves. They too preached and sang in the streets as a living testimony to the power of God.

In 1867, Booth had only 10 full-time workers. By 1874, the numbers had grown to 1,000 volunteers and 42 evangelists. They served under the name "The Christian Mission." Booth assumed the title of a General Superintendent. His followers called him "General." Known as the "Hallelujah Army,'" the converts spread out of the east end of London into neighboring areas and then to other cities.

Booth was reading a printer's proof of the 1878 Annual Report when the noticed the statement, '"The Christian Mission under the Superintendent's of the Rev. William Booth is a volunteer army. He crossed out the words "Volunteer Army'" and penned in "Salvation Army.'" From those words came the basis of the foundation deed of The Salvation Army which was adopted in August of that same year.

Converts became soldiers of Christ and are known as Salvationists. They launched an offensive throughout the British Isles. In some instances there were real battles as organized gangs mocked and attacked soldiers as they went about their work. In spite of the violence and persecution, some 250,000 persons were converted under the ministry of the Salvationists between 1881 and 1,885.

Meanwhile, the Army was gaining a foothold in the United States. Lieutenant Eliza Shirley had left England to join her parents who had migrated to America earlier in search of work. She held the first meeting of The Salvation Army in America in Philadelphia in 1879. The Salvationists were received enthusiastically. Shirley wrote to General Booth begging for reinforcements. None were available at first. Glowing reports of the work in Philadelphia convinced Booth to send an official group to pioneer the work in America in 1880.

On March 10, 1880, Commissioner George Scott Railton and seven women officers knelt on the dockside at Battery Park in New York City to give thanks for their safe arrival. This was to be their first official street meeting held in the United States. These pioneers were to be met with similar unfriendly actions, as was the case in Great Britain. They were ridiculed, arrested and attacked. Several officers and soldiers even gave their lives.

Three years later, Railton and the seven "Hallelujah Lassies"' had expanded their operation into California, Connecticut, Indiana, Kentucky, Maryland, Massachusetts, Michigan, Missouri, New Jersey, New York, Ohio and Pennsylvania.

President Grover Cleveland received a delegation of Salvation Army officers in 1886 and gave the organization a warm personal endorsement. This was the first recognition from the White House that was to be followed by similar receptions from succeeding presidents of the United States.

Termed as the "invasion of the United States," The Salvation Army movement expanded rapidly to Canada, Australia, France, Switzerland, India, South Africa, Iceland and Germany. Currently in the United States, there are more than 10,000 local neighborhood units, and The Salvation Army is active in virtually every corner of the world.

Restorationists

Restorationist organizations, which include Disciples of Christ, Churches of Christ, Independent Christian Churches/Churches of Christ, The Church of Jesus Christ of Latter Day Saints, Seventh-day Adventists, Jehovah's Witnesses, and others arose from the belief that the true pattern of the Christian religion died out through apostasy many years before and was finally restored by their churches. Some believe that they alone fully embody this restoration exclusively; others understand themselves as conforming to a rediscovered pattern of original Christianity that is now found in many churches, including their own (this is the official stance of the Christian Church (Disciples of Christ), for example). Some restorationist denominations go so far as to state that mainline Protestant groups, let alone Catholic or Orthodox churches, are not actually Christian.

The Great Apostasy

Restorationism is fundamentally based on a belief called the Great Apostasy. Essentially this is the claim that traditional Christianity has departed so far from the original Christian principles that it is not redeemable. Because of its divisions, errors, and compromises with the world, the claim is that the corrupted church fell out of line with the church founded by Jesus. If there were no apostasy-at-large and a church on the true-and-legitimate pattern was present, there would be no need for a Restoration. Thus, Restorationists can be compared to one another in their conviction that there has been an apostasy, which they undertook to correct.

Restoration Movement

Of these movements, the most optimistic about the then-present state of Christianity was the Stone-Campbell Restoration Movement, sometimes referred to as Campbellites. They called themselves the Christian Church, or the Church of Christ. They brought together many from Baptist, Congregationalist, Presbyterian, and Methodist churches, and other Christians across a spectrum of Evangelical and also Unitarian Christianity, at first with astounding success. But, as the movement progressed, it developed non-negotiable distinctives of its own, sometimes referred to disapprovingly as unwritten creeds, and fractured into four major groups—each of which has become a recognizable group (the term "denomination" still being unacceptable to many of them): the Churches of Christ (or "church of Christ"), the Independent Christian Churches and Churches of Christ, the International Church of Christ, and the Disciples of Christ.

Rise of sects in America

Latter Day Saints (Mormons)

The Church of Jesus Christ of Latter Day Saints or "Mormons" believe that Joseph Smith, Jr. was chosen not to reform, but restore in its fullness the original organization founded by Jesus Christ. According to Smith, God and Jesus appeared to him and instructed him that the churches of the day were all lacking authority and taught some incorrect doctrines, and that through him God would restore, or re-establish, the true church.

The Great Apostasy was complete, Smith taught, requiring a full restoration of the original church, which included a priesthood or authority, prophet, apostles, evangelists, and teachers in order for God's Kingdom on earth to be re-established. Joseph Smith founded the Church of Christ in 1830, serving as the first prophet believed to be appointed by Jesus Christ in the latter days. Sidney Rigdon, and several other preachers, left their Churches of Christ to join Smith.

As part of his prophetic mission, Smith published the Book of Mormon, said to be translated from Golden Plates as directed by an angel Moroni. Members of the Latter Day Saint movement (Mormonism) believe that the Book of Mormon contains doctrine of the original church of Jesus Christ given to people who lived on the American continents between about 600 BC and 421.

In addition, Smith claimed that he received the true authority or Priesthood directly from those who held it anciently, namely John the Baptist returned as an angel and gave him the authority to baptize (which he said had long been lost), and Peter, James and John, the ancient apostles, returned as angels and gave him the authority to lead the church just had they done anciently. The church was organized on April 6, 1830, in New York State.

Originally the church was called the "Church of Christ" due to the belief that it is the restored Church of Jesus Christ. Four years later, in April 1834, it was also referred to as the "Church of Latter Day Saints" to differentiate the church of this era from that of the New Testament. Then in April 1838, the full name was stated as the "The Church of Jesus Christ of Latter Day Saints".

Adventism

Adventism is a type of Christian eschatology which looks for the Second Coming of Jesus to inaugurate the Kingdom of God, usually in the near future. This view often involves belief that Jesus will return to receive only a small group of those true Christians who are expecting his return and in anticipation of it have made themselves ready.

Millerites and Sabbatarianism

The Millerites are the most well-known family of the Adventist movements. From the Millerites descended the Seventh-day Adventists. This group revived apocalyptic teachings anticipating the end of the world, and did not look for the unity of Christendom, but busied themselves in preparation for Christ's return. Millerites sought to restore a prophetic immediacy and uncompromising biblicism that they believed had long been rejected by mainstream Protestant and Catholic churches. The Worldwide Church of God movement belongs to this category because it sprang from the Seventh Day churches. The personal ministry of Herbert W. Armstrong became the Radio Church of God, which became the Worldwide Church of God. It later splintered into many other churches and groups when the Worldwide Church of God disassociated itself with the Restoration movements and made major attempts to join the Protestant branch of Christianity. More recently, the Nazarene (or using the Hebrew word Netzarim) movement claims that Jesus did not intend to replace the Torah, but only to demonstrate how to follow it. The Nazarenes generally hold to Aramaic Primacy, that the Christian New Testament was originally written in Aramaic, not Greek, and make their defense from Semitic languages.

Christadelphians

Dr John Thomas (April 12, 1805—March 5, 1871), was a devout convert to the Restorationist movement after a shipwreck at sea on his emigration journey to America brought to focus his inadequate understanding of the Bible and what would happen to him should he die. This awareness caused him to devote his life to the study of the Bible, which in turn brought him into contact with the teachings of Alexander Campbell. An independent mind and a sharp intellect inevitably led him to conflict with the teachings of Mr. Campbell, especially on matters concerning baptism and resurrection. Once the split with Mr. Campbell was inevitable, Dr. Thomas appealed to the churches of Christ both in America and in England and a growing movement emerged. A distinctive body of believers developed whose doctrine incorporated Adventism, anti-trinitarianism, objection to military service, a lay-membership with full participation by all members, as well as other doctrines consistent with the spirit of the Restorationist movement.

One consequence of objection to military service was the adoption of the name Christadelphians to distinguish this small community of believers and to be granted exemption from military service in the American civil war.

Jehovah's Witnesses

The Jehovah's Witnesses originated in the 1870s as a Bible study group founded by Charles Taze Russell. The Witnesses believe that they are True Christians and the Church generally departed in a Great Apostasy from the original faith on major points. Like the Millerites, the Witnesses believe that the original faith could be restored through a generally literal interpretation of the Bible, and a sincere commitment to follow its teachings. The Jehovah's Witnesses focused on the restoration of a number of key doctrinal points evident from their interpretation of the Bible, including the use of the commonly accepted, English, transliteration of the Tetragrammaton: "Jehovah", in reference to God; a rejection of trinitarianism in favor of a type of unitarianism; the rejection of the existence of hell; active proselytization; condemnation of the ingestion or transfusion of whole, allogeneic, blood; strict neutrality in political affairs; total abstinence from military service; and a belief in the imminent inauguration of the Kingdom of God on Earth.

Restorationist dates for the Great Apostasy

Restorationism is often criticized for rejecting the traditions followed by the early church, but different restoration groups have treated tradition differently. While some view all the Church Fathers as unreliable witnesses to the original Apostolic Church, others find in the earliest Church Fathers proof that the early church believed and practiced as some

Restorationists do, and the late Church Fathers differences as evidences of a gradual or sudden falling away. Common to all Restorationism is the belief that the Church Fathers or post-apostolic church leadership had no authorization to change the church's beliefs and practices, but did so nevertheless.

The Jehovah's Witnesses believe that the apostasy started after the death of the last apostle, John. They believe that the holy spirit held the apostasy back in full force but after John died the spirit let the apostasy grow. They believe that it came in full after the Council of Nicea. Still, they believe that throughout all that time there were true Christians alive until they believe the restoration began.

The Latter Day Saints (Mormons) date the apostasy among the earliest, beginning shortly after the deaths of the original Twelve Apostles at approximately 100 AD and certainly being in a full state of apostasy by the 4th century. With this early date, they claim the least need to reconcile known writings and practices of the early church and Church Fathers. Although their writings are sometimes cited to show reminiscences of earlier true practices, they are also used to demonstrate that doctrine and understanding had been already altered.

The Sabbatarians have generally agreed on the approximate date of AD 135 as the start of the apostasy. Justin Martyr in about AD 160 had specifically defended the first day assembly, and so is considered an apostate to Sabbatarians. Nevertheless, the early church history recorded the continued keeping of the Sabbath for creation and Sunday for the Resurrection in Hippolytus's time. They view the apostasy as not complete until the church stopped keeping the Sabbath sometime after Constantine.

The Stone-Campbell Restoration Movement views the Great Apostasy as a gradual process. Ignatius promoted obedience to the Bishop in about 100 AD, which is viewed by some as signaling the introduction of the idea of a professional clergy, who began to elevate themselves over the people, leading by a gradual process of corruption to the prophesied "man of lawlessness." Infant baptism, which restorationists condemned as coercive church membership, is a similar step toward apostasy. They believe that only adult baptism was practiced at least to the time of Tertullian, but that infant baptism was introduced locally around the time of Irenaeus. They often reject notions of original sin which entail a corruption of human nature, and admit only a defilement of mankind's habitual environment, traditions or culture. As do other Restorationists, they saw the church-state alliance under Constantine as a kind of taking captive of the church, through the foolishly centralized power of the bishops. And finally, the development of the idea of the supremacy and universal authority of the Bishop of Rome is considered the completing step of the Great Apostasy, from which the Protestant reformation only imperfectly recovered, but most nearly did so among the Anabaptists and the Baptists.

Wikipedia

Plymouth Brethren

During the winter of 1827–28, four Christian men – John Nelson Darby, Edward Cronin, John Bellett, and Francis Hutchinson – who had been concerned for some time about the condition of the professing church, agreed, after much prayer and conference, to come together on the Lord's Day and remember the Lord Jesus in the breaking of bread, as the early Christians did, counting on the Lord to be with them. Their first meeting was held in Francis Hutchinson's house in Dublin, Ireland. For some time previously, they and others had been meeting to study the Scriptures; in comparing what they found in the Word of God with existing conditions at the time, they found no expression of the nature and character of the church of God, either in the National Established churches or in the various dissenting bodies.

This led them to separate from these disparate ecclesiastical systems, and to come together in the name of the Lord Jesus. As they continued to meet, others in Dublin and elsewhere were added to their number. Among the many gatherings which sprang up, one at Plymouth, England became the most well-known and people in the district began to call them "brethren from Plymouth". This naturally resulted in the designation "Plymouth Brethren".

John Nelson Darby (1800–1882) later wrote, "What gave rise to the existence of so-called Plymouth Brethren is the grand truth, the great fact, of the descent of the Holy Spirit on the day of Pentecost, to form the body of Christ into one; then the coming of the Savior as the continual expectation of the Christian".

The Plymouth Brethren Movement

Christian Science

After publication in 1875 of Science and Health, Mary Baker Eddy's primary work on spirituality and healing, readers began meeting to discuss the ideas and share their healing results. Then, in 1879, Eddy established what became The First Church of Christ, Scientist (The Mother Church).

The Church is designed "to commemorate the word and works of our Master, which should reinstate primitive Christianity and its lost element of healing." (Church Manual, page 17). Eddy had a lifelong reverence for the life and teachings of Jesus Christ and a deep desire that his healing works be universally practiced.

It consists of The First Church of Christ, Scientist, in Boston, Massachusetts, and around 2,000 branch churches and societies of Christ, Scientist, worldwide.

The Church has no ordained clergy. In 1895, Eddy named the Bible and Science and Health with Key to the Scriptures as Pastor for worldwide Churches of Christ, Scientist.1879 Christian Science founded by Mary Baker Eddy. [The complete explanation of Christian Science is contained in the book Science and Health with Key to the Scriptures]

© 2007 The First Church of Christ, Scientist

The Vatican

Immaculate Conception

In the Constitution *Ineffabilis Deus* of 8 December, 1854, Pius IX pronounced and defined that the Blessed Virgin Mary "in the first instance of her conception, by a singular privilege and grace granted by God, in view of the merits of Jesus Christ, the Savior of the human race, was preserved exempt from all stain of original sin."

Pope Pius IX

It is astounding how fearlessly he fought, in the midst of many and severe trials, against the false liberalism which threatened to destroy the very essence of faith and religion. In his Encyclical "Quanta Cura" of 8 December, 1864, he condemned sixteen propositions touching on errors of the age. This Encyclical was accompanied by the famous "Syllabus errorum", a table of eighty previously censured propositions bearing on pantheism, naturalism, rationalism, indifferentism, socialism, communism, freemasonry, and the various kinds of religious liberalism. Though misunderstandings and malice combined in representing the Syllabus as a veritable embodiment of religious narrow-mindedness and cringing servility to papal authority, it has done an inestimable service to the Church and to society at large by unmasking the false liberalism which had begun to insinuate its subtle poison into the very marrow of Catholicism.

The First Vatican Council, 1869–1870

On 29 June, 1869, Pope Pius IX issued the Bull "Æterni Patris", convoking the Vatican Council which he opened in the presence of 700 bishops on 8 December., 1869. During its fourth solemn session, on 18 July, 1870, the papal infallibility was made a dogma of the Church. . . .

The fourth chapter contains the definition of papal infallibility. First, all the corresponding decrees of the Fourth Council of Constantinople, 680 (Sixth Ecumenical), of the Second Council of Lyons, 1274 (Fourteenth Ecumenical) and of the Council of Florence, 1439 (Seventeenth Ecumenical), are repeated and confirmed. It is pointed out, further, that at all times the popes, in the consciousness of their infallibility in matters of faith for the preservation of the purity of the Apostolic tradition, have acted as the court of last instance and have been called upon as such. Then follows the important tenet that the successors of St. Peter have been promised the Holy Ghost, not for the promulgation of new doctrines, but only for the preservation and interpretation of the Revelation delivered by the Apostles. The Constitution closes with the following words: Faithfully adhering, therefore, to the tradition inherited from the beginning of the Christian Faith, we, with the approbation of the sacred council, for the glory of God our Savior, for the exaltation of the Catholic religion, and the salvation of Christian peoples, teach and define, as a Divinely revealed dogma, that the Roman pontiff, when he speaks ex cathedra, that is, when he, in the exercise of his office as shepherd and teacher of all Christians, by virtue of his supreme Apostolic authority, decides that a doctrine concerning faith or morals is to be held by the entire Church, he possesses, in consequence of the Divine aid promised him in St. Peter, that infallibility with which the Divine Savior wished to have His Church furnished for the definition of doctrine concerning faith or morals; and that such definitions of the Roman pontiff are of themselves, and not in consequence of the Church's consent, irreformable.

New Advent Catholic Encyclopedia

PEOPLE

William Wilberforce (1759–1833)
William Carey (1761–1834)
Elizabeth Fry (1780–1845)
Charles Grandison Finney (1792–1875)
Søren Kierkegaard (1813 –1855)
David Livingstone (1813–1873)
C. H. Spurgeon (1834–1892)
D. L. Moody (1837–1899)

William Wilberforce

Dates
1759–1833

Famous for being
Abolitionist of the slave trade

Important writings
Real Christianity

One of his quotations
"Of all things, guard against neglecting God in the secret place of prayer."

William Wilberforce, the son of a wealthy merchant, was born in Hull in 1759. William's father died when he was young and for a time was brought up by an uncle and aunt. William came under the influence of his aunt, who was a strong supporter of John Wesley and the Methodist movement. Disturbed by these developments, Mrs. Wilberforce brought her son back to the family home.

At seventeen Wilberforce was sent to St. John's College, Cambridge. Wilberforce was shocked by the behavior of his fellow students and later wrote: "I was introduced on the very first night of my arrival to as licentious a set of men as can well be conceived. They drank hard, and their conversation was even worse than their lives." One of Wilberforce's friends at university was William Pitt, who was later to become Britain

Prime Minister.

William Wilberforce decided on a career in politics and soon after leaving universit the age of twenty, he decided to become a candidate in the forthcoming parliamentary election in Hull. His opponent was Lord Rockingham, a rich and powerful member of the nobility, and Wilberforce had to spend nearly £9,000 to become elected. In the House of Commons Wilberforce supported the Tory government led by William Pitt.

In 1784 Wilberforce became converted to Evangelical Christianity. He joined the Clapham Set, a group of evangelical members of the Anglican Church, centered around John Venn, rector of Clapham Church in London. As a result of this conversion, Wilberforce became interested in social reform and was eventually approached by Lady Middleton, to use his power as an MP to bring an end to the slave trade.

Society of Friends in Britain had been campaigning against the slave trade for many years. They had presented a petition to Parliament in 1783 and in 1787 had helped form the Society for the Abolition of the Slave Trade. Of the twelve members on the committee nine were Quakers. As a member of the evangelical movement, Wilberforce was sympathetic to Mrs. Middleton's request. In his letter of reply, Wilberforce wrote: "I feel the great importance of the subject and I think myself unequal to the task allotted to me." Despite these doubts, Wilberforce agreed to Mrs. Middleton's request, but soon afterwards, he became very ill and it was not until 12th May, 1789, that he made his first speech against the slave trade.

Wilberforce, along with Thomas Clarkson and Granville Sharp, was now seen as one of the leaders of the anti-slave trade movement. Most of Wilberforce's Tory colleagues in the House of Commons were opposed to any restrictions on the slave trade and at first he had to rely on the support of Whigs such as Charles Fox, Richard Brinsley Sheridan, William Grenville and Henry Brougham. When William Wilberforce presented his first bill to abolish the slave trade in 1791 it was easily defeated by 163 votes to 88.

Wilberforce refused to be beaten and in 1805 the House of Commons passed a bill to that made it unlawful for any British subject to transport slaves, but the measure was blocked by the House of Lords.

In February 1806, Lord Grenville formed a Whig administration. Grenville and his Foreign Secretary, Charles Fox, were strong opponents of the slave trade. Fox and Wilberforce led the campaign in the House of Commons, whereas Grenville, had the task of persuading the House of Lords to accept the measure.

Greenville made a passionate speech where he argued that the trade was "contrary to the principles of justice, humanity and sound policy" and criticized fellow members for "not having abolished the trade long ago". When the vote was taken the Abolition of the Slave Trade bill was passed in the House of Lords by 41 votes to 20. In the House of Commons it was carried by 114 to 15 and it become law on 25th March, 1807.

.ıt continuing the trade were fined £100 for every slave
.w did not stop the British slave trade. If slave-ships were
the British navy, captains often reduced the fines they had
.o be thrown into the sea.

ı the anti-slave trade campaign such as Thomas Fowell Buxton,
to end the suffering of the slaves was to make slavery illegal.
ıe believed that at this time slaves were not ready to be granted their
free... out in a pamphlet that he wrote in 1807 that: "It would be wrong to emancipate ... /es). To grant freedom to them immediately, would be to insure not only their masters' ruin, but their own. They must (first) be trained and educated for freedom."

In 1823 Thomas Fowell Buxton formed the Society for the Mitigation and Gradual Abolition of Slavery. Buxton eventually persuaded Wilberforce to join his campaign but as he had retired from the House of Commons in 1825, he did not play an important part in persuading Parliament to bring an end to slavery.

William Wilberforce died on 29th July, 1833. One month later, Parliament passed the Slavery Abolition Act that gave all slaves in the British Empire their freedom.

William Carey

Dates
1761–1834

Famous for being
"Father of modern missions"

Important writings
Forty translations of part of the Bible

One of his quotations
"Expect great things from God, attempt great things for God."

Summary

William Carey was an English Protestant missionary and Baptist minister, known as the "father of modern missions." Carey was one of the founders of the Baptist Missionary Society. As a missionary in Serampore, India, he translated the Bible into Bengali, Sanskrit, and numerous other languages and dialects.

"The number of languages into which the sacred Scriptures are translated, or under translation, are nearly forty."

"I do entertain the idea that I may possibly live to see the bible printed in all the languages of the East, especially those of Sangskrit origin."

Carey spent an active forty-one years serving the Lord in India. Carey never retu England.

Carey was born in a cottage in a small village called Paulerspury, about three miles fro Towcester, in Northampton, England. His father began life as a weaver; later he succeeded his father as parish-clerk and schoolmaster.

Carey's health did not allow him to engage in agricultural pursuits, so when he was sixteen years old he was apprenticed to a shoemaker at Hackleton. Later he himself became a shoemaker, an occupation of which he was never ashamed. Neither his trade nor his great poverty prevented him from the pursuit of knowledge, and for before he was thirty-one he could read the Bible in Latin, Greek, Hebrew, Dutch, French and English. It was during this period that Carey learned to love his Lord and became an earnest Christian.

Carey became a local Baptist preacher. It was during these days of humble living that he drew a crude map of the world, marking the places where the Gospel had not been preached, reading Cook's travels that so deeply impressed him, and praying the Lord of the harvest to send laborers into the great untouched portions of the world. Rev. Andrew Fuller's book, "The Gospel Worthy of All Acceptation," in which he declared that "if it is the duty of all men to believe whenever the Gospel is presented to them, it must be the duty of all who have received the Gospel to endeavor to make it universally known," settled his convictions.

Carey in his missionary ideas was far in advance of his age. When he began to reveal them some said, "How Utopian!" while others declared he was interfering with God's work. Once at a meeting Carey suggested as topic for discussion, "The conversion of the heathen."

Quickly a minister said, "Young man, sit down! When God pleases to convert the heathen, he will do it without your help or mine!" Such rebuffs did not dishearten him. Later his famous pamphlet entitled, "An Inquiry into the Obligation of Christians to Use Means for the Conversion of the Heathen," was published.

On May 30, 1792, he preached from Isaiah 54:2,3, and he laid down his two general arguments, which have since become a missionary motto, "Expect great things from God: attempt great things for God."

As a result of this agitation, on October 2, 1792, in a widow's home where twelve ministers were present, the Baptist Missionary Society was organized, the subscription there and then amounting to £13 2 shillings 6 pence.

John Thomas, recently home from Bengal and afire with missionary purposes, was appointed January 9, 1793, missionary to India, and Carey was asked to join him rather than go to any other land.

As Carey pressed his foot on India soil the longings and prayers of over seven years were being realized. He was now thirty-two years of age, and yet it proved that he was to have about forty years of service in bearing the good news to the heathen, before he would be called to his reward.

ımstances he left Calcutta and walked fifteen miles in the hot sun, ł a large lake, to the Sunderbund, a vast tract of land lying south ·ered villages in this region of jungle, tigers and malaria, Carey missionary work. Here Mr. Udny, a pious man and a friend of ..ım and offered him the superintendency of an indigo factory, at ın the district of Malda. Because this offer gave him ample support for his ..ıly, afforded him time to study, and gave him a regular congregation of natives who worked in the factory, to whom he could preach and teach, he accepted it and remained five years.

He visited villages, and translated the entire New Testament into the Bengalese dialect in order to reach the masses of the people. His first convert was of Portuguese descent, a whole-hearted Christian who built a church in 1797, and labored faithfully as a minister and missionary until his death in 1829. He left all his property to the mission.

Carey was a tireless worker. He got up at 5:45, reading a chapter in the Hebrew Bible, "private addresses to God," family prayers with the Bengali servants, reading Persian till tea, translating Scriptures in Hindustani from Sanskrit, teaching at the college from ten till two, correcting proof sheets of Bengali translating of Jeremiah, translating Matthew into Sanskrit, spending one hour with a pundit on Telinga, at seven collecting thoughts for a sermon, preaching at 7:30 to forty persons, translating Bengali till eleven, writing a letter home, reading a chapter from the Greek New Testament and commending himself to God as he lay down to sleep, is a sample of one day's work.

It would appear that Carey's chief work of life was to make translation of the Scriptures and it was his joy before the close of life to see "more than 213,000 volumes of the Divine Word, in forty different languages, issue from the Serampore press."

But this was but a part of his life work. About 1801 he was appointed professor of Sanskrit, Bengali and Marathi in Williams College, Calcutta, which position he held for thirty years. At first he received £600 per year.

When the last revised edition of the Bengali Bible came from the press he felt his labors were near the end. He had hosts of friends because to the very last he maintained a cheerful, hopeful disposition. Once he said to a friend, "There is nothing remarkable in what I have done. It has only required patience and perseverance." At another time he said, "When I compare things as they now are in India with what they were when I came here, I see that a great work has been accomplished, but how it has been accomplished, I know not."

To a friend who had expressed the hope that he might return to his loved work soon he said, "The passage which says, 'If we confess our sins, He is faithful and just to forgive us our sins, and to cleanse us from all unrighteousness,' gives me much comfort. For," he added further, "I am sure I confess my sins and if God forgives them and cleanses me from ALL unrighteousness, what more can I desire?" As his infirmities increased he was carried down into his study each morning, and sat by the desk where he did all his translating.

Here once Alexander Duff called on him. As he withdrew Dr. Carey said, "Mr. Duff, you have been talking about Dr. Carey, Dr. Carey; when I am gone, say nothing about Dr. Carey,—speak about Dr. Carey's Savior!"

Carey died on June 9, 1834. On the block of marble marking his last resting place in the Serampore Christian burial grounds are these words inscribed:

William Carey
Born August 17, 1761
Died June 9, 1834

"A wretched, poor, and helpless worm,
On Thy kind arms I fall."
"Mark the perfect man, and behold the upright, for
the end of that man is peace."

When Carey died there were in connection with the mission he founded some 30 missionaries, 40 native teachers, 45 stations and substations, and approximately 600 church members. In addition one must remember that he was the cause of the forming of the English Baptist Missionary Society, throughu whom Christ has been brought to thousands in different parts of the world . . . it may well be said he was the beginning of the present glorious day of world evangelization. He, whom Sydney Smith ridiculed and satirized in the Edinburgh Review in 1808, as a "consecrated cobbler" and "maniac," accomplished a work for which he is held, and will be held, forever, in high honor as a true friend and benefactor of India.

Chronology of Events in Carey's Life

1761 Born at Paulerspury, Northampton. England. August 17.
1777 Apprenticed to the shoemaking trade.
1779 Attended prayer meeting that changed his life, February 10.
1783 Baptized by Mr. Ryland, October 5.
1786 Called to the ministry at Olney, August 10.
1792 Pamphlet "An Inquiry" published;
Baptist Missionary Society in England formed, October 2.
1793 Appointed missionary to India, January 10;
Arrived in Calcutta, November 11.
1796 Baptized a Portuguese, his first convert.
1800 Moved to Serampore, January 10;
Baptized Krishna Pal, first Bengali convert, December 28;
Elected Professor of Sanskrit and Bengali languages in Williams College.

1801 Completed New Testament in Bengali, February 7.
1803 Self-supporting missionary organization founded.
1807 Doctor of Divinity conferred by Brown University of U.S.A.;
Member of Bengali Asiatic Society.
1808 New Testament in Sanskrit published.
1809 Completed translation of Bible in Bengali, June 24.
1811 New Testament in Marathi published.
1815 New Testament in Punjabi published.
1818 His father died, June 15.
1818 Old Testament in Sanskrit published.
1820 Founded the Agricultural and Horticultural Society, September 4;
Danish King granted charter for college at Serampore;
Marathi Old Testament published.
1821 Serampore college opened.
1825 Completed Dictionary of Bengali and English.
1826 Government gave Carey "Grant in Aid" for education.
1829 Suttee prohibited thru Carey's efforts, December 4.
1834 Died at Serampore, June 9.

Galen B. Royer, Christian Heroism in Heathen Lands, 1915

Elizabeth Fry

Dates
1780–1845

Famous for being
Prison reformer

Important writings
What owest thou unto thy Lord?

One of her quotations
"Punishment is not for revenge, but to lessen crime and reform the criminal."

Elizabeth Fry was a Quaker who became famous for her work to reform the prison system in Britain in the early nineteenth century. By her example she inspired other women to play a fuller role in society: it was unusual for women to have a voice outside the home. It was also unusual for a Quaker to be so prominent, because at that time the Quaker movement was going through a 'quietist' phase, and was very inward looking.

Elizabeth Fry was born on 21 May 1780, the third child of Joseph Gurney, a wealthy Quaker manufacturer, and his wife Catherine. Among the 'plain Quakers' of Goat Lane Meeting in Norwich, the Gurney family stood out because of their bright clothes and fashionable manners. At that time most Quakers were 'plain Quakers' who wore simple clothes without trimmings.

Throughout her life, Elizabeth struggled with her faith. She was not a great mystic, though prayer was a source of strength, but found it easier to be very practical. This led her to make great efforts to help other people. She started by running a Sunday school, in the laundry at the family home in Earlham. The children—many already working in Norwich factories—to whom she told Bible stories, and taught to read and write, were called 'Betsy's imps' by her sisters.

In 1812 she wrote in her diary 'I fear that my life is slipping away to little purpose'. Not long afterwards, Stephen Grellet came to see her to ask for help. He was a French aristocrat who had gone into exile because of the French Revolution. In America he had become a Quaker. While visiting Britain he had been given permission to visit some prisons, and had been horrified by the conditions he had seen in the women's prison in Newgate. He found prisoners lying on the bare stone floors, and some newborn babies without clothing. He went to Elizabeth Fry, who immediately sent out for warm material and asked other women Friends to help her make clothes for the babies.

The next day she went with her sister-in-law to Newgate prison. At first the turnkeys did not want to let her in as the women prisoners were wild and savage, but physical danger did not frighten her, in the way that public speaking and audiences did. Elizabeth and her sister-in-law did go in, and were very shocked at the conditions they found there—particularly when they saw two women stripping the clothes off a dead baby to give them to another child. They gave out the warm clothes for the babies and comforted the ill prisoners. Next day they returned with more warm clothes and with clean straw for the sick to lie on. On a third visit she prayed for the prisoners, who were moved by her sincere words of love for them.

Although she could not forget what she had seen in Newgate, she was unable to visit it for another four years for family reasons. Eventually she returned before Christmas in 1816. When she went in some of the women were fighting, and the turnkeys thought she would be in real danger. She went in calmly and, picking up a child, asked the mothers 'Is there not something we can do for these innocent little children?' She spoke to them as a mother herself, without fear. The women prisoners recognized her concern for them and began to listen. She suggested they might start a school for the children to give them a better chance in life. The prisoners suggested one of themselves to be the teacher and went on discussing the plan after she had gone. When she returned the next day she found a waiting crowd who had tried to tidy and clean the prison and themselves.

Elizabeth formed The Association for the Improvement of the Female Prisoners in Newgate. This group not only organized a school for the children, they arranged for a woman to be appointed as matron to supervise the prisoners, and promised to pay her wages. They also provided materials so that the prisoners could sew, knit and make goods for sale, in order to buy food, clothing and fresh straw for bedding. They took it in turns to visit the prison each day and to read from the Bible, believing that hearing the Bible had the power to reform people. When they applied to the Corporation of London for funding for the school, the Lord Mayor of London came to hear Elizabeth reading the Bible to the prisoners, and he agreed to pay part of the matron's wages.

This was the start of a period of Elizabeth Fry's life when she had extraordinary influence for a woman of her day. In 1818 she was asked to give evidence to a Committee of the House of Commons on London prisons, the first woman to do so. Her experience of Quaker Business Meetings meant she was able to give her evidence clearly and well. She described in detail the lives of the prisoners, and recommended that women, not men, should look after women prisoners, and stressed her belief in the importance of useful employment.

As well as her work with prisoners, Elizabeth Fry set up District Visiting Societies to work with the poor, libraries for coastguards and a training school for nurses. When a small boy was found frozen to death near her home, she set up another Ladies Committee to offer hot soup and a bed to homeless women and children.

News of what she had achieved at Newgate led to the setting up of Ladies Committees in other towns in Britain and in Europe. Some ladies at the Russian court set up a committee to visit prisoners. She also attracted the interest of Queen Victoria who made a donation of £50 and later gave Elizabeth Fry a royal 'audience'. Towards the end of her life she traveled in Europe and visited some of the royal families, talking with them about her work. The King of Prussia even visited her at home and dined with her.

Prison pioneer June Rose says:

> Through her personal courage and involvement, Elizabeth Fry alerted the nations of Europe to the cruelty and filth in the prisons and revealed the individual human faces behind the prison bars. Her own passionate desire to lead a useful life disturbed the placid, vapid existence of women in Victorian England and changed forever the confines of respectable femininity. The name of Elizabeth Fry broadened the appeal of the Quaker faith . . . Over two hundred years after her birth, she seems a brave and modern woman, battling with the injustices of her time.

Charles Grandison Finney

Dates

1792–1875

Famous for being
Revivalist and theologian

Important writings
Systematic Theology

One of his quotations
"You were made to think. It will do you good to think; to develop your powers by study. God designed that religion should require thought, intense thought, and should thoroughly develop our powers of thought."

Summary
Charles Grandison Finney, often called "America's foremost revivalist," was a major leader of the Second Great Awakening in America, which had a great impact on the social history of the United States.

Life and theology
Born in Warren, Connecticut as the youngest of seven children, Finney had humble beginnings. His parents were farmers, and Finney himself never attended college. However, his six foot two inch stature, piercing blue eyes, musical skill, and leadership abilities gained him good standing in his community. He studied as an apprentice to become a lawyer, but after a dramatic conversion experience in Adams, New York at the age of 29, Finney became a minister in the Presbyterian Church. Finney moved to New York City in 1832 where he pastored the Free Presbyterian Chatham Street Chapel and later founded and pastored the Broadway Tabernacle, known today as Broadway United Church of Christ. Finney's logical, clear presentation of his Gospel message reached thousands and promised renewing power and the love of Jesus. Some estimates are that his preaching led to the conversion of over 500,000 people.

Finney was known for his innovations in preaching and conducting religious meetings, such as allowing women to pray in public and the development of the "anxious bench," a place where those considering becoming Christians could come to receive prayer. Finney was also known for his use of extemporaneous preaching.

In addition to being a successful Christian evangelist, Finney was involved with the abolitionist movement and frequently denounced slavery from the pulpit. Beginning in the 1830s, he denied communion to slaveholders in his churches.

In 1835, he moved to Ohio where he would become a professor, and later President of Oberlin College from 1851–1866. Oberlin was a major cultivation ground for the early movement to end slavery. Oberlin was also the first American college to allow blacks and women into the same classrooms as white men.

Finney's place in the social history of the United States

As a new nation, the United States was undergoing massive social flux during the 19th century, and this period birthed quite a large number of independent, trans-denominational religious movements such as Mormonism (1830), as well as Millerism (1830's and beyond), and its offshoots the Jehovah's Witnesses (1870), and the Seventh-day Adventist Church (1863). The nation's westward expansion brought about untold opportunities and a readiness to dispense with old thinking, an attitude that influenced people's religious understanding.

The Burned-over district was a geographical area described by Finney himself the "hot bed" of religious revivalism, and it was in this area (largely western New York State) that he had much of his success. The lack of clergy from established churches ensured that religious activity in these areas was less influenced by traditional Christian teachings.

What Finney managed to achieve was to be the most successful religious revivalist during this period, and in this particular area. While groups such as the Jehovah's Witnesses, Mormons and Seventh-day Adventists became closed and exclusivist, Finney was widely admired and influential amongst more mainstream Christians. Finney never started his own denomination or church, and never claimed any form of special prophetic leadership that elevated himself above other evangelists and revivalists.

Finney's theology

Finney was a primary influence on the "revival" style of theology which emerged in the 19th century. Though coming from a Calvinistic background, Finney rejected several tenets of "Old Divinity" Calvinism which he felt were unbiblical and counter to evangelism and Christian mission.

Finney's rejection of Calvinism was not total. In his Systematic Theology, Finney fully embraced the Calvinist doctrine of the "Perseverance of the Saints." At the same time, he took the presence of unrepented sin in the life of a professing Christian as evidence that they must immediately repent or be lost. This type of teaching underscores the strong emphasis on personal holiness found in Finney's writings.

Wikipedia

Søren Aabye Kierkegaard

Dates

1813–1855

Famous for being

Existentialist philosopher

Important writings
Training in Christianity and Fear and Trembling

One of his quotations
"To stand on one leg and prove God's existence is a very different thing from going on one's knees and thanking Him."

Søren Aabye Kierkegaard was a 19th century Danish philosopher and theologian, generally recognized as the first existentialist philosopher. He bridged the gap that existed between Hegelian philosophy and what was to become Existentialism. Kierkegaard strongly criticized both the Hegelian philosophy of his time, and what he saw as the empty formalities of the Danish church. Much of his work deals with religious problems such as the nature of faith, the institution of the Christian Church, Christian ethics and theology, and the emotions and feelings of individuals when faced with existential choices. Because of this, Kierkegaard's work is sometimes characterized as Christian existentialism and existential psychology. Since he wrote most of his early work under various pseudonyms, which would often comment on and critique the works of his other pseudo-authors, it can be exceedingly difficult to distinguish between what Kierkegaard truly believed and what he was merely arguing for as part of a pseudo-author's position. Crossing the boundaries of philosophy, theology, psychology, and literature, Kierkegaard came to be regarded as a highly significant and influential figure in contemporary thought.

"I suppose the reason for evangelicals criticizing Kierkegaard is due to the danger of the philosophy of existentialism in the hands of faithless men. With the focus on the necessarily subjective experience of living, from the wrong frame of reference Kierkegaard could lead to excessive narcissism, self-centeredness, and moral relativity." Le Penseur Réfléchit, 2002

David Livingstone

Dates
1813–1873

Famous for being
Missionary and explorer

Important writings
Missionary Travels and Researches in South Africa

One of his quotations
"Fear God and work hard."

Summary

David Livingstone was a Scottish missionary, doctor and explorer who helped open the heart of Africa to missions. His travels covered one-third of the continent, from the Cape to near the Equator, and from the Atlantic to the Indian Ocean.

Early Life

David, the second son, was born on March 19, 1813. From childhood he showed unusual love for nature, and through great perseverance, which always characterized his life, gained prizes and excelled his playmates in many ways. At ten he made his own living in the cotton mills while spending his evenings in night school. Through reading Dick's "Philosophy of the Future State" he was led to confess Christ; the life of Henry Martyn, first modern missionary to Mohammedans, and Charles Gutslaff, medical missionary to China, fixed his life purpose.

"It is my desire to show my attachment to the cause of Him Who died for me by devoting my life to His service." Contact with Robert Moffat, pioneer missionary to Africa, prompted Livingstone to offer his services to this needy field. Ordained as a missionary in Albion Street Chapel, London, on November 8, 1840; Livingstone had only one night's visit home and that an all night's conference about missions. He was accompanied by his father to Broomiclaw, where they parted; never to meet again.

First Experiences in Africa

On December 8, 1840, Livingstone sailed for Africa. Going by Cape Town and Algoa Bay he was soon in the interior where Moffat was at work in the Bechuana territory. On the way he was incensed at the unkind treatment of the natives by Europeans. His had an intense desire that all natives should have an opportunity to embrace Christianity, so he started to work where no white man had previously worked, and this led him to locate at Mabotsa, northward in the interior. This locality was infested by lions; and one day one which the natives had wounded sprang out of the bushes, seized Livingstone by the shoulder, tore his flesh and broke his arm.

Marriage

In 1844 Livingstone married Mary Moffat, oldest daughter of Robert and Mary Moffat. To them six children were born, one dying in infancy. Few couples enjoyed living together better than this one; but for the sake of Africa they were often parted from each other. Thoughtless and unfriendly remarks about their separation caused them much heartache.

Self-Denial and Losses

Livingstone conceived the idea that, if a way were opened from the interior to the coast, Christianity, civilization and commerce would move freely to isolated peoples. But the undertaking involved fearful hardships and much self-denial. It was about this time that he wrote, "I place no value on anything I have or possess except in relation to the kingdom of Christ."

Taking his wife and children to Cape Town, where amidst many tears and heart struggles he saw them sail for England on April 23, 1852, he set his face to this new purpose. But he found many obstacles. The Dutch Boers, who had robbed and subjected the natives to the worst slavery, opposed his efforts. They even destroyed to the extent of his home. Undaunted, however, by any opposition, Livingstone continued exploring the regions preaching, teaching and healing,—making notes and observations of a geographical and scientific nature and forwarding them to England,—thus he sought to do the Father's will as he wrote, "As for me, I am determined to open up Africa or perish."

First Visit Home

After sixteen years of absence Livingstone made his first visit to England, arriving December 9, 1856. Had he risen from the grave he could not have been looked upon with more interest or loaded with more honors. Societies, colleges and others vied with each other in doing him honor. Mrs. Livingstone, who had heard the unfriendly criticism about their prolonged separation and her husband's exploring instead of doing regular missionary work, and who had endured the long, lonely months of waiting, stood by his side through all this flood of honor. Lord Shaftesbury on one occasion "paid her equal tribute with her husband and all England said 'Amen.'"

Extensive Explorations

On March 10, 1858, Dr. and Mrs. Livingstone, with their son Oswell, sailed from England. At Cape Town Mrs. Livingstone became so ill that she had to remain behind. After spending a year at the Cape, Mrs. Livingstone returned to England and placed her children in school. In 1862 she joined her husband in Africa, but died three months later. Of this time Livingstone wrote: "For the first time in my life I want to die."

His second return

After his second trip back to England Livingstone returned to Africa again. The next two years, July, 1869, to October, 1871, were spent in a journey from Ujiji to the river Lealaba and return, and were perhaps the saddest years of his life. He witnessed the thousand villages about which Moffat told, and which caused him to give his life to Africa. He, himself, preached to thousands and tens of thousands of natives. But his strength failed him in 1871. Feet sore from ulcers; teeth falling out through sickness; weary in body and sick of heart, he lay in his hut for eighty days, longing for home, now far beyond his reach. His sole comfort and help was his Bible, which he read through four times during this period, and upon the flyleaf of which he wrote these significant words: "No letters for three years. I have a sore longing to finish and go home, if God wills." Supplies and letters had been sent, but were intercepted by the Portuguese. The Royal Geographical Society had sent out a search party but failed to find him.

The Discoverer Discovered

Just at this moment of mystery about Livingstone's whereabouts, James Gordon Bennett, of the New York Herald, sent Henry M. Stanley to locate the explorer "at any cost." Stanley wrote, "No living man shall stop me. Only death can prevent me; but death,—not even this. I shall not die; I will not die; I cannot die. Something tells me that I shall find him. And I write it larger, find him, FIND HIM."

At last after forced marches he met Susi, who came to meet Stanley, and then soon the explorer himself. "Dr. Livingstone, I presume?" said Stanley, as he lifted his hat.

"Yes," replied the pale, weary, grey-haired missionary.

"I thank my God I am permitted to see you," said Stanley.

To this came the reply, "I feel thankful that I am here to welcome you."

It was a wonderful day for Livingstone. Letters and supplies were abundant and appreciated. He forgot his ailments and became overjoyed in this Good Samaritan act. Together the men spent four months exploring Lake Tanganyika. Stanley became a hero worshipper of his companion. Once he wrote, "I challenge any man to find a fault in his character . . . The secret is that his religion is a constant, earnest and sincere practice."

"Forward."

Once in his early life Livingstone said, "Anywhere, providing it is forward." Thus he was impelled even in old age. For, instead of returning with Stanley, he was now determined to continue his explorations. On March 19, 1872, when fifty-nine years old he wrote, "My birthday! My Jesus, my King, my Life, my All. I again dedicate my whole self to Thee." But the grey-haired, footsore explorer and missionary this time went forward thru swollen rivers and dismal swamps, every day of the march being marked with dysentery and most excruciating pain. At every convenient place he would have his carriers stop and let him rest. April 29 was his last day of travel. He had reached the village of Chitambo, in Ilala, on Lake Bangweolo.

Victory

He rested quietly on the 30th; but at four on the morning of May 1,1873, the boy who slept at Livingstone's door wakened, beheld his master, and fearing death, called Susi.

By the candle still burning they saw him, not in bed; but kneeling at the bedside, with his head buried in his hands upon the pillow. The sad, yet not unexpected truth soon became evident; he had passed away on the furthest of all his journeys, and without a single attendant. But he had died in the act of prayer,—prayer offered in that reverent attitude about which he was always so particular; commending his own spirit, with all his dear ones as he was wont, into the hands of his Savior; and commending Africa, his own dear Africa, with all her woes and sins and wrongs, to the Avenger of the oppressed and the Redeemer of the lost.

They removed the heart from the body of their dead leader and buried it under a tree near where he died. They dried the body in the sun, tied it to a pole and after nine months' march reached the coast and shipped it to England. On April 18, 1874, the remains were laid to rest, in Westminster Abbey, London.

Chronology of Events in Livingstone's Life

1813 Born at Blantyre, in Lanarkshire, Scotland, March 19.

1833 Real conversion took place in his life.

1838 Accepted by London Missionary Society, September.

1840 Ordained missionary in Albion St. Chapel, November 20

Sailed on H.M.S. "George" for Africa, December 8.

1841 Arrived at Kuruman, July 31.

1842 Extended tour of Bechuana country begun February 10.

1844 Marriage to Mary Moffat of Kuruman.

1848 Sechele, first convert, baptized, October 1.

1849 Lake 'Ngami discovered, August 1.

1850 Royal Geographical Society awarded royal donation, 25 guineas.

1851 Discovered the upper Zambesi, August 3.

1852 Mrs. Livingstone and four children sailed from Cape Town, April 23.

1853 Journey from Linyanti to west coast, November 11 to May 31, 1854.

1854 French Geographical Society awarded silver medal;

University of Glasgow conferred degree LL.D.;

Journey from west coast back to Linyanti, September 24 to September 11, 1855.

1855 Journey from Linyanti to Quilimane on east coast, November 3 to May 20, 1856;

Royal Geographical Society awarded Patron's Gold Medal.

1856 Arrived in London on first visit home, December 9.

1857 Freedom of cities of London, Glasgow, Edinburgh, Dundee and many other towns; Corresponding Member of American Geographical and Statistical Society, New York; Royal Geographical Society, London; Geographical Society of Paris; K. K. Geographical Society of Vienna; Honorary Fellow of Faculty and Physicians of Glasgow; Degree of D.C.L. by University of Oxford; elected F.H.S.; appointed Commander of Zambesi Expedition and her Majesty's Consul at Tette, Quilimane, Senna

1858 Returned with Mrs. Livingstone to Africa, March 10.

1859 River Shire explored and Lake Nyassa discovered, September 16.

1862 Mrs. Livingstone died at Shupanga, April 27;

Explored the Yovuma River.

1864 Arrived in Bombay, June 13; London, July 23.

1866 Arrived at Zanzibar, January 28.

1867 Discovered Lake Tanganyika April.

1868 Discovered Lake Bangweolo, July 18.

1869 Arrived at Ujiji, March 14.

1871 Reached Nyangwe, March 29; returned to Ujiji a "living skeleton," October 23.

Henry M. Stanley found him October 28.

1872 Gold Medal by Italian Geographical Society.

1873 Died in his tent at Ilala, May 1.

1874 Body buried with honors in Westminster Abbey, London, April 18.

Galen B. Royer, Christian Heroism in Heathen Lands 1915.

C. H. Spurgeon

Dates

1834–1892

Famous for being

Baptist preacher

Important writings

The Treasury of David

Sermons

Lectures to My Students

One of his quotations

"By perseverance the snail reached the ark."

Introduction

C. H. Spurgeon was to nineteenth-century England what D. L Moody was to America. Although Spurgeon never attended theological school, by the age of twenty-one he was the most popular preacher in London.

He preached to crowds of ten thousand at Exeter Hall and the Surrey Music Hall. Then when the Metropolitan Tabernacle was built, thousands gathered every Sunday for over forty years to hear his lively sermons.

In addition to his regular pastoral duties, he founded Sunday schools, churches, an orphanage, and the Pastor's College. He edited a monthly church magazine and promoted literature distribution.

Sincerely and straightforwardly he denounced error both in the Church of England and among his own Baptists. An ardent evangelical, he deplored the trend of the day toward biblical criticism.

Charles Haddon Spurgeon, preacher, came from a family of Dutch origin which sought refuge in England during the persecution of the Duke of Alva. Charles Haddon's grandfather, James Spurgeon (1776–1864), born at Halstead, Essex, was independent minister at Stambourne. His son, John Spurgeon, the father of Charles Haddon, born in 1811, was successively minister of the independent congregations of Tollesbury, Essex, of Cranbrook, Kent, of Fetter Lane, and of Upper Street, Islington.

Charles Haddon, elder son of John Spurgeon, by his wife, the youngest sister of Charles Parker Jarvis of Colchester, was born at Kelvedon, Essex, [England] on 19 June 1834. His early childhood was spent with his grandfather, James Spurgeon, but in 1841 he was sent to a school at Colchester conducted by Henry Lewis. In 1848 he spent a few months at an agricultural college at Maidstone. In the following year he became usher in a school at Newmarkert. His employer was a Baptist, and although Spurgeon had been reared an independent, and converted in a primitive Methodist chapel, he was baptised and formally joined the Baptist community at Isleham on 3 May 1850. In the same year he obtained a place in a school at Cambridge, recently founded by a former teacher and friend, Henry Leeding. There he became an active member of a Baptist congregation, and while a boy of sixteen, dressed in a jacket and turndown collar, preached his first sermon in a cottage at Teversham, near Cambridge.

His success was pronounced; his oratorical gifts were at once recognized, and in 1852 he became the pastor of the Baptist congregation at Waterbeach, Cambridgeshire. In April 1854 he was 'called' to the pulpit of the Baptist congregation at New Park Street, Southwark. Within a few months of his call his powers as a preacher made him famous. The chapel had been empty; before a year had passed the crowds that gathered to hear the country lad of twenty rendered its enlargement essential. Exeter Hall was used while the new building was in process of erection, but Exeter Hall could not contain Spurgeon's hearers. The enlarged chapel, when opened, at once proved too small, and a great tabernacle was projected. In the meantime Spurgeon preached at the Surrey Gardens music-hall, where his congregations numbered ten thousand. Men and women of all ranks flocked to his sermons. The newspapers, from the 'Times' downwards, discussed him and his influence.

Caricature and calumny played their part. On 19 Oct. 1856 a malicious alarm of fire raised while Spurgeon was preaching at the Surrey Gardens music-hall led to a panic which caused the death of seven persons and the injury of many others; but the preacher's position was not endangered. At twenty-two Spurgeon was the most popular preacher of the day.

In 1861 the Metropolitan Tabernacle in Newington Causeway was opened for service. It cost £31,000, and accommodated six thousand persons. There Spurgeon ministered until his death, and, until illness disabled him, fully maintained his popularity and power as a preacher. The Tabernacle quickly became, under Spurgeon's impressive personality, an energetic center of religious life. Many organizations grew up under his care and were affiliated to it. All are now flourishing institutions. A pastors' college, in which young men prepared for the ministry under his active guidance, was founded at Camberwell in 1856; it was removed to the Metropolitan Tabernacle in 1861, and is now located in Temple Street, Southwark. An orphanage, an unsectarian institution, was founded in 1867 at Stockwell for the maintenance and education of destitute orphan boys and girls . . . ; while a colportage association founded in 1866 to circulate 'religious and healthy literature among all classes' by means of colporteurs, who were to be paid a fixed salary and to devote all their time to the work, derived in 1891 over £11,000 by the sale of books and pamphlets.

A convinced Calvinist, staunchly adhering till the day of his death to every point in the system of theology in which he had been educated, Spurgeon was resolved to sacrifice nothing in the way of doctrine, even in the interests of peace among Christian churches. In 1864 he invited a controversy with the evangelical party in the church of England. In a powerful sermon on baptismal regeneration which he preached in that year he showed that that doctrine, to which he was strenuously hostile, was accepted in the church of England prayer-book, and he reproached evangelical churchmen, who in principle were equally antagonistic to the doctrine, with adhering to an organization which taught it. The attack occasioned much ferment. Three hundred thousand copies of Spurgeon's sermon were sold; and while high churchmen were elated by Spurgeon's admission that a doctrine, which they openly avowed, found a place in the prayer-book, low-churchmen were proportionately irritated. Numberless pamphlets set forth the views of the various parties. The most effective reply to Spurgeon was made by Baptist Wriothesley Noel, then a Baptist minister. In his 'Evangelical Clergy Defended,' Noel censured Spurgeon for introducing needless divisions among men of like faith. But Spurgeon remained obdurate, and emphasized his attitude by withdrawing from the Evangelical Alliance, which was largely supported by the low-church party of the church of England.

Spurgeon's strenuous and unbending faith in Calvinism loosened in course of time the bonds of sympathy between him and a large section of his own denomination. He long watched with misgivings the growth among Baptists of what he regarded as indifference to orthodoxy. He thought they laid too little stress on Christ's divine nature, and that the Arminian views which were spreading among them tended to Arianism. He keenly resented what he called the 'down grade' developments of modern biblical criticism, and the conviction grew on him that faith was decaying in all Christian churches. Consequently on 26 Oct. 1887 he announced his withdrawal from the Baptist Union, the central association of Baptist ministers, which declined to adopt the serious view that he took of the situation. Opposition to the rationalizing tendency of modern biblical criticism brought him in his later days into sympathy with many churchmen. It was perhaps on that account that he withdrew from the Liberation Society, of which he had been previously a vigorous supporter.

On the completion in 1879 of the twenty-fifth year of his pastorate at the Tabernacle, Spurgeon was presented with a testimonial of £6,263. During the latter part of his life he lived in some style at Norwood. He never practiced or affected to practice asceticism, but was generous in the use of the ample means with which his congregation supplied him. His opinions on social questions were always remarkable for sanity and common-sense. A liberal in politics, Spurgeon was, after 1886, a prominent supporter of the liberal-unionist party in its opposition to home rule for Ireland. Towards the end of his life he suffered severely from gout, and was repeatedly forced to take long rests. He died at Mentone on 31 Jan. 1892, and was buried at Norwood cemetery, London. The Memorial Hall at Stockwell and the Beulah Baptist Chapel at Bexhill (commenced in 1895) were erected in memory of him. The best portrait of Spurgeon is an oil painting in the pastor's vestry, Metropolitan Tabernacle, and there is a bust by Mr. Acton-Adams at the Pastors' College.

Spurgeon married, in 1856, Susannah, daughter of Robert Thompson of Falcon Square, London, by whom he had twin sons, Charles and Thomas. His widow and sons survived him.

Spurgeon's early fame as a preacher was largely due to his extreme youth, to the free play of his humor, and to the fervor of his unconventional appeals to the conscience. But he was by nature endowed with much oratorical power. He managed with the utmost skill a clear and sympathetic voice, while his gesture was easy and natural. Throughout life his matter united shrewd comment upon contemporary life with the expository treatment favored by the old puritan divines. In later life he spoke in the pulpit with somewhat less oratorical effect, but with an intenser earnestness. His humor was spontaneous; it marked his private as well as his public utterances.

Spurgeon was a prolific author, writing with the directness and earnestness that distinguished him as a speaker. From 1865 he conducted a monthly magazine, entitled 'Sword and Trowel.' From 1855 a sermon by him was published every week. These have been collected in numerous volumes, and many of them have been translated into the chief European languages. As many as 2,500 sermons are still on sale. Of his other works, nearly all of which ran into many editions, the most important were:

1. 'The Saint and his Savior,' 1857.
2. 'Morning by Morning,' 1866.
3. 'Evening by Evening,' 1868.
4. 'John Ploughman's Talks,' 1869.
5. 'The Treasury of David,' 1870–85.
6. 'Lectures to my Students,' 1st. ser. 1875; 2nd ser. 1877.
7. 'Commenting and Commentaries,' 1876.
8. 'John Ploughman's Pictures,' 1880.
9. 'My Sermon Notes,' 1884–7.

An autobiography compiled by his wife and the Rev. W. J. Harrald, his private secretary, from his dairy, letters, and records, appeared in four volumes in 1897–8.

Dictionary of National Biography, 1898

Timeline of C. H. Spurgeon

1834 Born at Kelvedon, Essex England, June 19

1850 Born again at Colchester, January 6

1850 Becomes a Baptist, May 3 (Baptized in the River Lark, at Isleham)

1850 Preaches first sermon, at a Cottage in Teversham

1851 Preached First Sermon at Waterbeach Baptist Chapel, October 12

1853 Preached First Sermon at New Park Street Chapel, London, December 18

1854 Accepts pastorate at New Park Street Chapel, April 28 (232 members then)

1855 First Sermon in the "New Park Street Pulpit" published, January 10

1856 MARRIAGE to Miss Susannah Thompson (born 1/15/1832), January 8

1856 Twin sons (not identical) Thomas and Charles Born, September 20

1856 Metropolitan Tabernacle Building Committee Begins, June

1856 Establishes The Pastor's College

1861 Metropolitan Tabernacle opens with a Great Prayer Meeting, March 18

1867 Stockwell Orphanage (Boy's side) Founded

1867 Foundation Stone Laid by Senior Deacon Thomas Olney for the Pastor's College Building, May 6 (with construction completed in March, 1868)

1871 Begins Annual Vacations to Southern France for Rest & Relaxation, December

1873 Foundation Stone Laid for a newer Pastor's College Building, October 14

1875 Mrs. Spurgeon's Book Fund Inaugurated

1879 Presentation of the Pastoral Silver Wedding Gift (offering) May 20

1879 Stockwell Orphanage (Girl's side) Founded

1884 Jubilee celebrations and Testimonials, June 18–19

1887 "Down Grade" Paper Published in The Sword & the Trowel, August

1888 Spurgeon's Mother Eliza dies

1891 Last sermon Delivered at Metropolitan Tabernacle, June 7

1891 As year ends, Tabernacle membership given as 5,311

1891 Suffers much pain and sickness during the months of June & July

1891 Travels to Mentone France again (for the Last Time), October 26. While there, becomes severely ill from his long-suffering combination of Rheumatism, Gout and Bright's disease (Kidney)

1892 Still Resting in Mentone, he Finally takes to bed, January 20

1892 Spurgeon dies, January 31

1892 Buried at Norwood Cemetery, February 11

D. L. Moody

Dates
1837–1899

Famous for being
Evangelist

Important writings
Sermons

One of his quotations
"Work as if everything depended on you and pray as if everything depended on God."

Summary
Dwight Lyman Moody was an American evangelist who founded the Northfield Schools in Massachusetts, Moody Church and Moody Bible Institute in Chicago, and the Colportage Association. Ira Sankey was solo singer/music director for their evangelistic campaigns in both the United States and Great Britain.

Dwight Lyman Moody was born at Northfield, Massachusetts. He was the sixth of the nine children of Edwin and Betsy Moody. His father, who was a mason, died in 1841 (aged 41) and the family was in very straitened circumstances for years. His mother died in 1895, aged ninety. Moody received his first religious impressions in the village Unitarian church and his first missionary work involved encouraging children to attend his own Sunday-school.

In September 1856, he went to Chicago and made a reputation as a salesman and traveler in the shoe trade. But while diligent in his business and uncommonly successful he became absorbed more and more in religious work. His energies were first spent upon the Sunday-school as teacher, as gatherer-in of new pupils, and most unpromising ones, who under his instruction improved marvelously, and then as superintendent of the North Market Hall Sunday-school which he built up until it had a membership of 1,500 and out of it in 1863 the Illinois Street Church was formed. In 1861 he gave up business and was an independent city missionary, then agent of the Christian Commission in the Civil War and after that again in Sunday-school work and the secretary of the Chicago Young Men's Christian Association. But as yet he had done nothing to give him international fame.

In 1867 he made a visit to Great Britain on account of his wife's health—he had married in 1862. He made some valuable acquaintances and did a little evangelistic work. One of his converts was John Kenneth Mackenzie. In 1872 he was again in Great Britain, held numerous meetings and won the esteem of prominent Evangelicals. From these he received an invitation to return for general revival work. He came the next year, bringing with him

Ira David Sankey, who was from then on linked with him in his revivalist work. They landed at Liverpool on June 17, 1873, and held their first services in York. Moody's downright preaching and Sankey's simple but soul stirring singing won attention, and as they passed from city to city they were heard by great crowds. They spent two years in this arduous labor, and then returned to America.

Moody had "consecrated common sense." He was honest, preached a Calvinistic creed which he accepted with all his heart, and was master of an effective style. His sermons and shorter addresses abound in personal allusions, and in shrewd remarks. He had no polish, little education, but he knew the English Bible and accepted it literally. He was fond of treating Bible characters very familiarly and enlivening his sermons by imaginary conversations with and between them. But that he was truly bent upon promoting the kingdom of God by the ways he thought most helpful there is no doubt. For sanity, sincerity, spirituality, and success Moody goes into the very first rank of revival preachers.

While Moody belonged to the independent Chicago Avenue Church, his activities he belonged to the Church universal.

The New Schaff-Herzog Encyclopedia of Religious Knowledge, 1910

Moody Bible Institute

Moody Bible Institute (MBI) was founded by evangelist and businessman Dwight Lyman Moody in 1886. The campus, founded by prayer in the heart of Chicago, has stood firm on the same property chosen by Moody more than 120 years ago.

History

In 1886 D. L. Moody established MBI, then know as the Chicago Evangelization Society, for the "the education and training of Christian workers, including teachers, ministers, missionaries and musicians who may completely and effectively proclaim the gospel of Jesus Christ."

Today

The Moody Bible Institute is a non-profit, fully accredited higher education institution, with related ministries in broadcasting, publishing, and conferences.

"Our flagship ministry is education, and we offer three different education divisions: undergraduate school, graduate school and distance learning. MBI trains students for full-time ministry in churches and para-church organizations."

Other Christian leaders in the Christian Church in the nineteenth century

Christmas Evans (1766–1838)
Adoniram Judson (1788–1850)
Robert Murray McCheyne (1813–1843)

Fanny Crosby (1820–1915)
James Hudson Taylor (1832–1905)
Frances Ridley Havergal (1836–1879)
Ira Sankey (1840–1908)

Christmas Evans (1766–1838)

Christmas Evans, one of the great Welsh preachers, was born on Christmas day 1766, at a place called Ysgaerwen, in the parish of Llandyssul, Cardiganshire [Wales]. His father, Samuel Evans, was a poor shoemaker, who, dying when his son was only nine years old, left him in a state of complete destitution. The next six years Christmas spent with his mother's uncle at Llanvihangel-ar-Arth in Carmarthenshire, "than whom," he says, "it would be difficult to find a more unconscionable man in the whole course of a wicked world." So he left him to become a farm servant at various places, and ultimately came under the influence of David Davies of Castellhywel, a well-known bard and schoolmaster, and the minister of a congregation of presbyterians at Llwynrhydowen. Evans joined Llwynrhydowen Chapel, was taught a little by Davies in his school, learnt how to read Welsh, and acquired some knowledge of English; became religious, and began to preach. But as the strict rules of the presbyterians required an academic education for their ministers, he gradually gravitated towards the Baptists, who had no such limitations, and in 1788 was baptised in the river Duar at Llanybyther in Carmarthenshire, and joined the Baptist congregation at Aberduar.

In 1789 Evans was ordained as a sort of missionary to the scattered Baptists of Lleyn, on the peninsula of Carnarvonshire. Here he married Catherine Jones, a member of his congregation. They had no family. While there he was "converted" during a preaching journey, and now began to preach with a power and earnestness of conviction that soon made him famous.

In 1792 he moved to Anglesey to act as minister to all the Baptist churches in the island. He lived at Llangevni, where the most important chapel was situated. Here he worked with great success, but a curious wave of Sandemanianism spread over Anglesey and greatly influenced rigid Calvinists like Evans.

Evans once commented, "The Sandemanian heresy afflicted me so much as to drive away the spirit of prayer for the salvation of sinners." After a time he regained his orthodoxy, and became the center of a great Baptist movement in Anglesey. Crowds flocked to hear his sermons. His humor sometimes threw a congregation into roars of laughter, often changed in a moment by his pathos into tears, and his startling power of declamation exercised extraordinary influence on all who heard him, whom his brethren called the "Bunyan of Wales." He remained in Anglesey more than thirty years.

While on a journey to South Wales he was suddenly taken ill, and died on 19 July 1838 at Swansea, where on 23 July he was buried with great honor in the burial-ground of the

Welsh Baptist chapel. His sermons were published in Welsh. He also wrote some hymns and tracts in Welsh, and assisted in translating into that language an exposition of the New Testament.

Dictionary of National Biography, 1889

Adoniram Judson (1788–1850)

Adoniram Judson was born at Malden, Massachusetts. Although his father was a Congregational minister, Judson embraced skeptical views of Christianity as a young man.

However, he went to Andover Theological Seminary where he was converted. The reading of Buchanan's "Star in the East," and the influence of his associates, Mills, Richards, and Hall, helped him decide to become a foreign missionary.

Judson, Hall, Newell, and Nott were sent as missionaries to Burmah. But Judson changed his beliefs about baptism so he and his wife were baptized by immersion on reaching Calcutta. The strained relations between England and America, England and Burmah, made their stay in Calcutta inadvisable, and they sailed to Mauritius, where they remained four months, doing missionary work among the English sailors of the garrison, and later left for Madras. On reaching their destination they learned of the order for the transportation of the American missionaries from Bombay to England, so they sailed at once for Rangoon, the principal port of the Burman empire, arriving there July, 1813. More than a year passed before Judson learned of the formation of the Baptist general convention, and that it had taken him under its care.

For three years he devoted himself to the study of the difficult Burmese language, and mastered it so thoroughly that he spoke with the freedom of a native; having practically abandoned the use of the English language, he both thought and spoke in Burmese, only allowing himself one English newspaper.

After six years his first convert was baptized. During this time he published tracts, translated the gospel of Matthew and the Epistle to the Ephesians, conducted public preaching, and worked indefatigably for the furtherance of his work, despite the unfriendly attitude of the Burmese monarch.

In 1824 he moved to Ava where he preached for a short time until war between the English and the Burmese broke out, which placed the missionaries in real danger and resulted in extreme hardships and suffering. Mr. Judson was imprisoned for two years at Ava, confined in the "death-prison," and subjected to the most extreme cruelty, being bound with either three or five pairs of fetters. In these straits he was only saved from actual starvation by the unwearying attentions of his faithful wife; for the prisoners were not supplied with food by the jailers. Mrs. Judson besought the officials to release and assist the missionaries; with her babe (born at this trying time), and a faithful Bengalese servant, following her husband who had been driven with the others, under the fierce sun, from one prison to another. Through the influence of Sir Archibald

Campbell, at the end of two years Mr. Judson was finally released, and with his wife left Ava for Amherst, the capital of the Provinces.

At the invitation of the British East India government Mr. Judson returned as interpreter with an embassy to Ava, to negotiate a new treaty between the English and the Burmese. Shortly after he died his wife died, in 1826, having become so weakened by her hardships and sufferings that she was unable to resist the fever which attacked her. Her child died soon after this, leaving the missionary alone. The record of Mrs. Judson's life and sufferings is well known and has hardly a parallel in female missionary annals.

In 1829 Judson joined the Boardmans at Maulmain, which became the chief seat of the Baptist mission in Burmah. Here schools and a house of worship were built, and a number of converts were added to the church.

About this time Judson thoroughly revised the New Testament in Burmese, and prepared twelve smaller works in the same tongue. In 1830 he visited central Burmah and gave away hundreds of tracts, besides making many converts, his boat at every landing being visited by natives anxious for books, and where his earlier converts greeted him. It was at this time also that he visited the Karen jungles, where his labors were so fruitful that during the next twenty-five years 20,000 Karen people converted to Christianity. Before returning to Maulmain he spent a year at Rangoon, and devoted himself to the work of the translation of the Scriptures into Burmese, which he completed in 1834, when he at once began the revision of the Scriptures, and completed this great labor in 1840. While in Rangoon he shut himself in an upper room to concentrate on his translation work.

The title of D.D. was given to Judson by Brown University in 1823. His literary works were a Burman dictionary, a Pali dictionary, a Burman grammar, and a complete Burman Bible. He was well known throughout India, being honored by English and native dignitaries alike, and the converts of his thirty-seven years of missionary labor deeply loved and revered him. He died April 12, 1850, three days out from Burmah, and was buried at sea.

The National Cyclopædia of American Biography, 1893

Robert Murray McCheyne (1813–1843)

Robert Murray McCheyne, Scottish divine, youngest son of Adam McCheyne, was born in Edinburgh, 21 May 1813. At the age of four he knew the characters of the Greek alphabet, and was able to sing and recite fluently. He entered high school in his eighth year, and matriculated in November 1827 at Edinburgh University, where he showed very versatile powers, and distinguished himself especially in poetical exercises, being awarded a special prize by Professor Wilson for a poem on 'The Covenanters.' In the winter of 1831 he commenced his studies in the Divinity Hall, under Dr. Chalmers and Dr. Welsh; and he was licensed as a preacher by the Annan presbytery on 1 July 1835.

In the following November he was appointed assistant to the Rev. John Bonar of Larbert and Dunipace, Stirlingshire. His health, which had never been robust, broke down under the strain of his new office; but his fame as a preacher spread through Scotland, and on 24 November 1836 he was ordained to the pastorate of St. Peter's Church, Dundee. The congregation numbered eleven hundred hearers, and McCheyne addressed himself to the work of the ministry with so much ardor that his health again gave way, and in December 1838 he was compelled to desist from all public duty.

At this time the general assembly of the church of Scotland decided to send a committee to Palestine to collect information respecting the Jews, and McCheyne was included in the number who set sail on 12 April 1839. The record of this journey was written jointly by McCheyne and his companion Andrew Bonar (died 1892), and was published in 1842. After his return at the end of 1839 McCheyne resumed his ministerial duties in Dundee with renewed energy. In the autumn of 1842 he visited the north of England on an evangelical mission, and made similar journeys to London and Aberdeenshire. On his return from the latter place he was seized with sudden illness, and died on Saturday, 25 March 1843. He was buried beside St. Peter's Church, Dundee, where an imposing tombstone marks his grave.

McCheyne devoted all his energies to preaching. He had refined musical taste, and was one of the first of the Scottish ministers to take an active part in the improvement of the congregational service of praise. Long after his death he was constantly referred to as 'the saintly McCheyne.'

His principal works are:

1. Narrative of a Mission of Inquiry to the Jews (jointly with Dr. Andrew Bonar)
2. Expositions of the Epistles to the Seven Churches of Asia
3. The Eternal Inheritance: the Believer's Portion, and Vessels of Wrath fitted to Destruction, two Discourses
4. Memoirs and Remains
5. Additional Remains, Sermons, and Lectures
6. Basket of Fragments, the substance of Sermons

Dictionary of National Biography, 1893

Fanny Crosby (1820–1915)

Hymn Writer and Poetess

Frances Jane Crosby, the daughter of John and Mercy Crosby, was born in Southeast, Putnam County, New York on March 24, 1820. She became blind at the age of six weeks from maltreatment of her eyes during a period of sickness.

Once time a preacher sympathetically remarked, "I think it is a great pity that the Master did not give you sight when He showered so many other gifts upon you."

She replied quickly, "Do you know that if at birth I had been able to make one petition, it would have been that I should be born blind?"

"Why?" asked the surprised clergyman.

"Because when I get to heaven, the first face that shall ever gladden my sight will be that of my Savior!"

At the age of fifteen she entered the New York Institution for the Blind, where she received a good education. She became a teacher in the Institution in 1847, and continued her work until March 1, 1858. She taught English grammar, rhetoric, Roman and American history. This was the great developing period in her life. During the vacations of 1852 and 1853, spent at North Reading, Massachusetts, she wrote the words to many songs for Dr. Geo. F. Root, then the teacher of music at the Institution.

In addition to the thousands of hymns that she has written wrote (about eight thousand poems in all), many of which have not been set to music, she has published four volumes of verses. The first was issued in 1844, and was entitled "The Blind Girl, and Other Poems"; a second volume, "Monterey, and Other Poems," followed in 1849, and the third, "A Wreath of Columbia's Flowers," in 1858.

Though these show the poetical bent of her mind, they have little to do with her world-wide fame. It is as a writer of Sunday-school songs and gospel hymns that she is known.

Since 1864 she has supported herself by writing hymns. She has resided in New York City nearly all her life, where, she saysaid, she iswas "a member of the Old John Street M. E. Church in good standing." She spendst regular hours on certain days at the office of The Biglow & Main Co., the firm for which she doesid most of her writing, and for whom she has composed over four thousand hymns.

Her hymns have been in great demand and have been used by many of our most popular composers, among whom may be mentioned Wm. B. Bradbury, Geo. F. Root, W. H. Doane, Rev. Robert Lowry, Ira, D. Sankey, J. R. Sweney, W. J. Kirkpatrick, H. P. Main, H. P. Danks, Philip Phillips, B. C. Unseld, and others.

Fanny loveds her work, and wasis happy in it. She wais always ready either to sympathize or join in a mirthful conversation, as the case may be. The secret of this contentment dateds from her first composition at the age of eight years. "It has been the motto of my life," she saysid. It is:

O what a happy soul am I!
  Although I cannot see,
I am resolved that in this world
  Contented I will be;

How many blessings I enjoy
  That other people don't!
To weep and sigh because I'm blind,
  I cannot, and I won't.

This has continued to be her philosophy. She saysid that had it not been for her affliction she might not have had so good an education, nor so great an influence, and certainly not so fine a memory. She kneows a great many portions of the Bible by heart, and had committed to memory the first four books of the Old Testament, and also the four Gospels before she was ten years of age.

Among her most widely-known hymns may be named the following: "There's a cry from 'Macedonia," "I feel like singing all the time," "Never be afraid to speak for Jesus," "Lord, at Thy mercy seat," "Jesus the water of life will give," "'Give,' said the little stream," "We are marching on with shield and banner bright," "Pass me not, O gentle Savior," "Jesus, keep me near the cross," "Rescue the Perishing," "Sing with a tuneful spirit," "Praise Him, praise Him," "To the work, to the work," "The Bright Forever," "Blessed Assurance," "Close to Thee," "Blessed Homeland," "Saved by Grace," "Thy Word is a lamp to my feet, O Lord," "Hast thou trimmed thy lamp, my brother?" "Never say goodbye."

Jacob H. Hall, Biography of Gospel

James Hudson Taylor (1832–1905)

James Hudson Taylor, founder of the China Inland Mission, was born at Barnsley (18 miles south. of Leeds), Yorkshire, England, on May 21, 1832; and he died at Changsha (340 miles north of Canton), China, on June 3, 1905. His father was an eloquent and able Methodist local preacher and his mother a woman who had a particularly sweet and patient spirit. Hudson Taylor combined the ability of his father with the gentle disposition of his mother. He was converted through the reading of a tract at the age of fifteen, and soon after this had a remarkable experience, when he dedicated himself to God for whatever service he should be guided to. Unknown to him, his father, who had been deeply interested in China, had prayed that his son might go to that land as a missionary, and very early, through the reading of Walter Henry Medhurst's China, the thoughts of young Taylor were directed to that country.

With a view to preparing himself for his lifework, he became an assistant to a doctor in Hull, and subsequently studied medicine at the London Hospital. The great interest awakened in China through the Taiping Rebellion, which was then erroneously supposed to be a mass movement toward Christianity, together with the glowing but exaggerated reports made by Carl Friedrich August Gutzlaff concerning China's accessibility, led to the founding of the China Evangelization Society. Hudson Taylor offered himself to this organization and on September 19, 1853, he sailed for China before the completion of his medical studies. The six years from 1854 to 1860 were spent in Shanghai, Swatow, and Ningpo, working sometimes in company with older missionaries of other societies and especially with William Chalmers Bums of the English Presbyterian Mission. During this period he left from the China Evangelization Society, which subsequently ceased to exist, and continued as an independent worker, trusting God to supply his need.

His experiences of God's faithfulness in meeting his own personal needs and the needs of a hospital at Ningpo, of which he had taken charge, had much to do with the subsequent step of founding the China Inland Mission. While at Ningpo he married Miss Maria Dyer, daughter of the Rev. Samuel Dyer of the London Missionary Society.

Invalided home in 1860, he spent the next five years in England, and with the Rev. Frederick Foster Gough of the Church Missionary Society, completed the revision of a version of the New Testament in the colloquial of Ningpo for the British and Foreign Bible Society, and also finished his medical course. To arouse interest in the great Middle Kingdom he published a book entitled China, its Spiritual Need and Claims in 1865.

In 1865, at Brighton, Taylor definitely dedicated himself to God for the founding of a new society to undertake the evangelization of inland China. In May, 1866, he, with his wife and children and a party of sixteen missionaries, sailed for China. Thus was definitely launched that organization which, on January 1, 1911, had 968 missionaries (including wives) connected with it, and in the support of which more than £1,471,000 had been contributed in answer to prayer and without public or private solicitation of funds. From the founding of the mission in 1865 Taylor's time became more and more occupied as general director of a growing work. His duties necessitated extensive journeys in China and frequent visits to the home country. In 1888 a wider ministry was started through the formation of a home center in North America. This arose through Taylor's presence at the Northfield Convention. Two years later another center was founded in Australasia. Various visits to the continent of Europe led to the inception of associate missions, which recognized Taylor as their general director on the field. In January, 1911, these associate missions had 216 workers on the field.

The constant pressure and increasing strain inseparable from such a work frequently threatened a serious breakdown; but Taylor, though far from strong as a child, manifested remarkable recuperative powers. In 1900, however, at the New York Conference, the first serious signs of failing health began to manifest themselves. Having already associated Dixon Edward Hoste with himself in the directorate of the mission, he slowly resigned his great responsibilities, still seeking to assist the work as consulting director while living quietly in retirement in Switzerland. His second wife (née Faulding), to whom he had been married in 1871, and by whom he had two children, died in the summer of 1904. Early in 1905 Taylor determined, though extremely feeble, to pay another visit to China. After visiting various centers he reached Changsha, the capital of the previously anti-foreign province of Hunan, where he suddenly and peacefully passed from his labors. His remains were interred at Chinkiang, by the side of his first wife and those of his children who had died in China.

As a Bible student Taylor was unique. Holding firmly to the plenary inspiration of the Scriptures and putting them to daily test in his life and work, he became a most helpful and remarkable expositor, his Bible readings being greatly appreciated at the various conventions held in Europe and North America. As a leader of men and careful organizer he had preeminent gifts. Being convinced of his duty, every detail was carefully thought out and arranged for, and then no subsequent difficulty or opposition was allowed to daunt him. Gifted with the power to command sleep whenever needed, he labored night and day, resting only when exhausted nature compelled him, No day, however, was entered upon without a period of quiet prayer and Bible study. James Hudson Taylor was, to quote the words of Prof. Gustav Warneck,

> A man full of the Holy Ghost and of faith, of entire surrender to God and his call, of great self-denial, heart-felt compassion, rare power in prayer, marvelous organizing faculty, energetic initiative, indefatigable perseverance, and of astonishing influence with men, and withal of child-like humility.

Taylor was the author of: Union and Communion; A Retrospect; Separation and Service; and A Ribband of Blue, and other Bible Studies.

The New Schaff-Herzog Encyclopedia of Religious Knowledge, 1911

Frances Ridley Havergal (1836–1879)

English Poet and Hymn Writer

Frances Ridley Havergal, daughter of the Rev. W. H. Havergal, was born at Astley, Worcestershire [England], December 14, 1836. Five years later her father moved to the Rectory of St. Nicholas, Worcester. In August, 1850, she went to Mrs. Teed's school, where Mrs Teed had a very positive influence over her. In the following year she says. "I committed my soul to the Savior, and earth and heaven seemed brighter from that moment." A short stay in Germany followed, and on her return she was confirmed in Worcester Cathedral, July 17, 1853. In 1860 she left Worcester on her father resigning the Rectory of St. Nicholas, and lived at different periods in Leamington, and at Caswall Bay, Swansea, broken by visits to Switzerland, Scotland, and North Wales. She died at Caswall Bay, Swansea, June 3, 1879.

Miss Havergal's scholastic acquirements were extensive, embracing several modem languages, together with Greek and Hebrew. She does not occupy, and did not claim for herself, a prominent place as a poet, but by her distinct individuality she carved out a niche which she alone could fill. Simply and sweetly she sang the love of God, and His way of salvation. To this end, and for this object, her whole life and all her powers were consecrated. She lives and speaks in every line of her poetry. Her poems are permeated with the fragrance of her passionate love of Jesus.

Her religious views and theological bias are distinctly set forth In her poems, and may be described as mildly Calvinistic, without the severe dogmatic tenet of reprobation. The burden of her writings is a free and full salvation, through the Redeemer's merits, for every sinner who will receive it, and her life was devoted to the proclamation of this truth by personal labors, literary efforts, and earnest interest in Foreign Missions.

'Take my life, and let it be'

This hymn was written at Areley House, Feb. 4, 1874, in 11 stanzas of 2 lines, and published in her Loyal Responses, 1878.

> "Perhaps you will be interested to know the origin of the Consecration hymn 'Take my life.' I went for a little visit of five days [to Areley House]. There were ten persons in the house, some unconverted and long prayed for, some converted, but not rejoicing Christians. He gave me the prayer 'Lord, give me all in this house!' And He just did! Before I left the house every one had got a blessing. The last night of my visit after I had retired, the governess asked me to go to the two daughters. They were crying, &c; then and there both of them trusted and rejoiced; it was nearly midnight. I was too happy to sleep, and passed most of the night in praise and renewal of my own consecration; and these little couplets formed themselves, and chimed in my heart one after another till they finished with 'Ever, ONLY, ALL for Thee!'"

Take my life, and let it be consecrated, Lord, to Thee.
Take my moments and my days; let them flow in ceaseless praise.
Take my hands, and let them move at the impulse of Thy love.
Take my feet, and let them be swift and beautiful for Thee.

Take my voice, and let me sing always, only, for my King.
Take my lips, and let them be filled with messages from Thee.
Take my silver and my gold; not a mite would I withhold.
Take my intellect, and use every power as Thou shalt choose.
Take my will, and make it Thine; it shall be no longer mine.
Take my heart, it is Thine own; it shall be Thy royal throne.
Take my love, my Lord, I pour at Thy feet its treasure store.
Take myself, and I will be ever, only, all for Thee.

A Dictionary of Hymnology, edited by John Julian, 1892

Ira Sankey (1840–1908)

Ira David Sankey, author, and evangelist, was born at Edinburgh, Lawrence County, Pennsylvania, August 28, 1840. His father, David Sankey, was a prominent citizen of western Pennsylvania in his day, having served as state senator for a number of years, after which he became in turn a banker and an editor, and was appointed by Abraham Lincoln a collector of internal revenue. He was a member of the Methodist Episcopal church, and although a man of business, was often called upon to address large audiences on religious subjects.

Ira was noted for his fondness for music and his ability to sing well even as a child; he joined the same church as his father and mother, when he was fifteen. He soon became leader of the choir, superintendent of the Sunday-school, and president of the Young Men's Christian Association. It was while filling these positions and in connection with various other Christian work that he developed his remarkable power of rendering sacred songs impressively.

At outbreak of the war in 1861, he was one of the first to enlist in the service of his country. On his return home he was appointed to a position in the U.S. Internal Revenue Service, which appointment did not, however, in any way interfere with his religious work, and as a singer of sacred songs he was in constant demand at all kinds of religious gatherings.

Having been sent as a delegate from New Castle, Pennsylvania, to the international convention of the Young Men's Christian Association, which met at Indianapolis in 1870, he met there Dwight L. Moody, a delegate from Chicago. When Moody heard Sankey sing, he invited him to come to Chicago, and assist him in his evangelic work there. Six months after their first meeting Sankey resigned from his Revenue work and joined Moody in Chicago.

In 1871, after the city had been destroyed by fire, they accepted an invitation to visit England, and commenced their work there in June, 1873. It was during this first visit to the old country that Sankey's singing began to give him an international reputation. His wonderful compass of voice, clear enunciation and evident sincerity made a deep impression throughout Great Britain, so much so that before he returned to America the names of "Moody and Sankey" had become household words throughout Europe.

Sankey is the author of one of the most popular hymn books in the English language, entitled "Sacred Songs and Solos." It was while he was on his first visit to Scotland that he wrote the words of his most famous song, "The Ninety and Nine."

He is the author of many popular tunes, and has written a number of hymns under various nom-de-plume. He is also the author of the popular book "Christian Endeavor Hymns," as used by the Society of Christian Endeavor in America, and of a number of Sunday-school hymnals, but it is on his gospel singing and life-long companionship with Mr. Moody that Mr. Sankey's reputation will chiefly rest.

The National Cyclopædia of American Biography

Classic Christian devotional books from the nineteenth century

William Wilberforce (1759–1833), *Real Christianity*

Charles Dickens (1812–1870), *The Life of Our Lord*

Søren Kierkegaard (1813–1855)

Crowd is Untruth

Provocations

J. C. Ryle (1816–1900), *Holiness*

Murray Andrew (1828–1917)

Absolute Surrender

With Christ in the School of Prayer

Frederic William Farrar (1831–1903), *The Life of Christ*

James Hudson Taylor (1832–1905), *Union and Communion*

D. L. Moody (1837–1899), *What Must I Do to be Saved?*

G. K. Chesterton (1847–1936), *Orthodoxy*

Thérèse of Lisieux (1873–1897), *Little Flower of Jesus*

Extracts from Classic Christian devotional books from the nineteenth century

William Wilberforce (1759–1833), *Real Christianity*

William Carey (1761–1834), *Enquiry*

Elizabeth Fry (1780–1845), *What Owest Thou unto Thy Lord?*

Charles Grandison Finney (1792–1875), *True and False Conversion*

Søren Kierkegaard (1813 –1855), *The Sickness unto Death*

C. H. Spurgeon (1834–1892), *Spurgeon's Autobiography; The Great Change—Conversion*

D. L. Moody (1837–1899), *Prevailing Prayer*

William Wilberforce (1759–1833)

Real Christianity

It is my opinion that the majority of Christians overlook, deny or, at the very least, minimize the problems of what it means to be a fallen human being. They might acknowledge that the world has always been filled with vice and wickedness and that human behavior tends toward the sensual and selfish. They might admit that the result of these facts is that in every age we can find innumerable instances of oppression, cruelty, dishonesty, jealousy and violence. They might also admit that we act this way even when we know better.

These facts are true; we don't deny them. They are so obvious that it is a mystery why so many still believe in the goodness of human nature. But even though the facts might be acknowledged, the source of the facts is often still denied.

These things are rationalized as small failures or periodic problems. Other explanations are given that fail to get to the heart of the matter. Human pride refuses to face the truth. Even the majority of professing Christians tend to think that the nature of humanity is basically good and is only thrown off course by the power of temptation. They believe that sin and evil are the exception, not the rule.

The Bible paints a much different picture. The language of Scripture is not for the faint of heart. It teaches that man is an apostate creature, fallen from his original innocence, degraded in his nature, depraved in his thinking, prone toward evil, not good, and impacted by sin to the very core of his being. The fact that we don't want to acknowledge these truths is evidence of their veracity. As Milton said in Paradise Lost:

Into what depth thou seest,
From what height fallen!

Think about the amazing capabilities of the human mind. We have the power to invent, reason, make judgments, remember the past, make decisions in the present and plan for the future. With the ability to discern, we do not merely understand an object; we can admire it, especially if it reflects something of the beauty of moral excellence. Emotionally, we have the ability to fear and hope, experience joy and sorrow, empathize and love. With the will, we can exercise courage to do hard tasks and exert patience to stay the course. With the power of conscience, we can monitor the thoughts and desires of our hearts and use reason to regulate our passions. We are truly amazing creatures. If aliens from another world observed us, they would be astonished at our ability to use all these faculties to be the best we can be. They would think that our Creator would delight in all the good we would choose to do with these marvelous attributes.

Unfortunately, we all know that this is not the way things are. Take a look at how we actually use these powers. Step back and take a look at the big picture of human history. What do we see? We see that human reason has become confused. Human desires have become twisted. Anger, envy, hatred and revenge rear their ugly heads. We have become slaves to our lower natures and seem unable to do good!

History confirms these tragedies of human nature. Ancient civilizations were not characterized by good. On the contrary, even the most advanced cultures were cloaked in moral darkness. We find superstition, the lack of natural affections, brutal excesses, unfeeling oppression and savage cruelty everywhere we look. Nowhere do we see decency and morality prevail. In the words of Paul, "Therefore God gave them over in the sinful desires of their hearts to sexual impurity for the degrading of their bodies with one another" (Rom. 1:24).

If we change our focus from the ancient to the modern, we find the same condition. One historian described America in the following way:

It is a compound of pride, and indolence, and selfishness, and cunning, and cruelty; full of a revenge that nothing could satiate, of a ferocity that nothing could soften; strangers to the most amiable sensibilities of nature. They appear incapable of conjugal affection, or parental fondness, or filial reverence, or social attachments; uniting too with their state of barbarism, many of the vices and weaknesses of polished society. Their horrid treatment of captives taken in war, on whose bodies they feasted, after putting them to death by the most cruel tortures, is so well known, that we may spare the disgusting recital. No commendable qualities relieve this gloomy picture, except fortitude, and perseverance, and zeal for the welfare of their little community, if this last quality, exercised and directed as it was, can be thought deserving of commendation.

Even in the most civilized of nations we see the truth of the fallen nature of humanity. In some of these nations, Christian influence has set the bar much higher than in what we might consider to be pagan nations. Generally, Christian influence in a nation has improved the character and comforts of society, especially in reference to the poor and the weak, who have always been accorded special attention by those professing Christian faith. This influence has created great blessings for many, even though these same people deny the truth of the Bible and do not accept its authority. But, even in those nations that have been influenced by biblical faith, we see many examples of human depravity.

When the true nature of man is revealed in situations where Christian influence once held sway, depravity becomes even more obvious. The laws and conscience of such societies have been designed to restrain these forces of human nature. When these laws are removed or violated, we see the most hideous and atrocious crimes perpetrated shamelessly and in broad daylight.

When you consider the biblical teaching concerning superior morality and obedience to the teachings of Christ combined with the truth that one day we will give account for our actions, it is a marvel that we have made so little progress in virtue. We still exhibit the characteristics attributed to less-informed societies; i.e., prosperity hardens the heart, unlimited power is always abused, bad habits develop naturally, while virtue, if obtained at all, is slow, hard work. Even moralists rarely practice what they preach. It seems the rule that people are more willing to suffer the negative consequences of vice than take advantage of the blessings of living a life of Christian obedience.

If we seek more evidence of the fallen nature of humanity, we need look no further than our own children. Even parents with the strongest Christian principles can testify how baffling it is to attempt to correct our children when they rebel against us in attitude and action.

Another example of the most twisted variety is how we can take the truth of the Bible and use it for the most hideous purposes. Christ gets vilified when those who bear His name use it as an excuse for cruelty or persecution. We must be careful to distinguish twisted zeal from true Christian commitment. History provides too many examples of people who called themselves Christians but were in fact devoid of the love and kindness of Christ. It is as if a healing medicine had become a deadly poison. How tragic that those of us who identify ourselves as followers of Jesus, who have the benefit of the revelation of God's Word, who have been exposed to the truth of the very nature of God, who profess that "in him we live and move and have our being" (Acts 17:28), who acknowledge His provision and blessing in our lives, and who have accepted the forgiveness provided by the death of Christ on the cross, continually forget His authority over our lives and become cold and uncaring about Him in our hearts.

Maybe the best testimony concerning depravity comes from those whose commitment to Christ is wholehearted. They can testify how difficult it is to fight against their fallen nature as they attempt to live lives of obedience. They will tell you that by observing their own lives and the way their minds work, they have discovered how corrupt the human heart really is. Every day this conviction grows. They will tell you of how poorly they are able to live out their convictions, how selfish their desires are, and how feeble and halfhearted are their attempts to do the right thing. They will acknowledge and confess that the biblical teaching about the two conflicting natures has proven true in their experience. In the words of Paul, "I have the desire to do what is good, but I cannot carry it out" (Rom. 7:18). As someone has said, even the spirituality we do possess is corrupted by our nature. We have nothing to brag about. On the contrary, God must always give us grace to bear with our faults and mercy to forgive our sins.

This is the true spiritual condition of humanity.

William Wilberforce, Real Christianity, Chapter 2

William Carey (1761–1834)
An Enquiry

Introduction

Many consider this book inaugurated the era of modern missions.

Full title

An Enquiry into the Obligations of Christians to use Means for the Conversion of the Heathens, by William Carey, 1792.

In which the religious state of the different nations of the
world, the success of former undertakings, and the practicability
of further undertakings, are considered.

For there is no difference between the Jew and the Greek: for the same Lord over all is rich unto all that call upon him. For whosoever shall call upon the name of the Lord shall be saved. How then shall they call on him in whom they have not believed? And how shall they believe in him of whom they have not heard? And how shall they hear without a preacher? And how shall they preach, except they be sent? Paul

Section 5

An enquiry into the duty of Christians in general, and what means ought to be used, in order to promote this work.

If the prophecies concerning the increase of Christ's kingdom be true, and if what has been advanced, concerning the commission given by him to his disciples being obligatory on us, be just, it must be inferred that all Christians ought heartily to concur with God in promoting his glorious designs, for he that is joined to the Lord is one spirit.

One of the first, and most important of those duties which are incumbent upon us, is fervent and united prayer. However the influence of the Holy Spirit may be set at nought, and run down by many, it will be found upon trial, that all means which we can use, without it, will be ineffectual. If a temple is raised for God in the heathen world, it will not be by might, nor by power, nor by the authority of the magistrate, or the eloquence of the orator; but by my Spirit, saith the Lord of Hosts. We must therefore be in real earnest in supplicating his blessing upon our labors.

The most glorious works of grace that have ever took place, have been in answer to prayer; and it is in this way, we have the greatest reason to suppose, that the glorious outpouring of the Spirit, which we expect at last, will be bestowed.

With respect to our own immediate connections, we have within these few years been favored with some tokens for good, granted in answer to prayer, which should encourage us to persist, and increase in that important duty. I trust our monthly prayer-meetings for the success of the gospel have not been in vain. It is true a want of importunity too generally attends our prayers; yet unimportunate, and feeble as they have been, it is to be believed that God has heard, and in a measure answered them. The churches that have engaged in the practice have in general since that time been evidently on the increase; some controversies which have long perplexed and divided the church, are more clearly stated than ever; there are calls to preach the gospel in many places where it has not been usually published; yea, a glorious door is opened, and is likely to be opened wider and wider, by the spread of civil and religious liberty, accompanied also by a diminution of the spirit of popery; a noble effort has been made to abolish the inhuman Slave Trade, and though at present it has not been so successful as might be wished, yet it is to be hoped it will be persevered in, till it is accomplished. In the mean time it is a satisfaction to consider that the late defeat of the abolition of the Slave-Trade has proved the occasion of a praiseworthy effort to introduce a free settlement, at Sierra Leona, on the coast of Africa; an effort which, if succeeded with a divine blessing, not only promises to open a way for honorable commerce with that extensive country, and for the civilization of its inhabitants, but may prove the happy mean of introducing amongst them the gospel of our Lord Jesus Christ.

These are events that ought not to be overlooked; they are not to be reckoned small things; and yet perhaps they are small compared with what might have been expected, if all had cordially entered into the spirit of the proposal, so as to have made the cause of Christ their own, or in other words to have been so solicitous about it, as if their own advantage depended upon its success. If an holy solicitude had prevailed in all the assemblies of Christians in behalf of their Redeemer's kingdom, we might probably have seen before now, not only an open door for the gospel, but many running to and fro, and knowledge increased; or a diligent use of those means which providence has put in our power, accompanied with a greater blessing than ordinary from heaven.

Many can do nothing but pray, and prayer is perhaps the only thing in which Christians of all denominations can cordially, and unreservedly unite; but in this we may all be one, and in this the strictest unanimity ought to prevail. Were the whole body thus animated by one soul, with what pleasure would Christians attend on all the duties of religion, and with what delight would their ministers attend on all the business of their calling.

We must not be contented however with praying, without exerting ourselves in the use of means for the obtaining of those things we pray for. Were the children of light, but as wise in their generation as the children of this world, they would stretch every nerve to gain so glorious a prize, nor ever imagine that it was to be obtained in any other way.

When a trading company have obtained their charter they usually go to its utmost limits; and their stocks, their ships, their officers, and men are so chosen, and regulated, as to be likely to answer their purpose; but they do not stop here, for encouraged by the prospect of success, they use every effort, cast their bread upon the waters, cultivate friendship with every one from whose information they expect the least advantage. They cross the widest and most tempestuous seas, and encounter the most unfavorable climates; they introduce themselves into the most barbarous nations, and sometimes undergo the most affecting hardships; their minds continue in a state of anxiety, and suspense, and a longer delay than usual in the arrival of their vessels agitates them with a thousand changeful thoughts, and foreboding apprehensions, which continue till the rich returns are safe arrived in port. But why these fears? Whence all these disquietudes, and this labor? Is it not because their souls enter into the spirit of the project, and their happiness in a manner depends on its success? -Christians are a body whose truest interest lies in the exaltation of the Messiah's kingdom. Their charter is very extensive, their encouragements exceeding great, and the returns promised infinitely superior to all the gains of the most lucrative fellowship. Let then every one in his station consider himself as bound to act with all his might, and in every possible way for God.

Suppose a company of serious Christians, ministers and private persons, were to form themselves into a society, and make a number of rules respecting the regulation of the plan, and the persons who are to be employed as missionaries, the means of defraying the expense, &c. This society must consist of persons whose hearts are in the work, men of serious religion, and possessing a spirit of perseverance; there must be a determination not to admit any person who is not of this description, or to retain him longer than he answers to it.

From such a society a committee might be appointed, whose business it should be to procure all the information they could upon the subject, to receive contributions, to enquire into the characters, tempers, abilities and religious views of the missionaries, and also to provide them with necessaries for their undertakings.

They must also pay a great attention to the views of those who undertake this work; for want of this the missions to the Spice Islands, sent by the Dutch East-India Company, were soon corrupted, many going more for the sake of settling in a place where temporal gain invited them, than of preaching to the poor Indians. This soon introduced a number of indolent, or profligate persons, whose lives were a scandal to the doctrines which they preached; and by means of whom the gospel was ejected from Ternate, in 1694, and Christianity fell into great disrepute in other places.

If there is any reason for me to hope that I shall have any influence upon any of my brethren, and fellow Christians, probably it may be more especially amongst them of my own denomination. I would therefore propose that such a society and committee should be formed amongst the particular Baptist denomination.

I do not mean by this, in any wise to confine it to one denomination of Christians. I wish with all my heart, that everyone who loves our Lord Jesus Christ in sincerity, would in some way or other engage in it. But in the present divided state of Christendom, it would be more likely for good to be done by each denomination engaging separately in the work, than if they were to embark in it conjointly. There is room enough for us all, without interfering with each other; and if no unfriendly interference took place, each denomination would bear good will to the other, and wish, and pray for its success, considering it as upon the whole friendly to the great cause of true religion; but if all were intermingled, it is likely their private discords might throw a damp upon their spirits, and much retard their public usefulness.

In respect to contributions for defraying the expenses, money will doubtless be wanting; and suppose the rich were to embark a portion of that wealth over which God has made them stewards, in this important undertaking, perhaps there are few ways that would turn to a better account at last. Nor ought it to be confined to the rich; if persons in more moderate circumstances were to devote a portion, suppose a tenth, of their annual increase to the Lord, it would not only correspond with the practice of the Israelites, who lived under the Mosaic Economy, but of the patriarchs Abraham, Isaac, and Jacob, before that dispensation commenced. Many of our most eminent fore-fathers amongst the Puritans followed that practice; and if that were but attended to now, there would not only be enough to support the ministry of the gospel at home, and to encourage village preaching in our respective neighborhoods, but to defray the expenses of carrying the gospel into the heathen world.

If congregations were to open subscriptions of one penny, or more per week, according to their circumstances, and deposit it as a fund for the propagation of the gospel, much might be raised in this way. By such simple means they might soon have it in their power to introduce the preaching of the gospel into most of the villages in England; where, though men are placed whose business it should be to give light to those who sit in darkness, it is well known that they have it not. Where there was no person to open his house for the reception of the gospel, some other building might be procured for a small sum, and even then something considerable might be spared for the Baptist, or other committees, for propagating the gospel amongst the heathen.

Many persons have of late left off the use of West-India sugar on account of the iniquitous manner in which it is obtained. Those families who have done so, and have not substituted anything else in its place, have not only cleansed their hands of blood, but have made a saving to their families, some of six pence, and some of a shilling a week. If this, or a part of this were appropriated to the uses before-mentioned, it would abundantly suffice. We have only to keep the end in view, and have our hearts thoroughly engaged in the pursuit of it, and means will not be very difficult.

We are exhorted to lay up treasure in heaven, where neither moth nor rust doth corrupt, nor thieves break through and steal. It is also declared that whatsoever a man soweth, that shall he also reap. These scriptures teach us that the enjoyments of the life to come, bear a near relation to that which now is; a relation similar to that of the harvest, and the seed. It is true all the reward is of mere grace, but it is nevertheless encouraging; what a treasure, what an harvest must await such characters as PAUL, and ELLIOT, and BRAINERD, and others, who have given themselves wholly to the work of the Lord. What a heaven will it be to see the many myriads of poor heathens, of Britons amongst the rest, who by their labors have been brought to the knowledge of God. Surely a crown of rejoicing like this is worth aspiring to. Surely it is worth while to lay ourselves out with all our might, in promoting the cause, and kingdom of Christ.

William Carey

Elizabeth Fry (1780–1845)

What Owest Thou Unto Thy Lord?

Are there not many here present whose desired are raised up to the living God, and to his kingdom of everlasting rest and peace, who are ready to adopt this language, "Oh Lord revive thy work in the midst of the years?" and are there not among you some of the bowed down, of the broken hearted, some who have many trials of faith and of patience, some of those conflicts which are much hidden from the eye of man? Oh! my friends, remember that we have to deal with a compassionate Father, who pitieth his children, who knoweth our frame, who remembereth that we are dust, who seeth us not as man seeth, who judgeth us not according to appearance, but according to the heart. Oh! my friends, whatever be the trials of your faith and of your patience, I sympathize with you; I desire that you may be upheld, that you may be strengthened, that you may find the grace of your Lord to be sufficient for you; and if we poor frail, feeble, unworthy mortals can feel as we do at seasons one for another, oh, what consolation is it to remember, that he who is infinite in mercy, infinite in love, and infinite in power also feels for us; we have a High Priest who is touched with the sense of our infirmities.

Oh, my friends, however many of you may be cast down for a season, however you may not know any peace, oh, trust in the Lord and stay yourselves on your God, for his tender mercies are over all his works. Oh, remember, that the very hairs of your head are all numbered; remember that not a sparrow falls to the ground without him, and you are of much more value than many sparrows. Were not these expressions made use of by our blessed Lord for the encouragement of his poor little tender ones, those who are brought very low before him? How consoling is it to remember that there is no desire however feeble after himself but he regards it, he is willing to strengthen it, and it rises before him even as a pure and acceptable sacrifice, therefore ye humble, broken-hearted, contrite, and afflicted ones, lift up your hearts and put your trust in him who suffered for you, who was despised and rejected of men, a man of sorrows and acquainted with grief.

Oh, how he did bear our sorrows; what an encouragement is it for us to remember this in all our tribulations, of whatever nature they may be, that the Lord can make all our trials, as well as all our blessing, work together for our good. Oh, may the language of our hearts increasingly be unto the Lord, "that which I know not, teach thou me; if I have done iniquity, I will do so no more." Oh, may we be strengthened to walk closer to God, to cleave very close unto him in spirit, to follow the Lamb our Savior withersoever he leadeth us, to make it the first business of our lives to be conformed to his will and to live to his glory, that whether we pass through heights or depths, whether prosperity or adversity be our portion, though our years pass away as a tale that is told, the blessings of the Most High will rest upon us, and through his unbounded love, and through his unmerited mercy in Christ Jesus, we may indeed humbly trust that when this passing scene is closed to our view, an entrance will be granted unto us, even abundantly ministered unto us, into the everlasting kingdom of our Lord and Savior Jesus Christ.

Indeed it is well for us, my friends, to enquire, "What owest thou unto thy Lord?" Ah, dear friends, is it not well for us to do this when we reflect on what he hath done for us, even He who was wounded for our transgressions, who was bruised for our iniquities; the chastisement of our peace, we may remember, was on him, and by his stripes we are healed. It is well for us to remember what he hath been from time to time doing for us in the visitations of his love unto our souls; how often have the proofs of his love been extended towards us to gather us and keep us within his sacred enclosure, even the revelation of the will of God through Jesus Christ our Lord, our hope of glory. Oh, then seeing, my brethren and sisters, that the work is a progressive one, the enquiry arose in the secret of my heart, is our salvation nearer than when we first believe? What do we owe unto the Lord? what can we rightly perform that he may be pleased to receive at our hands? and the language of the Psalmist came before the view of my mind with renewed instruction, whilst I have been led to believe that he, the Lord Almighty who dwelleth on high, is calling up us to go forward, to look not behind, to tarry not in the plain: "Who shall ascend unto the hill of the Lord, and who shall stand in his holy place? he that hath clean hands and a pure heart, who hath not lifted his soul unto vanity, nor sworn deceitfully; he shall receive the blessing from the Lord, and righteousness from the God of his salvation."

Elizabeth Fry, What Owest Thou Unto Thy Lord?

Charles Grandison Finney (1792–1875)
True and False Conversion

Text: Behold, all ye that kindle a fire, that compass yourselves about with sparks: walk in the light of your fire, and in the sparks that ye have kindled. This shall ye have of my hand; ye shall lie down in sorrow.

Isaiah 50.11.

I will now attempt to:

1. Show that the natural state of man is a state of pure selfishness.

2. Show that the character of the converted is that of benevolence.

3. Show that the New Birth consists in a change from selfishness to benevolence.

4. Point out some things wherein saints and sinners, or true and spurious converts, may agree, and some things in which they differ. And,

5. Answer some objections that may be offered against the view I have taken, and conclude with some remarks.

1. I am to show that the natural state of man, or that in which all men are found before conversion, is pure, unmingled selfishness.

By which I mean, that they have no gospel benevolence. Selfishness is regarding one's own happiness supremely, and seeking one's own good because it is his own. He who is selfish places his own happiness above other interests of greater value; such as the glory of God and the good of the universe. That mankind, before conversion, are in this state, is evident from many considerations.

Every man knows that all other men are selfish. All the dealings of mankind are conducted on this principle. If any man overlooks this, and undertakes to deal with mankind as if they were not selfish, but were disinterested, he will be thought deranged.

2. In a converted state, the character is that of benevolence.

An individual who is converted is benevolent, and not supremely selfish. Benevolence is loving the happiness of others, or rather, choosing the happiness of others. Benevolence is a compound word, that properly signifies good willing, or choosing the happiness of others. This is God's state of mind. We are told that God is love; that is, he is benevolent. Benevolence comprises his whole character. All his moral attributes are only so many modifications of benevolence. An individual who is converted is in this respect like God. I do not mean to be understood, that no one is converted, unless he is purely and perfectly benevolent, as God is; but that the balance of his mind, his prevailing choice is benevolent. He sincerely seeks the good of others, for its own sake. And, by disinterested benevolence I do not mean, that a person who is disinterested feels no interest in his object of pursuit, but that he seeks the happiness of others for its own sake, and not for the sake of its reaction on himself, in promoting his own happiness. He chooses to do good because he rejoices in the happiness of others, and desires their happiness for its own sake. God is purely and disinterestedly benevolent. He does not make his creatures happy for the sake of thereby promoting his own happiness, but because he loves their happiness and chooses it for its own sake. Not that he does not feel happy in promoting the happiness of his creatures, but that he does not do it for the sake of his own gratification. The man who is disinterested feels happy in doing good. Otherwise doing good itself would not be virtue in him. In other words, if he did not love to do good, and enjoy doing good, it would not be virtue in him.

Benevolence is holiness. It is what the Law of God requires: "Thou shalt love the Lord thy God, with all thy heart and soul and strength, and thy neighbor as thyself." Just as certainly as the converted man yields obedience to the law of God, and just as certainly as he is like God, he is benevolent. It is the leading feature of his character, that he is seeking the happiness of others, and not his own happiness, as his supreme end.

3. Show that true conversion is a change from a state of supreme selfishness to benevolence.

It is a change in the end of pursuit, and not a mere change in the means of attaining the end. It is not true that the converted and the unconverted differ only in the means they use, while both are aiming at the same end. It is not true that Gabriel and Satan are pursuing the same end, and both alike aiming at their own happiness, only pursuing a different way. Gabriel does not obey God for the sake of promoting his own happiness. A man may change his means, and yet have the same end, his own happiness. He may do good for the sake of the temporal benefit. He may not believe in religion, or in any eternity, and yet may see that doing good will be for his advantage in this world. Suppose, then, that his eyes are opened, and he sees the reality of eternity; and then he may take up religion as a means of happiness in eternity. Now, every one can see that there is no virtue in this. It is the design that gives character to the act, not the means employed to effect the design. The true and the false convert differ in this. The true convert chooses, as the end of his pursuit, the glory of God and the good of his kingdom. This end he chooses for its own sake, because he views this as the greatest good, as a greater good than his own individual happiness. Not that he is indifferent to his own happiness, but he prefers God's glory, because it is a greater good. He looks on the happiness of every individual according to its real importance, as far as he is capable of valuing it, and he chooses the greatest good as his supreme object.

4. Now I am to show some things in which true saints and deceived persons may agree, and some things in which they differ.

A. They may agree in leading a strictly moral life.

The difference is in their motives. The true saint leads a moral life from love to holiness; the deceived person from selfish considerations. He uses morality as a means to an end, to effect his own happiness. The true saint loves it as an end.

B. They may be equally prayerful, so far as the form of praying is concerned.

The difference is in their motives. The true saint loves to pray; the other prays because he hopes to derive some benefit to himself from praying. The true saint expects a benefit from praying, but that is not his leading motive. The other prays from no other motive.

C. They may be equally zealous in religion.

One may have great zeal, because his zeal is according to knowledge, and he sincerely desires and loves to promote religion, for its own sake. The other may show equal zeal, for the sake of having his own salvation more assured, and because he is afraid of going to hell if he does not work for the Lord, or to quiet his conscience, and not because he loves religion for its own sake.

D. They may be equally conscientious in the discharge of duty; the true convert because he loves to do duty, and the other because he dare not neglect it.

E. Both may pay equal regard to what is right; the true convert because he loves what is right, and the other because he knows he cannot be saved unless he does right. He is honest in his common business transactions, because it is the only way to secure his own interest. Verily, they have their reward. They get the reputation of being honest among men, but if they have no higher motive, they will have no reward from God.

F. They may agree in their desires, in many respects. They may agree in their desires to serve God; the true convert because he loves the service of God, and the deceived person for the reward, as the hired servant serves his master.

They may agree in their desires to be useful; the true convert desiring usefulness for its own sake, the deceived person because he knows that is the way to obtain the favor of God. And then in proportion as he is awakened to the importance of having God's favor, will be the intensity of his desires to be useful.

In desires for the conversion of souls; the true saint because it will glorify God; the deceived person to gain the favor of God. He will be actuated in this, just as he is in giving money. Who ever doubted that a person might give his money to the Bible Society, or the Missionary Society, from selfish motives alone, to procure happiness, or applause, or obtain the favor of God? He may just as well desire the conversion of souls, and labor to promote it, from motives purely selfish.

To glorify God; the true saint because he loves to see God glorified, and the deceived person because he knows that is the way to be saved. The true convert has his heart set on the glory of God, as his great end, and he desires to glorify God as an end, for its own sake.

The other desires it as a means to his great end, the benefit of himself.

To repent. The true convert abhors sin on account of its hateful nature, because it dishonors God, and therefore he desires to repent of it. The other desires to repent, because he knows that unless he does repent he will be damned.

To believe in Jesus Christ. The true saint desires it to glorify God, and because he loves the truth for its own sake. The other desires to believe, that he may have a stronger hope of going to heaven.

To obey God. The true saint that he may increase in holiness; the false professor because he desires the rewards of obedience.

In all these cases, the motives of one class are directly over against the other. The difference lies in the choice of different ends. One chooses his own interest, the other chooses God's interest, as his chief end. For a person to pretend that both these classes are aiming at the same end, is to say that an impenitent sinner is just as benevolent as a real Christian; or that a Christian is not benevolent like God, but is only seeking his own happiness, and seeking it in religion rather than in the world.

5. I am to answer some objections which are made against this view of the subject.

OBJECTION 1 "Am I not to have any regard to my own happiness?"

ANSWER. It is right to regard your own happiness according to its relative value. Put it in this scale, by the side of the glory of God and the good of the universe, and then decide, and give it the value which belongs to it. This is precisely what God does. And this is what he means, when he commands you to love your neighbor as yourself.

And again: You will in fact promote your own happiness, precisely in proportion as you leave it out of view. Your happiness will be in proportion to your disinterestedness. True happiness consists mainly in the gratification of virtuous desires. There may be pleasure in gratifying desires that are selfish, but it is not real happiness. But to be virtuous, your desires must be disinterested. Suppose a man meets a beggar in the street; there he sits on the curbstone, cold and hungry, without friends, and ready to perish. The man's feelings are touched, and he steps into a grocery near by, and buys him a loaf of bread. At once the countenance of the beggar lights up, and he looks unutterable gratitude. Now it is plain to see, that the gratification of the man in the act is precisely in proportion to the singleness of his motive. If he did it purely and solely out of benevolence, his gratification is complete in the act itself. But if he did it partly to have it known that he is a charitable and humane person, then his happiness is not complete until the deed is published to others. Suppose here is a sinner in his sins; he is very wicked and very wretched. Your compassion is moved, and you convert and save him. If your motive was to obtain honor among men and to secure the favor of God, you are not completely happy until the deed is told, and perhaps put in the newspaper. But if you wished purely to save a soul from death, then as soon as you see that done, your gratification is complete, and your joy is unmingled. So it is in all religious duties; your happiness is precisely in proportion as you are disinterested.

OBJECTION 2. "Did not Christ regard the joy set before him? And did not Moses also have respect unto the recompense of reward? And does not the Bible say we love God because he first loved us?"

ANSWER 1. It is true that Christ despised the shame and endured the cross, and had regard to the joy set before him. But what was the joy set before him? Not his own salvation, not his own happiness, but the great good he would do in the salvation of the world. He was perfectly happy in himself. But the happiness of others was what he aimed at. This was the joy set before him. And that he obtained.

OBJECTION 3. "Does not the Bible offer happiness as the reward of virtue?"

ANSWER. The Bible speaks of happiness as the result of virtue, but no where declares virtue to consist in the pursuit of one's own happiness. The Bible is every where inconsistent with this, and represents virtue to consist in doing good to others. We can see by the philosophy of the mind, that it must be so. If a person desires the good of others, he will be happy in proportion as he gratifies that desire. Happiness is the result of virtue, but virtue does not consist in the direct pursuit of one's own happiness, but is wholly inconsistent with it.

OBJECTION 4. "God aims at our happiness, and shall we be more benevolent than God? Should we not be like God? May we not aim at the same thing that God aims at? Should we not be seeking the same end that God seeks?"

ANSWER. This objection is specious, but futile and rotten. God is benevolent to others. He aims at the happiness of others, and at our happiness. And to be like him, we must aim at, that is, delight in his happiness and glory, and the honor and glory of the universe, according to their real value.

OBJECTION 5. "Why does the Bible appeal continually to the hopes and fears of men, if a regard to our own happiness is not a proper motive to action?"

ANSWER. The Bible appeals to the constitutional susceptibilities of men, not to their selfishness. Man dreads harm, and it is not wrong to avoid it. We may have a due regard to our own happiness, according to its value.

Conclusion

With two short remarks I will close:

1. We see, from this subject, why it is that professors of religion have such different views of the nature of the gospel.

Some view it as a mere matter of accommodation to mankind, by which God is rendered less strict than he was under the law; so that they may be fashionable or worldly, and the gospel will come in and make up the deficiencies and save them. The other class view the gospel as a provision of divine benevolence, having for its main design to destroy sin and promote holiness; and that therefore so far from making it proper for them to be less holy than they ought to be under the law, its whole value consists in its power to make them holy.

2. We see why some people are so much more anxious to convert sinners, than to see the church sanctified and God glorified by the good works of his people.

Many feel a natural sympathy for sinners, and wish to have them saved from hell; and if that is gained, they have no farther concern. But true saints are most affected by sin as dishonoring God. And they are more distressed to see Christians sin, because it dishonors God more. Some people seem to care but little how the church live, if they can only see the work of conversion go forward. They are not anxious to have God honored. It shows that they are not actuated by the love of holiness, but by mere compassion for sinners.

Charles G. Finney, Lectures To Professing Christians, Lecture 1, 1837

Søren Kierkegaard (1813 –1855)
The Sickness unto Death

The despairer understands that it is weakness to take the earthly so much to heart, that it is weakness to despair. But then, instead of veering sharply away from despair to faith, humbling himself before God for his weakness, he is more deeply absorbed in despair and despairs over his weakness. Therewith the whole point of view is inverted, he becomes now more clearly conscious of his despair, recognizing that he is in despair about the eternal, he despairs over himself that he could be weak enough to ascribe to the earthly such great importance, which now becomes his despairing expression for the fact that he has lost the eternal and himself.

Here is the scale of ascent. First, in consciousness of himself: for to despair about the eternal is impossible without having a conception about the self, that there is something eternal in it, or that it has had something eternal in it. And if a man is to despair over himself, he must indeed be conscious also of having a self; that, however, is the thing over which he despairs—not over the earthly or over something earthly, but over himself. Moreover there is in this case a greater consciousness of what despair is; for despair is precisely to have lost the eternal and oneself. As a matter of fact of f course there is greater consciousness of the fact that one's condition is that of despair. Furthermore, despair in this case is not merely passive suffering but action. For when the earthly is taken away from the self and a man despairs, it is as if despair came from without, though it comes nevertheless always from the self, indirectly-directly from the self, as counter-pressure (reaction), differing in this respect from defiance, which comes directly from the self. Finally, there is here again, though in another sense, a further advance. For just because this despair is more intensive, salvation is in a certain sense nearer. Such a despair will hardly forget, it is too deep; but despair is held open every instant, and there is thus possibility of salvation.

For all that, this despair is to be referred to the formula: in despair at not willing to be oneself. Just as a father disinherits a son, so the self is not willing to recognize itself after it has been so weak. In its despair it cannot forget this weakness, it hates itself in a way, it will not humble itself in faith under its weakness in order to gain itself again; no, in its despair it will not hear of itself, so to speak, will not know anything about itself.

Søren Kierkegaard

C. H. Spurgeon (1834–1892)
Spurgeon's Autobiography

The Great Change-Conversion

I have heard men tell the story of their conversion, and of their spiritual life, in such a way that my heart hath loathed them and their story, too, for they have told of their sins as if they did boast in the greatness of their crime, and they have mentioned the love of God, not with a tear of gratitude, not with the simple thanksgiving of the really humble heart, but as if they as much exalted themselves as they exalted God. Oh! when we tell the story of our own conversion, I would have it done with great sorrow, remembering what we used to be, and with great joy and gratitude, remembering how little we deserve these things. I was once preaching upon conversion and salvation, and I felt within myself, as preachers often do, that it was but dry work to tell this story, and a dull, dull tale it was to me; but, on a sudden, the thought crossed my mind, "Why, you are a poor, lost, ruined sinner yourself; tell it, tell it as you received it; begin to tell of the grace of God as you trust you feel it yourself." Why, then, my eyes began to be fountains of tears; those hearers who had nodded their heads began to brighten up, and they listened, because they were hearing something which the speaker himself felt, and which they recognized as being true to him if it was not true to them.

Can you not remember, dearly-beloved, that day of days, that best and brightest of hours, when first you saw the Lord, lost your burden, received the roll of promise, rejoiced in full salvation, and went on your way in peace? My soul can never forget that day. Dying, all but dead, diseased, pained, chained, scourged, bound in fetters of iron, in darkness and the shadow of death, Jesus appeared unto me. My eyes looked to Him; the disease was healed, the pains removed, chains were snapped, prison doors were opened, darkness gave place to light. What delight filled my soul! What mirth, what ecstasy, what sound of music and dancing, what soarings towards Heaven, what heights and depths of ineffable delight! Scarcely ever since then have I known joys which surpassed the rapture of that first hour.

C. H.S.

In my conversion, the very point lay in making the discovery that I had nothing to do but to look to Christ, and I should be saved. I believe that I had been a very good, attentive hearer; my own impression about myself was that nobody ever listened much better than I did. For years, as a child, I tried to learn the way of salvation; and either I did not hear it set forth, which I think cannot quite have been the case, or else I was spiritually blind and deaf, and could not see it and could not hear it; but the good news that I was, as a sinner, to look away from myself to Christ, as much startled me, and came as fresh to me, as any news ever heard in my life. Had I never read my Bible? Yes, and read it earnestly. Had I never been taught by Christian people? Yes, I had, by mother, and father, and others. Had I not heard the gospel? Yes, I think I had; and yet, somehow, it was like a new revelation to me that I was to "believe and live." I confess to have been tutored in piety, put into my cradle by prayerful bands, and lulled to sleep by songs concerning Jesus; but after having heard the gospel continually, with line upon line, precept upon precept, here much and there much, yet, when the Word of the Lord came to me with power, it was as new as if I had lived amid the unvisited tribes of Central Africa, and had never heard the tidings of the cleansing fountain filled with blood, drawn from the Savior's veins.

When, for the first time, I received the gospel to my soul's salvation, I thought that I had never really heard it before, and I began to think that the preachers to whom I had listened had not truly preached it. But, on looking back, I am inclined to believe that I had heard the gospel fully preached many hundreds of times before, and that this was the difference, that I then heard it as though I heard it not; and when I did hear it, the message may not have been any more clear in itself than it had been at former times, but the power of the Holy Spirit was present to open my ear, and to guide the message to my heart. I have no doubt that I heard, scores of times, such texts as these, "He that believeth and is baptized shall be saved;" "Look unto Me, and be ye saved, all the ends of the earth;" "As Moses lifted up the serpent in the wilderness, even so must the Son of man be lifted up: that whosoever believeth in Him should not perish, but have everlasting life;" yet I had no intelligent idea of what faith meant. When I first discovered what faith really was, and exercised it, for with me these two things came together, I believed as soon as ever I knew what believing meant, then I thought I had never before heard that truth preached. But, now, I am persuaded that the light often shone on my eyes, but I was blind, and therefore I thought that the light had never come there. The light was shining all the while, but there was no power to receive it; the eyeball of the soul was not sensitive to the Divine beams.

I could not believe that it was possible that my sins could be forgiven. I do not know why, but I seemed to be the odd person in the world. When the catalogue was made out, it appeared to me that, for some reason, I must have been left out. If God had saved me, and not the world, I should have wondered indeed; but if He had saved all the world except me, that would have seemed to me to be but right. And now, being saved by grace, I cannot help saying, "I am indeed a brand plucked out of the fire!" I believe that some of us who were kept by God a long while before we found Him, love Him better perhaps than we should have done if we had received Him directly; and we can preach better to others, we can speak more of His lovingkindness and tender mercy. John Bunyan could not have written as he did if he had not been dragged about by the devil for many years. I love that picture of dear old Christian. I know, when I first read The Pilgrim's Progress, and saw in it the woodcut of

Christian carrying the burden on his back, I felt so interested in the poor fellow, that I thought I should jump with joy when, after he had carried his heavy load so long, he at last got rid of it; and that was how I felt when the burden of guilt, which I had borne so long, was for ever rolled away from my shoulders and my heart.

I can recollect when, like the poor dove sent out by Noah from his hand, I flew over the wide expanse of waters, and hoped to find some place where I might rest my wearied wing. Up towards the North I flew; and my eye looked keenly through the mist and darkness, if perhaps it might find some floating substance on which my soul might rest its foot, but it found nothing. Again it turned its wing, and flapped it, but not so rapidly as before, across that deep water that knew no shore; but still there was no rest. The raven had found its resting-place upon a floating body, and was feeding itself upon the carrion of some drowned man's carcass; but my poor soul found no rest. I flew on; I fancied I saw a ship sailing out at sea; it was the ship of the law; and I thought I would put my feet on its canvas, or rest myself on its cordage for a time, and find some refuge. But, ah! it was an airy phantom, on which I could not rest; for my foot had no right to rest on the law; I had not kept it, and the soul that keepeth it not, must die. At last I saw the barque Christ Jesus, that happy ark; and I thought I would fly thither; but my poor wing was weary, I could fly no further, and down I sank; but, as providence would have it, when my wings were flagging, and I was falling into the flood to be drowned, just below me was the roof of the ark, and I saw a hand put out from it, and One took hold of me, and said, "I have loved thee with an everlasting love, therefore I have not delivered the soul of My turtle-dove unto the multitude of the wicked; come in, come in!" Then I found that I had in my mouth an olive leaf of peace with God, and peace with man, plucked off by Jesus' mighty power.

Once, God preached to me by a similitude in the depth of winter. The earth had been black, and there was scarcely a green thing or a flower to be seen. As I looked across the fields, there was nothing but barrenness, bare hedges and leafless trees, and black, black earth, wherever I gazed. On a sudden, God spake, and unlocked the treasures of the snow, and white flakes descended until there was no blackness to be seen, and all was one sheet of dazzling whiteness. It was at the time that I was seeking the Savior, and not long before I found Him; and I remember well that sermon which I saw before me in the snow: "Come now, and let us reason together, saith the Lord: though your sins be as scarlet, they shall be as white as snow; though they be red like crimson, they shall be as wool."

Personally, I have to bless God for many good books; I thank Him for Dr. Doddridge's Rise and Progress of Religion in the Soul; for Baxter's Call to the Unconverted; for Alleine's Alarm to Sinners; and for James's Anxious Enquirer; but my gratitude most of all is due to God, not for books, but for the preached Word, and that too addressed to me by a poor, uneducated man, a man who had never received any training for the ministry, and probably will never be heard of in this life, a man engaged in business, no doubt of a humble kind, during the week, but who had just enough of grace to say on the Sabbath, "Look unto Me, and be ye saved, all the ends of the earth." The books were good, but the man was better. The revealed Word awakened me; but it was the preached Word that saved me; and I must ever attach peculiar value to the hearing of the truth, for by it I received the joy and peace in which my soul delights. While under concern of soul, I resolved that I would attend all the places of worship in the town where I lived, in order that I might find out the way of salvation.

I was willing to do anything, and be anything, if God would only forgive my sin. I set off, determined to go round to all the chapels, and I did go to every place of worship; but for a long time I went in vain. I do not, however, blame the ministers. One man preached Divine Sovereignty; I could hear him with pleasure, but what was that sublime truth to a poor sinner who wished to know what he must do to be saved? There was another admirable man who always preached about the law; but what was the use of ploughing up ground that needed to be sown? Another was a practical preacher. I heard him, but it was very much like a commanding officer teaching the manoeuvres of war to a set of men without feet. What could I do? All his exhortations were lost on me. I knew it, was said, "Believe on the Lord Jesus Christ, and thou shalt be saved;" but I did not know what it was to believe on Christ. These good men all preached truths suited to many in their congregations who were spiritually-minded people; but what I wanted to know was, "How can I get my sins forgiven?" and they never told me that. I desired to hear how a poor sinner, under a sense of sin, might find peace with God; and when I went, I heard a sermon on "Be not deceived, God is not mocked," which cut me up still worse; but did not bring me into rest. I went again, another day, and the text was something about the glories of the righteous; nothing for poor me! I was like a dog under the table, not allowed to eat of the children's food. I went time after time, and I can honestly say that I do not know that I ever went without prayer to God, and I am sure there was not a more attentive hearer than myself in all the place, for I panted and longed to understand how I might be saved.

I sometimes think I might have been in darkness and despair until now had it not been for the goodness of God in sending a snowstorm, one Sunday morning, while I was going to a certain place of worship. When I could go no further, I turned down a side street, and came to a little Primitive Methodist Chapel. In that chapel there may have been a dozen or fifteen people. I had heard of the Primitive Methodists, how they sang so loudly that they made people's heads ache; but that did not matter to me. I wanted to know how I might be saved, and if they could tell me that, I did not care how much they made my head ache. The minister did not come that morning; he was snowed up, I suppose. At last, a very thin-looking man, [It is remarkable that no less than three persons claimed to have been the preacher on this occasion, but Mr. Spurgeon did not recognize any one of them as the man to whom he then listened.] a shoemaker, or tailor, or something of that sort, went up into the pulpit to preach. Now, it is well that preachers should be instructed; but this man was really stupid. He was obliged to stick to his text, for the simple reason that he had little else to say. The text was,

"LOOK UNTO ME, AND BE YE SAVED, ALL THE ENDS OF THE EARTH."

He did not even pronounce the words rightly, but that did not matter. There was, I thought, a glimpse of hope for me in that text. The preacher began thus: "My dear friends, this is a very simple text indeed. It says, 'Look.' Now lookin' don't take a deal of pains. It ain't liftin' your foot or your finger; it is just, 'Look.' Well, a man needn't go to College to learn to look. You may be the biggest fool, and yet you can look. A man needn't be worth a thousand a year to be able to look. Anyone can look; even a child can look. But then the text says, 'Look unto Me.' Ay!" said he, in broad Essex, "many on ye are lookin' to yourselves, but it's no use lookin' there. You'll never find any comfort in yourselves. Some look to God the Father. No, look to Him by-and-by. Jesus Christ says, 'Look unto Me.' Some on ye say, 'We must wait for the Spirit's workin'.' You have no business with that just now. Look to Christ. The text says, 'Look unto Me.'"

Then the good man followed up his text in this way: "Look unto Me; I am sweatin' great drops of blood. Look unto Me; I am hangin' on the cross. Look unto Me; I am dead and buried. Look unto Me; I rise again. Look unto Me; I ascend to Heaven. Look unto Me; I am sittin' at the Father's right hand. O poor sinner, look unto Me! look unto Me!

When he had gone to about that length, and managed to spin out ten minutes or so, he was at the end of his tether. Then he looked at me under the gallery, and I daresay, with so few present, he knew me to be a stranger. Just fixing his eyes on me, as if he knew all my heart, he said, "Young man, you look very miserable." Well, I did; but I had not been accustomed to have remarks made from the pulpit on my personal appearance before. However, it was a good blow, struck right home. He continued, "and you always will be miserable, miserable in life, and miserable in death, if you don't obey my text; but if you obey now, this moment, you will be saved."

Then, lifting up his hands, he shouted, as only a Primitive Methodist could do, "Young man, look to Jesus Christ. Look! Look! Look! You have nothin' to do but to look and live." I saw at once the way of salvation. I know not what else he said, I did not take much notice of it, I was so possessed with that one thought. Like as when the brazen serpent was lifted up, the people only looked and were healed, so it was with me. I had been waiting to do fifty things, but when I heard that word, "Look!" what a charming word it seemed to me! Oh! I looked until I could almost have looked my eyes away. There and then the cloud was gone, the darkness had rolled away, and that moment I saw the sun; and I could have risen that instant, and sung with the most enthusiastic of them, of the precious blood of Christ, and the simple faith which looks alone to Him. Oh, that somebody had told me this before, "Trust Christ, and you shall be saved." Yet it was, no doubt, all wisely ordered, and now I can say,

Ever since by faith I saw the stream
Thy flowing wounds supply,
Redeeming love has been my theme,
And shall be till I die.

I do from my soul confess that I never was satisfied till I came to Christ; when was yet a child, I had far more wretchedness than ever I have now; I will even add, more weariness, more care, more heart-ache than I know at this day. I may be singular in this confession, but I make it, and know it to be the truth. Since that dear hour when my soul cast itself on Jesus, I have found solid joy and peace; but before that, all those supposed gaieties of early youth, all the imagined ease and joy of boyhood, were but vanity and vexation of spirit to me. That happy day, when I found the Savior, and learned to cling to His dear feet, was a day never to be forgotten by me. An obscure child, unknown, unheard of, I listened to the Word of God; and that precious text led me to the cross of Christ. I can testify that the joy of that day was utterly indescribable. I could have leaped, I could have danced; there was no expression, however fanatical, which would have been out of keeping with the joy of my spirit at that hour. Many days of Christian experience have passed since then, but there has never been one which has had the full exhilaration, the sparkling delight which that first day had.

I thought I could have sprung from the seat on which I sat, and have called out with the wildest of those Methodist brethren who were present, "I am forgiven! I am forgiven! A monument of grace! A sinner saved by blood! "My spirit saw its chains broken to pieces, I felt that I was an emancipated soul, an heir of Heaven, a forgiven one, accepted in Christ Jesus, plucked out of the miry clay and out of the horrible pit, with my feet set upon a rock, and my goings established. I thought I could dance all the way home. I could understand what John Bunyan meant, when he declared he wanted to tell the crows on the ploughed land all about his conversion. He was too full to hold, he felt he must tell somebody.

It is not everyone who can remember the very day and hour of his, deliverance; but, as Richard Knill said, "At such a time of the day, clang went every harp in Heaven, for Richard Knill was born again," it was e'en so with me. [It is definitely known that the date of Mr. Spurgeon's conversion was January 6th, 1850, for preaching at New Park Street Chapel, on Lord's-day morning, January 6th, 1856, from Isaiah 45:22, he said that, six years before, that very day, and at that very hour, lie had been led to look to Christ, by a sermon from that text.] The clock of mercy struck in Heaven the hour and moment of my emancipation, for the time had come. Between half-past ten o'clock, when I entered that chapel, and half-past twelve o'clock, when I was back again at home, what a change had taken place in me! I had passed from darkness into marvelous light, from death to life. Simply by looking to Jesus, I had been delivered from despair, and I was brought into such a joyous state of mind that, when they saw me at home, they said to me, "Something wonderful has happened to you;"

and I was eager to tell them all about it. Oh! there was joy in the household that day, when all heard that the eldest son had found the Savior, and knew himself to be forgiven, bliss compared with which all earth's joys are less than nothing and vanity. Yes, I had looked to Jesus as I was, and found in Him my Savior. Thus had the eternal purpose of Jehovah decreed it; and as, the moment before, there was none more wretched than I was, so, within that second, there was none more joyous. It took no longer time than does the lightning-flash; it was done, and never has it been undone. I looked, and lived, and leaped in joyful liberty as I beheld my sin punished upon the great Substitute, and put away for ever. I looked unto Him, as He bled upon that tree; His eyes darted a glance of love unutterable into my spirit, and in a moment, I was saved. [On one of the foundation stones of the School-Chapel erected at Bexhill-on-Sea in ever-loving memory of Mr. Spurgeon, the following inscription has been cut, in the hope that passersby may find salvation through reading the passage of Scripture which was blessed to his conversion.]

HOW C. H. SPURGEON FOUND CHRIST.
"I looked to Him;
He looked on me;
And we were one for ever."
C. H. S.

"Look unto Me, and be ye Saved, all the ends of the earth; for I am God, and there is none else."

Isaiah 45:22

C. H. Spurgeon

D. L. Moody (1837–1899)

Prevailing Prayer

There was a mother in Connecticut who had a son in the army, and it almost broke her heart when he left, because he was not a Christian. Day after day she lifted up her voice in prayer for her boy. She afterward learned that he had been taken to the hospital, and there died. but she could not find out anything about how he had died. Years passed, and one day a friend came to see some member of the family on business. There was a picture of the soldier boy upon the wall. He looked at it, and said, "Did you know that young man?" The mother said, "That young man was my son. He died in the late war." The man replied, "I knew him very well; he was in my company." The mother then asked, "Do you know anything about his end?" The man said, "I was in the hospital, and he died a most peaceful death, triumphant in the faith." The mother had given up hope of ever hearing of her boy; but before she went hence she had the satisfaction of knowing that her prayers had prevailed with God.

I think we shall find a great many of our prayers that we thought unanswered answered when we get to heaven. If it is the true prayer of faith, God will not disappoint us. Let us not doubt God. On one occasion, at a meeting I attended, a gentleman pointed out an individual and said, "Do you see that man over there? That is one of the leaders of an infidel club." I sat down beside him, when the infidel said, "I am not a Christian. You have been humbugging these people long enough, and making some of these old women believe that you get answers to prayer. Try it on me." I prayed, and when I got up, the infidel said with a good deal of sarcasm, "I am not converted; God has not answered your prayer!" I said, "But you may be converted yet." Some time afterwards I received a letter from a friend, stating that he had been converted and was at work in the meetings.

Jeremiah prayed, and said: "Ah, Lord God! Behold Thou hast made the heaven and the earth by Thy great power and stretched out Arm, and there is nothing too hard for Thee." Nothing is too hard for God; that is a good thing to take for a motto. I believe this is a time of great blessing in the world, and we may expect great things. While the blessing is falling all around, let us arise and share in it. God has said, "Call unto Me, and I will answer thee, and show thee great and mighty things which thou knowest not." Now let us call on the Lord; and let us pray that it may be done for Christ's sake—not our own.

At a Christian convention a number of years ago, a leading man got up and spoke—his subject being "For Christ's Sake"—and he threw new light upon that passage. I had never seen it in that way before. When the war broke out the gentleman's only son had enlisted, and he never saw a company of soldiers but his heart went right out after them. They started a Soldiers' Home in the city where that gentleman lived, and he gladly went on the committee, and acted as President. Some time afterward he said to his wife, "I have given so much time to these soldiers that I have neglected my business," and he went down to his office with the fixed determination that he would not be disturbed by any soldiers that day. The door opened soon after, and he saw a soldier entering. He never minded him, but kept on writing; and the poor fellow stood for some time. At last the soldier put down an old soiled piece of paper on which there was writing. The gentleman observed that it was the handwriting of his son, and he seized the letter at once and read it. It was something to this effect: "Dear father, this young man belongs to my company. He has lost his health in defense of his country, and he is on his way home to his mother to die. Treat him kindly for Charlie's sake." The gentleman at once dropped his work and took the soldier to his house, where he was kindly cared for until he was able to be sent home to his mother; then he took him to the station, and sent him home with a "God bless you, for Charlie's sake!"

Let our prayers, then, be for Christ's sake. If we want our sons and daughters converted, let us pray that it be done for Christ's sake. If that is the motive, our prayers will be answered. If God gave up Christ for the world, what will He not give us? If He gave Christ to the murderers and blasphemers, and the rebels of a world lying in wickedness and sin, what would He not give to those who go to Him for Christ's sake? Let our prayer be that

God may advance His work, not for our glory—not for our sake—but for the sake of His beloved Son whom He hath sent.

So let us remember that when we pray we ought to expect an answer. Let us be looking for it. I remember at the close of a meeting in one of our Southern cities near the close of the war, a man came up to me weeping and trembling. I thought something I had said had aroused him, and I began to question him as to what it was. I found, however, that he could not tell a word of what I had said. "My friend," said I, "what is the trouble?" He put his hand into his pocket, and brought out a letter, all soiled, as if his tears had fallen on it. "I got that letter," he said, "from my sister last night. She tells me that every night she goes on her knees and prays to God for me. I think I am the worst man in all the Army of the Cumberland. I have been perfectly wretched today." That sister was six hundred miles away, but she had brought her brother to his knees in answer to her earnest, believing prayer. It was a hard case, but God heard and answered the prayer of this Godly sister, so that the man was as clay in the hands of the potter. He was soon brought into the Kingdom of God—all through his sister's prayers.

I went off some thirty miles to another place, where I told this story. A young man, a lieutenant in the army, sprang to his feet and said, "That reminds me of the last letter I got from my mother. She told me that every night as the sun went down she prayed for me. She begged of me, when I got her letter, to go away alone, and yield myself to God. I put the letter in my pocket, thinking there would be plenty of time." He went on to say that the next news that came from home was that that mother was gone. He went out into the woods alone, and cried to his mother's God to have mercy upon him. As he stood in the meeting with his face shining, that lieutenant said: "My mother's prayers are answered; and my only regret is that she did not live to know it; but I will meet her by-and-by." So, though we may not live to see the answer to our prayers, if we cry mightily to God, the answer will come.

In Scotland, a good many years ago, there lived a man with his wife and three children—two girls and a boy. He was in the habit of getting drunk, and thus losing his situation. At last, he said he would take Johnnie, and go off to America, where he would be away from his old associates, and where he could commence life over again. He took the little fellow, seven years old, and went away. Soon after he arrived in America, he went into a saloon and got drunk. He got separated from his boy in the streets, and he has never been seen by his friends since. The little fellow was placed in an institution, and afterward apprenticed in Massachusetts. After he had been there some time he became discontented, and went off to sea; finally, he came to Chicago to work on the lakes. He had been a roving spirit, had gone over sea and land, and now he was in Chicago. When the vessel came into port, one time, he was invited to a Gospel meeting. The joyful sound of the Gospel reached him, and he became a Christian.

After he had been a Christian a little while, he became very anxious to find his mother. He wrote to different places in Scotland, but could not find out where she was. One day he read in the Psalms—"No good thing will He withhold from them that walk uprightly." He closed his Bible, got down on his knees, and said: "O God, I have been trying to walk uprightly for months past; help me to find my mother." It came into his mind to write back to the place in Massachusetts from which he had run away years before. It turned out that a letter from Scotland had been waiting for him there for seven years. He wrote at once to the place in Scotland, and found that his mother was still living; the answer came back immediately. I would like you to have seen him when he got that letter. He brought it to me; and the tears flowed so that he could scarcely read it. His sister had written on behalf of the mother; she had been so overcome by the tidings of her long lost boy that she could not write.

The sister said that all the nineteen years he had been away, his mother had prayed to God day and night that he might be saved, and that she might live to know what had become of him, and see him—once more. Now, said the sister, she was so overjoyed, not only that he was alive, but that he had become a Christian. It was not long before the mother and sisters came out to Chicago to meet him.

D. L. Moody, Prevailing Prayer, Chapter 11

History of Bible translations

Number of languages Bible had been translated into during this period

1800

67 languages

1900

573 languages (in its complete form or portions of it)

Examples of Bible translation during the nineteenth century

1808 Jane Aitken's Bible (Daughter of Robert Aitken); The First Bible to be Printed by a Woman.

1833 Noah Webster's Bible; After Producing his Famous Dictionary, Webster Printed his Own Revision of the King James Bible.

1841 English Hexapla New Testament; an Early Textual Comparison showing the Greek and 6 Famous English Translations in Parallel Columns.

1846 The Illuminated Bible; The Most Lavishly Illustrated Bible printed in America. A King James Version.

1885 The "Revised Version" Bible; The First Major English Revision of the King James Bible.

Other American Bible Firsts

1800—First Greek New Testament printed in America

1814—First Hebrew Bible printed in America

1815—First French Bible printed in America

1824—First Spanish Bible printed in America

1842—First Bible printed for the blind in America

CHAPTER 8

THE CHRISTIAN CHURCH IN THE TWENTIETH CENTURY

B. B. Warfield to Wolfhart Pannenberg
AD 1900–1999

Important dates in the time of the Christian Church in the Twentieth Century

1906 Albert Schweitzer publishes *The Quest of the Historical Jesus*

1906–1909 Azusa Street Revival in Los Angeles and modern Pentecostal movement

1909 Scofield Reference Bible first published

1910 Edinburgh Missionary Conference launches modern missions movement and modern ecumenical movement

1910–1915 *The Fundamentals*, a 12-volume collection of essays by 64 British and American scholars and preachers, becomes the foundation of Fundamentalism and demonstrates the great divide in American Christianity known as the "Modernist-Fundamentalist" controversy

1913 *Catholic Encyclopedia* published

1916 Father Divine founded International Peace Mission movement

1917 True Jesus Church founded in Beijing

1919 Karl Barth's *Commentary on Romans* is published, criticizing Liberal Christianity and beginning the neo-orthodox movement

1921 Oxford Group founded at Oxford

1921 First Christian radio broadcast over KDKA in Pittsburgh

1931 Christ the Redeemer (statue) in Rio de Janeiro, Brazil

1933 Catholic Worker Movement founded

1934 Herbert W. Armstrong founded Radio Church of God, Worldwide Church of God

1935 Dr. Frank C. Laubach, known as "The Apostle to the Illiterates," working in the Philippines, develops his literacy program

1935 Billy Sunday, early U.S. radio evangelist

1939 Southern and Northern US branches of the Methodist Episcopal Church, along with the Methodist Protestant Church reunite to form The Methodist Church

1939 Theodore Epp airs the first Back to the Bible program

1940 Monumento Nacional de Santa Cruz del Valle de los Caidos, world's largest cross, 152.4 meters high, erected

1940 Wycliffe Bible Translators founded
1940 Jack Wyrtzen founded Word of Life ministry
1942 National Association of Evangelicals founded
1945 Dietrich Bonhoeffer is executed by the Nazis on Hitler's order
1947 *Uneasy Conscience of Modern Fundamentalism* by Carl F. H. Henry, a landmark of Evangelicalism versus Fundamentalism in US
1947 Oral Roberts founded Evangelistic Association
1948 World Council of Churches is founded
1949 Billy Graham preaches his first Los Angeles crusade
1950 Pope Pius XII proclaims the Assumption of the Blessed Virgin Mary to be dogma
1950 Missionaries of Charity founded by Mother Teresa
1951 Campus Crusade for Christ founded at UCLA
1952 *Novum Testamentum Graece*, critical edition of Greek New Testament published, basis of modern translations
1952 C. S. Lewis's *Mere Christianity* is published
1954 Moonies: Sun M. Moon
1955 Founding of L'Abri by Francis and Edith Schaeffer
1956 In God We Trust designated U.S. national motto
1956 Jim Elliot, Nate Saint, and three other missionaries killed by the Auca Indians
1957 United Church of Christ founded by ecumenical union of Congregationalists and Evangelical and Reformed, representing Calvinists and Lutherans
1960 Election of John F. Kennedy, first Catholic United States President
1960 Growth of charismatic renewal, going across denominational lines
1962–1965 Catholic Second Vatican Council produced 16 documents which became official Roman Catholic teaching
1963 Martin Luther King leads a civil rights march in Washington, D.C.
1964 Roman Catholic Church in United States changes from Latin to English in the Mass
1965 China church grows despite Cultural Revolution
1968 United Methodist Church formed with union of Methodist Church & Evangelical United Brethren Church, becoming the largest Methodist/Wesleyan church in the world
1969 Children of God: David "Mo" Berg
1970s The Jesus movement takes hold in the U.S.
1971 New American Standard Bible first published
1974 Jim Bakker founds PTL television ministry
1977 Focus on the Family founded by James Dobson
1978 New International Version of the Bible first published
1978–2005 Pope John Paul II, reaffirmed moral traditions (*The Splendor of Truth*)

1979 Moral Majority founded by Jerry Falwell
1983 Martin Luther King Jr. Day established in the United States
1988 Christian Coalition
1989 New Revised Standard Version
1992 Catechism of the Catholic Church
1999 Oct 31 signing of the Joint Declaration on the Doctrine of Justification between the Lutheran World Federation and the Catholic Church

Introduction

Christianity in the 20th century was characterized by accelerating fragmentation. The century saw the rise of both liberal and conservative splinter groups, as well as a general secularization of Western society. The Roman Catholic Church instituted many reforms in order to modernize. Missionaries also made inroads in the Far East, establishing further followings in China, Taiwan, and Japan. At the same time, state-promoted atheism in Communist Eastern Europe and the Soviet Union brought many Eastern Orthodox Christians to Western Europe and the United States, leading to greatly increased contact between Western and Eastern Christianity. Nevertheless, church attendance declined more in Western Europe than it did in the East. Christian ecumenism grew in importance, beginning at the Edinburgh Missionary Conference in 1910. Liturgical Movement became significant in both Catholic and Protestant Christianity.

Wikipedia

EVENTS

Important events in the Christian Church in the twentieth century

Emergence of charismatic Christian sects.
Rise of the ecumenical movement.
Revision of the Roman Catholic liturgy.
Missions reach virtually every region of the world.
New translation methods put the Bible into the languages of 95% of humankind.
Dramatic increase in number of Christians martyred.
Decline of church attendance in Western world contrasts with revivals in Africa and South America and explosive growth of Chinese Christianity.

PEOPLE

Christian leaders in the Church in the twentieth century

B. B. Warfield (1851–1921)
Karl Barth (1886–1968)

Dietrich Bonhoeffer (1906–1945)

C. S. Lewis (1898–1963)

Francis A. Schaeffer (1912–1984)

Mother Teresa of Calcutta (1910–1997)

Billy Graham (b. 1918)

Religious Americanism

I. The nation after the war

After the World War II, America displayed a conservative mood and it remained so for 15 years. Church membership rose dramatically.

1800 - 15% 1950 - 55%

1900 - 36% 1956 - 62%

1920 - 43% 1960 - 69%

1940 - 49% 1972 - 70% (40% attended church regularly)

Most Americans considered church attendance appropriate—even intellectuals.

Billy Graham

Billy Graham best characterizes the conservative religious mood. In 1957, Graham went to New York. Copying Billy Sunday's organizational techniques, but preaching like D. L. Moody, Graham had his most significant meeting. The New York revival lasted three and a half months and counted 56,000 public decisions with television decisions estimated at 60,000. Huge crowds gathered in Times Square to hear Graham and at least 100,000 came to Yankee Stadium each night for the services.

Graham peppered his sermons with, "The Bible says, . . . "His simple Bible messages appealed to "generic" Christians. He avoided controversial doctrinal issues preaching a message of sin and salvation. Movie stars, sports figures and underworld figures who professed conversion added to Graham's fame.

The Graham organization led in establishing the conservative journal, *Christianity Today*, and produces Christian films.

II. The secularizing of religion

In spite of increasing church membership secular attitudes and values gripped America. Most Americans conformed outwardly to traditional American values, inwardly they were pushed aside.

Norman Vincent Peale

Norman Vincent Peale's ministry illustrates the growth of empty Christianity. Peale kicked off the whole self-help and positive thinking industry in 1948 when he wrote *Guide to Positive Thinking*. The book became a best seller.

Following Peale, came Dale Carnegie. You can see his self-help approach in *How to Win Friends and Influence People.* The self-help/positive thinking fad ties religion to the old American values of success, individualism, industry and self-reliance. Peale's second book, *The Power of Positive Thinking*, continued the fad. None have any genuine theological value. Robert Schuller continues Peale's approach at Los Angeles' Garden Grove Community Church.

John Sutherlin Bonnell secularized religion in 1956 with his tremendously successful "Dial a Prayer" idea. Religious themes permeated American society at all levels. Popular music included such hits as "He" and "Have You Talked to the Man Upstairs." *Moviescreen Magazine* published a series of articles on how movie stars "found their faith." It was a deep faith, too. Jane Russell once said, "God is a living doll!" How profound!

Dwight David Eisenhower

In 1952, Dwight David Eisenhower ran for the presidency against Adali E. Stevenson. Ike, the war, hero received America's adulation and her vote. Ike represented solid American values. Eisenhower reflected America's prevailing religious attitudes. He once said America had to be built on faith—any faith! He did not mean a commitment to biblical faith but a commitment to democracy's moral values. After World War II, Ike had said he was intensely religious. He said, "No man goes through six years of war without faith." Eisenhower did not belong to any church. His faith rested in democracy, in the American way!

Communism and the cold war

After World War II, America and the Soviet Union entered a cold war. Russia's communistic system challenged the American free enterprise capitalistic system. Christianity said "man has worth and value," communism stressed the priority of the state over the individual. Eisenhower said democracy cannot exist without a religious base so it is essential to be "Christian." Americans elected Ike partly because he recognized the value of a commitment to "religious humanism." Religion and Americanism became inexorably linked. Americans believed you couldn't be a good American without being religious. During Eisenhower's presidency we added the phrase, "under God," to the Pledge of Allegiance. American coins have carried the phrase, "In God We Trust," since 1865 but it was not the nation's motto until 1956.

House Un-American Activities Committee

Other significant events which occurred after World War II include the formation of the House Un-American Activities Committee. What does it mean to be un-American? No one knew. The ambiguity led to Joseph McCarthy's witch hunts and conservative American preachers preached strong anticommunist messages. In 1947 the Supreme Court ruled that

Bible classes in public schools might be a violation of the first amendment. In 1962 the court ruled public schools could not write a prayer and force students to recite it.

Baby Boomers

Something else happened after the war. In 1946, America began a baby boom that did not end until 1964, adding 75,000,000 to our population.(1) The bulk of the Baby Boomers reached college during the 1960s. Os Guinness and other Christian observers note a shift in American culture in the 1960s. Several factors shaped this generation:

During the fifteen years from 1940–1955 American personal income soared 293%. Their parents had suffered through the Depression and World War II and they wanted their children to enjoy their plenty. The standard of living rose accordingly and most American young people grew accustomed to the amenities and luxuries of life. Baby Boomers, themselves, became a major market force.

The Baby Boomers became the best educated generation in American history. In fact, they had the best schools money could buy. Education became the nation's secular religion. In 1950, the United States had spent $6.6 billion on our elementary and secondary schools. A decade later the total rose to $18.6 billion. In 1958 alone, the U.S. built 62,000 new classrooms at an average of $40,000 each.(2)

The Baby Boomers were the first generation to be raised with television. Television itself created change. Baby Boomers became used to excellence with messages communicated in "sound bites." Attention spans reduced and the small screen promoted the expectation of smooth transition with little time drag.

As Landon Jones put it:

> In the new world inhabited by children three or four hours a day—call it Televisionland—there was violence but rarely blood or pain. There was death but never emptiness. People did not work regularly but were rarely hungry or in need. In fact, economic realities were not present at all. There was little unemployment in Televisionland and no food stamps. Fathers were not wage earners but hapless buffoons, outwitted by both their children and their wives. There was desire in Televisionland, but lust and greed were somehow mixed up with cravings for prettier hair and whiter laundry.(3)

In recent years Baby Boomers discovered their great expectations have fallen down around their ears. Expecting great things from life they have discovered reality. The Baby Boomer hates hypocrisy worse than heresy and honors genuine commitment over lip service even though they often demonstrate an uncertainty of what real commitment means.

Today churches face their most difficult . . . and potentially most rewarding times. You will face some challenging times for the scholars tell us those following the Baby Boom do not have their desire for excellence.

Footnotes

1. Landon Y. Jones, Great Expectations: America and the Baby Boom Generation (New York: Ballantyne Books, 1980), p. 39.

2. Ibid., p. 58.

3. Ibid., p. 140–141.

Michael Hines, Christian Chronicler

Theological movements

Process theology

Process theology departs from traditional Christian beliefs mainly because of its view of the nature of God and His relationship to the universe. Many critics relate this deviance to the low view of Scripture held by Process theologians who by and large deny the divine inspiration of the Bible. Others critique Process theology as panentheism which says that God is to the world as a soul is to a body. It is believed that God is not the universe as in pantheism, but that God is apart from the universe, yet also in it. As the world is in the process of changing, so is God, and he is in the process of becoming all that he can be.

Process theology and God

In Process theology, God has two poles:

A primordial pole—this pole is eternal, unchanging, and not of this world.

And a consequent pole—this pole is temporal, changing, and of this world.

The primordial pole is what God could be, or what his potential is.

Thus, the consequent pole is what God is at this very moment. This means that God is not perfect, and in order for him to become perfect he needs our help. Because God is limited within his consequent pole, he is not omnipotent (he does not know everything). Thus he cannot control evil and cannot guarantee that it will ever be conquered. Once again, this leaves God relying on humans to help him with his creation.

Feminism

Feminism, based on a belief in the fundamental equality of the sexes, specifically promotes the rights and interests of women. Within Christianity, feminism is primarily concerned with the role of women in the church. A distinction may be made between two groups:

"Liberal-Christian feminists" who work from the standpoint of a commitment to the Christian faith but accept the authority of Scripture in only a limited way, and

"Evangelical feminists" who have a high view of Scripture and believe that the Bible teaches the full equality of men and women without role distinctions based on gender.

To many, liberal-Christian feminism and evangelical feminism are both seen as included in the idea of Christian egalitarianism (gender equality)—the difference being primarily in how they each deal with the Scriptures.

To the liberal-Christian, the Bible is not viewed as infallible or inerrant, and therefore its authority is limited. The patriarchal framework of the Old Testament and the New Testament teaching of Paul (which seems to limit the role of women) are simply viewed as culturally obsolete and wrong.

The evangelical feminist, who generally accepts the infallibility of Scripture, seeks hermeneutical (or interpretational) means, in addition to issues of cultural limitation, to argue for egalitarianism. However, they attempt to do so while remaining faithful to the text of Scripture.

Postmodernism

Within the context of Christianity, postmodernism is a rebuttal to orthodox doctrines of God and ecclesiology, questioning historical Christian notions of objective truth and epistemology through postmodern philosophy. Postmodern Christianity emphasizes the otherness and incomprehensibility of God and the transcendental nature of faith as an attempt to satisfy a postmodern position while offering a rebuttal to secular accusations against Christian religion and spirituality.

Theopedia

Liberation theology

Liberation theology focuses on Jesus as not only Savior but also as Liberator.

Liberation is a movement to reform theology "from below," from the perspective of the poor, for the sake of radical social change.

Liberation theology sought freedom from oppression.

Liberation theology addresses systemic issues such as class conflict, racism, and sexism. It arose in Africa, to reject colonialism and apartheid, and in Latin America, to reject political, military, and economic oppression. In Latin America it has played a role in church and state conflicts. In 1973, the English translation of Gustavo Gutierrez's A Theology for Liberation helped spread liberation theology to North America, where it has been taken up by some African-American and feminist theologians. Major themes in liberation theology include: God's favoring of the poor and the oppressed; Jesus' identification with the poor; the imperative for Christians to act with and for the poor; biblical mandates for justice; necessity of confrontation or conflict to bring about justice.

Luther Seminary

Evangelicalism and Fundamentalism

Introduction

Evangelicalism is the term applied to a number of related movements within Protestantism. They are bound together by a common emphasis on what they believe to be a personal relationship with Jesus Christ and a commitment to the demands of the New Testament. Evangelicalism is usually associated with a type of preaching that calls on the hearer to confess his or her sin and believe in Christ's forgiveness.

During the late 17th century and throughout the 18th, Pietism was the mainspring of the so-called evangelical revival in Germany. Its counterpart in Great Britain and the United States was Methodism, which contributed to the series of revivals called the Great Awakening that swept 18th century America. The common purpose of evangelical movements was to revitalize the churches spiritually. In the late 18th and early 19th centuries, Evangelicals in the Church of England—especially William Wilberforce and other members of the group known as the Clapham Sect—played a leading role in the movement to abolish slavery in the British colonies.

Since about 1950 the term evangelical frequently has been applied in the United States to the inheritors and proponents of Fundamentalism.

Paul Merritt Bassett

Evangelicalism

Evangelicalism is a movement in modern Anglo-American Protestantism (and in nations influenced by Britain and North America) that emphasizes personal commitment to Christ and the authority of the Bible. It is represented in most Protestant denominations.

Evangelicals believe that each individual has a need for spiritual rebirth and personal commitment to Jesus Christ as savior, through faith in his atoning death on the cross (commonly, although not necessarily, through a specific conversion experience). They emphasize strict orthodoxy on cardinal doctrines, morals, and especially on the authority of the Bible. Many Evangelicals follow a traditional, precritical interpretation of the Bible and insist on its inerrancy (freedom from error in history as well as in faith and morals).

The term Evangelicalism has been a source of controversy, and the precise relationship or distinction between Evangelicalism and Fundamentalism has been disputed. Liberal Protestants often oppose the use of Evangelical to refer only to the strict traditionalists.

In the general sense, evangelical (from the New Testament Greek *euangelion*, "good news") means simply pertaining to the Gospel. The word identified the early leaders of the Reformation, who emphasized the biblical message and rejected the official interpretation of dogma by the Roman Catholic church. Thus, Evangelical often simply means Protestant in continental Europe and in the names of churches elsewhere. In Germany, it once identified Lutherans in contrast to the Reformed (Calvinist) churches. Nevertheless, the large union body, the Evangelical Church in Germany, today encompasses most Protestants, whether Lutheran or Calvinist, liberal or conservative. The term has also been applied to the Low Church wing of Anglicanism, which stresses biblical preaching, as opposed to sacramentalism and belief in the authority of church tradition.

The emergence of theological Modernism during the 19th century, particularly historical criticism of the Bible, produced a movement of reaction within many denominations. From 1910 to 1915 conservative scholars produced a series of booklets entitled The Fundamentals, and in 1920 a conservative northern Baptist journal coined the designation Fundamentalist for the defenders of orthodoxy.

The term Fundamentalism gradually came to designate only the most uncompromising and militant wing of the movement, however, and more moderate Protestant conservatives began to adopt the older designation of Evangelical. They created the National Association of Evangelicals in the U.S. (1942) and the World Evangelical Fellowship (1951), the latter reviving an international body formed under Britain's Evangelical Alliance (founded 1846). The constituencies of these bodies are largely outside the World and National Councils of Churches, but large numbers of Evangelicals exist within the mainstream ecumenical denominations.

The largest U.S. Protestant body, the Southern Baptist Convention, embraces Evangelical tenets; other components of Evangelicalism include Pentecostalists, the Charismatic Renewal (including its Roman Catholic wing), Arminian-Holiness churches, conservative confessionalists such as the Lutheran Church-Missouri Synod, and numerous black Baptists, as well as independent "faith missions" and interdenominational ministries such as InterVarsity Christian Fellowship, Campus Crusade for Christ, and World Vision. Current Evangelicalism bridges two elements that were, for the most part, antithetical in the 19th century, the doctrinaire conservatives and the revivalists.

Evangelical educational materials are produced by a number of publishing houses, and such publications as *Christianity Today* are widely read. Evangelical preachers have long made extensive use of radio broadcasts, and during the 1970s evangelical programs on television proliferated, reaching an audience of more than 20 million. According to a recent estimate, there are about 157 million Evangelicals throughout the world, including about 59 million in the United States.

Richard N. Ostling

(Christian) Fundamentalism

Introduction

Fundamentalism was a movement among American evangelicals to assert biblical authority as over-against several aspects of modernity.

"The best description of fundamentalism, as it appears in the late nineteenth and early twentieth century, is to recognize it as orthodox Christianity. Fundamentalists continued biblical and supernatural Christianity when many denominations defected." Michael Hines

American revivalist Dwight L. Moody (1837–1899) was an inspiration to many in the early Fundamentalist movement

"Fundamentalism" is so named for five beliefs, deemed fundamental to Christianity:

inerrancy of Scripture,
the virgin birth of Christ,
the substitutionary atonement of Christ,
the authenticity of miracles, and
the resurrection of Christ.

In the late nineteenth century, fundamentalism formed as a coalition of Christians, concerned that liberalism, biblical criticism, and Darwinism were penetrating schools and churches. They believed that biblical authority and the Christian message were at stake. Upon losing many battles for control of religious and public institutions, most fundamentalists withdrew to build their own networks of schools, churches and publications. Beginning in the 1950s, moderate evangelicals chafed under a fundamentalist ethos which was separatistic and combative; these moderates followed Billy Graham and other leaders into a broader evangelicalism. In the late twentieth century fundamentalism reentered the public arena, debating such issues as evolution, abortion, and the prohibition of prayer in the public schools.

Luther Seminary

Fundamentalism

Fundamentalism is a term popularly used to describe strict adherence to Christian doctrines based on a literal interpretation of the Bible. This usage derives from a late 19th and early 20th century transdenominational Protestant movement that opposed the accommodation of Christian doctrine to modern scientific theory and philosophy. With some differences among themselves, fundamentalists insist on belief in the inerrancy of the Bible, the virgin birth and divinity of Jesus Christ, the vicarious and atoning character of his death, his bodily resurrection, and his second coming as the irreducible minimum of authentic Christianity. This minimum was reflected in such early declarations as the 14 point creed of the Niagara Bible Conference of 1878 and the 5 point statement of the Presbyterian General Assembly of 1910.

Two immediate doctrinal sources for fundamentalist thought were Millenarianism and biblical inerrancy. Millenarianism, belief in the physical return of Christ to establish a 1,000 year earthly reign of blessedness, was a doctrine prevalent in English speaking Protestantism by the 1870s. At the same time, powerful conservative forces led by Charles Hodge and Benjamin Warfield opposed the growing use of literary and historical criticism in biblical studies, defending biblical inspiration and the inerrant authority of the Bible.

The name fundamentalist was coined in 1920 to designate those "doing battle royal for the Fundamentals." Also figuring in the name was The Fundamentals, a 12 volume collection of essays written in the period 1910—15 by 64 British and American scholars and preachers. Three million copies of these volumes and the founding of the World's Christian Fundamentals Association in 1919 gave sharp identity to fundamentalism as it moved into the 1920s. Leadership moved across the years from such men as A T Pierson, A J Gordon, and C I Scofield to A C Dixon and Reuben Torrey, William Jennings Bryan, and J Gresham Machen.

As fundamentalism developed, most Protestant denominations in the United States felt the division between liberalism and fundamentalism. The Baptists, Presbyterians, and Disciples of Christ were more affected than others. Nevertheless, talk of schism was much more common than schism itself. Perhaps the lack of a central organization and a normative creed, certainly the caricature of fundamentalism arising from the Scopes Trial (1925), the popularization of the liberal response by representatives like Harry Emerson Fosdick, well publicized divisions among fundamentalists themselves, and preoccupations with the Depression of the 1930s and World War II curtailed fundamentalism's appeal. By 1950 it was either isolated and muted or had taken on the more moderate tones of Evangelicalism.

In the 1970s and 1980s, however, fundamentalism again became an influential force in the United States. Promoted by popular television evangelists and represented by such groups as the Moral Majority, the new politically oriented "religious right" opposes the influence of liberalism and secularism in American life. The term fundamentalist has also been used to describe members of militant Islamic groups.

Paul Merritt Bassett

Dispensationalism and premillennialism

One new factor contributes to fundamentalism's growth. It is the interest in dispensationalism. Dispensationalism and premillennialism go together but aren't synonymous. (Dispensational premillennialism is just one form of premillennial eschatology.)

Dispensationalism is associated with John Nelson Darby, the founder of the Plymouth Brethren in Plymouth, England about 1830. Darby promoted a dispensational premillennial theology; a theology he reportedly obtained from Margaret McDonald. McDonald, who participated in a Scottish charismatic revival about the same time, received dispensationalism as part of a charismatic prophecy.

One of Darby's students, C. I. Scofield, developed and popularized the view with his *Scofield Reference Bible.*

Michael Hines, Christian Chronicler

Princeton theologians

Princeton Theological Seminary and the Princeton theologians demonstrated consistent biblical orthodoxy during the later nineteenth century. Professors Charles Hodge and B. B. Warfield develop what became known as the "Princeton School." It is a mindset which is conservative, biblical and orthodox. These two erudite men emphasize biblical inspiration, authority and inerrancy, positions which stand out in stark contrast to the Liberal and critical attacks on biblical veracity.

By the 1890s, the "Princeton School" and the dispensationalists come together. Organizers of the prophecy conferences invite Hodge, Warfield, and others to speak. In 1895 the conferences issued a list of five points which they held as fundamental to the faith. Two wealthy businessmen provide funds for the production of twelve large tracts called "The Fundamentals." According to these scholars, Christianity's five fundamental points include:

Verbal inerrancy of the Scripture.
Christ's deity and virgin birth.
The substitutionary atonement.
The bodily physical resurrection of Christ.
The bodily return of Christ.

Conservative Christians accepted these principles without question; even some of the mainline denominations formally accepted these points. The General Assembly of the Northern Presbyterian Church continued their affirmation of these standards until 1910.

Itinerant evangelists also repudiate Liberalism. I don't classify D. L. Moody as a fundamentalist although he attended some of the prophecy conferences and identified with them. One of the best known evangelists is Reuben A. Torrey, a northern theologian and intellectual. We know Torrey best for his later move to the west coast where he established a "Moody Seminary" on the west coast, the Bible Institute of Los Angeles (BIOLA). Other evangelists recognized as fundamentalists include J. Wilbur Chapman and Rodney "Gipsey" Smith.

The decline of fundamentalism

Fundamentalism took on negative overtones after World War I and lost much of its influence. Fundamentalism's doom occurred simultaneously with the fall of Princeton Theological Seminary in 1927. Liberals challenged J. Gresham Machen on his position of inerrancy and the school reorganized along Liberal lines in 1929. For many years fundamentalism was synonymous with anti-intellectualism and narrow thinking. Fundamentalism all but disappeared until the late 1970s. Jerry Falwell led the resurgence of fundamentalism with his publication *Fundamentalist Journal.* Modern fundamentalism combines basic conservative orthodox theology with dispensational premillennialism and an insistence on local autonomy.

Michael Hines, Christian Chronicler

The Origins of the Pentecostal Movement

Introduction

The Pentecostal movement is by far the largest and most important religious movement to originate in the United States. Beginning in 1901 with only a handful of students in a Bible School in Topeka, Kansas, the number of Pentecostals increased steadily throughout the world during the Twentieth Century until by 1993 they had become the largest family of Protestants in the world. With over 200,000,000 members designated as denominational Pentecostals, this group surpassed the Orthodox churches as the second largest denominational family of Christians, surpassed only by the Roman Catholics. In addition to these "Classical denominational Pentecostals," there were over 200,000,000 "Charismatic" Pentecostals in the mainline denominations and independent charismatic churches, both Catholic and Protestant, which placed the number of both Pentecostals and charismatics at well over 420,000,000 persons in 1993. This explosive growth has forced the Christian world to pay increasing attention to the entire movement and to attempt to discover the root causes of this growth.

Although the Pentecostal movement had its beginnings in the United States, it owed much of its basic theology to earlier British perfectionistic and charismatic movements. At least three of these, the Methodist/Holiness movement, the Catholic Apostolic movement of Edward Irving, and the British Keswick "Higher Life" movement prepared the way for what appeared to be a spontaneous outpouring of the Holy Spirit in America.

Perhaps the most important immediate precursor to Pentecostalism was the Holiness movement which issued from the heart of Methodism at the end of the Nineteenth Century. From John Wesley, the Pentecostals inherited the idea of a subsequent crisis experience variously called "entire sanctification,"" perfect love," "Christian perfection," or "heart purity." It was John Wesley who posited such a possibility in his influential tract, A Plain Account of Christian Perfection (1766). It was from Wesley that the Holiness Movement developed the theology of a "second blessing." It was Wesley's colleague, John Fletcher, however, who first called this second blessing a "baptism in the Holy Spirit," an experience which brought spiritual power to the recipient as well as inner cleansing. This was explained in his major work, Checks to Antinominianism (1771). During the Nineteenth Century, thousands of Methodists claimed to receive this experience, although no one at the time saw any connection with this spirituality and speaking in tongues or any of the other charisms.

In the following century, Edward Irving and his friends in London suggested the possibility of a restoration of the charisms in the modern church. A popular Presbyterian pastor in London, Irving led the first attempt at "charismatic renewal" in his Regents Square Presbyterian Church in 1831. Although tongues and prophecies were experienced in his church, Irving was not successful in his quest for a restoration of New Testament

Christianity. In the end, the "Catholic Apostolic Church" which was founded by his followers, attempted to restore the "five-fold ministries" (of apostles, prophets, evangelists, pastors, and teachers) in addition to the charisms. While his movement failed in England, Irving did succeed in pointing to glossolalia as the "standing sign" of the baptism in the Holy Spirit, a major facet in the future theology of the Pentecostals.

Another predecessor to Pentecostalism was the Keswick "Higher Life" movement which flourished in England after 1875. Led at first by American holiness teachers such as Hannah Whitall Smith and William E. Boardman, the Keswick teachers soon changed the goal and content of the "second blessing" from the Wesleyan emphasis on "heart purity" to that of an "enduement of spiritual power for service." Thus, by the time of the Pentecostal outbreak in America in 1901, there had been at least a century of movements emphasizing a second blessing called the "baptism in the Holy Spirit" with various interpretations concerning the content and results of the experience. In America, such Keswick teachers as A. B. Simpson and A. J. Gordon also added to the movement at large an emphasis on divine healing "as in the atonement" and the premillenial rapture of the church.

Origins of Pentecostalism

The first "Pentecostals" in the modern sense appeared on the scene in 1901 in the city of Topeka, Kansas in a Bible school conducted by Charles Fox Parham, a holiness teacher and former Methodist pastor. In spite of controversy over the origins and timing of Parham's emphasis on glossolalia, all historians agree that the movement began during the first days of 1901 just as the world entered the Twentieth Century. The first person to be baptized in the Holy Spirit accompanied by speaking in tongues was Agnes Ozman, one of Parham's Bible School students, who spoke in tongues on the very first day of the new century, January 1, 1901. According to J. Roswell Flower, the founding Secretary of the Assemblies of God, Ozman's experience was the "touch felt round the world," an event which "made the Pentecostal Movement of the Twentieth Century."

As a result of this Topeka Pentecost, Parham formulated the doctrine that tongues was the "Bible evidence" of the baptism in the Holy Spirit. He also taught that tongues was a supernatural impartation of human languages (xenoglossolalia) for the purpose of world evangelization. Henceforth, he taught, missionaries need not study foreign languages since they would be able to preach in miraculous tongues all over the world. Armed with this new theology, Parham founded a church movement which he called the "Apostolic Faith" and began a whirlwind revival tour of the American middle west to promote his exciting new experience.

It was not until 1906, however, that Pentecostalism achieved worldwide attention through the Azusa Street revival in Los Angeles led by the African-American preacher William Joseph Seymour. He learned about the tongues-attested baptism in a Bible school that Parham conducted in Houston, Texas in 1905. Invited to pastor a black holiness church in Los Angeles in 1906, Seymour opened the historic meeting in April, 1906 in a former African Methodist Episcopal (AME) church building at 312 Azusa Street in downtown Los Angeles.

What happened at Azusa Street has fascinated church historians for decades and has yet to be fully understood and explained. For over three years, the Azusa Street "Apostolic Faith Mission" conducted three services a day, seven days a week, where thousands of seekers received the tongues baptism. Word of the revival was spread abroad through The Apostolic Faith, a paper that Seymour sent free of charge to some 50,000 subscribers. From Azusa Street Pentecostalism spread rapidly around the world and began its advance toward becoming a major force in Christendom.

The Azusa Street movement seems to have been a merger of white American holiness religion with worship styles derived from the African-American Christian tradition which had developed since the days of chattel slavery in the South. The expressive worship and praise at Azusa Street, which included shouting and dancing, had been common among Appalachian whites as well as Southern blacks. The admixture of tongues and other charisms with black music and worship styles created a new and indigenous form of Pentecostalism that was to prove extremely attractive to disinherited and deprived people, both in America and other nations of the world.

The interracial aspects of the movement in Los Angeles were a striking exception to the racism and segregation of the times. The phenomenon of blacks and whites worshipping together under a black pastor seemed incredible to many observers. The ethos of the meeting was captured by Frank Bartleman, a white Azusa participant, when he said of Azusa Street, "The color line was washed away in the blood." Indeed, people from all the ethnic minorities of Los Angeles, a city which Bartleman called "the American Jerusalem," were represented at Azusa Street.

The place of William Seymour as an important religious leader now seems to be assured. As early as 1972 Sidney Ahlstrom, the noted church historian from Yale University, said that Seymour was "the most influential black leader in American religious history." Seymour, along with Charles Parham, could well be called the "co-founders" of world Pentecostalism.

American Pentecostal Pioneers

The first wave of "Azusa pilgrims" journeyed throughout the United States spreading the Pentecostal fire, primarily in holiness churches, missions, and camp meetings. For some time, it was thought that it was necessary to journey to California to receive the "blessing." Soon, however, people received the tongues experience wherever they lived.

American Pentecostal pioneers who received tongues at Azusa Street went back to their homes to spread the movement among their own people, at times against great opposition. One of the first was Gaston Barnabas Cashwell of North Carolina, who spoke in tongues in

1906. His six-month preaching tour of the South in 1907 resulted in major inroads among southern holiness folk. Under his ministry, Cashwell saw several holiness denominations swept into the new movement, including the Church of God (Cleveland, Tennessee), the Pentecostal Holiness Church, the Fire-Baptized Holiness Church, and the Pentecostal Free-Will Baptist Church.

Also in 1906, Charles Harrison Mason journeyed to Azusa Street and returned to Memphis, Tennessee to spread the Pentecostal fire in the Church of God in Christ. Mason and the church he founded were made up of African-Americans only one generation removed from slavery. (The parents of both Seymour and Mason had been born as southern slaves). Although tongues caused a split in the church in 1907, the Church of God in Christ experienced such explosive growth that by 1993, it was by far the largest Pentecostal denomination in North America, claiming some 5,500,000 members in 15,300 local churches. Another Azusa pilgrim was William H. Durham of Chicago. After receiving his tongues experience at Azusa Street in 1907, he returned to Chicago, where he led thousands of mid-western Americans and Canadians into the Pentecostal movement. His "finished work" theology of gradual progressive sanctification, which he announced in 1910, led to the formation of the Assemblies of God in 1914. Since many white pastors had formerly been part of Mason's church, the beginnings of the Assemblies of God was also partially a racial separation. In time the Assemblies of God church was destined to become the largest Pentecostal denominational church in the world, claiming by 1993 over 2,000,000 members in the U.S. and some 25,000,000 adherents in 150 nations of the world.

Missionaries of the One-Way Ticket

In addition to the ministers who received their Pentecostal experience at Azusa Street, there were thousands of others who were indirectly influenced by the revival in Los Angeles. Among these was Thomas Ball Barratt of Norway, a Methodist pastor later to be known as the Pentecostal apostle to northern and western Europe. Receiving a glossolalic baptism in the Spirit in New York City in 1906, he returned to Oslo where he conducted the first Pentecostal services in Europe in December of 1906. From Norway, Barratt traveled to Sweden, England, France, and Germany, where he sparked other national Pentecostal movements. Under Barratt such leaders as Lewi Pethrus in Sweden, Jonathan Paul in Germany, and Alexander Boddy in England were brought into the movement.

From Chicago, through the influence of William Durham, the movement spread quickly to Italy and South America. Thriving Italian Pentecostal movements were founded after 1908 in the USA, Brazil, Argentina, and Italy by two Italian immigrants to Chicago, Luigi Francescon and Giacomo Lombardy. Also, in South Bend, Indiana (near Chicago) two Swedish Baptist immigrants, Daniel Berg and Gunnar Vingren, received the pentecostal experience and felt a prophetic call to Brazil. Their missionary trip in 1910 resulted in the formation of the Brazilian Assemblies of God, which developed into the largest national pentecostal movement in the world, claiming some 15,000,000 members by 1993. Also hailing from Chicago was Willis C. Hoover, the Methodist missionary to Chile who in 1909 led a pentecostal revival in the Chilean Methodist Episcopal Church. After being excommunicated from the Methodist Episcopal Church, Hoover and 37 of his followers organized the "Pentecostal Methodist Church" which by 1993 grew to number some 1,500,000 adherents in Chile.

African Pentecostalism owed its origins to the work of John Graham Lake (1870–1935), who began his ministry as a Methodist preacher but who later prospered in the business world as an insurance executive. In 1898 his wife was miraculously healed of tuberculosis under the ministry of divine healer Alexander Dowie, founder of a religious community called "Zion City" near Chicago, Illinois. Joining with Dowie, Lake became an elder in the "Zion Catholic Apostolic Church." At one point, Lake testified to an instant experience of entire sanctification in the home of Fred Bosworth, an early leader in the Assemblies of God. In 1907, he received the Pentecostal experience and spoke in tongues under the ministry of Charles Parham, who visited Zion while the aging Dowie was losing control of his ministry. Out of Zion also came a host of almost 500 preachers who entered the ranks of the Pentecostal movement, chief of whom was John G. Lake.

After his Pentecostal experience, Lake abandoned the insurance business in order to answer a long-standing call to minister in South Africa. In April 1908, he led a large missionary party to Johannesburg, where he began to spread the Pentecostal message throughout the nation. Coming with him was his wife and seven children as well as Holiness evangelists Thomas Hezmalhalch and J. C. Lehman. Only Lehman had been to Africa before 1908, having served for five years as a missionary to the Zulus. Hezmalhalch, lovingly known as "Brother Tom," was born in England and was sixty years of age when he arrived in South Africa. Before the end of his first year in South Africa Lake's wife died, some believed through malnutrition. Lake nevertheless succeeded in founding two large and influential Pentecostal churches in Southern Africa. The white branch took the name "Apostolic Faith Mission" (AFM) in 1910, borrowed from the name of the famous mission on Azusa Street. This is the church that eventually gave David duPlessis to the world as "Mr. Pentecost." The black branch eventually developed into the "Zion Christian Church" (ZCC) which by 1993 claimed no less than 6,000,000 members and, despite some doctrinal and cultural variations, was recognized as the largest Christian church in the nation. In its annual Easter conference at Pietersburg, this church gathers upwards of 2,000,000 worshippers, the largest annual gathering of Christians on earth.

After his African missionary tour of 1908–1912, Lake returned to the United States where he founded churches and healing homes in Spokane, Washington, and Portland, Oregon, before his death in 1935. Throughout the rest of the century, Pentecostal denominational missionaries from many nations spread the movement to all parts of Africa. In addition to the AFM and ZCC churches, the Pentecostal Holiness Church in South Africa was founded in 1913 under the leadership of Lehman, who had come with Lake in 1908. In 1917, the Assemblies of God entered South Africa when the American church accepted the mission already established by R. M. Turney. The Church of God (Cleveland, Tennessee) came to the country in 1951 through amalgamation with the Full Gospel Church. In retrospect, the work of Lake was the most influential and enduring of all the South African Pentecostal missions endeavors. According to Cecil Rhodes, the South African "Empire Builder," "His (Lake's) message has swept Africa. He has done more toward South Africa's future peace than any other man." Perhaps the highest accolade was given by no less a personage than Mahatma Ghandi who said of Lake, "Dr. Lake's teachings will eventually be accepted by the entire world."

Soon after Lake returned to the United States, the movement reached the Slavic world through the ministry of a Russian-born Baptist pastor, Ivan Voronaev who received the Pentecostal experience in New York City in 1919. Through prophecies, he was led to take his family with him to Odessa in the Ukraine in 1922, where he established the first Pentecostal church in the Soviet Union. Although he was arrested, imprisoned, and martyred in a communist prison in 1943, Voronaev's churches survived incredible persecution to become a major religious force in Russia and the former Soviet Union by 1993.

Neo-Pentecostals and Charismatics

This first wave of Pentecostal pioneer missionaries produced what has become known as the "Classical Pentecostal Movement" with over 11,000 Pentecostal denominations throughout the world. These continued to proliferate at an amazing rate as the century came to an end. In retrospect, the pattern established in South Africa was repeated in many other nations as the movement spread around the world. That is, an enterprising Pentecostal pioneer such as Lake broke the ground for a new movement which was initially despised and rejected by the existing churches. This phase was followed by organized Pentecostal denominational missions efforts which produced fast-growing missions and indigenous churches. The final phase was the penetration of Pentecostalism into the mainline Protestant and Catholic churches as "charismatic renewal" movements with the aim of renewing and reviving the historic churches.

Strangely enough, these newer "waves" also originated largely in the United States. These included the Protestant "Neo-pentecostal" movement which began in 1960 in Van Nuys, California, under the ministry of Dennis Bennett, Rector of St. Marks Episcopal (Anglican) Church. Within a decade, this movement had spread to all the 150 major Protestant families of the world reaching a total of 55,000,000 people by 1990. The Catholic Charismatic Renewal movement had its beginnings in Pittsburgh, Pennsylvania, in 1967 among students and faculty of DuQuesne University. In the more than thirty years since its inception, the Catholic movement has touched the lives of over 70,000,000 Catholics in over 120 nations of the world. Added to these is the newest category, the "Third Wave" of the Spirit, which originated at Fuller Theological Seminary in 1981 under the classroom ministry of John Wimber. These consisted of mainline Evangelicals who moved in signs and wonders, but who disdained labels such as "pentecostal" or "charismatic." By 1990 this group numbered some 33,000,000 members in the world.

In summary, all these movements, both Pentecostal and charismatic, have come to constitute a major force in Christendom throughout the world with explosive growth rates not seen before in modern times. By 1990, The Pentecostals and their charismatic brothers and sisters in the mainline Protestant and Catholic churches were turning their attention toward world evangelization. Only time will reveal the ultimate results of this movement which has greatly impacted the world during the Twentieth Century.

Vinson Synan

Vatican II

A Roman Catholic view

"The Second Vatican Council is the most important Christian event since the schism between the Churches of East and West in 1054 AD. Vatican II opens the way forward to heal that schism. It also aims to heal the rifts of the sixteenth century Reformation. By means of the Council Pope John sought to promote unity between Christians, greater openness and Aggiornamento (updating) within the Catholic Church itself. His hope also was for dialogue with other religions, and to relate better to the whole world, which the Church serves."

Voice of the Church

[A very different view comes at the conclusion of this article, by Hans Küng.]

Introduction

The First Vatican Council was adjourned in 1870, following the solemn definition of papal infallibility. Only a part of its task had been accomplished, but it was destined never to meet again. Pope Pius IX died in 1878, and five popes had come and gone before the Second Vatican Council was proclaimed by Pope John XXIII.

Pope John announced his intention of summoning the Ecumenical Council in January, 1959, within three months of his election to the Chair of Peter; he signed the Apostolic Constitution, *Humane Salutis*, on Christmas Day in 1961. Meanwhile, ten commissions had been formed to prepare draft decrees to be debated in the Council. At first, seventy decrees were proposed, but gradually their number was reduced to seventeen.

Summary

The Second Vatican Council, or Vatican II, was an ecclesial, theological, and ecumenical congress convened in the autumns of the four years from 1962 through 1965. Pope John

XXIII convoked the Council on October 11, 1962, and with bishops from all over the world, sought to define the nature, scope, and mission of the Church. Of the 2,908 clergy entitled to attend the Council, 2,450 did so. The Council closed December 8, 1965.

The Council produced 16 documents some of which are described as the greatest expressions of Catholic social teaching in church history.

Facts and contents of Vatican II
Second Ecumenical Council of the Vatican
Date 1962–1965
Convoked by Pope John XXIII
Presided by Pope John XXIII, Pope Paul VI
Attendance up to 2540
Topics of discussion: the Church in itself, in relation to ecumenism and other religions, in relation to the modern world, renewal, liturgy, etc.

Documents
4 Constitutions:
Dei Verbum (Dogmatic Constitution on Divine Revelation)
Lumen Gentium (Dogmatic Constitution on the Church)
Gaudium et Spes (Pastoral Constitution on the Church in the Modern World)
Sacrosanctum Concilium (Constitution on the Sacred Liturgy)

9 decrees
Ad Gentes (Mission Activity)
Apostolicam Actuositatem (Lay People)
Christus Dominus (Bishops in the Church)
Inter Mirifica (Social Communication)
Optatam Totius (Priestly Training)
Orientalium Ecclesiarum (Eastern Churches)
Perfectæ Caritatis (Renewal of Religious Life)
Presbyterorum Ordinis (Life of Priests)
Unitatis Redintegratio (Ecumenism)

3 declarations
Dignitatis Humanæ (Religious Freedom)
Gravissimum Educationis (Christian Education)
Nostra Ætate (Relations with Non-Christians)

The Second Ecumenical Council of the Vatican, or Vatican II, was an Ecumenical Council of the Roman Catholic Church opened under Pope John XXIII in 1962 and closed under Pope Paul VI in 1965.

First Session (Autumn 1962)

Pope John opened the Council on October 11, 1962 in a public session which included the Council Fathers as well as representatives of 86 governments and international bodies. Following a Mass, the Pope read an address to the assembled bishops entitled *Gaudet Mater Ecclesia* (Latin for "Mother Church Rejoices"). In the speech, he rejected the thoughts of "prophets of doom who are always forecasting disaster" in the world and in the future of the Church. Pope John stressed the pastoral, not doctrinal, nature of the Council: The Church did not need to repeat or reformulate existing doctrines and dogmata but rather had to teach Christ's message in light of the modern world's ever-changing trends. He exhorted the Council Fathers "to use the medicine of mercy rather than the weapons of severity" in the documents they would produce.

In their first working session, issues considered included::

liturgy,

mass communications,

the Eastern Catholic churches, and

the nature of revelation.

Most notably, the schema on revelation was rejected by a majority of bishops, and Pope John intervened to require its rewriting.

Second Session (Autumn 1963)

Pope Paul's opening address on September 29, 1963 stressed the pastoral nature of the council, and set out four purposes for it:

to more fully define the nature of the church and the role of the bishop;

to renew the church;

to restore unity among all Christians, including seeking pardon for Catholic contributions to separation;

and to start a dialogue with the contemporary world.

During this period, the bishops approved the constitution on the liturgy (Sacrosanctum Concilium) and the decree on the media of social communication (Inter Mirifica). Work went forward with the schemata on the Church, bishops and dioceses, and ecumenism. On November 8, 1963, Cardinal Joseph Frings criticized the Holy Office (known before 1908 as the Holy Roman and Universal Inquisition), and drew an articulate and impassioned defense by its Secretary, Alfredo Cardinal Ottaviani. This exchange is often considered the most dramatic of the council. (Cardinal Frings's theological advisor was the young Joseph

Ratzinger, now Pope Benedict XVI, who would later, as Cardinal, head the same department of the Holy See.) The second session ended on December 4.

Third Session (Autumn 1964)

During this session the Council Fathers worked through a large volume of proposals. Schemata on ecumenism (*Unitatis Redintegratio*), the Eastern Rite churches (*Orientalium Ecclesiarum*), and the constitution of the Church (*Lumen Gentium*) were approved and promulgated by the Pope.

A votum or statement concerning the sacrament of marriage for the guidance of the commission revising the Code of Canon Law regarding a wide variety of juridicial, ceremonial, and pastoral issues. The bishops submitted this schema with a request for speedy approval, but the Pope did not act during the council. Pope Paul also instructed the bishops to defer the topic of artificial contraception (birth control) to a commission of clerical and lay experts that he had appointed.

Fourth Session (Autumn 1965)

Eleven schemata remained unfinished at the end of the third period, and commissions worked to give them their final form. Schema 13, on the Church in the modern world, was revised by a commission that worked with the assistance of laymen.

Pope Paul opened the last session of the Council on September 14, 1965 with the establishment of a Synod of Bishops. This more permanent structure was intended to preserve close cooperation of the bishops with the Pope after the council.

The first business of the fourth period was the consideration of the decree on religious freedom, which may be the most controversial of the conciliar documents. The vote was 1,997 for to 224 against (a margin that widened even farther by the time the bishop's final signing of the decree (*Dignitatis Humanæ*)). The principal work of the rest of the period was work on three documents, all of which were approved by the council fathers. The lengthened and revised pastoral constitution on the Church in the modern world (*Gaudium et Spes*), was followed by decrees on missionary activity (*Ad Gentes*) and the ministry and life of priests (*Presbyterorum Ordinis*).

One of the most controversial documents was *Nostra Ætate*, which affirmed, as did the documents of the 16th century Council of Trent, that the Jews of the time of Christ, taken indiscriminately, and all Jews today are no more responsible for the death of Christ than Christians. From Nostra Ætate:

> True, the Jewish authorities and those who followed their lead pressed for the death of Christ; still, what happened in His passion cannot be charged against all the Jews, without distinction, then alive, nor against the Jews of today. Although the Church is the new people of God, the Jews should not be presented as rejected or accursed by

God, as if this followed from the Holy Scriptures. All should see to it, then, that in catechetical work or in the preaching of the word of God they do not teach anything that does not conform to the truth of the Gospel and the spirit of Christ. Furthermore, in her rejection of every persecution against any man, the Church, mindful of the patrimony she shares with the Jews and moved not by political reasons but by the Gospel's spiritual love, decries hatred, persecutions, displays of anti-Semitism, directed against Jews at any time and by anyone.

A major event of the final days of the council was the act of Pope Paul and Orthodox Patriarch Athenagoras of a joint expression of regret for many of the past actions that had led up to the Great Schism between the western and eastern churches, expressed as the Catholic-Orthodox Joint declaration of 1965.

On December 8, the Second Vatican Council was formally closed, with the bishops professing their obedience to the Council's decrees.

Wikipedia

Interview with Hans Küng

Towards a "Continual Reform of the Church"

Interview by Laura Sheahen with Hans Küng

In this interview the controversial Catholic theologian talks about birth control, the pope, ecumenism and the unfulfilled promise of Vatican II

Introduction

February 2004

Hans Küng is a Christian theologian whose influential writings have been criticized by the Vatican, which in 1979 stripped him of his right to teach as a representative of the Church. Ordained a priest in 1954, Küng was the youngest theologian to participate in Vatican II, the council which dramatically modernized aspects of the Catholic Church. He spoke with Beliefnet recently about his new memoir and about his concerns with the Curia, the Rome-based departments and officials through which the pope governs the Church.

Laura Sheahen

Your book focuses on the years of Vatican II–you say the Council's promise has not been fulfilled. What was your most severe disappointment relating to Vatican II?

Hans Küng

The most severe disappointment for me was that the Council never really [was] free and was not able to control the curial machinery, but was constantly hindered, corrected, and sometimes even obstructed by the Roman Curia.

That is the reason why a lot of basic, very important questions were not resolved by the Council. I mention just a few:

Birth control as a matter of personal responsibility;

Priestly celibacy in the Latin church;

The regulation of the question of mixed marriages—validity of the marriage . . .

Meaning marriages between Catholics and non-Catholics.

Between Catholics and non-Catholics, especially with regard to the upbringing of children.

The involvement of Church regions concerned in the appointment of bishops;

The election of the pope by the synod of bishops, which would be more representative of the Church then the College of Cardinals, who are all appointed by the pope in the way of absolutist regimes.

Laura Sheahen

So you think all these things could have been settled by Vatican II, but were not?

Hans Küng

Yes, they could have been settled by Vatican II. The proof is that we had the same obstruction against [the document on] religious freedom and the Declaration on the Jews [in *Nostra Aetate*].

The Curia opposed both vigorously, but because the Council in this case really was strong enough, [it] was able to resolve these questions. And if the Council had not been hindered—after one morning of discussion—in going on with the discussion on the Pill, the Council would certainly have given a positive answer to that.

Laura Sheahen

So you're saying that in the space of just a few days, the question on birth control could have been decided in a way you approved of?

Hans Küng

Well, that was always a process. If you had a discussion that would have been frank and unhindered, then this would have been discussed in the commission, and the commission would have made a proposal. And I am sure it would have been possible to resolve it. It's a rather easy question, because the principles are already stated in the Constitution on the Church in the Modern World.

But the Curia was able to add, especially in the notes, the reactionary documents of Pius XI and Pius XII. So they based *Humanae Vitae* [the 1968 birth control document] on these reactionary documents.

In the text itself, you have a clear affirmation of the responsibility of the parents, but that is only one example of how the Council suffered on the compromises. The result of the compromises was that after the Council, the Curia was able to interpret these compromises in its own way, so we got *Humanae Vitae*.

Laura Sheahen

Towards the end of your book, there is a brief mention of [John Paul II], who at that time was the Archbishop of Krakow. When you're speaking about birth control and the papal Pill commission, you say that he—Karol Wojtyla—"engag[ed] in intrigue behind the backs of the progressive majority." What did you mean?

Hans Küng

I did not use this word. I just stated the facts that he never participated in the [Pill] commission, but [rather] sent letters to the Vatican. You may call this an intrigue.

That's how it's translated in the English version of your book. Perhaps it's a translation question.

For me, this was already an indication that this pope is not interested in serious scholarly discussions on controversial issues, dogma, and morals, but just in the decision making process by authoritarian means. Imposing doctrines as he has done now during his 25 years of the pontificate. This was already an indication of his methods.

Laura Sheahen

On the more positive side, of the Vatican II reforms that were implemented, which reforms pleased you most?

Hans Küng

First, the importance of the Bible being valued highly in the liturgy, in theology, and in the whole life of the Church.

Second, we also got a more authentic liturgy of the people of God, in the vernacular language. It is an absolutely unique success of the church community to have introduced such an epoch-making change, in just a few years, without having a serious division.

And a third thing is the understanding of the Church as a community, a communion which is just a hierarchy but the people of God, whose servants are the priests and bishops. That is a result which has daily consequences in our parishes.

Laura Sheahen

What do you think about *Dominus Iesus* [the Vatican's 2001 statement on other denominations and religions]?

Hans Küng

The Council's decree *Nostra Aetate*—On World Religions—is a very open decree which does not offend anybody but which estimates highly all the other religions.

[*Nostra Aetate* is not] definitive in a way that you could not go on developing practical relations with other religions and also having a further theological elucidation of the other world religions.

Dominus Iesus has affirmations which are on the old line, the old proconciliar line, of considering the Christian religion as an absolute, and the other religions—as they say explicitly—as "deficient" forms of religion. That is an offense for all the other religions, and it's arrogance on the side of the Catholic Church to think that we are not at all deficient. As a matter of fact, you have deficiencies in all religions, but you have truth in all religions.

There are points where I think, for instance, Judaism or Buddhism are more constructive than the Catholic position, and vice versa.

Laura Sheahen

Do you see hope for ecumenism now, or do you think *Dominus Iesus* has been a major setback?

Hans Küng

We are certainly at an impasse, because on the grassroots level, we have a lot of ecumenical understanding, encounter, cooperation, even liturgy. But from the point of view of the hierarchy, they do everything to hinder, for instance, Eucharistic Communion.

Let me recall only one fact: the first big, national, ecumenical meeting of the Catholic Church and the churches of the Reformation in Berlin [in 2003], public opinion polls showed that more or less 85 percent of German Catholics and Protestants wanted to have intercommunion. But that was absolutely no argument for the bishops, because the bishops in the present system say only what Rome says, and they just ignored it. That gave a great deal of anger, and is only one example of how Rome, the pope, the Curia, is hindering progress in ecumenism. They are very strong in words and gestures and they are always saying we are very ecumenical, but practically speaking, they are hindering it.

Laura Sheahen

But hasn't John Paul II given Communion to non-Catholics, making exceptions every now and then?

Hans Küng

Of course he made exceptions, and probably also Cardinal Ratzinger [now Pope Benedict XVI] has made exceptions. That is the Roman way: to give favors to the favorites.

It is an indication that they are not honest in this issue. If they would be honest, they would permit the others what they do themselves.

Laura Sheahen

Speaking of Cardinal Ratzinger, what do you think of recent statements from the Congregation for the Doctrine of the Faith? The 2003 statement on homosexual unions, for example?

Hans Küng

Let me say first a general statement. Because of the compromises made in the Second Vatican Council, the Roman Curia has done everything to get control of the Church again in a preconciliar way. For that, they follow two methods.

One is to publish one document after the other, affirming traditional theology and practice. And the second is to appoint bishops who have to sign . . . who have to agree beforehand that they are for *Humanae Vitae*, that they are for the law of celibacy, that they are against the ordination of women.

In the question of homosexuality, the Vatican was rather permissive or lenient, with regard to all these crimes of sexual abuse.

Laura Sheahen

You're talking about the clergy abuse scandals?

Hans Küng

Yes, the church abuse scandals. They have been rather permissive. They permitted that these priests have been transferred. They knew quite well what was going on. They are always well informed.

Laura Sheahen

Some American Catholics think Rome didn't know that much.

Hans Küng

That's because American Catholics are sometimes a little naive. I'm sorry to say that, but I think it's a fact. Can you imagine that in Rome they do not know? They get a lot of denunciations. Everybody is allowed to write to the Congregation for the Doctrine of Faith; [the CDF] receives denunciations and sometimes accusations that are true. They know quite well what is going on in the different dioceses. They have nuncios, they have in every episcopal conference a fifth column which is always reporting to the Curia what is going on.

Now, after all this was discovered, and especially after the fact that this was brought to courts, the Vatican—who said that's not our business, it's the American church who has to see that.

I was in the States when this happened. I remember the Curia said, that's up to the American bishops, not up to Rome. Afterwards they saw that the anger and the protests were so hard that finally the Vatican said, yes we have to make an . . . And now finally they have published a document on homosexuals.

Laura Sheahen

You're saying there's a connection between the clergy abuse scandal and the Vatican's decision to publish a document on homosexual unions?

Hans Küng

It's a connection because both are on homosexuality. It's a question of fact. They want to justify themselves by a strong statement. They had been rather lenient before, you didn't hear very much about all these scandals that existed already in America. [It's] not a new phenomenon, and [is] in other countries, in Europe—in Ireland, in Poland and also in Germany.

But now they make an affirmation, which is in many ways, not very understanding for homosexuals. But I am not a specialist in this matter; I have not studied this document thoroughly. About the document itself, I would have to study it more carefully.

The document seems to concern consenting adult homosexual relationships, whereas the clergy abuse scandal involved young people: non-consenting relationships. But you seem to draw some parallels.

One partner is always an adult, isn't it? And to think that this has no relation is just not possible. It's both on homosexuality.

In Rome, of course, they always have the tendency to say that these are all different questions. It's the same [when] they say that this sexual abuse has nothing to do with clerical celibacy. But of course it has to do. If priests were allowed to marry, if this would be an optional thing, and if he could have wife and children, he would certainly have less temptation to satisfy certain sexual impulses with minors.

Laura Sheahen

On a personal level, what do you like best and least about being Catholic?

Hans Küng

I like most that I belong to the whole universal comprehensive Catholic church and that it is not just a national church. I like the catholicity in time: our tradition is one of 2,000 years. And I like the catholicity in space, because it's a universality of faith and a community of faith which embraces all groups, nations, and regions.

But I have to add—and this answers your other question—this catholicity in time and in space is only meaningful for me if there is, at the same time, a concentration on the Gospel. If [the Church] includes everything, and has no criteria for what is really Christian or not, then Catholicism becomes a syncretism of all sorts of superstitions and abuses. The Gospel has to be the norm. I am evangelical and am for a continual reform of the Church, which was affirmed by the Second Vatican Council.

Laura Sheahen

Where do you see the Catholic Church not concentrating on the Gospel or becoming superstitious?

Hans Küng

For instance, this whole thing about Fatima. Popes going to Fatima and preaching there—the Gospel of Fatima is exaggerated.

Laura Sheahen

Which books of the Bible are your favorite?

Hans Küng

Well, the whole history of Jesus—we need what exegetes call source Q. The Sermon on the Mount. The gospels and the authentic epistles of Paul, I like very much. The Epistle to the Romans is an extremely important synthesis of the whole theology of St. Paul.

Laura Sheahen

What about from the Old Testament-is there a book you especially love to re-read?

Hans Küng

I prefer everything that the Jews themselves call the Torah, the five books of Moses.

Laura Sheahen

What in the Roman Catholic Church today do you think Jesus would approve of? What do you think is right with the Catholic Church?

Hans Küng

He would certainly not be very interested in Church dogmas and medieval canon law, but he would be interested to see where his spirit is alive. It is active in individual Christians who are working and acting in the spirit of Christ himself.

Beliefnet, Towards a "Continual Reform of the Church": Laura Sheahen's interview with Hans Küng

The Lausanne Covenant

Introduction

One of the issues debated by evangelicals in the twentieth century was the social gospel and the social implications of the Gospel. Paragraph 5 of the Lausanne Covenant confronts this issue head on and makes its position very clear, as it affirms that, "evangelism and socio-political involvement are both part of our Christian duty."

The Lausanne Covenant is a declaration agreed upon by more than 2,300 evangelicals during the 1974 International Congress to be more intentional about world evangelization. Since then, the Covenant has challenged churches and Christian organizations to work together to make Jesus Christ known throughout the world.

Fifteen years later in July 1989, the more than 3,000 participants in the Second International Congress on World Evangelization (Lausanne II) in Manila, Philippines produced another important document: *The Manila Manifesto.*

INTRODUCTION

We, members of the Church of Jesus Christ, from more than 150 nations, participants in the International Congress on World Evangelization at Lausanne, praise God for his great salvation and rejoice in the fellowship he has given us with himself and with each other. We are deeply stirred by what God is doing in our day, moved to penitence by our failures and challenged by the unfinished task of evangelization. We believe the Gospel is God's good news for the whole world, and we are determined by his grace to obey Christ's commission to proclaim it to all mankind and to make disciples of every nation. We desire, therefore, to affirm our faith and our resolve, and to make public our covenant.

4. THE NATURE OF EVANGELISM

To evangelize is to spread the good news that Jesus Christ died for our sins and was raised from the dead according to the Scriptures, and that as the reigning Lord he now offers the forgiveness of sins and the liberating gifts of the Spirit to all who repent and believe. Our Christian presence in the world is indispensable to evangelism, and so is that kind of dialogue whose purpose is to listen sensitively in order to understand. But evangelism itself is the proclamation of the historical, biblical Christ as Savior and Lord, with a view to persuading people to come to him personally and so be reconciled to God. In issuing the gospel invitation we have no liberty to conceal the cost of discipleship. Jesus still calls all who would follow him to deny themselves, take up their cross, and identify themselves with his new community. The results of evangelism include obedience to Christ, incorporation into his Church and responsible service in the world.

(I Cor. 15:3,4; Acts 2: 32–39; John 20:21; I Cor. 1:23; II Cor. 4:5; 5:11,20; Luke 14:25–33; Mark 8:34; 10:43–45; Acts 2:40,47)

5. CHRISTIAN SOCIAL RESPONSIBILITY

We affirm that God is both the Creator and the Judge of all men. We therefore should share his concern for justice and reconciliation throughout human society and for the liberation of men and women from every kind of oppression. Because men and women are made in the image of God, every person, regardless of race, religion, color, culture, class, sex or age, has an intrinsic dignity because of which he or she should be respected and served, not exploited. Here too we express penitence both for our neglect and for having sometimes regarded evangelism and social concern as mutually exclusive. Although reconciliation with other people is not reconciliation with God, nor is social action evangelism, nor is political liberation salvation, nevertheless we affirm that evangelism and socio-political involvement are both part of our Christian duty. For both are necessary expressions of our doctrines of God and man, our love for our neighbor and our obedience to Jesus Christ. The message of salvation implies also a message of judgment upon every form of alienation, oppression and discrimination, and we should not be afraid to denounce evil and injustice wherever they exist. When people receive Christ they are born again into his kingdom and must seek not only to exhibit but also to spread its righteousness in the midst of an unrighteous world. The salvation we claim should be transforming us in the totality of our personal and social responsibilities. Faith without works is dead.

(Acts 17:26,31; Gen. 18:25; Isa. 1:17; Psa. 45:7; Gen. 1:26,27; Jas. 3:9; Lev. 19:18; Luke 6:27,35; Jas. 2:14–26; Joh. 3:3,5; Matt. 5:20; 6:33; II Cor. 3:18; Jas. 2:20)

6. THE CHURCH AND EVANGELISM

We affirm that Christ sends his redeemed people into the world as the Father sent him, and that this calls for a similar deep and costly penetration of the world. We need to break out of our ecclesiastical ghettos and permeate non-Christian society. In the Church's mission of sacrificial service evangelism is primary. World evangelization requires the whole Church to take the whole gospel to the whole world. The Church is at the very center of God's cosmic purpose and is his appointed means of spreading the gospel. But a church which preaches the cross must itself be marked by the cross. It becomes a stumbling block to evangelism when it betrays the gospel or lacks a living faith in God, a genuine love for people, or scrupulous honesty in all things including promotion and finance. The church is the community of God's people rather than an institution, and must not be identified with any particular culture, social or political system, or human ideology.

(John 17:18; 20:21; Matt. 28:19,20; Acts 1:8; 20:27; Eph. 1:9,10; 3:9–11; Gal. 6:14,17; II Cor. 6:3,4; II Tim. 2:19–21; Phil. 1:27)

9. THE URGENCY OF THE EVANGELISTIC TASK

More than 2,700 million people, which is more than two-thirds of all humanity, have yet to be evangelized. We are ashamed that so many have been neglected; it is a standing rebuke to us and to the whole Church. There is now, however, in many parts of the world an unprecedented receptivity to the Lord Jesus Christ. We are convinced that this is the time for churches and para-church agencies to pray earnestly for the salvation of the unreached and to launch new efforts to achieve world evangelization. A reduction of foreign missionaries and money in an evangelized country may sometimes be necessary to facilitate the national church's growth in self-reliance and to release resources for unevangelised areas. Missionaries should flow ever more freely from and to all six continents in a spirit of humble service. The goal should be, by all available means and at the earliest possible time, that every person will have the opportunity to hear, understand, and to receive the good news. We cannot hope to attain this goal without sacrifice. All of us are shocked by the poverty of millions and disturbed by the injustices which cause it. Those of us who live in affluent circumstances accept our duty to develop a simple life-style in order to contribute more generously to both relief and evangelism.

(John 9:4; Matt. 9:35–38; Rom. 9:1–3; I Cor. 9:19–23; Mark 16:15; Isa. 58:6,7; Jas. 1:27; 2:1–9; Matt. 25:31–46; Acts 2:44,45; 4:34,35)

12. SPIRITUAL CONFLICT

We believe that we are engaged in constant spiritual warfare with the principalities and powers of evil, who are seeking to overthrow the Church and frustrate its task of world evangelization. We know our need to equip ourselves with God's armor and to fight this battle with the spiritual weapons of truth and prayer. For we detect the activity of our enemy, not only in false ideologies outside the Church, but also inside it in false gospels which twist Scripture and put people in the place of God. We need both watchfulness and discernment to safeguard the biblical gospel. We acknowledge that we ourselves are not immune to worldliness of thoughts and action, that is, to a surrender to secularism. For example, although careful studies of church growth, both numerical and spiritual, are right and valuable, we have sometimes neglected them. At other times, desirous to ensure a response to the gospel, we have compromised our message, manipulated our hearers through pressure techniques, and become unduly preoccupied with statistics or even dishonest in our use of them. All this is worldly. The Church must be in the world; the world must not be in the Church.

(Eph. 6:12; II Cor. 4:3,4; Eph. 6:11,13–18; II Cor. 10:3–5; I John 2:18–26; 4:1–3; Gal. 1:6–9; II Cor. 2:17; 4:2; John 17:15)

CONCLUSION

Therefore, in the light of this our faith and our resolve, we enter into a solemn covenant with God and with each other, to pray, to plan and to work together for the evangelization of the whole world. We call upon others to join us. May God help us by his grace and for his glory to be faithful to this our covenant! Amen, Alleluia!

The Lausanne Covenant

Taizé

(See also: Other Christian leaders in the twentieth century, Brother Roger)

Taizé, in the south of Burgundy, France, is the home of an international, ecumenical community, founded there in 1940 by Brother Roger. The brothers are committed for their whole life to material and spiritual sharing, to celibacy, and to a great simplicity of life. Today, the community is made up of over a hundred brothers, Catholics and from various Protestant backgrounds, from more than twenty-five nations.

At the heart of daily life in Taizé are three times of prayer together. The brothers live by their own work. They do not accept gifts or donations for themselves. Some of the brothers are living in small groups – "fraternities"—among the very poor.

Since the late 1950s, many thousands of young adults from many countries have found their way to Taizé to take part in weekly meetings of prayer and reflection. In addition, Taizé brothers make visits and lead meetings, large and small, in Africa, North and South America, Asia, and in Europe, as part of a "pilgrimage of trust on earth".

Christians persecuted

State-sponsored or permitted suppression of Christianity in modern times; or cultural attitudes that encourage anti-Christian violence or discrimination.

Throughout the modern era, hundreds of thousands of Christians have become martyrs. Persecutions have occurred in France, Japan, Korea, and China; between 1895–1910 thousands of Armenian Christians were massacred under Turkish rule. In Germany the Confessing Church and others who resisted Hitler were persecuted; and many, like Dietrich Bonhoeffer, were killed. In the Soviet Union the government tried for decades to destroy Christianity; in El Salvador Archbishop Oscar Romero was killed for his beliefs. In the United States the death of Martin Luther King Jr. is widely recognized as a martyrdom. In some parts of Africa, Asia, and Latin America, persecution continues. According to one estimate there were 160,000 Christian martyrs a year before the close of the twentieth century. It is also reckoned that there were more Christians martyrs in the twentieth century than in the first 1900 years of Christianity.

Christian mission in China

OMF

OMF International (formerly Overseas Missionary Fellowship and before that the China Inland Mission before 1964) is an interdenominational Protestant Christian missionary society, founded by English missionary Hudson Taylor on 25 June 1865.

Overview

The non-sectarian China Inland Mission was founded on principles of faith and prayer. From the beginning it recruited missionaries from the working class as well as single women, which was a new practice for a large agency. Even today, no appeals for funds are made, instead a reliance upon God is practiced to move people through prayer alone. The goal of the mission that began dedicated to China has grown to include bringing the Gospel to the millions of inhabitants of East Asia who have never heard or had access to the message of Jesus Christ. Reluctantly, along with the departure of all foreign Christian workers in the early 1950s, the China Inland Mission redirected all of its missionaries to other parts of east Asia, to continue the work and maintain a ministry to China and the Chinese. The name was officially changed to Overseas Missionary Fellowship in 1964. A quote from the OMF website in 2006 summarizes the current organization:

> The goal of OMF International is to glorify God through the urgent evangelization of East Asia's peoples. Overseas Missionary Fellowship is a global network of Christians proclaiming the glory of Jesus Christ among East Asia`s peoples through fervent prayer, loving service and personal witness. Through God's grace and power we work to see a biblical church movement in each people group of East Asia. Started as the China Inland Mission by Hudson Taylor, OMF serves throughout East Asia in a variety of ministries, including evangelism and discipleship, starting new churches, tentmaking, student ministry, English teaching and mobilizing and equipping Asian churches for world missions. Our relationships with national churches provide meaningful opportunities for partnership in long-term and short-term outreach activities. OMF currently has around 1,100 workers from more than 25 countries.

Missiological Distinctives

Priority is given to unreached inland provinces while seeking to evangelize the whole of China.

No solicitation of finance, or indebtedness; looking to God alone; pooling support in life of corporate faith

Identification with Chinese by wearing Chinese dress and queue (pigtail), worshipping in Chinese houses

Indigenization through training Chinese co-workers in self-governing, self-supporting and self-propagating principles

Recruitment of missionaries not based on education or ecclesiastical ordination, but spiritual qualification; deployment of single women in the interior and Christian professionals

Interdenominational-International Membership

Headquarters on the field, director rule; leaders and workers serving shoulder to shoulder

"We wish to see churches and Christian Chinese presided over by pastors and officers of their own countrymen, worshipping the true God in the land of their fathers, in the costume of their fathers, in their own tongue wherein they were born, and in edifices of a thoroughly Chinese style of architecture." (-J. Hudson Taylor)

Boxer Crisis of 1900

In 1900, attacks took place across China in connection with the Boxer Rebellion which targeted Christians and foreigners. The China Inland Mission lost more members than any other agency: 58 adults and 21 children were killed. (See the List of the Martyred Missionaries of the China Inland Mission in 1900). However, in 1901, when the allied nations were demanding compensation from the Chinese government, Hudson Taylor refused to accept payment for loss of property or life in order to demonstrate the meekness of Christ to the Chinese. In the same year, Dixon Edward Hoste was appointed to the directorship of the mission.

Growth amid War and Revolution

The early 1900s saw great expansion of missionary activity in China following the Boxer Rebellion and during the Revolution of 1912 and the establishment of the Chinese Republic. William Whiting Borden, wealthy heir of the Borden Milk Products family, who graduated from Yale in 1909, left behind a comfortable life in America to respond to the call for workers with the Muslims of northwest China. He died in Egypt while still in training.

A musician and an engineer named James O. Fraser was the first to bring the Gospel message to the Lisu tribes of Yunnan in southwest China. This resulted in phenomenal church growth among the various tribes in the area that endured to the 21st century.

The Warlord period brought widespread lawlessness to China and missionary work was often dangerous or deadly. John and Betty Stam were a young couple who were murdered in 1934 by Communist soldiers. Their biography "The Triumph of John and Betty Stam" inspired a generation of missionaries to follow in the same steps of service despite the trials of war and persecution that raged in China in the 1930's and 1940's.

The Japanese invasion further complicated efforts as the Japanese distrusted anyone with British or American Nationalities. When the Japanese invaded China in World War II, the China Inland Mission moved its headquarters up the Yangzi River to Chongqing. Many missionaries were put into concentration camps until the end of the war. One such camp was at Weifang. The entire Chefoo School run by the mission at Yantai was imprisoned at a concentration camp. The students were separated from their parents for more than 5 years.

In 1900 there were an estimated 100,000 Christians in China. It multiplied to seven times that number by 1950 (700,000). The Chinese church began to be an indigenous movement helped by strong leaders such as John Sung, Wang Ming-Dao, David Yang, Watchman Nee, and Andrew Gih.

From C.I.M. to O.M.F

Phyllis Thompson wrote that between 1949 and 1952, after the victory of the Communist armies, there was a "reluctant exodus" of all of the members of the China Inland Mission. The leaders met at Bournemouth, England to discuss the situation and the decision was made to re-deploy all of the missionaries into the rest of East Asia. Headquarters were moved to Singapore and work commenced in Japan, Taiwan, Hong Kong, the Philippines, Thailand, Malaysia, Singapore, Vietnam, Cambodia, Laos, and Indonesia. In addition to reducing some languages to written form, the Bible was translated, and basic theological education was given to neglected tribal groups. The publication and distribution of Christian literature were prioritized among both the rural tribes people and the urban working classes and students. The goal remained for every community to have a church in East Asia and thereby the Gospel would be preached "to every creature". The proclamation of the Christian message also included medical work. Three hospitals were opened in rural Thailand as well as a leprosy control program. Many of the patients were refugees. In the Philippines, community development programs were launched. Alcoholic rehabilitation began in Japan, and rehabilitation work among prostitutes was begun in Taipei and Bangkok.

In 1980, Hudson Taylor's great grandson, James Hudson Taylor III, became General Director of the mission work. According to Taylor in 1989,

> The fellowship has no desire to re-establish itself there (in China) in the form it used to have", but he also affirmed that "OMF is still deeply committed to the Chinese people. We can never forget that we came into existence as the China Inland Mission. Ever since our 'reluctant exodus' we have called the church worldwide to prayer for our brothers and sisters in China, and to share in proclaiming the gospel and nurturing millions of new believers through radio broadcasts and the provision of Bibles and Christian literature.
>
> The work continues to the present day. Patrick Fung, a Chinese Christian appointed in 2005, is the first Asian to lead the mission.

Chronology of CIM/OMF in China

1900s

Boxer Rebellion of 1900 claims 58 missionaries and 21 children killed from the China Inland Mission.

In 1901 Hudson Taylor refused to accept compensation payment from the Chinese government for loss of property or life, to show the 'meekness and gentleness of Christ'

Dixon Edward Hoste appointed acting General Director in 1901

James Hudson Taylor Resigned as Director of the China Inland Mission November 1902

James Hudson Taylor died 3 June 1905 in Changsha, Hunan, China

Empress Dowager Dies in 1908

China Inland Mission sent relief team to flood and famine in Jiangsu, Anhui, and Henan

1910s

J. O. Fraser arrived in China in 1910

60,000 Christians in West Yunnan, China tribal region

1911 Benjamin Broomhall died after Anti-Opium Campaign succeeds

Chinese Republic Established in 1912

In 1912 membership in the China Inland Mission exceeds 1000, now the largest mission agency working in China

1920s

The Chinese Civil War forced a temporary evacuation of nearly all of the missionaries

1927–1932 200 missionaries selected from over 1200 applicants

1930s

Headquarters in Shanghai move to Sinza Road in 1930

John and Betty Stam executed in South Anhui in 1934

World War II forced many of the missionaries further inland—or they were captured by the Japanese and detained until the end of the war

1940s

November 1942 China Inland Mission School at Chefoo (Yantai) is closed and all students and staff imprisoned.

August 1945 China Inland Mission School at Chefoo (Yantai) is liberated by American paratroopers

October 1 1949 Mao Zedong proclaims People's Republic of China in Beijing

1950s

After the "Christian Manifesto", the China Inland Mission began to withdraw its missionaries ending in 1953

Re-deployment of all missionaries to East Asia

1951 Three-Self Patriotic Movement launched allowing government control of Christian assembly

In November 1951, a new headquarters was set up in Singapore, and the organization's name was changed to The China Inland Mission Overseas Missionary Fellowship

1960s

China Inland Mission re-named Overseas Missionary Fellowship in 1964

Chinese Cultural Revolution 1966–1972: all Christians silenced including the Three-

Self Patriotic Movement

Medical work begun in rural Thailand

1970s and 1980s

Chinese Church reaches 21.5 million baptized members, over 52 million including Christian families and adherents

1990s

Overseas Missionary Fellowship renamed OMF International

Wikipedia

PEOPLE

B. B. Warfield (1851–1921)

Karl Barth (1886–1968)

Dietrich Bonhoeffer (1906–1945)

C. S. Lewis (1898–1963)

Francis A. Schaeffer (1912–1984)

Mother Teresa of Calcutta (1910–1997)

Billy Graham (b. 1918)

B. B. Warfield

Dates

1851–1921

Famous for being

Princeton Theologian

Important writings

The Plan of Salvation

The Inspiration and Authority of the Bible

One of his quotations

"Calvinism is just religion in its purity. We have only, therefore to conceive of religion in its purity, and that is Calvinism."

Benjamin Breckinridge Warfield was the principal of Princeton Seminary from 1887 to 1921. He is considered the last great Princeton theologian before the split in 1929 that formed Westminster Seminary and the Orthodox Presbyterian Church.

Education

Like many children born into a wealthy family, Warfield's childhood education was private. Warfield entered Princeton University in 1868 and graduated in 1871 with high honors. After this he entered Princeton Seminary in 1873, in order to train for Presbyterian ministry. He graduated in 1876.

Ministry

For a short time in 1876 he preached in Presbyterian churches in Concord, Kentucky and Dayton, Ohio as a "supply pastor"—the latter church calling him to be their ordained minister (which he politely refused). In late 1876 Warfield and his new wife moved to Germany where he studied under Ernst Luthardt and Franz Delitzsch. Warfield was the assistant pastor of First Presbyterian Church in Baltimore, Maryland for a short time. Then he became an instructor at Western Theological Seminary, which is now called Pittsburgh Theological Seminary. He was ordained on April 26, 1879.

In 1881 Warfield wrote a joint article with A. A. Hodge on the inspiration of the Bible. It drew attention because of its scholarly and forceful defense of the inerrancy of the Bible. In many of his writings, Warfield attempted to demonstrate that the doctrine of Biblical inerrancy was simply orthodox Christian teaching, and not merely a concept invented in the nineteenth century. His passion was to refute the liberal element within Presbyterianism and within Christianity at large.

At Princeton

In 1887 Warfield was appointed to the Charles Hodge Chair at Princeton Theological Seminary, where he succeeded Hodge's son A. A. Hodge. Warfield remained there until his death. As the last conservative successor to Hodge to live prior to the re-organization of Princeton Seminary, Warfield is often regarded as the last of the Princeton theologians.

The Bible

During his tenure, his primary thrust (and that of the seminary) was an authoritative view of the Bible. This view was held in contrast to the emotionalism of the revival movements, the rationalism of higher criticism, and the heterodox teachings of various New religious movements that were emerging. The seminary held fast to the Reformed confessional tradition—that is, it faithfully followed the Westminster Confession of Faith.

Warfield believed that modernist theology was problematic, since it relied upon the thoughts of the Biblical interpreter rather than upon the divine author of Scripture. He therefore preached and believed the doctrine of *sola scriptura*—that the Bible is God's inspired word and is sufficient for the Christian to live his or her faith.

Much of Warfield's work centered upon the Bible's "inspiration" by God—that while the authors of the Bible were men, the ultimate author was God himself. The growing influence of modernist theology denied that the Bible was inspired, and alternative theories of the origin of the Christian faith were being explored.

Because of the Bible's style of writing, many modernist scholars had pointed out the unquestionably "human" traits of certain Biblical books. Grammatical and linguistic styles were contrasted and compared, which proved beyond doubt that humans wrote the text of the Bible. Unfortunately for Warfield and other conservatives, some resulted in a belief that the Bible was therefore not written by God at all, but by men. Warfield was instrumental in countering this by arguing that the supernatural work of the Holy Spirit did not lead to a form of "mechanical" inspiration (whereby the human authors merely wrote down what God dictated to them) but one in which the human author's intellect was fully able to express itself linguistically, while at the same time being supervised by the Holy Spirit to ensure its inspiration. This important argument is used by many Reformed and Evangelical Christians today as part of their understanding of what the Bible is.

Calvinism

Underpinning much of Warfield's theology was his adherence to Calvinism as espoused by the Westminster Confession of Faith. It is sometimes forgotten that, in his battles against Modernism on the one hand, and against revivalism on the other, that he was simply expressing the Reformed faith when applied to certain situations.

It was Warfield's belief that the 16th century Reformers, as well as the 17th century Confessional writers, were merely summarizing the content and application of scripture. New revelations, whether from the minds of celebrated scholars or popular revivalists, were therefore inconsistent with these confessional statements (and therefore inconsistent with Scripture). Throughout his ministry, Warfield contended that modern world events and thinking could never render such confessions obsolete. Such an attitude still prevails today in many Reformed churches and Christians who embrace Calvinism.

Theopedia

Karl Barth

Dates

1886–1968

Famous for being

Leading twentieth century theologian

Important writings

Church Dogmatics

One of his quotations
"Conscience is the perfect interpreter of life."

Summary
Karl Barth was a German Protestant theologian who was active in the resistance to the Nazis. He was instrumental in the development of neo-orthodoxy, which represented a return to the scriptures as the basis for religion.

"Barth's theological revolution was a dynamic, non-fundamentalistic recovery of the biblical message as the proclamation of the unique self-disclosure of God to man in Jesus Christ. He believed that Christian theology ought always to derive its entire thinking on God, man, sin, ethics, and society from what can actually be seen in Jesus as witnessed by the Old and New Testaments rather than from sources independent of this revelation. His voluminous writings explore the inexhaustibly fruitful implications of his total Christ-centeredness."

Encyclopedia of World Biography. ©2005–2006 Thomson Gale

Karl Barth is considered by some the greatest Protestant theologian of the 20th century and possibly the greatest since the Reformation. More than anyone else, Barth inspired and led the renaissance of theology that took place from about 1920 to 1950. The son of the Swiss Reformed minister and New Testament scholar Fritz Barth, Karl Barth was born in Basel, May 10, 1886, and was reared in Bern, where his father taught. From 1904 to 1909, he studied theology at the universities of Bern, Berlin, Tübingen, and Marburg. In 1913 he married Nelly Hoffman; they had five children. Barth became known as a radical critic both of the prevailing liberal theology and of the social order. Liberal theology, Barth believed, had accommodated Christianity to modern culture.

Barth held professorships successively at Göttingen and Münster universities from 1923 to 1930, when he was appointed professor of systematic theology at the University of Bonn. He engaged in controversy with Adolf von Harnack, holding that the latter's scientific theology is only a preliminary to the true task of theology, which is identical with that of preaching. He opposed the Hitler regime in Germany and supported church-sponsored movements against National Socialism; he was the chief author of the Barmen Declaration, six articles that defined Christian opposition to National Socialist ideology and practice. In 1934 he was expelled from Bonn and returned to Switzerland; from 1935 until his retirement in 1962 was professor at Basel, exercising a worldwide influence. During this period he worked on his *Church Dogmatics* (1932–68), a multivolume work of great richness that was unfinished at his death. He remained in Basel until his death, December 10, 1968.

The principal emphasis in Barth's work, known as neoorthodoxy and crisis theology, is on:

the sinfulness of humanity,
God's absolute transcendence, and
the human inability to know God except through revelation.

His objective was to lead theology away from the influence of modern religious philosophy back to the principles of the Reformation and the prophetic teachings of the Bible. He regarded the Bible, however, not as the actual revelation of God but as only the record of that revelation. For Barth, God's sole revelation of himself is in Jesus Christ. God is the "wholly other," totally unlike mankind, who are utterly dependent on an encounter with the divine for any understanding of ultimate reality. Barth saw the task of the church as that of proclaiming the "good word" of God and as serving as the "place of encounter" between God and mankind. Barth regarded all human activity as being under the judgment of that encounter.

Church Dogmatics

The *Church Dogmatics* is in four "volumes," each comprising between two and four large tomes.

Volume I is on the doctrine of the Word of God. Volume I/1 is about the three forms of the Word of God (preached, written, and revealed) and the nature of the Trinity. Volume I/2 treats the three forms in more detail—the revealed form in the incarnation of the Word of Jesus Christ, the written form in Scripture and the preached form in church proclamation.

Volume II is on the doctrine of God. Volume II/1 treats the knowledge of God, the main emphasis being on God's initiative in revealing himself. Then Barth treats the reality of God. He describes God as "one who loves in freedom," and there is an exposition of the "perfections of the divine loving" (grace, holiness, mercy, righteousness, patience, and wisdom), and the "perfections of the divine freedom" (unity, omnipresence, constancy, omnipotence, eternity, and glory). Volume II/2 is on the election of God, Barth's term for predestination. Barth transforms the doctrine of his own Calvinist tradition of double predestination by centering rejection and election in Jesus Christ, who takes all rejection on himself and also both elects all and is himself elected. Christ's election leads to the election of the community of Israel and the church, and only in that context is it right to talk about the election or rejection of the individual.

Volume III is on the doctrine of creation. Volume III/1 is on God's work of creation, its goodness and the relation of creation to God's covenant. Volume III/2 is on human being. Jesus Christ is the "real" human being and the criterion for true humanity. Volume III/3 covers providence, evil as an "impossible possibility" which has no future, and heaven, angels, and demons. Volume III/4 treats the ethical side of the doctrine of creation. God gives the freedom to live in gratitude before God, with other people, in respect for life and in limitation.

Volume IV considers the doctrine of reconciliation, in Volume IV he interweaves the themes of Christology, sin, soteriology, pneumatology, ecclesiology, justification, sanctification, and vocation. Christ is the servant, the judge who is judged in our place and who empties himself, the royal man who is raised up by God; He is the true witness, the victor over all that opposes him, and the light of life. Specific aspects of sin are exposed by each aspect of Christ—pride resists accepting what God become man does for us; sloth refuses to take an active part in the new life given by Christ; falsehood resists and distorts the witness of Christ. The way of human salvation is justification by faith through which the Christian community is gathered, sanctification in love through which the community is built up, and vocation in hope, which sends the community out as witnesses in word and life.

Among Barth's other better known works are *The Word of God and the Word of Man* (1924; trans. 1928), *Credo* (1935; trans. 1936), and *Evangelical Theology, an Introduction* (1962; trans. 1963). His works have influenced many theologians positively and negatively, including Rudolf Bultmann, Paul Tillich, Hans Urs von Balthasar, Hans Küng, Jürgen Moltmann, Wolfhart Pannenberg, Eberhard Jüngel, and many theologians from beyond continental Europe.

Island of Freedom

Dietrich Bonhoeffer

Dates
1906–1945

Famous for being
Pastor and theologian

Important writings
The Cost of Discipleship

One of his quotations
"Christianity without discipleship is always Christianity without Christ."

Dietrich Bonhoeffer—along with his twin sister, Sabine—was born on February 4, 1906, in Breslau, Germany. Later a student in Tübingen, Berlin, and at Union Theological Seminary in New York—as well as a participant in the European ecumenical movement—Bonhoeffer became known as one of the few figures of the 1930s with a comprehensive grasp of both German- and English-language theology.

His works resonate with a prescience, subtlety and maturity that continually belies the youth of their author. He wrote his dissertation, *Sanctorum Communio*, at the end of three years at the University of Berlin (1924–1927) and was awarded his doctorate with honors. Act and Being, his *Habilitationsschrift*, or qualifying thesis, allowing him to teach at the University of Berlin, was accepted in July 1930. The following year, 1930–1931, Bonhoeffer spent a postgraduate year at Union Theological Seminary in New York. He assumed his post as a lecturer in theology at the University of Berlin in August 1931. In the winter semester 1931–1932 Bonhoeffer presented the lectures that were published as *Creation and Fall.*

His final lecture courses at Berlin—published as *Christ the Center*—along with a seminar on the philosopher G. W. F. Hegel, were taught in the summer of 1933. His authorization to teach on the faculty of the University of Berlin was finally withdrawn on August 5, 1936. Bonhoeffer served as a curate for a German congregation in Barcelona during 1929–1930. Following his ordination at St. Matthias Church, Berlin, in November 1931, he was to help organize the Pastors' Emergency League in September 1933, prior to assuming the pastorate of the German Evangelical Church, Sydenham, and the Reformed Church of St. Paul in London.

During his sojourn in England, Bonhoeffer became a close friend and confidant of the influential Anglican Bishop, George Bell. After the Confessing Church was organized in May 1934 at Barmen, Germany, Bonhoeffer returned from England in the spring of 1935 to assume leadership of the Confessing Church's seminary at Zingst by the Baltic Sea—a school relocated later that year to Finkenwalde in Pomerania. Out of the experiences at Finkenwalde emerged his two well-known books, *The Cost of Discipleship* and *Life Together*, as well as his lesser known writings on pastoral ministry such as Spiritual Care. His work to prepare pastors in the Confessing Church continued all the way to 1939.

Bonhoeffer's early travel to Rome, his curacy in Barcelona and his post-doctoral year in New York (including regular work at Abyssinian Baptist Church in Harlem, as well as travel to Cuba and Mexico), opened Bonhoeffer to the ecumenical church. In 1931 he as appointed youth secretary of the World Alliance for Promoting International Friendship through the Churches, and in 1934 he became a member of the Universal Christian Council for Life and Work. At conferences throughout Europe he vigorously represented the cause of the Confessing Church and challenged the ecumenical movement about its theological foundations and its responsibility for peace.

Bonhoeffer's theologically rooted opposition to National Socialism first made him a leader, along with Martin Niemueller and Karl Barth, in the Confessing Church (*bekennende Kirche*), and an advocate on behalf of the Jews. Indeed, his efforts to help a group of Jews escape to Switzerland were what first led to his arrest and imprisonment in the spring 1943. His leadership in the anti-Nazi Confessing Church and his participation in the Abwehr resistance circle (beginning in February 1938) make his works a unique source for understanding the interaction of religion, politics, and culture among those few Christians who actively opposed National Socialism, as is particularly evident in his drafts for a posthumously published Ethics.

His thought provides not only an example of intellectual preparation for the reconstruction of German society after the war but also a rare insight into the vanishing social and academic world that had preceded it. Bonhoeffer was also a spiritual writer, a musician and an author of fiction and poetry. The integrity of his Christian faith and life, and the international appeal of his writings, have led to a broad consensus that he is the one theologian of his time to lead future generations of Christians into the new millennium.

He was hanged in the concentration camp at Flossenbürg on April 9, 1945, one of four members of his immediate family to die at the hands of the Nazi regime for their participation in the small Protestant resistance movement. The letters he wrote during these final two years of his life were posthumously published by his student and friend, Eberhard Bethge, as *Letters and Papers from Prison*. His correspondence with his fiancée, Maria von Wedermeyer, has been published as *Love Letters from Cell* 92.

The International Dietrich Bonhoeffer Society

C. S. Lewis

Dates

1898–1963

Famous for being

Author and Christian apologist

Important writings

Mere Christianity and the Narnia Chronicles

One of his quotations

"As St. Paul points out, Christ never meant that we were to remain children in intelligence: on the contrary, He told us to be not only 'as harmless as doves' but also 'as wise as serpents.' He wants a child's heart, but a grown-up's head."

Summary

The English scholar, science-fiction writer, and Christian apologist Clive Staples Lewis was born in Belfast, Ireland. He was educated privately and at the University of Oxford, and was a member of The Inklings, a group of Oxford writers including J. R. R. Tolkien and Charles Williams. A fellow and tutor at Oxford from 1925 to 1954, he was subsequently professor of medieval and Renaissance English literature at the University of Cambridge.

Clive Staples Lewis, commonly referred to as C. S. Lewis, was an Irish author and scholar. Lewis is known for his work on medieval literature, Christian apologetics, literary criticism and fiction. He is best known today for his children's series *The Chronicles of Narnia*.

Lewis was a close friend of J. R. R. Tolkien, the author of *The Lord of the Rings*, and both were leading figures in the English faculty at Oxford University and in the informal Oxford literary group known as the "Inklings". Due in part to Tolkien's influence, Lewis converted to Christianity becoming "a very ordinary layman of the Church of England". His conversion had a profound effect on his work, and his wartime radio broadcasts on the subject of Christianity brought him wide acclaim. Late in life he married the American writer Joy Gresham, who died of bone cancer four years later at the age of 45.

Lewis's works have been translated into over 30 languages and continue to sell over a million copies a year; the books that comprise The Chronicles of Narnia have sold over 100 million copies. A number of stage and screen adaptations of Lewis's works have also been produced, the most notable of which is the 2005 Disney film adaptation of *The Lion, the Witch and the Wardrobe* which grossed US$745,000,000 worldwide.

Childhood

Clive Staples Lewis was born in Belfast, Ireland (now the capital of Northern Ireland) on November 29, 1898. His father was Albert James Lewis (1863–1929), a solicitor whose father had come to Ireland from Wales. His mother was Flora Augusta Hamilton Lewis (1862–1908), the daughter of a Church of Ireland priest. He had one older brother, Warren Hamilton Lewis (Warnie). At the age of four, shortly after his dog Jacksie was hit by a car, Lewis announced that his name was now Jacksie. At first he would answer to no other name, but later accepted Jacks which became Jack, the name by which he was known to friends and family for the rest of his life. At six his family moved into "Little Lea", the house the elder Mr. Lewis built for Mrs. Lewis, in Strandtown, Northern Ireland.

World War I

Having won a scholarship to University College, Oxford in 1916, Lewis enlisted the following year in the British Army as World War I raged on, and was commissioned an officer in the third Battalion, Somerset Light Infantry. Lewis arrived at the front line in the Somme Valley in France on his nineteenth birthday.

On 15 April 1917, Lewis was wounded during the Battle of Arras, and suffered some depression during his convalescence, due in part to missing his Irish home. On his recovery in October, he was assigned to duty in Andover, England. He was discharged in December 1918, and soon returned to his studies. Lewis received a First in Honor Moderations (Greek and Latin Literature) in 1920, a First in Greats (Philosophy and Ancient History) in 1922, and a First in English in 1923.

Conversion to Christianity

Although raised in a church-going family in the Church of Ireland, Lewis became an atheist at the age of 13, and remained as such until he was 31 years old. His separation from Christianity began when he started to view his religion as a chore and as a duty; around this time he also gained an interest in the occult as his studies expanded to include such topics. Lewis quoted Lucretius as having one of the strongest arguments for atheism:

Had God designed the world, it would not be
A world so frail and faulty as we see.

Though an atheist at the time, Lewis later described his young self (in Surprised by Joy) as being paradoxically "very angry with God for not existing".

Influenced by arguments with his Oxford colleague and friend J. R. R. Tolkien, and by the book The Everlasting Man by Roman Catholic convert G. K. Chesterton, he slowly rediscovered Christianity. He fought greatly up to the moment of his conversion noting, "I came into Christianity kicking and screaming." He described his last struggle in Surprised by Joy:

You must picture me alone in that room in Magdalen, night after night, feeling, whenever my mind lifted even for a second from my work, the steady, unrelenting approach of Him whom I so earnestly desired not to meet. That which I greatly feared had at last come upon me. In the Trinity Term of 1929 I gave in, and admitted that God was God, and knelt and prayed: perhaps, that night, the most dejected and reluctant convert in all England. (Lewis 1966)

After his conversion to theism in 1929, Lewis converted to Christianity in 1931. Following a long discussion and late-night walk with his close friends Tolkien and Hugo Dyson, he records making a specific commitment to Christian belief while on his way to the zoo with his brother. He became a member of the Church of England—somewhat to the regret of the devout Catholic Tolkien, who had hoped he would convert to Roman Catholicism.

Joy Gresham

In Lewis's later life, he corresponded with and later met Joy Davidman Gresham, an American writer of Jewish background and a convert from atheistic communism to Christianity. She was separated from her husband and came to England with her two sons, David and Douglas Gresham. Lewis at first regarded her as an agreeable intellectual companion and personal friend, and it was at least overtly on this level that he agreed to enter into a civil marriage contract with her so that she could continue to live in the UK.

However, after complaining of a painful hip, she was diagnosed with terminal bone cancer, and the relationship developed to the point that they sought a Christian marriage. Since she was divorced, this was not straightforward in the Church of England at the time, but a friend, the Rev. Peter Bide, performed the ceremony at Joy's hospital bed in 1956.

Joy's cancer soon went into a remarkable yet brief remission, and the couple lived as a family (together with Warren Lewis) until her eventual relapse and death in 1960. Lewis's book *A Grief Observed* describes his experience of bereavement in such a raw and personal fashion that Lewis originally released it under the pseudonym N. W. Clerk to keep readers from associating the book with him. However, so many friends recommended the book to Lewis as a method for dealing with his own grief that he made his authorship public.

Illness and death

In early June 1961, Lewis began experiencing medical problems and was diagnosed with inflammation of the kidneys which resulted in blood poisoning. His illness caused him to miss the autumn term at Cambridge, though his health gradually began improving in 1962 and he returned that April. Lewis's health continued to improve, and according to his friend George Sayer, Lewis was fully himself by the spring of 1963. However, on July 15, 1963 he fell ill and was admitted to hospital. The next day at 5:00 pm, Lewis suffered a heart attack and lapsed into a coma, unexpectedly awaking the following day at 2:00 pm. After he was discharged from hospital, Lewis returned to the Kilns though he was too ill to return to work. As a result, he resigned from his post at Cambridge in August. Lewis's condition continued to decline and in mid-November, he was diagnosed with end stage renal failure. On November 22, 1963, Lewis collapsed in his bedroom at 5:30 pm and died a few minutes later, exactly one week before his 65th birthday. He is buried in the churchyard of Holy Trinity Church, Headington, Oxford.

The author

In addition to his scholarly work, Lewis wrote a number of popular novels, including his science fiction Space Trilogy and his fantasy Narnia books, most dealing implicitly with Christian themes such as sin, the Fall, and redemption.

Major Works:

The Pilgrim's Regress (1933)

The Allegory of Love (1936)

Out of the Silent Planet (1938)

The Problem of Pain (1940)

The Screwtape Letters (1942)

Mere Christianity (1942)

The Abolition of Man (1943)

Perelandra (1943)

That Hideous Strength (1945)
Miracles (1947)
The Narnia Chronicles (1951–56)
English Literature in the Sixteenth Century (1954)
Surprised by Joy (1955)
The Four Loves (1960)

The Christian apologist

In addition to his career as an English professor and an author of fiction, Lewis is regarded by many as one of the most influential Christian apologists of his time; *Mere Christianity* was voted best book of the twentieth century by *Christianity Today* magazine in 2000. Lewis was very much interested in presenting a reasonable case for the truth of Christianity. *Mere Christianity, The Problem of Pain*, and *Miracles* were all concerned, to one degree or another, with refuting popular objections to Christianity.

Due to Lewis's approach to religious belief as a skeptic, and his following conversion by the evidence, he has become popularly known as The Apostle to the Skeptics. Consequently, his books on Christianity examine common difficulties in accepting Christianity, such as "How could a good God allow pain to exist in the world?", which he examined in detail in *The Problem of Pain*.

Lewis also wrote an autobiography entitled *Surprised by Joy*, which places special emphasis on his own conversion. His essays and public speeches on Christian belief, many of which were collected in *God in the Dock* and *The Weight of Glory* and *Other Addresses*, remain popular today.

His most famous works, the *Chronicles of Narnia*, contain many strong Christian messages and are often considered allegory. Lewis, an expert on the subject of allegory, maintained that the books were not allegory, and preferred to call the Christian aspects of them "suppositional".

Trilemma

In the book *Mere Christianity*, Lewis famously criticized the idea that Jesus was a great moral teacher whose claims to divinity were false:

> I am trying here to prevent anyone saying the really foolish thing that people often say about Him: I'm ready to accept Jesus as a great moral teacher, but I don't accept his claim to be God. That is the one thing we must not say. A man who was merely a man and said the sort of things Jesus said would not be a great moral teacher. He would either be a lunatic—on the level with the man who says he is a poached egg—or else he would be the Devil of Hell. You must make your choice. Either this man was, and is, the Son of God, or else a madman or something worse. You can shut him up for a fool, you

can spit at him and kill him as a demon or you can fall at his feet and call him Lord and God, but let us not come with any patronizing nonsense about his being a great human teacher. He has not left that open to us. He did not intend to. (*Mere Christianity, pp. 43*)

According to the argument, most people are willing to accept Jesus Christ as a great moral teacher, but the Gospels record that Jesus made many claims to divinity, either explicitly—("I and the father are one." John 10:30; when asked by the High priest whether he was the Son of God, Jesus replied "It is as you said" Matthew 26:64)—or implicitly, by assuming authority only God could have ("the Son of Man has authority on earth to forgive sins" Matthew 9:6). Lewis said there are three options:

Jesus was telling falsehoods and knew it, and so he was a liar.
Jesus was telling falsehoods but believed he was telling the truth, and so he was insane.
Jesus was telling the truth, and so he was divine.

Lewis's "trilemma" appeared at a time when secular scholars, such as David Friedrich Strauss, had portrayed Jesus' miracles and resurrection as myths. The concept that Jesus was not God but a wise man had gained ground in academic circles. The trilemma opposes the idea that Jesus was a wise mortal teacher without relying on miracles to prove it. In accepting the premise that Jesus had claimed divinity, he contradicted a viewpoint, popularized by H. G. Wells in his Outline of History, that Jesus had made no such claim.

Wikipedia

Timeline of C. S. Lewis

1898 November 29, born in Belfast, Ireland
1913 Discovers Norse mythology and decides that Christianity is an inferior mythology
1917 Goes to France with the Somerset Light Infantry
1918 April 15, wounded by an exploding shell in the Battle of Arras
1919 Takes first class degrees in classics, philosophy, and English
1925–1954 Fellow of English language and literature at Magdalen College, Oxford
1926 Meets J. R. R. Tolkien at a gathering of the English faculty at Merton College
1929 Comes to believe in the existence of some sort of god
1931 Converts to Christianity
1955 Professor of medieval and renaissance literature at Magdalene College, Cambridge
1956 marries Joy Gresham
1960 Wife Joy Gresham dies of cancer at the age of 45
1963 November 22, dies in Oxford, England

Francis Schaeffer

Dates
1912–1984

Famous for being
Christian apologist

Important writings
The God Who Is There
He Is There and He Is Not Silent

One of his quotations
"Art is a reflection of God's creativity, an evidence that we are made in the image of God."

Introduction

Francis Schaeffer was a Presbyterian minister with an ability to see how the questions of meaning, morals, and value being dealt with by philosophy, were the same questions that the Bible dealt with, only in different language. Once an agnostic, Schaeffer came to the conclusion that Biblical Christianity not only gave sufficient answers to the big questions, but that they were the only answers that were both self-consistent and livable. With this conviction he became a man of conversation.

Schaeffer taught that God is really there and He is not silent. He had spoken to man in the Bible as and a result we could have "true truth" about God and man. Knowing the dignity of man created in God's image, he placed a high value on creativity as an expression of that image. He opened his Swiss home to travelers to discuss these things. Later he began lecturing in universities and writing a number of books. Perhaps no other Christian thinker of the twentieth century, besides C. S. Lewis, has had more influence on thinking people.

The unique contribution of Dr. Francis Schaeffer on a whole generation was the ability to communicate the truth of historic Biblical Christianity in a way that combined intellectual integrity with practical, loving care. This grew out of his extensive understanding of the Bible from a deep commitment to Jesus Christ as his Lord and Savior and a critical study of the world of man. These two pillars supported his inquisitive and analytical mind on the solid reality of the truth of God's creation and of his revelation. He understood the roots of modern thinking in its rejection of reality and rationality and pointed out the logical conclusions in a wide range of disciplines and in society.

Dr. Schaeffer understood that what a person believes will influence the way he acts in history and individual situations. There is a relationship between a person's view of truth and life, between philosophy and practice, between faulty ideas and foolish choices. Dr. Schaeffer discussed the truth of reality with anyone in many settings. This in turn brought students, professionals, scholars and others from around the world to his home to learn from his insights. They returned with them to their own world and applied them to their circle of life and work. The ideas continue to bear fruit and to stimulate discussions and discoveries through more than 25 books, several films, taped seminars and lectures at leading universities in Europe, the US and abroad. The result has been a profound and enduring impact upon many thousands, who have themselves gone to make their own mark in history.

The central thrust of Dr. Schaeffer's teaching is that Biblical Christianity is the truth about the real world. The only reason to be a Christian is an acknowledgement of what is objectively true about human beings, the real world and the basic human predicaments. The Bible is true in all that it affirms. This emphasis is not so much the summary of academic instructions or doctrinal positions. It is the result of a searching mind, of being exposed to human history, the European culture and art, and of in-depth discussions with knowledgeable people for a life time of study, observation and work.

With the Bible as his base and a profound interest in human beings, Dr. Schaeffer's insights were developed through the experience of the Rijksmuseum in Amsterdam, the study of Florentine society and art, in lectures followed by tough discussions at modern Cambridge, in rude exposure to the slums of Bombay and in probing questions of people from a great variety of backgrounds, in abortion protests, in response to life in the wider arena of human need and pervasive intellectual confusion in our world.

Udo W. Middelmann, President, The Francis A. Schaeffer Foundation

Writings of Francis A. Schaeffer

Art and the Bible
Back to Freedom and Dignity
Basic Bible Studies
Christian Manifesto, A
Church at the End of the Twentieth Century, The
Church before the Watching World, The: A Practical Ecclesiology
Corruption Vs. True Spirituality
Death in the City
Escape from Reason
Everybody Can Know
Finished Work of Christ, The : The Truth of Romans 1–8
Genesis in Space and Time: The Flow of Biblical History

Great Evangelical Disaster, The
God Who Is There, The
He Is There and He Is Not Silent
How Should We Then Live?
Joshua and the Flow of Biblical History
Letters of Francis Schaeffer
Mark of the Christian, The
New Super-Spirituality, The
No Final Conflict
No Little People
Pollution and the Death of Man: A Christian View of Ecology
True Spirituality
Two Contents, Two Realities
Whatever Happened to the Human Race?
Who Is For Life?
Who Is For Peace?

Mother Teresa of Calcutta

Dates
1910–1997

Famous for being
"A mother to the poor"

Important writings
My Life for the Poor

One of her quotations
"The most terrible poverty is loneliness, and the feeling of being unloved."

Birth name: Agnes Gonxha Bojaxhiu
Place of Birth: Skopje, Yugoslavia (what is now Macedonia)
Residence: Calcutta, India

"By blood, I am Albanian. By citizenship, an Indian. By faith, I am a Catholic nun. As to my calling, I belong to the world. As to my heart, I belong entirely to the Heart of Jesus."

Small of stature, rocklike in faith, Mother Teresa of Calcutta was entrusted with the mission of proclaiming God's thirsting love for humanity, especially for the poorest of the poor. "God still loves the world and He sends you and me to be His love and His compassion to the poor." She was a soul filled with the light of Christ, on fire with love for Him and burning with one desire: "to quench His thirst for love and for souls."

This luminous messenger of God's love was born on 26 August 1910 in Skopje, a city situated at the crossroads of Balkan history. The youngest of the children born to Nikola and Drane Bojaxhiu, she was baptized Gonxha Agnes, received her First Communion at the age of five and a half and was confirmed in November 1916. From the day of her First Holy Communion, a love for souls was within her. Her father's sudden death when Gonxha was about eight years old left in the family in financial straits. Drane raised her children firmly and lovingly, greatly influencing her daughter's character and vocation. Gonxha's religious formation was further assisted by the vibrant Jesuit parish of the Sacred Heart in which she was much involved.

At the age of eighteen, moved by a desire to become a missionary, Gonxha left her home in September 1928 to join the Institute of the Blessed Virgin Mary, known as the Sisters of Loreto, in Ireland. There she received the name Sister Mary Teresa after St. Thérèse of Lisieux. In December, she departed for India, arriving in Calcutta on 6 January 1929. After making her First Profession of Vows in May 1931, Sister Teresa was assigned to the Loreto Entally community in Calcutta and taught at St. Mary's School for girls. On 24 May 1937, Sister Teresa made her Final Profession of Vows, becoming, as she said, the "spouse of Jesus" for "all eternity." From that time on she was called Mother Teresa. She continued teaching at St. Mary's and in 1944 became the school's principal. A person of profound prayer and deep love for her religious sisters and her students, Mother Teresa's twenty years in Loreto were filled with profound happiness. Noted for her charity, unselfishness and courage, her capacity for hard work and a natural talent for organization, she lived out her consecration to Jesus, in the midst of her companions, with fidelity and joy.

On 10 September 1946 during the train ride from Calcutta to Darjeeling for her annual retreat, Mother Teresa received her "inspiration," her "call within a call." On that day, in a way she would never explain, Jesus' thirst for love and for souls took hold of her heart and the desire to satiate His thirst became the driving force of her life. Over the course of the next weeks and months, by means of interior locutions and visions, Jesus revealed to her the desire of His heart for "victims of love" who would "radiate His love on souls." "Come be My light," He begged her. "I cannot go alone." He revealed His pain at the neglect of the poor, His sorrow at their ignorance of Him and His longing for their love. He asked Mother Teresa to establish a religious community, Missionaries of Charity, dedicated to the service of the poorest of the poor. Nearly two years of testing and discernment passed before Mother Teresa received permission to begin. On August 17, 1948, she dressed for the first time in a white, blue-bordered sari and passed through the gates of her beloved Loreto convent to enter the world of the poor.

After a short course with the Medical Mission Sisters in Patna, Mother Teresa returned to Calcutta and found temporary lodging with the Little Sisters of the Poor. On 21 December she went for the first time to the slums. She visited families, washed the sores of some children, cared for an old man lying sick on the road and nursed a woman dying of hunger and TB. She started each day in communion with Jesus in the Eucharist and then went out, rosary in her hand, to find and serve Him in "the unwanted, the unloved, the uncared for." After some months, she was joined, one by one, by her former students.

On 7 October 1950 the new congregation of the Missionaries of Charity was officially established in the Archdiocese of Calcutta. By the early 1960s, Mother Teresa began to send her Sisters to other parts of India. The Decree of Praise granted to the Congregation by Pope Paul VI in February 1965 encouraged her to open a house in Venezuela. It was soon followed by foundations in Rome and Tanzania and, eventually, on every continent. Starting in 1980 and continuing through the 1990s, Mother Teresa opened houses in almost all of the communist countries, including the former Soviet Union, Albania and Cuba.

In order to respond better to both the physical and spiritual needs of the poor, Mother Teresa founded the Missionaries of Charity Brothers in 1963, in 1976 the contemplative branch of the Sisters, in 1979 the Contemplative Brothers, and in 1984 the Missionaries of Charity Fathers. Yet her inspiration was not limited to those with religious vocations. She formed the Co-Workers of Mother Teresa and the Sick and Suffering Co-Workers, people of many faiths and nationalities with whom she shared her spirit of prayer, simplicity, sacrifice and her apostolate of humble works of love. This spirit later inspired the Lay Missionaries of Charity. In answer to the requests of many priests, in 1981 Mother Teresa also began the Corpus Christi Movement for Priests as a "little way of holiness" for those who desire to share in her charism and spirit.

During the years of rapid growth the world began to turn its eyes towards Mother Teresa and the work she had started. Numerous awards, beginning with the Indian Padmashri Award in 1962 and notably the Nobel Peace Prize in 1979, honored her work, while an increasingly interested media began to follow her activities. She received both prizes and attention "for the glory of God and in the name of the poor."

The whole of Mother Teresa's life and labor bore witness to the joy of loving, the greatness and dignity of every human person, the value of little things done faithfully and with love, and the surpassing worth of friendship with God. But there was another heroic side of this great woman that was revealed only after her death. Hidden from all eyes, hidden even from those closest to her, was her interior life marked by an experience of a deep, painful and abiding feeling of being separated from God, even rejected by Him, along with an ever-increasing longing for His love. She called her inner experience, "the darkness." The "painful night" of her soul, which began around the time she started her work for the poor and continued to the end of her life, led Mother Teresa to an ever more profound union with God. Through the darkness she mystically participated in the thirst of Jesus, in His painful and burning longing for love, and she shared in the interior desolation of the poor.

During the last years of her life, despite increasingly severe health problems, Mother Teresa continued to govern her Society and respond to the needs of the poor and the Church. By 1997, Mother Teresa's Sisters numbered nearly 4,000 members and were established in 610 foundations in 123 countries of the world. In March 1997 she blessed her newly-elected successor as Superior General of the Missionaries of Charity and then made one more trip abroad. After meeting Pope John Paul II for the last time, she returned to Calcutta and spent her final weeks receiving visitors and instructing her Sisters.

On 5 September Mother Teresa's earthly life came to an end. She was given the honor of a state funeral by the Government of India and her body was buried in the Mother House of the Missionaries of Charity. Her tomb quickly became a place of pilgrimage and prayer for people of all faiths, rich and poor alike. Mother Teresa left a testament of unshakable faith, invincible hope and extraordinary charity. Her response to Jesus' plea, "Come be My light," made her a Missionary of Charity, a "mother to the poor," a symbol of compassion to the world, and a living witness to the thirsting love of God.

Vatican News

One of Mother Teresa's prayers

> Dear Jesus, help me to spread Thy fragrance everywhere I go. Flood my soul with Thy spirit and love. Penetrate and possess my whole being so utterly that all my life may only be a radiance of Thine. Shine through me and be so in me that every soul I come in contact with may feel Thy presence in my soul. Let them look up and see no longer me but only Jesus. Stay with me and then I shall begin to shine as you shine, so to shine as to be a light to others.

Timeline of Mother Teresa

1928 Went to India and taught at a convent school in Calcutta

1937 Took her final vows

1948 Left the convent to work alone in the slums; received some medical training in Paris

1950 The Missionaries of Charity (Mother Teresa's sisterhood) started

1952 House for the Dying opened

1957 The Missionaries of Charity started work with lepers and in many disaster areas of the world

1971 Awarded the Pope John XXIII Peace Prize

1979 Awarded Nobel Peace Prize

Billy Graham

Dates

1918-present

Famous for being

Evangelist

Important writings

Peace with God

Answers to Life's Problems

One of his quotations

"My one purpose in life is to help people find a personal relationship with God, which, I believe, comes through knowing Christ."

Evangelist Billy Graham took Christ literally when He said in Mark 16:15, "Go ye into all the world and preach the Gospel to every creature."

Mr. Graham has preached the Gospel to more people in live audiences than anyone else in history—over 210 million people in more than 185 countries and territories—through various meetings, including Mission World and Global Mission. Hundreds of millions more have been reached through television, video, film, and webcasts.

Since the 1949 Los Angeles crusade vaulted Mr. Graham into the public eye, he has led hundreds of thousands of individuals to make personal decisions to live for Christ, which is the main thrust of his ministry.

Born November 7, 1918, four days before the Armistice ended World War I, Mr. Graham was reared on a dairy farm in Charlotte, North Carolina. Growing up during the Depression, he learned the value of hard work on the family farm, but he also found time to spend many hours in the hayloft reading books on a wide variety of subjects.

In the fall of 1934, at age 16, Mr. Graham made a personal commitment to Christ through the ministry of Mordecai Ham, a traveling evangelist, who visited Charlotte for a series of revival meetings.

Ordained in 1939 by a church in the Southern Baptist Convention, Mr. Graham received a solid foundation in the Scriptures at Florida Bible Institute (now Trinity College in Florida). In 1943 he was graduated from Wheaton College in Illinois and married fellow student Ruth McCue Bell, daughter of a missionary surgeon, who spent the first 17 years of her life in China.

After graduating from college, Mr. Graham pastored the First Baptist Church in Western Springs, Illinois, before joining Youth for Christ, an organization founded for ministry to youth and servicemen during World War II. He preached throughout the

United States and in Europe in the immediate post war era, emerging as a rising young evangelist.

The Los Angeles crusade in 1949 launched Mr. Graham into international prominence. Scheduled for three weeks, the meetings were extended to more than eight weeks, with overflow crowds filling a tent erected downtown each night.

Many of his subsequent early crusades were similarly extended, including one in London which lasted 12 weeks, and a New York City crusade in Madison Square Garden in 1957 which ran nightly for 16 weeks.

Billy Graham and his ministry are known around the globe. He has preached in remote African villages and in the heart of New York City, and those to whom he has ministered have ranged from heads of state to the simple living bushmen of Australia and the wandering tribes of Africa and the Middle East. Since 1977, Mr. Graham has been accorded the opportunity to conduct preaching missions in virtually every country of the former Eastern bloc, including the former Soviet Union.

Mr. Graham founded the Billy Graham Evangelistic Association (BGEA) in 1950 which was headquartered in Minneapolis, Minnesota, until relocating to Charlotte, North Carolina in 2003. He conducts his ministry through the BGEA, including:

the weekly "Hour of Decision" radio program broadcast around the world on Sundays for over 50 years.

television specials featuring Billy Graham Crusades and Franklin Graham Festivals which are broadcast in prime time on an average of 150 stations across the United States and Canada five to seven times annually.

a syndicated newspaper column, "My Answer," which is carried by newspapers both nationally and internationally.

"Decision" magazine, the official publication of the Association, which has a circulation of more than 600,000 and is available in English and German versions, with special editions available in Braille and on cassette tape for the visually impaired.

World Wide Pictures which has produced and distributed over 125 productions, making it one of the foremost producers of evangelistic films in the world. Films have been translated into 38 languages and viewed by more than 250 million people worldwide and are available for showing in prisons and correctional facilities nationwide.

Mr. Graham has written 25 books, many of which have become top sellers. His memoirs, "Just As I Am," published in 1997, achieved a "triple crown," appearing simultaneously on the three top best-seller lists in one week. In it Mr. Graham reflects on his life, including more than 60 years of ministry around the world. From humble beginnings as the son of a dairy farmer in North Carolina, he shares how his unwavering faith in Christ formed and shaped his career.

Of his other books, "Approaching Hoofbeats: The Four Horsemen of the Apocalypse" (1983) was listed for several weeks on The New York Times best seller list; "How to Be Born Again" (1977) had the largest first printing in publishing history with 800,000 copies; "Angels: God's Secret Agents" (1975) sold one million copies within 90 days; and "The Jesus Generation" (1971) sold 200,000 copies in the first two weeks.

Mr. Graham's counsel has been sought by presidents, and his appeal in both the secular and religious arenas is evidenced by the wide range of groups that have honored him, including numerous honorary doctorates from many institutions in the U. S. and abroad.

Recognitions include the Ronald Reagan Presidential Foundation Freedom Award (2000) for contributions to the cause of freedom; the Congressional Gold Medal (1996); the Templeton Foundation Prize for Progress in Religion (1982); and the Big Brother Award for his work on behalf of the welfare of children (1966). In 1964 he received the Speaker of the Year Award and was cited by the George Washington Carver Memorial Institute for his contributions to race relations. He was recognized by the Anti-Defamation League of the B'nai B'rith in 1969 and the National Conference of Christians and Jews in 1971 for his efforts to foster a better understanding among all faiths. In December 2001 he was presented with an honorary knighthood, Honorary Knight Commander of the Order of the British Empire (KBE), for his international contribution to civic and religious life over 60 years.

Mr. Graham is regularly listed by the Gallup organization as one of the "Ten Most Admired Men in the World," whom it described as the dominant figure in that poll since 1948—making an unparalleled 48th appearance and 41st consecutive appearance. He has also appeared on the covers of Time, Newsweek, Life, U.S. News and World Report, Parade, and numerous other magazines and has been the subject of many newspaper and magazine feature articles and books.

He and his wife, Ruth, have three daughters, two sons, 19 grandchildren and numerous great grandchildren. The Grahams make their home in the mountains of western North Carolina.

Billy Graham Evangelistic Association

Other Christian leaders in the twentieth century

1. Theologians in the twentieth century

Rudolf Bultmann (1884–1976)

Paul Tillich (1886–1965)

Emil Brunner (1889–1966)

Karl Rahner (1904 – 1984)

Jürgen Moltmann (b. 1926)

Hans Küng (b. 1928)
Wolfhart Pannenberg (b. 1928)

2. Missionaries in the twentieth century
The Cambridge Seven
Jim Elliot (1927–1956)

3. Other Christian leaders
Billy Sunday (1862–1935)
Martin Luther King, Jr. (1929–1968)
Brother Roger (1915–2005)

1. Theologians in the twentieth century

Rudolf Karl Bultmann (1884–1976)

Rudolf Karl Bultmann was a German theologian of Lutheran background, who was for three decades professor of New Testament studies at the University of Marburg. His *History of the Synoptic Tradition* (1921) is still highly regarded as an essential tool for gospel research, even by scholars who reject his analyses of the conventional rhetorical tropes or narrative units of which the Gospels are assembled, and the historically-oriented principles called "form criticism," of which Bultmann has been the most influential exponent:

> The aim of form-criticism is to determine the original form of a piece of narrative, a dominical saying or a parable. In the process we learn to distinguish secondary additions and forms, and these in turn lead to important results for the history of the tradition.

In 1941, he applied form criticism to the Gospel of John, in which he distinguished the presence of a lost Signs Gospel on which John, alone of the evangelists, depended. This monograph, highly controversial at the time, is a milestone in research into the historical Jesus. The same year his lecture *New Testament and Mythology: The Problem of Demythologizing the New Testament Message* called on interpreters to replace traditional theology with the philosophy of Bultmann's colleague, Martin Heidegger, an endeavor to make accessible to a literate modern audience the reality of Jesus' teachings. Bultmann remained convinced the narratives of the life of Jesus were offering theology in story form. Lessons were taught in the familiar language of myth. They were not to be excluded, but given explanation so they could be understood for today. Bultmann thought faith should become a present day reality. To Bultmann, the people of the world appeared to be always in disappointment and turmoil. Faith must be a determined vital act of will, not a culling and extolling of "ancient proofs".

Some scholars criticized Bultmann and other critics for excessive skepticism regarding the historical reliability of the gospel narratives.

Wikipedia

Paul Tillich (1886–1965)

Introduction

Paul Johannes Tillich was a German-American theologian and Christian existentialist philosopher. Tillich was, along with contemporary Karl Barth, one of the more influential Protestant theologians of the twentieth century.

Biography

Paul Tillich was born on August 20, 1886, in the province of Brandenburg in eastern Germany in the small village of Starzeddel. Paul's Prussian father was a Lutheran pastor and his mother was from the Rhineland and more liberal, influenced heavily by Calvinist thinking. At an early age Paul held an appreciation for nature and the countryside into which he had been born.

When Paul was 17 his mother died of cancer. Tillich studied at a number of German universities—those of Berlin, Tübingen, Halle, and Breslau—before finally obtaining a degree. Shortly thereafter, in 1912, he was ordained minister in the Lutheran Church, and soon took up a career as professor. Except for an interlude as chaplain in the German army during World War I, he taught at a number of universities throughout Germany over the next two decades. Tillich taught theology at the universities of Berlin, Marburg, Dresden, and Leipzig, and philosophy at Frankfurt. However, his opposition to the Nazis cost him his job: he was fired in 1933 and replaced by philosopher Arnold Gehlen, who had joined the Nazi Party that year. Finding himself thus barred from German universities, Tillich accepted an invitation from Reinhold Niebuhr to teach at the Union Theological Seminary in the United States, where he emigrated later that year. Tillich became a US citizen in 1940.

It is at the Union Theological Seminary that Tillich earned his reputation, publishing a series of books that outlined his particular synthesis of Protestant Christian theology with existentialist philosophy (drawing on research in psychology in the process). Between 1952 and 1954 Tillich gave the Gifford lectures at the University of Aberdeen, which resulted in the comprehensive three volume Systematic Theology. A 1952 book outlining many of his views on existentialism, The Courage to Be, proved popular even outside philosophical and religious circles, earning him considerable acclaim and influence. These works led to a prestigious appointment at Harvard University in 1954, where he wrote another popularly acclaimed book, Dynamics of Faith (1957). He was also a very important contributor to modern Just War thought. In 1962, he moved to the University of Chicago, where he continued until his death in Chicago in 1965. Tillich's ashes were interred in 1965 in the Paul Tillich Park in New Harmony, Indiana.

Theology

Tillich's approach to Protestant theology was highly systematic. He sought to correlate culture and faith such that "faith need not be unacceptable to contemporary culture and contemporary culture need not be unacceptable to faith". Consequently, Tillich's orientation is apologetic, seeking to make concrete theological answers that are applicable to ordinary daily life. This contributed to his popularity because it made him easily accessible to lay readers. In a broader perspective, revelation is understood as the fountainhead of religion. Tillich sought to reconcile revelation and reason by arguing that revelation never runs counter to reason (affirming Thomas Aquinas who said that faith is eminently rational), but both poles of the subjective human experience are complementary.

In his metaphysical approach, Tillich was a staunch existentialist, focusing on the nature of being. Nothingness is a major motif of existentialist philosophy which Tillich employed as a means of reifying being itself. Tillich argued that anxiety of non-being (existential anguish) is inherent in the experience of being itself. Put simply, people are afraid of their own deaths. Following a line similar to Søren Kierkegaard and almost identical to that of Sigmund Freud, Tillich says that in our most introspective moments we face the terror of our own nothingness. That is, we "realize our mortality", that we are finite beings. The question which naturally arises in the mind of one in this introspective mood is what causes us to "be" in the first place. Tillich concludes that radically finite beings (which are, at least potentially, infinite in variation) cannot be sustained or caused by another finite or existing being. What can sustain finite beings is being itself, or the "ground of being". This Tillich identifies as God. Much of Tillich's phenomenological language with regard to being can be traced back to Martin Heidegger, with whom Tillich was in contact prior to 1933. Tillich also utilized some of the basic framework of Heidegger's fundamental ontology in the discussion on Being and God in the Systematic Theology.

Tillich's radical departure from traditional Christian theology is his view of Christ. According to Tillich, Christ is the "New Being", who rectifies in himself the alienation between essence and existence. Essence fully shows itself within Christ, but Christ is also a finite man. This indicates, for Tillich, a revolution in the very nature of being. The gap is healed and essence can now be found within existence. Thus for Tillich, Christ is not God per se in himself, but Christ is the revelation of God. Whereas traditional Christianity regards Christ as wholly man and wholly God, Tillich believed that Christ was the emblem of the highest goal of man, what God wants men to become. Thus to be a Christian is to make oneself progressively "Christ-like", a very possible goal in Tillich's eyes. In other words, Christ is not God in the traditional sense, but reveals the essence inherent in all existence, including mine and your own. Thus Christ is not different from you or me except insofar as he fully reveals God within his own finitude, something you and I can also do in principle.

"God does not exist. He is being itself beyond essence and existence. Therefore to argue that God exists is to deny him."

This Tillich quotation summarizes his conception of God. He does not think of God as a being which exists in time and space, because that constrains God, and makes God finite. But all beings are finite, and if God is the Creator of all beings, God cannot logically be finite since a finite being cannot be the sustainer of an infinite variety of finite things. Thus God is considered beyond being, above finitude and limitation, the power or essence of being itself.

Tillich stated that since things in existence are corrupt and therefore ambiguous, no finite thing can be (by itself) infinite. All that is possible is for the finite to be a vehicle for revealing the infinite, but the two should never be confused. This leaves religion in the situation where it should not be taken too dogmatically, because of its conceptual and therefore finite and imperfect nature. True religion is that which correctly reveals the infinite, but no religion can ever do so in any way other than through metaphor and symbol. Thus the whole of the Bible should be understood symbolically, and all spiritual and theological knowledge cannot be other than symbol. This idea is used by theologians as an effective counterpoint to religious fundamentalism. Tillich argued that symbols are immensely important to faith because "faith is the state of being ultimately concerned." Faith without symbols is a form of idolatry. It is faith in something finite, something that can be expressed without symbols, and something that is fundamentally less than the ultimate

Wikipedia

Emil Brunner (1889 –1966)

Introduction

Emil Brunner was an eminent and highly influential Swiss theologian. Along with Karl Barth, he is commonly associated with the neo-orthodoxy or dialectical theology movement.

Biography

Emil Brunner was born near Zurich.

He studied at both the universities of Zurich and Berlin, receiving his doctorate in theology from Zurich in 1913. The title of his doctoral dissertation was: *The Symbolic Element in Religious Knowledge*. Brunner served as pastor from 1916–1917 in the mountain village of Obstalden in the Canton of Glarus. He spent a year in New York, USA at Union Theological Seminary studying (1919–1920).

In 1921 Brunner wrote what he considered a second dissertation: *Experience, Knowledge and Faith*. Soon, another book followed: *Mysticism and the Word*. This work was a devastating critique of the liberal theology of Friedrich Schleiermacher. Brunner was rewarded for his literary efforts with the appointment as the professor of Systematic and Practical Theology at the University of Zurich from 1924–1955. In the next few years his reputation continued to increase particularly with the publication of two more books, the first *The Philosophy of Religion from the Standpoint of Protestant Theology*, and second *The Mediator*.

In 1932, following a few years of receiving invitations to visit and lecture across Europe and the United States, and accepting them, Brunner wrote *God and Man and The Divine Imperative*. Brunner continued his theological output with *Man in Revolt and Truth as Encounter* in 1937. In 1938–1939 he again visited the US when he agreed to a visiting professorship at Princeton Theological Seminary.

His teaching career concluded in 1953–1955 at what was then the new International Christian University in Tokyo, Japan, but not before the publication of his three volume *Dogmatics*. Volume One was titled: *The Christian Doctrine of God*. Volume Two was titled: *The Christian Doctrine of Creation and Redemption*, and the final volume was titled: *The Christian Doctrine of the Church, Faith, and Consummation*. On the return journey from Japan to Europe, Brunner suffered a cerebral hemorrhage and was physically impaired weakening his ability to work productively. Though there were times when he felt better during the next nine years, he suffered further strokes off and on, finally succumbing to death in 1966.

Brunner undoubtedly holds a place of prominence in Protestant theology in the 20th century and was one of the four or five system builders.

Theology

Brunner rejected liberal theology's portrait of Jesus Christ as merely a highly-respected human being. Instead, Brunner insisted that Jesus was God incarnate and central to salvation. Brunner also attempted to find a middle position within the ongoing Arminian and Calvinist debate, stating that Christ stood between God's sovereign approach to humankind and our free acceptance of God's gift of salvation. Although Brunner re-emphasized the centrality of Christ, conservative theologians have often been hesitant to accept Brunner's other teachings, including his rejection of certain "miraculous" elements of the Scriptures and his questioning of the usefulness of the doctrine of the inspiration of Scripture.

Wikipedia

Karl Rahner (1904 – 1984)

Karl Rahner, was one of the most influential Roman Catholic theologians of the 20th century. He was born in Freiburg, Germany, and died in Innsbruck, Austria. His theology influenced the Second Vatican Council and is ground-breaking for a modern understanding of Catholic faith. Written near the end of his life, Rahner's Foundations of Christian Faith is the most developed and systematic of his works, most of which was published in the form of theological essays.

The basis for Rahner's theology is that all human beings have a latent ("unthematic") experience of God in any experiences of meaning or "transcendental experience." It is only because of this proto-revelation that recognizing a specifically special revelation (such as the Christian gospel) is possible.

The philosophical sources for Rahner's theology include Thomas Aquinas, read from the aspect of contemporary continental philosophy. Rahner attended lectures by Heidegger in Freiburg.

Wikipedia

Jürgen Moltmann (b. 1926)

Jürgen Moltmann is a German theologian and Professor Emeritus of Systematic Theology at the University of Tübingen, Germany. He is most noted as a proponent of his "theology of hope" and for his incorporation of insights from liberation theology and ecology into mainstream trinitarian theology.

Theology

As a prisoner of war in a British camp during World War II, Moltmann observed that his fellow prisoners who had hope fared the best. After the war, it seemed to him Christianity was ignoring the hope offered in its promise of a future life.

Moltmann is known as one of the leading proponents of the theology of hope. He believes that God's promise to act in the future is more important than the fact that he has acted in the past. What is implied by this focus on the future, however, is not withdrawal from the world in the hope that a better world will somehow evolve, but active participation in the world in order to aid in the coming of that better world.

The most influential work by Moltmann is his *Theology of Hope*, published in English in 1967. Moltmann proposes that Christian hope should be the central motivating factor in the life and thought of the church and of each Christian. For Moltmann, the whole creation longs for the renewal by the "God of Hope." Empowered by hope, the Christian's response should therefore involve: mission of the church to all nations, the hunger for righteousness in the world, and love for the true life of the imperiled and impaired creation.

Although Moltmann is perhaps most conspicuous, he is not the only theologian of hope. His theology is in concert with that of Lutheran theologian Wolfhart Pannenberg, who has become quite well known in the United States since the late 60s and in whose essay "Dogmatic Theses on the Doctrine of Revelation" is found a similar emphasis on understanding of all reality in terms of the *eschaton*.

Wikipedia

Hans Küng (b. 1928)

Introduction

Hans Küng is the most published, translated, and read Catholic theologian of the 20th century.

Hans Küng was born March 19, 1928, in Sursee, Switzerland, studied for the priesthood in Rome, and earned a Th.D. at the Institut Catholique in Paris. After his doctoral dissertation comparing the doctrine of justification in the theology of the then most influential Protestant theologian, Karl Barth, with that of the Council of Trent in the 16th century (finding them compatible!), his fame earned him a call in 1960 to the University of Tübingen as the successor to my Doktorvater Professor Heinrich Fries, who had moved to Munich.

The following year Hans published a small book urging reform at Vatican Council II (1962–65), which brought him not only further fame, but also "notoriety." As a consequence, when he was invited to lecture in the U.S. in the spring of 1963, on freedom in the Catholic Church, it was like a triumphant tour (spiced with his being forbidden to speak in several dioceses—including Philadelphia). He was made an expert (*peritus*) at the Council and played a significant role in that watershed experience.

After the death of John XXIII, Hans often ran into difficulties with the conservatives of the Vatican. This reached its apogee December 18, 1979, when the Vatican declared that he could no longer be considered a Catholic theologian. This had a dramatic result. Instead of 150 students at his lectures, he then had 1500! Hans had always worked for the reform of the Catholic Church and for ecumenism. Then he turned more and more of his energy to dialogue with world religions, and since 1990 to Global Ethics. It is for these two poles of his life—Reform of the Catholic Church and Interreligious Dialogue, and their intimate linkage, that we honor him.

Leonard Swidler

Wolfhart Pannenberg (b. 1928)

Wolfhart Pannenberg (born 1928) is a German Christian theologian. Pannenberg was born in Stettin, Germany (which is now Szczecin Poland) and was baptized at as an infant into the Lutheran Church. Despite his baptism, Pannenberg had virtually no contact with the church in his early years. Some time in his youth though, he did have an intensely religious experience that he called his "light experience." Pannenberg wanted to understand this experience and began to search through the works of great philosophers and religious thinkers. While in High School Pannenberg encountered a literature teacher who had been a part of the Confessing Church during World War II who encouraged Pannenberg to take a hard look at Christianity. At this time Pannenberg experienced an "intellectual conversion" when he decided that Christianity was the best available religious option. This propelled him into his vocation as a theologian.

Education

Pannenberg began his theological studies at the University of Berlin after World War II and also studied at the University of Göttingen and the University of Basel. He completed his doctoral dissertation at the University of Heidleberg. He studied under theologians Karl Barth and Edmund Schlink, among others.

Theology

Pannenberg's theology draws together religion and science. He published his magnum opus, a three-volume *Systematic Theology* in the 1990s.

Theopedia

Statements of some modern theologians

"The Bible gives to every man and every era such answers to their questions as they deserve. We shall always find in it as much as we seek and no more: high and divine content if it is high and divine content that we seek; transitory and historical content if it is transitory and historical content that we seek."

Karl Barth

"It is not the right human thoughts about God which form the content of the Bible, but the right divine thoughts about men."

Karl Barth

"... the Biblical idea of the Creation is never expanded into a cosmogony. It is intended for a solemn marking of the distance between the cosmos and the Creator, and precisely not for a metaphysical explanation of the world. God said, Let there be! That is all."

Karl Barth

"The Bible tells us more, or less, according to the much or little that he are able to hear and translate into deed and truth ... But the source even of our sense of problem is in God."

Karl Barth

"Theology, above all, must leave to science the description of the whole of objects and their interdependence and history."

Paul Tillich

"When the Scriptures are viewed as a court of last resort for determining what is and what is not Christian doctrine, it becomes necessary to make sure of the Scriptures historically and critically."

Søren Kierkegaard

"The six days of creation and the narrative of the creation of man are, as we are well aware today, images which do not describe the scientific course of the origin of the world; they proclaim-and still proclaim to man even today-the splendor and uniqueness of the Creator and the greatness, simplicity, and goodness of His work."

Hans Küng

"If you cannot see that divinity includes male and female characteristics and at the same time transcends them, you have bad consequences. Rome and Cardinal O'Connor base the exclusion of women priests on the idea that God is the father and Jesus is his son, there were only male disciples, etc. They are defending a patriarchal church with a patriarchal God. We must fight the patriarchal misunderstanding of God."

Hans Küng, Newsweek interview, July 8, 1991

"Everyone agrees the celibacy rule is just a church law dating from the 11th century, not a divine command."

Hans Küng, Newsweek interview, July 8, 1991

"We must put in the forefront of our concrete preoccupations the systematic arrangement and exploration of our universe. The time has come to realize that research is the highest form of function, embracing the spirit of conflict and bright with the splendor of religion. To keep up a constant pressure on the real, is not that the supreme posture of faith in Being and therefore the highest form of adoration?"

Pierre Teilhard de Chardin

"Though frightened for a moment by evolution, the Christian now perceives that what it offers him is nothing but a means of feeling more at one with God and of giving himself more to him."

Pierre Teilhard de Chardin

"Then God said 'Let us make man in our image, after our likeness'. This has nothing at all to do with Darwinism. We certainly have no wish to deny our connection with the animal world; rather it is just the opposite."

Dietrich Bonhoeffer

2. Missionaries in the twentieth century

The Cambridge Seven

The Cambridge Seven were seven students from Cambridge University, who in 1885, decided to become missionaries in China; the seven were:

C. T. Studd
Montagu Harry Proctor Beauchamp
Stanley P. Smith
Arthur T. Polhill-Turner
Dixon Edward Hoste
Cecil H. Polhill-Turner
William Wharton Cassels

Having been accepted as missionaries by Hudson Taylor of the China Inland Mission the seven were scheduled to leave for China in early February 1885. Before leaving the seven held a farewell tour to spread the message across the country—it was during this tour that someone dubbed them "The Cambridge Seven."

For the next month, the seven toured the University campuses of England and Scotland, holding meetings for the students. Queen Victoria was pleased to receive their booklet containing The Cambridge Seven's testimonies. The record of their departure is recorded in "The Evangelization of the World: A Missionary Band". It became a national bestseller. Their influence extended to America where it led to the formation of Robert Wilder's Student Volunteer Movement.

All seven had become born-again Christians and were moved by their beliefs to go to China in 1885 to spread these beliefs and to help the local population; most remained in or connected to missionary work for the rest of their lives. They were greatly influenced by Taylor's book "China's Spiritual Need and Claims". After their acceptance into the China Inland Mission, the seven toured England and Scotland, preaching and appealing to their listeners to follow their example and follow Christ. Charles Studd's brother Kynaston helped the seven in their preparations for departure.

Assessment

The conversion and example of the seven, was one of the grand gestures of 19th century missions—making them religious celebrities; as a result their story was published as "The Evangelization of the World" and was distributed to every YMCA and YWCA throughout the British Empire and the USA.

Though their time together was brief, they helped catapult the China Inland Mission from obscurity to "almost embarrassing prominence," and their work helped to inspire many recruits for the CIM and other mission societies. In 1885, when the Seven first arrived in China, the CIM had 163 missionaries; this had doubled by 1890 and reached some 800 by 1900—which represented one-third of the entire Protestant missionary force.

The Seven's work

William Wharton Cassels worked in China for ten years and then returned to England in 1895 where he was consecrated as the new Bishop of a new diocese in Western China. He then returned to Western China—he lived here until his death in 1925.

Stanley Peregrine Smith was sent to North China. Here he learned Chinese language and soon became as fluent a preacher in Chinese as he was in English. He died in China on January 31, 1931.

Charles Studd, one of the famous Studd brothers, who was before his missionary work well known as an England cricketer—having played in the famous Ashes series against Australia, was probably the best the known of "The Cambridge Seven,". He was sent home because of ill health in 1894. Later he worked in India and Africa and was the founder of WEC. He died in 1931.

Arthur Polhill-Turner was ordained as a minister in 1888 and moved to the densely populated countryside to reach as many people as he could. He remained in China throughout the uprisings against foreigners at the turn of the century and did not leave there until 1928, when he retired and returned to England. He died in 1935.

Cecil Polhill-Turner, stayed in the same province with the others for a while before moving to the northwest, in the direction of Tibet. During a violent riot there he and his wife were both nearly killed in 1892. In 1900, his health failed and he was sent home to England and where he was forbidden to return to China. Despite this ban, his heart remained there and throughout the rest of his life, he made seven prolonged missionary visits. He died in England in 1938.

In 1900 Montagu Harry Proctor Beauchamp was evacuated from China because of the uprisings but returned again to China in 1902. He then returned again to England in 1911 and served as a chaplain with the British Army. His son became a second-generation missionary in China and in 1935 he went back to China; he died at his son's mission station in 1939.

Dixon Hoste succeeded Hudson Taylor as the Director of the China Inland Mission and for thirty years, he led the Mission. He retired in 1935 but remained in China until 1945, when he was interned by the Japanese. He died in London, in May 1946 and was the last remaining member of the "The Cambridge Seven" to die.

Wikipedia

Jim Elliot (1927–1956)

Philip James Elliot was an evangelical Christian missionary to Ecuador who, along with four others, was killed while attempting to evangelize the Huaorani people during what may be referred to as Operation Auca.

Wheaton

Jim's burden for missions solidified during years at Wheaton. At the beginning of Jim's third year at Wheaton, he decided to pursue a major in Greek, believing that it would both help him in his personal study of the Bible and make it easier to translate the Scriptures into the language of a people group unreached by missionaries.

Preparation

Jim graduated from Wheaton in 1949 and returned to his family's home in Portland early in the summer. He felt no immediate leading toward missions work and instead devoted more time to reading and study of the Bible. He engaged himself in some odd jobs at his church and worked as a substitute teacher at a local Christian school, but his lack of consistent employment was met with the disapproval of some of his neighbors. He maintained correspondence with Wilfred Tidmarsh, a missionary to the Quechua of Ecuador, as well as Rowland Hill, a missionary in Bangalore, India, who wanted Jim to teach biblical Greek in a Bible school he intended to found. Jim was not sure of which path to take and decided instead to wait.

In January 1950, Jim was accepted to attend Camp Wycliffe, a summer linguistics program sponsored by the Summer Institute of Linguistics and the University of Oklahoma. While not sure whether to attend, his focus on missions was steady—he got involved in InterVarsity, attending many group meetings and conferences during the spring. In April, he turned down an offer of full-time employment for the school in which he had been a substitute teacher, and soon after he decided to attend Camp Wycliffe.

Leaving for Ecuador

While at Camp Wycliffe, Jim practiced the skills necessary for writing down a language for the first time by working with a former missionary to the Quechua people. The missionary told him of the Auca people, an indigenous people group in Ecuador that had never had friendly contact with the outside world. Jim remained unsure about whether to go to Ecuador or India until July, when he became convinced that God was leading him to Ecuador. His parents and friends wondered if he might instead be more effective in youth ministry in the United States, but considering the home church "well-fed", he felt that international missions should take precedence.

Ecuador

He arrived in Ecuador on February 21, 1952, with the purpose of evangelizing Ecuador's Quechua Indians. On October 8, 1953, he married fellow Wheaton alumna and missionary Elisabeth Howard in Quito, Ecuador. Their only child, Valerie, was born February 27, 1955. While working with the Quechua Indians, Elliot began preparing to reach the violent Huaorani Indian tribe which were known at the time as the Aucas.

He and four other missionaries, Ed McCully, Roger Youderian, Peter Fleming, and their pilot, Nate Saint, made contact from their airplane with the Huaorani Indians using a loudspeaker and a basket to pass down gifts. After several months, the men decided to build a base a short distance from the Indian tribe, along the Curaray River. There they were approached one time by a small group of Huaorani Indians and even gave an airplane ride to one curious Huaorani whom they called "George" (his real name was Naenkiwi). Encouraged by these friendly encounters, they began plans to visit the Huaorani, but their plans were preempted by the arrival of a larger group of 10 Huaorani men, who killed Elliot and his four companions on January 8, 1956. Elliot's mutilated body was found downstream, along with those of the other men, except that of Ed McCully.

His journal entry for October 28, 1949, contains his now famous quotation, expressing his belief that missions work was more important than his life.

"He is no fool who gives what he cannot keep to gain that which he cannot lose."

Elliot and his friends became instantly known worldwide as martyrs, and Life Magazine published a ten-page article on their mission and death. They are credited with sparking an interest in Christian missions among the youth of their time and are still considered an encouragement to Christian missionaries working throughout the world. After her husband's death, Elisabeth Elliot and other missionaries began working among the Auca (Huaorani) Indians, where they had a profound impact and won many converts. She later published two books, *Shadow of the Almighty: The Life and Testament of Jim Elliot* and *Through Gates of Splendor*, which describe the life and death of her husband.

In 2005, a documentary based on the story was released entitled *Beyond the Gates of Splendor*. In 2006, a theatrical movie was released *End of the Spear*, based on the story of the pilot, Nate Saint, and the return trip of Saint's son attempting to reach the natives of Ecuador.

Wikipedia

3. Other Christian leaders

Billy Sunday (1862–1935)

William Ashley Sunday was born November 19, 1862, in Ames, Iowa, to a middle class family. Sunday's father enlisted to fight in the Civil War. When Sunday was a month old, his father died in Missouri of camp disease. His mother tried to keep the family together but ultimately sent Billy to a soldier's orphanage. Sunday ran away to his grandfather's farm. He didn't like the farm any better, however, so he ran off again and worked his way through high school as a janitor.

Sunday developed an interest in sports during high school. He played high school baseball but soon joined a semi-pro team in Marshalltown, Iowa. Sunday contributed to the team's victory in the Central Iowa League championship. Sunday, who had speed, kept pitchers unsettled constantly with zany antics once on base. His antics and his speed enabled him to steal base after base. On several occasions he stole home to score.

Cap Anson, a former big leaguer and Chicago Whitestockings (now the Cubs) scout, lived in Marshalltown. Anson saw Sunday play and, when asked, agreed to a try out with the Whitestockings. Anson believed Sunday a bush-leaguer so he lined him up for a race against the Whitestockings' fastest player. In a 100 yard dash Sunday beat his opponent by 15 feet. The Chicago team signed Sunday on the spot.

Sunday played professional baseball for eight years. He began with unimpressive statistics but he ended his career with a lifetime batting average of .257 although he once hit a high of .350. A terror once on base, Sunday stole 94 bases in one 116 game season. In a game against the Philadelphia Athletics in Chicago, with the game tied 0-0 at the top of the ninth, Sunday caught three fly balls to retire the side. He led off and walked. On the first pitch to the next batter Sunday stole second, on the next pitch he stole third and on the next pitch he stole home. One other item of useless trivia, Billy Sunday was the first professional baseball player to circle the bases in 14 seconds.

Sunday starred on the diamond, off the field he was a "rounder." In 1886, while on a drinking spree with friends, he found himself "in the gutter"—literally! A rescue mission band went by playing hymns. Reminded of his mother, Sunday picked himself up out of the gutter and followed the band to Chicago's Pacific Garden Mission. Mission workers ultimately led Sunday to Christ and he began attending a nearby Presbyterian Church.

After his conversion, Sunday worked with the YMCA. In 1891, Sunday decided to go full time with the "Y" even though the Philadelphia Athletics offered him $500 a month to play ball. Sunday turned the offer down to take an $83.33 monthly salary at the "Y". Even then Sunday often found himself behind in salary. Nonetheless, he continued to work spending much time in Chicago bars inviting men to come to church. No, he didn't drink; he had become a tee-totaller.

When the famous midwestern evangelist J. Wilbur Chapman needed an assistant he selected Sunday on the "Y's" recommendation. Sunday worked as Chapman's advance man. He made all the advance arrangements for Chapman's revivals. In the process he learned the "revival business" from the ground up. When Chapman took a ministry in Philadelphia in 1895, he had one revival meeting left—in Garner, Iowa. The Iowans asked Sunday to fill the date since Chapman was in Philadelphia. Sunday went and the rest is, as they say, history. Garner is today a small community of only 2300 in north central Iowa. By the end of Sunday's first meeting some 286 made decisions.

Sunday's initial success convinced him to launch into full time evangelism. He first copied Chapman's style but soon developed his own. He watched other evangelists and adapted some of their styles to himself. By 1900, larger communities outside Iowa invited him to hold meetings. In 1901 he hired a singer and insisted revival organizers erect a wooden tabernacle for his meetings. In 1904, he had hired his own advance man as well as an architect to design the tabernacles and supervise their construction. Each tabernacle was inexpensively built with dirt floors. To keep down the dust, organizers covered the floors with sawdust, thus the phrase, "Hitting the sawdust trail." In 1909, he hired Homer Rodeheaver as his song evangelist; they spent 22 years together.

Sunday preached a crude style. He referred to himself as the "rube of rubes" because of his rural background. He gestured wildly and every sermon became a pantomime. He ran, jumped, skipped and gyrated all over the place. He even smashed chairs in a "rage against Satan." He perspired freely. In an effort to cool off, he often removed his coat, tie and vest, and then rolled up his shirt sleeves. He mocked and chided the "dandy" preachers with their conservative style and demeanor. Sunday boldly attacked saloons striking out at them in nearly every sermon. After a campaign in Wilkes-Barre, Pennsylvania, bars closed for lack of business. He linked his message to patriotism. In one sermon, in no uncertain terms, he called upon God to damn the Germans (it was during World War I). When the government announced registration for the draft, Sunday purchased $25,000 worth of liberty bonds. In another sermon, he announced that if hell could be turned over it would be stamped, "Made in Germany!"

By the 1930s, Sunday's influence waned until many considered him a laughable hold over from the past. During his heyday, however, he was a force to be reckoned with. On November 6, 1935, Sunday died of an heart attack.

Michael Hines, Christian Chronicler

Timeline of Billy Sunday

1862 November 19: William Ashley Sunday born in Ames, Iowa.

December 22: Sunday's father, William Ashley Sunday, dies of pneumonia at army camp in Patterson, Missouri. Sunday never knew his father. Later, when Sunday was a young child, his mother sent him and brother George to orphanage.

1883 May 22: Sunday begins baseball career with Chicago White Stockings; strikes out his first 13 times at bat.

1886 Sunday led to the Lord by Mrs. Sarah "Ma" Clarke at the Pacific Garden Mission in Chicago.

1887 Winter: Sunday coaches baseball team at Northwestern University.

December 31: Sunday proposes to Helen Amelia Thompson.

1888 Sunday traded from the White Stockings to the Pittsburgh Pirates.

September 5: Billy Sunday and Helen Thompson married at the Thompson home in Chicago; Helen subsequently known as "Ma Sunday."

1889 Daughter Helen Sunday born.

1891 Sunday sets record of 90 bases stolen in 116 games.

Philadelphia Phillies offer Sunday $400/month.

Cincinatti offers $500/month.

Sunday takes "secretary of religious department" job at YMCA for $83/month.

1892 Son George Sunday born.

1894 Pittsburgh Pirates offer Sunday $2,000/month.

Evangelist J. Wilbur Chapman visits Sunday and hires him as advance man for $40/week.

1896 J. Wilbur Chapman takes a church and leaves his nationwide evangelism ministry.

1897 January: Sunday holds his first revival meeting at Garner, Iowa; nearly 100 people accept Christ during the week of meetings.

1903 Sunday ordained by the Presbyterian Church.

1907 Ma Sunday begins traveling with Sunday, handling his campaign planning and finances, and speaking at women's meetings.

1909 Homer Rodeheaver joins Sunday as soloist and song leader.

1917 Sunday's famous ten-week New York Campaign; the love offering (over $100,000) was given by him to the Red Cross and other World War I charities; over 98,000 came forward to accept Christ.

1920 Ma Sunday survives serious car accident.

1933 Sunday collapses while preaching in Des Moinse, Iowa.

Son George commits suicide.

1935 October 27: Sunday preaches his last sermon, at First Methodist Church, Mishawaka, Indiana; 44 people respond.

November 6: Sunday dies of heart attack.

November 9: Memorial Service at Moody Memorial Church, Chicago, attended by thousands.

Martin Luther King, Jr. (1929–1968)

Raised in Atlanta, Georgia as the son and grandson of Baptist ministers, King had deep roots in African-American Churches. After seminary studies to prepare for ministry, King went on to graduate studies in systematic theology at Boston University; his studies included the work of Walter Rauschenbusch. In 1954 King became pastor of a Baptist church in Montgomery, Alabama. Soon he led the Montgomery Bus Boycott, an effort to end racial segregation on public transportation. King later became a pastor at Ebenezer Baptist church in Atlanta, where he continued leading the civil rights movement for social change through non-violent protest. In 1957 King became president of the Southern Christian Leadership Conference (SCLC) which sought to register African-American voters and to desegregate public accommodations. In many southern cities King led protests, marches, and campaigns to focus national attention on the need for racial and economic justice. In 1963 King led a march on Washington D.C., where he delivered the famous "I Have a Dream" speech, calling America to live up to its promise of equality for all citizens. In 1964 he was awarded the Nobel Peace Prize. In later years he denounced the Vietnam War and became more radical in his critique of American society. On April 4, 1968, King was assassinated in Memphis, Tennessee; his birthday became a national holiday in 1986.

Luther Seminary

Timeline of Martin Luther King, Jr.

1929

Born at noon on January 15, 1929.

Parents: The Reverend and Mrs. Martin Luther King, Sr.

1944

Graduated from Booker T. Washington High School and was admitted to Morehouse College at age 15.

1948

Graduates from Morehouse College and enters Crozer Theological Seminary.

Ordained to the Baptist ministry, February 25, 1948, at age 19.

1951

Enters Boston University for graduate studies.

1953

Marries Coretta Scott and settles in Montgomery, Alabama.

1955

Received Doctorate of Philosophy in Systematic Theology from Boston University, Boston, Massachusetts on June 5, 1955.

Dissertation Title: A Comparison of God in the Thinking of Paul Tillich and Henry Wiseman.

Joins the bus boycott after Rosa Parks was arrested on December 1. On December 5, he is elected president of the Montgomery Improvement Association, making him the official spokesman for the boycott.

1956

On November 13, the Supreme Court rules that bus segregation is illegal, ensuring victory for the boycott.

1957

King forms the Southern Christian Leadership Conference to fight segregation and achieve civil rights. On May 17, Dr. King speaks to a crowd of 15,000 in Washington, D.C.

1958

The U.S. Congress passed the first Civil Rights Act since reconstruction. King's first book, *Stride Toward Freedom*, is published.

On a speaking tour, Martin Luther King, Jr. is nearly killed when stabbed by an assailant in Harlem. Met with President Dwight D. Eisenhower, along with Roy Wilkins, A. Philip Randolph, and Lester Grange on problems affecting black Americans.

1959

Visited India to study Mohandas Gandhi's philosophy of nonviolence.

Resigns from pastoring the Dexter Avenue Baptist Church to concentrate on civil rights full time. He moved to Atlanta to direct the activities of the Southern Christian Leadership Conference.

1960

Becomes co-pastor with his father at the Ebenezer Baptist Church in Atlanta, Georgia.

Lunch counter sit-ins began in Greensboro, North Carolina. In Atlanta, King is arrested during a sit-in waiting to be served at a restaurant. He is sentenced to four months in jail, but after intervention by John Kennedy and Robert Kennedy, he is released.

Student Non-Violent Coordinating Committee founded to coordinate protests at Shaw University, Raleigh, North Carolina.

1961

In November, the Interstate Commerce Commission bans segregation in interstate travel due to work of Martin Luther King, Jr. and the Freedom Riders.

Congress on Racial Equality (CORE) began first Freedom Ride through the South, in a Greyhound bus, after the U.S. Supreme Court outlawed segregation in interstate transportation.

1962

During the unsuccessful Albany, Georgia movement, King is arrested on July 27 and jailed.

1963

On Good Friday, April 12, King is arrested with Ralph Abernathy by Police Commissioner Eugene "Bull" Connor for demonstrating without a permit.

On April 13, the Birmingham Campaign is launched. This would prove to be the turning point in the war to end segregation in the South.

During the eleven days he spent in jail, MLK writes his famous "Letter from Birmingham Jail."

On May 10, the Birmingham agreement is announced. The stores, restaurants, and schools will be desegregated, hiring of blacks implemented, and charges dropped.

On June 23, MLK leads 125,000 people on a Freedom Walk in Detroit.

The March on Washington held August 28 is the largest civil rights demonstration in history with nearly 250,000 people in attendance.

At the march, King makes his famous *I Have a Dream* speech.

On November 22, President Kennedy is assassinated.

1964

On January 3, King appears on the cover of Time magazine as its Man of the Year.

King attends the signing ceremony of the Civil Rights Act of 1964 at the White House on July 2.

During the summer, King experiences his first hurtful rejection by black people when he is stoned by Black Muslims in Harlem.

King is awarded the Nobel Peace Prize on December 10. Dr. King is the youngest person to be awarded the Nobel Peace Prize for Peace at age 35.

1965

On February 2, King is arrested in Selma, Alabama during a voting rights demonstration.

After President Johnson signs the Voting Rights Act into law, Martin Luther King, Jr. turns to socioeconomic problems.

1966

On January 22, King moves into a Chicago slum tenement to attract attention to the living conditions of the poor.

In June, King and others begin the March Against Fear through the South.

On July 10, King initiates a campaign to end discrimination in housing, employment, and schools in Chicago.

1967

The Supreme Court upholds a conviction of MLK by a Birmingham court for demonstrating without a permit. King spends four days in Birmingham jail.

On November 27, King announces the inception of the Poor People's Campaign focusing on jobs and freedom for the poor of all races.

1968

King announces that the Poor People's Campaign will culminate in a March on Washington demanding a $12 billion Economic Bill of Rights guaranteeing employment to the able-bodied, incomes to those unable to work, and an end to housing discrimination.

Dr. King marches in support of sanitation workers on strike in Memphis, Tennessee.

On March 28, King lead a march that turns violent. This was the first time one of his events had turned violent.

Delivered *I've Been to the Mountaintop speech.*

At sunset on April 4, Martin Luther King, Jr. is fatally shot while standing on the balcony of the Lorraine Motel in Memphis, Tennessee.

There are riots and disturbances in 130 American cities. There were twenty thousand arrests.

King's funeral on April 9 is an international event.

Within a week of the assassination, the Open Housing Act is passed by Congress.

1986

On November 2, a national holiday is proclaimed in King's honor.

Brother Roger of Taizé (1915 – 2005)

Everything began in great solitude. In 1940, at the age of 25, Brother Roger left his native Switzerland in order to live in France, the country of his mother. For several years he had borne within him a calling to begin a community where reconciliation between Christians would be lived out in daily life. A community where "kindness of heart would be a matter of practical experience, and where love would be at the heart of all things". He wanted this community to be present in the midst of the suffering of the time, and thus it was that he made his home in the small village of Taizé, in Burgundy, just a few miles from the demarcation line which cut France in two during the first years of the war. There he was able to hide refugees (Jews in particular), who had fled the occupied zone in the knowledge that they could find refuge in his house.

After the war he was joined by others, and on Easter Day, 1949, the first brothers of the community made their commitment to a life in celibacy, to community of possessions, and to simplicity of life.

During a long silent retreat in the winter of 1952–3, Brother Roger wrote "The Rule of Taizé" which expressed the "things necessary for living in community".

From the 1950s onwards some of the brothers went to live in areas of deprivation in order to share the life of the poor.

At the end of 1950s the number of young people visiting Taizé started to increase noticeably. And from 1962 onwards, brothers, as well as young people sent by the community, made continual visits in Eastern European countries. They made these journeys with great discretion so as not to compromise those whom they were visiting.

Between 1962 and 1989, Brother Roger visited most of the Eastern European countries himself. Sometimes he went for youth gatherings which were authorized but under surveillance, sometimes he went for simple visits, with no permission to speak in public. "I will be silent with you", he said to the Christians he visited in those countries.

In 1966 some of the Sisters of St. Andrew, an international Catholic community, founded over seven centuries ago, came to live in the neighboring village. They have taken on part of the work for the meetings at Taizé. In recent years Polish Ursuline sisters have also come to give their help.

Today the Taizé Community is made up of over a hundred brothers, Catholics and from various Protestant backgrounds, coming from more than twenty-five nations. The community's existence is in itself a sign of reconciliation between divided Christians and divided nations.

In one of his recent books, "God is Love Alone" (Continuum [UK] and GIA Publications [USA]), Brother Roger describes the shaping of his ecumenism in this way:

Can I recall here that my maternal grandmother discovered intuitively a sort of key to the ecumenical vocation, and that she opened for me a way to put it into practice? Marked by the witness of her life, while I was still very young, following her I found my own Christian identity by reconciling within myself the faith of my origins with the mystery of the Catholic faith, without breaking fellowship with anyone.

The brothers accept no donations or gifts. Furthermore, if a brother inherits something from his family, it is given by the community for the very poor. The community earns its living by the brothers' work.

Today, small groups of brothers are present in Asia, Africa and South America. As far as possible they share the living conditions of those who surround them, striving to be a presence of love among the very poor, street children, prisoners, the dying, and those who are wounded in their depths by broken relationships, by being abandoned.

Every week from early spring to late autumn, young adults from different continents arrive on the hill of Taizé. They are searching for meaning in their lives, in communion with many others. By going to the wellsprings of trust in God, they set out on an inner pilgrimage that encourages them to build relationships of trust among human beings. Some weeks in the summer months, more than 5000 young people from 75 different countries thus take part in a common adventure. And this adventure continues when they return home. It is expressed in their concern to deepen an inner life and by their readiness to take on responsibilities in order to make the world a better place to live in.

Church leaders also come to Taizé. The community has welcomed Pope John Paul II, three Archbishops of Canterbury, Orthodox metropolitans, the fourteen Lutheran bishops of Sweden, and countless pastors from all over the world.

To support young people the community has undertaken a "pilgrimage of trust on earth". This does not mean organizing a movement around the community. Each person is invited, after his or her stay at Taizé, to live out in their own situation what they have understood, with greater awareness of the inner life within them as well as of their bonds with many others who are involved in a similar search for what really matters. At the end of every year, Taizé leads a large meeting in one of the major cities of Europe, East or West. Tens of thousands of young adults take part, from all over Europe and from other continents. These meetings are stages in the "pilgrimage of trust on earth".

At the time of these European meetings, Brother Roger wrote a "letter" every year. These letters were translated into over fifty languages and used as a text for reflection by many young people, both at home and during the meetings at Taizé. Brother Roger often wrote these letters during extended stays in regions of poverty (in Calcutta, Chile, Haiti, Ethiopia, the Philippines, South Africa).

Today, throughout the world, Taizé's name evokes peace, reconciliation, communion and the ardent expectation of a springtime of the Church: "When the Church listens, heals, reconciles, then she becomes what she is in her most radiant aspect: a crystal-clear reflection of a love." (Brother Roger)

The death of Brother Roger

During evening prayer on Tuesday 16 August 2005, in the middle of the crowd surrounding the community in the Church of Reconciliation, a mentally disturbed woman struck Brother Roger violently with knife blows. He died a few moments later.

The funeral was held on Tuesday 23 August.

In 1998, Brother Roger had designated Brother Alois to succeed him after his death, as animator of the community. Brother Alois entered straight away into his ministry as servant of communion at the heart of the community.

Brother Roger received the following awards

The Templeton Prize, London

Peace Prize of the German Book Trade, Frankfurt

UNESCO Prize for Peace Education, Paris

Charlemagne Prize, Aix-la-Chapelle

Robert Schuman Prize, Strasbourg

Notre Dame Award for International Humanitarian Service, Notre Dame University, Indiana, USA

Dignitas Humana Award, Saint John's School of Theology Seminary, Collegeville, Minnesota, USA

Classic Christian devotional books from the twentieth century

E. M. Bounds (1835–1913)

Power Through Prayer

Necessity of Prayer

A. T. Pierson (1837–1911)

George Muller of Bristol

In Christ Jesus

F. B. Meyer (1847–1929), *Way Into the Holiest*

C. M. Sheldon (1857–1946), *In His Steps*

James Denney (1856–1917), *Death of Christ*

R. A. Torrey (1856–1928), *How To Pray*

Oswald Chambers (1874–1917), *My Utmost for His Highest*

G. K. Chesterton (1874–1936), *Orthodoxy*

Sadhu Sundar Singh (1889–1929), *At the Feet of the Master*

A. W. Tozer (1897–1963), *The Pursuit of God*

C. S. Lewis (1898–1963)

Nonfiction

The Allegory of Love: A Study in Medieval Tradition (1936)

The Problem of Pain (1940)

The Abolition of Man (1943)

Beyond Personality (1944)

Miracles: A Preliminary Study (1947, revised 1960)

Mere Christianity (1952; based on radio talks of 1941–1944)

Surprised by Joy: The Shape of My Early Life (1955; autobiography)

Reflections on the Psalms (1958)

The Four Loves (1960)

A Grief Observed (1961; first published under the pseudonym «N. W. Clerk»)

Prayer: Letters to Malcolm (1964)

Letters to an American Lady (1967)

God in the Dock: Essays on Theology and Ethics (1970), = Undeceptions (1971)

Fiction

The Pilgrim's Regress (1933)

Space Trilogy

Out of the Silent Planet (1938)

Perelandra (1943)

That Hideous Strength (1946)

The Screwtape Letters (1942)

The Great Divorce (1946)

The Chronicles of Narnia

The Lion, the Witch and the Wardrobe (1950)

Prince Caspian (1951)

The Voyage of the Dawn Treader (1952)

The Silver Chair (1953)

The Horse and His Boy (1954)
The Magician's Nephew (1955)
The Last Battle (1956)
Till We Have Faces (1956)
Screwtape Proposes a Toast (1961) (an addition to The Screwtape Letters)
The Dark Tower and other stories (1977)

David Martyn Lloyd-Jones (1899–1981)
Studies in the Sermon on the Mount
Spiritual Depression: Its Causes and Cure
Why Does God Allow War?
Preaching and Preachers

Watchman Nee (1903–1972), *The Normal Christian Life*

Billy Graham (b. 1918)
Angels: God's secret agents
Just as I am: the autobiography of Billy Graham
Peace with God
The Holy Spirit
Approaching Hoofbeats: the four horsemen of the Apocalypse
Facing death and the life after
How to be born again
Answers to Life's Problems
The Secret of Happiness

Extracts from Classic Christian devotional books from Medieval Christianity

Benjamin B. Warfield (1851–1921), *The Theology of John Calvin*
Billy Sunday (1862–1935), *Why Delay Your Real Conversion?*
Billy Graham (b. 1918), *Peace With God*

Benjamin B. Warfield (1851–1921)

The Theology of John Calvin

I wish to speak about Calvinism, that great system of religious thought which bears John Calvin's name.

In the first place, the doctrine of predestination is not the formative principle of Calvinism, it is only its logical implication. It is not the root from which Calvinism springs, it is one of the branches which it has inevitably thrown out. And so little is it the peculiarity of Calvinism, that it underlay and gave its form and power to the whole Reformation movement—which was, as from the spiritual point of view a great revival of religion, so from the doctrinal point of view a great revival of Augustinianism. There was, accordingly, no difference among the Reformers on this point; Luther and Melanchthon and the compromising Butzer were no less zealous for absolute predestination than Zwingli and Calvin.

Just as little can the doctrine of justification by faith be represented as specifically Lutheran. It is as central to the Reformed as to the Lutheran system. Nay, it is only in the Reformed system that it retains the purity of its conception and resists the tendency to make it a doctrine of justification on account of; instead of by, faith. It is true that Lutheranism is prone to rest in faith as a kind of ultimate fact, while Calvinism penetrates to its causes, and places faith in its due relation to the other products of God's activity looking to the salvation of man. And this difference may, on due consideration, conduct us back to the formative principle of each type of thought. But it, too, is rather an outgrowth of the divergent formative principles than the embodiment of them.

The "five points of Calvinism," we have no doubt learned to call them, and not without justice. They are, each and every one of them, essential elements in the Calvinistic system, the denial of which in any of their essential details is logically the rejection of the entirety of Calvinism; and in their sum they provide what is far from being a bad epitome of the Calvinistic system.

> The sovereignty of the election of God,
> the substitutive definiteness of the atonement of Christ,
> the inability of the sinful will to good,
> the creative energy of the saving grace of the Spirit,
> the safety of the redeemed soul in the keeping of its Redeemer,—

are not these the distinctive teachings of Calvinism, as precious to every Calvinist's heart as they are necessary to the integrity of the system?

The exact formulation of the formative principle of Calvinism lies in a profound apprehension of God in His majesty, with the poignant realization which inevitably accompanies this apprehension, of the relation sustained to God by the creature as such, and particularly by the sinful creature. The Calvinist is the man who has seen God, and who, having seen God in His glory, is filled on the one hand, with a sense of his own unworthiness to stand in God's sight as a creature, and much more as a sinner, and on the other hand, with adoring wonder that nevertheless this God is a God who receives sinners. He who believes in God without reserve and is determined that God shall be God to him, in all his thinking, feeling, willing—in the entire compass of his life activities, intellectual, moral, spiritual—throughout all his individual, social, religious relations—is, by the force of that strictest of all logic which presides over the outworking of principles into thought and life, by the very necessity of the case, a Calvinist.

If we wish to reduce this statement to a more formal theoretical form, we may say perhaps, that Calvinism in its fundamental idea implies three things. In it, objectively speaking, theism comes to its rights;

subjectively speaking, the religious relation attains its purity;

soteriologically speaking, evangelical religion finds at length its full expression and its secure stability.

Theism comes to its rights only in a teleological view of the universe, which recognizes in the whole course of events the orderly working out of the plan of God, whose will is consequently conceived as the ultimate cause of all things. The religious relation attains its purity only when an attitude of absolute dependence on God is not merely assumed, as in the act, say, of prayer, but is sustained through all the activities of life, intellectual, emotional, executive. And evangelical religion reaches its full manifestation and its stable form only when the sinful soul rests in humble, self-emptying trust purely on the God of grace as the immediate and sole source of all the efficiency which enters into its salvation. From these things shine out upon us the formative principle of Calvinism. The Calvinist is the man who sees God behind all phenomena, and in all that occurs recognizes the hand of God, working out His will; who makes the attitude of the soul to God in prayer the permanent attitude in all its life activities; and who casts himself on the grace of God alone, excluding every trace of dependence on self from the whole work of his salvation.

Calvinism comes forward simply as pure theism, religion, evangelicalism, as over against less pure theism, religion, evangelicalism. It does not take its position then by the side of other types of these things; it takes its place over them, as what they too ought to be. It has no difficulty thus, in recognizing the theistic character of all truly theistic thought, the religious note in all really religious manifestations, the evangelical quality of all actual evangelical faith. It refuses to be set antagonistically over against these where they really exist in any degree. It claims them in every instance of their emergence as its own, and seeks only to give them their due place in thought and life. Whoever believes in God, whoever recognizes his dependence on God, whoever hears in his heart the echo of the *Soli Deo gloria* of the evangelical profession—by whatever name he may call himself; by whatever logical puzzles his understanding may be confused—Calvinism recognizes such as its own, and as only requiring to give full validity to those fundamental principles which underlie and give its body to all true religion to become explicitly a Calvinist.

Calvinism is born, we perceive, of the sense of God. God fills the whole horizon of the Calvinist's feeling and thought. One of the consequences which flow from this is the high supernaturalism which informs at once his religious consciousness and his doctrinal construction. Calvinism indeed would not be badly defined as the tendency which is determined to do justice to the immediately supernatural, as in the first so in the second creation. The strength and purity of its apprehension of the supernatural Fact (which is God) removes all embarrassment from it in the presence of the supernatural act (which is miracle). In everything which enters into the process of the recovery of sinful man to good and to God, it is impelled by the force of its first principle to assign the initiative to God. A supernatural revelation in which God makes known to man His will and His purposes of grace; a supernatural record of the revelation in a supernaturally given Book, in which God gives His revelation permanence and extension,—such things are to the Calvinist matters of course. And above all things, he can but insist with the utmost strenuousness on the immediate supernaturalness of the actual work of redemption; this of course, in its impetration. It is no strain to his faith to believe in a supernatural Redeemer, breaking His way to earth through a Virgin's womb, bursting the bonds of death and returning to His Father's side to share the glory which He had with the Father before the world was. Nor can he doubt that this supernaturally purchased redemption is applied to the soul in an equally supernatural work of the Holy Spirit.

Thus it comes about that monergistic regeneration—"irresistible grace," "effectual calling," our older theologians called it,—becomes the hinge of the Calvinistic soteriology, and lies much more deeply imbedded in the system than many a doctrine more closely connected with it in the popular mind. Indeed, the soteriological significance of predestination itself consists to the Calvinist largely in the safeguard it affords to the immediate supernaturalness of salvation. What lies at the heart of his soteriology is absolute exclusion of creaturely efficiency in the induction of the saving process, that the pure grace of God in salvation may be magnified. Only so could he express his sense of men's complete dependence as sinners on the free mercy of a saving God; or extrude the evil leaven of synergism, by which God is robbed of His glory and man is encouraged to attribute to some power, some act, some initiative of his own, his participation in that salvation which in reality has come to him from pure grace.

Calvinism however, is not merely a soteriology. Deep as its interest is in salvation, it cannot escape the question—"Why should God thus intervene in the lives of sinners to rescue them from the consequences of their sin?"

And it cannot miss the answer—"Because it is to the praise of the glory of His grace."

Thus it cannot pause until it places the scheme of salvation itself in relation with a complete world-view in which it becomes subsidiary to the glory of the Lord God Almighty. If all things are from God, so to Calvinism all things are also unto God, and to it God will be all in all. It is born of the reflection in the heart of man of the glory of a God who will not give His honor to another, and draws its life from constant gaze upon this great image. And let us not fail punctually to note, that "it is the only system in which the whole order of the world is thus brought into a rational unity with the doctrine of grace, and in which the glorification of God is carried out with absolute completeness."

Therefore the future of Christianity—as its past has done—lies in its hands. For, it is certainly true, as has been said by a profound thinker of our own time, that "it is only with such a universal conception of God, established in a living way, that we can face with hope of complete conquest all the spiritual dangers and terrors of our times."

"It, however," as the same thinker continues, "is deep enough and large enough and divine enough, rightly understood, to confront them and do battle with them all in vindication of the Creator, Preserver and Governor of the world, and of the Justice and Love of the divine Personality."

This is the system of doctrine to the elaboration and defense of which John Calvin gave all his powers nearly four hundred years ago. And it is chiefly because he gave all his powers to commending to us this system of doctrine, that we are here today to thank God for giving to the world the man who has given to the world this precious gift.

B. B. Warfield

Billy Sunday (1862–1935)

Why Delay Your Real Conversion?

What does converted mean? It means completely changed. Converted is not synonymous with reformed. Reforms are from without—conversion from within. Conversion is a complete surrender to Jesus. It's a willingness to do what he wants you to do. Unless you have made a complete surrender and are doing his will it will avail you nothing if you've reformed a thousand times and have your name on fifty church records.

Believe on the Lord Jesus Christ, in your heart and confess him with your mouth and you will be saved. God is good. The plan of salvation is presented to you in two parts. Believe in your heart and confess with your mouth. Many of you here probably do believe. Why don't you confess? Now own up. The truth is that you have a yellow streak. Own up, business men, and business women, and all of you others. Isn't it so? Haven't you got a little saffron? Brave old Elijah ran like a scared deer when he heard old Jezebel had said she would have his head, and he beat it. And he ran to Beersheba and lay down under a juniper tree and cried to the Lord to let him die. The Lord answered his prayer, but not in the way he expected. If he had let him die he would have died with nothing but the wind moaning through the trees as his funeral dirge. But the Lord had something better for Elijah. He had a chariot of fire and it swooped down and carried him into glory without his ever seeing death. (2 Chronicles 21:12).

So he says he has something better for you—salvation if he can get you to see it. You've kept your church membership locked up. You've smiled at a smutty story. When God and the Church were scoffed at you never peeped, and when asked to stand up here you've sneaked out the back way and beat it. You're afraid and God despises a coward—a mutt. You cannot be converted by thinking so and sitting still.

Maybe you're a drunkard, an adulterer, a prostitute, a liar; won't admit you are lost; are proud. Maybe you're even proud you're not proud, and Jesus has a time of it.

Jesus said: "Come to me," not to the Church; to me, not to a creed; to me, not to a preacher; to me, not to an evangelist; to me, not to a priest; to me, not to a pope; "Come to me and I will give you rest." Faith in Jesus Christ saves you, not faith in the Church.

You can join church, pay your share of the preacher's salary, attend the services, teach Sunday school, return thanks and do everything that would apparently stamp you as a Christian—even pray—but you won't ever be a Christian—until you do what God tells you to do.

That's the road, and that's the only one mapped out for you and for me. God treats all alike. He doesn't furnish one plan for the banker and another for the janitor who sweeps out the bank. He has the same plan for one that he has for another. It's the law—you may not approve of it, but that doesn't make any difference.

Salvation a Personal Matter

The first thing to remember about being saved is that salvation is a personal matter. "Seek ye the Lord"—that means every one must seek for himself. It won't do for the parent to seek for the children; it won't do for the children to seek for the parent. If you were sick all the medicine I might take wouldn't do you any good. Salvation is a personal matter that no one else can do for you; you must attend to it yourself.

Some persons have lived manly or womanly lives, and they lack but one thing—open confession of the Lord Jesus Christ. Some men think, that they must come to him in a certain way—that they must be stirred by emotion or something like that.

Some people have a deeper conviction of sin before they are converted than after they are converted. With some it is the other way. Some know when they are converted and others don't.

Some people are emotional. Some are demonstrative. Some will cry easily. Some are cold and can't be moved to emotion. A man jumped up in a meeting and asked whether he could be saved when he hadn't shed a tear in forty years. Even as he spoke he began to shed tears. It's all a matter of how you're constituted. I am vehement, and I serve God with the same vehemence that I served the devil when I went down the line.

Some of you say that in order to accept Jesus you must have different surroundings. You think you could do it better in some other place. You can be saved where you areas well as anyplace on earth. I say, "My watch doesn't run. It needs new surroundings. I'll put it in this other pocket, or I'll put it here, or here on these flowers." It doesn't need new surroundings. It needs a new mainspring; and that's what the sinner needs. You need a new heart, not a new suit.

What can I do to keep out of hell? "Believe on the Lord Jesus Christ and thou shalt be saved."

The Philippian jailer was converted. He had put the disciples into the stocks when they came to the prison, but after his conversion he stooped down and washed the blood from their stripes.

Now, leave God out of the proposition for a minute. Never mind about the new birth—that's his business. Jesus Christ became a man, bone of our bone, flesh of our flesh. He died on the cross for us, so that we might escape the penalty pronounced on us. Now, never mind about anything but our part in salvation. Here it is: "Believe on the Lord Jesus Christ, and thou shalt be saved."

You say, "Mr. Sunday, the Church is full of hypocrites." So's hell. I say to you if you don't want to go to hell and live with that whole bunch forever, come into the Church, where you won't have to associate with them very long. There are no hypocrites in heaven.

You say, "Mr. Sunday, I can be a Christian and go to heaven without joining a church." Yes, and you can go to Europe without getting on board a steamer. The swimming's good—but the sharks are laying for fellows who take that route. I don't believe you. If a man is truly saved he will hunt for a church right away.

You say, "It's so mysterious. I don't understand." You'll be surprised to find out how little you know. You plant a seed in the ground—that's your part. You don't understand how it grows. How God makes that seed grow is mysterious to you.

Some people think that they can't be converted unless they go down on their knees in the straw at a camp-meeting, unless they pray all hours of the night, and all nights of the week, while some old brother storms heaven in prayer. Some think a man must lose sleep, must come down the aisle with a haggard look, and he must froth at the mouth and dance and shout. Some get it that way, and they don't think that the work I do is genuine unless conversions are made in the same way that they have got religion.

I want you to see what God put in black and white; that there can be a sound, thorough conversion in an instant; that man can be converted as quietly as the coming of day and never backslide. I do not find fault with the way other people get religion. What I want and preach is the fact that a man can be converted without any fuss.

If a man wants to shout and clap his hands in joy over his wife's conversion, or if a wife wants to cry when her husband is converted, I am not going to turn the hose on them, or put them in a strait-jacket. When a man turns to God truly in conversion, I don't care what form his conversion takes. I wasn't converted that way, but I do not rush around and say, with gall and bitterness, that you are not saved because you did not get religion the way I did. If we all got religion in the same way, the devil might go to sleep with a regular Rip Van Winkle snooze and still be on the job.

Look at Nicodemus. You could never get a man with the temperament of Nicodemus near a camp meeting, to kneel down in the straw, or to shout and sing. He was a quiet, thoughtful, honest, sincere and cautious man. He wanted to know the truth and he was willing to walk in the light when he found it.

Look at the man at the pool of Bethesda. He was a big sinner and was in a lot of trouble which his sins had made for him. He had been in that condition for a long time. It didn't take him three minutes to say "Yes," when the Lord spoke to him. See how quietly he was converted.

Matthew stood in the presence of Christ and he realized what it would be to be without Christ, to be without hope, and it brought him to a quick decision. "And he arose and followed him."

How long did that conversion take? How long did it take him to accept Christ after he had made up his mind? And you tell me you can't make an instant decision to please God? The decision of Matthew proves that you can. While he was sitting at his desk he was not a disciple. The instant he arose he was. That move changed his attitude toward God. Then he ceased to do evil and commenced to do good. You can be converted just as quickly as Matthew was.

God says: "Let the wicked man forsake his way." The instant that is done, no matter if the man has been a life-long sinner, he is safe. There is no need of struggling for hours—or for days—do it now. Who are you struggling with? Not God. God's mind was made up long before the foundations of the earth were laid. The plan of salvation was made long before there was any sin in the world. Electricity existed long before there was any car wheel for it to drive. "Let the wicked man forsake his way." When? Within a month, within a week, within a day, within an hour? No! Now! The instant you yield, God's plan of salvation is thrown into gear. You will be saved before you know it, like a child being born.

Rising and following Christ switched Matthew from the broad to the narrow way. He must have counted the cost as he would have balanced his cash book. He put one side against the other. The life he was living led to all chance of gain. On the other side there was Jesus, and Jesus outweighs all else. He saw the balance turn as the tide of a battle turns and then it ended with his decision. The sinner died and the disciple was born.

I believe that the reason the story of Matthew was written was to show how a man could be converted quickly and quietly. It didn't take him five or ten years to begin to do something—he got busy right away.

You don't believe in quick conversions? There have been a dozen men of modern times who have been powers for God whose conversion was as quiet as Matthew's. Charles G. Finney never went to a camp meeting. He was out in the woods alone, praying, when he was converted. Sam Jones, a mighty man of God, was converted at the bedside of his dying father. Moody accepted Christ while waiting on a customer in a boot and shoe store. Dr. Chapman was converted as a boy in a Sunday school. All the other boys in the class had accepted Christ, and only Wilbur remained. The teacher turned to him and said, "And how about you, Wilbur?" He said, "I will," and he turned to Christ and has been one of his most powerful evangelists for many years. Gipsy Smith was converted in his father's tent. Torrey was an agnostic, and in comparing agnosticism, infidelity and Christianity, he found the scale tipped toward Christ. Luther was converted as he crawled up a flight of stairs in Rome.

Seemingly the men who have moved the world for Christ have been converted in a quiet manner. The way to judge a tree is by its fruit. Judge a tree of quiet conversion in this way.

Another lesson. When conversion compels people to forsake their previous calling, God gives them a better job. Luke said, "He left all." Little did he [Matthew] dream that his influence would be world-reaching and eternity-covering. His position as tax-collector seemed like a big job, but it was picking up pins compared to the job God gave him. Some of you may be holding back for fear of being put out of your job. If you do right God will see that you do not suffer. He has given plenty of promises, and if you plant your feet on them you can defy the poor-house. Trust in the Lord means that God will feed you. Following Christ you may discover a gold mine of ability that you never dreamed of possessing. There was a saloon-keeper, converted in a meeting at New Castle, who won hundreds of people to Christ by his testimony and his preaching.

You do not need to be in the church before the voice comes to you; you don't need to be reading the Bible; you don't need to be rich or poor or learned. Wherever Christ comes follow. You may be converted while engaged in your daily business. Men cannot put up a wall and keep Jesus away. The still small voice will find you.

Right where the two roads through life diverge God has put Calvary. There he put up a cross, the stumbling block over which the love of God said, "I'll touch the heart of man with the thought of father and son." He thought that would win the world to him, but for nineteen hundred years men have climbed the Mount of Calvary and trampled into the earth the tenderest teachings of God.

You are on the devil's side. How are you going to cross over?

So you cross the line and God won't issue any extradition papers. Some of you want to cross. If you believe, then say so, and step across. I'll bet there are hundreds that are on the edge of the line and many are standing straddling it. But that won't save you. You believe in your heart—confess him with your mouth. With his heart man believes and with his mouth he confesses. Then confess and receive salvation full, free, perfect and external. God will not grant any extradition papers. Get over the old line. A man isn't a soldier because he wears a uniform, carries a gun, or carries a canteen. He is a soldier when he makes a definite enlistment. All of the others can be bought without enlisting. When a man becomes a soldier he goes out on muster day and takes an oath to defend his country. It's the oath that makes him a soldier. Going to church doesn't make you a Christian any more than going to a garage makes you an automobile, but public definite enlistment for Christ makes you a Christian.

"Oh," a woman said to me out in Iowa, "Mr. Sunday, I don't think I have to confess with my mouth." I said: "You're putting up your thought against God's."

M-o-u-t-h doesn't spell intellect. It spells mouth and you must confess with your mouth. The mouth is the biggest part about most people, anyhow.

What must I do?

Philosophy doesn't answer it. Infidelity doesn't answer it. First, "believe on the Lord Jesus Christ and thou shalt be saved." Believe on the Lord. Lord—that's his kingly name. That's the name he reigns under. "Thou shalt call his name Jesus." It takes that kind of a confession. Give me a Savior with a sympathetic eye to watch me so I shall not slander. Give me a Savior with a strong arm to catch me if I stumble. Give me a Savior that will hear my slightest moan.

Believe on the Lord Jesus Christ and be saved. Christ is his resurrection name. He is sitting at the right hand of the Father interceding for us.

Because of his divinity he understands God's side of it and because of his humanity he understands our side of it. Who is better qualified to be the mediator? He's a mediator. What is that? A lawyer is a mediator between the jury and the defendant. A retail merchant is a mediator between the wholesale dealer and the consumer. Therefore, Jesus Christ is the Mediator between God and man. Believe on the Lord. He's ruling today. Believe on the Lord Jesus. He died to save us. Believe on the Lord Jesus Christ. He's the Mediator.

Her majesty, Queen Victoria, was traveling in Scotland when a storm came up and she took refuge in a little hut of a Highlander. She stayed there for an hour and when she went the good wife said to her husband, "We'll tie a ribbon on that chair because her majesty has sat on it and no one else will ever sit on it." A friend of mine was there later and was going to sit in the chair when the man cried: "Nae, nae, mon. Dinna sit there. Her majesty spent an hour with us once and she sat on that chair and we tied a ribbon on it and no one else will ever sit on it." They were honored that her majesty had spent the hour with them. It brought unspeakable joy to them.

It's great that Jesus Christ will sit on the throne of my heart, not for an hour, but here to sway his power forever and ever.

"He Died for Me"

In the [civil] war there was a band of guerillas—Quantrell's band—that had been ordered to be shot on sight. They had burned a town in Iowa and they had been caught. One long ditch was dug and they were lined up in front of it and blindfolded and tied, and just as the firing squad was ready to present arms a young man dashed through the bushes and cried, "Stop!" He told the commander of the firing squad that he was as guilty as any of the others, but he had escaped and had come of his own free will, and pointed to one man in the line and asked to take his place. "I'm single," he said, "while he has a wife and babies." The commander of that firing squad was an usher in one of the cities in which I held meetings, and he told me how the young fellow was blindfolded and bound and the guns rang out and he fell dead.

Time went on and one day a man came upon another in a graveyard in Missouri weeping and shaping the grave into form. The first man asked who was buried there and the other said, "The best friend I ever had." Then he told how he had not gone far away but had come back and got the body of his friend after he had been shot and buried it; so he knew he had the right body. And he had brought a withered bouquet all the way from his home to put on the grave. He was poor then and could not afford anything costly, but he had placed a slab of wood on the pliable earth with these words on it: "He died for me."

Major Whittle stood by the grave some time later and saw the same monument. If you go there now you will see something different. The man became rich and today there is a marble monument fifteen feet high and on it this inscription:

SACRED TO THE MEMORY OF
WILLIE LEE
HE TOOK MY PLACE IN THE LINE
HE DIED FOR ME

Sacred to the memory of Jesus Christ. He took our place on the cross and gave his life that we might live, and go to heaven and reign with him.

"Believe on the Lord Jesus Christ, confess him with thy mouth, and thou shalt be saved and thy house."

It is a great salvation that can reach down into the quagmire of filth, pull a young man out and send him out to hunt [for] his mother and fill her days with sunshine. It is a great salvation, for it saves from great sin.

The way to salvation is not Harvard, Yale, Princeton, Vassar or Wellesley. Environment and culture can't put you into heaven without you accept Jesus Christ.

It's great. I want to tell you that the way to heaven is a blood-stained way. No man has ever reached it without Jesus Christ and he never will.

Billy Sunday

Billy Graham (b.1918)

Peace with God

The greatest warfare going on in the world today is between mankind and God. People may not realize that they're at war with God. But if they don't know Jesus Christ as Savior, and if they haven't surrendered to Him as Lord, God considers them to be at war with Him. That chasm has been caused by sin. The Bible says that all have "sinned and come short of the glory of God" (Romans 3:23). "Oh," people say, "I have joined the church. I have been baptized." But has Jesus come to live in their hearts? Not only as Savior, but as Lord?

It would be the greatest tragedy if I didn't tell you that unless you repent of your sins and receive Christ as your Savior, you are going to be lost.

"For God so loved the world, that he gave his only begotten Son, that whosoever [that "whosoever" is you] believes in him should not perish, but have everlasting life" (John 3:16). It's not just head-belief. It's heart-belief too. It's total trust, total commitment. We bring everything to the cross where the Lord Jesus Christ died for our sins. He made peace with God by His death on the cross. If we turn our backs on Him, and don't commit our lives to Him, we will have no hope in the future.

For one to have peace with God, it cost the blood of His Son. "With the precious blood of Christ, as of a lamb without blemish and without spot," said Peter (1 Peter 1:19). If I were the only person in all the world, Jesus would have died for me, because He loves me. And He loves you! His love is pouring out from the cross.

"Meet Me in Heaven"

I read a biography of Queen Victoria, and I learned that the queen would sometimes go to the slums of London. She went into one home to have tea with an older lady, and when the queen rose to leave, she asked, "Is there anything I can do for you?" And the woman said, "Yes, ma'am, Your Majesty, you can meet me in heaven." The queen turned to her and said softly, "Yes. I'll be there, but only because of the blood that was shed on the cross for you and for me."

Copyright 1984, by Billy Graham, Peace with God

History of Bible translations

Number of languages Bible had been translated into during this period.

AD 1900

573 languages (In its complete form or portions of it)

AD 1997

2,167 languages (In its complete form or portions of it)

AD 1998

2,197 languages (In its complete form or portions of it)

AD 1999

2,212 languages (In its complete form or portions of it)

Examples of Bible translation from the twentieth century

New International Version (NIV)

Copyright © 1973, 1978, 1984 by International Bible Society

Matthew 5

The Beatitudes

1Now when he saw the crowds, he went up on a mountainside and sat down. His disciples came to him, 2and he began to teach them saying:

3"Blessed are the poor in spirit,
for theirs is the kingdom of heaven.
4Blessed are those who mourn,
for they will be comforted.
5Blessed are the meek,
for they will inherit the earth.

6Blessed are those who hunger and thirst for righteousness,
for they will be filled.
7Blessed are the merciful,
for they will be shown mercy.
8Blessed are the pure in heart,
for they will see God.
9Blessed are the peacemakers,
for they will be called sons of God.
10Blessed are those who are persecuted because of righteousness,
for theirs is the kingdom of heaven.
11"Blessed are you when people insult you, persecute you and falsely say all kinds of evil
against you because of me. 12Rejoice and be glad, because great is your reward in heaven,
for in the same way they persecuted the prophets who were before you.

Salt and Light

13"You are the salt of the earth. But if the salt loses its saltiness, how can it be made salty again? It is no longer good for anything, except to be thrown out and trampled by men.

14"You are the light of the world. A city on a hill cannot be hidden. 15Neither do people
light a lamp and put it under a bowl. Instead they put it on its stand, and it gives light to
everyone in the house. 16In the same way, let your light shine before men, that they may see
your good deeds and praise your Father in heaven.

The Message (MSG)

Matthew 5

You're Blessed

1–2 When Jesus saw his ministry drawing huge crowds, he climbed a hillside. Those who were apprenticed to him, the committed, climbed with him. Arriving at a quiet place, he sat down and taught his climbing companions. This is what he said:

3"You're blessed when you're at the end of your rope. With less of you there is more of God and his rule.

4"You're blessed when you feel you've lost what is most dear to you. Only then can you be embraced by the One most dear to you.

5"You're blessed when you're content with just who you are—no more, no less. That's the moment you find yourselves proud owners of everything that can't be bought.

6"You're blessed when you've worked up a good appetite for God. He's food and drink in the best meal you'll ever eat.

7"You're blessed when you care. At the moment of being 'care-full,' you find yourselves cared for.

8"You're blessed when you get your inside world—your mind and heart—put right. Then you can see God in the outside world.

9"You're blessed when you can show people how to cooperate instead of compete or fight. That's when you discover who you really are, and your place in God's family.

10"You're blessed when your commitment to God provokes persecution. The persecution drives you even deeper into God's kingdom.

11–12"Not only that—count yourselves blessed every time people put you down or throw you out or speak lies about you to discredit me. What it means is that the truth is too close for comfort and they are uncomfortable. You can be glad when that happens—give a cheer, even!—for though they don't like it, I do! And all heaven applauds. And know that you are in good company. My prophets and witnesses have always gotten into this kind of trouble.

Salt and Light

13"Let me tell you why you are here. You're here to be salt-seasoning that brings out the God-flavors of this earth. If you lose your saltiness, how will people taste godliness? You've lost your usefulness and will end up in the garbage.

14–16"Here's another way to put it: You're here to be light, bringing out the God-colors in the world. God is not a secret to be kept. We're going public with this, as public as a city on a hill. If I make you light-bearers, you don't think I'm going to hide you under a bucket, do you? I'm putting you on a light stand. Now that I've put you there on a hilltop, on a light stand—shine! Keep open house; be generous with your lives. By opening up to others, you'll prompt people to open up with God, this generous Father in heaven.

New Living Translation (NLT)

Matthew 5

The Sermon on the Mount

1 One day as he saw the crowds gathering, Jesus went up on the mountainside and sat down. His disciples gathered around him, 2 and he began to teach them.

The Beatitudes

3 "God blesses those who are poor and realize their need for him,[a]
for the Kingdom of Heaven is theirs.
4 God blesses those who mourn,
for they will be comforted.
5 God blesses those who are humble,
for they will inherit the whole earth.
6 God blesses those who hunger and thirst for justice,[b]
for they will be satisfied.

7 God blesses those who are merciful,
for they will be shown mercy.
8 God blesses those whose hearts are pure,
for they will see God.
9 God blesses those who work for peace,
for they will be called the children of God.
10 God blesses those who are persecuted for doing right,
for the Kingdom of Heaven is theirs.
11 "God blesses you when people mock you and persecute you and lie about you[c] and
say all sorts of evil things against you because you are my followers. 12 Be happy about it!
Be very glad! For a great reward awaits you in heaven. And remember, the ancient prophets
were persecuted in the same way.

Teaching about Salt and Light

13 "You are the salt of the earth. But what good is salt if it has lost its flavor? Can you
make it salty again? It will be thrown out and trampled underfoot as worthless.
14 "You are the light of the world—like a city on a hilltop that cannot be hidden. 15 No
one lights a lamp and then puts it under a basket. Instead, a lamp is placed on a stand, where
it gives light to everyone in the house. 16 In the same way, let your good deeds shine out for
all to see, so that everyone will praise your heavenly Father.

Footnotes:

Matthew 5:3 Greek poor in spirit.

Matthew 5:6 Or for righteousness.

Matthew 5:11 Some manuscripts omit and lie about you.

GLOSSARY OF TERMS

A

Abbey

A community of monks or nuns, ruled by an abbot or abbess. Usually founded by a monastic order.

Abjuration

Renunciation, under oath, of heresy to the Christian faith, made by a Christian wishing to be reconciled with the Church.

Accidie

Term used in ascetical literature for spiritual sloth, boredom, and discouragement.

Aisle

Lateral division of the nave or chancel of a church.

Alexandrian School

School of thought associated with Alexandria, Egypt. It was influenced by Platonic philosophy and tended to emphasize the divinity of Christ over his humanity and interpret scripture allegorically. Compare with the Antiochene School. Notable Alexandrians include Clement and Origen.

Amen

The final word of a prayer; means "so be it".

Amish (also Amish Mennonites)

Conservative group in the USA and Canada arising from a division within the Swiss Brethren in Alsace under the leadership of Jakob Ammann (c. 1656–1730). Further divisions occurred after the Amish migrated to North America, but most are members of the Old Order Amish Mennonite Church. Amish are similar to other Mennonites in doctrine and practice, but the former worship in private homes instead of a church, wear "plain" dress and retain the use of German in their services. There were about 35,000 baptized members in 1984.

Anabaptist:

One of a sect that arose in Zurich in 1523 among the followers of Zwingli, who started the Reformation in Switzerland and advocated opposition to infant baptism, and believed that only such persons as had been baptized after a confession of faith in Christ constituted a real church.

Anathema

Condemnation of heretics, similar to major excommunication.

Anchoret (Anchorite, Anchoress)

A hermit, or recluse.

Anglican (Communion)

A worldwide branch of the Protestant church led by the Archbishop of Canterbury.

Annihilationism

The doctrine that the finally impenitent will be totally annihilated after death.

Ante-Nicene

Predating the Council of Nicea (325 AD).

Antiphon

A sentence, or versicle, from Scripture, sung as an introduction to a psalm or canticle.

Apocalypse

Another name for the book of Revelation, the last book of the New Testament.

Apocrypha

(Lit. Greek "out of the writings"). Books not included in the Hebrew canon of the Old Testament, but included in the Greek Septuagint. Catholic and Orthodox Christians include the Apocrypha in the canon of scripture; Protestant Christians do not. Apocryphal books are:

1 and 2 Esdras
Tobit
Judith
Wisdom of Solomon
Ecclesiasticus
Baruch

Song of the Three Children
Susanna
Bel and the Dragon
The Prayer of Manasseh
1, 2, 3, and 4 Maccabees
Additions to Esther

Apology

A theological term to describe a contention made in defense of the Christian faith. It is derived from the Greek, *apologia,* meaning "a defense in conduct or procedure." Apologetics is the study of this explanation or defense.

Apostate

Term used to describe a person who leaves religious orders after making solemn profession.

Apostle

(Greek *apostolos,* "one sent out"). Missionaries sent out by Jesus, including the disciples and Paul.

Apostles' Creed

The oldest statement of belief in the church, based on the teachings of the Apostles.

Apostolic Fathers

Group of Christian leaders and writers from the late first and early second centuries AD. These authors were not apostles themselves, but had close proximity to the apostles, either by personal relationship or close connection with apostolic teaching. Examples include Clement of Rome, Ignatius, Polycarp, Papias, Pseudo-Barnabas, the Didache, the Second Epistle of Clement, the Shepherd of Hermas, and The Apostles' Creed.

Apostolic succession

Doctrine that the authority of ordained clergy (to perform valid sacraments and teach right doctrine) derives from an unbroken succession of valid ordinations beginning with the apostles.

Aramaic

One of the languages used by people in Jesus' time, probably the language that Jesus and the disciples would have spoken to each other.

Arianism

Belief, taught by Arius in the 4th century, that Christ was created by the Father, and although greater than man he is inferior to the Father. Athanasius, Bishop of Alexandria, wrote and campaigned against Arianism. It was declared a heresy at the Council of Nicea in 325.

Armageddon

In Biblical prophecy, the scene of a great battle between the forces of good and evil, to occur at the end of the world.

Asceticism

The belief that one can attain to a high intellectual or spiritual level through solitude, mortification of the flesh, and devotional contemplation.

Ash Wednesday

The first day of Lent. The day after Shrove Tuesday.

Assumption of Mary

The doctrine that the Virgin Mary was bodily taken up into heaven at her death.

Atheist

One who denies or disbelieves in the existence of God.

Atonement

The reconciliation between God and man effected by Christ's death.

B

Baptism

The entry rite into the Christian church, which can take place as a baby or as an adult.

Baptists

One of the largest Protestant denominations, with 40 million members (and many more non-member adherents) worldwide and 26.7 million in the United States. The Baptist tradition has its roots in the Anabaptist movement of the Reformation and English Puritan John Smyth (1554–1612). Its most notable distinction is its rejection of infant baptism. Today, most Baptists in American belong either to the Southern Baptist Convention or the American Baptist Convention.

Beatification

In the Roman Catholic church, an act of the Pope declaring a deceased person beatified (declared as blessed) and worthy of a certain degree of public honor, usually the last step toward canonization

Beatitudes

Eight declarations of special blessedness pronounced by Jesus in the Sermon on the Mount, Matthew chapter 5.

Benedictine Order

Monastic order founded by St. Benedict. Monks take vows of personal poverty, chastity and obedience to their abbot and the Benedictine Rule.

Born-again

The state of being born in the Spirit, resulting from placing faith in Jesus Christ.

Breviary

A book containing the Divine Office (lessons, psalms, hymns, etc.) for each day.

BVM

Blessed Virgin Mary.

C

Calvinism a system of belief, named after the French reformer John Calvin (1509–64) whose chief tenets are that scripture is the only rule of faith, that man is justified by faith not works, and that there is absolute predestination of the elect to salvation and of the reprobate to damnation.

Canon

(Greek *kanon*, "rule" or "reference point").

The body of scriptures accepted as authoritative.

A priest who serves on the staff of a cathedral.

Canon law

Body of law related to the organization, discipline, and belief of the church and enforced by church authority.

Canonical Hours

The services sung or recited at the fixed times of the day: matins, lauds, prime, tierce, sext, none, vespers, compline.

Cappadocian Fathers

Three theologians from the region of Cappadocia in modern-day Turkey:

Basil of Caesarea (c. 330–379),

Gregory of Nazianzus (329–389) and

Gregory of Nyssa (330–395)—whose development of Trinitarian doctrine remains highly influential in Orthodox Christianity.

Catechism

A short treatise given in catechistic (question and answer) form an outline of the fundamental principles of a religious creed

Catechumen

(Greek *katachesis*, "instruction"). One who is being instructed in the basics of Christian doctrine, usually in preparation for confirmation or baptism.

Catharism

The aiming at or proclaiming peculiar purity of life or doctrine as practiced by the Novatians (3rd century), the Albigenses (12th century), among others.

Catholic

A Latin term taken from the Greek, *katholikos*, meaning "universal," referring to all believers.

Chancel

Part of a church to the east of the crossing, containing the main altar and choir.

Chapter

The daily assembly of a monastic community at which a chapter of the Rule was read, faults were confessed, and business was transacted. Also the term for a body of clergy serving a cathedral.

Charismatic

Comes from the Greek word *charismata* which means gifted. A Christian who believes in or practices speaking in tongues and the present-day operation of the spiritual gifts.

Christ

(Greek *christos*, "messiah" or "anointed one"). Title applied to Jesus identifying him as the figure predicted by the Hebrew prophets.

Church

(Greek *kuriakon*, "belonging to the Lord"). The worldwide body of Christian believers, a particular denomination or congregation, or the building in which they meet. The study of the nature of the church is ecclesiology.

Collect

A short prayer appointed for a particular day (hence "collect-books").

Compline

The last service of the day, being the final canonical hour, about 9 p.m.

Congregationalism

A form of churchmanship depending on the independence and autonomy of the local gathered church, but without insistence on believers' baptism.

Coptic Orthodox Church

The principal Christian church in Egypt.

Council of Trent

The 19th ecumenical council of the Catholic Church, which took place over the period 1545–63. A very important council in that it reformed numerous aspects of church practice (e.g., abolished the sale of indulgences) and clarified Catholic doctrine in response to the challenges by Reformers.

Counter Reformation

The revival of the Roman Catholic Church in Europe in the sixteenth and seventeenth centuries, which was stimulated by the Protestant Reformation. The Jesuits were at the forefront of the revival.

Creed

A formal summary of religious belief; an authoritative statement of doctrine.

Crusades

(Lat. "cross-marked") Wars fought against enemies of the Christian faith, primarily the Muslim Turks in the period 1095 to 1291, but later against other infidels and heretics.

D

Decalogue

A reference to the ten commandments.

Deist

One who subscribes to or professes the belief in the existence of a personal God, based solely on the testimony of reason and rejecting any supernatural revelation; also believing that God created the world and set it into motion, subject to natural laws, but takes no interest in it

Deus volt!

(Latin "God wills it"). The battle cry of the Crusaders.

Dissenter

A general term for those Christians (not including Roman Catholics) outside the Established Church.

Docetism

(Greek "to seem"). The belief that Christ only appeared to have a human body. Associated with Gnosticism and based on the dualistic belief that matter is evil and only spirit is good.

Dogma

A belief which is held as authoritative and indisputable by a religious body.

Donatists

Fourth century North African Christian faction, named for Bishop Donatus. The Donatists believed the church should be pure, and therefore church leaders who had handed over scripture during persecution (*traditores*) should not retain their positions. They were opposed most notably by Augustine.

Doxology

(Greek *doxa*, "glory"). A short hymn glorifying God.

E

Ebionites

(Hebrew *ebionim*, "poor men"). An ascetic sect of Jewish Christians that taught Jesus was only a human prophet who had received the Holy Spirit at his baptism. Rejected Paul, and held that the law of Moses must be obeyed by Christians.

Ecclesiology

(Greek *ekklesia*, "church"). Branch of theology dealing with the doctrine of the church.

Ecumenical council

A council of the Christian church at which representatives from several regions are present. To be distinguished from a "synod," which is a meeting of the local church.

ELCA

Evangelical Lutheran Church in America. The largest Lutheran church body in the U.S. and more liberal than the LCMS.

Eschatology

Branch of theology dealing with end times or last things. Includes such subjects as the afterlife, the Day of Judgment, the Second Coming, and the end of the world.

Eucharist

A sacrament recognized by all branches of Christianity. Commemorates the Last Supper of Christ with the sharing of bread and wine. See also transubstantiation and Real Presence.

Evangelical

Group or church placing particular emphasis on the gospel and the scriptures as the path to salvation.

Excommunication

A penalty imposed by the Catholic Church prohibiting a person from receiving or administering sacraments or holding church office.

Ex cathedra

(Latin "from the throne.") Authoritative statements made by the Pope in Roman Catholicism.

F

Fall, the

Disobedience of Adam and Eve (chronicled in Genesis 3) that resulted in ill effects for the remainder of humanity.

Fasting

Going without food, wholly or in part, as in observance of a religious duty.

Flagellation

Self-scourging as a means of religious discipline.

Foot washing

A religious ceremony performed by certain sects in remembrance of the washing of the disciples' feet by Jesus.

Franciscans

Monastic order founded by Francis of Assisi in 1210 AD.

Free Churches

Non-conformist denominations, free from state control.

Friars

They are like the monks but ready to move from place to place at any time if needed for evangelical or apostolic purposes. Started with St. Dominic and St. Francis of Assisi in the 13th century, and today there are over 2,000 orders of friars and nuns, many of them with thousands of members

G

Glossolalia

Speaking in tongues, a striking phenomenon of primitive Christianity.

Gnosticism

A complex of religious movements rooted in both paganism and Judaism. By about the second century AD, Gnosticism had developed and was labeled a heresy by the established church. Distinctive Gnostic beliefs include:

two separate divine beings (the unknowable supreme deity and an inferior, evil creator god);

the inherent goodness of spirit and evil of matter;

the importance of gnosis, or special knowledge, for salvation; and

a view of Christ as a messenger of the supreme deity who only appeared to take on a body.

Major Gnostic teachers include Valentinus, Basilides, and Marcion.

Gospel

(Greek *evangelion*; Old English *godspel*, "good news"). The content of Christian preaching; that is, that Christ died to save humans from the penalty of sin and reunite them with God. When capitalized, the word usually refers to one of the first four books of the New Testament, which relate the life of Christ.

Gospels

The narrative of Christ's life and teaching as given in the first four books of the New Testament

Grace

The undeserved gift of divine favor in the justification and then sanctification of sinners. The Greek term *charis*, usually translated in English as "grace," is about 150 times in the New Testament, mostly in the Pauline epistles.

Grayfriars

Name given to the Franciscans in England because of their gray robes.

H

Hagiography

A biography of a saint, usually written from an admiring and idealized perspective.

Heresy

A doctrinal view of belief at variance with the recognized tenets of a system, church, school, or party.

Hermeneutics

The science or art of interpretation, especially of the Scriptures.

Hermits

They lived alone usually in caves. St. Paul the Hermit was the first Hermit in 251.

High Church

A general term, normally applied to those Anglicans who stress the authority of the Church and its bishops, and who place high value on the sacraments.

Homiletics

The branch of rhetoric that treats of the composition and delivery of sermons.

Homily

A message delivered to lay Christians for their edification; sermon.

Homoousios

(Greek, "one substance" or "one in being"). The Christological doctrine introduced by Athanasius and accepted as orthodox at the Council of Nicea in 325. The doctrine arose in the context of the heresy of Arius, who contented that Christ was created by the Father and was thus not fully divine.

Huguenots

In the 16th and 17th centuries, the name Huguenot was applied to a member of the Protestant Reformed Church of France, historically known as the French Calvinists.

I

Icon

In the Greek Church, a holy picture, mosaic, or related object.

Immaculate Conception

In the Roman Catholic Church, the doctrine that the Virgin Mary was conceived in her mother's womb without the stain of original sin.

Incarnation

The assumption of the human nature by Jesus Christ as the second person of the Trinity

Indulgences

In the Roman Catholic Church, remission, by those authorized, of the temporal punishment still due to sin after sacramental absolution, either in this world or in purgatory.

Inquisition

A court or tribunal of the Roman Catholic Church for the discovery, examination, and punishment of heretics; specifically, the ecclesiastical tribunal for the discovery and punishment of heretics, active in central and southern Europe in the 13th century.

Indulgences

A commutation of a certain period of canonical penance, authorized by a bishop, enabling the penitent who had repented and confessed his sin to substitute for his penance

J

Jansenism

The doctrines taught by Cornelis Jansen, emphasizing predestination and the irresistibility of God's grace, and denying free will.

Johannine

Pertaining to the apostle John.

Justification

The act by which God moves a sinner from a state of sin to a state of grace or, especially in Protestantism, the act by which God declares a sinner righteous.

K

Kerygma

(Gk.) Term coined by Rudolf Bultmann to indicate the essential message (or gospel) of the New Testament church.

L

Laity

The laymen and laywomen or non-clergy members of the church.

Lauds

The service of the divine office immediately following Matins. Sometimes it is called "Matins" in medieval texts. It was observed about 3 a.m.

Lollards

Originally, followers of John Wycliffe (14th cent.), who emphasized personal faith, predestination and the Bible. The word was later applied to anyone seriously critical of the Church.

M

Manicheism

A dualistic religious philosophy developed by the Persian Manes and his followers in which goodness, typified as light, God, or the soul, is represented as in conflict with evil, typified by darkness, Satan, or the body: taught from the 3rd to the 7th century.

Mariology

The whole body of religious belief and dogma relating to the Virgin Mary.

Martyrology

A list of the martyrs

Matins

The first office of the day, sung during the night about midnight, commonly called the Nocturns in medieval texts.

Michaelmass

Feast of St. Michael on September 29.

Modernism

The humanistic tendency in religious thought to supplement old theological creeds and dogmas by new scientific and philosophical learning and thus to place emphasis on practical ethics and world-wide social justice: distinguished from fundamentalism.

Monks

They are hermits but living in community, usually all their lives in the same monastery. St. Anthony Abbot (251–356) began the first monastic community in Egypt at the end of the 3rd century.

Monophysite churches

Christian sects originating in the 5th century which affirms that Christ had but one nature, the divine alone or a single compounded nature, and not two natures so united as to preserve their distinctness.

Monotheism

The belief in one God.

Moravians

A group of Christians from central Europe, formed by Count von Zinzendorf in 1722 but with roots going back much further. Strong elements in their tradition include missionary enterprise, hymn-singing, fellowship meals and general simplicity of approach to life. They influenced John Wesley.

Mysticism

The belief that knowledge of divine truth or the soul's union with the divine is attainable by spiritual insight or ecstatic contemplation without the medium of the senses or reason.

N

Nantes, Edict of

Edict signed by Henry IV at Nantes on April 13, 1598, after the end of the French wars of religion. It granted extensive rights to the Huguenots (French Calvinists). The edict was revoked by Louis XIV n the Edict of Fontainebleau on October 18, 1685.

Nestorianism

The doctrine, named for Nestorius (d. c. 451), Patriarch of Constantinople, that there were two separate persons in the incarnate Christ, one divine and the other human. Nestorius preached against Apollinarianism and objected to the term Theotokos ("God-Bearer") as a title for the Virgin Mary, and was opposed by St. Cyril of Alexandria.

Nimbus

Another word for halo.

Non-conformist

A general term for those who do not assent to the Established Church. Much the same as Dissenter, but the word is much more negative. The sequence Puritan—Dissenter—Nonconformist is significant of a decline in intensity.

Nones

The liturgical office sung or recited at the ninth hour of the day, i.e., about 3 p.m.

Norman

Term applied to the style of architecture which flourished in England from about 1050 to about 1200.

Novice

A member of a monastic community under training who has not yet taken vows.

O

Original Sin

The doctrine that Adam's sin was passed on to all mankind. Human beings are thus 'born in sin' and universally in need of redemption.

Orthodox

(Greek *orthos*, "correct"). The correct or majority view.

Orthodox

The branch of Christianity prevalent in Greece, Russia and Eastern Europe. Originates as a separate body when the Eastern (Orthodox) church split from the Western (Catholic) church in 1054 AD. Orthodox Christians do not recognize the authority of the Pope, but rather the Patriarch of Constantinople. The Seven Ecumenical Councils are also of special authoritative importance. Orthodox Christianity is characterized by emphasis on icons.

P

Passion

(Latin *passio*, "suffering"). The crucifixion of Jesus and the events leading up to it.

Patristics

(Lat. *pater*, "father") Branch of Christian theology and history concerned with the church "fathers" (*patres*), usually understood to refer to the period from the later first century to the mid-fifth century.

Pelagianism

Belief system, attacked by Augustine and declared a heresy in, which denies original sin and asserts the ability of humans to choose good over evil with only external assistance from God.

Penance

A sacramental rite involving contrition, confession to a priest, the acceptance of penalties, and absolution.

Pietism

A movement in the Lutheran Church in Germany during the latter 17th century, advocating a revival of the devotional ideal.

Pilgrimage

A long journey, especially one made to a shrine or sacred place.

Presbyterian

An adherent of a form of church government through elders.

Prime

A liturgical office sung or recited at the first hour of the day, i.e., at sunrise.

Protestant

A major division of the Church protesting against Roman Catholic belief and practice as distinct from Orthodox and Roman Catholic Churches.

Psalter

The psalms appointed to be read or sung at any given service.

Purgatory

In Roman Catholic theology, a state or place where the soul of those who have died penitent are made fit for paradise by expiating venial sins and undergoing any punishment remaining for previously forgiven sins.

Q

"Q"

The hypothetical source that many biblical critics suggest was used by the authors of the Gospels of Matthew and Luke. It consists of all passages Matthew and Luke have in common that are not found in Mark.

Quakers

A nickname for members of the Society of Friends.

Quietism

17th-century movement emphasizing complete passivity and the "prayer of quiet" before God. The ideal is to abandon all desires, even for virtue, love of Christ, or salvation, as well as all outward acts of devotion, and simply rest in the presence of God. Notable Quietist writers include de Molinos, Guyon, and Archbishop Fenelon.

R

Real Presence

In Catholic and some Protestant churches, the physical and spiritual presence of the body and blood of Christ in the bread and wine of the Eucharist.

Reformation

A sixteenth century reform movement which led to the formation of Protestant Churches.

Reredos

A screen, usually carved and painted, behind and above the altar.

Requiem

Any musical hymn, composition, or service for the dead.

Roman Catholic

Major division of the Church, owing loyalty to Rome, as distinct from Orthodox and Protestant Churches.

Rosary

Catholic devotional practice in which 15 sets of ten Hail Marys are recited, each set preceded by the Lord's Prayer and followed by the *Gloria Patri*. A string of beads is used to count the prayers. The number of sets represents the 15 "mysteries" (five joyful, five sorrowful, five glorious), which are events in the lives of Jesus and Mary.

S

Sabellianism

Modalist belief system attributed to Sabellius, in which God consists of a single person who reveals himself in different modes. Thus the Son is divine and the same as the Father. Essentially synonymous with patripassianism and modalist monarchianism.

Sacrament

A solemn Christian ritual believed to be a means of grace, a sign of faith, or obedience to Christ's commands. The Anglican catechism defines a sacrament as "an outward and visible sign of an inward and spiritual grace . . . ordained by Christ himself." In the Catholic and Orthodox churches, there are seven sacraments: baptism, confirmation, the eucharist (communion), penance, extreme unction, ordination and marriage. In Protestant churches, only baptism and the eucharist are regarded as sacraments.

Scholasticism

(Latin *scholastici*, "schoolmen"). A medieval movement which emphasized the rational justification of religious.

Scriptorium

Room in a monastery set aside for the use of scribes copying manuscripts.

Slain in the Spirit

An extrabiblical term used to describe a phenomenon which brings about an overwhelming awareness of the Holy Spirit, causing a person to fall prostrate.

Socinianism

The teachings of the [two] Italian theologians named Socinus, as the denial of the Trinity, of the depravity of man, of vicarious atonement, and the efficacy of sacraments.

Sola fide

(Latin, "faith alone"). Martin Luther's doctrine that faith is all that is necessary for salvation.

Sola scriptura

(Latin, "scripture alone"). Martin Luther's doctrine that Scripture is the only authority for Christians (i.e., church tradition and papal doctrine are unnecessary and inferior to direct reading of the Scripture).

Soteriology

Branch of Christian theology dealing with salvation.

Stations of the Cross

Series of fourteen events in the passion of Christ, beginning with Jesus' condemnation and ending with his body being laid in the tomb (for list, see Christianity by the Numbers). The stations are a subject of public and private devotion in Catholicism, especially during Lent.

Stigmata

The wounds that Christ received during the Passion and Crucifixion.

Synoptic Gospels

(Greek synopsis, "single view "). The New Testament books of Matthew, Mark and Luke, which offer similar views of the life of Christ (compared with the unique perspective of the Gospel of John).

T

Terce

The liturgical office sung or recited at the third hour of the day, i.e., about 9 a.m.

Theotokos

(Greek, "God-bearer"). Title of the Virgin Mary in the Orthodox tradition, used from the time of Origen (early 3rd century) onwards as an affirmation of Christ's divinity.

Transubstantiation

The doctrine that the bread and wine of the Eucharist actually becomes the body and blood of Christ, although it continues to have the appearance of bread and wine. Transubstantiation was rejected in different degrees by the Reformers.

Trinity

The Christian doctrine of the unity of Father, Son and Holy Spirit as three persons in one Godhead.

Trinitarian

Holding or professing belief in the Trinity.

U

Unitarianism

The doctrine of a Protestant denomination which rejects the Trinity, but accepts the ethical teachings of Jesus and emphasizes complete freedom of religious opinion, the importance of personal character, and the independence of each local congregation. In 1961, Unitarians jointed with the Univeralists to form the Unitarian Universalist Association.

Universalism

The belief that all souls will be saved by God in the end. Hell either does not exist or is temporary.

V

Vatican

The residence of the Pope in Rome and the administrative center of the Roman Catholic Church.

Vespers

The liturgical office of the evening, otherwise called Evensong.

Vigils

In early monastic literature the term for Matins, i.e., the office sung during the watches of the night.

Virgin Birth

Belief that Jesus Christ had no human father, but was conceived by the power of the Holy Spirit coming upon the Blessed Virgin Mary. It is based on Matthew 1 and Luke 1 in the New Testament and is implied in the Apostles' and Nicene Creeds.

W

Waldensianism

Pertaining to, or a member of, a sect of religious dissenters founded about 1170 by Peter Waldo.

Wounds, Five Sacred

The five wounds Christ suffered during the Passion: the piercing of his hands, feet and side. Devotion to the Five Wounds developed in the Middle Ages.

GENERAL INDEX

B

C

D

H

I

K

L

M

N

O

P

Q

R

S

T